TURN UP THE VOLUME!

Brass band at the Odwira festival. Photograph by Doran H. Ross, Abeadze Dominase, Ghana, 1975.

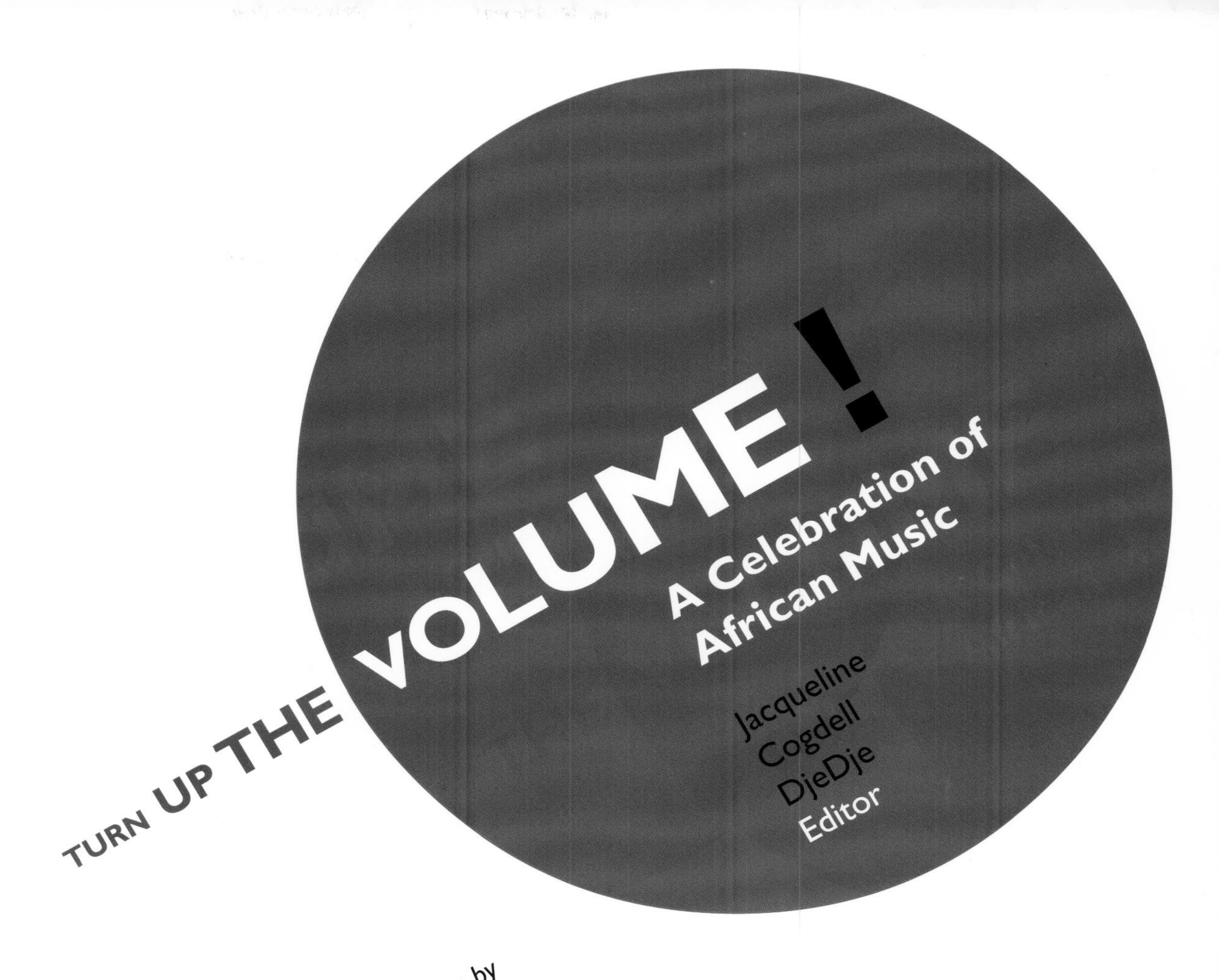

TURN UP THE VOLUME!

A Celebration of African Music

Jacqueline Cogdell DjeDje
Editor

With contributions by

Ernest D. Brown Jr.
Kimasi L. Browne
Leigh Creighton
Akin Euba
Clarence Bernard Henry
Christian Dowu Jayeola Horton
Cheryl L. Keyes
Jean Ngoya Kidula
Cynthia Tse Kimberlin
Gerhard Kubik
Heather A. Maxwell
Eddie S. Meadows
Lester P. Monts
Kazadi wa Mukuna
Ali Jihad Racy
Victoria Simmons

UCLA Fowler Museum of Cultural History
Los Angeles

Supported by the National Endowment for the Humanities dedicated to expanding American understanding of history and culture

NATIONAL ENDOWMENT FOR THE HUMANITIES

Major funding for this publication has been provided by

National Endowment for the Humanities

The Jerome L. Joss Foundation
The Ahmanson Foundation
Manus, the support group of the UCLA Fowler Museum of Cultural History

---

The Fowler Museum is part of UCLA's School of the Arts and Architecture

Lynne Kostman, Managing Editor
Lynne Kostman, Greg Dobie, and Michelle Ghaffari, Manuscript Editors
Ann Molvik, Editorial Assistant
Patrick Fitzgerald, Designer
Don Cole, Principal Photographer
Daniel R. Brauer, Production Manager

UCLA Fowler Museum of Cultural History
Box 951549
Los Angeles, California 90095-1549

Maps (pp. 17, 24, 35): © David L. Fuller

Printed and bound in Hong Kong by South Sea International Press, Ltd.

Library of Congress Cataloging-in-Publication Data

Turn up the volume: a celebration of African music/Jacqueline
Cogdell DjeDje, editor : with contributions by Ernest Brown . . . [et
al.].
p. cm.
Essays and a catalog serving three exhibits: Music in the Life of
Africa (UCLA Fowler Museum of Cultural History), The Fine Art of African Musical
Instruments (Los Angeles County Museum of Art), and African Instruments in the
Diaspora (California African American Museum).
Includes bibliographical references.
Contents : African life and music — Africa and the diaspora :
cross-cultural influences — catalog
ISBN 0-930741-76-5. — ISBN 0-930741-77-3 (softcover)
1. Music—Africa exhibitions. 2. Musical instruments—Africa.
3. Music—African influences, 4. Music—Africa Cross-cultural studies. 5. Blacks—
Music—History and criticism. I. DjeDje, Jacqueline Cogdell. II. Brown, Ernest. III.
University of California, Los Angeles. Fowler Museum of Cultural History
ML141.L7U557 1999
780'.89'96—dc21 99-42125
CIP

Cover and page 4: Photographs by Don Cole

Kuba slit-gong player. Photograph by Elisabeth L. Cameron, Nkoshi, Democratic Republic of the Congo, July 23, 1989.

Contents

Part Two: Africa and the Diaspora: Cross-Cultural Influences

PARTICIPANT
PARTICIPANT

Foreword

This publication was designed as a companion to an ambitious exhibition collaboration between the California African American Museum (CAAM), the Los Angeles County Museum of Art (LACMA), and the UCLA Fowler Museum of Cultural History (FMCH). Under the umbrella title *The Heritage of African Music*, each museum mounted an exhibition that ran through most of the school year: *Rhythms of the Soul: African Instruments in the Diaspora* at CAAM, *Music for the Eyes: The Fine Art of African Musical Instruments* at LACMA, and *Music in the Life of Africa* at FMCH. This citywide celebration of the musical legacy of Africa included extensive teacher-training workshops, a school tour program that encouraged visits to all three exhibitions, a substantial performing arts component, and an array of lectures, symposia, and instrument-building activities.

Although such African-influenced genres as jazz, blues, rock and roll, rap, and hip-hop have held widely recognized positions in the global music scene for some time, it is somewhat ironic that the trendy category of "World Music" has risen to prominence only over the last ten years of the millennium. Of course, world music has always been around, but only recently has it been aggressively marketed to Euro-American consumers. Propelled by popular guidebooks, specialized magazines, numerous local and national radio programs, live concerts and music festivals, and booming sales of recorded music, the richly diverse musics of Asia, the Pacific, Latin America, and especially Africa have become increasingly accessible to wider audiences. No longer the sole province of ethnomusicologists, the musics of Africa and the rest of the "non-Western world" are now also part of the popular arts of the United States and Europe.

While this volume is intended as a freestanding work and not an overview or catalog for the three exhibitions, it does provide an opportunity to acknowledge the efforts of individuals at all three institutions who contributed to this unprecedented collaboration. I would especially like to thank Elisabeth Cameron, former associate curator of LACMA, and Rick Moss, the curator of history at CAAM, for their dedication and hard work. Their consistent leadership kept the project moving forward and ensured whatever successes it has achieved. I am also grateful to Andrea Rich, President, and Director Graham Beal of LACMA, and to Director Jai Henderson of CAAM for maintaining their strong commitment to this project. The education departments at the three museums deserve special recognition. An initiative called *An African Musical Journey*, a collaborative arts and music project between the three museums and the Los Angeles Unified School District (LAUSD), was led by Evelyn Carter and Mar Hollingsworth at CAAM; Elisabeth Cameron, Liz Caffry, and Bridget Cooks at LACMA; Betsy D. Quick, Amy Frame, and Joy Chase at FMCH; and Esther Taira, Don Doyle, and Lynne Hickey at LAUSD. The Curriculum Resource Unit published to complement the three exhibitions was developed by Betsy Quick, Lyn Avins, Bradley Shank, Bridget Cooks, Evelyn Carter, and Liz Caffry; it was designed by Anthony A. G. Kluck. We would also like to thank Alicia Katano, Gianna Carotenuto, Craig Woodson, Ilana Gatti, and Natalie Sanderson for their development of FMCH school services and public programs.

Support for the three-institution collaboration was generously provided by the National Endowment for the Humanities, dedicated to expanding American understanding of history and culture. We are extremely grateful for the counsel and encouragement of Nancy Rogers, Director, Division of Public Programs, and Program Officer John Meredith. We would also like to thank Morris A. Kaplan and the Jerome L. Joss Foundation for their continuing support of the Fowler Museum publication program. The City of Los Angeles Cultural Affairs Department and Sony Pictures Entertainment also provided funding for this project.

The essays in this volume were selected and organized by Jacqueline DjeDje, professor of Ethnomusicology at UCLA. We are grateful to Jackie and all the authors for their contributions. Lynne Kostman handled the considerable responsibility of managing the editing of this volume. Her attention to detail and her commitment to keeping the project on schedule were critical and greatly appreciated. Editors Greg Dobie and Michelle Ghaffari are also deserving of thanks for their careful and thoughtful work, as is editorial assistant Ann Molvik. Patrick Fitzgerald designed the publication with sensitivity and insight. Object photography was beautifully executed by Don Cole with the assistance of Jonathan Molvik. As he has for the past eleven years, Danny Brauer supervised the production of this volume as director of Fowler Museum publications.

The catalog section of this volume and the Los Angeles County Museum of Art exhibition are substantially based on a collection of 144 African musical instruments given to the Fowler Museum in 1991 and 1992 by Helen and Dr. Robert Kuhn. This collection was assembled primarily on aesthetic grounds—each instrument a work of art in itself. The generosity of Helen and Bob has sustained many exhibitions of African art in the Los Angeles area and elsewhere over the past thirty years. We are grateful for their long-standing interest in the expressive culture of Africa.

Doran H. Ross
Director
UCLA Fowler Museum of Cultural History

Visiting drummers from Suriname at the third Pan-African Historical Theatre Festival. Photograph by Doran H. Ross, Cape Coast, Ghana, 1997.

Introduction

JACQUELINE COGDELL DJEDJE

At the dawn of the twenty-first century, African music in all of its manifestations has become a global phenomenon. From Asia and the Pacific to Europe and the Americas, musical elements from Africa can be heard in blues, jazz, rap, gospel, rock, country, salsa, reggae, rumba, samba, calypso, *rai*, noise (a fusion of art and popular music), and many other world music genres. Not only do African features serve as the root worldwide for most commercial, secular popular music styles, many sacred music genres include African elements (e.g., lining-out hymns, spirituals, and gospel quartet music).

Although African culture has been enormously influential, the continent continues to be an area of the world that is often ridiculed and belittled, rarely adequately acknowledged for its creations and contributions. Comments made by David Lamb in the 1980s still hold true today:

> No continent has been more mistreated, misunderstood and misreported over the years than Africa. Ask an American to mention four things he associates with Africa and the answer is likely to be "pygmies, jungle, heat and lions." Yet pygmies have been all but extinct for decades, jungle is now as uncommon as snow in Southern California, the heat is no more intolerable than that in Washington, D.C., on a summer's day, and lions are so few in number that most Africans have never seen one. [Lamb 1984, xii]

Without realizing it, many in other cultures embrace African-derived musical traits, particularly when these have been re-created or refashioned into forms that suit their own aesthetic preferences (e.g., jazz and tango). Yet when these same characteristics are used within a context or sensibility that is clearly associated with Africa, much debate arises about the significance or worthiness of the forms (e.g., rap). What accounts for this schizophrenic attitude toward the continent that is considered to be the birthplace of human life? In other words, why are people around the globe at once so attracted to African music and culture and so very critical of it? The central question is: What gives African music its power? It is impossible to give a single answer to this question, and in fact it generates a plethora of others. Do individuals find African and African-derived musics appealing because they permit and encourage freedom of expression, experimentation, and individual interpretation? Is it because African music reflects the spirit of a people who have survived in spite of oppression and suffering? To what extent has African and African-derived music become a mouthpiece for protest? When the Berlin Wall came tumbling down, why did Europeans sing "We Shall Overcome"? To what extent have the media influenced the popularity and power of the music? When African music is adopted and/or appropriated, which African elements are maintained? Which are discarded? To what extent has the fusion of African and European music helped or hindered the popularity of African-derived genres? How have people on the African continent responded to influences from other parts of the world? By no means can the essays in this volume hope to address all these questions. Rather, it is hoped that the material presented here will stimulate discourse and more reflection on these and other issues related to African expressive culture.

This volume has two objectives. First, it is presented as a celebration of African music and culture. *Celebration*, according to *Webster's*, means "to sound the praises of; extol; to make known publicly; proclaim." The decision to use *celebration* in our title aligns this volume with several other works on music, published in the last two decades of the twentieth century that also include the word in their titles: *Repercussions: A Celebration of African-American Music* (1985), *Music of the Common Tongue: Survival and Celebration in Afro-American Music* (1987), and *Africa O-Ye! A Celebration of African Music* (1991). My intent is not to emulate, however, but rather to use a title that captures the meaning and spirit of what Africa represents to world culture. Like me, the authors and editors of these works obviously felt that African music deserved to be praised and honored. In the introduction to *Music of the Common Tongue*, Christopher Small states:

> I have been prompted to write this book by two impulses, one public and general and the other personal and specific, which are inextricably intertwined with each other. The first is a conviction that the time has come, if it is not well overdue, for a recognition, a celebration even, of the central contribution which Africans and people of African descent scattered over the face of the earth have made to the very mainstream of human culture, that is, to the human race's awareness of itself and of the way in which we relate to the world in which we live. [Small 1987, 1]

Dennis Marks, one of the editors of *Repercussions*, indicates that while the book's main title was chosen with some reservations, the subtitle, which includes the word *celebration*, seemed to fit the spirit of what was occurring at the time the television series and book were produced: "It seemed to mirror one aspect of the subject—the increased assurance with which Afro-Americans were reclaiming and celebrating their African heritage" (Marks 1985, 179). Although Graeme Ewens, editor of *Africa O-Ye!*, does not give a reason for the use of the term *celebration*, he states, "'Celebration of African Music' looks at the development of those styles which have crossed over cultural boundaries to find an audience in other parts of Africa or farther afield" (1991, 8).

Our main title, *Turn Up the Volume!*, is for me also related to the concept of celebration, although it can suggest several meanings or interpretations. In Ernest Brown's essay, from which the phrase is borrowed, "turning up the volume in music ...is an essential part of creating...public and psychological ritual spaces" for participants in Trinidad Carnival. For me, "turn up the volume" is a metaphor for individuals heightening their senses, becoming more cognizant, listening more carefully, being more sensitive to the sounds and sights in world culture that are African and African derived. One of the primary reasons Africa is rarely acknowledged is because many people do not know or care to learn about the history, culture, and life of African people. Lamb suggests that Africa's complexity may account for it being so misunderstood:

> If Africa is much discussed and little understood these days, it is hardly surprising, for the continent is as diverse and complex as it is huge. Africa is four times larger than the United States and has twice as many people. It spans seven time zones, and to fly from Nairobi in the east to Dakar, Senegal, in the west takes longer than to fly from New York to London. It is inhabited by 2,000...ethnic groups, most of which have a specific language or dialect. In many capitals you can have lunch with an Oxford-educated businessman who wears three-piece Western suits and asks you about last year's Superbowl game, then drive a few hours and dine on a recently slaughtered goat with...herdsmen who hunt with bows and arrows, live on a barter economy and think all white men are missionaries or doctors. [Lamb 1984, xiii]

Turning up the volume, heightening our awareness, allows us to appreciate and to celebrate the richness and diversity of African cultures that Lamb describes.

A second objective of this publication is to present a panoramic view—geographically and culturally—of the African world through music. Within the last two decades, only a few works, to my knowledge, have attempted to present a holistic discussion of African and

African-derived musics: John Storm Roberts's *Black Music of Two Worlds* (1998 [1972]); Irene V. Jackson's *More Than Drumming: Essays on African and Afro-Latin American Music and Musicians* (1985) and *More Than Dancing: Essays on Afro-American Music and Musicians* (1985); Geoffrey Haydon and Dennis Marks's *Repercussions: A Celebration of African-American Music* (1985); and Ruth M. Stone's *Africa: The Garland Encyclopedia of World Music* (1998). The first of these, *Black Music of Two Worlds*, is written by a single author who relies primarily on secondary sources to present and interpret information. This has advantages in that one person is able to synthesize the material using a single theme or approach, thereby making the discussion clear in terms of its objectives and organization. Because the focus is on African-derived cultures in the Americas, however, Roberts's discussion of Africa as an independent entity is limited. Rather, he treats Africa, Europe, and the Islamic world collectively in an effort to explain the roots for the developments and the syncretism that occurred in the Americas. Although a second edition of *Black Music of Two Worlds* was published in 1998 with a new introduction and many more photographs, it is still essentially a work based on material that was available twenty-five years ago. Irene V. Jackson's two volumes are the most ambitious and comprehensive works published to date. With the first volume focusing on Africa, South America, and the Caribbean, and the second volume centered on the United States, the two provide an extensive amount of information about Africa and developments in the Americas. The only shortcoming is that the amount of material on the Caribbean and South America is limited, and no discussion is included of the African presence in the Arab world or Asia. *Repercussions* is a collection of essays based on the British television series of the same name. With a number of authors who have various disciplinary backgrounds, the work is multivoiced but nonetheless very selective in its coverage of the African world. Three articles focus on Blacks in the United States, and one deals with the Caribbean. Only one region, West Africa, is represented, and Latin America is not included at all. The advantage of this book over others, however, is that each article is accompanied by an excellent video that provides important visual and aural material augmenting the written text. Ruth M. Stone's *Africa* is the most compre-hensive work to date focusing on the continent as an entity. The work is groundbreaking in that North Africa is not partitioned off and treated with Southwest Asia but is instead presented as part of the continent in a holistic manner. Because the primary focus is on developments in Africa, no attempt has been made to investigate areas of the world where African influence can be found. One has to look to the other volumes in the ten-volume series of *The Garland Encyclopedia of World Music* for information on developments in the African Diasporas.

Turn Up the Volume! is distinctive for several reasons. Not only are the majority of articles written by scholars who have training in ethnomusicology, most authors have intimate knowledge about their subjects based on their fieldwork or are themselves culture bearers.[1] Because the volume also accompanies three major exhibitions (*Music in the Life of Africa* at the UCLA Fowler Museum of Cultural History; *Music for the Eyes: The Fine Art of African Musical Instruments* at the Los Angeles County Museum of Art; *and Rhythms of the Soul: African Instruments in the Diaspora* at the California African American Museum), several articles deal with musical instruments. However, unlike Marie-Thérèse Brincard's *Sounding Forms: African Musical Instruments*, which focuses almost entirely on the sculptural aspects of African musical instruments, *Turn Up the Volume!* includes essays that look at the history, morphology, and function of musical instruments; how instruments are used as symbols of culture and identity and as objects for understanding cross-cultural influences; and the use of instruments as the producers of sounds.

The geographical coverage of material in *Turn Up the Volume!* is broad. In addition to information on the major regions in Africa, articles on the Arab Gulf, the Caribbean, and South and North America are featured; these help the reader to recognize African influence as global. Although there has been much debate about cross-cultural influences between Africa and Asia, music scholarship[2] dealing with the impact of African culture on various parts of Asia is still in its infancy.[3] When Roberts first published *Black Music of Two Worlds* in 1972, the most important question was whether Africanisms were still apparent in the culture of the United States. Fortunately, this is no longer an issue; enough research[4] has been presented to demonstrate that African concepts continue to be manifested in the expressive culture of the Americas regardless of the time elapsed since their introduction. Transforming, reinterpreting, and re-creating concepts and features that are African derived continues, because many people of African ancestry intuitively find that the *process* of making music tends to be more important than the product. When one keeps this in mind, it becomes very clear that Africa is not a static entity, nor should African culture and people be regarded as monolithic.

In the performance of African or African-derived musics, it is common for a melody, rhythm, or any other musical idea to be repeated. As the music gains momentum through repetition, this heightens the intensity level of the performance and the involvement of participants. In addition, the repetition lays a foundation for variation or improvisation, which may occur concurrently during the performance. Thus, the cycle is an organizing principle often used for many African musical forms. Although a continuous repetition does not occur, the organization of the essays in this work also forms a circle. The first few essays in *Turn Up the Volume!* begin with Africa. From there, we move to the various African Diasporas. The last two essays deal with the return of Africa-derived musics to the homeland, the source of origin. Through a process of feedback (Collins 1987), Africa becomes an extension or a part of the Diasporas, functioning as a source *and* as an entity within them. With time, the cycle will begin again when the reinvented or syncretic form that has been reintroduced to Africa is reappropriated and re-created by those outside the Motherland.[5] Thus, the subject matter of the essays comes full circle, demonstrating the dynamic and innovative power of African music.

The essays in part one, "Music in African Life," can be subdivided into three groups: (1) musical instruments, (2) musical events, and (3) music and musical instruments as symbols of culture. The three essays in the first group provide extensive information on the history, function, and aesthetic qualities of individual instruments and groups of instruments. The first essay, "African and African American Lamellophones" by Gerhard Kubik, deals with the lamellophone, an instrumental type indigenous to the African continent. Kubik states that these instruments "have no counterparts in other musical cultures. Their invention and development in very specific areas of sub-Saharan Africa can be taken for certain." Kubik's work is remarkable for its thoroughness; he discusses terminology, construction, classification, tunings, playing techniques, and history, as well as the instrument's distribution within Africa and the Americas. From his work, one derives a complete picture of the lamellophone and its development in Africa and the Americas.

Although the xylophone, or *balafon*, can be found in various parts of Central, East, and Southeast Africa, Heather

Maxwell's essay focuses on the use of the instrument among Mande and Voltaic peoples who live in the savanna regions of West Africa. Her essay includes some discussion of the history, distribution, terminology, and tunings of the xylophone, but her primary focus is on how individuals interact with the instrument: "people use them, appreciate them, and create them." For Maxwell, "learning about xylophone music culture provides a window into the diverse complexity of West African societies and worldviews." Not only does Maxwell draw on the personal narratives of musicians to discuss tuning, classification, and performance aesthetics, she uses their voices to explain how the instrument "speaks" (communicates) with the spiritual and human world at performance events.

In "African Traditional Musical Instruments in Neo-African Idioms and Contexts," Akin Euba explains that traditional music and ritual arts are alive and well in modern Africa. Instead of bemoaning the death of traditional practices and ritual arts, Euba believes that many can and have been saved through secularization. His article includes discussion of new idioms (church music, popular music, music theater, and modern art music) in which traditional music is now employed, and he indicates as well that traditional musical instruments will continue to survive because of their use in modern contexts. While these changes are not without problems, Euba feels that there are benefits. African music survives because the adaptation of instruments creates new functions and new voices, which lead to a new aesthetic. Eventually, the innovations become traditions. Thus, neo-African idioms serve as a conduit for the maintenance of tradition.

In many African societies, events of the life cycle (e.g., birth, initiation, marriage, death) provide opportunities to participate in music making as well as to establish greater social cohesion within the community. Thus, the celebration of a rite of passage serves several functions:

> The performance of music in such contexts, therefore, assumes a multiple role in relation to the community: it provides at once an opportunity for sharing in creative experience, for participating in music as a form of community experience, and for using music as an avenue for the expression of group sentiments. [Nketia 1974, 22]

The essays by Lester Monts and Jean Kidula deal with two different events or rites of passage: the funeral and the initiation. In "Ritual, Lore, and Music in the Pre-Islamic Vai Funerary Sequence," Monts not only discusses Vai philosophies and myths about death, he presents information on funeral musical practices and the roles of ancestors, musicians, and other specialists who participate in funeral activities. Although Monts makes note of changes that have taken place in Vai culture as a result of the fusion of Islamic and traditional culture, the most important aspect of the essay is his discussion of the funerary sequence. He gives detailed descriptions of each stage of the event and comments on the significance of the rituals and changes that have occurred over time. Because musical instruments and other forms of musical material culture have always played primary roles in the celebration of death, a comparison of the present-day Islamic rites with those from the pre-Islamic period provides an important source for reconstructing African music history.

In "*Ingolole:* Then We Shall See," Jean Kidula discusses her encounter with *ingolole*—the mask worn by young males among the Tiriki people of Kenya during their initiation rites. She begins with her earliest childhood recollection of the events surrounding the mask and the transformative effects wearing it had in her village. Her discussion is presented from the perspective of a spectator—a female and member of another cultural group. The initiation, which is the most important rite of passage for males, signifies physically (through circumcision) and symbolically the adolescent's transition to adulthood. As Kidula aptly demonstrates, music and dance play integral roles at virtually every step in this process.

The final group of essays in part one is concerned with the deeper meaning and function of music making in society. In "The Fulbe Fiddle In The Gambia: A Symbol of Ethnic Identity," I explain that the fiddle is one of the few instruments in Senegambia that is identified with Fulbe culture. This is significant as the Fulbe have always lived in multicultural settings where they rarely constitute a majority. In contexts where intercultural contacts are commonplace, individuals create markers or symbols to distinguish themselves from others. For the Fulbe, the fiddle serves this function. Therefore, knowledge about the fiddle allows one, in turn, to learn more about Fulbe culture, history, and identity. Included in the essay are an ethnography of Fulbe music and culture and a more detailed analysis of the Fulbe fiddle tradition; together they clarify ways in which intercultural relations can affect the history and development of a musical tradition.

In "The *Luŋa* Drum as Social Mediator among the Dagbamba of Ghana," Leigh Creighton discusses the importance of the drum as a conduit for the transmission of cultural information between members of the community. Unlike other musical forms in which the transferral of textual information is conducted mainly through the voice, Dagbamba musicians make their instruments speak. She explains that the Dagbamba have created a system of human surrogation in which important cultural information is imparted not from person to person but from musical instrument to person. Her description of the Damba festival, an important performance event at which the *luŋa* and other instruments within the ensemble are used, clearly shows how the instrument functions and how praise songs and proverbs are used to deal with topics that might be deemed too sensitive or offensive in direct communication. The role of the *luŋa* has interesting parallels with that of the linguist in many African societies.

Cynthia Tse Kimberlin's work on Ethiopia allows us to see how war and political and social upheaval, which have become more and more commonplace in many parts of Africa in the late twentieth century, have affected music making and expressive culture. Not only has political and social strife given rise to a new song repertoire, vocal performance style, and innovations in the construction and use of instruments, the marketing and distribution of music have changed and musical genres that were once forbidden or banned are now openly performed. For example, between 1974 and 1991, the *bagana* (also *begena, begenna*), the ten-string plucked lyre reputed to be descended from David's harp, as well as the performance of solo religious songs, was forbidden in public and not to be mentioned in the media. Since the ban on religious worship has been lifted, the *bagana* and religious music are performed in public with overflowing attendance at churches. This article forces us to keep in perspective the myriad factors that can affect musical change in modern Africa. It also shows how the creative essence within the human spirit helps individuals to conquer forces that are socially devastating.

Part two of *Turn Up the Volume!* focuses on the music of the African Diaspora(s) and cross-cultural influences. The essays treat four areas: the Arab Gulf, the Caribbean and South America, the United States, and Africa itself. As Ali Jihad Racy indicates, "cross-cultural studies ...make us more conscious of the individuality of musical cultures." As musical traditions are modified when they move from place to place, it is important to determine what remains the same, what changes, and why innovations take place.

Modifications may occur in instrumental construction, repertoire, symbolic meaning, and social function. To date, as noted previously, most research on the African Diaspora has been concerned with developments in the Americas; only minimal attention has been given to African influence in Asia. The reason why people of African ancestry in Asia have not been more visible or vocal in discoursing about their association with their homeland is an issue that needs to be discussed. It is only recently that scholars have begun to investigate how the movement of Africans into various parts of Asia has affected music making there.

Instead of limiting their discussion to survivals and retentions, the majority of authors here are more interested in other stages in the process; most show how African elements have been transformed and reinterpreted into other traditions. Whether individuals consciously recognize or acknowledge their African ancestry is not the issue. Rather, it is fascinating to observe that an African "feel" continues to be present as people *unconsciously* perform and create their music. As Ernest Brown explains, "It [Trinidad Carnival] incorporates innovation, yet does not abandon older traditions." Also, whereas African practices and performance were once ridiculed, they are now gaining acceptance. Vodou, for example, has survived to the point that it is now accepted as a legitimate religion in Haiti.

In "The Lyre of the Arab Gulf," Racy not only discusses the history of the lyre but explains that the instrument used in the Gulf is closely related to that played by Africans in Ethiopia, Uganda, and Kenya. Similarities appear in the number of strings, playing technique, construction, tuning, and decoration. More importantly, the use of the Arab Gulf lyre for healing and treating those thought to be possessed by spirits provides additional evidence of its connection to groups in East Africa: "The distribution of the lyre can shed light over the various ethnic, political, and artistic contacts between Southwest Asia and East Africa. Indeed, the return of the ancient lyre to the Arab Gulf and southern Iraq in the form of the *tanbūrah* can be viewed as the completion of an old geographical and historical cycle."

Brown's essay, "'Turn Up the Volume!' The African Aesthetic in Trinidad's Carnival Music," explains that even with the creation of new genres and performance traditions, African influence continues to be an important aspect of expressive culture in the Americas. He discovers that although the musical sounds used to fuel Trinidad Carnival parades may have changed over the past 150 years, the aesthetic goals of the enslaved Africans who were brought to Trinidad are still being realized, albeit through different means. From African drumming to quieter tamboo bamboo bands and Venezuelan-style string and wind bands, from the steelbands to the massive sound trucks playing prerecorded music or carrying live bands, African elements continue to dominate. Instead of lamenting the loss of old traditions or criticizing the electronic and technological advances that seem to be encroaching on "traditional" musical practices, Brown's article demonstrates that scholars need to be more sensitive in their study of innovations. What on the surface may appear to be an aberration (e.g., electronic and other types of technological developments now used in music), may in fact be a new and different manifestation of an African aesthetic.

Articles by Victoria Simmons ("The Voice of Ginen: Drums in Haitian Religion, History, and Identity") and Clarence Henry ("The African Legacy: The Use of Music and Musical Instruments in the Candomblé Religion of Salvador da Bahia, Brazil") complement each other, for both focus on the use of African-derived instruments in the sacred world. Whereas Simmons is more concerned with the history of the religion and how it interfaces with class in Haiti, however, Henry tends to focus on the city of Salvador as the context for the development of religion. Together, the articles by Simmons and Henry show what happens to new creations when major or subtle differences exist in the history, culture, and ethnic origin of the involved groups.

Simmons's article includes much historical information on Vodou in Haiti, noting the ambivalence that the Haitian elite (who, during the early twentieth century, identified more closely with Europe than Africa) maintained toward the religion, as well as the persecution that Vodou adherents experienced. Although many similarities exist in African-derived religious practices in the Americas, Simmons notes that Haitian Vodou differs from other African-derived religions because the ethnicity of African groups that had the greatest influence in Haiti differed from that of groups in other areas. Whereas Yorùbá culture was the dominating force in music and religious practices in Cuba and Brazil, the Fon of Benin (formerly known as Dahomey) had the greatest impact on the developments in Haiti. Her study makes us realize that scholars need to be aware of the differentiation that exists in Africa (Ginen) and to include this as a factor for understanding what occurred in the Americas. The varied conditions that Africans endured in slavery (European attitudes, type of work, social conditions, etc.) also affected what they were able to transform and the manner in which they were able to create new traditions in the Americas.

Henry's study of Candomblé gives much detailed information on the structure and ritual practices used, as well as the role of music and dance in the religion. As a result of commercialization, Candomblé has become an important part of Brazilian culture, serving as a national symbol for the country and its people. What is particularly fascinating is his discussion of how the religion has become a mediator between the rich and poor, the upper and lower classes, the rulers and ruled. In addition, Henry provides a detailed account of an actual Candomblé ceremony.

Together, the essays by Brown, Simmons, and Henry show how Africans in the respective countries have used African elements to suit their aesthetic preferences. Because the common element in the three countries under consideration is Catholicism, one would think that parallel developments would have occurred. However, because the European populations were different (Spanish and English in Trinidad, French in Haiti, and Portuguese in Brazil), their attitudes toward slavery differed, the history of Africans in the three countries differed, the development of the physical spaces differed, and the ethnic origin of the religions (e.g., Fon in Haiti and Yorùbá in Brazil) differed. This makes the reinterpretation of African traits in the various parts of the Americas quite distinct. Yet in the secular and sacred world, Africa continues to be pervasive in many aspects of these societies.

Kazadi wa Mukuna's "Ethno-musicology and the study of Africanisms in the Music of Latin America" outlines the different approaches that scholars have used to study Latin American music from the eighteenth century to the present. During the period of awakening interest, European travelers reported on African music and dances using Europe as a frame of reference. While they provided eyewitness accounts of various geographical regions, their reports were not interpretive but rather important for the iconographic details about instruments that they provided. Kazadi suggests that scholars began to identify and describe music and dance during the early twentieth century as a reflection of trends occurring in the field of ethnomusicology (or comparative musicology as it was referred to at that time). It was not until the mid-twentieth century that researchers became interested in identifying and describing the function of idioms found in Latin America and relating these to an African origin. Great emphasis was placed on the degree to which elements were maintained and reinterpreted in the Americas. Finally, as Kazadi suggests, scholars began to approach the material holistically, and conceptual and contextual analysis began to occur. While some took an anthropological approach, many were grounded in ethnomusicology.

The essays by Gerhard Kubik and Eddie Meadows also complement each other. Both authors argue that the performance practices associated with instruments used by Blacks in the United States have their origin in Africa. Interestingly, both deal with individuals and instrumental traditions from the Mississippi Delta region, Mississippi and Louisiana, respectively—areas of the country where African presence is believed to be very strong. Both use the family history of a single individual as a basis for analyzing the resilience and transformation of the instrumental tradition.

In "Reflections on Eli Owens's Mouth-Bow: African American One-Stringed Instrumental Traditions and Their African Backgrounds," Gerhard Kubik presents an interesting discussion of the maintenance of the musical bow and monochord zither in the Americas. Particularly noteworthy are his report on the history and distribution of the instrument and his discussion of how the musical bow has been transformed in construction and function. Inspired by the family history of Eli Owens, a Mississippian able to trace his mouth-bow playing technique to family members who lived during the nineteenth century, Kubik compares traits found in the American version to those observed in Africa. While Kubik is not able to trace the musical bow to any specific African bow tradition, his analysis provides a convincing argument that features associated with the American mouth-bow can be found among groups in several African regions.

The conditions of slavery experienced by Africans brought to the United States did not permit the survival of Africanisms to the same extent that is evident in the Caribbean and Latin America. Because of this, one must look beyond questions of origins, precursors, and survivals in studying Black music in North America. In "Africa and Jazz: The Melo-Rhythmic Essence of Warren 'Baby' Dodds," Meadows does not attempt to draw a direct connection between Dodds's music and a particular African performance tradition. Rather, he argues that there is sufficient family resemblance to *suggest* that the music of Dodds is African derived. By analyzing Dodds's family history (his maternal great grandfather played African drums in New Orleans's Congo Square during the mid-nineteenth century and taught him to make the drums "talk"), Meadows provides the necessary link between Africa and Dodds. In addition to discussing Dodds's learning period, philosophy, and the uniqueness of his drum set, Meadows shows how Dodds's drumming techniques and performance style relate to Meki Nzewi's concept of melo-rhythm. A selected discography of Dodds's recordings accompanies the article.

The last three essays concern specific popular music genres in three areas of the Diaspora: the United States, West Africa, and Southern Africa/ United States. Although it began in the Bronx, rap music has become one of the most important musical creations of the late twentieth century. Not only is it a vehicle for protest and a means of personal expression for urban youth, the media and commercial world have capitalized on the idiom as it has gained popularity worldwide. In "Musical Collages of Sound: Technologizing the Band in the Rap Music Tradition," Cheryl Keyes explains how the mixing of records by mobile disc jockeys became a competitive art that transformed the record turntable into a musical instrument. Her essay explores the impact of music technology on rap music and describes the aesthetic choices rap disc jockeys make in producing simulated instrumental sounds. These developments in rap, in many ways, parallel the new technological innovations in music that are occurring in Trinidad. Juxtaposing the Keyes and Brown articles allows us to see how individuals who are impacted by some of the same life forces respond by creating something similar yet different.

In "The Introduction As Signature: An Analysis of Western Musical Instruments in *Chimurenga, Mbaqanga,* and *Motown,*" Kimasi Browne examines the use of Western instruments in the introductions of popular music in Zimbabwe, South Africa, and the United States. After presenting the historical background and context for the development of commercial popular music in the three countries, Browne looks at what one can learn from the musical introduction of a song. Through the analysis of selected pieces, Browne finds that popular musicians in the three countries use similar but nonetheless distinct techniques to introduce their compositions. The intention is not to tell us that one is directly related to the other; rather, the essay provides an interesting discussion of how musicians creatively organize their material.

The *gumbe* frame drum, usually identified with Jamaica but found as well in several Caribbean cultures, provides the first evidence of the feedback process or return of African expressive culture to the continent. In his article "The Role of the *Gumbe* in Popular Music and Dance Styles in Sierra Leone," Christian Horton discusses the historical linkages and cross-cultural influences that tie the *gumbe* to Africa. He then focuses on the readaptation of the instrument in popular music and dance styles in Sierra Leone. The return of the instrument to Sierra Leone has sparked new musical creations and helped several musicians to become important innovators.

The articles in *Turn Up the Volume!* deal with a number of themes: history and ethnography; resilience and transformation; the sacred and the secular; tradition and innovation; popular music and art music; the rural and the urban; the acoustic and the technological; the individual and the collective; identity, ethnicity, and class; instruments as physical objects and instruments as symbols of culture; idioms that are traditional or ethnic and those formed from interethnic or national ties. In addition, the book focuses on several regions of the world where African presence has made a significant impact musically. It is hoped that this volume not only celebrates Africa and African music but will help the reader to gain a better understanding of the African world and its complexities. Though there is enormous diversity, a significant unity also exists. As various cultures and groups in the world continue to be affected by Africa, new creations and new aesthetics will develop and eventually return to their source of origin where the cycle begins again. Thus, African music will continue to be a global phenomenon, a dynamic and living force that gives and receives life as it reinvents itself.

Tunisia
Morocco
Algeria
Libya
Egypt
Western Sahara
Mauritania
Mali
Niger
Chad
Sudan
Eritrea
Djibouti
The Gambia
Senegal
Guinea Bissau
Guinea
Burkina Faso
Benin
Togo
Nigeria
Sierra Leone
Côte d'Ivoire
Ghana
Liberia
Ethiopia
Central African Republic
Cameroon
Somalia
Equatorial Guinea
São Tomé and Príncipe
Gabon
Republic of the Congo
Uganda
Kenya
Rwanda
Democratic Republic of the Congo
Burundi
Indian Ocean
Atlantic Ocean
Tanzania
Comoros
Angola
Malawi
Zambia
Mozambique
Zimbabwe
Madagascar
Namibia
Botswana
Swaziland
Lesotho
South Africa
0
300 mi
0
600 km

PART ONE:
Music in African Life

Atumpan drummer at the Odwira festival. Photograph by Doran H. Ross, Abeadze Dominase, Ghana, 1975.

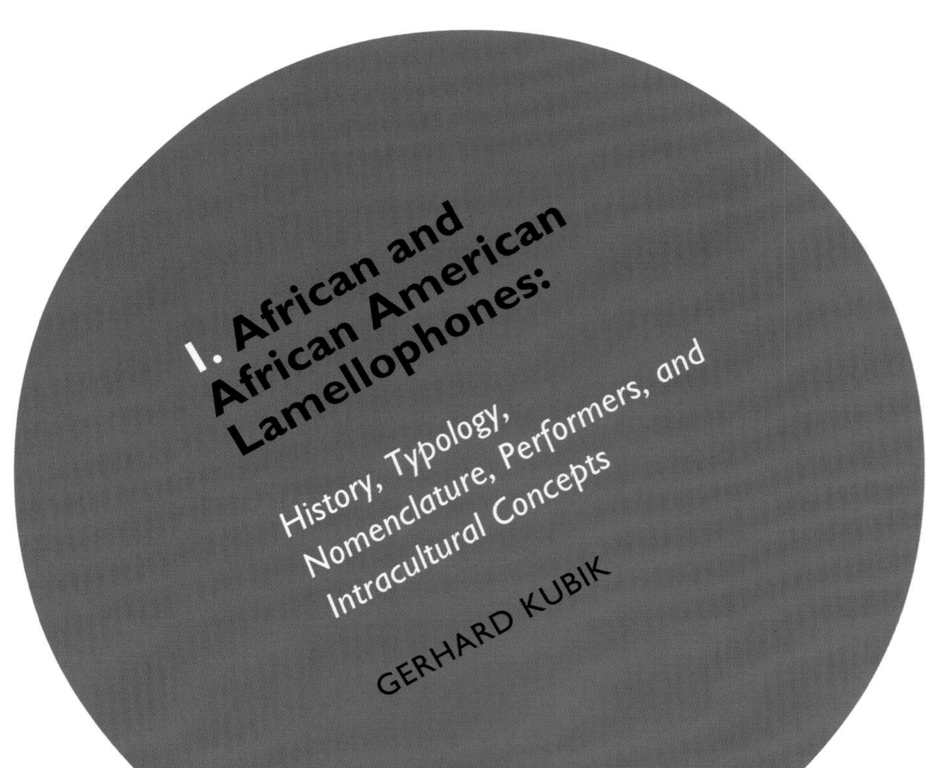

Lamellophones constitute a particularly important and ramified family of African musical instruments. In the Hornbostel/Sachs worldwide classification of musical instruments (1914) they are characterized as *Zupfidiophone* (in translation, "plucked idiophones," see Baines and Wachsmann 1961). "Lamellae, i.e., elastic plaques, fixed at one end, are flexed and then released to return to their position of rest" (Hornbostel/Sachs 1914, trans. Baines and Wachsmann 1961, 16).

General Characteristics

Lamellae can be fastened to a soundboard or frame using a variety of methods. The sound-producing principle of a lamellophone is the actuation with a finger of the freely vibrating *end* of a lamella. This is not "plucking," however, in the sense of a picking or pulling action, as when playing a stringed instrument. As Hornbostel and Sachs suggested, the action of playing can be more accurately described as depressing and releasing a lamella's free end with a finger, usually the thumb. In Zimbabwe and central Cameroon, performers often use thumbs and index fingers. In these cases the index finger "plucks" one of the outer lamellae of the arrangement in an upward movement.

The principles of actuation of a lamella are universally known. In cultures outside Africa, the Jew's harp, or guimbard, for example, could be described as a one-note lamellophone. Only in sub-Saharan Africa, however, was the technology developed to make multinote instruments of complex design. The basic idea of the African lamellophone is that a variable number of manufactured lamellae are attached to a (mostly wooden) body that constitutes a soundboard and may also form a resonator. For manufacturing the lamellae, steel from a variety of sources or vegetable materials—such as the epidermis of a raffia stem leaf, cane, or bamboo—are used. Most lamellophones surviving in museum collections have iron lamellae. It has never been clarified, however, which surviving specimens have iron lamellae that were indeed manufactured by a blacksmith from locally melted iron ore. Most of the specimens collected in the second half of the nineteenth and first half of the twentieth century were manufactured using a variety of nonindigenous sources, such as old nails, springs, umbrella ribs, sheet metal, etc.

There are several methods of attaching the lamellae to the soundboard, all of which are intended to facilitate the tuning process. In most lamellophones the various methods allow for periodic retuning of the instrument by its owner. A common and simple method is illustrated in figure 1.1. Here several lamellae are laid out on a soundboard (in this particular case with a hollowed-out wooden body) across two parallel, horizontal bars. The upper bar is a piece of wood, and it is called the "backrest" in English, following a proposal by Andrew Tracey (1969). The lower bar can be S- or U-shaped in order to prevent it from moving, or it can be inserted into a groove across the soundboard. It is made of iron and called a "bridge." To hold the lamellae in position, an iron pressure bar (also called "straining bar" in the literature) is fastened horizontally on top of the lamellae, between bridge and backrest. A variety of methods can be used to attach the straining bar, depending on local tradition. The method shown in figure 1.1—a commonly used one—entails binding it with strong wire threaded through tiny holes in the soundboard. The lamellae stick out at different lengths over the bridge. They are fastened firmly enough to prevent them from moving out of position during playing, but they can still be shifted and adjusted by the performer, if the need arises to retune the instrument.

In the process of tuning, the vibrating section of a lamella is pulled at an appropriate length over the bridge. The greater the length, the deeper the pitch. Pitch and sound spectrum are also influenced by factors other than length. These include shape (e.g., straight or spatula-shaped), width (broad or thin), thickness. and flexibility (see Andrew Tracey 1969 on the results of his experiments with *mbira* notes). Another method of tuning, which is often used in combination with the former, is found in several lamellophones from Angola and central Cameroon. This entails attaching a lump of black beeswax in an appropriate quantity under the protruding end of the

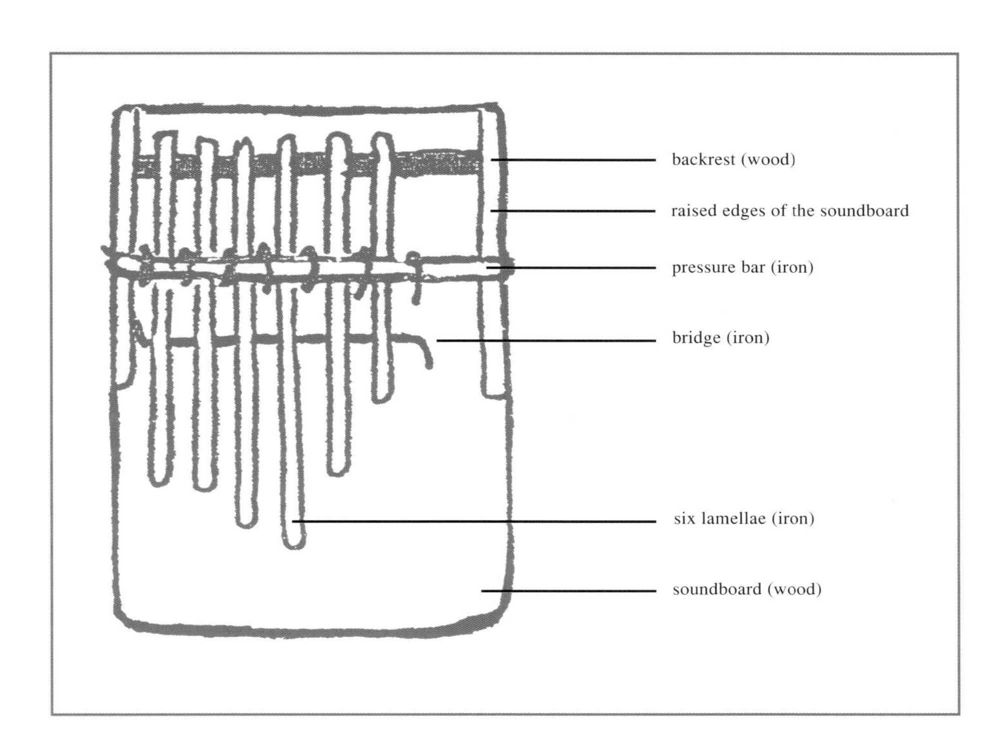

1.1 Basic construction design of a lamellophone. This example is a *sansi* with six iron notes and a shallowly hollowed-out, tray-shaped body. It was recorded as played by N. G. Murimanthewe, about fifty-five years old, at Chakumbira village, north of Mwanza, Malawi, April 1967 (orig. tape no. 30 and notes Djenda/Kubik, Museum für Völkerkunde, Berlin). Drawing by Gerhard Kubik.

1.2 A blacksmith makes a new lamella (*ngeya*) in a workshop inside the *ndzango*, the men's assembly place, in a Mbwela/Nkhangala village of southeastern Angola. He works at his small iron anvil (*lisiki*), which rests on an oblong foundation of wood. Holding the lamella with the special pincers in his left hand, he files the metal to produce an even spatula shape, thereby also eliminating the possibility of distracting overtones. The new lamella will replace one that was broken on the *cisanzi calungandu* that leans against the log. Photograph by Gerhard Kubik, Sangombe village, north of Kwitu-Kwanavale, Kwandu Kuvangu Province, southeastern Angola, September 1965.

lamella. The more wax one applies, the lower the pitch becomes. Elsewhere, in Indonesia for example (see Jones 1963), a related technique is used for xylophones.

In the cultures of sub-Saharan Africa, the basic principles that I have outlined have been combined, creatively modified, expanded, and supplemented by additional technical devices, giving rise to a fascinating typological variety underlining the long history of this instrument. Before the permanent extinction of many types and the ongoing decrease in the diversity of forms that has occurred since the mid-twentieth century, there existed in Africa an impressive wealth of forms with unheard-of technical innovations and sometimes idiosyncratic playing techniques. This is evident from the systematic study of the thousands of specimens preserved in American, European, and other museums and private collections, as well as from systematic work in the field.

African lamellophones have no counterparts in other musical cultures. Their invention and development in very specific areas of sub-Saharan Africa can be taken for certain. From the sixteenth to the nineteenth century a few types spread to the Americas with the slave trade, particularly to the Caribbean and South America where they gave rise to the development of new varieties.

Western Terminology

Up to the early 1960s this class of instruments was summarized in museum notes and writings under the designation *sansa* (see Ankermann 1901), or *sanza* in French (Laurenty 1962). This misnomer originated with David Livingstone's (1865; 1875) misspelling of the Nyungwe and Maŋanja terms *nsansi* and *sansi,* respectively, which are used in the lower Zambezi/Shire River areas of Mozambique (see Hugh Tracey 1961; Kubik 1999).

To resolve this problem, Hugh Tracey (1953; 1961) proposed to use *mbira* as a generic term in instrument classification. The geographical distribution of this term, however, is limited to Zimbabwe and adjacent areas, and as a word stem it is also used to form xylophone designations. Meanwhile, the indiscriminate use of the term *mbira* in writings about lamellophones from regions as far off as Ghana—and even with reference to specimens from the Caribbean (see Thompson 1975/76) and Brazil (Thiermann 1972), where both the term and the types of lamellophones associated with it are unknown—has created some confusion. It can also seriously affect conclusions about the history of area-specific types and their paths of migration. Generally, it is advisable *not* to use names in African languages with their specific meanings and regional distribution in a universal instrument classification system, as this distorts and corrupts the original semantic fields. Similar problems were created by the defective use of another Southeast African term, *marimba,* especially in early ethnomusicological writings (see Husmann 1936).

In 1966 I suggested therefore that we use the designation *lamellophone* as a neutral term for this family of instruments in the major European languages (see Kubik 1966a, 277; 1966b, 42, English and French version; Kubik 1966c, 153). This would also replace other misnomers such as "thumb piano," "hand piano," and the like.

The African Nomenclature and What We Can Learn from It

Designations for lamellophones in African languages vary with the language, its phonetics, the geographical area, the type of instrument, local classification systems,[1] and, more rarely, with the social context. The study of variations and naming practices is not only an important part of cognitively oriented research in African music, it also gives us clues for the reconstruction of cross-regional relationships, migration routes, typological genealogies, and chronological patterns in the sequence of inventions. Some of the current designations of lamellophones are shared with other instrument types, a fact that is in itself conclusive. The chart shown at the right (fig. 1.3) introduces us to a few common designations in African languages, the types to which they refer, and their areas of distribution.

1.3 Common Designations for Lamellophones in a Variety of African Languages

Designation	Organological type	Ethnic-linguistic group	Distribution area (country, etc.)
mbira or *mbila*	nonspecific, also for one-note xylophone; lamellophones usually with many lamellae in two ranks	-Shona and other peoples in southeast Africa (T.11–15 Bantu)	Zimbabwe; central Mozambique
malimba or *marimba*	nonspecific; also (on the Tanzanian coast) for xylophones	(a) -Dzimba, -Phodzo (b) -Kisi, -Pangwa, -Bena, etc. (c) -Zaramo (D.15, N.46, G.67. 65.64:33 Bantu)	Mozambique; southern Malawi; coast of Tanzania, southwestern Tanzania
nsansi or *sansi*	nonspecific, but exclusively used for lamellophones; preferably large types with up to 36 lamellae in two ranks, and gourd resonator	-Nyungwe and other ethnic groups	Central Mozambique; southern Malawi
kalimba	small specimens (a) with a fan-shaped soundboard (b) with a box resonator; some with mirliton	(a) -Chewa, -Lala, etc. (b) -Tumbuka (N.3lb, M.52, N.21a, Bantu)	Malawi; Zambia
ilimba	box-resonated, large with spider-web mirliton; rattle rings slung round the lamellae; reference lamellae for tuning	-Gogo (G.11, Bantu)	central Tanzania
likembe (pl. *ma-*)	box-resonated, specific shape with cut-out section at the back; rattle rings; vibrato hole; mostly 8 to 12 lamellae	many ethnic groups across Central Africa	Congo/Zaire; Republic of Congo; Angola; northwestern Zambia; Central African Republic; etc.
kadongo (pl. *bu-*)	derivative of the *likembe*; oval resonator made of sheet iron; vibrato hole; 12 lamellae	-Soga; -Gwere (E.16, E.17, Bantu)	Uganda
cisanzi (pl. *vi-*)	generic designation for several lamellophone types; mostly board- or tray-shaped	-Mbwela, -Nkhangala, -Lucazi, and other languages (K.13, Bantu)	Angola; northwestern Zambia
kaŋombyo	"Caprivi" type; fan-shaped soundboard; two ranks of lamellae	-Subia, -Lozi (K.42, K.21, Bantu)	Namibia; western Zambia
mucapata (also *cisaji camucapata*) (pl. *mi-*)	bell-shaped resonator; specific arrangement of lamellae	-Cokwe (K.11, Bantu)	Angola, southern Congo/Zaire
mbø ŋgo	raffia lamellophone, with raft-shaped soundboard	Tikar (I.A.5, Benue-Congo)	Cameroon
timbrh	lamellophone with raffia notes, raft- or box-shaped resonator; use of black wax for tuning	Vute (I.A.5, Benue-Congo)	Cameroon
agidigbo	lamellophone with large box; broad lamellae from sheet iron; few lamellae	Yorùbá (I.A.4, Kwa)	Nigeria

The data in this chart come from my own field notes (1959–1993) in the countries concerned. Ethnic-linguistic groups speaking Bantu languages have been identified according to Malcolm Guthrie (1948) as to language zone and group, e.g., T.11 indicates zone T, group 10, language 11. Speakers of non-Bantu languages and those otherwise classed as Semi-Bantu or Bantoid are listed according to Joseph Greenberg's universal classification of African languages (1966), e.g., I.A.4, Kwa. In Greenberg's classification, all Bantu languages fall under I.A.5, Benue-Congo.

Although African lamellophone nomenclature is diversified, patterns and recurrent strands can be observed:

1. Very few designations are restricted to a single language. Normally they are shared by speakers of neighboring languages with small variation in pronunciation or syllable construction. Many terms have regionally definable distribution areas.
2. In Bantu-language speaking parts of Africa, that is, in most of the subcontinent, many designations can be reduced to variations of *four* particularly recurrent word stems of nouns to which different prefixes are attached, according to the class system of the local language and desired meanings (see Kubik 1964b; 1965). These four most widely distributed word stems are -LIMBA (-RIMBA), -MBILA (-MBIRA), -SANSI (-SANJI, -SANZI), and -KEMBE. It should be noted that [l] and [r] are interchangeable in many Bantu languages, forming one and the same phoneme.

The -LIMBA/-RIMBA Stem

Equipped with different prefixes, this word stem is concentrated in Southeast Africa with extensions into Tanzania, Angola, and the southern Democratic Republic of the Congo (fig. 1.4). It is used both for lamellophones and xylophones. In some languages of Bantu language zone N, group 30, such as Cinyanja, Chicheŵa, and Chimaŋanja, there is a verb *kulimba,* meaning "to be firm, hard, strong," etc., properties that would apply to the characteristics of a xylophone key or a lamellophone note. Whether the noun stem -LIMBA/-RIMBA can be linked to the semantics of this verb, as proposed by George T. Nurse (1970, 34), however, is still controversial.

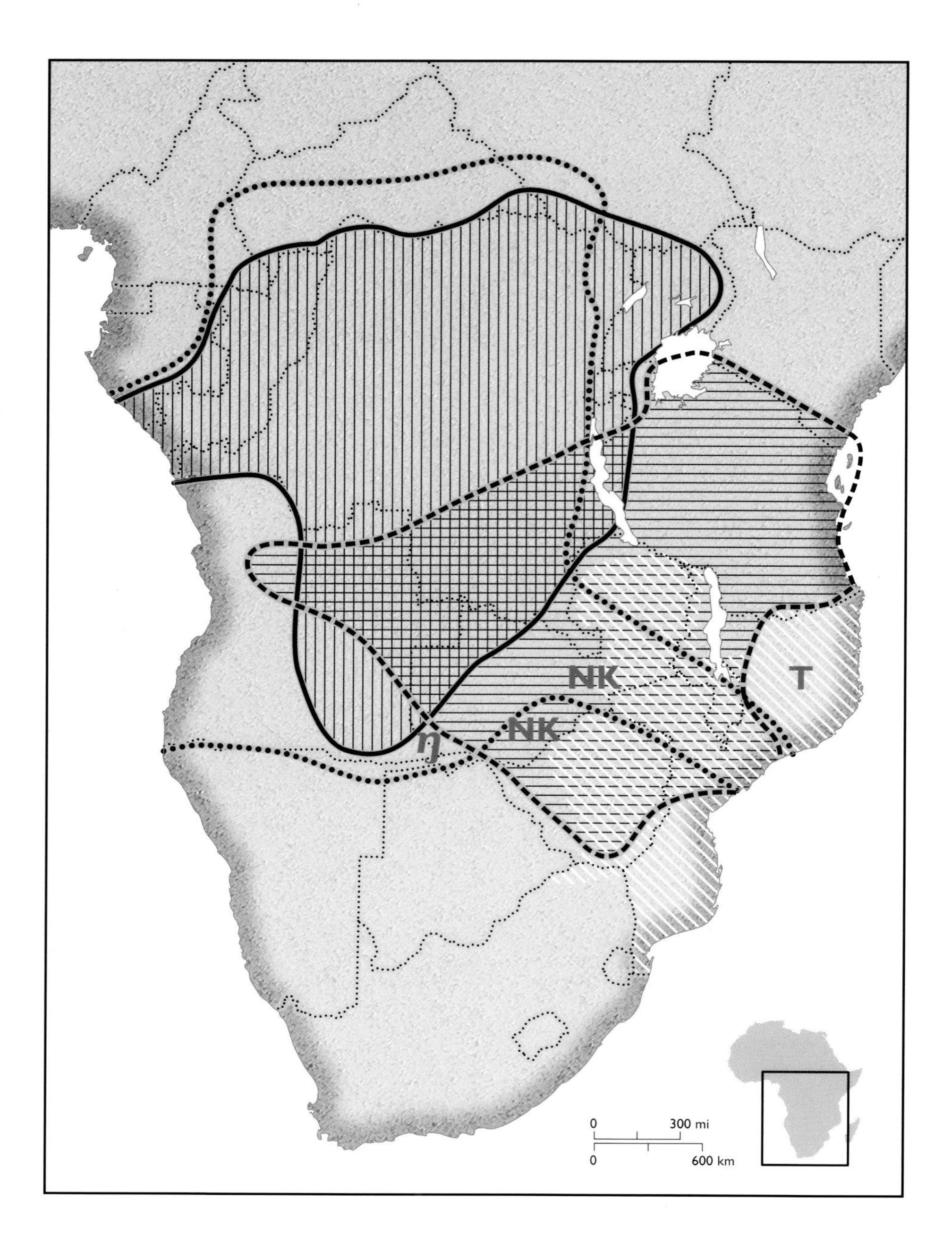

1.4 Geographical distribution of four prominent noun stems used in lamellophone names by the mid-twentieth century. Based on data from fieldwork by Hugh Tracey (1961; 1969; 1973), Andrew Tracey (1972), Margot Dias (1986), Maurice Djenda, Gerhard Kubik, and Moya A. Malamusi (field notes to recordings archived in the Museum für Völkerkunde, Berlin).

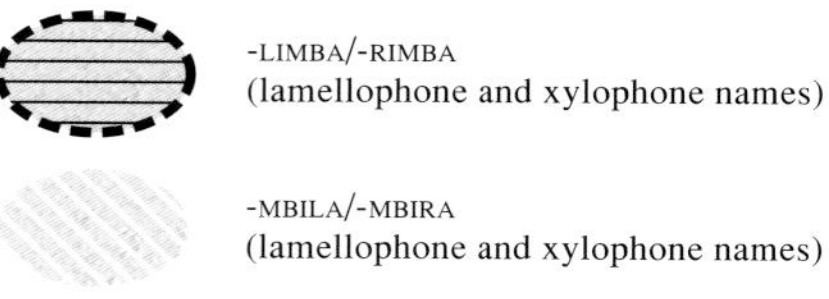

-LIMBA/-RIMBA
(lamellophone and xylophone names)

-MBILA/-MBIRA
(lamellophone and xylophone names)

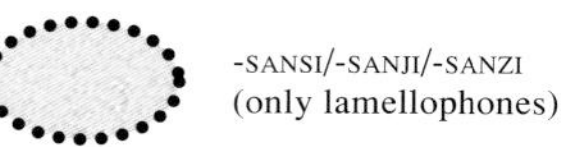

-SANSI/-SANJI/-SANZI
(only lamellophones)

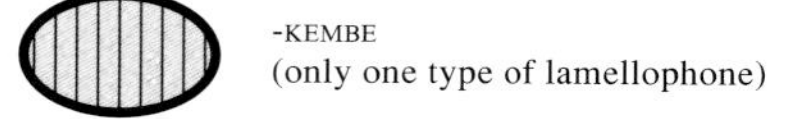

-KEMBE
(only one type of lamellophone)

Approximate areas
of three additional designations:
T = *shitata* or *shityatya*
ŋ = *kaŋombyo*
NK = *kankobele*

A one-note, gourd-resonated xylophone common among the -Maŋanja as an instrument connected to the reverence of ancestral spirits is called *limba*. Several of these one-note xylophones are played together and are then called *alimba* (field notes Lidiya Malamusi/G. Kubik, Bwanansompho village, Blantyre District, Malawi, 1987). One-note xylophones spread as far north as Katanga with eighteenth-century trading connections; among the -Luba they are known as *didimbàdimbà* (pl. *ma-*, see Gansemans 1980, 39), which demonstrates some of the modifications the -LIMBA stem can undergo, in this particular case by reduplication of the word stem and phonetic shift, [l] transformed into [d], as well as the addition of the prefix *di-* (a phonetic variation of the common *li-* prefix in other Bantu languages).

Among the -Dzimba and -Phodzo of central Mozambique and the southern tip of Malawi, *malimba* is the term for a large bell-shaped and gourd-resonated lamellophone with twenty-six, even thirty-six iron notes (see double album MC 15, *Opeka Nyimbo*, Kubik/Malamusi 1989, items A5-6 and B-5). In the same culture area, among the -Sena, *valimba* is the term for a twenty- to twenty-two-note, gourd-resonated xylophone on a stand.

The prefix *ma-* is a cumulative prefix in Bantu languages and conveys the idea of an assemblage of objects or people, even abstract ideas. Thus *limba* is one xylophone or lamellophone note, *malimba* an assemblage. *Ka-* is a diminutive prefix. Hence, *kalimba* among the -Nsenga of Zambia and many other ethnic groups in Southeast Africa refers to a small lamellophone with a fan-shaped body (Blacking 1961); similarly among the -Tumbuka of northern Malawi it designates a small box-resonated lamellophone. There is, however, no cross-cultural consistency in the choice of terms. Among the -Pangwa, -Kisi, -Kinga, -Bena, -Nyakyusa, and others in southwestern Tanzania, the same type of instrument is simply called *malimba* without any apparent need for the distinction expressed by the *ka-* prefix. (Kubik 1978a; Kubik et al. 1982, 164–65).

Among the -Lozi of western Zambia and in the Caprivi Strip of Namibia, a tablelike gourd-resonated xylophone is called *silimba*, whereas lamellophone terminology is based on a different noun stem; and *jinjimba* among the -Luvale of northwestern Zambia is a two-note xylophone. Among the -Gogo of central Tanzania large lamellophones with a sound hole that is equipped with the vibrating membrane of a spider's nest covering are known as *ilimba* (see Kubik et al. 1982, 136–39). On the Tanzanian coast and on the island of Zanzibar, *marimba* refers to a box-resonated xylophone in the Kiswahili language; if a lamellophone is meant the term is descriptively modified to *marimba madogo* (i.e., "small xylophone"). Not only does this demonstrate the association between the two instrument types from a local perspective, it also suggests a historical sequence, namely that the xylophone was in this region first and that lamellophones came later. The name for xylophone was then projected upon the new instrument. In this particular case verification is possible. We know from oral tradition and other historical sources (see the distribution map in Ankermann 1901) that with the exception of southernmost Tanzania (the *ulimba* of the -Mwera and -Makonde), lamellophones were unknown in the whole of East Africa until shortly before the turn of the nineteenth/twentieth century. They were introduced from Congo along the caravan trade routes.

The -MBILA/-MBIRA Stem

Similarly, the stem -MBILA/-MBIRA is used to construct designations for both lamellophones and xylophones. In the Shona language of Zimbabwe, *mbira* (sing. and pl.) is the generic term for large lamellophones of complex design and playing technique, such as the *mbira dza vadzimu* (lamellophone of the ancestors), historically one of the oldest types and one that has become part of the popular culture since the 1970s (see Andrew Tracey 1963; 1970a; Berliner 1975; 1976; 1978; and others). Andrew Tracey (1972, 88) has mentioned three lamellophone types in Zimbabwe that incorporate the term *mbira:* (1) *mbira dza vadzimu* (also *mbira dze midzimu* according to dialect), (2) *mbila deza*, and (3) *mbira dza vandau*. Though generally referred to as *mbira*, all other lamellophone types in Zimbabwe and adjacent areas are usually called by specific names, such as *njari, njari huru, nyonganyonga, hera, matepe* etc.

Further north, in Zambia, the designation *mbila* is used among the -Bemba, -Bisa, -Nsenga, and -Shila for one-note xylophones of the same type as the *limba* of the -Maŋanja in Malawi. This xylophone type spread in history as far north as Katanga (Shaba Province, Democratic Republic of the Congo) where the -LIMBA stem reappears (see above). This demonstrates another important fact: the interchangeability of the word stems -LIMBA/-RIMBA and -MBILA/-MBIRA. George T. Nurse (1970, 34) even suggested that the two noun stems are one and the same, owing their separate existence to metathesis:

L – I – MB – A ⟶ MB – I – L – A
1 2 3 4 reshuffled 3 2 1 4

In the Chopi language of southern Mozambique *mbila* means one xylophone key, *timbila* (pl.) designates xylophones, as well as their art form in general. Among the -Khokola of Malawi the prefix *ma-*, joined with the stem –MBIRA, results in the term *mambira* referring to a log xylophone, while among the -Cuambo the same term refers to a trough-resonated xylophone (see Kubik 1968; Kubik et al. 1982, 110–11). Among the -Lomwe of northern Mozambique and southeastern Malawi a part of the word stem is reduplicated: *mambirira* denotes a log xylophone. Among the -Makonde *dimbila* also refers to a log xylophone, while a characteristic Mwera/Makonde lamellophone is called *ulimba* (Dias 1986, 35–37).

The -SANSI/-SANJI/-SANZI Stem

As far as we can reconstruct, the word stem -SANSI originated in Bantu languages of the lower Zambezi area. Its rise was probably stimulated by a need to use a term that was *not* shared with xylophones, at a time when lamellophones in the lower Zambezi culture area had increasingly become an independent tradition. It is a specific term for lamellophones only, even more specifically referring to relatively small board-shaped or tray-shaped types with an external (gourd) resonator. Most certainly, in the migratory history of this type of instrument, the semantic field of the stem -SANSI was occasionally modified, so that other organological types were included under the -SANSI stem. But the original meaning is still detectable. In the languages of the lower Zambezi and Shire River areas in southeast Africa, the word stem is a class-IV noun (sing. and pl. without a prefix), hence *sansi* in Cinyanja/Chichewâ, *nsansi* among the -Nyungwe of Tete (Mozambique), or *sasi* among the -Khokola, in this case for a very large type with fifteen to sixteen lamellae and a bell-shaped resonator.

This word stem was originally concentrated in southeast Africa, and it only spread across central Africa into the Democratic Republic of the Congo, Angola, and neighboring countries during the last four to five hundred years. This has been reconstructed in a painstaking manner from written sources, oral tradition, linguistic comparisons, and comparison of the organological details of the instruments involved (see Kubik 1964b; 1965; 1999). The word stem -SANSI in the course of its migration has assumed many phonetic variants, for example, *thishanji* (pronounced: θiʃandʒi) in the Mbukushu language of the Okavango region of Namibia (Kubik 1994b, 195). It has also undergone sound shifts as in *ndandi* for a lamellophone of the -Lala of Zambia (Jones 1949).

As this word stem traveled from the lower Zambezi region to Central Africa, another significant modification occurred with the addition of a class-III prefix, for example, KI-/VI-, CI-/VI-, CI-/ZI, all across the southern savanna from Katanga into Angola. New designations, preferably referring to board-shaped (or tray-shaped) varieties, also became generic terms for lamellophones in certain areas, notably in Angola, for example, *kisanji* in Kimbundu, *ocisanji* in Umbundu, *cisanzi* in the Ngangela group of languages, *cisaji* in Cokwe, etc. Further up in central Africa, toward the northwestern Bantu borderland, the trend of adding prefixes was reversed, and they were dropped again. While *esanzi* is a common term in the Republic of the Congo, the term in Mpyemɔ̃, a Bantu language spoken in the area of Nola, Central African Republic, is just *sanji*. The instrument was introduced into this area early in the twentieth century. And where the name crossed linguistic borders, for example into I.A.6 (Adamawa-Eastern) languages (see Greenberg 1966 for classification), the prefix was also lost, as in the Zande designation *sanzu* (Kubik 1994a, 99) or the *sanje* among the Gbaya-Bokoto, Central African Republic, a box-resonated variety (see field notes 1964/Kubik, rec. orig. -tape no. R 41/II/5–10, Museum für Völkerkunde, Berlin).

a

The -KEMBE Stem

As yet, nothing certain can be said about the etymology and origins of the term *likembe* (pl. *makembe*), which is associated across Central Africa with one specific, box-resonated type of lamellophone (fig. 1.5a–d). The term is so widespread (see fig. 1.4) because the associated instrument—invented somewhere in the lower Congo area—spread like wildfire within decades. The invention of the *likembe* dates only to the nineteenth century, as is suggested by the total absence of this type in earlier reports and from the specific stages of its spread, which have been reconstructed.

The *likembe* is characterized by the following organological traits : (1) it has a box-shaped resonator; (2) the iron bridge is mostly U-shaped; (3) from eight to twelve relatively thin, iron lamellae are attached to the sound board in a V-shaped or VI-shaped layout, so that the longest deep-tuned note is in the middle, and most often a second deep-tuned note is found at the far right of the arrangement; (4) looked at from the back, the *likembe* is characterized by a cutout section at the top to facilitate attachment of wire slung around the pressure bar, holding down the lamellae; (5) most characteristic is the sound hole at the back of the resonator, which is operated by the player with his left middle finger to create wow effects; another sound hole is cut at the small end of the box directed toward the player; (6) rattle rings are slung around all or some of the lamellae between bridge and straining bar.

b

c

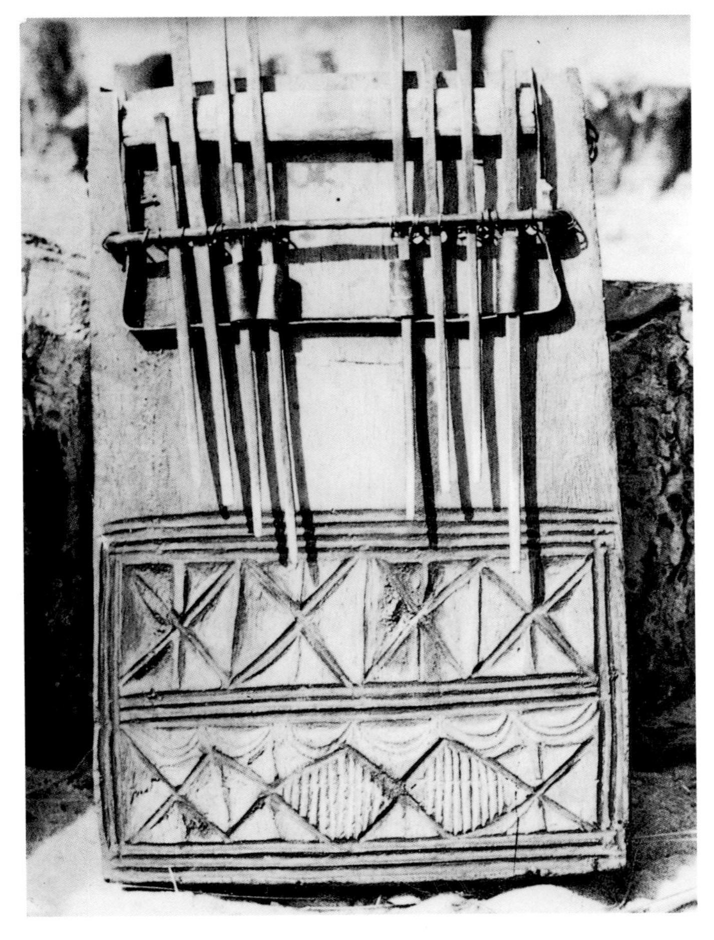

d

1.5a–d These photographs show the organology and playing technique of the *likembe*, an eight-note lamellophone. It is played by the late Kufuna Kandonga, who was fifteen years old at the time. In addition to sounding the iron lamellae with the thumbs, he operated the sound hole on the back of the *likembe* with the left middle finger to create timbre melodies and wow effects (see figs. 1.5b,c). Photographs by Gerhard Kubik, Chisende and Mupeku villages, Longa District, Kwandu Kuvangu Province, southeastern Angola, November 1965.

In addition to the four prominent word stems, some other lamellophone designations with regional distribution areas—though on a much smaller scale—must be mentioned. Cases in point are names such as *shitata* among the -Lomwe and their neighbors in northern Mozambique and—no doubt related to it—*shityatya* among the -Makonde (see Dos Santos Jr. 1958; Dias 1986, 80–83). The term *kankobele* is widespread in central Zambia (Davidson 1970), and *kaŋombyo* is well established among the -Subia, -Lozi, and others in northeastern Namibia.

Outside Bantu-language areas, designations abound that are unrelated to any Bantu-language name. The Vute term *timbrh* for raffia lamellophones in central Cameroon, although mispronounced by neighbors as *timbili* (see Kubik 1966c) is *not* related to the Chopi term *timbila*. Among the Tikar, another Cameroon grassland people, the generic term *mbø* is applied to stringed instruments and lamellophones, for example, *mbø loya* is a polyidiochord stick zither, *mbø toŋ* and *mbø ŋgo* are raffia-manufactured lamellophones (the distinction referring to different music/dance genres), while mbø menjyãŋ refers to a secret type of lamellophone with up to eighteen raffia lamellae and vibration needles over an oval wooden resonator, somewhat similar to old-style Vute lamellophones. This instrument is only played inside the ancestral shrine at Ngambe for the dead Tikar chiefs. Strangely, the attribute *menjyãŋ* to narrow down the semantic field of the term *mbø*, is quite obviously lifted from the name for xylophone found among the Tikar's southern, Bantu-language speaking neighbors (see Kubik et al. 1989, 56–61).

Typology, Tunings, and Playing Techniques

In Hugh Tracey's *Handbook for Librarians* (1948, 72), lamellophones are classified comparatively according to the presence or absence of a variety of traits:

a. According to the arrangement of notes in one, two, or three superimposed ranks (Tracey: "one manual," "two manuals," or "three manuals").
b. According to the general disposition of pitches, for example, "bass notes central, sequence regular" or "bass notes on the left, sequence irregular," and so forth.
c. According to presence or absence of a mirliton, that is, a buzzing device in which the membrane of a common house-spider's nest covering is glued over a sound hole, as also in gourd-resonated xylophones.
d. According to the shape of the soundboard and the type of resonator used. Here, Hugh Tracey distinguishes five basic types
   1. Board, rectangular
      Board, rectangular with external resonator
   2. Fan-shaped or scallop-shell board
      Fan-shaped or scallop-shell board with external resonator
   3. Bell
      Bell with external resonator
   4. Box
      Box with external resonator
   5. Other shape, raft or irregular pattern

Hugh Tracey's classification has been widely accepted, and it is now common to speak of "board-shaped," "fan-shaped," "bell-type," and "box-resonated" lamellophones. Tracey's "external resonator" is almost always a gourd. It is sometimes used in addition to an "internal" bell-shaped or box resonator, as for example in the Phodzo *malimba* (central Mozambique) or the Mpyɛmɔ̃ *kembe* (Central African Republic).

Classification according to the presence or absence of buzzing devices can be considerably expanded, however, because there are many more devices than the spider-web mirliton. The most important include rattle rings fastened to a bar at the thin front part of the soundboard, affixed inside the orifice of a bell-shaped resonator, or slung around the lamellae between straining bar and bridge. Chains of beads or an iron chain can be laid across the lamellae; snail shells or bottle tops can be attached to the soundboard or the resonating gourd. In westernmost Africa (Sierra Leone, Côte d'Ivoire, etc.) a piece of sheet iron dotted with small buzzing rings is attached at the top of many lamellophones, and in central Cameroon vibration needles provide the characteristic sound of raffia-made lamellophones. There are many more of these ingenious devices whose function by sympathetic vibration is threefold: (1) to lengthen the duration of a note; (2) to amplify the sound (this has been particularly stressed by performers of the Vute *timbrh*, Kubik 1966c; Kubik et al. 1989, 50); (3) to modify the sound spectrum of individual notes to help create subjective auditory patterns, an illusion effect (see Kubik 1989), and thereby stimulate a meditative mood in solo players who "talk" to the instrument from which the voices of spirits may seem to emanate.

The organological and technological properties of lamellophones can also be classified further according to: the shape of the lamellae, for example, thin prongs, spatula shape, etc.; the method of their attachment; the method of tuning (adjusting the length and/or attaching tuning wax); the presence or absence and position of sound holes and their function (e.g., played upon or not); the materials used for manufacture (e.g., wood, iron, raffia, bamboo, industrial debris); and the specific tools used in the manufacturing process.

Lamellophones can also be classified by sociocultural usages, for example, by minstrels, by travelers as a pastime, for self-enjoyment, for purposes of meditation, for conversation with a spirit, in group performances for entertainment, for ritual and/or religious ceremonies, as part of a homogenous instrumental set (e.g., lamellophones with one or two accompanying instruments), or as part of an ensemble with several other instrument types.

Working in close cooperation with musicians and their conceptual worlds, Andrew Tracey discovered during his research in Zimbabwe that by far the most definitive distinguishing factor of a lamellophone type is not the kind of resonator, nor is it the tuning, but the tuning layout (Andrew Tracey 1972). In contrast to actual pitch sequences, which can be measured by various electronic and other devices (e.g., Stroboconn, Korg tuner, set of tuning forks, etc.) but may show considerable fluctuation from occasion to occasion, instrument to instrument, and musician to musician—reflecting culturally and individually conditioned margins of pitch tolerance—the general layout of the intervals is usually stable. Andrew Tracey has introduced a notational system that allows comparison of the tuning layout of lamellophones and other musical instruments cross-culturally without getting diverted by minute pitch differences. The scheme adopts horizontal lines to present *tonemes*, that is, pitch-values considered by the musician as identical. The octaves are represented by reinforced horizontal lines. In heptatonic systems every seventh line will be reinforced, in pentatonic systems every fifth. The notational system is relative, but the results of measurements in Hertz (c.p.s.) can be added at the beginning of each line, if the need arises. In this way it is possible to recognize with one glance the difference between the concept of a thirty-six-note Phodzo *malimba*, a twenty-two-note *mbira dza vadzimu* from Zimbabwe, a *mucapata* from Angola, and a *kadongo* from Uganda. (figs. 1.6–1.9)

Figures 1.6–1.9: Tuning layouts on the instruments of four prominent lamellophone players in Africa.

1.6 *Malimba* with thirty-six iron lamellae arranged in two ranks; bell-shaped body and gourd resonator. Performer: Dzingo Chiningamphale, male, about seventy years old; ethnic group: -Phodzo from central Mozambique. Recorded by Maurice Djenda and Gerhard Kubik, Chambuluka, south of Muona, Nsanje District, Malawi, June 1967. Published song "Kabutera" in Kubik/Malamusi 1989, LP item B-5. Tonal system: equiheptatonic.

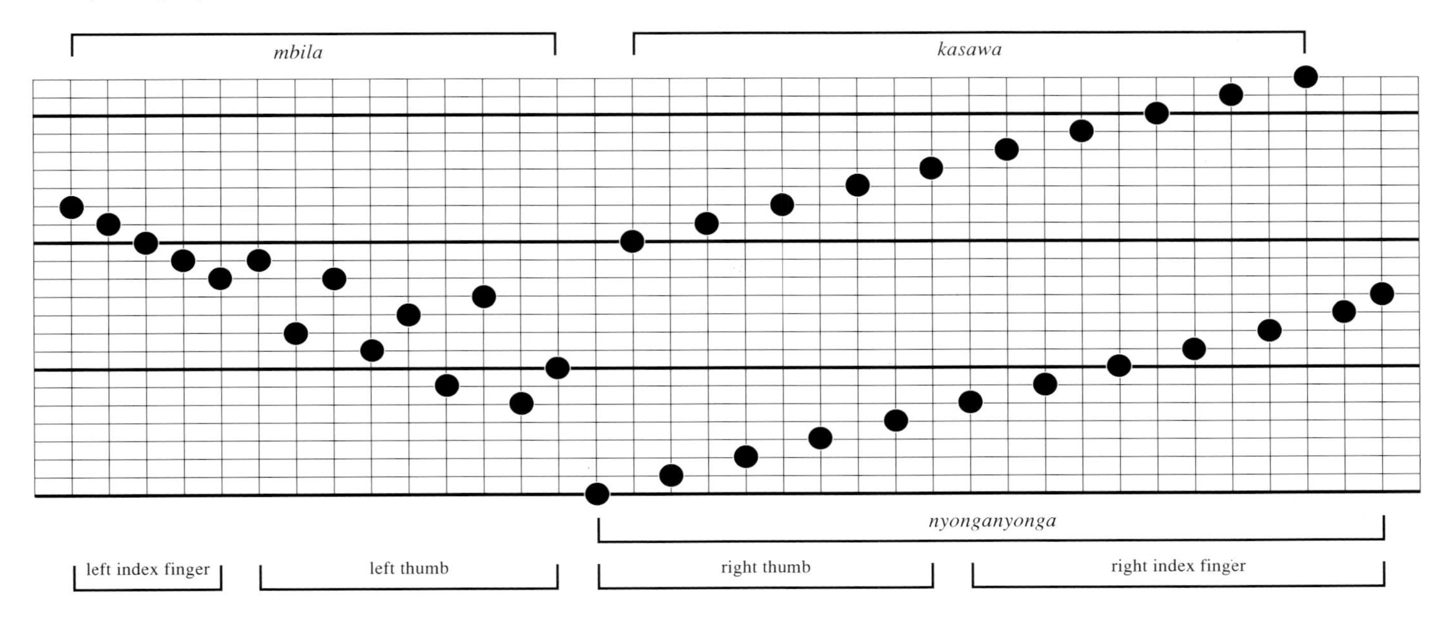

1.7 *Mbira dza vadzimu* with twenty-two iron lamellae arranged in two ranks; tray-shaped body and gourd resonator. Performer: Beuler Dyoko, female, born 1945 in Mozambique. Language now used: Shona. Recorded by Gerhard Kubik, Chitungwiza township, Harare, Zimbabwe, July 16, 1989. Published song "Kuzanga" in Kubik 1994a, CD item 26. Tonal system: heptatonic with two roots a major third apart.

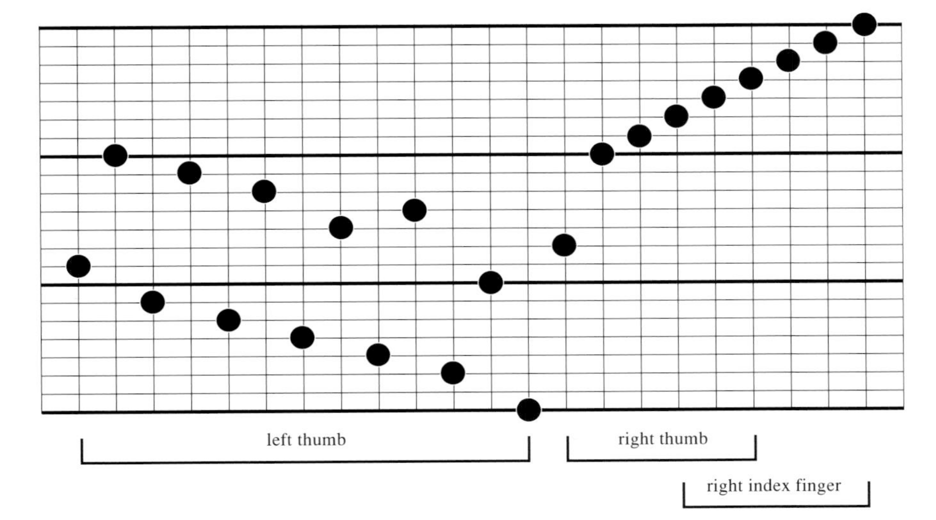

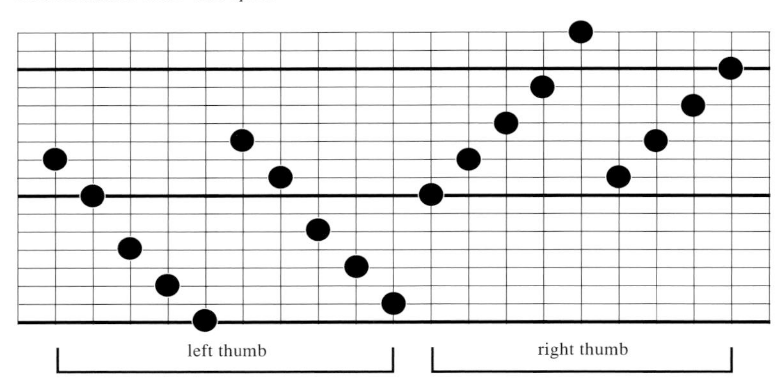

1.8 *Mucapata* with nineteen iron lamellae arranged in sections; bell-shaped body; no external resonator. Performer: Sachiteta, male, born circa 1895. Ethnic group and language: Cokwe. Recorded by Gerhard Kubik, Chisende village, Longa District, southeast Angola, October 1965. Published song "Sangu waya mama," in Kubik 1999, CD item 26. Tonal system: equiheptatonic temperament of an originally hexatonic system derived from partials four to six over two fundamentals a whole-tone apart.

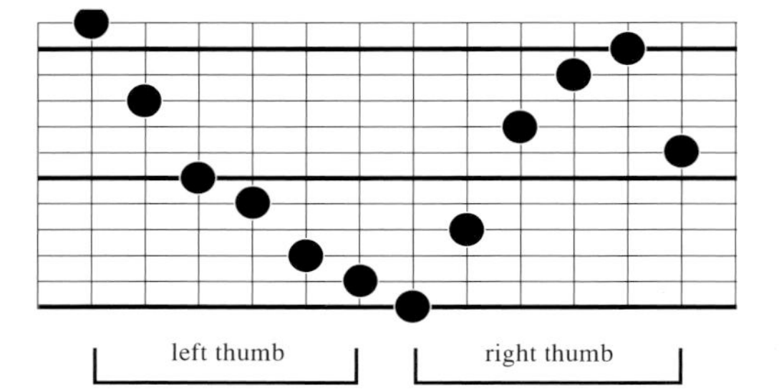

1.9 *Kadongo* twelve iron lamellae arranged in VI-shape; the distribution of tones (from top to bottom) following this pattern of left-right alternations : l - r - r, l - r - r, l - l - r, l - l - r. Performer: Daudi Mukama, male, about eighteen years old, blind. Ethnic group: -Gwere. Recorded by Gerhard Kubik, Salama, south of Mukono, Uganda, March 1960. Published song"Malaya mukadde" in Kubik 1999, CD item 19. Tonal System: equipentatonic.

Numerous tonal arrangements may be observed in lamellophones across Africa. The many types characteristic of just one region, Zimbabwe, are illustrated in Andrew Tracey (1972). All the different tuning layouts have their own compelling logic, reflecting trial and error, selection and adaptation in long-term historical processes. Obviously, the kind of arrangement reflects regional and individual tonal/harmonic concepts and the techniques adopted to give them audible expression. As much as the superimposed ranks of the sections called *kasawa* and *nyonganyonga* on Dzingo's *malimba* (fig. 1.6) reflect the concept of an ascending equiheptatonic scale, so does the major third interval at the basis of the *mbira dza vadzimu* (fig. 1.7) give us a clue to the Shona tonal system with its progressions in bichords of fourths and fifths (see Andrew Tracey 1970b; 1989a; and Kubik 1994a for further analysis). Sachiteta's tuning layout on his *mucapata* (fig. 1.8) plainly reveals that his tonal/harmonic concepts are linked to the two deep notes in the left-thumb playing area representing two fundamentals a whole-tone apart with partials four to six over either fundamental used in the formation of harmonic columns. Cokwe culture is a formidable area of homophonic multipart singing in chord clusters of thirds-plus-fifths. While Cokwe tunings have long been near-equiheptatonic, the tuning layout in a *mucapata* such as Sachiteta's reveals their origin in a partials-derived hexatonic scale. And the arrangement on Mukama's twelve-note *kadongo* (fig. 1.9) in an equi*penta*tonic tuning with no other simultaneous sounds than octaves is structured so that parallel octaves can be played comfortably using left and right thumbs; in addition a rhythm pattern in left-right thumb alternations is hidden in this layout. It comes to the surface if one plays all the twelve notes downward or upward as a scale.

The figures also demonstrate the interrelationship between tuning layout and playing areas. Most lamellophones in Africa are played with the thumbs, actually the thumbnails, and the "keyboard" is divided in half to form a left-thumb and right-thumb playing area (see figs. 1.8, 1.9, *mucapata* and *kadongo*). In many lower Zambezi/Zimbabwe lamellophones with more than twenty lamellae arranged in two ranks, the work is divided between more than two fingers, whereby only thumbs depress their lamellae downward, all other fingers involved "pluck" them upward. Dzingo Chiningamphale used thumbs and index fingers of both hands on his thirty-six-note *malimba; mbira dza vadzimu* players use the two thumbs and the right index fingers. Among the -Khokola five fingers are involved in the playing technique of the large *sasi*: thumbs, index fingers, and the little finger of the left hand (field notes 1967/Djenda/Kubik, Malawi; Museum für Völkerkunde, Berlin). Among the Vute of central Cameroon, the thumb of each hand of a *timbrh* player depresses *two* adjacent lamellae tuned in octave pairs at once. By contrast, Tikar musicians use thumbs and index fingers of both hands in playing *mbø toŋ* and *mbø ŋgo*, like their Zambezi counterparts. The most unusual playing techniques can be found along the Guinea Coast. While lamellophones all over the subcontinent are played so that the ends of the lamellae point toward the performer, in West Africa from the Fõ of Togo with their *gidiŋbo* up to Sierra Leone stretches a zone where lamellophones are often held with the lamellae pointing away from the player in which case they are played with the thumbs. If they are played with the ends directed toward the player, they are often played with the index fingers.

1.10 "Marimba de Cafri," a late sixteenth- or early seventeenth-century lamellophone player depicted as plate CXLIV in Fillipo Bonanni's *Gabinetto Armónico* (1716; 2d ed. 1723). Reproduced from Bonanni 1964, no. 144.

Early Historical Sources

Lamellophones made of vegetable materials cannot survive in the strata excavated by archaeologists. Even iron objects are subject to considerable corrosion. This shuts off most effectively much of the earliest history of this instrument family from our knowledge. "Prehistoric" sources, such as rock paintings, have not given us any yield either, which only confirms that their authors belonged to cultures and times that we do not associate with the invention of the lamellophone. Even more recent African iconographic sources, such as the terra-cotta pots excavated by Frank Willet in Ife (dated between the eleventh and fourteenth centuries C.E.) and showing reliefs of drums, bells, and horns), give no clues about lamellophones. They are also absent in Benin bronzes of which no less than 295 objects have been counted that contain very naturalistic depictions of musical instruments (Dark and Hill 1971, 66). This suggests that the Yorùbá/Benin cluster was outside the key areas of Africa where lamellophones were developed.

Archaeological finds that have been interpreted tentatively as iron prongs of lamellophones are available from northern Katanga (Democratic Republic of the Congo), Zambia, and Zimbabwe. At Kumadzulo on the Zambezi, Joseph O. Vogel excavated iron prongs that could be lamellophone notes. Radiocarbon dating has suggested a time span between the fifth and seventh centuries C.E. (Vogel 1971, 40; Gansemans/Schmidt-Wrenger 1986). By comparison, some excavations of similar iron objects at Kalamo and Kalundu by Brian M. Fagan were dated to the tenth/eleventh centuries C.E. (Gansemans/Schmidt-Wrenger 1986, 12–13). Iron objects that might be *mbira* lamellae were also uncovered in Zimbabwe. Some of them are preserved in the Great Zimbabwe Site Museum.

Written sources begin in the sixteenth century with a famous text by the Portuguese missionary Frei João dos Santos (1609) who visited the Kingdom of Kiteve, on the Mozambique coast along the Sofala River, in 1586. He described a lamellophone with nine notes called "ambira" (dos Santos's spelling; see pp. 74–75 of the 1891 edition of his work). He mentions that this instrument was generally played in the king's palace and that the lamellae were sounded with the thumbnails, so a performer would let them grow longer than usual. He describes how the iron lamellae were hammered out and stresses that the resulting music was gentle and soft. This is not only the first known written description of a lamellophone, it is also the first record of the term *mbira* (the *a-* in dos Santos's spelling should not be mistaken for a prefix; it derives from the Portuguese's phonetic reinterpretation of the African name).

In a treatise on musical instruments from many cultures, Fillipo Bonanni in his *Gabinetto Armónico* (1723) depicts a lamellophone player with the caption "Marimba de Cafri" (fig. 1.10). Bonanni was born in Rome in 1658; he was a Jesuit priest and in 1698 he became curator of the collection of antiquities at the Jesuit College. His book was first published in 1716; the revised version in 1723. He never traveled to Africa, and some of his African illustrations were no doubt inspired by previous Italian publications now lost. The ultimate source of his picture "Marimba de Cafri" (174, no.CXLIV) is not known. Details of the instrument are only vaguely represented by the illustrator, but the use of the thumbs as agents is clear. The caption "Marimba de Cafri" suggests that the illustrator must have had southeastern Africa in mind, because the term *kaffir* (from the Arabic) was commonly used along the Indian Ocean coast by Omani Arabs and others to categorize the non-Islamized people. Omani influence starting in the tenth century C.E. reached as far south as Sofala in Mozambique. The lamellophone player is shown on what looks like a beach, and his clothing reveals that cotton cloth was available. The player seems to dance, and his leg rattles are suggestive of the life of minstrels playing in public, a phenomenon that continued into the mid-twentieth century in northern Mozambique, also in connection with other solo instruments, such as one-stringed fiddles (field notes 1962/Kubik on the *takare* bowed lute; Museum für Völkerkunde, Berlin). Significantly the two adjacent illustrations in Bonanni, "Arco de Cafri" and "Violino de Cafri," confirm this impression and fit well into the area of Mozambique between Mozambique Island and Sofala. Finally, the term *marimba* (although it was also reported in connection with xylophones from Angola in the seventeenth century) corroborates the likely Southeast African origin of the information transmitted by Bonanni's early eighteenth-century illustration. Southeast Africa was a most important area in the historical development of complex lamellophone types (see the testimonies by Hugh Tracey 1969; 1973; Andrew Tracey 1961; 1963; 1970a; 1970b; 1972; 1989a,b). Therefore, it is somewhat reassuring that the two oldest accounts have come from there.

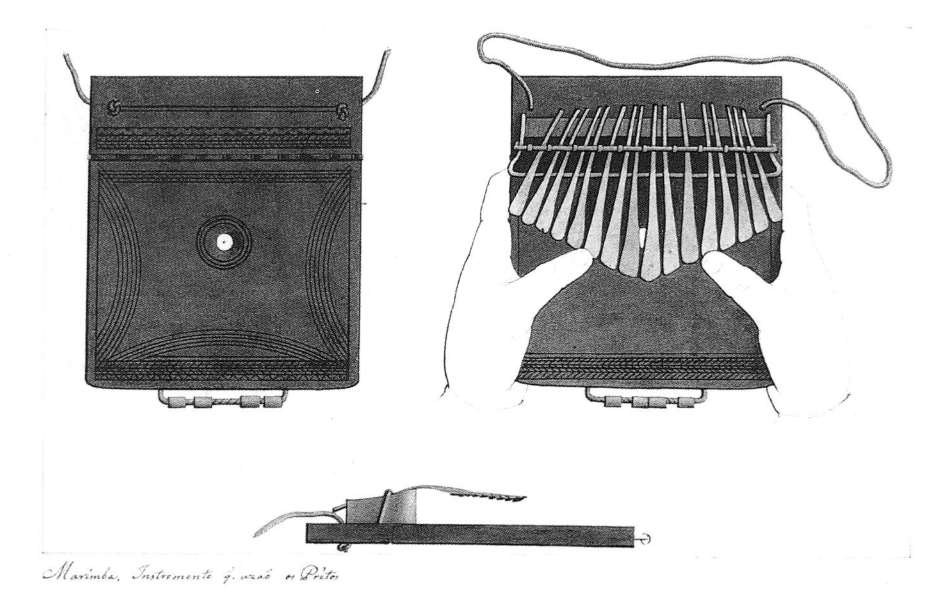

1.11 Alexandre Rodrigues Ferreira's late eighteenth-century illustration of a southwestern Angolan type of board lamellophone with sixteen iron tongues, which was played by an Angolan slave in northern Brazil (the area of Belem). The original caption reads: "Marimba, Instrumento q. uzão os Prétos" (Marimba, an instrument that the Blacks use). Reproduced from Ferreira's *Philosophical Journey . . . , 1783–1792*. (For further analysis of this picture see Kubik 1979; 1999).

The next source in the chronology dates from the late eighteenth century. Although it does *not* come from Africa, it is extremely important for the reconstruction of the history of lamellophones. An Angolan type of lamellophone manufactured by an Angolan slave in northern Brazil, probably in or near Belem, is shown in fascinating detail. Alexandre Rodrigues Ferreira on his "philosophical journey to the flagships of Grão-Pará, Rio Negro, Mato Grosso and Cuiabá, 1783–1792," depicts a sixteen-note board lamellophone with a V-shaped layout of its spatula-shaped lamellae (fig. 1.11). The method of tuning with lumps of black wax is clearly testified by the drawings, which were made by two of Ferreira's companions. The accuracy and detail of the front, side, and back views compensate for the paucity of information in the caption, which says only "Marimba que uzão os pretos" (Marimba that the Blacks use). I have analyzed this iconographic source in my book *Angolan Traits in Black Music, Games, and Dances of Brazil* (1979) and was able to compare it with identical twentieth-century instruments from the southwestern Angolan provinces of Huíla (Wila) and Namibe (figs. 12a–c), which were collected for the Museu de Etnologia in Lisbon (especially specimens AP-824, AG-847, and AG-850). In 1965 I also recorded this type of sixteen-note board lamellophone with a gourd resonator in southwestern Angola, the area where it is concentrated (see Kubik 1999: CD item no. 2 "Elamba" by Docota, male, thirty-two years old, at Munengole village, Dinde/Quilengues, July 15, 1965). It is called *ocisanzi* (or just *cisanzi*) in that area. According to my Angolan colleague Marcelina Gomes (personal communication, Luanda, February 17, 1982), it can also be called *ocihumba* (with the name of the pluriarc or bow-lute) especially in the Municipiós Cipungu and Eyo where it seems to be a relatively recent import. The name "marimba" in Ferreira's eighteenth-century account, is therefore to be read as a Portuguese designation and not as a retention of an Angolan name. The term *marimba* had long been accepted in the Portuguese language as a loanword, and we know from many other sources in Brazil that it had quickly become a common designation in Portuguese for both xylophones and lamellophones as played by African slaves.

The implications of my comparisons are far-reaching. One startling result is that the organological and technological details of this type of sixteen-note board lamellophone must have remained stable for some two hundred years. In light of the enormous innovative powers displayed by lamellophone history in Africa, this throws up general questions about the circumstances favoring stability or triggering mutation. I think that once a type has been invented and developed to satisfy musicians' needs, it tends to remain stable and that the innovative power in lamellophone history was mainly programmed to the creation of technologically new types that would satisfy the needs of younger generations and underline their separate identities, rather than modify the old types. The latter then tended to continue as a parallel tradition. This model would explain why a specific southwestern Angolan type that must have been established there at least by the mid-eighteenth century—if the knowledge could have reached Brazil with a captive probably taken out of Angola through the port of Benguela—did not change in its homeland up until the twentieth century. My idea, however, should not be abused as a generalization. It seems to work specifically for instrumental traditions whose original distribution area remained stationary. When a certain type begins to migrate and is adopted by ethnic neighbors and travelers, modifications inevitably take place after time. In addition to the local invention of new types as a result of young people's delight in experimentation and their secessionist social spirit, a second important channel leading to innovative changes of a device seems to be migratory innovation, whereby a core of conservative attitudes is often preserved.

1.12a–c A twentieth-century southwestern Angolan specimen, virtually identical to Ferreira's late eighteenth-century find (see fig. 1.11), is the *ocisanzi* that was collected by Ernesto Veiga de Oliveira from a Kwisi musician near Namibe, southwestern Angola, in 1971. Like Ferreira's instrument, it originally also had an iron bar with rattle rings, which was attached to the edge of the board directed toward the player's chest. Proof that this has been lost are two small holes that can be seen at the edge of the specimen in Lisbon. Museu de Etnologia, Lisbon, inv. no. AP-824, photographs by Gerhard Kubik.

Alexandre Rodrigues Ferreira's drawings not only add historical depth to the history of lamellophones that were exported to the Americas, but indirectly to their African histories as well. It is unlikely that the Angolan prototype of Ferreira's instrument had significantly shifted its Angolan distribution area, if it has not done so during the last 150 years, being still rooted in the provinces of Wila and Namibe, and perhaps Benguela. This was an area whose population had been drained by the slave trade of the Ovimbundu. The owner of the lamellophone Ferreira reports from in or near Belem, Brazil, must thus have come from southwestern Angola and from nowhere else. This is corroborated by the fact that Ferreira depicts yet another musical instrument that he probably found with the same player or the same group of slaves in the Brazilian household where he stayed: a pluriarc or bow-lute of the Nkhumbi/Handa type. The distribution area of this particular type of bow-lute is also restricted to the same southwestern Angolan provinces (see Kubik 1979 for further analysis).

While sixteenth- to eighteenth-century sources on lamellophones are scarce, though some more may yet be discovered, a marked increase in the availability of sources occurs in the nineteenth century. Beginning in the early nineteenth century, there are many more testimonies about African lamellophones played by slaves in Brazil, and two specimens that were apparently collected in Brazil have survived (see below). Written sources from Africa on lamellophones, however, only become numerous from the mid-nineteenth century on, the most prominent being David Livingstone (1865; 1875) for the lower Zambezi valley, Carl Mauch (1872) for Zimbabwe, Capello and Ivens (1881) for Angola, Paul B. Du Chaillu (1861) for west-central equatorial Africa, Camille Coquilhat (1888) for the upper Congo River area and many others. Carl Mauch attempted the first notations of the playing of a *mbira dze midzimu* with twenty-nine lamellae by a Shona-Karanga musician whom he met near the ruins of Great Zimbabwe on March 13, 1872 (see Mauch 1969; Kubik 1971 for analysis).

Collectors' notes in museums, accompanying the several thousand specimens of African lamellophones that were collected between the 1860s and 1950s, form the largest bulk of our historical information. In addition to the better-known collections in European museums, there are smaller ones in private hands, in Christian mission centers, and in the circuits of the art trade. Contemporaneous photographs showing musicians in action, sometimes accompany the specimens. The systematic evaluation of museum collections of African musical instruments began in 1901 with the work of Bernhard Ankermann (1901) in Berlin, whose book contains a most informative chapter on lamellophones. Later works include Jean-Sebastian Laurenty (1962) in Tervuren, Francois Borel (1986) on the collections in Neuchâtel, Margot Dias (1986) on Mozambique, Erich Tremmel (1986) on the collections in the mission center St. Ottilien, Germany (1986), Anneliese Gnielinski (1986) on those in the National Museum of Tanzania, and that of our own team in the Museu de Etnologia, Lisbon, the Musikinstrumenten-Museum/Münchener Stadtmuseum, Munich (cf. Kubik/Malamusi 1985–1987), the Museum für Völkerkunde, Berlin (Kubik 1999), and the Metropolitan Museum of Art, New York, carried out with an Andrew W. Mellon Senior Research Fellowship in 1993 (see Manuscript G. Kubik/Moya A. Malamusi 1993, deposited in the museum).

Reconstructing the Remote History of African Lamellophones

We do not know precisely where and when the African lamellophone was invented, but the recorded typology, technological properties, recent histories, migration routes, nomenclature, and playing techniques suggest certain likelihoods.

1. We are pretty sure that simple lamellophones made of cane or raffia were invented and first used by speakers of I.A.5 (Benue-Congo) languages, perhaps some three thousand years ago. Only much later did this knowledge spread to speakers of other languages, notably to the eastern branch of the I.A.4 (Kwa) languages, east of the Niger River, and to I.A.6 (Adamawa-Eastern) speakers in northern central Africa.
2. We are also quite certain that in its initial stages the knowledge of making lamellophone notes must have spread with human migration, in particular with southward migrations during the period 1000 to 200 B.C.E. of early Bantu-language speakers from the so-called Bantu Nucleus, assumed to be in the eastern Nigeria/western Cameroon area.
3. In conformity with these postulates, it appears that the lamellophone was developed before the onset of the use of iron metallurgy in the area of the Bantu Nucleus, that is, long before 500–200 B.C.E. within a critical ecological background that could be called the *raffia intensity zone*. Today, this zone—wherein local technology from house building to the manufacture of furniture, household articles, toys, and musical instruments is heavily based on the use of the raffia palm tree (*Raphia farinifera*)—covers southeastern Nigeria, central and southern Cameroon, Gabon, Equatorial Guinea, and northern parts of the Republic of the Congo and the Democratic Republic of the Congo. Strips cut from the epidermis of a raffia stem leaf almost automatically lend themselves to discovery of the principle of the lamellophone. The diversity of raffia-manufactured lamellophone types from Cameroon and Gabon as demonstrated in museum collections (see Ankermann 1901; Kubik/Malamusi 1985–87; Kubik 1999) confirms the picture of long-term developments. Instruments with iron lamellae in this zone are of relatively recent (nineteenth- to twentieth-century) introduction. The west central African raffia zone also saw in southern Cameroon and Gabon, among the Beti/Bulu/ Faŋ cluster of peoples, the historical development of other raffia-based musical instruments not found anywhere else in Africa, such as the polyidiochord stick zither variously called *mvet, ebenza, ngombi*, and so forth.
4. The knowledge of making lamellophones with notes cut from the epidermis of a raffia-palm leaf probably spread across the subcontinent with the migration of western-stream Bantu-language speakers during the first centuries of our era. From Katanga it eventually reached the lower Zambezi valley and the Nyasa/Ruvuma culture area in Southeast Africa. Today, lamellophones with raffia notes, or—in the absence of raffia—with tongues of cane or bamboo can be found in a scattered distribution picture from the -Cokwe in the Kasai area of the southern Democratic Republic of the Congo and northeastern Angola to the Zambezi valley and Lake Malawi where they are often used as children's instruments.
5. With the advent of iron technology, lamellophones with iron notes began to appear during the first millennium C.E. in three specific areas of the

subcontinent. Possible stimulus diffusion between these three areas, and even extra-African influences in areas *b* and *c* cannot be excluded:

a. the Katanga area (Shaba Province, Democratic Republic of the Congo) archaeologically covered by Pierre de Maret (1978) and others;
b. the middle Zambezi/Zimbabwe area, that is, southern Zambia, Zimbabwe, and central Mozambique, the iron-age archaeology of which was documented by Brian Fagan, 1965; Joseph O. Vogel 1971; João Morais 1986; 1988; and others;
c. the lower Ruvuma area and highlands of the Makonde Plateau on the Indian Ocean coast in northeastern Mozambique and southeastern Tanzania, where a very unusual type of lamellophone with iron notes has survived until the present.

6. With the refinement of iron technology beginning around 1000–1100 C.E. (see Phillipson 1977), the Zimbabwe/Zambezi culture area became a new center in lamellophone technology, and it is here that the most complex, multinote instruments were developed. The great variety of types developed here is second only to the diversity of raffia lamellophones in the northwestern part of the I.A.5 (Benue-Congo) language area. The proliferation of forms began about one millennium ago, an inference from the general archaeological picture of the "Later Iron Age" in this region (Garlake 1973) and the evolutionary steps suggested by Andrew Tracey's "family tree" of Zimbabwe/Zambezi lamellophones (see Tracey 1972, 89).
7. From the fifteenth century on the Zimbabwe/Zambezi culture area became a new dispersal zone for lamellophone technology through the developing trading contacts into Central Africa from Portuguese posts on the Zambezi (fig. 1.13)

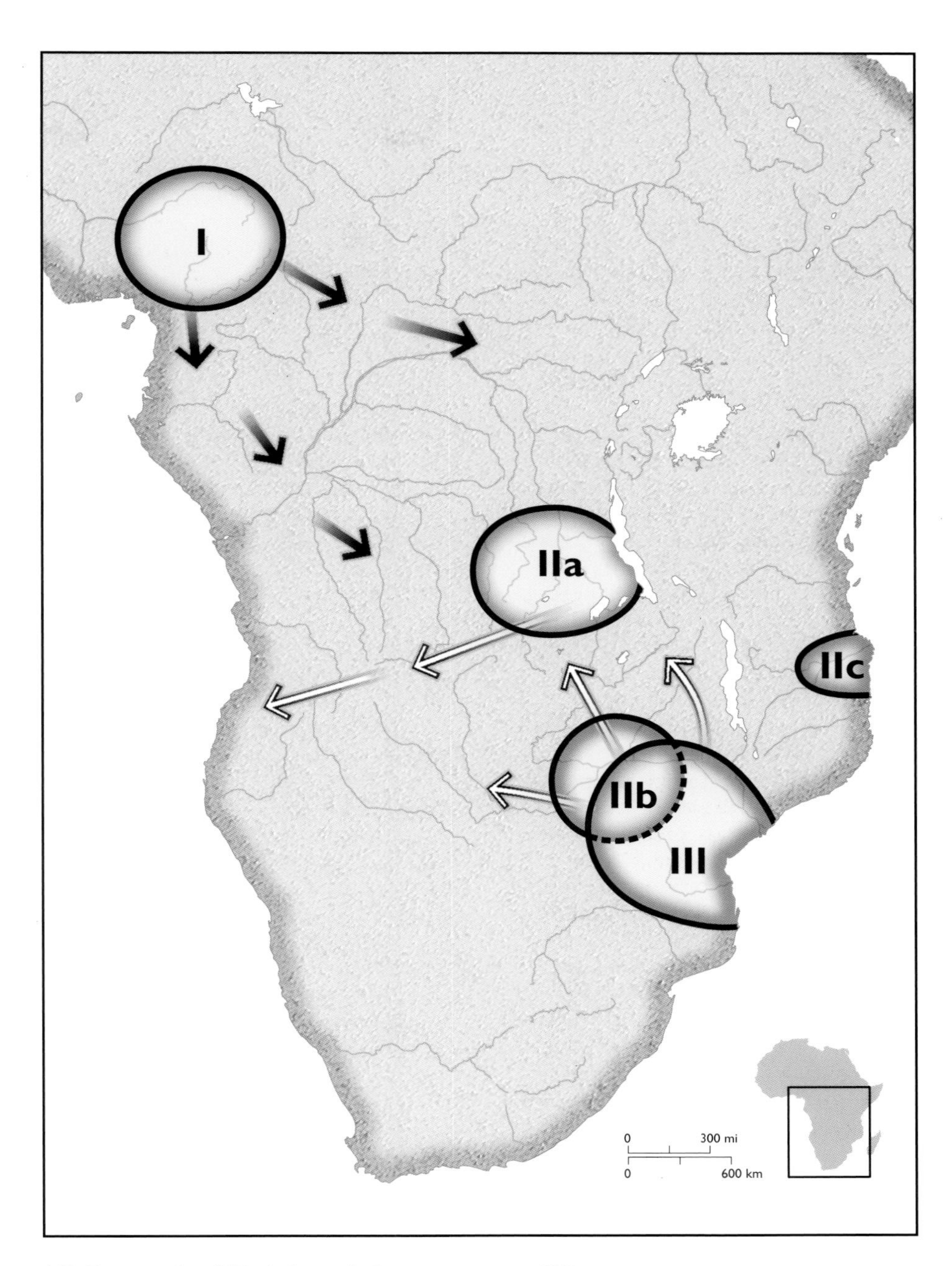

1.13 Reconstruction of historical stages in the invention, spread, and development of lamellophone technology, circa 1000 B.C.E. to 1600 C.E.

Rise of three centers of early iron age technology in which lamellophones with iron tongues were developed between circa 700 and 1000 C.E.

Area of likely invention of lamellophones of raffia or cane (before 1000 B.C.E.) and principal dispersal center.

Area of development of multinote, complex lamellophones with advanced iron-working technology, beginning circa 1000 C.E.

Major directions of the spread of raffia (cane, bamboo) lamellophone technology during the first centuries of our era.

Spread of Zimbabwe/Zambezi lamellophone technology into Central Africa with increasing trading contacts from the fifteenth/sixteenth century on.

While the earliest stages of the development of lamellophones made of vegetable materials (see map, fig. 1.13, area I) probably occurred independently of xylophone development, there is much evidence that during the later stages, especially in areas IIc and III in Southeast Africa (refer to map), a considerable flow of information in concepts and compositional principles took place between xylophone and iron-note lamellophone traditions. This does not imply any evolutionary sequence *from* xylophones *to* lamellophones, but rather conceptual associations, as suggested in the terminology especially for Southeast Africa—an area where xylophones and lamellophone technology have both attained levels of refinement unheard-of in other places (see Hugh Tracey 1948b; Andrew Tracey 1991; Malamusi 1993). Some small lamellophones in this region—and my case in point is the Makonde *ulimba* (see below)—were probably conceptually influenced by xylophone knowledge in a quest for constructing a "portable xyolophone."

In a remarkable letter to the editor of the journal *African Music*, A. M. Jones (1973/74, 97) demonstrated the process—illustrated by a drawing—whereby two imaginary xylophone players seem to be merged into a single person in some lamellophone playing styles, with the left-hand beater of one xylophone player transformed into the left thumb, the right-hand beater of the other player becoming the lamellophone player's right thumb. Although highly speculative, Jones's scheme has a compelling logic. It would also connect well with the fact that in Southeast Africa the word stems -LIMBA/-RIMBA and -MBILA/-MBIRA have been used in the formation of both xylophone and lamellophone names. On the Tanzanian coast the relationship is verbally attested by the expression *marimba madogo* (small xylophone).

An ingenious method for historical reconstruction was tried out by Andrew Tracey. In his article "The Original African *Mbira*" (1972), he tried to reconstruct a genealogy of all the complex Zimbabwean and Zambezi types that are obviously related historically. His method is not based on organological comparisons, but on the comparison of one trait, which, from an intracultural standpoint, identifies a type and distinguishes it from another: the *tuning layout* (see above). Comparing lamellophones from his father's (Hugh Tracey's) research in the 1930s and his own, he discovered that somewhere *hidden* in manifold tunings of these complex instruments, there was always a sort of core that consisted of a constant and specific layout of eight notes in a hexatonic tuning over two roots a major third apart. Characteristically, this scale is spread over one octave and two more steps (fig. 1.14). Andrew Tracey then went on to show how the "basic *kalimba* core" can be detected and traced through the other types of Zimbabwean lamellophones, for example, in the twenty-five-note "south bank karimba" (fig. 1.15; "south bank" refers to the southern bank of Zambezi). After a thoughtful excursion through the various lamellophone types in this culture area, Andrew Tracey arrived at a genealogy of the lamellophones in Southeast Africa (fig. 1.16). His table shows that *karimba, mbira dza vadzimu,* and *ndandi* should be relatively early developments in that culture area, *njari huru, hera,* and *nyonganyonga* the most recent.

In a sense, Andrew Tracey's genealogy is a classic evolutionistic developmental series such as Langfox Pitt Rivers, for example, had postulated at the turn of the nineteenth/twentieth century for the bow and arrow (though on a universal basis, while Tracey's scheme is regional). The silent assumption and possible weakness of any such scheme is that evolutionary direction in the development of new technological forms would have had to be always from "simple" to "more complex," whereby complexity often remains insufficiently defined. There is evidence that seventeenth- to eighteenth-century economic conditions north of the Zambezi River in connection with the caravan trade from Tete (a Portuguese post on the Zambezi since 1532) to the Maravi Empire and further north to Lunda-Kazembe, etc., favored the development of small, portable types with a fan-shaped soundboard and relatively few notes. Whether this is merely the reversal of an evolutionary trend with the makers of these small instruments falling back on earlier forms or the unbroken retention of a truly ancestral type (Andrew Tracey's eight-note *kalimba* as "the original African *mbira*," A. Tracey [1972], 85) cannot be said at the moment.

With this caveat in mind, however, Andrew Tracey's family tree fascinates by its inner logic and originality of thought. If we estimate that each development of a new form would have unfolded over a period of roughly two hundred years, Andrew Tracey's relative chronology would cover a time span of about eight hundred years from the ancestral *kalimba* to the *nyonganyonga* and *hera* and one evolutionary branch leading to the *mbila deza*; and six hundred years to the *njari huru*. Whether my two-hundred-year estimate can serve as a "genetic clock" in instrumental development schemes remains to be tested. In a somewhat different endeavour I have been able to unravel the logic of the sound structure in Andrew Tracey's *kalimba* core and have reached the startling conclusion that it is based on lower harmonics over *four* fundamentals that can be written as C, E, G, and A, resulting in the typical Nsenga/Shona bichord progressions, such as, for example:

g → b → d → g → b → e
C   E   G   C   E   A

These are the tones and their harmonic relationships making up the "basic *kalimba* core." It was further brought to light, that—independent of musical instrument history—the tonal system that constitutes the *kalimba* core and indeed the tonal/harmonic world of the -Shona, -Nsenga, -Lala, -Manyika, and others in the Zimbabwe/Zambezi culture area might have remote roots in the music of Khoisan speakers (see Kubik 1988a, reprinted in 1994a; comments from Andrew Tracey 1989a, 47–48).

The Twentieth Century: Typographical Overview by Regions

Lamellophone technology has declined in most parts of Africa during the second half of the twentieth century; the immense variety of types has seriously decreased, and a significant number are extinct. My regional overview will therefore be based mainly on late nineteenth- to early twentieth-century instruments preserved in museums or recorded in the field up to the 1970s (with some exceptions recorded later). According to their typology and cultural and historical relationships, lamellophones can be discussed in an overview of eight major regions including the West African and American Diasporas.

1. Eastern Nigeria and the Cameroon Grasslands

As has already been suggested, it was probably in eastern Nigeria and the Cameroon grasslands that lamellophones made of cane or materials derived from the raffia palm were developed in ancient times. The area still displays some types and construction principles that might perpetuate ancient models, as in the Tikar *mbø toŋ* and *mbø ŋgo,* which are played with thumbs and index fingers of both hands (figs. 1.17a,b), and the instruments found among the Mbum and Vute

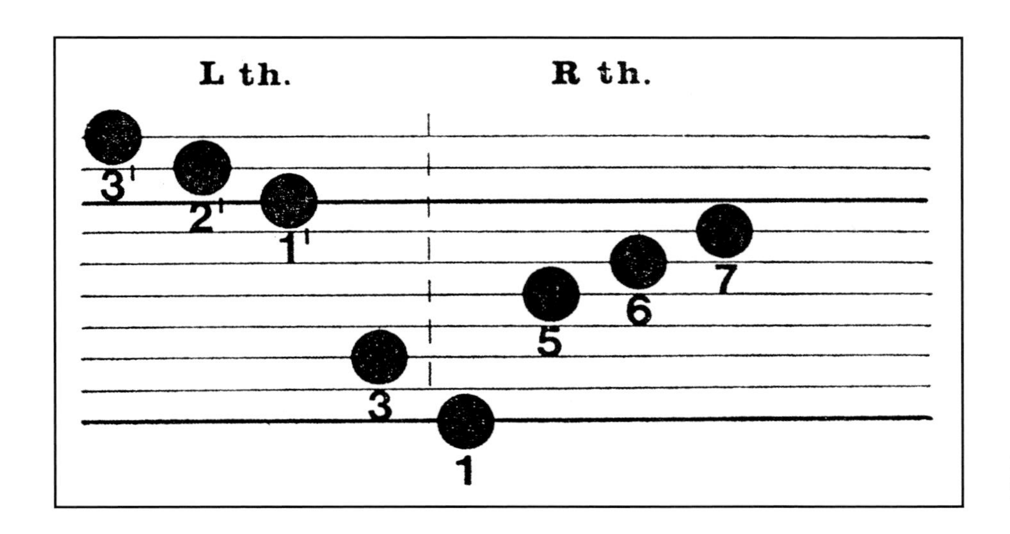

1.14 Andrew Tracey's "basic kalimba core" in the Zimbabwe/Zambezi culture area. Reproduced from A. Tracey 1972, 88.

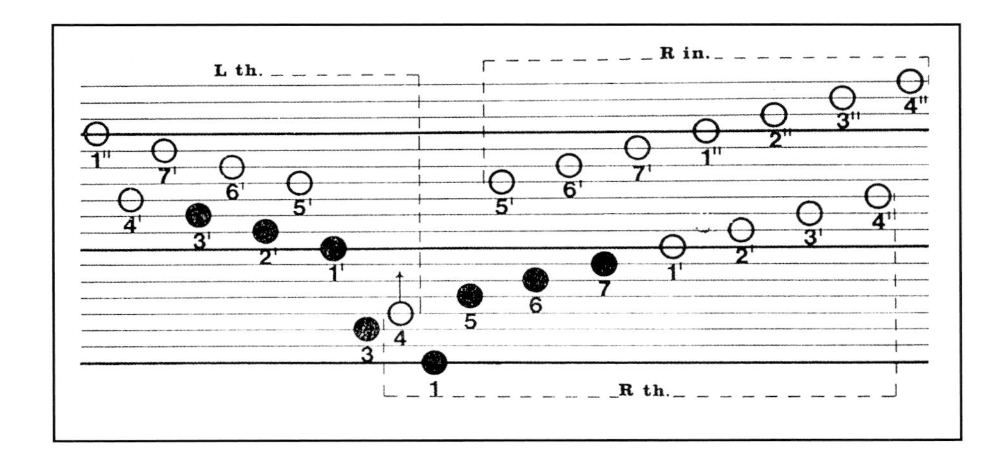

1.15 The "basic kalimba core" contained in the tuning layout of the twenty-five–note *karimba*, as played by - Nyungwe and others south of the middle Zambezi. Reproduced from A. Tracey 1972, 90.

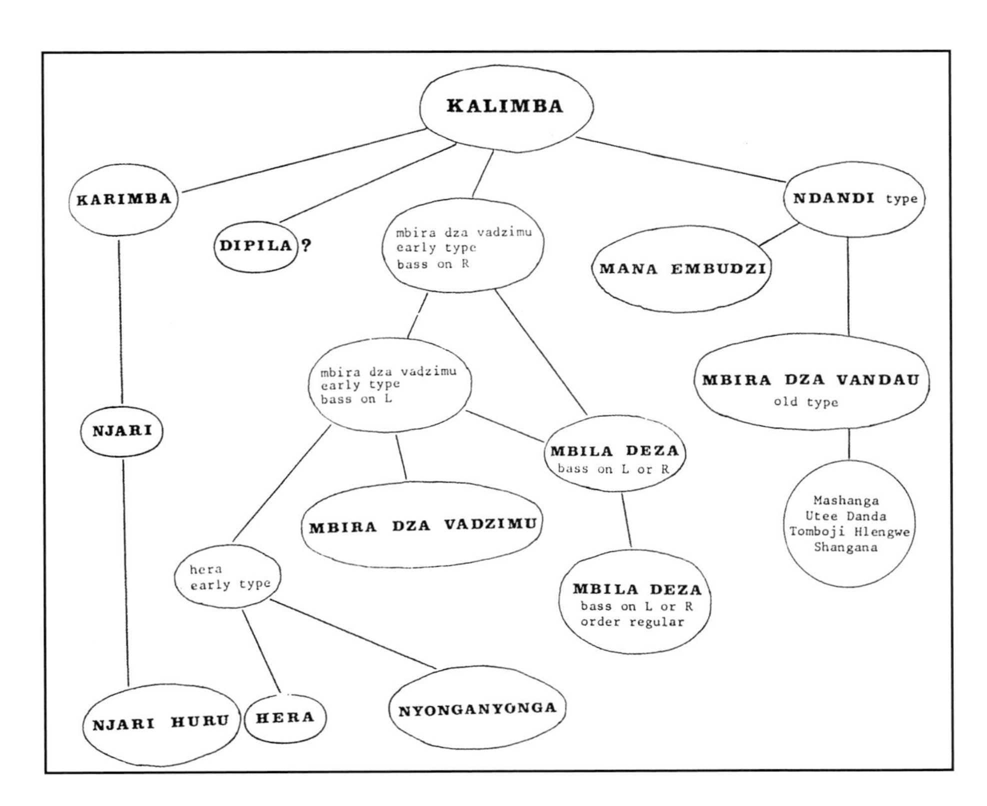

1.16 Andrew Tracey's family tree of lamellophones in the Zimbabwe/Zambezi culture area showing how and in which order all the presently known types could have descended from an ancestral eight-note *kalimba* with a specific tuning layout (see fig. 1.14). Reproduced from A. Tracey 1972, 89.

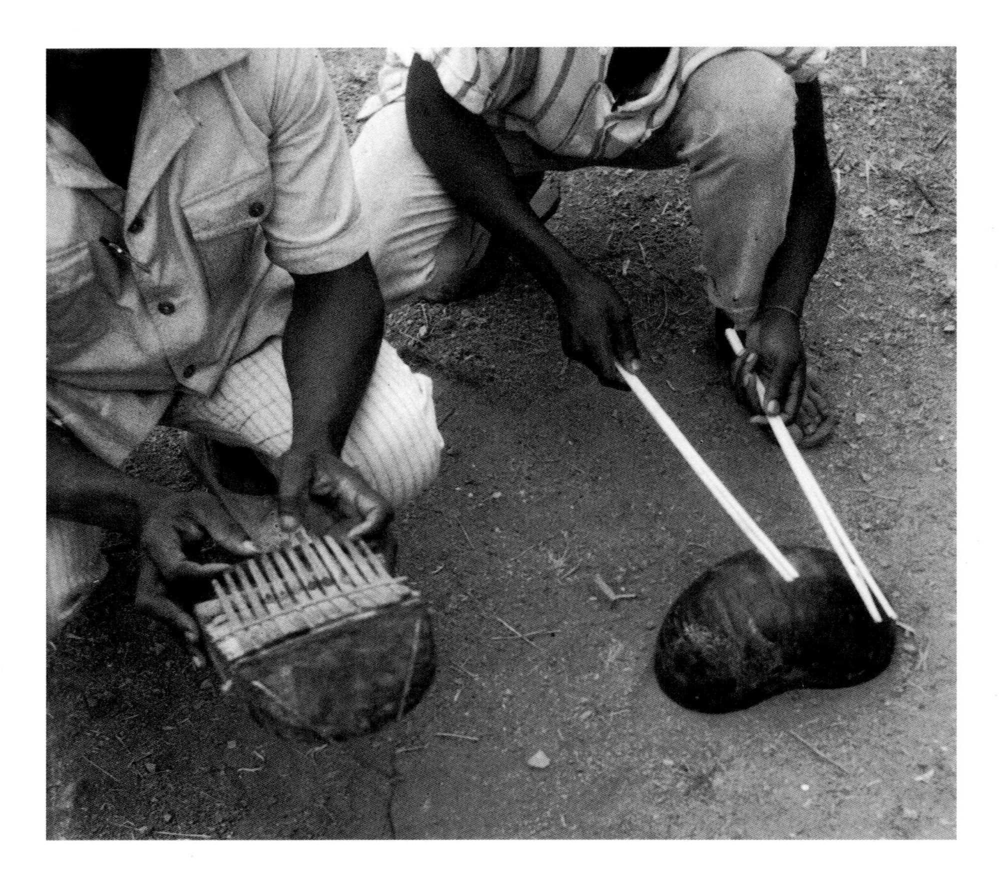

1.17a,b Playing technique of a Tikar *mbø ŋgo* with thumbs and index fingers of both hands. The instrument has twelve lamellae cut from the epidermis of a raffia stem leaf. Six deep-tuned lamellae in the middle of the V-shaped layout have vibration needles. The performer, Mekubueŋ, about forty-five years old, is accompanied by a second musician with a rhythm pattern struck on an inverted gourd. Photograph by Gerhard Kubik, Ngambe village, central Cameroon, February 16, 1964.

(Ankermann 1901, 33), which were primarily collected in the late nineteenth century. This is all the more surprising as the western Cameroon grassland highlands are an ancient area of metal working in bronze and iron. Giant single- and double-flange welded bells were produced in the Kingdom of Bamum, and high furnaces were used throughout the region. But in lamellophones raffia technology persisted.

The mid-rib of a raffia stem leaf serves as the universal material for manufacturing both the body and the lamellae. Two to three split raffia mid-ribs are cut and joined to form a "raft." The lamellae to be mounted on the raft are obtained from the hard surface, or epidermis, of the same raffia branch (fig. 1.18). In some lamellophones a resonator is formed by hollowing out the raffia mid-ribs to form two or three tubes that are joined by inserting thin sticks crosswise into the tubes to hold them together. A variety of methods exist for mounting the lamellae between the bridge and the backrest, which are also cut from the same raffia material. The most frequently encountered involves threading or plaiting either the pressure bar or the individual lamellae to the soundboard using rattan or other plant materials. Some methods of attaching lamellae are so specific that their geographical distribution across the raffia zone can serve as a diagnostic marker for historical connections between the types concerned.

A lamellophone constructed entirely of plant materials does not produce a penetrating sound. The sounds tend to be short, fading away quickly. An ingenious solution to this problem is to be found in the use of vibration needles, also cut from the epidermis of a raffia stem leaf. These are attached lengthwise on top of some (or all) lamellae with the same black wax used for tuning. The pointed ends of the needles stand off the surface of the lamellae less than a millimeter. When the musician depresses and releases a lamella, its vibration induces a sympathetic vibration of the attached needle resulting in the prolongation and considerable amplification of the sound.

The eastern Nigeria/central Cameroon region displays a stunning variety of forms and ideas in lamellophone technique. At one time, in southeastern Nigeria, there existed—in addition to sculptured versions—"double lamellophones" in which two eight-note V-shaped sets are mounted next to each other on a large soundboard of balsa wood. An example is specimen no. 1900.1.5 collected by Sir C. E. Peek in Old Calabar at the end of the nineteenth century and now preserved in

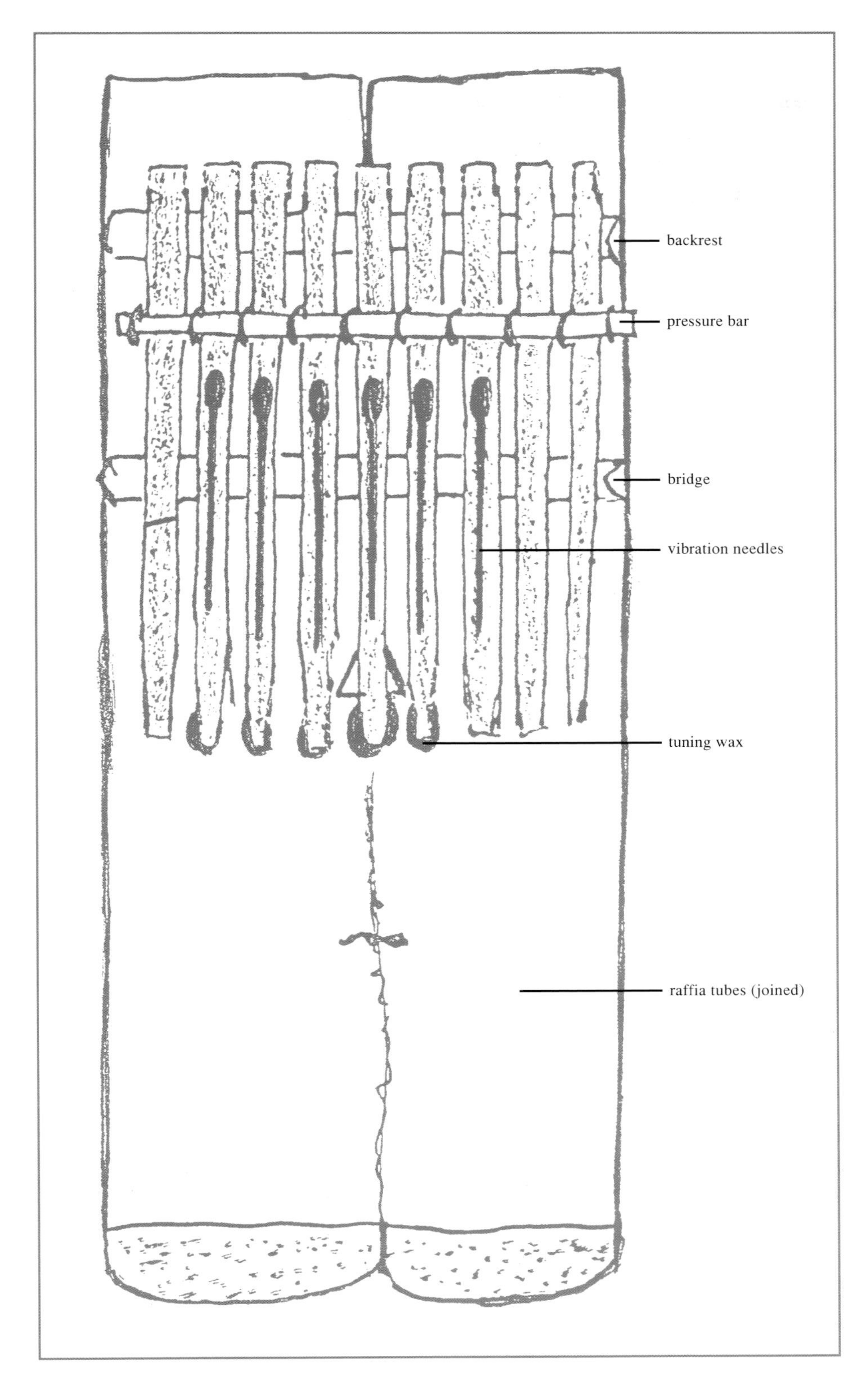

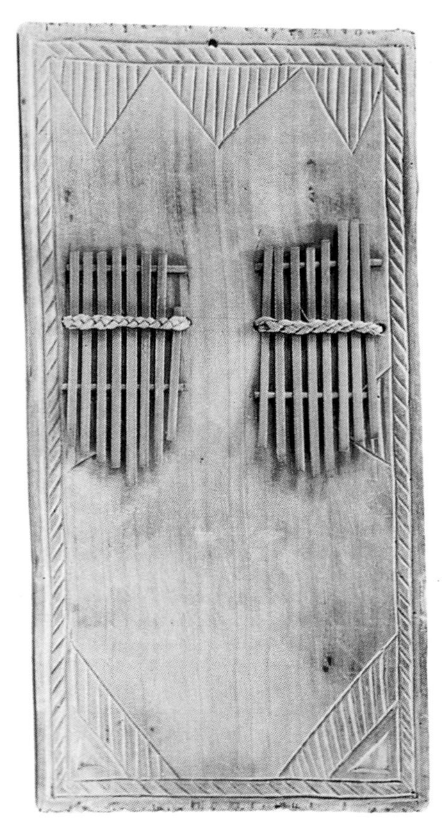

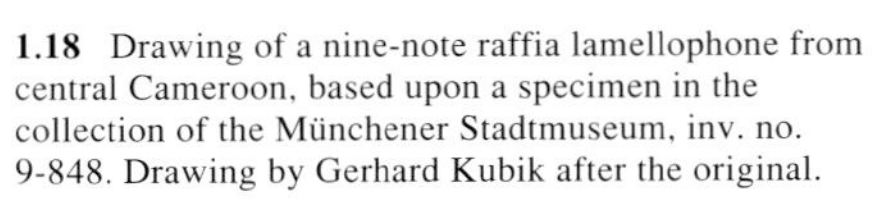

1.18 Drawing of a nine-note raffia lamellophone from central Cameroon, based upon a specimen in the collection of the Münchener Stadtmuseum, inv. no. 9-848. Drawing by Gerhard Kubik after the original.

1.19 "Double lamellophone" collected by Sir C. E. Peek in Old Calabar before 1900. © The Pitt Rivers Museum, University of Oxford, inv. no. 1900.1.5.

1.20 Calabar lamellophone with engraved *nsibidi* ideogram referring to conjugal happiness. In abstraction a married couple is depicted in a state of complete merger with a pillow to the right and to the left of them. Münchener Stadtmuseum, instrument inv. no. 40-100.

the Pitt Rivers Museum, Oxford (fig. 1.19). Another type, which was developed in the area of Calabar, is characterized by a flat, box-shaped resonator that looks like an old-style cigar box, with fire-incised decoration all over. Some specimens such as inv. nos. 40-100 and 41-301 in the Münchener Stadtmuseum, Munich, have *nsibidi* ideograms engraved (fig. 1.20). *Nsibidi* was the old ideographic script of Efik, Ekom, and others in southeastern Nigeria, and it is still used by the Ekpe secret society among the Igbo (personal communication from Dr. Azuka Tuburu, January 26, 1987). These Calabar lamellophones usually have eight raffia lamellae in a VI -shaped layout.

Another significant development in this zone is the *ubɔ aka* of the Igbo (Thieme 1967, 43, 45–46; Kubik et al. 1989, 74–75), with eight iron notes in a VI -shaped layout, and—like the other eastern Nigerian lamellophones—played with the thumbs. Its salient characteristic is a soundboard tightly fitted into the circumference of a gourd resonator with two sections cut out so that the player can insert his hands comfortably. An analogous instrument is mentioned by Roger Blench (1987, 46) from the Idoma (who, like the Igbo, are I.A.4, or Kwa, speakers) under the name *ògwúmògwú*. He describes it as a board lamellophone "set into a hemispherical gourd played by men for their personal amusement." He mentions that today the notes are always iron but that they were made of cane in the past. Describing the playing technique, which seems to be identical to that of the *ubɔ aka*, Blench writes, "In the face of the table are set two crescent-shaped resonating holes that enable the player to grip the instrument firmly while plucking the keys with the thumbs" (Blench 1987, 46).

The eastern Nigeria/central Cameroon area has displayed an enormous potential for innovation. In central Cameroon from the early decades of the twentieth century, Vute lamellophones (*timbrh*) began to be constructed with a large box resonator and a crescent shaped sound hole in the middle. On top there are two carved arrowheads that recall the hunting past of the Vute (figs. 1.21a–c). The tuning of these instruments is tetratonic and in pairs of octaves with the thumbs sounding two neighboring lamellae at once. The music, normally performed with two to three *timbrh* of different size and an accompanying raft rattle (*kara*) displays a fabulous swing. Figures 1.22a–c show the structure of one composition in cipher notation.

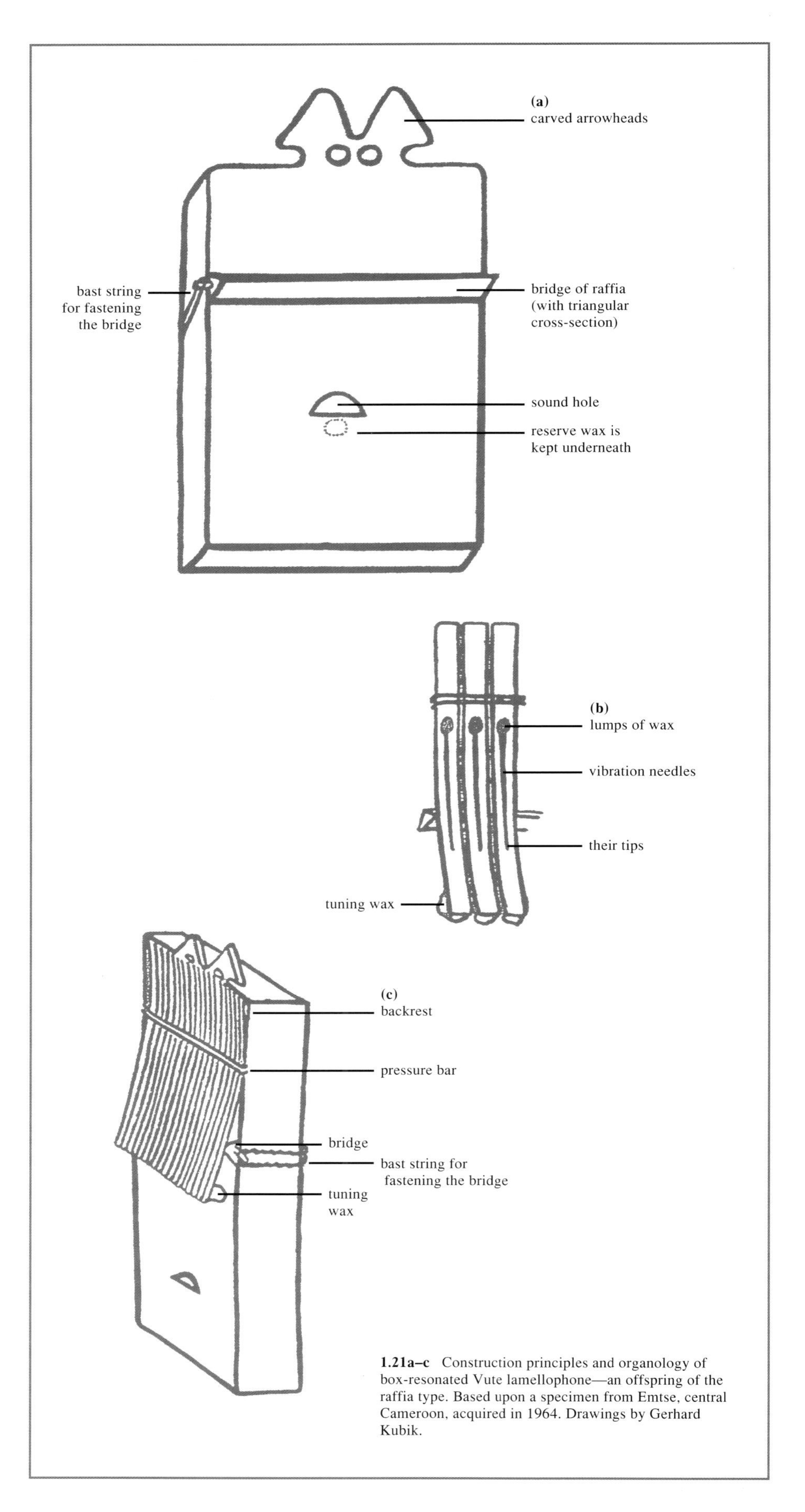

1.21a–c Construction principles and organology of box-resonated Vute lamellophone—an offspring of the raffia type. Based upon a specimen from Emtse, central Cameroon, acquired in 1964. Drawings by Gerhard Kubik.

1.22a–c Transcription in cipher notation of the basic cycle of the instrumental piece "Manengombe," which was played by Omaru Sanda, male, about thirty years old, at the chief's court in Emtse, north of Nanga-Eboko, Cameroon, February 1964. Recording: B 8893/Kubik, Phonogrammarchiv Vienna.

1.22a Tuning: Tetratonic. Ciphers 1, 2, 3, 4 correspond approximately to C, E, G, A (relative) in Western notation. Lower octaves are shown by underlining a cipher, higher ones by a line on top. Layout: in octave pairs, eighteen notes.

$\overline{1}$	1	$\underline{3}$	3	$\underline{4}$	4	$\underline{2}$	$\underline{2}$	2	2	4	$\underline{4}$	1	$\underline{1}$	$\underline{3}$	3	4	$\overline{2}$
left thumb area							right thumb area										

1.22b The piece "Manengombe":

right thumb

$2 . 1 . 3 . 1 . 2 . 4 . | 1 . 1 . 3 . 1 . 1 . 4 .$

$\underline{2} . \underline{1} . \underline{3} . \underline{1} . \underline{2} . \underline{4} . | \underline{1} . \underline{1} . \underline{3} . \underline{1} . \underline{1} . \underline{4} .$

(12) etc.

left thumb

$. 2 . 3 . \overline{1} . 2 . \overline{1} . \overline{1} | . 2 . 3 . \overline{1} . 2 . \overline{1} . \overline{1}$

$. \underline{2} . \underline{3} . 1 . \underline{2} . 1 . 1 | . \underline{2} . \underline{3} . 1 . \underline{2} . 1 . 1$

1.22c From these cyclic structures human auditory perception (in both listeners and performers) isolates so-called inherent patterns combining pitches close to each other. The effect is intended by the composers, but the arising patterns are a subjective perceptual phenomenon, a kind of auditory illusion. These are the patterns that arise from the played cycles transcribed above (aligned with ciphers on top):

Auditory image: some inherent patterns isolated by the ear.

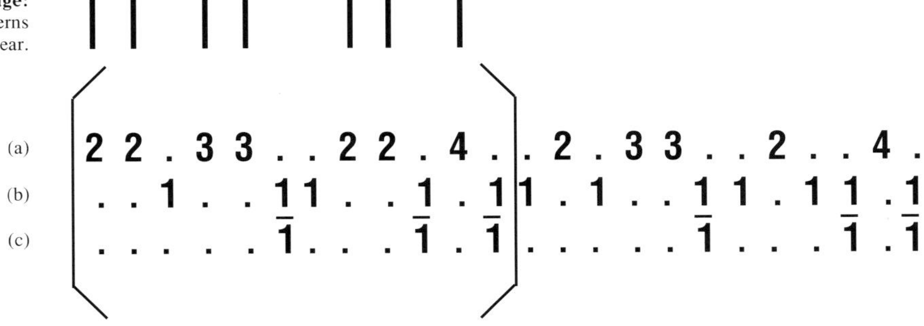

2. West-Central Equatorial Africa (from Gabon to the Eastern Parts of the Democratic Republic of the Congo)

Ecologically this area is well within the raffia intensity zone. A peculiar type of lamellophone is found among the Faŋ of Gabon; it has a curved resonator that looks like a cradle that could be rocked. A typical example is specimen no. 41-296 (coll. Dr. Neupert, Nuremberg) in the Musikinstrumenten-Museum/Münchener Stadtmuseum, illustrated in figures 23a,b below. This seven-note instrument corresponds in almost every detail to one collected late in the nineteenth century among the Faŋ and shown in Ankermann (1901, 32). The body of these instruments is made of light balsa-type wood with relatively few lamellae from raffia or similar material mounted between two identical bridges. The lamellae are fastened to the soundboard in a characteristic binding pattern using two straps of rattan or similar material.

The lamellae in the Faŋ-type lamellophone stick out across the bridges at almost equal length in both directions. A triangular sound hole is usually cut into one of the sides of the resonator. Sometimes the bottom of the resonator has raised edges that seem to form rails, as if to facilitate the imaginary rocking movement (see details of specimen no. III C 240, Museum für Völkerkunde, Berlin, collected in 1867! [Kubik 1999]).

These instruments look archaic; whether they are an archaic survival cannot be decided at this stage. That the lamellae are laid out across identical bars, instead of bars differentiated as "bridge" and "backrest," is perhaps also an archaic trait. It can be found in raffia or cane lamellophones across the raffia intensity zone and even in other areas of Africa to which the raffia technology spread. Occasionally, such lamellophones look as if the lamellae had been laid across two bars like the keys of a log xylophone.

Similar to region 1 (above) an abundance of forms developed in the west-central equatorial region, all using vegetable materials (see Ankermann 1901; Laurenty 1962; Kubik 1999). Conversely, lamellophones with iron notes are limited to very few types, and they are clearly a relatively recent introduction from the south (the combined territory of both Congos). Raffia-based lamellophones are found as far north as the Azande. For the Democratic Republic of the Congo, Laurenty (1962) has classified them as "type Haute-Uele." Many have an oval-shaped resonator of light balsa-type wood that looks like an egg cut in half. In 1964 I recorded one such instrument with nine cane lamellae, arranged in a V-shape and "plaited" to the soundboard, as played by a Zande musician, Bameke Gaston, aged around sixty, as far north as Djema in the Central African Republic. The oval soundboard was glued onto the resonator. (Recordings May 1964/Kubik, orig. tape no. 47/II, Museum für Völkerkunde, Berlin).

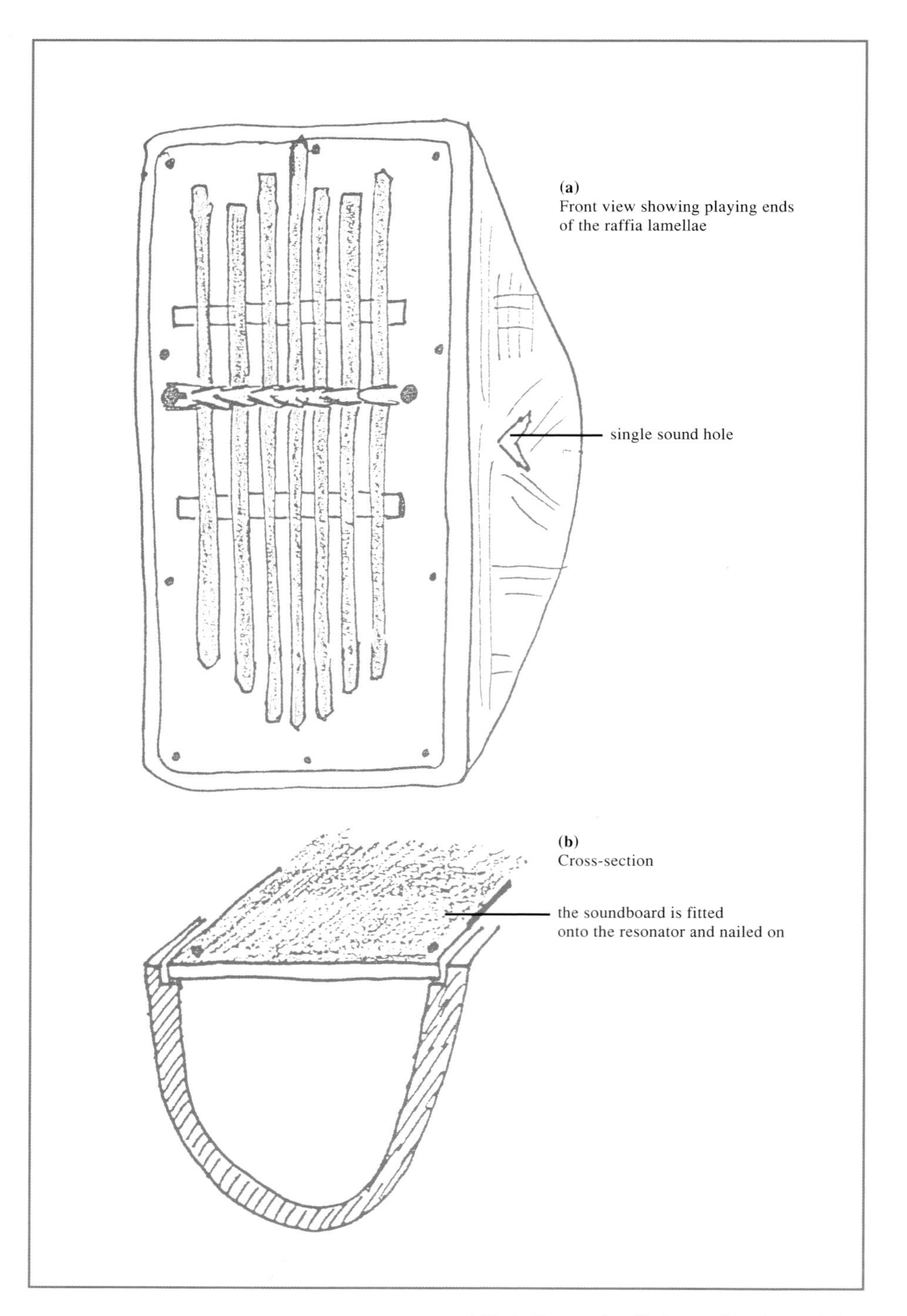

1.23a,b Faŋ-type lamellophone and its characteristics. Drawings by Gerhard Kubik from the original specimen, collection of Dr. Neupert, Nuremberg, Münchener Stadtmuseum, Munich, no. 41-296.

Original types of lamellophones using iron developed in the more southern parts of equatorial Africa, south of the rain forest. Perhaps the most specific type is the one with a bell-shaped resonator and linear arrangement of notes developed among the -Fioti, -Manyombe, and neighboring groups on the Loango coast, that is, in Cabinda, and the Atlantic seaboard of Congo (see Maes 1921, 3ff.; Laurenty 1962). These instruments are sometimes called *mbishi* (see Stephen Chauvet [1929] who depicts specimens with a carved head). The bell-shaped resonating body is cut from a single piece of wood to a shape that looks like a Capuchin monk wearing his garment and cowl. The resonator's orifice is characteristically shaped and directed toward the performer. The most frequent is crescent-shaped probably with religious meanings. Further north, in the Bwiti religion of Gabon the highest transcendental being, a female, is thought of as emerging from a half-moon (see painting by the priest André Mvome in Kubik 1986, 112). The anthropomorphic idea behind this type of lamellophone is also confirmed by the fact that several specimens were collected with a sculptured head replacing the "hood" (see Chauvet 1929). This type of lamellophone usually has from seven to nine iron notes arranged as a scale rising from left to right. Between the U-shaped bridge and the pressure bar, iron rings may be slung as buzzers around some of the lamellae. In many types there is no backrest, but the upper ends of the iron lamellae rest comfortably on the top part, slightly bent upward; a small piece of leather may also serve as a backrest. A typical example of these Loango-type lamellophones is listed as specimen no. 8669 in the collections of the Museu da Sociedade de Geografia de Lisboa, Lisbon, though it is erroneously listed under "Sofala." Most probably it came from Cabinda (see also comments by Margot Dias 1986, 100–101). A slightly variant type of the Loango lamellophone is also depicted in Dias (1986, 99). The main difference is in the shaping of the orifice (both lamellophones are listed under the no. 8669). See figures 24a–d.

An unusual, large lamellophone that looks like a cello was collected by Adolf Bastian on the Loango coast during a stay from June to December of 1873. It is preserved in the Museum für Völkerkunde, Berlin, inv. no. IIIC 350 (see Kubik 1999). This specimen is 92 cm long, 28 cm wide, and 23 cm high. It demonstrates the extraordinary developments that took place in this region only to disappear again—not being pursued further.

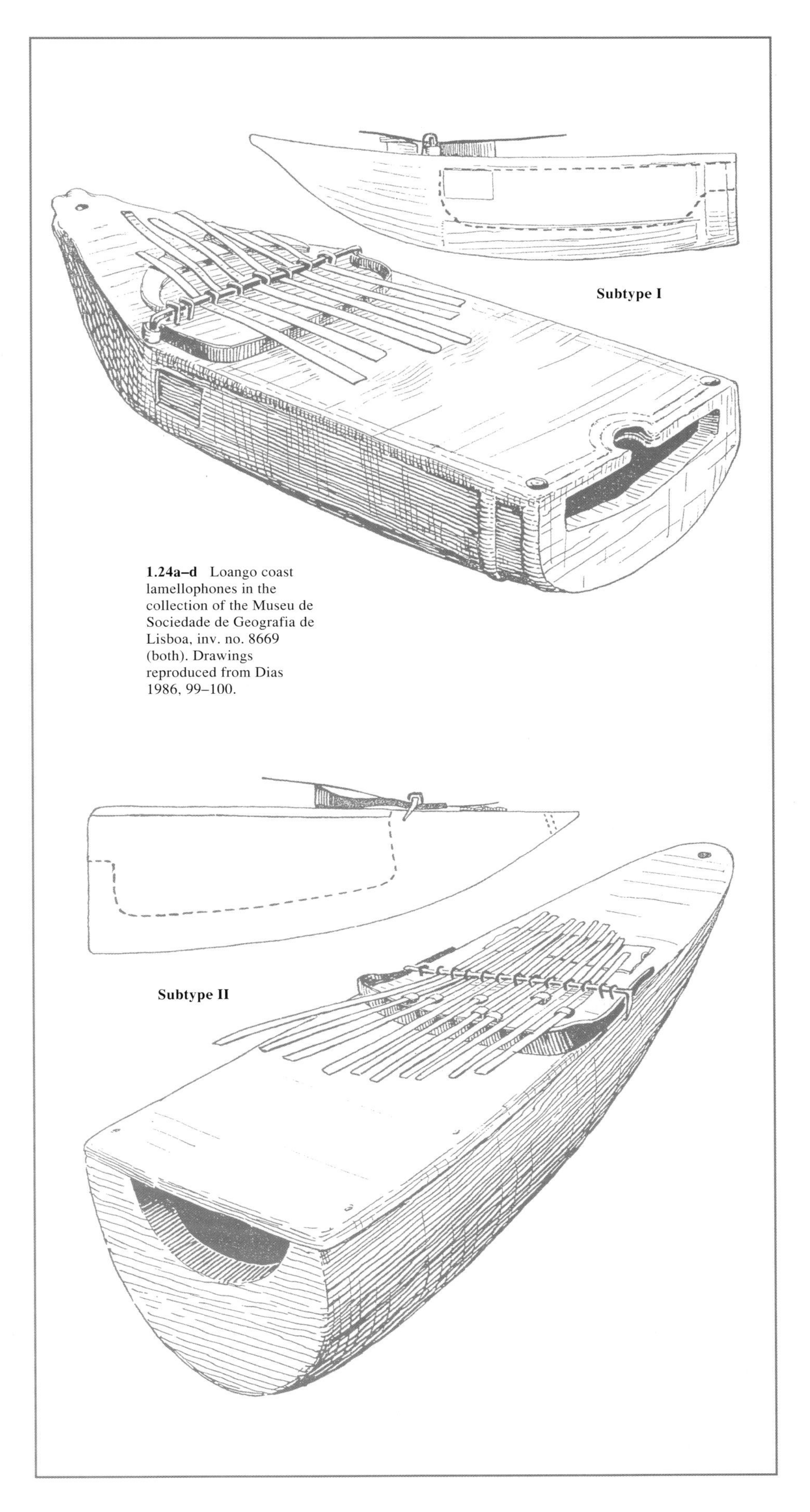

1.24a–d Loango coast lamellophones in the collection of the Museu de Sociedade de Geografia de Lisboa, inv. no. 8669 (both). Drawings reproduced from Dias 1986, 99–100.

In the early to mid-nineteenth century the southwestern part of the equatorial region, often referred to as the lower Congo, gave rise to a new type of lamellophone that turned out to be very suitable for travel. The new instrument incorporated a technical novelty: two sound holes, one at the narrow front end of the box resonator, the other at the back of the box to be controlled by the right middle finger and used for creating timbre modifications and wow effects. (See the more detailed description, above, under -KEMBE).

This instrument became interregionally known as the *likembe,* and it spread like wildfire among porters and employees in the Belgian colonial service throughout the French and the Belgian Congo, thus paralleling the spread of the trade language Lingala, which initially traveled along the major navigable rivers, such as the Congo. Camille Coquilhat described the *likembe* from the area near Kisangani in his work published 1888. Among the -Teke in the Republic of the Congo the *likembe* was firmly established during the second half of the nineteenth century, and it appears in many museum collections. The Teke specimens feature cheap, imported, blue, hexagonal beads used as buzzers slung around the lamellae and brass nails employed as decoration on the body (see for example specimen no. III C 2093, Museum für Völkerkunde, Berlin; Kubik 1999). In the decade before World War I, the *likembe* was established all along the Congo River among the -Kongo, -Mfinu, etc., and it was known among the Loi and Mbuja near Kisangani; it had also spread along the Ubangi River, where it was collected between 1911 and 1913 several times among the Ngbaka. This is evident from data in the Musée Royal de l'Afrique Centrale, Tervuren (see Collaer 1968; Laurenty 1962). In 1913 a specimen called *ikimbe* with eleven lamellae was acquired as far north as the Kadei River, near Ngundi in the present-day Central African Republic (inv. no. III C 29925, Museum für Völkerkunde, Berlin, coll. Von Ramsay). It conforms in all details with instruments that I recorded among the Mpyεmɔ̃ west of Nola, Central African Republic in 1964 and 1966 (see "Asɔε mɔ mεri" by Marcel Mogaya, CD item no. 14 in Kubik 1999).

Although the *likembe* was a fascinating original invention, some of its traits, such as the U-shaped iron bridge and the mode of attachment of the straining bar may have been inspired locally from the Loango-type lamellophone, while the idea of a box resonator and the VI -shaped layout of eight iron notes in many specimens may even have come from southeastern Nigerian models, such as the Calabar box-resonated types and the *ubɔ aka*. Maritime contacts all along the west and west central African coast have been important since the sixteenth century, contributing to the exchange of ideas. However, in the *likembe*, even the general idea of a box resonator was creatively modified, because the *likembe* box resonator is shorter than its soundboard ending exactly where a series of holes is to be bored into the latter horizontally to thread through the wire for attaching the straining bar. As a result, looked at from the back, the *likembe* seems to have a characteristic cut-out section.

3. The South Central African Savanna (Democratic Republic of the Congo, Angola, Northern Parts of Zambia, and the Central Region of Malawi)

It is striking that the lamellophone nomenclature in the western parts of this region is mostly dominated by the word stem -SANSI (with its variants and various prefixes), and in the eastern parts by -LIMBA. This suggests ancient connections to the Zambezi valley. It is well known that from the seventeenth century on, small fan-shaped, portable lamellophones became popular with porters who accompanied traders from the Portuguese settlements on the Zambezi, Tete, and Sena, north into the ancient Maravi Empire and further on to Lake Mweru. Eventually the trade routes crossed southern Africa from points in Angola, via the Lunda Empire, to the Lunda-Kazembe chieftaincy on Lake Mweru, and south into Mozambique. Two famous *pombeiros* (Afro-Portuguese traders) accomplished the whole route and the return trip in a few years at the beginning of the nineteenth century (see Bastin 1961).

But long before that, the Zambezi valley had become an important dispersal center for lamellophones. Small fan-shaped and tray-shaped types, held into a gourd-resonator during performance and featuring a mirliton-covered central hole, were swept northward into the area of the Maravi Empire (central Malawi, eastern Zambia). In 1987 we were still able to record two such instruments under the names *nsansi* and *kalimba* near Lilongwe. (See field recordings 1987/Kubik/Malamusi at village headman Nchenche, near Likuni, Lilongwe area, orig. tape no. 87/34, Museum für Völkerkunde, Berlin). A spectacular derivative with an oblong tray-shaped board whose raised sides often ended on the top in two sculptured heads was developed among the -Shila and their neighbors west of Lake Mweru, probably by the eighteenth century. In spite of a spectacular mutational leap, the "Zambezi connection" is still recognizable in these instruments. A few specimens were collected for museums, but it has not always been possible to trace their precise origins. A marvelous specimen is the one collected by Heinrich von Wissmann in 1887 for the Museum für Völkerkunde, Berlin (inv. no. III E 2109; reproduced in Brincard 1989 and Dias 1986). The museum card notes give "Sambesi" as regional origin, which—in light of the much-treaded caravan route from Lake Mweru down to Tete—is not necessarily wrong as the place where this specimen would have been collected. In Katanga R. P. Bultereys collected a related type with two heads, which obviously depict slave traders from the Indian Ocean coast, in 1936 (see Laurenty 1962, specimen no. 439). Finally, Placide Tempels collected a specimen without sculptural extensions in Katanga from the -Shila near Lake Mweru, Bantu-language speakers of zone M group 40, related to Taabwa (see Guthrie 1948, 57; Laurenty 1962, specimen no. 442; both the Bultereys and Tempels examples are housed in the Musée Royal de l'Afrique Centrale).

Using only nineteenth- and early twentieth-century specimens, one can almost reconstruct step-by-step how the organological details of the Zambezi fan-shaped and tray-shaped lamellophones gradually transformed along the migration route north to Lake Mweru, then west through Luba-speaking territory in Katanga, where many traits of the Shila-type were retained—such as the curved, broad U-shape of the iron bridge and the mode of attachment of the straining bar—and into Angola. At every juncture new types and modifications of known types were developed. Among the -Luba of Katanga board lamellophones with a gourd resonator were once very popular (see the many specimens preserved in the Musée Royal de l'Afrique Centrale; Laurenty 1962). Today, they are mostly obsolete (Gansemans 1980, 27). Jos Gansemans mentions two types from his fieldwork among the -Luba in the 1970s: *kisanzi* and a small-size version of the former called *kawaya*. Among the -Lunda farther west, board lamellophones are called *cisanj* (with the ending vowel characteristically eliminated).

In Angola board lamellophones are universally distributed. Among the -Mbondo (a Kimbundu-speaking group) specimens with twelve iron lamellae, called *kisanji* were still played in Malanji Province in 1982 (see recordings 1982/Kubik at Kixingambambi, Município de Kunda, February 6, 1982, orig. tape no. A 137, Museum für Völkerkunde, Berlin). Among the -Holo a small type was played called *kitutu* and also *sartela* (a designation that derives from Portuguese *salterio,* or psaltery). Obviously, this is an instance of a projection of a European name onto an African instrument, analogous to "hand piano," etc. But the psaltery is an ancient European instrument with strings stretched over a board, and it is played with the fingers; this explains the association. Because the psaltery was only popular in Portugal, and possibly with Portuguese in Luanda, until the eighteenth century, the projection must have occurred at that time (see Kubik 1997). Indirectly, this suggests that lamellophones were known among the -Holo in the eighteenth century, which links well with the ascertained presence of the sixteen-note varieties in southwestern Angola during that period.

The greatest variety in the lamellophones of Angola is concentrated in the eastern half of the country, among the -Cokwe, -Lwena (-Luvale), -Lucazi, -Mbwela, etc., all peoples within Bantu-language zone K, group 10. All these types have reached a high degree of independence, and only occasionally can a remote echo of the Zambezi valley be discerned amidst some other "echos" from the north and northwest. As a case in point the inventory of lamellophones among the -Cokwe includes five types (Barbosa 1989; Bastin 1992; Laurenty 1962; Kubik 1965; 1998, 678):

a. *Cisaji cakele*—a raffia-manufactured lamellophone of oblong shape and few notes. Some types have a board; others feature the original raft composed of two or three raffia tubes (see also Laurenty's "sanza en radeau type Kwango-Kasayi," Laurenty 1962) reminiscent of central Cameroonian types.
b. *Cisaji cakakolondondo*—a board lamellophone with somewhat raised side parts giving it a tray shape. Rattle rings serving as buzzers are attached on a bar at the thin front part of the board that is directed toward the musician. The usual ten lamellae are spatula-shaped and arranged in a V-shaped layout.
c. *Cisaji calungandu* or *cisaji camandumbwa*—a twelve- to thirteen-note board lamellophone similar in shape to the *cisaji cakakolondondo* but with its spatula-shaped lamellae tuned by means of lumps of black wax and the pitches arranged in two ranks, rising from left to right, according to this scheme (figs. 1.25a,b, 1.26).
d. *Mucapata*—a lamellophone with a bell-shaped resonator; rattle rings on a bar fixed across the orifice; and seventeen, nineteen, or more iron lamellae in a characteristic arrangement forming chord columns (see fig. 1.8).
e. *Likembe*—a box-resonated lamellophone (already described under -KEMBE, above). Among the -Cokwe this type is often elaborately decorated.

1.25a, b *Cisaji calungandu* with thirteen lamellae in two ranks played by the blind Lwena musician, Kaumbu, about twenty-five years old. The music is based on a sixteen-pulse time-line pattern known as *kacaca*, struck gently on the gourd resonator by Musumali, sixty years old, who was also a notable lamellophone player. Photographs by Gerhard Kubik, Sakatuta village, near Kazombo, Alto Zambezi Province, northeastern Angola, December 1965.

1.26 Tuning layout of a *cisaji calungandu* with thirteen notes played by Kaumbu, a blind Lwena musician, about twenty-five years old, recorded at Sakatuta village, Alto Zambezi, Angola, December 1965, orig. tape no. 80/Kubik.

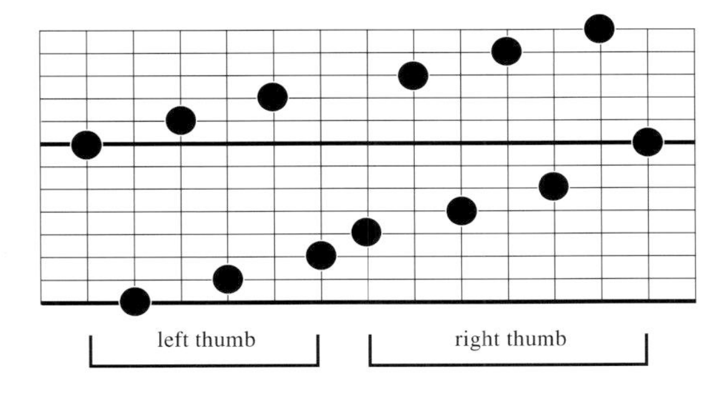

Except where iron-note lamellophones such as the *mucapata* have been copied with raffia materials (as in a specimen collected by Hermann Baumann in the 1930s, see Museum für Völkerkunde, Berlin, inv. no. III C 35457), the Cokwe raffia lamellophones have few notes mounted on a raft composed of two, three, or four parts of a raffia mid-rib, sometimes arranged in an anthropomorphic shape with two "legs." The Kasai area where the -Cokwe live is the southernmost point of the otherwise dense distribution of raffia lamellophones, and these simple types could be an old heritage among the -Cokwe.

The *cisaji cakakolondondo* and the *cisaji calungandu* have remote links to the Zambezi valley with intermediate developmental stages in the Lake Mweru and Luba-speaking areas of southern Congo. The *lungandu* is actually the only Congo/Angolan lamellophone type showing an arrangement of the lamellae in two ranks, a trait par excellence of the Zimbabwe/Zambezi cluster. But the use of tuning wax (*vulongo*) points to a different heritage.

The *mucapata,* which has been played by -Cokwe and -Mbangala musicians (the latter to the west of the -Cokwe) has an altogether different heritage (figs. 1.27a–d). Some traits like the upward-bent shape of the head portion, promoting the absence of a backrest or its symbolic presence in form of a leather strap, might even link it as far west as the Loango-types, but other elements such as specific shapes, might also point to the Luba cluster; while the types of buzzers and the way they are attached could also demonstrate a remote Zimbabwe/Zambezi background. In any case, the *mucapata* is the nineteenth- and twentieth-century outcome of genealogical links that might reach far into the past and are difficult to disentangle.

The tuning of both Luba and Cokwe lamellophones is in principle hexatonic. The scale is perfectly demonstrated in the *lungandu* layout shown in fig. 1.26, above. The *mucapata* layout (see fig. 1.8) especially reveals that this system is based on two roots approximately a whole-tone apart, which suggests a remote inspiration in mouth-bows with reinforcement of partials four–six over each fundamental. Among the -Cokwe, -Luvale, and other peoples in zone K, group 10, this system has long been expanded into heptatonism, and a tuning temperament was developed.

The Angolan types—with the exception of the *likembe* imported recently from the lower Congo—are the developmental result of a western branch of diffusion and ideas from the lower Zambezi valley. Characteristically, none of these types have retained the spider-web mirliton,

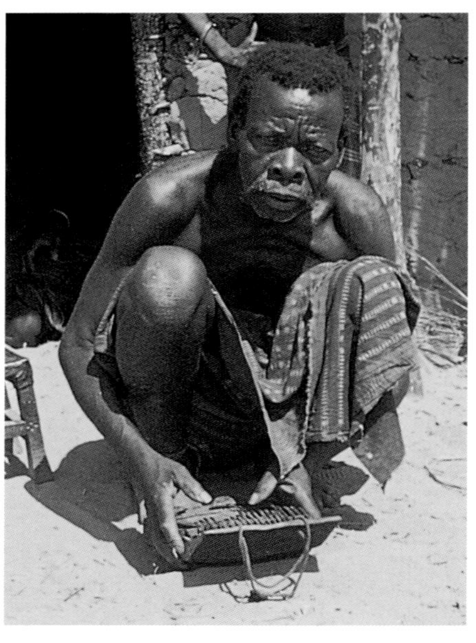

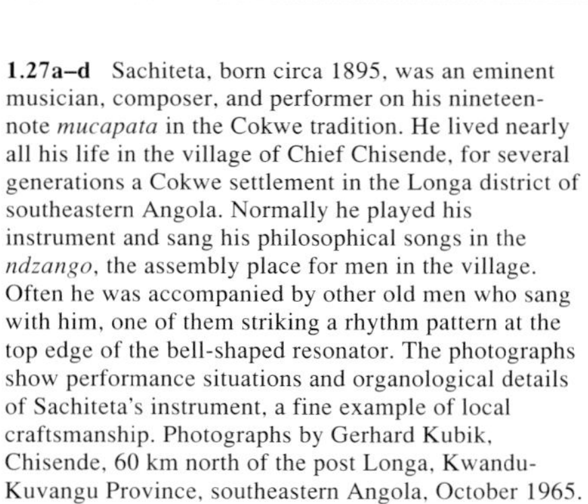

1.27a–d Sachiteta, born circa 1895, was an eminent musician, composer, and performer on his nineteen-note *mucapata* in the Cokwe tradition. He lived nearly all his life in the village of Chief Chisende, for several generations a Cokwe settlement in the Longa district of southeastern Angola. Normally he played his instrument and sang his philosophical songs in the *ndzango*, the assembly place for men in the village. Often he was accompanied by other old men who sang with him, one of them striking a rhythm pattern at the top edge of the bell-shaped resonator. The photographs show performance situations and organological details of Sachiteta's instrument, a fine example of local craftsmanship. Photographs by Gerhard Kubik, Chisende, 60 km north of the post Longa, Kwandu-Kuvangu Province, southeastern Angola, October 1965.

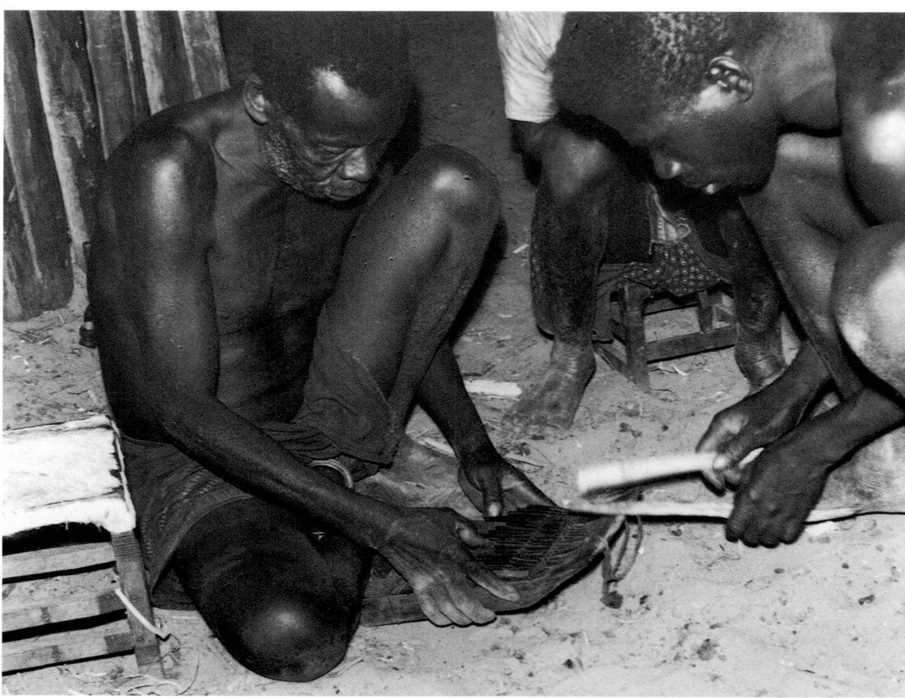

though the central hole in the soundboard, which could have accommodated this buzzing device, is retained in most of the board-shaped Angolan varieties. The idea of the mirliton, however, has continued in what could be called the northern/northeastern branch of the diffusion. It did spread from eastern Zambia as far north as Lake Mweru and from there with the eastern caravan trade in the nineteenth century to Tanzania where it reappears in the lamellophones of the -Gogo of central Tanzania.

4. The Zimbabwe/Lower Zambezi Culture Area (Zimbabwe, Central Mozambique, and Adjacent Territories)

This is one of the most prolific and probably ancient areas of the establishment of complex iron-note lamellophones. It is also one of the best researched thanks to the indefatigable work of Hugh Tracey beginning in the 1920s and continued by his son Andrew Tracey and other researchers, such as Paul Berliner (1975; 1976; 1978; 1980), Margot Dias (1986), Keith Goddard (1996), Robert Kauffman (1969), and others.

Lamellophones in this culture area have a body that is either a tray-shaped board, such as the *mbira dza vadzimu*, or forms a bell-shaped resonator, such as the *nyonganyonga, matepe,* etc. The redesign of the soundboard into fan-shaped forms characteristic of the smaller instruments found north of the Zambezi River seems to be based on the historical need during the times of the caravan trade to create lamellophones suitable for travel along the trade routes from Tete and Sena to the north.

The body of the Zimbabwe/Zambezi lamellophones is always cut from a single piece of wood, primarily *Pterocarpus angolensis* (in Shona, *mubvamaropa*). Andrew Tracey considers the *mbira dza vadzimu* to be one of the oldest complex types (Andrew Tracey 1972, 89). He distinguishes an early type with the bass notes in the playing area of the right hand from a somewhat later type with the bass notes to the left, a pattern that continues up to the present forms (fig. 1.28). The *mbira dza vadzimu*, as is suggested by its name (*dza vadzimu*, or "of the ancestral spirits") was used long ago in the context of religious ceremonies for the ancestors. When playing, it is held into a gourd resonator (*deze*), the name of which is sometimes also used to designate the instrument itself. The body is a rectangular, almost square-shaped, tray with raised edges; it most usually has twenty-two to twenty-three lamellae arranged in three rows. For playing, three fingers are used: the thumbs of both hands and the index finger of the right hand. The action of playing is described as *kukwenya* (scratching) rather than "plucking." The right index finger operates on the six highest-tuned lamellae at the outside right and moves upward from below.

Like other Shona music in Zimbabwe, the music of the *mbira dza vadzimu* is based on harmonic progressions between six bichords (octaves, fourths, or fifths according to context) to form cycles. The cycles can be segmented in various ways (see Beuler Dyoko's segmentation 36 = 4 times 9 elementary pulses in her song "Kuzanga," see Kubik 1994a, CD item no. 26). In ritual contexts the instrument was often accompanied by a rattle (*hosho*). Today two are often played together in a duet. While the *mbira dza vadzimu* was almost extinct in the 1930s, it saw a spectacular revival in Zimbabwe in the context of the national liberation struggle (*chimurenga*) from the 1950s on. It has been incorporated, together with the characteristic Shona harmonic patterns, into new Zimbabwean dance music, especially by Thomas Mapfumo. Originally played by males, women such as Beuler Dyoko have taken up the art.

Among the -Chikunda of the lower Zambezi valley the most important lamellophone type is the *njari huru*, among the -Korekore the *hera,* among the Sena/Tonga the *matepe* and *mana embudzi,* and among the Barwe and Gorongozi *nyonganyonga* are predominant (Andrew Tracey 1972, 96–100). Among the -Dzimba and -Phodzo the type otherwise called *nyonganyonga* goes by the name *malimba* (figs. 1.29a,b; see Kubik 1967, 29; recordings in Kubik/Malamusi 1989, items A5, A6 and B5).

North of the town of Sena, toward Lake Chilwa, a large bell-resonated type played with five fingers—thumbs, index fingers, and the left little finger plucking upward—was developed among the -Khokola. It is called *sasi*. In 1967 Maurice Djenda and I recorded this unusual instrument on two occasions, a fifteen-note variety from Chief Kolowiko (figs. 1.30a–f), then about fifty years old, at Kolowiko, near Lake Chilwa (orig. tape no. 50) and a sixteen-note variety from Julias Chikopa, about sixty years old at Chiwalo, in Mulanje District, Malawi (orig. tape no. 52). Both specimens were more than 40 cm high and had large bell-shaped resonators with rattle rings attached inside on a bar. The playing technique was identical in both musicians. Chief Kolowiko gave me this

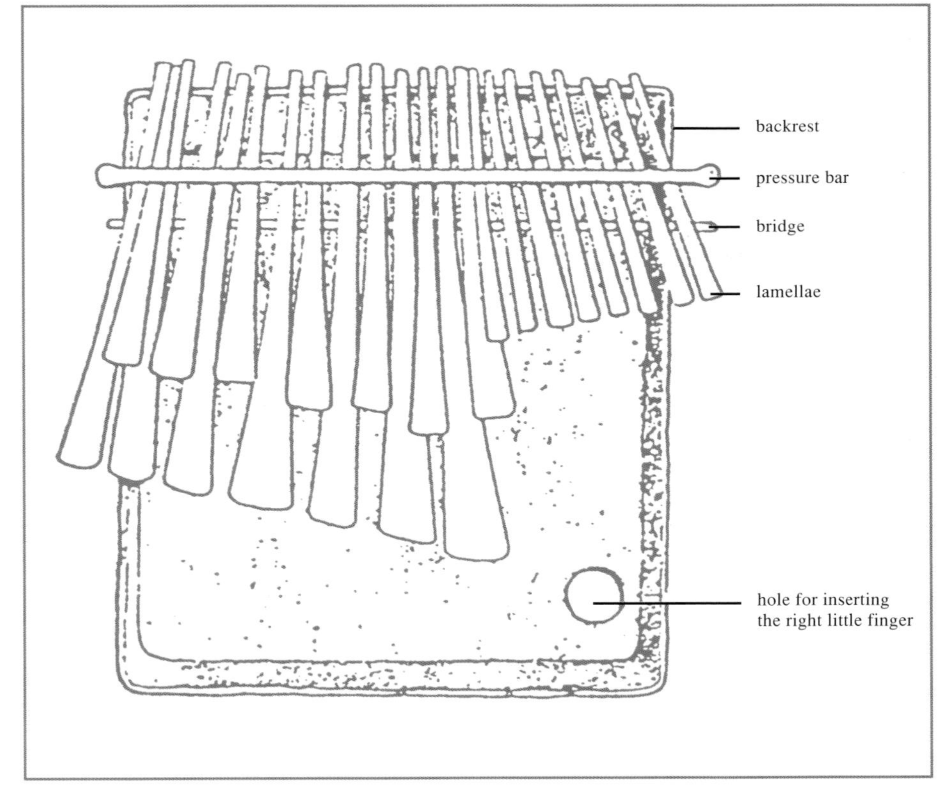

1.28 Drawing of a *mbira dza vadzimu* by Andrew Tracey. Reproduced from A. Tracey 1970a.

1.29a,b Dayi Masitine, born circa 1882, of the Adzimba ethnic group in the Zambezi valley area, Mozambique, was a living cultural monument when we recorded him on two occasions in 1967. His twenty-six–note *malimba*, a bell-shaped complex lamellophone with the notes arranged in two ranks was held into a large gourd, still dotted round its rim with the traditional snail shells sewn on. He had constructed the very instrument that accompanied him through his life before World War I, and he had traveled with it from place to place during the war years, 1914–1918. Only the gourd resonator had to be replaced once or twice. Dayi's music (see Kubik/Malamusi 1989, LP, items A5–6) incorporates some unusual rhythms reminiscent a bit of ragtime. Photographs by Djenda/Kubik, Ndamera, Nsanje District, Malawi, March 1967.

1.30a–f Khokola-chief Kolowiko, about fifty years old, with his fifteen-note *sasi*, one of the largest types of lamellophones ever recorded in Africa, and an unusual member of the Zimbabwe/Zambezi family. The pictures show the size, organology, fingering set, and performance context of this instrument. Chief Kolowiko used to play it sitting on a mat with the orifice of the bell-shaped resonator comfortably placed on the ground; at his left and his right sit rattle players accompanying him. His songs contain extensive local chronicles, news, social criticism, and gossip, often expressed symbolically. Photographs by Gerhard Kubik, Chief Kolowiko's headquarters, near Lake Chilwa, Mulanje District, Malawi, May 1967.

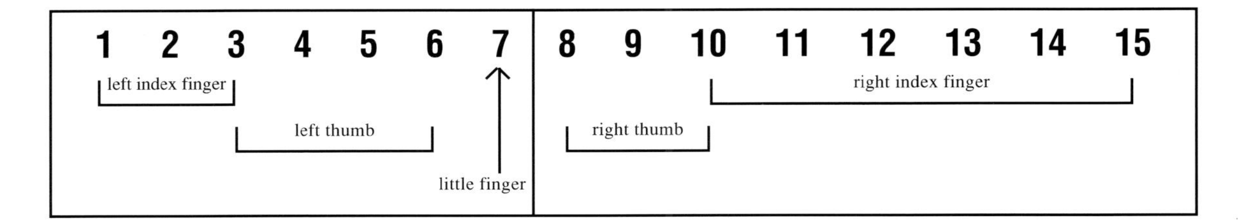

1.31 Left- and right-hand playing areas of Chief Kolowiko's *sasi* (see figs. 1.30a–g).

scheme shown in figure 1.31 of the left- and right-hand playing areas (the deepest-tuned lamellae are in the middle; the tuning layout is V-shaped).

To the best of my knowledge this type of lamellophone, no doubt an offspring of the Zimbabwe/Zambezi cluster, has never been seen again. Moya A. Malamusi, who has screened southern Malawi virtually village-by-village since 1989, has never reported it (field notes in the African Music Archive Wolfgang Bender, Institut für Ethnologie und Afrika-Studien, University of Mainz). Earlier in this century, however, a comparable instrument was acquired from a chief at Namarral, near Mossuril in northern Mozambique, just opposite Mozambique Island (inv. no. 6197, collections of the Museu da Sociedade de Geografia de Lisboa, Portugal; see Dias 1986, 90).

All this suggests that perhaps some more unusual types were developed in the history of the Zimbabwe/Zambezi culture area but have disappeared without trace. The Portuguese source in the museum gives the name "cavirá" (pronounced *kavira*) for this sixteen-note specimen from Namarral. One could speculate whether this name might be related to *bira* or *mbira*, and also whether any kind of relationship might have existed in the remote history between this type and the -Makonde/Mwera type (see below). Arrangements of little sound holes to form patterns such as a cross in the case of the "cavirá" also appear in northeastern Mozambiquan decorative art, but they are also found in some Angolan lamellophones, such as the *ocisanzi* (inv. no. AP 824, Museu de Etnologia, Lisbon) discussed earlier.

Small fan-shaped types, it seems, were developed in the eighteenth century, particularly in the Nyungwe-speaking environment of Tete, which was founded by the Portuguese in 1532. Some of these instruments still have arrangements of notes in two ranks, as was recorded by Moya A. Malamusi from a young Mozambiquan refugee, Kwitenti Wirison, fifteen years old, in 1989 (orig. tape no. 89/12, Oral Literature Research Program, Chileka, Malawi). An analogous instrument from Tete is found in the Museu de Etnologia, Lisbon, inv. no. AO 138 (see Margot Dias 1986, 87)

Fan-shaped types also spread westward from the lower Zambezi into Zambia, where characteristic modifications took place among the -Lala (see Jones 1950 and the *kankobele* discussed by Marjory Davidson 1970). Characteristic form modifications into a shovel shape took place among the -Lozi of western Zambia, the top part of the body functioning as a backrest (see specimens in Borel 1986, 108–14). Related instruments, but with two ranks, can be found among the -Subia of the Caprivi Strip in Namibia under the name *kaŋombyo* (notes of the field research project Kubik/Malamusi Namibia 1991–1993; see also Kubik 1994b).

5. Northern Mozambique and the Ruvuma Valley

Relatively few types of lamellophones are known in this region, the most prominent being the gourd-resonated *shitata* among the -Lomwe (see dos Santos Jr. 1958, 349), called *shityatya* among the -Makonde, and the box-resonated Mwera/Makonde *ulimba*, also called *lulimba* among the -Mwera of Tanzania according to field notes by Uta Reuster Jahn, Institut für Ethnologie und Afrika-Studien, University of Mainz (personal communication, June 29, 1999). The latter is a very unusual instrument within the lamellophone family and cannot be linked genealogically to any other type. Some of its traits, however—the polished red-brown box, etc.—may have influenced the development of the *malimba* among the -Pangwa and others east of Lake Malawi, possibly through -Yao intermediate contacts. But the Pangwa/Bena *malimba* is not a derivative of the Mwera/Makonde *ulimba*. The latter stands out in the history of southeastern Africa as a very special, possibly ancient, and independent development. It also has no place within the Zimbabwe/Zambezi genealogical tree. Some thoughts on its history have already been stated (see Kubik/Malamusi 1985–87, 72–79; Kubik 1999; and for its detailed description, Dias 1986, 83–84; 1988).

One of the salient traits of the *ulimba* or *lulimba* is that the iron lamellae, usually seven and relatively broad, are hooked with their pointed ends into the thick, steeply rising wall of the instrument's top part. It is the only type of lamellophone, so far, found in Africa that is devoid of bridge, backrest, and pressure bar. Another characteristic is the shape of the box resonator, the top part of which is reminiscent of a gabled roof. The box is also often covered with a board from behind and not from the front. Actually, the whole design of the *ulimba* looks as if it were a miniaturized version of a Javanese *saron barung* with one wall of its trough resonator cut off and the seven metal keys turned lengthwise (figs. 1.32a,b). *Saron* keys are called *wilah* in

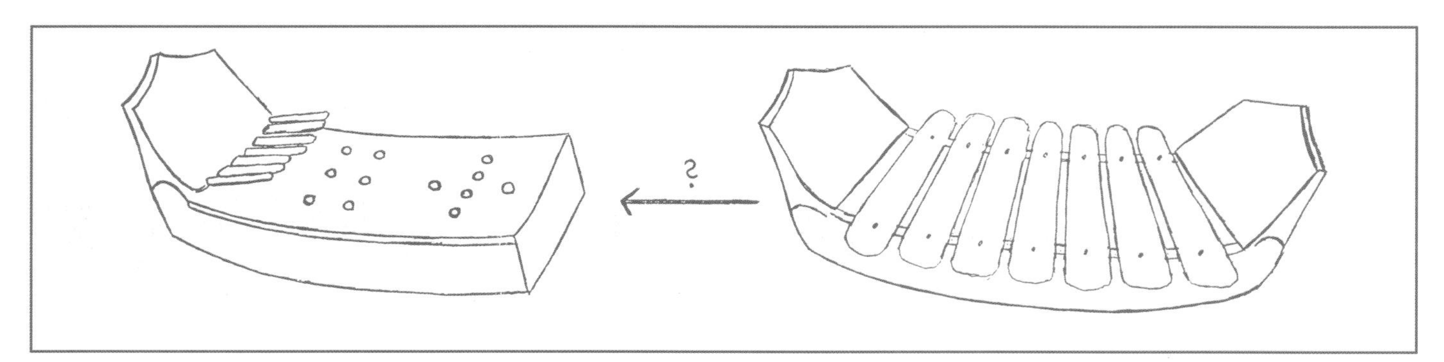

1.32a,b Does the Mwera/Makonde *ulimba* (left) represent a portable miniature *saron* (right)? Drawing by Gerhard Kubik.

Java and are cast from a copper-tin alloy, but they can also be iron.

While working with one of the *ulimba* lamellophones (inv. no. 9-461) in the Münchener Stadtmuseum in 1985, Moya A. Malamusi and I had a strange experience. By chance while I was trying to measure the (preserved) tuning of the *ulimba*, Mr. Varsanyi of the museum played a seven-note *saron barung* (inv. no. 60–64) in the hall. To our amazement we discovered that the two instruments could play together. Not only were both instruments tuned to a *slendro*-type pentatonic scale (the *saron* one octave higher than the *ulimba*), but they also matched with each other in their pitch range from $A^{\#}_{L}$-45 to $C^{\#}_{H}$ (*ulimba* tuning), see Kubik/Malamusi 1985–87, 76–79 for discussion and complete results.

A. M. Jones, whose book *Africa and Indonesia* (1964, 2d enlarged ed. 1971) has stimulated some controversy, would be delighted to read these paragraphs. Of course, speculation is not necessarily a negative undertaking if one acts with restraint and declares it as such. Although we lack factual historical sources, and thereby also a timescale for reconstructing the history of the Mwera/Makonde *ulimba*, it is legitimate to express at least the possibility that the idea behind the invention of this unusual lamellophone type in an area close to the Indian Ocean coast could have been to make a toy *saron*. Archaeological evidence pointing to the intensity of the Indian Ocean trading network from circa. 700 C.E. on is abundant, in addition to Arab and other written sources of (see the summary in Davidson 1984, 117–26, map on p. 120 showing the extent of the east coast trade to the Arabian Peninsula, India, Indonesia, and even China). The magnificent ruins of the palace of Husuni Kubwa at Kilwa and the great mosque completed in 1450 present a vivid testimony. Nothing would have prevented the knowledge of Southeast Asian metallophones from reaching the coasts of Tanzania and Mozambique, in light of other instruments, such as the *sese* flat-bar zither and the one and two-stringed bowed spike-lutes with their Asiatic bourdon tones, that were implanted there and gradually spread inland (see Kubik et al. 1982). Among the -Zaramo on the Tanzanian coast, box-resonated xylophones are common (Hyslop 1974), and trough-resonated xylophones (*mambira*), even closer to Indonesian models in organology and in the three-point mode of fixation of the keys (see Kubik et al. 1982, 110–11; Jones 1971, 126 for discussion of this trait) are found among the -Cuambo on the northern Mozambique coast. In 1962 I documented one such specimen as far inland as Lake Chilwa (on the Mozambique side of the border), and in 1987 Lidiya Malamusi and I recorded and filmed another Cuambo performer, a refugee from Mozambique near Mulanje in Malawi (cinematographic document no. 70 at Chief Safari, July 8, 1987, archived in the Museum für Völkerkunde, Berlin).

The *ulimba* was reported and collected by German researchers, such as Karl Weule (1908), at the turn of the nineteenth/twentieth century. Meinulf Küsters made cylinder recordings in 1927/28 (see W6 and W7 cylinders in the Museum für Völkerkunde, Berlin). Considerable research was carried out on this instrument by Margot Dias (1982; 1986; 1988). But only in the early 1990s was it possible for Uta Reuster-Jahn, University of Mainz, to make field recordings of actual performances among the -Mwera in southern Tanzania (copies in the African Music Archive Wolfgang Bender, Insitut für Ethnologie und Afrika-Studien, University of Mainz).

6. East Africa (Uganda, Tanzania)

In Bernhard Ankermann's distribution map of lamellophones (1901) East Africa is still blank. Indeed, lamellophones were only introduced to East Africa toward the end of the nineteenth century. During the second half of the nineteenth century, the newly invented *likembe*, well-established at that time among the -Teke in (French) Congo had spread with Belgian colonial penetration all along the Congo River upstream to Kisangani. From there it spread on into northeastern Congo crossing the linguistic border between Bantu and eastern Sudanic (II.E.1) languages. Soon it was adopted by porters and workers among the Logo (figs. 1.33a,b), then around the turn of the nineteenth/twentieth century by the Alur, then by the Acooli who modified the name to become *lukeme*. Klaus Wachsmann (1971), basing his findings on oral traditions, suggested that it entered Uganda

1.33a,b Logo migrant workers from northeastern Congo with *kidongo*, a ten-note *likembe* derivative. The lamellophone player on the left, Joseph Nyako, and his friend accompanying with a time-line pattern struck on a beer bottle, had come across the border into northern Uganda to join Acooli and other workers employed under an Italian foreman in the repair of a bridge at Weiga, Murchison Falls National Park. The pictures testify to a typical social milieu of men in colonial service who spread this instrument across the Congo in the early twentieth century. Photographs by Gerhard Kubik, Weiga, Murchison Falls (now Kabalega Falls) National Park, northern Uganda, February 1960.

probably at two points, in West-Nile Province and also in the Ruwenzori area of western Uganda. Alur and Acooli who were recruited to work on plantations in southern Uganda and especially on the construction of the railway through Jinja and Kampala to Kasese introduced the instrument to Busoga by 1912 (interview with Ephraim Bisase in Kubik 1978). There it was adopted by the -Soga and -Gwere who projected the term for the lyre, *endongo*, on the newcomer. Basoga musicians transferred the compositional experience of their *embaire* log xylophones to the new instrument and created a new music perpetuating their traditional *slendro*-type equipentatonic tonal system. In the early 1960s there were many eminent personalities who composed for and performed on this instrument, either solo or in partnership with one or two other musicians. They included the blind musician-composers Daudi Mukama (see recording in Kubik 1999, CD item 19 "Malaya mukadde") and Waiswa Lubogo (see LP record *The Blind Musicians of Salama*, A.I.T. records Nairobi, GK 02, items II/5 and 6, "Kirembemani," etc.). See figures 1.34a–d.

In the 1950s, and possibly before, -Soga musicians developed a small version entirely made of metal with an oval resonator hammered out of sheet iron, usually from a Coca-Cola advertising dish. The new device was called *kadongo* (*ka-* being a diminutive prefix). The plural is *budongo*, and *budongo* groups incorporating the treble instrument with twelve notes (see fig. 1.9) with one or two deeper-tuned instruments with a wooden resonator became the hallmark of Soga music. For sociopsychological reasons, the Baganda, western neighbors of the Basoga who had previously incorporated so much of the Soga musical genius into their court music, did not adopt the *budongo*. But in northern Uganda, *likembe* derivatives, such as the *lukeme* among the Acooli and *okembe* among the Langi (all speakers of II.E.1, Eastern Sudanic languages), have continued an independent existence.

Another route of imports into East Africa was from Ujiji at Lake Tanganyika to Tabora, seat of the powerful Mnyamwezi paramount chief who controlled the nineteenth-century trade route from Bagamoyo on the Tanzanian coast across his territory into the Congo as far as Kisangani. In Henry Morton Stanley's time -Nyamwezi porters introduced box-resonated lamellophones, which had incorporated some traits from Zambezi fan-shaped types such as the central hole covered with a mirliton, from northern Katanga into Tanzania. Among the -Gogo of central Tanzania—along the Ujiji/Bagamoyo caravan route—spectacular developments took place. The newcomer was soon tuned to the local tonal system, the characteristic Gogo scale, which is based on speech-derived harmonics over a *single* fundamental, with the use of the series from partial four to nine (more rarely up to ten) in the formation of pitch lines in characteristic bichords of fourths, fifths, thirds, and diminished fifths (see Kubik 1994a, 175–84 for a comprehensive analysis). The Gogo *ilimba* with a relatively large box resonator normally has from twenty to twenty-three lamellae, out of which a central section functions as a tuning reference. This section is not to be played upon (see Kubik 1994a, 181). In the 1970s the famous Mgogo musician, Hukwe Zawose, constructed *ilimba* lamellophones with over fifty iron notes.

1.34a–c Livingstone Waiswa Lubogo, twenty-four years old, on the treble *kadongo*, and Gatangayire Abonnyo Ntalo, fourteen years old, on a deep-tuned *endongo*—both of them blind—were two fabulous Basoga musicians, composers, singers, and lamellophone players in the early 1960s. Ntalo's large instrument with a wooden box resonator and the characteristic cut-out section perpetuates the ancestral Congolese shape, but Waiswa's small instrument, in shape and in its sound quality almost like a metallophone, was an innovative breakthrough in southern Uganda. By the time Waiswa took up his art, the treble *kadongo* had already been established for a long time. Photographs by Hillegeist/Kubik, Salama, south of Mukono, southern Uganda, May 1962.

A third entry point into East Africa was from Zambia into the area of Tukuyu in southwestern Tanzania, which became an important center for the production of small box-resonated lamellophones with a vibrato hole at the back, eight lamellae made from umbrella ribs, and a chain of beads or iron laid across them. These instruments called *malimba* became popular among the -Nyakyusa, -Kinga, -Pangwa, -Bena, and -Kisi northeast of Lake Malawi during the first two decades of the twentieth century (according to Father Leonhard Wüst of Madunda Mission who was there in 1912; personal communication at Madunda Mission in 1960). Among the -Kisi, a people of fishers and potters on the northeast shores of Lake Malawi a fascinating expertise on the wow-producing sound hole at the back of the instrument was developed (see recording by Laurenti, ca. thirty years old in 1962; see Simon, ed., 1983 Cassette I/1/1, rec. by Hillegeist/Kubik).

7. The West African Lamellophone Diaspora

Lamellophones were not known along the Guinea Coast west of the Niger River prior to the eighteenth century; and even in the late nineteenth century they had been reported mostly from Liberia and Sierra Leone. Writing on the geographical distribution of lamellophones in Africa, Bernhard Ankermann (1901, 86–89) stated that outside the compact distribution area between Niger, Zambezi, and Kunene, they were only found in Liberia, quoting Büttikofer (II: 336). Ankermann (1901, 87–88) suspects that it was the Kru working as seamen on European ships and cruising the West African Coast, who picked the instrument and brought it to Liberia. The Kru have been known ever since as catalysts in the diffusion of instruments, notably the guitar from West Africa to the Congo earlier this century (see Schmidt 1998).

No lamellophones can be seen in Benin bronze art (see Dark and Hill 1971) in contrast to another individual Bini (Ẹdo) instrument, the *akpata* (pluriarc), which is depicted in a bronze plaque preserved in the British Museum (see Ben-Amos 1975, 32). Dan Ben-Amos (1975, 33) states that the *asologun*, a box-resonated lamellophone with nine notes made from umbrella stays, "is mentioned neither in eyewitness accounts nor does it appear on indigenous commemorative art. This is not accidental, for even today there is a ban on the *asologun* in Benin City itself, and the instrument appears only in rural surroundings. Moreover, quite a few village chiefs bar it from their territories." He continues to explain that "the reason for the restrictions is related to the instrument's symbolic significance," and he quotes an informant saying that the *asologun* "is the instrument of witches" (p. 47).

I interpret these data to suggest that the *asologun* is a relative newcomer to Benin City from eastern Nigeria and that it was associated with despised foreigners, who were also accused of practicing witchcraft. Organological details of the *asologun* can be compared to Calabar box-resonated types in the identity of "backrest" and "bridge" and the pattern of binding the lamellae to the soundboard. The use of umbrella stays demonstrates the recent modification of an instrument that in its

earlier forms probably had lamellae cut from cane. The type of umbrella from which the notes of the *asologun* are obtained was very popular earlier in the twentieth century in British colonial territories.

In the early nineteenth century maritime pathways triggered the spread of specific types of lamellophones from areas in southeastern Nigeria, southern Cameroon, and Gabon to Freetown (Sierra Leone), a major resettlement point for liberated slaves after 1815. But in the evolving multicultural Krio society and among its indigenous neighbors, the new knowledge was strangely reinterpreted with curious playing postures adopted that seem to be based on a misunderstanding of how lamellophones were played in the areas where they had come from. Sierra Leonean developments include the *kɔndi* or *kututen* among the Limba and the *budoma* among the Loko and others (see van Oven 1973/74). One new tradition that has become characteristic of lamellophone playing of the West African Diaspora is that some instruments are played with the free ends of the lamellae pointing away from the player's body. In this position the instrument is played with the thumbs (see picture of a *budoma* performance in Borel 1986, 16). The *budoma* and many of its derivatives across Liberia into Côte d'Ivoire incorporate a characteristic buzzing device attached to what (in this playing position) is the top part. It is an ear-shaped piece of sheet iron dotted all around with small holes through which iron rings are threaded; when the lamellae are sounded the rings serve as buzzers by virtue of their sympathetic resonance. This device is also found on drums all over the area (see Mose Yotamu's picture in Kubik et al. 1989, 171). On the Ivory Coast the Sierra Leonean type was modified in the sense that iron lamellae are attached in the middle of a large, thick oval board with a grip accommodating the buzzer, which points away from the player. The resonator is a large gourd, loosely attached to the board with thick strings (see Kubik et al. 1989, 172–73).

Further east, among the Fon in Togo, a small portable lamellophone with the notes mounted on a wooden board that is inserted into an oval resonator made from an old fish can is played in two ways: (a) with the thumbs like the Sierra Leonean type mentioned; (b) with the index fingers, for which purpose the instrument is set up vertically in the player's lap with the free ends of the lamellae pointing upward and the soundboard directed away from the musician's body (see Kubik et al. 1989, 138). The first is the "walking" way of playing, the second the "seated" position. The Fon instrument is called *gidigbo* (a Yorùbá name). Its organology, playing techniques, and name demonstrate historical connections in *both* directions, west and east, along the Guinea Coast. The same can be said of the Ghanaian lamellophones, for example the *atabo* among the northern Ewe in the Volta River region, documented by Urban Bareis (see Kubik 1999, 72–73). It has a large box and four bamboo lamellae. It is related to the *prempensua* of the Asante, and its playing technique includes percussive action suggesting affinities to the Yorùbá *agidigbo*.

The history of the various Guinea Coast models is intertwined and has yet to be written up in a manner that fully details the diffusion of traits, reinterpretation, and innovation. A case in point is the Yorùbá *agidigbo* of five or more notes. It has broad lamellae cut from materials such as old saws, springs, or sheet iron, which are then attached to a large wooden packing case with a metal bridge and a piece of sheet iron serving as a "straining bar" nailed to the soundboard. This type is manufactured entirely from industrial debris, and its history is an interesting issue. From the 1960s on, the *agidigbo*, which can be played solo and "talk" *oriki* praise poetry (see a performance by the Yorùbá poet Bakare Gbadamosi, recorded 1960/Kubik, CD item no. 23, in Kubik 1999) has also been equipped with electric amplification and used in *apala* and *juju* groups.

Darius L. Thieme (1967, 43) mentions gourd-resonated lamellophones that apparently preceded the *agidigbo* among the Yorùbá and were given the Hausa name *molo*. These are very curious instruments, however, and cannot be directly related to the *agidigbo*. As stated by Thieme (1967, 43) and shown in his photograph, the Yorùbá *molo* consists of an inverted calabash: "the tongues are inserted directly into and through the outside surface of the calabash." There seems to be no relationship between this device and lamellophones in the eastern Nigeria/central Cameroon nuclear dispersal area. It might well demonstrate an archaic principle perhaps developed in the savanna hinterlands of Nigeria (the Hausa name *molo* is probably not coincidental). According to Thieme (1967) its geographical distribution seems to be associated with the kingdom of Ọ̀yọ́.

If the *molo* was the predecessor of the *agidigbo*, most certainly it was not its ancestor. The *agidigbo*'s ancestral relationships have to be looked for somewhere else. According to Valentine Ojo from Ondo-Yoruba (personal communication March 19, 1973) the term *gidigbo* in Yorùbá refers to a wrestling game. According to oral tradition the Yorùbá *agidigbo* lamellophone was formerly used to accompany such shows. This makes one even think of Brazilian "Capoeira," an idea perhaps not totally absurd in view of the known resettlement of Afro-Brazilian "returnees" in Lagos after 1888 when slavery had been abolished in Brazil. The Brazilians introduced a new architectural twist into Yorubaland, which spread quickly to all towns of western Nigeria where houses of wealthy citizens were built in the "Brazilian architectural style."

In its construction and organological details, the Yorùbá *agidigbo* is largely identical to the Caribbean *marimbula*, which spread nearly everywhere in the Caribbean and to northern parts of South America. Its introduction to Lagos at the turn of the nineteenth/twentieth century, where it would give rise to the development of a Yorùbá version that should become known as *agidigbo* is a very likely scenario.

8. African American Lamellophones

The slave trade brought the knowledge of lamellophones from several parts of Africa to the Americas. Most of the African types, however, became extinct, before the end of the nineteenth century with the exception of one derivative, the *marimbula*, a large box-resonated lamellophone that also became known as the "rumba box," and variously served as a bass instrument in dance ensembles. It was comprehensively documented in Cuba by Fernando Ortiz (1955, 5: 86–116) with many specimens compared that were collected during the first half of the twentieth century.

The remote history of the *marimbula* is obscure, but we are pretty certain that it was an Afro-Cuban development. In Walter Goodman's *The Pearl of the Antilles; or, An Artist in Cuba* (1873, 124), there is an early description of "a primitive instrument formed out of a square box upon which are arranged strips of flexible iron of different length and tone." Donald Thompson (1975/76, 140) cites a dictionary published in 1862 in which the *marimbula* is mentioned. But even earlier than that, a painting by Paul Harro-Harring (1840) from Brazil called *Dancing Negroes* depicts a man playing a relatively large, box-resonated lamellophone with the index fingers. This shows that antecedents of the *marimbula* were probably around early in the nineteenth century. The remote inspiration for the *marimbula* probably came from raffia-manufactured lamellophones of southeastern Nigeria. A clue is contained in the illustration by

Fernando Ortiz of a "marimbula de güira" (1955, 5: 99) with a circular resonator and two identical bars functioning as bridge and backrest for twelve broad tongues laid out across them like the keys of a log xylophone. These traits are common in the raffia intensity zone of west central Africa. Ortiz's specimen could even be an American offspring of an ancestral southeastern Nigerian type that also preceded the development of the *ubɔ aka*. Whatever might be discovered eventually, it is clear that the ancestry of the *marimbula* cannot be connected to Congo/Angola lamellophone types but rather to those in the hinterland of the coastal towns of Bonny, Calabar, Victoria, and so forth, with the island of Biyogo (Fernando Po) the turntable. In the early twentieth century the popular *marimbula* spread to nearly every country of the Caribbean. George List (1968; 1983) has reported it from Colombia; Angelina Pollak-Eltz (1978) from Venezuela; Donald Thompson (1975/76) has described its use in Puerto Rico; and Jos Gansemans (1989) from the Dutch Antilles (Aruba, Bonaire and Curaçao). Gansemans (1989, 126) writes that it was seamen from Bonaire who discovered the *marimbula* in Cuba at the turn of the nineteenth/twentieth century and incorporated it into their own musical groups. Gansemans has also learned from informants that the *marimbula* was introduced in Aruba around 1922 when workers returned from Cuba, and it was introduced during the period from 1925 to 1930 in Bonaire. The *marimbula* is frequently played in a "vertical" position. The large quadrangular wooden box is placed on the ground with the performer sitting on it; the ends of the lamellae, which he operates with the index (and sometimes several) fingers, point up toward him, and the soundboard faces away from him. A most important trait is that a free hand also strikes percussive patterns on the box, a trait that has continued in the *marimbula*'s Nigerian derivative (see above).

In the nineteenth century there existed many more types of lamellophones in the Americas. One remarkable specimen was collected by Mrs. Braithwaite Batty in northern South America, probably Dutch Guiana (Suriname) in the early twentieth century (fig. 1.35); it was acquired by the Pitt Rivers Museum in July 1917 (inv. no. 1917.14.6). This instrument has nine bamboo lamellae in a characteristic Ѵl-shaped layout, mounted on a small, rectangular soundboard nailed to a box. Bridge and backrest are identical horizontal bars, also of vegetable material, and the straining bar is bound to the soundboard in the same manner as some Calabar lamellophones, the Ẹdo *asologun*, and the Igbo *ubɔ aka*. This establishes convincingly the ancestry of this specimen in southeastern Nigeria or any other place on the West African Coast where southeastern Nigerian lamellophone technology had spread before this type became known in Suriname. Only the decoration carved into the balsa-type wood of the soundbox with a shell shows a pattern that may be based in local (Suriname) decorative art. This does not exclude the possibility that a comparable southeastern Nigerian decorative style might still be found.

Lamellophones even made it to New Orleans in the early nineteenth century. Apparently with the influx of people from the Caribbean to Louisiana under Spanish and French administrations (Louisiana was sold by Napoleon Bonaparte to the United States in 1803), the knowledge of at least one or two types of lamellophones spread to New Orleans. George Washington Cable (1886, reprinted in Katz, ed., 1969, 34) mentions it under the strange name *marimba brett*. This name is a mystery because "brett," if this is the spelling, is a German word, meaning "board." Cable describes the instrument as small with a series of reeds mounted on a board or box resonator and played with the thumbnails.

The most important recipient of African lamellophones in the Americas was Brazil. This is not so by chance. Particularly during its late stages, the slave trade brought many people from Angola, Cabinda (today a part of the Republic of Angola), and adjacent areas to Brazil via the island of São Tomé. By the mid-eighteenth century these had become key areas for the exportation of lamellophone types and techniques. Apart from the earliest known Brazilian source, Alexandre Rodrigues Ferreira (1783–1792), already discussed, there are ample written and pictorial sources testifying to the early nineteenth-century presence of Angolan

1.35a,b Lamellophone with box resonator, nine notes of bamboo in Ѵl-shape layout, and decorative engravings collected in northern South America, probably Dutch Guiana (Suriname). © The Pitt Rivers Museum, University of Oxford, inv. no. 1917.14.6 (collection Batty).

board lamellophones in Brazil, especially in the area of Rio de Janeiro. This was first pointed out by David Thiermann (1971) and later researched systematically (see Kubik 1979; Pinto, ed., 1986; etc.). Afro-Brazilian cultural activities had attracted the attention of many European painters who settled in Rio de Janeiro to paint the "picturesque" scenes. Jean-Baptiste Debret (1834) who was in Brazil from 1816 to 1832 depicted the performance of gourd-resonated lamellophones from Angola in several of his paintings. Although they lack detail, it is clear that they were board lamellophones held into a gourd resonator. They were used either as a solo instrument, such as in Debret's painting *L'aveugle chanteur* (Debret 1834) or played in a duet—with two instruments of different size and a scraper—to accompany a group of dancers and singers as in his painting *La promenade du Dimanche Midi*, depicting a leisurely Sunday lunchtime walk by a group of slaves in fanciful dress in Rio de Janeiro. Thomas Ewbank (1856, 111–12) who visited Brazil in 1846 also describes and depicts the playing of a gourd-resonated lamellophone. Angolan lamellophones even made it to areas further south. Fernando Ortiz (1952–55, 89) cites a Spanish-language source testifying that the "quisanche" (Spanish transliteration of the Angolan name *kisanji*) was used in the area of the Río de la Plata, Montevideo, Uruguay in carnivals during the nineteenth century.

To Richard Graham of Memphis, I owe the discovery of a German-language article by a certain G. W. Finck, published in the *Allgemeine musikalische Zeitung* (35, no. 2, January 1833). The author wrote about music and dance practices in Brazil without specifying any locations but apparently as an eyewitness as he states that he was invited to rehearsals by Afro-Brazilians in military ensembles (p. 20). He then describes a board lamellophone with five-to-seven iron notes, the board apparently glued to a coconut shell, which served as a resonator. He gives the name *loangobania*, mentioning the different lengths of the "iron springs" and their attachment on one side with a piece of wood (most certainly the bridge) pushed under so that the "springs" stand off the board about 1/2 an inch. He also describes a mouth-bow called *benta* and the use of a scraper and a rattle. Since such names are not mentioned in any early nineteenth-century sources from southern Brazil, my preliminary estimate is that the author, who also mentions places where wood for house construction was piled up, saw these instruments in equatorial areas, close to Guyana.

At least two specimens of lamellophones made by Africans in Brazil seem to have survived in collections. Most surprisingly, both belong to the Loango type whose distribution in Africa is restricted to the Loango coast (Cabinda, etc., see above). The most spectacular specimen is preserved in the Museum für Völkerkunde, Vienna (inv. no. 12.066); see figures 1.36a–d. It was part of a collection of mostly North American ethnographic materials in possession of Johann Georg Schwarz who was a fur trader in North America from 1820 to 1821 and American consul in Vienna from 1827 to 1848. He died in 1867. The objects he had collected were kept until 1880 in the Vienna Museum for Art and Industry and were eventually incorporated into the Museum für Völkerkunde. No details about Schwarz's Brazilian contacts are known, but the instrument appears in his collection declared as "Sansa brazilianischer Neger."

The specimen is the work of an expert. It has seven iron lamellae—originally it could have had nine—in a typical Loango-type arrangement as a scale rising from left to right. The body is of the bell-type; the orifice of the resonator crescent-shaped. It is decorated all over with brass nails. If it was manufactured in Brazil, then the slave must have come from the Loango coast, and he must have been a great expert in wood carving and instrument making. The seated figure carved at the top of the instrument with her hands directed toward her breasts is a great work of art.

It is not certain, however, that the Vienna specimen really is Brazilian; it could also be a stray specimen from the Loango coast. The controversy can probably be solved by a thorough investigation of the materials by a team involving wood and iron specialists. In the meantime, a second comparable specimen has come to light which is Brazilian (fig. 1.37). It is preserved in the Pitt Rivers Museum, Oxford (inv. no. 1906.20.106). The documentation in the files is scarce, but it informs us that this comes from the upper Amazon and was part of the S.W. Silver collection, d.d. Mrs. S. W. Silver in March 1906. This instrument is an eight-note Loango-type lamellophone, of much more rudimentary manufacture than the Vienna specimen but also with an anthropomorphic feature, in this case a carved head in a style difficult to associate with the Loango coast.

This nineteenth-century Loango-type lamellophone from a remote region of the Amazon basin has, of course, raised the probability that the Vienna specimen might indeed be Brazilian, as is claimed in the inventory of the Schwarz collection. No doubt, it is also much older. It must have been manufactured at least in the early nineteenth century, if not in the eighteenth. Modern technologies for dating have not yet been tried, however, as far as I know. On the other hand, the specimen in the Pitt Rivers Museum, which shows that carpenter's wood was used in its manufacture could have been made in Brazil by a second- or third-generation descendent from the Loango coast or even by an Amerindian. It is well-known from oral testimonies and organological evidence that in the Americas, African musical instruments had regularly "drifted" into the Amerindian population during the era of slavery and later. David Thiermann (1971, 74) reports that an old German musician in Rio de Janeiro told him that he had seen Brazilian Indians living in the interior town of Goiana, near Brasilia, playing lamellophones about ten years earlier.

In the meantime, the instrument seems to "come back" in Brazil as a result of a new historical consciousness and the activities of so-called Blocos Afro. Pop groups have used a commercialized model made in South Africa, and historical reconstructions, even recreations of small board-lamellophones with a gourd resonator, have been produced by a certain maker in Bahia and are sold regularly to tourists in the famous Mercado Modelo of Salvador/Bahia. Such attempts at recuperating and rewriting history are common these days in many parts of the Americas, and they are part of movements to reconstruct and reconstitute African American cultures.

1.37 Nineteenth-century Loango-type lamellophone with eight iron notes. Collected in the upper Amazon area of Brazil. © The Pitt Rivers Museum, University of Oxford, inv. no. 1906.20.106.

1.36a–d Nineteenth-century Loango-type lamellophone with seven iron notes (originally possibly nine) of Brazilian provenance according to museum records. Museum für Völkerkunde, Vienna, inv. no. 12.066.

Xylophones are among the most commonly used and appreciated musical instruments in West Africa. They exist in many shapes, sizes, and sonorizations, including trough xylophones, leg xylophones, frame xylophones, and both free and fixed xylophones. Their range can extend from a mere one and one-half octaves to three octaves of five- or seven-note scales, with timbres anywhere from high and hollow to low and resonant. By far the most prevalent xylophones, those considered here, are the ones with fixed keys and frames from the Mande and Voltaic regions. Although every West African language and dialect has its own local name for xylophones, they are commonly known in French-speaking countries by the term *balafon* and in English-speaking countries by their English name.

Because of their special sound and deep connection to regional and ethnic identity, xylophones are highly valued by most sectors of society. Spiritualists, oral historians, politicians, women, and boisterous youth all employ the xylophone for their various life activities. The instrument is used to animate dances, weddings, and storytelling events; to broadcast social commentary; and as a symbol of national, ethnic, and individual identity.[1] Xylophones and xylophonists are often attributed important roles in the rise and fall of West African civilizations, and their continued performance in contemporary life keeps these memories alive. The well-known Malian epic *Sundiata*, for example, which is told and retold through the songs of Mande oral historians known as *griots* or *jeli*, depicts the xylophone's critical role in the establishment of the Malian Empire in the thirteenth century.

While xylophones are discussed in this paper in relation to particular ethnic and lingual groups, there are incredibly active trade routes between these groups, who exchange musical ideas, practices, and instruments. In fact, the entire relevance as to which ethnic or lingual group plays x or y xylophone and in x or y fashion is less important in this study than how people use them, appreciate them, and create them. Learning about xylophone music culture provides a window into the diverse complexity of West African societies and worldviews. Thus, I invite the reader to explore the world of xylophones by focusing on its artists, musical aesthetics, and importance as a social tool for spiritual and human communication.

The Mande and Voltaic Peoples

The Mande and Voltaic peoples covered in this study encompass millions of individuals in the West African savanna regions. The Manding constitute the majority of the population in Mali, Guinea, Guinea-Bissau, and The Gambia.[2] Manding peoples are also numerous in Côte d'Ivoire, Senegal, Sierra Leone, Ghana, and Burkina Faso; smaller groups are found in Liberia, Benin, Nigeria, and Niger. The Mande people include such ethnic groups as the Bambara, Dogon, Gouro, Jula, Kassonke, Malinke, Mandinka, Maninka, Soninke, Sossou, Wangara, Wassulun, Yacouba, etc. (School of Oriental and African Studies 1972, vol. 3). The Voltaics (Birifor, Bobo, Bwa, Bwamu, Dagara, Lobi, Minyanka, Samo, Senufo, Sisaala, etc.) are located in the areas of southeastern Mali, northern and northeastern Côte d'Ivoire, northwestern Ghana, and southern Burkina Faso.

In West Africa, the system of ethnicity is complex, and in order to understand it, one must take into account three main points: (1) the ecological and political changes (such as grand empires, long-distance trade across the Sahara Desert, and their impact on population movements); (2) the influence of the different slavery systems, mainly domestic captivity (the most important before the slave trade by Western countries); and (3) the alliances during wars and periods of penury. These have all contributed to the creation of new ethnicities (such as the Wassulun, Gouro, and Jula, for example) and the redefinition of others.

This flexibility and negotiability of ethnic identity was already in progress for centuries before colonialism imposed itself and fixed its own criteria for ethnic identity on top of those already in existence. In many cases, the colonial criteria for determining and documenting ethnic groups was completely unrelated to the ways that the people defined themselves. The Lobi from northern Ghana, for example, found their name used as an umbrella term for several smaller ethnic groups during the colonial era. Thus, like the "overnight" creation of countries belonging to the French, English, or Portuguese colonies, which disregarded and often cut across native ethnic and political territories, many ethnic groups were created.[3]

In certain regions some Mande peoples share the scalar system of the Voltaics. This simple fact concerning xylophones brings to light an important aspect of ethnicity in West Africa that is often overlooked. Ethnic groups define and redefine themselves in response to different social, economic, religious, and political forces.

Xylophones and Xylophonists

Technically speaking, Mande and Voltaic xylophones consist of wooden sets of multitone keys with individual gourd resonators. The keys are mounted and fixed over a wooden, rectangular frame and consist of a series of pitched tones from low to high. Xylophones are played by striking or tapping the keys with mallets made from light wooden sticks and soft rubber heads. The instruments are, with only few exceptions, played by men, sometimes as solo instruments accompanying vocal music or in ensembles consisting of several xylophones and other instruments. Depending on the context, xylophone music may treat a wide range of secular, religious, and historical topics.[4] Both Mande and Voltaic xylophones also play a critical role in ritual and sacred events, which, out of respect, are generally not revealed openly to international and public view. It is however, common knowledge in several regions in West Africa that funerals and spiritual communication seances (or possession) cannot proceed without xylophone music.

The structure of xylophone frames exists in two basic forms: the keys are either built parallel to the ground or at an angle, with one end higher than the other by several inches. Since the keys are fixed to the frame, the tonal arrangement of pitches and intervals on each instrument remains constant (as opposed to other African xylophones with "free keys" that can be moved around). The tonal organization of most flat-framed xylophones is based on the equidistant heptatonic division of the octave (the octave is divided into seven equal intervals). The octave in the angular frames is pentatonic (divided into five intervals). These intervals may be equidistant or arranged in steps that correspond roughly to Western intervals of major and minor seconds, thirds, fourths, and so on. In both cases, the player sits or stands facing the xylophone so that the keys to his left have the greatest length and lowest pitch. With the slanted frame, the smallest and highest-pitched keys are at the low end of the frame, on the right (fig. 2.1).

In general, the flat-framed, heptatonic xylophone is played by most Mande groups found in Mali, Senegal, The Gambia, and Sierra Leone (Malinke, Mandinka, and Maninka). The angled-frame, pentatonic xylophone is mostly found among the Voltaic peoples in regions of Mali, Côte d'Ivoire, Ghana, and Burkina Faso (Bobo, Bwamu, Dagara, Lobi, Senufo, and Sisaala).[5] Exceptions to this general scheme are, of course, not uncommon, given the high rate of interaction between various groups in West Africa. Bambara xylophonists from Mali, for example, who are a Mande people, play the angled-frame type (*balaniw* or *balabaw*) similar to their southern Senufo and Minyanka neighbors.

In Mande and Voltaic xylophone traditions, the most experienced and respected players build their own instruments, those for their students, and others for individuals who commission them for various reasons. Xylophonists also play the important role of general band leader. In short, they are the bearers of their region's xylophone music repertoire and performance practices. Since music is not written down, xylophonists must remember all of its aspects, from song texts (folk, secular, sacred, and historical), to xylophone patterns and rhythms to other instrumental and percussion parts within the total ensemble. In addition to these responsibilities, the best players are also the innovators and animators of new styles and social contexts.

Who are xylophonists and how do they learn their skills? Xylophone players all have certain shared characteristics, but there are also regional and individual differences. In the Mande culture, for example, almost all xylophonists come from a professional class of musician families. Most xylophonists from Voltaic culture groups, however, may come from any family. Although there are always exceptions to "rules of tradition" in every culture, the Voltaic tradition offers a much broader spectrum of possibilities for individuals who want to become xylophonists, both in terms of who is eligible and how one learns.

The relatively strict social rules regarding who can and cannot be a xylophonist among the Mande (especially

2.1 Xylophone. Bambara and Minyanka peoples, Central Mali. Constructed by Duga Koro Diarra, 1991. Stands roughly 14 in. high from the ground at the left end and gradually slopes down to reach 8 in. at the right end. The bass keys (positioned to the left side of the player) measure approximately 23 in. long; the highest soprano key is about 12 in. long. Photograph by Heather A. Maxwell, 1995.

the Bambara, Malinke, and Maninka groups) is explained in large part by mythical accounts of the first *balafon* in *Sundiata*. Believed to have been a gift from a spirit (*jin*) to the king of Sosso, Soumangourou Kante, the xylophone was discovered by one of his adversary's messengers (a *griot* named Kouyate) while the king was absent. The *griot* began to play it and was so enchanted with its sound that he did not notice the king's surprise return. Soumangourou, who had promised the *jin* to kill anyone who touched the instrument, was so impressed by Kouyate's talent that he forgot his promise and said to Kouyate, "*Balafo segue*" (Continue playing! Continue). From that time on, Kouyate was called *balafo segue*, and the *balafon* naturally became the instrument of the *griots*. Most non-*griots* (determined by family name) do not touch the *balafon*, and in the case where a non-*griot* individual insists on becoming a musician, he normally chooses another instrument to play.

Personal narratives of several xylophonists from Voltaic regions reveal that among the Dagara, Lobi, and Sisaala groups some individuals are believed to be born with the talent and will to be xylophonists, while others choose to learn it as their primary instrument or to be well-rounded musicians. The story of one such xylophonist, a man from the upper west region of Ghana named Bernard (Sogolinso) Woma, describes how his unusual birth position was a signal to his family and the community that a predestined xylophonist had been born.

In an interview with Woma in 1996 he explained that knowing how to play the xylophone just "came with him." When he was born, his thumbs were folded in his fists, with just the tips protruding through his index and middle fingers. His father, who was alarmed by the hand position of his newborn, took him to a spiritualist for consultation. The spiritualist quickly explained that Woma was destined to be a xylophone player and instructed his father to buy two xylophones and keep them in the house for his son. At the age of two, Woma began to play. Xylophonists in this region hold their mallets in-between their index and middle fingers as illustrated in figure 2.2.

Minyanka xylophonists, who have assimilated aspects of xylophone music culture from their Mande neighbors, have an even more liberal set of "rules." Like the Voltaics, they are not exclusive to particular clans or families and are thus free to play whichever instrument they wish. Going one step beyond this freedom, Minyanka people do not consider ethnicity as a relevant criterion. They do not have to be Minyanka nor do they have to live in Minyankala to be part of Minyanka xylophone music culture. According to Duga Koro Diarra, a Bambara xylophonist from the Minyanka area and my teacher, any man is technically eligible to become a xylophonist provided that he possesses talent, discipline, and desire.[6]

Within most Mande groups xylophonists learn to play within their *griot* families. They grow up surrounded by xylophone

2.2 Xylophonist Kakraba Lobi, from northern Ghana, singing the secular song "Cat and Mouse." Photograph by Heather A. Maxwell, Accra, Ghana, 1986.

music and begin learning and playing at a very early age. Assimilationist groups like the Minyanka, and most Voltaics, have a wider variety of types of instruction. For example, in Diarra's region, young xylophonists must go through years of apprenticeship before they are acknowledged as genuine players. When a student has shown sufficient knowledge and skill, Diarra constructs him a xylophone, hand-carries it to the graduate's house, and places it publicly in his home, declaring thus that the apprenticeship is concluded and the student has become a master in his own right. In other parts of Minyankala, xylophonists simply learn to play by watching, experimenting, and applying self-discipline.

Kakraba Lobi, from northern Ghana, learned on his own by watching xylophonists for several years until one day he simply began playing. People took notice of his enormous talent immediately, and since that time he has been a xylophone player. Woma learned on his own mostly by listening to other people's songs. He would then go home and play them. Most of the time the music "just sticks in his head" and is "all there" when he wants to play it for the first time (personal communication, 1997).

Building a Xylophone

Since xylophones are not mass-produced in the sense of modern technology and calibrated machines, building a xylophone is a specialized art. Xylophonists must choose their materials carefully. Everything used to build a xylophone comes from the natural environment, so this activity is closely connected to environmental and climatic changes. For most xylophonists, cutting down trees for the wood is something for which they are personally accountable, and thus requires special sacrifices that thank nature for providing the necessary materials.

During my own field research and apprenticeship from 1989 to 1991 with Diarra, I followed him along through the process of constructing a xylophone. Choosing the wood for the keys is an activity that requires a highly specialized knowledge of the forest and trees. During one visit with Diarra, he took me to the *bala jiri yoro la* (the place of the *bala* trees) to show me where the wood for the keys originates and how the trees look. Locally known as *n'goni*, these trees were all growing together in what appeared to be a naturally formed orchard. He explained that these trees grew only in this particular place in and around Sineni and that the next largest grouping existed near N'Tòssoni, a village some thirty-five miles away.

I admired the trees, tried to memorize their form, and then asked Diarra how he determined which ones would make good xylophones. He explained very simply that they tell him when they're ready. *"U bè fo ne ma dè"* (They tell me), he said. To demonstrate what he meant by this, Diarra approached the nearest tree, placed one ear on the trunk, paused, and said, *"A ma sè folo"* (It's not ready yet). He continued this process until, a few trees later, he apparently heard one that sounded ready.

When he needs to build a xylophone, Diarra explained, he comes to this orchard, cuts down a tree, and then chops the wood up into slabs of approximate key sizes. It is usually during this time that he sacrifices something to show his respect and thanks for having cut the tree. As is common throughout West African xylophone construction practice, Diarra used the key measurements of an already existing xylophone as the model for his new one. Once the keys are cut, he places them in a special oven, which cures them by smoke and fire over approximately one week. During this time the frame is constructed, and when the keys are ready, they are mounted and securely tied to the frame with goatskin.

Gourds are another important feature of West African xylophones that xylophonists must select and treat carefully are gourds. Each key has a corresponding gourd tied carefully beneath it. Depending on the regional crop and seasonal conditions, the gourds are round or oval and range in size from very small to extremely large (3 to 15 inches in diameter). The tops are cut off at the narrowest part, then the gourds are cleaned out and fastened tightly to the supporting frame structure so as to fit snugly just underneath each key. The smallest gourds correspond to the smallest and highest-pitched keys, and the largest to the bass keys (figs. 2.3a,b).

Because the gourds function primarily as resonating chambers, their size and

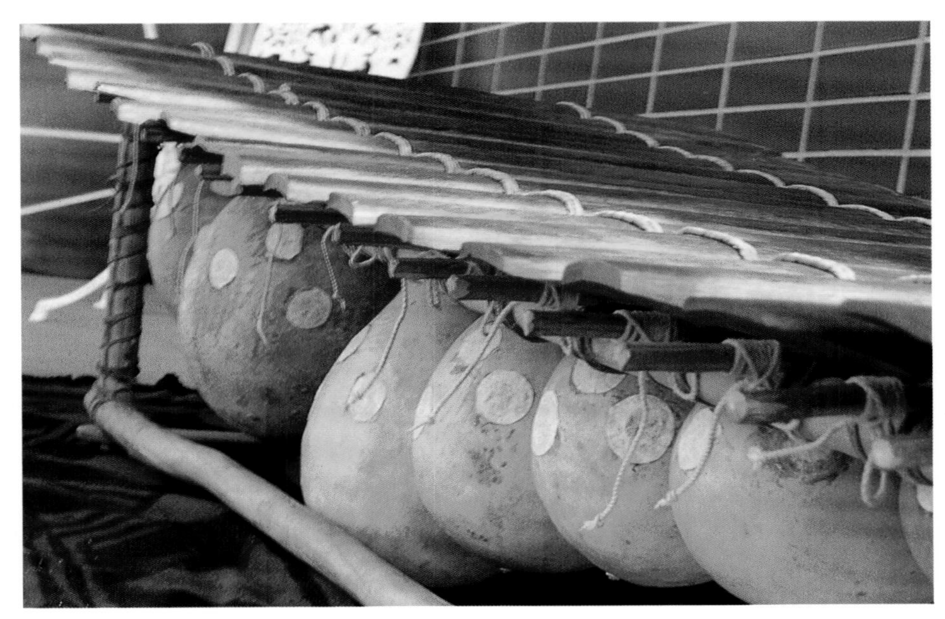

2.3a,b Xylophone gourds. Bambara and Minyanka peoples, Central Mali. Photographs by Heather A. Maxwell, Bloomington, Indiana, 1995.

shape are important factors in selection. The gourds that Diarra used for the xylophone he was constructing came from the surrounding bush. When the frame and keys were mounted, children brought Diarra a large pile of gourds with the tops cut off and the interior cleared out. He selected sixteen gourds (since there are sixteen keys) that ranged from small to large by gradual increments and that had a well-formed roundness so as to emphasize and properly resonate the gradation of pitched keys. In addition to visually examining the gourds, Diarra also listened to them. He picked up each gourd, tapped it on his knee, and put its open end next to his ear.

After selecting the gourds, Diarra drew three small circles on the surface of each one with pencil, which served as the outline for holes that I and other less-experienced participants cut out. After attaching the gourds to the frame and tuning the keys, the holes in the gourds were covered with a spider egg-sac membrane, which was affixed permanently with glue from melted tree sap. The vibration of these membranes produces a buzzing effect when the keys are struck, much like the sound of a kazoo. Today, cigarette paper or tissue paper for wrapping gifts and clothes is also used in place of the spider egg-sacs.

Woma's method of tuning the gourds to the wood is slightly different from Diarra's, but it has the same effect. He is careful in how he cuts the tops off the gourds because the wider the gourd is cut, the higher the sound. He explains that he has difficulty sometimes finding good gourds to use for the lower-registered notes because the quality of gourds for xylophones depends on the season and the harvest. If the smaller gourds do not "line up" with the pitch of the bass key, Woma adds cow dung and glue to the hole to make it smaller, and thus lower pitched. The gourds on his xylophone are thirty-two years old and in perfect condition. They can last, he says, providing that they are well protected and cared for.

The number of xylophone keys on West African instruments ranges anywhere from eleven to twenty-one depending on regional cultural preferences and ecological factors. Techniques and systems of tuning the keys are particularly interesting because they show how xylophonists tune their instruments primarily in terms of relationships, rather than to specific pitches as measured by a constant, universal tone such as the tuning fork in most Western music traditions. By learning what xylophonists listen for when they tune, we also discover that musical sound can be culturally constructed, which sometimes prevents people of one culture from literally "hearing" important musical sounds of another.

In Mali, Diarra's system of tuning a new xylophone involved a long and concentrated series of alternate tapping and striking, from one key on the model xylophone (one I brought to him from further south) to its counterpart on the new one, and from adjacent intervals on the model, back and forth several times to the new one. He started from the highest-pitched keys and worked his way to the lowest. He adjusted the pitches (and intervals) by scraping either the top end of the keys, the underside, or the top middle of the key. After this process, which lasted several hours, Diarra and I affixed the egg-sac membranes onto the holes in the gourds, and the xylophone was complete.

Considering the significant care and amount of time Diarra used in tuning the xylophone, one might assume that precision of pitch and interval agreement is what he was trying to achieve. However, during my discussions with him, I discovered that pitch was not necessarily his primary concern. In this case, keys are identified by their spatial relationship to the ground, rather than by their pitch.

During the construction process, there was great confusion surrounding the identification of the keys. I referred to the higher-pitched keys as "*san fè*" (which can mean "toward the sky" or "high," depending on the context). Yet, when I did so, Diarra, Issah (Diarra's apprentice), and others present repeatedly turned their attention to the lower-pitched keys. After discussing the

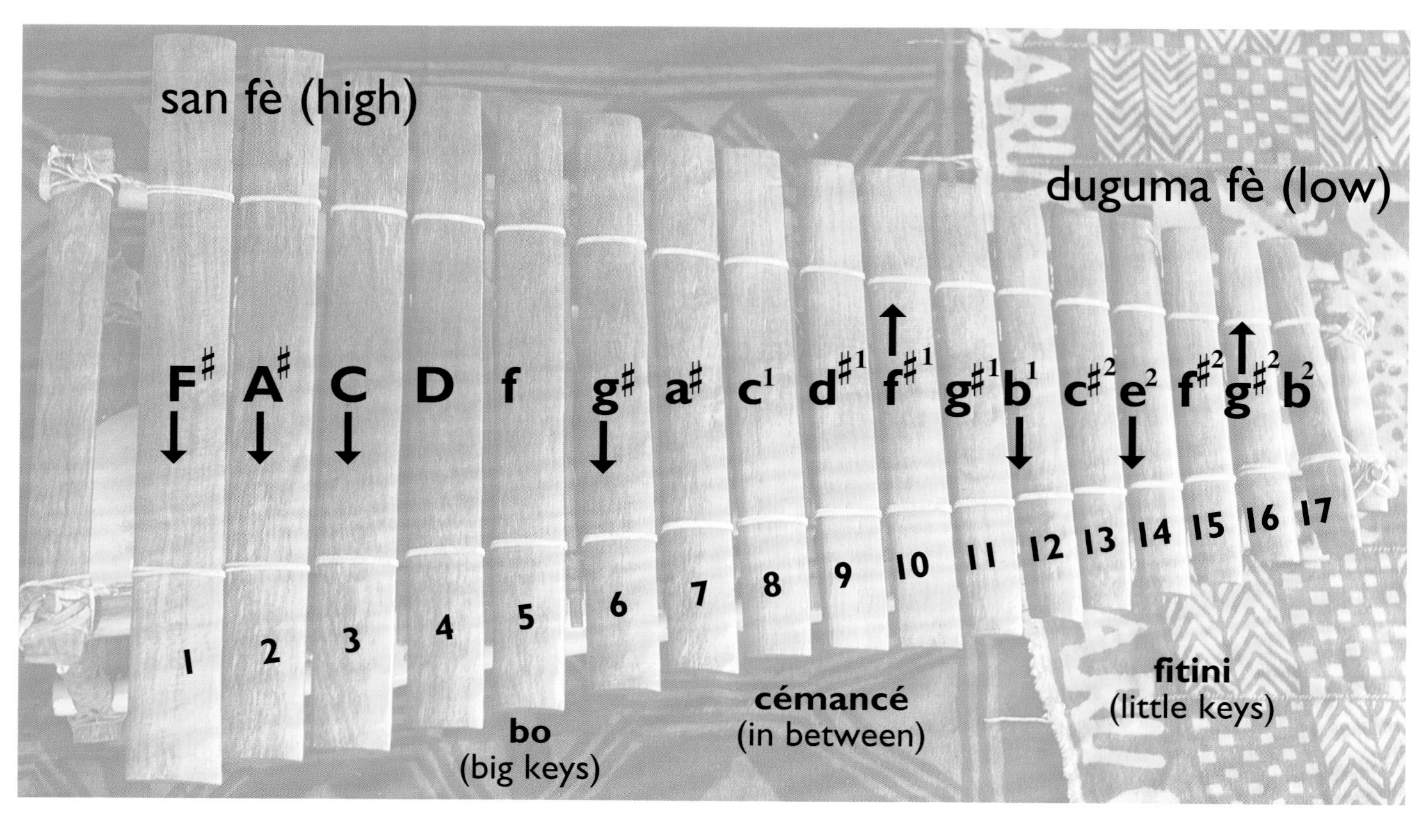

2.4 Approximate pitch measurements of xylophone keys in Minyanka and Western tuning systems. Bambara and Minyanka peoples, Central Mali. Original photograph and analysis by Heather A. Maxwell, Indiana University, 1995.

conflict, I learned that the higher-pitched keys were referred to as "*duguma fè*" (toward the ground) and the lower-pitched keys "*san fè*" (toward the sky) because of their relative physical proximity to the earth and the sky. (Remember that the frame is tallest or closest "toward the sky" at the bass-key end, and it slopes down "toward the ground" as the keys get smaller and higher pitched). As figure 2.4 illustrates, the words used to describe the sound of these keys are *fitini* (little) for the high-pitched keys and *bo* (big) for those with low pitches. This situation suggests that pitch is certainly recognized in the keys, but that it is not necessarily the primary criterion by which keys are identified and considered.

Woma's method for tuning utilizes even more conceptual tools than Diarra's. Woma's relationships include spatial as well as tonal family ones. He also refers to his "high" and "low" keys in terms of their physical height from the ground, but in addition his conceptual tools include a set of two-syllable words whose tonal contour (like high-low or low-low) match the tonal contour of the intervals comprised in the scale, and a set of relationships defined in terms of family members that are used as models for intervals. Thus the two work to reinforce each other, incorporating both concrete sounds and abstract concepts to tune the xylophone.

Beginning from the bass key (his "high"), the tonal contour of the word *tig-be* should match the tonal contour of the intervals between keys 1 and 2. The word for key 2 is *kye-gya*, and from key 3 up to the octave the words are *gang-kye*, *kpng-kpng*, *pog-zre*, and then back to *tig-be* again with the octave. The last key of the xylophone, regardless of how many keys it has, is either *zag-bal* (with no resonating gourd), or *zag-bal tuure* (with gourd). In both types, the keys are not usually played by the mallet but reserved for the stick part to tap out rhythms.

For an explanation of the family kinship concept involved in tuning his xylophones, a direct quotation from one of my interviews with Woma captures the sense better than paraphrasing.

> The most important intervals are "friend" and "senior brother." You always tune each key to the next using the same concept of "friend." You never tune say the first and third key by its interval. Just move from one note to its neighbor, tuning it according to the same friend interval. They should be exactly alike. When you arrive at the senior brother, you check it with its brother (the one you started from.) If they are not "in line" then you decide which note doesn't sound quite right between the two, and correct it. But you never touch the other intervals in between the octave because they are already fine. Just adjust one of the brothers.
>
> To finally recheck, you play the two senior brothers together to make sure that they are "in line." After the first "set" (octave) is checked, then the rest of the octaves are easy. You can check each note by its relative senior brother, which has already been laid out in the first octave. So you could then play the second key of the second octave with its senior brother from the first octave (personal communication, 1997).

As we were communicating on the phone, Woma quickly stopped talking and started playing his xylophone over the line so I could hear and understand how this tool worked.

During my participation in Diarra's tuning session in Mali, I discovered that in some local xylophone traditions there are pitches and sounds that people not familiar with Minyanka xylophone music culture do not automatically hear. This short anecdote of my personal experience with Diarra shows that musicians hear pitches that are "hidden" in the sense that first, they are not actually embodied in a physical key but are produced by the simultaneous strike of two adjacent pitches. Second, although acoustically produced, some pitches are perceived differently, depending on cultural orientation or familiarity of the listener.

While living in N'Tòssoni, one of my biggest frustrations with playing and studying the xylophone was that I experienced great difficulty in trying to notate the music. Interested in practical matters like notating songs and pieces for memorization purposes and composing new pieces on my own, I was not only unable to determine the appropriate intervals on which to base a particular piece but also had trouble transposing blues songs into the tonal system of the xylophones, namely the bass octaves.

One day in particular, when I could not locate a minor third near the bass notes, I remarked to my instructor, Brehman Mallè, that the xylophone was "missing" the minor third from the lowest A-sharp (there is no C-sharp key on the instrument). I played the third pitch, then the fourth, and then sang the interval in between that I wanted to play. I said, "You see, you don't have this note!" Mallè quickly looked at me, smiled, and said, "Oh yes we do, it's here!" He played notes 3 (C) and 4 (D) together and what resulted was a clear C-sharp. He asked me if I could hear it then, and after a few repetitions (and several other influencing voices), I finally did. Once having heard it, I noticed that it was quite clear.

Computer-generated analysis of this phenomenon shows that this "hidden" pitch is intentionally created through skillful tuning techniques to produce an acoustic behavior know as beating.[7] It allows the players more melodic flexibility within the constraints of their fixed-keyed instrument, so that if a C-sharp is desired, it can be played although it does not physically exist on the actual keyboard. This phenomenon raises theoretical questions about whether or not these particular xylophones are in fact pentatonic, but that is the subject of another paper.

Classification Types

With the advancement of ethnomusicological research over the past few decades, scholars have discovered several local systems of classifying musical instruments that are based on different principals than the Western system established by E. M. von Hornbostel and Curt Sachs. With the xylophone, and all other instruments of the world, the Hornbostel/Sachs system classifies musical instruments first by the principal resonating material, and then more specifically by the type of materials and action used to set the sound in motion (Myers 1992, 450–52).[8] Since the gourds are not the primary resonating material, they do not figure into this system of classification. However, since they are an essential part of the sound aesthetic of West African xylophones, they should be included in the classification analysis. In the class of membranophones (instruments where sound is excited by tightly stretched membranes), xylophone gourds are referred to as "adulterated tube kazoos" (Myers 1992, 455), because currents of air resulting from the impact of the mallet on the keys pass through them and the membranes and produce a loud, buzzing quality.

Local terms in West Africa for the xylophone are especially interesting because, by understanding how and why xylophones are defined the way they are by the people who make and use them, we can learn what features are most salient by their own standards. This ethnographic perspective of xylophone names provides a reflection of the way people order and make sense of their musical world. Furthermore, differences in orthography of the instrument reflect intra- and extra-streams of communication and cultural contact between different groups of people.

Most names for xylophones are similar because Mande languages are mutually intelligible. The most common terms are *balafon* (also spelled *balaphone, balafone*), *bala, balangi,* and *mala-kelen. Balafon,* actually the French term for *bala fo,* which means in Bambara to "make the *bala* speak," has been reappropriated and integrated into contemporary Mande language use. Among the Voltaic peoples the xylophone is called *balafon* and *xylophone* depending on which colonial language is in use. It is called *gyil (jil), jengsi,* and *kogyil (kur jil)* in Birifor groups who occupy Volta River regions in northern Ghana and southwestern Burkina Faso; *cholu* and *balam* in Bobo and Bwamu groups in Burkina Faso; and *kpoye* and *dylegbaha* in Senufo groups in the northern Côte d'Ivoire and southern Mali.

Local Classification Systems

In most local classification systems, the number of keys, pitch areas (that is pitches that cluster around distinct registers such as bass or soprano), and the performance context and function are essential criteria for categorizing xylophone types. The Minyanka and Bambara xylophones, for example, differentiate between sixteen keys (*balanin*) and eighteen keys (*balaba*). In addition to the difference in keys, the *balanin* has a higher pitch center than the *balaba* and is used for social dance events associated with youths. The *balaba*, by contrast, is normally reserved for religious and ceremonial contexts and with an older, more mature age group. Also in Mali, but among the Malinke, sacred xylophones have seventeen keys.

Among the Senufo of Mali and Côte d'Ivoire, two types of xylophones are differentiated by the number of keys they carry and how they are played. The large xylophones (eighteen to twenty keys) are played on the ground, and the twelve-keyed xylophones are suspended from the player's shoulders. They are also categorized by usage: the *ncimuoyin* (big xylophone) is used during major social and religious gatherings and as accompaniment to singers who comment on important social facets of life. The *ncizaare* is played in strictly instrumental ensembles and those of youths (Sanogo 1997, 14–15).

In my own system of differentiation, I use the shape of the frame and the tonal organization (pentatonic or equiheptatonic) based on ethnographic data from musicians about their own and other xylophones and on my own compatibility tests of playing my own Bambara/Minyanka xylophones with those from Voltaic players in Ghana. Woma, when asked to comment on differences he heard between his Dagara xylophones and the Bambara/Minyanka ones I had from Mali said that they were "the same dialect" and that if he had to go play music in Mali without his xylophones, he would be able to do it using theirs without any problem. "Dialect," he said, is "the flow of music which comes out of speaking."

When playing my own xylophones from central Mali to recorded music from Burkina Faso, I am able to replicate the pieces without any trouble. The only difference is that they are about one-half step lower and transposition is necessary. On the other hand, it is virtually impossible to play pentatonic xylophones with heptatonic ones, and there have been no musical recordings from West African xylophonists who have attempted this endeavor. Heptatonic xylophones, the Malinke type, are often played with Western instruments and in popular, electronic music ensembles because the scale, if moderated slightly, works with the Western tempered scale. Pentatonic xylophones, however, have not yet been featured as functional parts of Western music or world music ensembles because their tuning is highly incompatible with tempered tuning.

A Different Sense of Aesthetics

Aside from the tonal organization of the heptatonic and pentatonic types, generally speaking, xylophone aesthetics throughout West Africa value thick, timbral textures, resonance, "buzzing" (as was seen in the analysis of gourds), and a certain degree of ambiguity. Precise and matching pitches, or what Westerners would call being "in tune," are much less important than other musical qualities. In Malinke xylophone cultures, where xylophones most often serve as accompaniment to singing praises, oral history, and sometimes social commentary, aesthetics of melo-rhythmic tension and ambiguity are foregrounded. Xylophonists achieve this aesthetic of tension and ambiguity by playing complex polyrhythms in both hands (thus tension and ambiguity in motion) and through the sound of wide and variable pitch margins (Harris 1992).

In Voltaic contexts, loudness, prolonged duration of constant sound, and inharmoniousness in both timbral and tonal features are essential aesthetic components in addition to melo-rhythmic tension and ambiguity. These aesthetic priorities enable musicians to motivate dancers in social dance events, to communicate with the natural and spiritual worlds in sacred events such as possessions and funerals, and to accompany singing with a matching sound aesthetic. Understanding xylophone music aesthetics can, in turn, inform us about important values in a society.

Aesthetics can be understood by the way artists and participants describe what is a "good" and "bad" performance, instrument, and sound. Aesthetic quality can be identified in field and commercial music recordings throughout the region, live performance events, and even by computer-generated analysis. Conversations with Woma and Diarra reveal that a good xylophone is a matter of degree. According to both specialists and nonspecialists, all *balaw* are good if they produce a sound that emphasizes loudness, resonance, and a noisy timbre. By noisy I mean a sound that features high degrees of inharmoniousness, buzzing, and strike tones. When I asked my mentors how they would like the sound of the xylophone without the buzzing sound, they both replied that without the buzz, it is not good. Diarra went even further in stating that without the buzzing sound, it is not the *bala* but rather a different type of xylophone altogether.

For Woma, a xylophone would not sound good for one of two reasons: (1) if the wood is "good" but not well tuned, or (2) if the wood is "bad" but well tuned. He said that if the relationship of the wood to the tuning, the song to the tuning, and the gourds to the tuning are good, then the xylophone is good. Again, the concept of relationships surfaces in terms of musical aesthetics.

Evaluations of good performers are also important criteria for xylophone music aesthetics. The celebrated Ghanaian ethnomusicologist J. H. Nketia states that intensity is a general prerequisite of good performers and an attribute of performance (Nketia 1988, 53–89). According to musician informants from Sineni and N'Tòssoni in Central Mali, the same holds true for xylophonists in Minyankala. The criteria by which one identifies a master xylophonist is an extensive knowledge of repertoire, ability to communicate with and inspire dancers, stamina, and a unique playing style. Stamina, or playing with power (*fanga*), translates in performance as the ability to lead the musicians and dancers for extended lengths of time—sometimes from nightfall till dawn—and producing consistent loudness, resonance, and a high degree of timbral noise. Diarra used to tell me that the best players are particularly pleased when they can keep people dancing all night by continuous playing. The most common expression used by everyone in the community to describe a good player is "strong" (*fanga b' a la*). In fact, for his performances Diarra procured for himself and applied on his forearms a traditional "medicine" (whose name and location he refused to divulge), which he claimed gave him extra power to play for so long without fatigue.

Finally, individual expression is another important aesthetic in xylophone music. Diarra, Issah and other xylophonists from N'Tòssoni explained on several different occasions that master xylophonists build the best instruments and are recognized by and admired for their uniqueness. Since Diarra is regarded as the greatest master by most people in the greater region of northern Minyankala, his xylophones operate as the standing prototype. Thus, his students and their signature instruments, which Diarra builds and hand-carries to their respective home regions, represent the Diarra school, if you will. He used to say to me with great satisfaction that when xylophones are being played, if one of them is his, people will say with pleasure, "Ah, that is Duga's *bala*."

After spending several years in West Africa, I returned to Indiana University to find that the descriptions of aesthetics given to me by various artists and people in the field were further confirmed through analysis of the xylophone's sound behavior. Through computer-generated analyses of the effects certain parts of the xylophone have on the overall sound, we can see how these aesthetics are built. The *bala's* amplitude, for example, is affected by the gourds, as figures 2.5a,b show.

Noise and inharmoniousness are also important features in both xylophone types. One aspect of pitch in African pentatonic xylophones, which enhances inharmonic sounds, or "noise," is the strike tone. A strike tone is the initial higher-pitched sound produced by contact between the mallet and the key, which is separate from the resonating tone that results from vibrations from the key passing through its resonator. The strike tone produces distinctly different pitches than the primary tone. This became evident when using the Korg Pitch analyzer, which registered the pitch of both the mallet against the wood as well as that of the deeper sustained tone (figs. 2.6a,b).

When the Xylophone Speaks

Players often say their xylophones speak. This can have two meanings: (1) myths of origin about the xylophone, and (2) messages given by the xylophone during music performance events. Both Voltaic and Mande myths concerning the origins of the xylophone revere the first xylophones for their spiritual birth and "speaking power." In this case, "speaking" is understood in the literal sense, but this power is generally believed to have been lost over the centuries. In performance, xylophones "speak" at marriages, funerals, and spirit possessions. According to some, they communicate with creatures of the natural world. In this sense, "speaking" means communicating to human and spiritual audiences through playing but not necessarily in literal terms. One finds a wide variety of performance events throughout West Africa, several of which are beautifully illustrated in ethnomusicology literature (Stone 1982). I have selected one example from central Mali.

The xylophone "speaks" in social events usually to dancers through musical interaction. In Minyankala, xylophone dance events are important because they maintain and fortify Minyanka social identity. People of the community are able to celebrate both their individuality and their collective identity. In short, it is one of the most important ways Minyanka people express their "sense of belonging." In secular dances, the xylophone speaks by encouraging and engaging its audiences in a plethora of participatory roles, such as dancing, playing instruments, improvising, observing, and courting.

The general physical placement of these events is characteristic of many West African dance events. From a bird's-eye view, the event occurs in a circular formation. Figures 2.7a,b show this formation with dancers, xylophone players, and other musicians in Kakraba Lobi's dance ensemble in Ghana. Xylophone music is generally accompanied by songs patterned on call and response where the leader (*balafokela*) calls the songs and is answered by the response of the other musicians. These songs, often self-composed or re-created, include repertoire from other regions in West Africa and even from other regions of the world. The participants in these events, outside of the musicians, vary depending on a number of factors, such as particular occasion, size, and composition of village members. Social dance events for youths (*soirées*) are organized by occupational and social associations (*tons*) composed of various gender, age, and special interest groups. *Soirées* resemble a middle American high school dance but without chaperones.

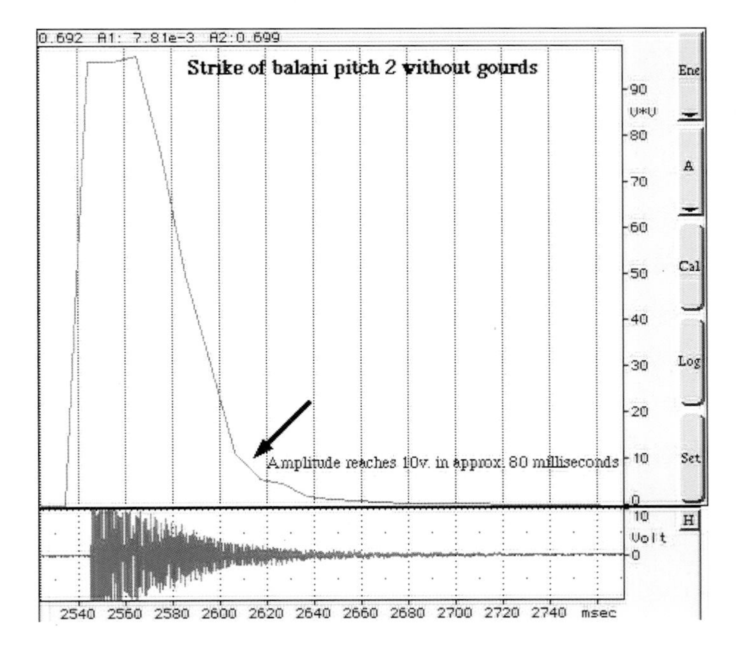

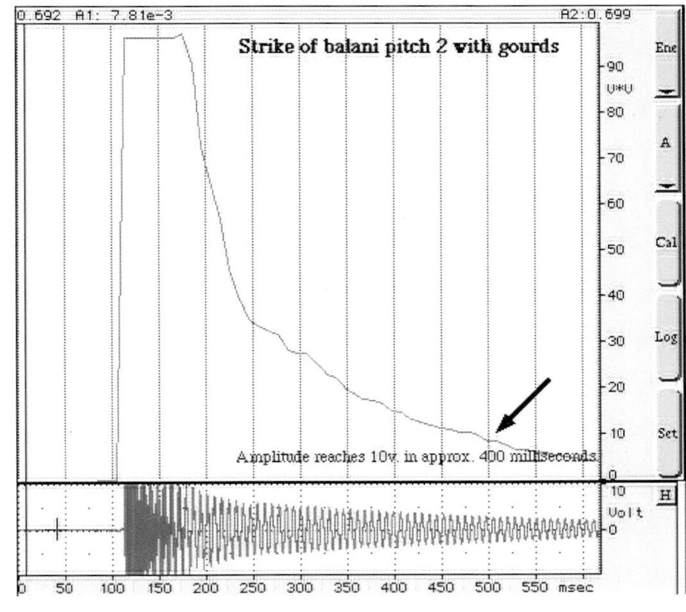

2.5a,b Rise and Decay of *bala* tones. These graphs compare the amplitude of a tone produced without and with a gourd. The amplitude in the tone without the gourd (fig. 2.5a) drops dramatically and rapidly. In figure 2.5b the amplitude of the same tone with the gourd drops and then maintains its amplitude level for a few milliseconds before dropping off like the other.

Xylophonists are responsible for keeping people dancing and in a state of experiential intensity until they themselves get tired. They are expected to provide high-intensity music throughout the night to play loud, hard, and fast almost constantly. Since buzzing and rattling devices serve as intensifiers, *balafokelaw* also wear wrist bracelets to which are attached pieces of metal that vibrate when they play. They also use medicines to improve strength and stamina.

Xylophones speak to the dancers by engaging indirect "conversation" between the *balafokela* and each dancer who comes to dance in front of him. The musician is expected to follow the dancers completely, as long as the dancers respect the basic steps and rhythmic structures that the xylophonist provides. An excerpt from Yaya Diallo's narrative accounts of situational events helps illustrate this point:

> When a person comes to the center of the circle to dance, the musicians must follow the dancer. The dancer can take as long as necessary to feel satisfied. The whole night is available for dancing. The musicians alternately relate the tempo of their playing to the circle and to the individuals who come to the center. A person who weighs 300 pounds cannot be expected to dance at the same speed as one who weighs 100 pounds. A grandfather of sixty-five years will move differently from a youth of eighteen. The Minianka feel that a music of standardized speed does not take human differences into account and thereby fails to show adequate respect for the individual. If a trembling elder enters the circle to do a dance he knows, the musicians honor him by following him (Diallo 1989, 114).

I found this same type of communication and respect in Sineni, Mali, with Diarra. In addition, part of the delight of these events is the individual character of the dancers which, when demonstrated, is highly applauded. During one event in Sineni, a group of boys had just finished up their personality dances when, after a moment's pause, one of the very old men who was back in the shadows of the crowd slowly entered the circle. Approaching the center in a stylistic rhythmic walk, he prompted squeals of excitement and

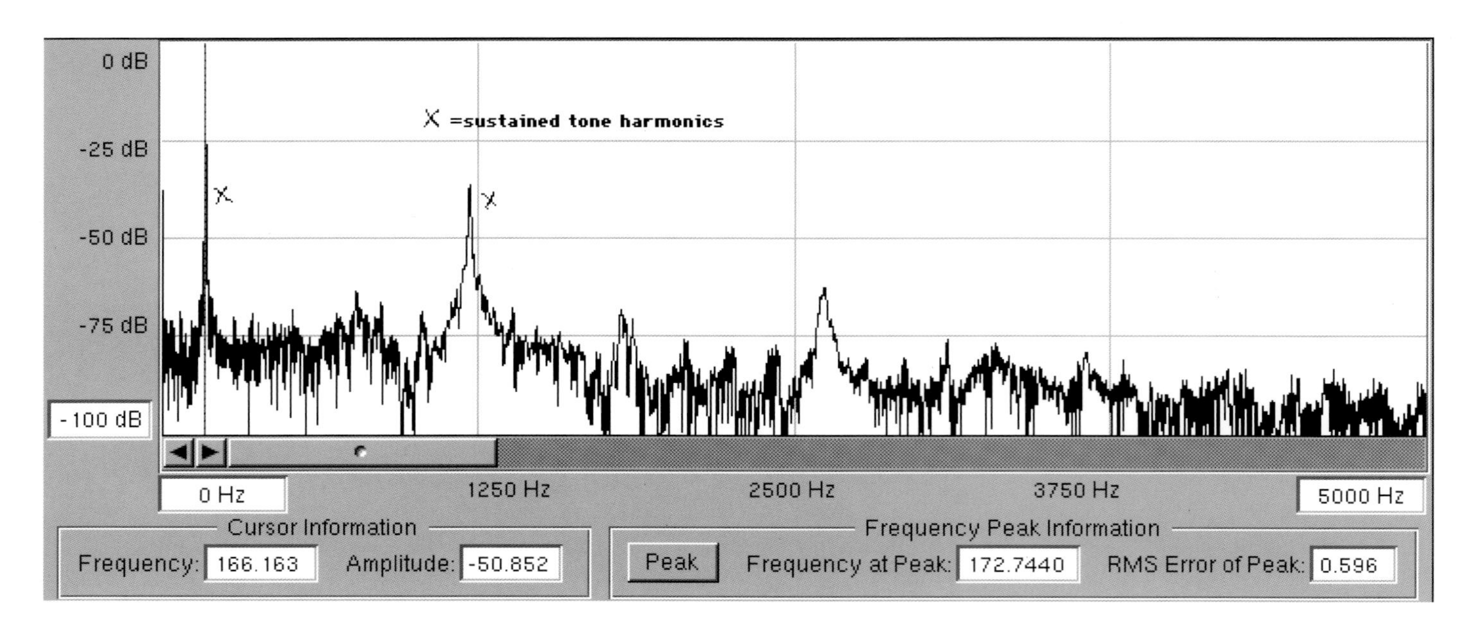

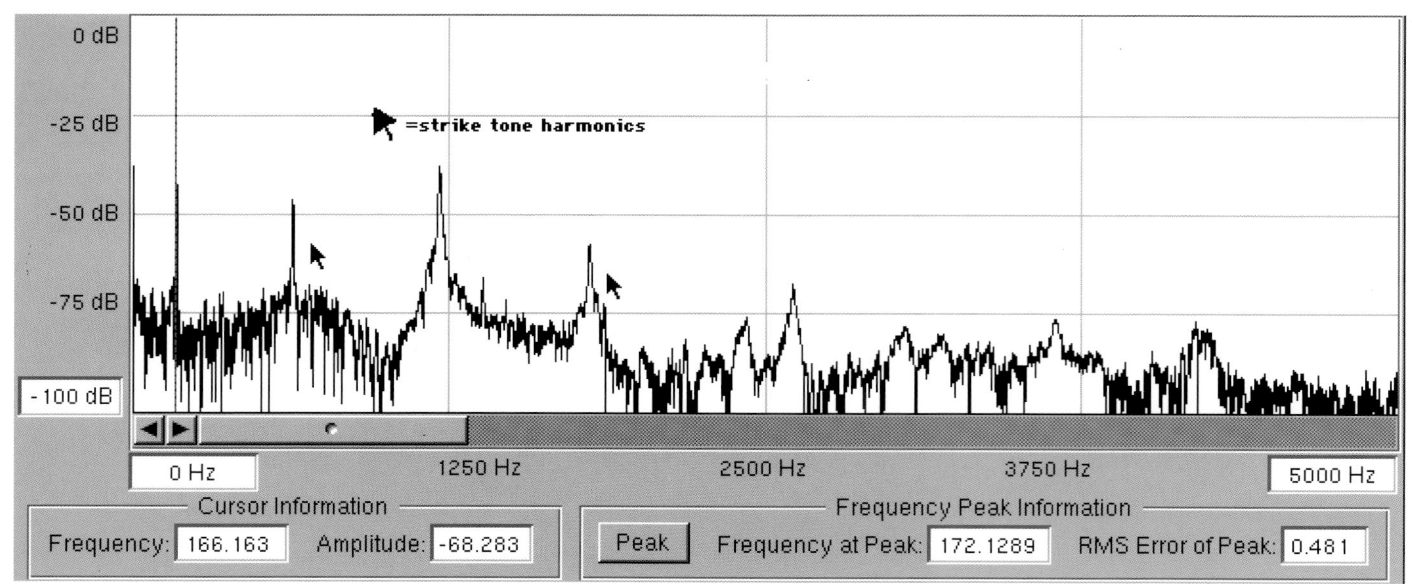

2.6a,b Analysis of amplitudes of sustained and strike tones on Bambara/Minyanka xylophone keys.

encouragement from the crowd, and the women let out high-pitched ululations that, characteristic of many African and Middle Eastern societies, are a sound that only women make to express intense emotion such as joy, warning, or excitement.

As we can see, "speaking" the xylophone in both esoteric and secular dance performance contexts requires a complex and delicate symbiosis between xylophonists and dancers, individual personality and community solidarity. The xylophonist's critical role in the success of these events, and the multiple skills (builder, player, singer, and communicator) he masters, demonstrate his profound understanding and integration in contemporary society. The fact of being well integrated in society, however, does not mean that master xylophonists are not also international, "world-class" artists.

Woma is one of many such cases. He is the principal xylophonist for the Ghana National Dance Ensemble (GNDE) and also performs professionally as a solo artist. He travels extensively, performing both independently and with the GNDE each year. In 1995, for example, he went to Japan, Indonesia, America, and twice to Germany with the GNDE alone. When he returned home after the visit to the United States, he was scheduled to spend only two days in Ghana before touring in Denmark. During an American tour in 1986 he came through Bloomington, Indiana. I was able to talk with him several times about how his xylophone "speaks" in this international setting.

Woma "speaks" his xylophones by communicating the "logic" in the music, by communicating with international audiences the common feelings that all people share. He believes that his playing brings people from all ends of the globe together. Though he is a "traditional" xylophone player from northern Ghana, Woma is an international artist who plays and composes xylophone music according to principles based on creative processes more than anything else. He wants his international audiences to appreciate the beauty of xylophone music and the expressive emotions that it invokes (personal communication, 1997).

Conclusion

To conclude this article, I want to emphasize once more the importance of cultural particularity and specificity and the significance of these aspects as viewed by the people in each xylophone music community. Such a perspective is enriching for those interested in musical cultures, as long as the analysis does not exoticize and marginalize the people under study. My personal conviction is that every culture participates, in one way or another, in the universal culture of humanity. The existence of people like Bernard Woma and other xylophonists proves that successful integation in one's own society does not exclude the ability to share that society's principal values with other civilizations. In conclusion, I leave the readers to reflect on this axiom of the celebrated writer Aimé Césaire: "There are two ways someone can lose him or herself: by segregation walled up in particularity, or by dilution in 'universality'" (1956).

2.7a,b Rehearsal of Kakraba Lobi's Dance Ensemble. Photographs by Heather A. Maxwell, Accra, Ghana 1987.

3. African Traditional Musical Instruments in Neo-African Idioms and Contexts

AKIN EUBA

Among persons claiming an interest in the survival of African music, it is doubtful that many continue to see "survival" in terms of fossilization as opposed to growth and innovation. Over the centuries many changes have occurred in the music of Africa, and it is through this dynamism and vitality that the various forms we know today have survived. In the process of preserving African performing arts, therefore, the museum must be a support system rather than the sole repository of these living traditions.

Change can engender crises, especially when its consequences are not immediately perceived. Some become afraid of parting with the status quo, forgetting, or perhaps unaware, that society is constantly in flux and that previous changes have been well accommodated. Currently Africans are confronted with a crisis stemming from the decline in the practice of traditional religions, a crisis that I believe can be partly resolved through artistic innovation. If we cannot prevent religious rituals from dying, we can at least save ritual arts by secularizing them. The works of many African artists who are presently doing just that suggest the tremendous potential of this approach. Composers, writers, and visual artists often employ ritual motifs in works that are not intended for ritual ceremonies. An obvious example is Dúró Ládípọ̀'s folk opera *Ọba Kòso*, a dramatization of the life of Ṣàngó, a fifteenth-century king of Ọ̀yọ́ in Yorubaland—worshiped today by the Yorùbá as the god of thunder and lightning. Audiences who are unable to observe actual ceremonies for Ṣàngó are able to appreciate the artistic forms associated with them through Ládípọ̀'s folk opera. This example and others like it—occurring in a variety of musical contexts—constitute what might best be referred to as "neo-African idioms." In addition to these idioms, traditional instruments are now being used in new contexts—national dance ensembles, educational institutions, and the Diaspora. I will discuss these new contexts below. It should be noted that while many of the examples cited in this essay are drawn from Nigeria, they nonetheless typify the trends occurring in many other African cultures as well.

3.1 CD cover from Akin Euba's opera *Chaka* with a painting by Nigerian artist Moyọ̀ Okédìjì.

Neo-African Idioms

Neo-African idioms are nontraditional types of music that developed in response to new social contexts encountered during the colonial era. They have since become increasingly dominant. They reflect African contacts with Arab and Western cultures and include: (a) church music, (b) popular music (such as *highlife* and *jùjú*), (c) music theater (e.g., the Yorùbá folk opera and plays written by African authors in vernacular and nonvernacular languages), (d) modern art music (e.g., the works of composers trained in Western schools of music). In this study I will discuss new idioms that feature traditional instruments as well as the institutions and contexts that have given rise to them.

Church Music

Although "drums and other percussion instruments were used in the Ethiopian church, which had been established in the fourth century A.D.," their use in West African and other churches south of the Sahara was forbidden when Christianity arrived in those parts in the nineteenth century (Nketia 1974, 15). All things pertaining to traditional arts and culture (including musical instruments) were regarded by Christian missionaries as "pagan." As missionary influence declined, however, African churches began to adopt elements of African culture.

In Yorubaland, there were three main reasons why traditional instruments found their way into the church. First, from around the beginning of the twentieth century, the Yorùbá began to protest European domination of their religious institutions; this led prominent Yorùbá to break away from Western denominations and found their own churches. These were the first indigenous (African) churches of the Yorùbá. Second, the resistance to European domination within the church paralleled a general cultural reawakening, which witnessed the use of traditional performing arts in the emergent neo-African theater. Third, the political movements that culminated in national independence in various parts of Africa were accompanied in Yorubaland by a general return to African cultural practices among members of the new Yorùbá elite who had previously embraced Western lifestyles.

Before all of this took place, the musical instruments most commonly used in Yorùbá churches were the pipe organ and the harmonium. When the churches initially adopted African instruments (consisting mainly of drums and other percussion), these were simply combined with the organ or harmonium. In recent decades, the African churches in Yorubaland (commonly called *aládùrà*, i.e., "prayer" churches) have adopted idioms from modern Yorùbá popular music (such as *highlife* and *jùjú*) as a way of promoting evangelism. Consequently they use international pop instruments such as guitars, saxophones, electric keyboards, and drum kit, in combination with Yorùbá drums and other percussion.

Interestingly, however, the Yorùbá churches have retained in part the attitude of the early missionaries toward traditional musical instruments. On the one hand, they disallow the use of instruments associated with indigenous ritual ceremonies (e.g., *bàtá* drums used by the devotees of Ṣàngó, the god of thunder and lightning and *ìgbìn* drums used by the devotees of Ọbàtálá, the god of creation).[1] On the other hand, the double-headed hourglass tension drum (a secular instrument with no specific ritual or institutional associations) is now a very prominent member of the church ensemble. Other regularly used instruments include the small, beaded gourd rattle (*ṣẹ̀kẹ̀rẹ̀*), the iron bell (*agogo*), and a set of single-headed fixed-pitch drums (*àkúbà*), whose immediate prototype is the Latin American conga (commonly used in *jùjú* and *highlife*) but whose ultimate origin is the traditional single-headed fixed-pitch drums of the Yorùbá.

Popular Music

The term "popular music" is problematic when applied to Africa where in traditional cultures, all music is "popular" in that it always attracts a sizable audience. This includes such difficult musical genres as *pípè òrìṣà*, or "calling the divinities," which consists of poetry in praise of Yorùbá gods. Although the term "popular" is not easily applicable to the music of traditional cultures, it is useful when dealing with modern types of music, such as *jùjú*, *highlife*, and *taarab*, which are functionally and stylistically similar to Western popular music.

Popular music is designed for entertainment and is most frequently performed (either live or recorded) at weddings and funeral parties or in venues that typically serve alcoholic or other beverages (e.g., bars, cafes, nightclubs, beer parlors). As noted earlier, popular music was developed in response to such social contexts, which emerged during the colonial era. The new social contexts were designed to cater to the needs of persons moving from their traditional home bases into modern urban conditions. For example, among the Yorùbá the role of the traditional praise singer (accompanied by traditional instruments) was taken over by the *jùjú* singer (accompanied by guitars combined with traditional instruments). Much of the style of "popular" music has been derived from European (and in some cases Arab) culture. Nonetheless, the most successful types are those that include strong African elements and a definite African identity. In establishing an African identity, the musicians employ: (a) stylistic elements of traditional music, (b) local (indigenous) languages for song texts, and (c) indigenous musical instruments, among other devices. Language and instruments have a high profile and are often crucial to establishing an African identity. There are, however, many well-known masters of popular music who have managed to create a credible African sound while excluding African instruments from their ensembles or making minimal use of them. A notable example is Fẹlá Aníkúlápó-Kútì, who, as far as I know, did not feature African instruments in the ensembles of his mature period.[2]

Among the types of popular music that feature African instruments is the *jùjú* ensemble, whose idiom is largely defined by the Western guitar and the hourglass talking drum. *Jùjú* music was created by Yorùbá musicians of southwestern Nigeria, and its texts are in the vernacular and focus on validating the status and enhancing the prestige of its patrons. In 1986 King Sunny Ade (one of the leading *jùjú* artists) and his Golden Mercury ensemble, featured three hourglass talking drums, one *agogo* (iron bell), and one *ṣẹ̀kẹ̀rẹ̀* (gourd rattle), together with eight guitars (including a Hawaiian guitar) and various other standard instruments of the international popular ensemble (Ade 1986).[3] Interestingly, the *highlife* ensemble, another well-known type of West African popular music, was modeled on the big band of Glenn Miller. In the 1960s (when "classical" *highlife* was at its peak in Nigeria) Roy Chicago introduced the use of the hourglass talking drum, and this became quite fashionable.[4] While *jùjú* is mainly performed by Yorùbá musicians, *highlife* was the first pan-ethnic form of modern "popular" music in Ghana and Nigeria, and today it enjoys wide distribution all over West Africa.

Minstrelsy is a contemporary art form among the Igbo of southeastern Nigeria. The minstrels recite "texts in which they comment on questions of everyday life and (articulate) the hopes and concerns of the population" (Bender 1991, 99). According to Bender (1991, 104–5), the typical minstrel accompanies himself on the *ubo* (a thumb piano) but sometimes uses a larger ensemble. In addition to the *ubo*, Ezigbo Obiligbo sometimes includes a rattle consisting of fruit shells tied together, a small slit drum, and the *udu* (a plosive idiophone consisting of a clay pot struck at the mouth with a fibrous beater).

Taarab is another musical genre in which traditional instruments feature prominently. Writing about its practice in Kiswahili-speaking East Africa and the region bordering the Indian Ocean, Davis (1990, 188) describes *taarab* as being "essentially a non-participatory entertainment music embracing a diverse spectrum of regional styles, vocal and instrumental combinations, and performance contexts, which in turn reflect, in varying degrees and proportions, 'the overall influence of Indian film tracks, Egyptian and Lebanese music and popular Latin music of various periods.' " In one of the LPs reviewed by Davis, the two artists, Seif Salim Saheh and Abdullah Mussa Ahmed, played the *'ūd* (a short-necked plucked lute), the *qānūn* (a plucked box-zither or psaltery), and the *duff* (a single-headed frame drum). These three instruments are members of the Egyptian *takht* ensemble. The second LP features the Ikhwani Safaa Musical Club, a much larger ensemble, comprising the *takht* group already mentioned together with the *nay* (a Middle Eastern flute), several violins, cello, double bass, accordion, and electric guitar.[5]

Music Theater

One of the major developments in African performing arts in the twentieth century is the creation of a neo-African theater in which spoken dialogue in a European language is juxtaposed with song, dance, and instrumental music derived from traditional culture. One of the foremost exponents of this idiom is the 1986 Nobel laureate in literature Wọlé Ṣóyinká. I have thus far been unable to ascertain the date of the earliest instance of an African play in a European language, but by the 1960s, when Nigerian playwrights Ṣóyinká and J. P. Clark first become prominent, this type of theater had become an established aspect of African culture.

Death and the King's Horseman, one of Ṣóyinká's most important works for the stage, is set in 1940s Ọ̀yọ́ (a leading center of the Yorùbá cultural heritage) during the colonial era and focuses on kingly traditions. It is logical therefore that Ṣóyinká employs elements deeply embedded in Yorùbá culture—including traditional musical instruments—for dramatic effect. Hourglass tension drums are characteristic of the traditional music of central Yorubaland, and these are prominently deployed in *Death and the King's Horseman*.

Another example of modern theater that features traditional instruments is the Yorùbá folk opera, a genre that dates from about 1903. Folk opera originated as part of the general trend toward Africanization of modern theater (noted above) and has strong connections with the church. Consequently, elements in the idiom of Yorùbá church music are among its stylistic characteristics. Also characteristic are features of Yorùbá traditional performing arts, including musical instruments. The typical ensemble of the Yorùbá folk opera includes hourglass tension drums combined with *àkúbà* drums, iron bell, and gourd rattle. In Dúró Ládípọ̀'s *Ọba Kòso* (noted previously) prominence is given to *bàtá* drums (double-headed, conically shaped membrane drums), which are today identified with the devotees of Ṣàngó and of his wife Ọya (goddess of the River Niger).[6]

Modern Art Music

Musical instruments are very effective in establishing musical identity. For example, the symphonic idiom gains much of its identity from the particular choice of instruments that constitute the orchestra; similarly, the jazz idiom is identified with certain kinds of instruments (although I should point out that nontypical instruments often appear in jazz). This principle may be equally applied to the music of Africa, and, inasmuch as there is a unity of approach in the music of Africa south of the Sahara (or north of the Sahara), this music is to a great extent distinguished from other world musics by virtue of the types of musical instruments involved in its making.

In an earlier study (Euba 1989, 128) I identified four categories of neo-African art music, ranging from the more Western-oriented (such as Ayọ̀ Bankọ́lé's *Toccata* for organ and my own *String Quartet*) to the more African-oriented (such as Dúró Ládípọ̀'s previously remarked folk opera *Ọba Kòso*). Before the coming of the Europeans, Africans had indigenous types of art music, that is, idioms in which the focus was on contemplative listening rather than ceremonial activity or dance. The types under discussion in this essay, however, had their origin in contact between Africa and Europe, and more specifically in the Christian influence in Africa. For one thing, European missionaries introduced staff notation (primarily to enhance the abilities of African organists and choirmasters), and this facilitated African access to European types of music that rely on notation, including Western classical music.[7]

African composers trained in Western conservatories have not routinely employed African instruments in their works but have often sought to establish an African identity through other means. For example, J. H. Kwabena Nketia, apart from a collection of pedagogical pieces for Ghanaian *atenteben* (bamboo flutes), has not typically composed music for African instruments. Nevertheless, his music for Western instruments has a strong African identity resulting from a deep knowledge of the stylistic organization of African music.

Nonetheless, some composers of modern art music have made copious use of African instruments. It is to this group that I will now turn my attention. "Kyrie" from *Missa Maleng* (1976) by the Ugandan Anthony Okelo is scored for four-part choir (SATB) with *aja* (a gourd rattle) and three membrane drums (*latin bwul*, *lakele*, and *min bwul*), and the drumming style employed is that of the *larakaraka* dance of the Acholi of Uganda. Okelo is a Roman Catholic priest, and the idiom of his sacred choral works is in conventional four-part harmony. In spite of this, his "Kyrie" commands attention because of its novel use of African instruments where one would ordinarily expect a church organ.

Solomon Mbabi-Katana, also from Uganda, composed a work that is a model for persons interested in writing for African instruments. Titled *Midday Dream*, Mbabi-Katana's work is scored for wood block, cow bells, small drum, big drum, rattle, xylophone, bow-lutes, flutes, thumb pianos, scraper, pan pipes, and slit drum. Mbabi-Katana, who is also an ethnomusicologist, provided detailed notes in the score describing the instruments and how they are played. He also made diagrams showing the tuning systems of the xylophone, thumb pianos, flutes, and bow-lutes.

Midday Dream is a pedagogical work written for the students of the Department of Music, Dance, and Drama at Makerere University, Uganda, where Mbabi-Katana taught. Composers who write for African instruments sometimes devise a new notation that accommodates the techniques of those instruments or otherwise adapt the Western staff notation in one form or another. One such composer, Halim El-Dabh from Egypt, designed a notation that allows him to express the African and Egyptian elements in his works (Daniel 1980, 103).

In order to facilitate the performance of these works, El-Dabh (1965b) published a drumming tutor, *The Derabucca: Hand Techniques in the Art of Drumming*, in which his special notation is explained. According to the author, the *derabucca* "is the Arabic name of an African drum known in the Nile and Niger regions, mostly in Egypt, Mali, Guinea and Senegal." In Upper Egypt the name refers to a single-headed, vase-shaped membrane drum, with a shell made of terra-cotta (El-Dabh 1965b, 1). El-Dabh uses the *derabucca* in some of his works, namely *Fantasia-Tahmeel* for *derabucca* (or timpani) and string orchestra and *Sonic* nos. 7 and 10 for *derabucca* (or multiple drums).

I would like to further exemplify the use of African instruments in neo-African composition by citing my own work, *Chaka*—an opera in two chants for soloists, Yorùbá chanter, chorus, dancers, and an ensemble of Western and African instruments—from a dramatic poem of the same name by Léopold Sédar Senghor. The ensemble used in *Chaka* consists of the following African instruments: five *atenteben* (At), bamboo flutes in C; one *agogo* (Ag), a double bell; two slit drums (St.D I–II); one *ṣẹ̀kẹ̀rẹ̀* (Skr), a gourd rattle; three Yorùbá hourglass tensions drums (TD I–III); one gúdúgúdú (Gd), a small Yorùbá kettle drum with tuning paste; three single-headed, fixed-pitch membrane drums (SHD I–III) of unspecified origin. (In a live performance of 1995 and subsequent CD recording, drums of the Ewe of Ghana were used.) The rest of the ensemble comprises the following Western instruments: one flute, one clarinet in B-flat, one bassoon, one trumpet in B-flat, one horn in F, one bass trombone, one double bass, one xylophone, five timpani, bass drum, cymbals, triangle, and synthesizer keyboard. There is no place in the entire score where all of the instruments (African and Western) play together, but illustrated in this essay (fig. 3.3) is a segment near the end of the prelude (beginning from measure 428), which gives a good idea how the African instruments in *Chaka* are deployed. The following instruments are featured in the excerpt: *atenteben*, trumpet in B-flat, horn in F, trombone, *gúdúgúdú*, slit drums I and II, and single-headed drum III.

3.2 *Chaka* by Akin Euba as performed by the City of Birmingham Touring Opera at Symphony Hall, Birmingham, England, 1995. From left to right: Yorùbá chanter (Jolaade Pratt), leader of the chorus (Louis de Costa Johnson), and Chaka (Devon Harrison). Photograph reproduced courtesy of Richard H. Smith, London.

3.3 Excerpt from *Chaka* by Akin Euba.

Ag	*agogo*
At	*atenteben*
Bn	bassoon
Cl	clarinet
Fl	flute
Gd	*gúdúgúdú*
Hn	horn in F
SHD	single-headed drum
St.D	slit drum
Tpt	trumpet in B-flat
Trom	trombone

At
Tpt
Hn
Gd
St.D I
St.D II
SHD III
440
con sord.
mp
S
H
444
448
Trom

Neo-African Contexts

National Dance Ensembles

The idea of national dance ensembles (probably pioneered by the Francophone countries of West Africa) belongs to the postcolonial era. The typical national dance ensemble seeks to portray the diversity of music and dance traditions of a given country in the most economical way possible. Instead of hiring complete mini-ensembles from the different ethnic groups existing in a given country, the national troupe hires individual master musicians and master dancers from various ethnic groups who then teach the other members of the national troupe (drawn from as many different ethnic groups as possible) to perform traditions of music and dance from their own and other ethnic groups within the country.[8] The basic idea is that all members of the troupe can learn to perform one another's music and dance traditions. The national dance ensembles provide alternative sources of income for musicians and dancers who had previously earned their living mainly from ceremonies and other social contexts in their own areas of the country.

In the postcolonial era, one of the most pressing problems of newly independent African states was that of welding diverse ethnic groups into unified nations with a common purpose and identity. In order to solve this problem, African governments needed to promote interethnic understanding, and national dance ensembles provided an effective means of doing so. Moreover, these ensembles are a medium for showcasing the nation's traditions abroad.

The Ghana Dance Ensemble is a good example of the concept of national dance ensembles. Previously existing within the School of Performing Arts in the University of Ghana, Legon, the ensemble now operates under the Ghana National Theatre. A typical program presented by the Ghana Dance Ensemble would include dances from various traditions around the country, each using the same resources (costumes, musical instruments, etc.) that are characteristic of the given dance in its original context. In other words, the dance and resources are traditional, but they are rearranged to suit the new context of a staged performance. A program presented by the Ghana Dance Ensemble gives the observer an overview of the instrumental resources available in Ghana and how they are used in different ceremonies and contexts.

Pedagogical Developments

In traditional culture south of the Sahara, talent for some types of music is thought to reside within selected families. The Yorùbá for example acknowledge *ilé ìlù* (drumming families), which are believed to be the direct descendants of Ayan, the first Yorùbá drummer and patron god of drummers.[9] In Yorùbá culture, only persons born into drumming families may learn or practice the art of drumming, and this is true of other African societies as well.[10]

In modern times, new educational priorities have changed somewhat the traditional concept of musical talent. Departments of music in African universities typically include the teaching of African instruments in their curricula, and the criteria used in admitting students to their programs disregard traditional practice. For example, in the University of Ghana, where I have often served as an external examiner, female students pursuing music courses are often required to acquire some competence in the performance of *atumpan* (single-headed, goblet-shaped talking drums of the Akan) even though, in traditional culture, these drums are customarily played by men.

In Nigeria high schools usually have music and dance troupes in which students from different parts of the country learn one another's traditions. In an all-girl school, the troupe's instrumentalists are invariably girls who often play instruments that are normally assigned to men—instruments that they would not be permitted to play in their original contexts.

African Instruments in the Diaspora

In order to illustrate the increasing presence of African instruments and instrumentalists outside Africa, I would like to cite a personal experience that occurred during AFRICA 95 (an important celebration of African arts and culture that was held in the United Kingdom during the last quarter of 1995 and featured a performance of my opera *Chaka* by the City of Birmingham Touring Opera; see fig. 3.2).

As previously discussed, *Chaka* uses a number of African instruments, and in preliminary discussions with the officials of AFRICA 95, a budget was arrived at that included the costs of bringing performers and instruments from Nigeria. By the time the performance took place, however, I discovered to my surprise that all of the African instruments featured in the score of *Chaka*, as well as competent performers of them, were available in the United Kingdom and that it was unnecessary to bring them from Nigeria.

In recent years, the presence of African instruments and instrumentalists outside Africa, particularly in Europe and the United States, has increased dramatically, and there are various reasons for this. First of all, beginning with the example of Mantle Hood (former director of the Institute of Ethnomusicology at the University of California, Los Angeles), ethnomusicologists have come to accept the idea that scholars gain a better insight into the musics that they are studying when they actually learn to perform them. Although Hood may not have been the first to articulate this theory,[11] he was, I believe, the first to practice it on an institutional basis. Today, in addition to that of UCLA, notable programs of African music performance include those at the University of West Virginia (led by the Ghanaian Paschal Younge) and the University of Pittsburgh (led by Sylvia Nanyonga-Tamusuza of Uganda).[12]

There are other African music and dance ensembles that function outside academia. In the United Kingdom a number of organizations have emerged with the uniform aim of disseminating African arts and culture. Consistent with this aim, they typically feature the performing arts, including storytelling, music, and dance. Contexts of presentation include workshops, demonstrations, and full-blown concerts. The directors of such projects are not necessarily persons who would qualify in Africa as specialists in traditional music or dance, but they usually have sufficient expertise (however acquired) to operate as "professionals" in the African Diaspora. This statement is not meant to imply that "anything goes" in the Diaspora but simply to establish that there are persons living outside Africa who have the competence to fill vacuums existing in Diaspora culture. The picture in the United Kingdom corresponds to that of the United States.

There are also expatriate artists working in the Diaspora who, while having recognition at home as specialists, choose to operate either totally or partially abroad. Such persons cater to a wide variety of needs; for example they could create their own ensembles or join those created by others. They are also useful as instructors in primary, secondary, and tertiary institutions of learning. Furthermore, they frequently appear in live and recorded performances featuring African music or so-called fusion music. The opportunities existing for highly qualified instrumentalists in the Diaspora are extensive.

Among the most widely traveled African instruments are the *djembe*, also known as *jembe* (a single-headed fixed-pitch membrane drum whose original home is in the Mande-speaking areas of West Africa, comprising Guinea, The Gambia, Mali, and Senegal) and the *atenteben* (a bamboo flute). Traditionally, the *atenteben* belongs to a family of end-blown flutes that also includes the *odurugya*—these are played for the kings of Ashanti. Using the traditional prototype, Ephraim Amu (a well-known Ghanaian composer and teacher) constructed a modern version of the *atenteben* that is tuned to the Western diatonic system and is available in either C or B-flat. Amu's version is used extensively in pedagogical contexts in Ghana (serving the same purpose as the recorder in Europe) and in neo-African ensembles. Like Nketia, Amu also wrote numerous pedagogical pieces for the *atenteben*. This instrument has traveled to other parts of West Africa and is used by Ghanaian musicians resident in Europe and probably also in the United States.

Problems of Performance

Composers of music that features African instruments face problems relating to the availability of instruments and/or players whenever there is a need to stage performances outside the immediate cultures to which such instruments belong. It is a safe assumption that the great majority of African musical instruments existing outside Africa are to be found in museums and private collections where they are used as decorative objects and are not necessarily in performance-ready condition. Moreover, Africa has an almost infinite variety of musical instruments, and although there are some basic common features within classes of instruments, significant differences exist in terms of tuning systems, structural features, types of materials used in construction, timbres, methods of performance, and so forth. For example, when a work uses a xylophone, the composer may need to specify its ethnic origin, structural characteristics, and tuning. Furthermore, the double-headed hourglass tension drums of the Yorùbá of Nigeria (several types of which exist) are not exactly the same as the double-headed hourglass tension drums of the Dagbamba of Ghana (even though they belong to the same class); and it is not enough for a composer to indicate a double-headed[13] hourglass tension drum in a score without at least giving its ethnic origin.

I am not suggesting that works involving African instruments should be written in the finely honed style of orchestration typical of Western art music (especially in the twentieth century); imprecision and a certain degree of generalization (which are typical of African traditional music) may be a desirable feature of neo-African music. Some degree of compromise invariably takes place when works in which African instruments are used are performed outside the immediate cultures from which the instruments originate. It is for this reason that Halim El-Dabh indicates in advance possible alternatives for the non-Western instruments that he features in his compositions.[14]

Conclusion

The spread of African musical instruments into new idioms and contexts has some important implications. To begin with, there is clearly an economic advantage resulting from an increase in demand for the instruments, but what is less clear is who will derive benefit from this advantage. As long as African craftsmen continue to produce enough instruments to meet local and international demands, they will be active participants in what could become a lucrative industry. If supply from African sources fails to meet demand, then the industry could be invaded by foreigners who may then find a way to maximize profits by mass-producing instruments that have hitherto been handcrafted. Some African musicians might even come to prefer foreign versions of African instruments because of perceived technological improvements (for example, greater durability), thereby further jeopardizing the local industries.

Currently, there are various sources in Europe and the United States from which one can purchase musical instruments imported from Africa. These are not tourist specimens for decoration but specimens that African musicians would be happy playing. Among the most readily available are Ewe drums from Ghana. What is more, whenever drums need to be repaired, there are persons in the United States (who are not necessarily of African origin) who can handle the job competently.

The aesthetic implications of the migration of African musical instruments to other parts of the world are difficult to assess. If such instruments become fully integrated into their new cultures and are actually manufactured abroad, some people may expect them to perform the same functions in the new context that they did in the original one and may well be disappointed if the new instruments do not measure up to the old. A more positive way to view innovation (in the making of musical instruments as in other things) is that new instruments will have new functions and speak with new voices. Their success should therefore be judged in terms of how well they perform their new functions. For example, there is evidence that hourglass tension drums found in West Africa derived from a common source in the Middle East (Euba 1990,43). There are differences, however, in the timbres of the hourglass tension drums of the Yorùbá and the Hausa (both of Nigeria) and the Dagbamba of Ghana. The sounds of the Yorùbá drums are well suited to the music they perform, and those of the Dagbamba and Hausa similarly well suited to the musics that they perform. While I very much enjoy hearing the Dagbamba hourglass tension drum in the context of Dagbamba music, it would not be appropriate for the performance of Yorùbá drum music and vice versa. The point is that when the hourglass drum migrated into Yorùbá, Hausa, and Dagbamba cultures, it adapted to the new cultures and developed new voices suited to them. Music and dance troupes in Europe and the United States that specialize in African traditions have actually adapted these traditions to suit the needs of audiences in the Diaspora and cannot be expected to be strictly faithful to what Africans perform in Africa. We must therefore discover an aesthetic that is appropriate for evaluating them rather than try to force on them values that exist on the African continent. Finally, the migration of music and musical instruments is a historical truism that has produced many important intercultural traditions all over the world, and these are valuable precedents for the new developments that we are witnessing today. There is no reason to presume that today's innovations will not in future become traditions in their own right.

An Interview with Akin Euba

On May 28, 1999, Lynne Kostman of the Fowler Museum of Cultural History had the opportunity to conduct a brief interview with Akin Euba who was then attending a conference at the Department of Ethnomusicology on the UCLA campus.

LK: In a recent article in the *New York Times* [April 25, 1999],Wọlé Ṣóyinká commented that growing up in western Nigeria, he was "weaned on opera," by which he meant African opera. I'm wondering if you as a fellow Nigerian had a similar experience.

AE: In high school we were exposed to what was known at that time as "native air opera." It dealt primarily with Christian subject matter, but I must say my memories of my first encounters with these native air operas are very vague. By the way, "air" in this case means "melody." Much later, when I returned to Nigeria after my college studies in the UK, I became familiar with the term "folk opera." Ulli Beier supposedly coined this term to replace "native air opera." He wrote what I think was the first article on "folk opera." It was supposedly derived from Yorùbá tradition; I don't think it spread to the Igbo or the Hausa.

LK: It evolved from Yorùbá tradition, but the themes were Christian?

AE: I should perhaps insert a bit of my own background here to clarify. It was really only after I came to UCLA to study ethnomusicology that I began to look at music from a cultural or sociological perspective, and it was at that point that I became more interested in folk opera and actually began to study it seriously. The first folk opera was composed around 1903, and a number of events in the last years of the nineteenth century led up to it. Western-educated Yorùbá and Christian "returnees" from Brazil had a growing desire to discover their own cultural traditions. They had accepted Western music, Western culture, Western dress, but they had begun to realize that there was an indigenous African culture, and they wanted to bring elements of that culture into forms of entertainment, theater, music. Leaders in the community also became unhappy about the domination of the church by European missionaries. So some of them broke away and started their own African churches. They introduced drums and other traditional Yorùbá instruments, and at holiday times, Easter, Christmas, and so forth, they would stage biblical stories with music.

LK: How elaborately were these folk operas staged?

AE: I think initially the format was very simple. They would use costumes they thought reflected the dress of biblical times. Gradually, however, these operas began to focus more on Yorùbá history, Yorùbá mythology, Yorùbá traditions; and contemporary life. Then, of course, the costuming became traditional, and there was free use of the symbols of Yorùbá culture.

LK: Did your parents have more exposure to traditional Yorùbá culture?

AE: Not necessarily. In fact some of the most popular forms of entertainment in those days were things like Gilbert and Sullivan. My mother who was born in 1909 even told me that in school she performed in Samuel Coleridge-Taylor's setting of Longfellow's *Hiawatha.*

LK: So you yourself actually had very little exposure as a child to Yorùbá performance outside the context of the church.

AE: There was always a lot of drumming to be heard in Lagos in those days, but I did not myself play drums. I was in fact brought up on the piano. My father's family were "returnees," and they lived apart from the more traditional area of Lagos, as did many "returnees." My exposure was primarily to Western music. I started learning the piano when I was eight and grew up on a diet of Beethoven and other Western classical composers. In fact, as I often tell people the first time that I actually played African drums was right here at UCLA in 1962 or 1963 as part of an African drumming ensemble.

LK: I'm curious as to what prompted you to select Chaka, a nineteenth-century Zulu king and warrior, as the protagonist of your opera?

AE: As a matter of fact, the answer to that is quite simple. A friend of mine Abíọ́lá Irele, who is now a professor of African literature at Ohio State University, suggested in the late 1960s that I take a look at [Léopold Sédar] Senghor's poem *Chaka*. He thought it would lend itself to treatment as an opera. I looked at it, and I agreed! I set to work, and the first performance took place in 1970. In those days we had an Ifẹ̀ Festival of the Arts [held at the University of Ifẹ̀, now Ọbáfẹ́mi Awólọ́wọ̀ University, Ilé-Ifẹ̀]. The festival was very ambitious, and we brought in international scholars and performers. We sometimes had a symposium going on at the same time. *Chaka* was presented at the Festival of the Arts in December 1970. A group from the Daniel Sorano Theater in Dakar, Senegal, was attending, and when they went back home, they invited us to do a performance in 1972 in Dakar.

LK: Have you always been attracted to opera as a musical form?

AE: Throughout my career I have been drawn to music theater. Even within modern African society, we cannot jump completely away from African traditions. We need to integrate dance, music, and theater. In African traditional culture you cannot easily separate music from the other performing arts; you don't have absolute music. The concept of, say, a string quartet is very distant from the way we think; it is not likely to succeed with an African audience. I thought it was better to start with music theater. It could be modern, it could be traditional, whatever, but I wanted to start with something that had a dramatic visual element. It was no wonder I was drawn to Irele's suggestion.

LK: Has Chaka always been a well-known historical figure throughout Africa? Would you, for example, have studied about Chaka at school?

AE: I had no contact at all with the historical figure of Chaka, nor did I have contact with Senghor's poem. I left school in Nigeria in 1951 and traveled to the UK for studies in 1952, and that was long before African literature was introduced into the curriculum. Even when I came back to Nigeria in 1957, it was still too early. I remember somebody in the Department of English at the University of Ìbàdàn, trying to introduce African literature and finding it impossible because the faculty of the department were not ready for it. It was only later, much later, that African literature was introduced into the curriculum. My generation had no contact with it in a school setting. Interestingly, last year I got a copy of a new translation of the Chaka story originally written in Zulu by Thomas Mofolo, and I read it very closely. I found that I had to change my opinion of Chaka because he was clearly guilty of human rights abuses. I couldn't see the Senghor poem in the same way I had earlier.

LK: You mentioned translation, and I am interested in the many layers of translation involved in this project. First Senghor was writing in French—a Senegalese author writing about a Zulu chieftain—and you were working with an English translation of Senghor. Then you have created a Yorùbá opera.

AE: The theme is Yorùbá, the musical conception is Yorùbá. Thus far the opera has been produced with minimal dancing; but I feel that dance is an essential part of it. I think we will do a live performance probably next year. We will then have dances that will also be based on Yorùbá dance. You're right, there are many levels of translation. As a matter of fact, when Irele who had introduced me to Senghor's poem received the CD, he said it was a pity that I didn't draw on the rich tradition of Zulu music. But I don't know Zulu music; I know Yorùbá music; it is natural to me. I have studied the music. If I were to use Zulu music, it would not be with the same conviction. I believe that the theme of *Chaka* is a universal one; so it doesn't really matter if I use Zulu or Yorùbá. In fact a more broadly based concept would be better so all Africans can see how it relates to them.

LK: There is also an aspect of translation involved in your taking material from traditional Yorùbá talking drums.

AE: I did my doctoral research on Yorùbá drumming, which is very heavily poetry based. The drums are talking all the time. The speech aspect is so crucial to the drums that I had to study Yorùbá poetry, the construction of Yorùbá poetry, and then I had to make recordings of drum music, then transcribe both music and text. With regard to the text, I played the recordings back to the drummers so that they could tell me line-by-line what text was being played by the talking drum. In the course of this I collected a number of poems. When we did the first version of *Chaka* in 1970 I looked for a Yorùbá praise chanter who could praise Chaka. I located a traditional chanter from Osogbo and told him that I wanted a poem in praise of a king who was a hero and warrior as well. Although the first performance was recorded, something happened to that part of the recording. As a result, I had to create a new praise poem for Chaka when the opera was performed in Birmingham in the UK in 1995. I did this by adapting the praise poems of two deceased Yorùbá kings, His Highness Ọba Sir Adésọjí Adérẹmí, Ọ̀ọ̀ni of Ifẹ̀, and His Highness Ọba Adétóyèṣe Láoyè, Tìmì of Ẹdẹ. These poems were part of the materials that I collected in the course of my doctoral research.

LK: Let me ask you about the difficulties you have had in getting *Chaka* staged. I would be interested in finding out just what you have had to go through to get it produced.

AE: Well considering that the first performance was in 1970, it has taken almost thirty years to get a CD produced. There were two performances in the 1970s, and with each one, changes were made. We did two performances in the UK in 1986. One was done with a Black theater company in Brixton. The company invited me to do a workshop based on *Chaka*. In order to better relate to the company and their target audience, I decided to do a more popular version, using jazz motifs, motifs from pop music, to make it more engaging for the audience.

LK: *Chaka* has been through more permutations than I realized. What was the reaction in Brixton?

AE: The reaction was good; the performance was a success. Following the two performances in 1986, I wanted to establish a more definitive version. For the 1970 performance very few musical notes were ever written down. The chance to do this came in 1995 for the performance by the City of Birmingham Touring Opera, which was part of the Africa 95 festival held in the UK.

LK : The final question I would like to ask you is how you conceive the definitive version of *Chaka*. How would you ideally like to see it staged?

AE : When I worked on the CD I thought this would be the definitive version, but once the CD was done I decided that this was not yet it. A definitive version would include Yorùbá and other types of West African dance. Following the live performance of the opera in September 1995, I decided to revise the work in preparation for the CD recording. I worked on the revision off and on for two years, and it was only between 22 and 31 December 1997 that I was able to complete it. Anyway in the course of this work I found that elements of Chinese music had crept in. I also began to envision an Indonesian element—in terms of dance and costume—as appearing in the second half. *Chaka* in a way seems to want to escape a definitive version, to be a work that continuously evolves and changes.

4. Ritual, Lore, and Music in the Pre-Islamic Vai Funerary Sequence

LESTER P. MONTS

249.

III A Specimen of the Vei Writing.

4.1 A specimen of the Vai script from Koelle (1854, 246).

It is difficult to determine when Islam was first introduced to the Vai. By the beginning of the nineteenth century, Muslims were observed in the coastal region of present-day Liberia (Cates 1819, 63), and by the late 1840s, the Vai had assimilated many of Islam's social ideas and religious practices (Koelle 1854, 13). Islam did not, however, completely overtake traditional ritual and ceremonial life; many practices continue, even to the present day. During the late nineteenth and early twentieth centuries, a marked religious dualism existed among the Vai, characterized by two separate yet potent religious forces, traditional and Islamic. In practice, Islam developed along the periphery of Vai life and was far from being the main religious orientation, though many people at the time claimed to be Muslims. The sodalities Póró and Sàndè, which operated under the guidance of the ancestors and lineage leaders, persevered as the most powerful spiritual elements in Vai life.[1] Throughout this era, the influence of Islam was narrowly circumscribed. The rituals and ceremonies surrounding the celebration of death, for example, fell clearly within the purview of the traditional religious system.

Reconstructing these past traditions can help to reveal the socioreligious bases from which Vai musical and religious syncretism with Islam developed. The literature on this part of Africa provides little evidence of the early music and ritual structures used by the Vai and neighboring ethnic groups. Several studies contribute to our knowledge of past social, political, and linguistic developments in the region,[2] but only a few mention early music practices. This results in an imbalance in the data, creating difficulties for comparative analyses between pre-Islamic and contemporary music practices.[3] The purpose of this paper is to present a view of the traditional lore and socio-musical practices associated with death in pre-Islamic Vai society. Using data derived from written and oral sources, the discussion focuses on Vai philosophies and myths about death and dying, the perceived role of ancestors, rituals in the funerary sequence, associated musical practices, and the roles of musicians and other ritual specialists in the funerary activities.

Today, traditional beliefs and practices surrounding death have absorbed new proscriptions. Contemporary Vai deathways are an amalgam of both Islamic and traditional influences. Many Vais are unaware of the traditional roots of their funerary practices, and when presented with some early accounts of them, they attribute such ritual activities to the neighboring Gola people, where these practices still exist. While the Vai once shared many cultural traits with the neighboring Mende, Gola, and Dei peoples, a number of factors made their culture and traditions of origin unique.

The Vai people have lived in the coastal region of present-day northern Liberia and southern Sierra Leone for over four hundred years. As inhabitants of the Guinea Coast, they represent the southwesternmost dispersal of northern Mande-speaking peoples who migrated at various times from the upper Niger region (Welmers 1960, 21). Ethnohistorians postulate that the Vai began arriving on the coast sometime between 1500 and 1550 (Holsoe 1967, 67–68). Despite a period of over four hundred years of geographic isolation from the so-called Nuclear Mande homeland of the Western Sudan, the Vai kept their history alive (Murdock 1959, 259). Their traditions of origin and migration tell of a close cultural affinity with the Kono people of northern Sierra Leone. One version of the tradition

> refers to a king[4] called Jomani Kamara, whose hunters wandered from the Maninka country to the sea and brought back salt. Each Maninka monarch under Jomani then sent a son or nephew with followers to visit the sea, led by Jomani's son, Kamara II. When they reached what is now Kono country, some wanted to stop for a while. Kamara said *ŋkɔnɔ tallu fai* ("Wait for me, I go bravely"). Thus those who "waited" or stayed behind acquired the name Kono, whilst those who "went bravely" became the Vai. [Jones 1981, 165]

Similar traditions have existed in Vai and Kono lore for several generations,[5] although some ethnohistorians have cast doubts on their reliability.[6] The Manding-Kono-Vai relationship is confirmed, however, in modern linguistic studies (Welmers 1960, 21). The Vai are best known for their nineteenth-century development of an indigenous system of writing, the first by a sub-Saharan ethnic group (fig. 4.1).

For the first Vai immigrants, the forested coastal region presented an ecological and cultural environment that was different from their purported upper Niger homeland. To orient themselves to their new surroundings,[7] they adopted from their neighbors the Gola, Dei, and later the Mende, several primary cultural traits, foremost among which were coastal versions of the Póró and Sàndè secret societies (d'Azevedo 1962, 516; Holsoe 1967, 23–28). Religious practices among these groups were also similar. Hence, the secret societies, trade activities, and religion became the main channels through which cultural traits were diffused in the forest region.

Vai participation in coastal commerce may have begun as early as the sixteenth century. Some traditions speak of hunters penetrating the forest and coming upon the sea by chance, while others claim that the main objective was to set up a coast-to-interior salt and kola nut trade enterprise. By the early nineteenth century, Manding immigrants had congregated at Bopolo—located in the region to the east of Cape Mount—to participate in foreign and domestic trade. The Vai collaborated with these more recent Manding immigrants, mainly the Muslim Koniaka traders originally from the Musadu region of modern Guinea,[8] to become the entrepreneurs and middlemen in coastal commerce.

Another distinction for the Vai was their early acceptance of Islam;[9] they were the first people occupying the coastal region to do so. Within the context of Islam-induced change, the Vai have made dramatic shifts away from many cultural practices that were once shared with the Mende and Gola. With these changes, the Vai, along with the Koniaka, developed a notoriety that has distinguished them among the coastal inhabitants, as has been noted by both modern and early observers.

> From the earliest colonial period, the Mandingo [Koniaka] and the Vai were considered among the most "civilized" native peoples of the western region. Their wealth, their skill and dominance in trade, and their apparent close connection with Islam and legendary civilizations of the far African interior, were contributing elements to the view of these people as superior. [d'Azevedo 1970/71, 14]

A similar report came from a Bishop Payne, a churchman in the Cape Mount region during the 1870s.

> They [the Vai] are the most intelligent of any on the West Coast. It was this people who, some fifteen years ago, invented a syllabic alphabet. They hold constant intercourse with the Mandingoes [Koniakas] and other Muhammedan tribes in the interior. And these intelligent neighbors are fast converting them to their false faith. [Blyden 1974, 101]

Payne's appraisal, like many others of the period, makes a connection between the Vai and the Mandingo through commerce, language, culture, or religion. Thus, it was the Vai/Mandingo "intelligence" and "advanced culture" that separated them from other peoples in the region and brought praise and notoriety from the Americo-Liberian settlers and other foreign travelers. These accounts are derived in part from aspects of culture the Vai wished to exhibit to foreign observers. Evidence suggests that the Vai adopted Western traits and behaviors in order to appeal to foreigners and to African American settlers for political and economic gain.[10] Beneath this "advanced" facade, however, was a sociocultural system only marginally influenced by the values praised by early writers. A deeper look into the lifeways of Vai people during the late nineteenth and early twentieth centuries reveals that traditional practices, not Western or Islamic ones, dominated funerary rites and the music employed therein.

Pre-Islamic Myths and Philosophies about Death and Afterlife

To understand the Vai response to death and its accompanying rituals, it is necessary to examine the beliefs surrounding these events. To the Vai, illness and death were charged with deep significance—these conditions were not simply common occurrences. To understand death, the Vai needed to learn to predict the will of supernatural entities. The rituals surrounding death mobilized Vai society in a profound way, consuming a disproportionate amount of family and community resources. Struggling to cope with the mystery, fear, and ambivalence of the unknown, they approached death from within a conceptual framework that included myth, legend, and song. The nature of those concepts stemmed from the basic moral principles that controlled the Vais' destiny, which included trust, respect, and psychological bonding between themselves and ancestral spirits. These virtues accentuated the authoritative role of spiritual forces and helped the society remember the past.

The Vai belief in the role of ancestors (*fòé-nú*) as mediators and protectors expressed the notion that death is not the final state of existence.[11] Though preventive measures were used to prolong life, the Vai were comforted by their conviction that there was life after death and eternal solace in the spirit world. Death was seen as a mysterious aspect of reality, and Vai mythology sought to explain the natural order of things and the origin of death. As the giver of all things, *kàŋ-bà* (God; literally, "big sky") was the source of life and death. The commonly told story of the two messengers explains how *kàŋ-bà* sent death to the world.

> Before the coming of death on earth, God chose Dog and Frog and sent them on an errand to a distant town with two separate messages. Dog was to announce "lasting life," and Frog was to proclaim the coming of "death." The first to arrive in the town would give God's message that would serve mankind forever. Dog and Frog departed together to deliver the message. Dog, as you know, runs faster than Frog. Dog took the lead with a difference of about five miles. Before reaching the town with about one-fourth mile remaining, Dog came upon a dump site where the people had left lots of bones and food. Sensing that he had a substantial lead on the Frog and that he was hungry and weary from his long journey, Dog decided to stop and eat. While Dog continued to eat at the dump, Frog passed him. Frog reached the town first and announced the message that death was coming. The sun began to set, and Dog finally realized the passage of time. Running as fast as he could to the town, he hoped that Frog had not yet arrived. When he told the people of his mission, he was shunned and hated, for Frog had already told them that death was coming. This is how death came to the world and why people do not like dogs today.[12]

The Vai believed that life manifests itself as a convergence of the body and soul. Death, however, separated the two, returning the body to the earth and sending the soul to the metaphysical world.[13] During a person's lifetime, the body works in synergy with the soul, and that which affects one affects the other. Hence, death may result from ailments affecting the body, the soul, or both. The Vai believed that everyone has a soul and that it always survives death. Only those who disciplined their lives according to *kàŋ-bà*' s law enjoyed eternal peace; the souls of witches suffered eternal torment. If a postmortem examination exposed the hidden identity of a witch, all after-death ceremonies were abandoned, and the body was unceremoniously discarded.

Death by natural causes was not a part of Vai conceptualization. Although death could seem to result from an accident, childbirth, personal conflict, or capital punishment, some other force brought forth by an ancestral spirit or retribution by a malevolent force was the underlying cause. Death may also result from breaking taboos: violating the laws protecting the ritual elements of the women's initiation society, Sàndè; not heeding the warnings of ancestral spirits; or breaking the oaths of secret medicine societies.

Recognizing the inevitability of death, and realizing its profound destructiveness in depriving family and society of its members, the Vai worldview provided psychological comfort through the positive notion that life continues at a spiritual level. The rituals and ceremonies surrounding death served an important purpose in society by making this bewildering phenomenon understandable. Otherwise, the pain, grief, and agony associated with death would remain unexplained, resulting in traumatic disillusionment and a breakdown of communal order. Death was comprehended as a transition from mortal to immortal. And though a person's physical presence was lost, the deceased continued to live in spirit form, which had potential benefit for the living. At sacrifices and during periods of discontent, the dead were called by name. They were propitiated—approached reverently, symbolically fed their special foods, and praised with their favorite songs. Though death ended direct communion with the family and community, it began a higher level of interaction with the spirits. The death of high-ranking secret society leaders or chiefs often had far-reaching social and political implications. During the period immediately following a chief's death, a temporary breakdown in political authority was common.[14]

The fear and anxiety surrounding death influenced pre-Islamic funerary rites.[15] The living were comforted by the presumption that a recently deceased person was potentially their new agent in the spirit world. But they also believed that the dead could return as malevolent ghosts or witches. Therefore, the Vai staged rituals to ensure that the deceased became benevolent spirits. Sawyerr and Harris's explanation of the ambiguity surrounding this belief among the neighboring Mende people is equally applicable to the Vai.

> The belief in witchcraft is based on the [read Vai] conception of human personality. The witch-element or force is talked of as something that lives in a person's abdomen, but functions independently of the host while assuming its form. So if a witch dies, the witch-element, if not removed from the host before its burial, survives as a witch-spirit, which may then wander at large to cause all manner of harm, without being deterred by any protective charm his victim may use. Thus whilst the witch-element is talked of in one context as a foreign power in symbiosis with its *host*, it is also referred to in another context in

> language which suggests that it is a spiritual replica of the *host*. It is therefore difficult, almost impossible, to grasp the full nature of the belief in witchcraft among the [read Vai]. [1968, 73]

The Vai attributed many mental and physical disorders to witches. They believed witches caused epileptic seizures by riding their victims; and they caused wet dreams by having sexual intercourse with men during sleep. A witch could cause death through a variety of ailments including tuberculosis, hernia, and malaria. Protective measures in the form of amulets (*gree-grees*), divination, and countersorcery, were taken to combat the malevolent forces of the dead.[16] The first essential step to prevent malevolence, however, was a proper burial to send a person's soul on its journey to the spirit world. Hence, after-death ceremonies were held in order to restore equilibrium to the social relations upon which the society stood.

Of the four major rites of passage—birth, initiation, marriage, and death—the ceremonies connected with death were the largest, only occasionally equaled by the "coming out" events of the secret societies or the seating of a paramount chief (*ɓóló mànjà*). Today, the Vai have largely forgotten details on the role of music at these occasions. Only rarely does one encounter an elder or oral historian (*kó kɔ́lɔ́ fɔ́-mɔ́ɔ́*) who can provide specific information on the music and funerary rites of the distant past. Documentary sources complement the oral data.

Early Accounts of Pre-Islamic Music and Funerary Rites

Documentary sources dating back to the 1600s contain a wealth of ethnographic data on the societies of the Guinea Coast region, including information on major social institutions and practices (i.e., the secret societies, political leadership, and ritual practices). These sources provide brief accounts of the role of music in ritual and ceremonial occasions. However, the descriptions of pre-Islamic funerary rites contribute only cursory evidence and often fail to provide the data needed to determine the continuity of a particular practice. Early accounts on the Vai for the years 1700 to 1850 are especially sketchy. Conversely, the documentary evidence on the coastal region since the late nineteenth century is rich and germane to the present study. By combining information from all of these sources with recently collected oral data, we can begin to reconstruct past ritual and ceremonial practices related to death. The combined use of this evidence requires a sensitivity to methodology, since the reliability of both written and oral data is problematic. Hence, special efforts to corroborate the extant data are required, especially when dealing with the ubiquitous cultural phenomenon of music. Through a careful examination of the ethnomusicological present, another useful analytic tool emerges. Data derived from field observations of music and celebrations of death in present-day Vai society can be compared effectively with accounts contained in early historical sources and recent oral accounts to determine the continuity and change in key musical and social features.[17] Nketia explains:

> Music history in Africa must begin with a sensitive study of the *historic* present, since the present, to a large extent, encapsulates the past, which continues to have contemporary relevance. The *historic* (which might also be referred to as the ethnographic present) becomes *historical* when stylistic layers or phases become evident from analysis, or when the historical factors that account for aspects of the musical tradition are identified. We can never move from the historic to the historical until we have evidence that enables us to take one or more steps backward into the past. [Nketia 1982, 97]

Dapper's work of 1668 is the earliest documentary record of Vai life and culture.[18] It is invaluable to researchers attempting to trace the histories, language affiliations, and migratory patterns of peoples now occupying the region. This work is an especially important source of information on music and funerary activities among the Vai. The description of the coastal region includes references to music performances at funerals, communal dances, and secret society rituals and ceremonies. From Ogilby's translation of the Dapper account, we learn of the use of song and dance at an early Vai funeral.

> When a man dies according to the course of nature, or by mischance, presently all his friends and acquaintances meet, and encompassing the corpse, sing elegies and epicediums, wherein they set forth at large the praises and actions of the deceased in several languages, everyone choosing that wherein he thinks himself best skilled and able with most excellence to express his fancy.... For they account it a great honor to have such a funeral-elegy composed and spoken in a high strain and lofty style.... Some of his nearest kindred come and play [dance] with bows and arrows before him. [Ogilby 1670, 395]

From Dapper, we move to an account of 1843 by Captain Theophile Conneau (sometimes spelled "Canot"), the infamous slave trader who operated in the Vai region. Conneau maintained a slave factory at Cape Mount and befriended King Fana Toro, the powerful Vai chief at Toso who was a major figure in coastal trade and the main supplier of slaves in the Cape Mount region. The following excerpt from Conneau's account of the funeral for Prince Graye, King Fana Toro's son and Conneau's close friend, sheds further light on Vai funerary practices:

> On the appointed day, the body was brought from the hut.... His wives had their heads shaven and were wearing but just enough cloth round their loins to replace the fig leaf; the more affectionate ones showing less regard to hide their charms, estimating them valueless since the death of their husband. The oldest wife appeared covered with bruises, gashes, and burns, self-inflicted to denote her sorrow, and chanting in chorus with the others the praises of the defunct. [1976, 328]

Another account from this era was written in 1891 by Thomas Besolow, a Vai raised in the Cape Mount region and educated in the United States. Here he describes the music-making activities at a common funeral and at the funeral of his father:

> His body was treated with the utmost respect.... Musicians with drums and clappers played airs as doleful and woeful as you can imagine. I remember those who had no drums came with tin pans and sharply polished sticks. An appropriate song was sung. [1891, 92]

> After father was laid out in state, and his body anointed with oils and ointments, and arrayed in his finest habiliments, songs were chanted over him mournfully. [1891, 129]

The final report is from George Ellis, an African American assigned to the United States diplomatic mission in Monrovia. Ellis apparently admired the Vai and made frequent trips to the interior to observe their culture. He reports that "whenever a death occurs among the important men and women of the tribe it is always followed by a 'Big Play.' The maids dress and march through the streets. The singers sing, and the drums announce the merriment of the day" (Ellis 1914, 69–70).

These brief accounts reveal that music performance at funerary activities attracted the attention of several observers over a three-hundred-year period. From this scant information, along with oral data from present-day informants, we can begin to reconstruct the role of music and ritual procedures in past celebrations of death.

Vai funerary rites seem to have passed through several stages, merging various features over time.[19] The first stage, common in the distant past, consisted of three major ceremonies: the burial, which took place within forty-eight hours of death;[20] a sacrificial offering and feast on the third day (female) and another on the fourth day (male); and a large-scale celebration, typically held one year later.[21] The final celebration often depended on the wealth and social and political importance of the person. Such occasions were customarily reserved for chiefs, leaders of the secret societies, and warriors.[22] These ceremonies marked key junctures in the deceased's journey into the world of the ancestors.

The Pre-Islamic Funerary Sequence

From the time a person died and throughout the funerary sequence, a series of rituals were enacted. By the early nineteenth century, three ceremonies comprised the sequence: *sìtòá*, the burial; *dìbɔ̀ɔ̀*, "pulling the cry"; and *jítìɛ́*, "crossing the water." These occasions were interspersed with several small-scale, yet important, events.

When the death of a person seemed imminent, a succession of events commenced. Kinsmen first sought information about any evil the ailing person had done. The patient was given cold water and asked to confess past sins in order to avoid torture by vengeful spirits. If the life-threatening ailment was determined by a diviner or through some other means to be linked to *súà* or *súkɛ̀* (witchcraft), the confession would rid the person of its effects. The Vai believed that an admission of past iniquities was the only cure and that once wrongdoings were divulged, many patients would survive. Accounts of deathbed confession are widespread even today. The following was provided as an example of the practice:

> In the early 1970s, there was a monthlong outburst of mosquitoes in the town of Jɔni [Gawula chiefdom]. There were so many mosquitoes that people found it difficult to sleep, and half the town came down with fever [malaria]. Several people died. Then in 1975, a big elder/clan chief who was sick for about two years, confessed that he went to a friend in Buluma to engage in witchcraft business. He asked the friend to give him some mosquitoes that would make his hometown adversary become ill. He took the mosquitoes back to Jɔni in a small parcel with the intention of putting them in the house of his enemy, but a small boy opened the parcel and the mosquitoes spread all over town. The man also confessed that he had used other witchcraft to cause another man's blindness, because the man had been loving to his wife.[23]

When life left the body, surgery would be performed to determine if the deceased was a witch (*súà-mɔ̀ɔ̀*) even before an announcement of death was made. The operation was necessary for several reasons. First, the powers of a witch could be repelled with medicines and other protective items. However, if a witch went about life unnoticed and was allowed to become a spirit-witch after death, its power was immune to any medicine, amulet, or counteragent. Second, witches were not accorded a normal burial or after-death sacrifices. Third, the Vai believed that witches live in families and that a witch's malevolent attributes were inherited. Therefore, a positive determination alerted the society to monitor the behavior of the person's relatives.

The surgery centered on the spleen (or milt), the organ where the "witch-potential" was believed to reside. Removal and proper disposal of the spleen rendered the spirit harmless. To determine the person's after-death status, the extracted spleen was placed in a pot of water with special herbs. If it sank, the person was declared a witch. The spleen was then cut into small pieces and buried with the body in an isolated part of the forest. The surgeons reported the results to the town. The customary after-death ceremonies were not held, and family members were forbidden to mourn openly. A floating spleen, however, indicated the person was free of witchcraft. The body was returned for the ritual washing, and the towncrier (*jèlè ɗɔ́ŋ ɓɔ́-mɔ́ɔ́*) announced the death. Townspeople rushed to the home of the deceased to offer condolences and to assist with the burial. Póró or Sàndè (depending on the gender of the deceased) morticians washed the body with special herbs, wrapped it with layers of cloth (*kásáŋgí*), and laid it in a bed or "hung" it in a hammock inside a "kitchen."[24] As a sign of sorrow, close female kin shaved their heads and smeared their bodies with mud from kaolinitic clay. A wake or "death sitting" (*ɗìfì-jɔ́ndɔ́*) followed. Wailing and singing at the death sitting continued while other men, normally the town elders or secret society officials, made preparations for the burial and post-burial activities.

According to my Vai teachers, the style of wailing has changed little over time. A typical wail is characterized by a long-held, piercing pitch followed by rapid utterance of short exclamations, followed by another elongated pitch. The extreme emotion expressed between sobs makes it difficult to decipher the words uttered. However, the themes of wailing may be placed into four broad categories: messages, skepticism, prophetic anecdotes, and queries.

ì a ŋdá mbá ó
Oh, my mother.

ŋ na mbé mà í à ó
What did I do to you?

féŋ gbí sɔ́ à à ì bɛ̀ á wá kɛ̀
Whatever stands, falls.

í á (ŋ) tò jɔ́ ì è
With whom did you leave me?

jɔ́ wá ì è (ŋ) kù mà fé à wɛ̀
Who is going to take care of me now?

í á fálé ŋ ná mbá sùà
When you go, greet my mother for me.

ó kàmbá í á mbé wá ŋdà kɛ̀
Oh, God. What did you do to me so?

kàmbá ŋ ná mbé mà
What did I do, God?

kòngò bélè mbé jí mà
A good gourd does not last on the water.

bàí í à mú tò
Bai you have left us.

Ritual wailing was interspersed with or followed by the singing of praise songs. These songs were musical eulogies, acknowledging the deceased's contribution to family and community and/or his exploits as a hunter, warrior, or musician. The genealogies of warriors, chiefs, and lineage heads were extolled in song. The performance of praise songs focused on the unique talents of a female music specialist bearing the title *kéngâì*, whose musical responsibilities were also connected with the Sàndè Society. The *kéngâì* accompanied herself with a shaken gourd rattle called *sásáá*, an instrument common to women's musical roles throughout the region (Monts 1982, 104–5).[25]

The following are examples of pre-Islamic praise songs collected in 1977. Though these songs are no longer used in present-day funerary activities, a few elderly Vai women remembered them.[26]

jà jà sì kòò, jàsì kòò
"Song words" (untranslatable vocables)

mɔ̀ bélé í á mɔ̀ mà nɔ́é-nɔ́e
'One does not mistreat your

kὲ nú tá mɔ̀ɔ̀ á kóà ò
relative for the next man.

ò ó kàí mὲ
Oh, This man.

mɔ̀ bélé kàà à kàí mὲ ɗàó
This man is an adult. One does not mind this man. This man is a big man.

ò ó ŋyɔ̀jáà féŋ mù
Oh! Hatred. Hatred is a worthless thing.

mɔ bélé kàà à nyɔ̀jáá
Pay no attention to hatred.

ŋyɔ̀jàa̋ kàsàà feŋ mù ò
Hatred is a worthless thing.

The final example is a praise song that was formerly performed by large groups. Women stated that it used to be sung during the "death sitting" or during the performance of *ŋgèlè*, a communal recreational dance commonly associated with pre-Islamic death feasts.

à mò nàndòɗé
"Songwords" (untranslatable vocables)

kàmbá ì à ŋὲìmá nàndò óó yà à ó
May God grace Nando's soul.

Some mourning songs do not have worded texts. Singers intimate that the occasions for which these songs are performed are so sad that they, as singers, are often unable to find the appropriate words. Instead, the vocables used as text consist of the typical performative utterances used by women during periods of mourning.

Each stage of the funerary sequence (*sìtóà, dìbɔ́ɔ́,* and *jíťìé)* involved a sacrifice, and one of the essential foodstuffs was a specially prepared rice known as *ɗὲὲ*, "rice dust" or "rice powder." To make *ɗὲὲ*, sweetened and dampened rice was placed in a mortar and pulverized with pestles (fig. 4.2). This work was supervised by an elderly female member of the deceased's family. As an act of respect and a gesture of goodwill, women from all parts of the town brought their own pestles to assist. They considered it an honor to participate. The pounding of foodstuffs, accompanied by song, was a daily occurrence, but the preparation of *ɗὲὲ* called for special songs. These could be songs of praise, similar to those cited above or, when the deceased was a woman, Sàndè songs. The following are typical of rice-pounding song texts.

mɔ̀èìá ŋ tó
Molly left me.

áíjénὲ mɔ́é à ŋ tó ŋdɔ́kpéì
Heavenly Molly left me alone.

jènì ɓáɓá ŋ ná mànjá ɗé ó
Jeni Baba, my chief.

ó ŋ nà mánjá ɗè wé
Oh, where is my chief.

ɓàɓà ò ŋ ná mànjá ɗé ó
Baba, where is my chief.

à ó í á á kɔ́ó á bàŋɗɔ́ ó ì ì ó
Ah, Kɔi has divorced me.

kɔ̀i; báŋdɔ́ ó ò tátà bómbóì
Kɔi has divorced me, Tata.

ò kὲ nà wὲ ô
Bomboi hasn't come yet.

ò ó ó kùlà gbègbè
Oh! Kula Gbegbe.

kùlà tálá wáì è ò ò
Kula has left.

4.2 Women preparing the sacrificial rice mixture *ɗὲὲ*. In the past, praise songs in Vai were sung as part of these events. In modern Islamic society, the songs are in Arabic or in mixtures of Arabic, Koniaka, and Vai. Photograph by Lester P. Monts, Bulumi, 1988.

Rice-pounding songs sung for a high-ranking man typically consisted of short melodic and textual phrases. Women reportedly composed many songs extemporaneously, commenting on their relationship with the deceased, his military prowess, how he treated his spouses, and the number of children he fathered.

When the preparation of *ɗɛ̀ɛ̀* was complete, women placed their pestles in the mortars and pointed them in the direction of the cemetery. As they stood around the mortars, the eldest woman remarked with words similar to these: "Let this body be the last death here, and let it carry all trouble away with it. Let death go on that side [to the cemetery]. Let it not come here again." Afterwards, with their pestles stamping the ground, the women paraded (singing songs and dancing) around the town to obtain small gratuities for their work. The procession returned to the home of the deceased where the head elder presented them with a "white kola," a symbol of the family's gratitude.

Sìtóà, the Burial

The next stage in the procedure was interment of the body. Individuals and groups were called upon to perform prescribed duties in this elaborate ritual drama. Grave diggers (*kàbú sèŋ*) looked for a suitable spot in the town cemetery. Graves were commonly dug near a young sapling so that the burial site could be easily determined in future years. The body was placed on a bier for its journey to the grave. An entourage of family and townspeople accompanied the body in a slow procession, singing funeral dirges along the way.[27] At the graveside men conducted sacrifices while women and children stood by. To rid the soul of sin and debt toward others, speeches were made over the body, recounting past relationships with those still living. Money and other personal articles were placed in the grave to assist the deceased on his journey to the spirit world.[28]

The body was committed to the grave, accompanied by subtle wailing. A rock-lined perimeter and a large headstone marked the grave. The "offering giver" (*síèkɛ̀-mɔ̀ɔ̀)* invoked the ancestors to watch over the deceased. Male kin threw small amounts of dirt onto the grave as a sign of their cooperation in the burial activity. After the burial, the family met to make post-burial arrangements. Once decisions were made, family elders and the *síèkɛ̀-mɔ̀ɔ̀* returned to the grave site to offer another sacrifice of rice dust and water. They spoke to the deceased and summoned the ancestors to attend the *dìbɔ̀ɔ̀* with words similar to these:[29] "We have come to let you know we haven't forgotten you. We are going to give you food before you undertake your long journey, so you must wait for us in the morning" (Alldridge 1910, 200).

Through the night, groups bearing food, money, and other gifts visited the bereaved family. Participation in the events held immediately after death were mainly confined to townspeople. At subsequent celebrations—on the third or fourth days—gifts to the bereaved family were made by out-of-town relatives, friends, and political leaders.

Dìbɔ̀ɔ̀, "Pulling the Cry"

Early the following day, townspeople gathered at the graveside for the *dìbɔ̀ɔ̀*, ritual wailing, or "pulling the cry."[30] This was one of several occasions in the funerary sequence in which wailing, especially by widows, was expected.[31] As a symbol of mourning during *dìbɔ̀ɔ̀* or of general bereavement, participants wore plaited grass around their heads and necks or across their chests. Male elders offered eulogies and appealed to the ancestors on behalf of the deceased. They addressed the ancestors by name, asking them to provide protection and guidance. As the body was committed to the grave, local hunters fired their guns into the forest to frighten away malevolent spirits. Cannons provided by European traders were fired for chiefs and the wealthy (fig. 4.3). This signaled the beginning of the graveside wailing. Intense wailing followed each gun (or cannon) volley. After all eulogies were delivered, the occasion turned from sadness to jubilation. Drummers and singers accompanied energetic dancing around the grave, celebrating the beginning of the deceased's journey to the spirit world (fig. 4.4). Upon their return to town, the family of the deceased were presented with rice and a portion of the animals killed for the sacrifice.

Jítìɛ́, "Crossing the River," the Three- or Four-Day Feast

The Vai believed that to pass over into the world of the spirits, the soul had to traverse a turbulent river. The journey to the river bank required four days (three days for women).[32] On the third or fourth day after burial (depending on the gender of the deceased), a ceremony was held to assist the soul on its journey. Here again, fear was an underlying factor in the proceedings. These ceremonies had to be performed properly; otherwise, the ancestors would seek retribution from those responsible. Generally, segments of the entire community played roles in these festivities. People were expected to give of their time and labor unselfishly. For events surrounding the *jítìɛ́* celebration, the town elders assigned individuals to coordinate food and lodging for visitors. Specialty services were provided by drummers, butchers, cooks, and messengers. Overall, it was the supportive response and social consciousness surrounding death that made it a communal affair.

Before crossing the river, a person's soul was believed to be tormented by the revenge-seeking souls of those whom he had mistreated during his lifetime. The deceased's relatives could make good any evil done to the living by paying debts or returning stolen property, but they could not make good the evils of which they had no knowledge. Only those of the spirit world were aware of such injustices and sought vengeance. Once the spirits were convinced that restitution for misdeeds had been attained, the soul was allowed to cross the river into the spirit world *àlìjɛ́nɛ̀* (Welmers 1974, 1) or *igenie* (Besolow 1891, 129). Those souls unable to provide restitution were denied entry and became ghosts, wandering aimlessly in space.

As part of the third- or fourth-day observance, family members and townspeople returned to the grave for a sacrifice and to plead to the ancestors on behalf of the deceased. A white chicken, rice dust, and kola nuts were offered as a sacrifice (fig. 4.5). The blood of the chicken was spilled on the headstone of the grave. Placed around the headstone were four of the chicken's feathers (three for women). The chicken was cooked and designated portions were returned to the grave site for the final offering. The *síèkɛ̀-mɔ̀ɔ̀* or a male kinsman made the offering by placing the food on a leaf beside the grave. After the sacrifice, the feet, head, heart, liver, and gizzard of the chicken, along with palm oil and rice, were eaten by

4.3 A nineteenth-century cannon brought by European traders to the coastal region and used by the Vai to protect their commodities and trade routes. Photograph by Lester P. Monts, Gɔn, 1988.

4.4 A covered grave site at an in-town family compound. In some Vai towns, the use of in-town graves is reserved for high-ranking religious and political leaders. Photograph by Lester P. Monts, Makbouma, 1988.

4.5 The sacrificial items common in the pre-Islamic celebrations of death are still used today—a white chicken, kola nuts, silver coins, and pulverized rice called *ɗɛ̀ɛ̀*. Photograph by Lester P. Monts, Bulumi, 1988.

family members. Activities taking place during the *jítìɛ́* celebration ranged from dancing in a particular quarter in the town to a large celebration involving the community at large. Depending on the sociopolitical status of the deceased, celebrations might last for several weeks.

Communal dances at the *jítìɛ́* celebration, such as *ŋgɛ̀lɛ̀* helped overcome grief and brought a period of calm to the community. Communal dances were also held in praise of the deceased. Secret society dances, such as *zìàwá* emphasized the fraternal or sororal bond among members of a corporate unit, in essence defying the notion that it could be broken by death. At the feast of a war chief (*kɛ̀lɛ́ mànjà*), his fellow warriors performed war dances (*kɛ̀lɛ́ tɔ̀mbɔ̀-nú*) that expressed and symbolized the chief's leadership and courage in battle. The fundamental function of these forms of dance was catharsis—the need to release tension associated with fear and sorrow and the "need to confront death with an assertion of life" (Huntington and Metcalf 1979, 39). In this regard, dances at pre-Islamic funerary rites were as much celebrations of life's vitality as they were of death's morbidity.

The wealth and power of the deceased were often measured by the presence of professional musicians and dancers at these occasions. Powerful kings, warriors, and wealthy men often retained the services of non-Vai music specialists, both male and female. Vai men have long admired Gola women for their beauty, obedience, and singing. Vai kings prided themselves by marrying Gola women who were celebrated singers.[33] Male musicians of Bandi, Loma, and Kissi ethnicity were under the patronage of Vai chiefs to serve as praise singers and as drummers for war rituals, performing on hourglass-shaped drums called *fàŋgà* and singing in their languages.[34] Except for perhaps Gola, the other languages—Bandi, Loma, and Kissi—were unintelligible to most Vai. Hence, it seems the language of the praise songs' texts was less important than the prestige non-Vai musicians brought their patrons.[35] Upon the death of a patron, imported musicians played an important role in the funerary rites. Because of the prestige court musicians afforded, the question as to which of a man's male survivors would inherit the musicians' services was often controversial.[36]

The performance of songs and acts of praise at funerary rites, however, was not the exclusive domain of specialists. Groups of secret society members performed songs they used to perform with the deceased. Visitors from neighboring towns paid homage to the deceased as soloists and in groups. Locally based quasi-secret associations called *gbɔ̀njí*,[37] whose membership included masquerades, drummers, carvers, and singers, performed acts of praise (figs. 4.6, 4.7).

The House Visit

Dancing and singing were expressions of communal solidarity in the wake of disorder. Amid the boisterousness at the wider *jítìɛ́* celebration were a number of smaller events. People bearing gifts and words of praise formed in processions to visit the house of the deceased (fig. 4.8). These small assemblages of townfolk included a *kàí-bá* ("big man"—a man of some social or political prominence), the deceased's close kin, and musicians. The somnambulistic movement of their procession was accompanied by subtle dirgelike songs.

ó ó wéí ó ó múá ná ó ó
Oh! We have come.

ó ó wéí ó ó múá ná ó ó
Oh! We have come.

Members of the deceased's family sat in waiting to receive the "house visitors," who entered singing or with singers. The "big man" greeted the mourning family with gestures of sorrow. He signaled a stop to the music and commenced to offer condolences on behalf of his family or followers.[38] He then made a speech before which words similar to these would be spoken, *kàmbá yɛ́ wɔ́ bàlò* (May God bless you all). The accompanying group responded with *kàmbá ì á tòàmà* (God let it remain so). Then singers interceded with:

kàmbá wálà bááká-bá kɛ́ à í ɗɔ̀
God will put strength in you in abundance.

bááká-bà kɛ́ à í ɗɔ̀
Abundant strength in you.

Such songs were sung at the beginning of a speech to praise the speaker and to give him inspiration and courage to express properly the group's sentiments.[39] Singers often intervened with a song when the speaker became exceedingly profound in his delivery. The Vai say that when a "big man" is praised in this manner, he is not only encouraged to speak well but is also inclined to be more generous with his gifts.

Western observers were often perplexed by the behavior displayed at these celebrations. Why did people dance and rejoice when indeed the main focus of the occasion was death? Certain components of Vai funerary celebrations appeared joyous and dynamic, lacking the conventional Western signs of grief and bereavement. A closer look, however, reveals that these dances exhibited a wide range of emotions tied directly and indirectly to death. Oral and written sources describe a variety of dances performed at Vai funerals. War dances, secret society dances, masked dancing, and communal dances were all common in the pre-Islamic funerary sequence. Since these practices are no longer customary, details are sketchy. The documentary sources note wide variations in the funerary activities for chiefs, barren women, infants, and lepers.[40] My Vai teachers spoke of ceremonies for chiefs lasting as long as a month, and of similar large-scale celebrations one year after death. Much of what occurred during the funerary rites of secret society leaders was held in strict secrecy, however. The death of a *dà-zóó*, the sacred head of the Póró Society, was not announced; he was said to have gone "to pick leaves" (Johnson 1954, 36, 87).

The documentary sources describe funerary rites for chiefs, princes, and kings as "special," requiring the full deployment of a community's resources. Why did the death of a chief or "king" warrant so much celebratory attention? As in other societies, "the death of the king undermines the integrative symbol of political stability and makes all too palpable the danger of an outbreak of political violence" (Huntington and Metcalf 1979, 154). A Vai chief was seen as a protector, and upon his death his constituents often felt defenseless against rival war chiefs who sat waiting to exploit the occasion. To avoid attack, people often sought refuge under another chief, requiring a move from one locale to another. In exchange for protection, the chief was given a share of the crops and certain portions of game killed (Johnson 1954, 68–70). In a country plagued by constant fear of war and slave raiding, these measures provided people their best chance for peace and stability.

4.6 The male masquerade (*náfàlí*), with a dancer sponsored by the quasi-secret society called *gbɔ̀njí*. Photograph by Jeanne Monts, Senjenama, 1978.

4.7 *Zóó-ɓà*, the Sàndè Society masquerade, was an integral part of pre-Islamic funerary rites, especially at the celebrations for high-ranking Sàndè women. Photograph by Jeanne Monts, Bulumi, 1977.

4.8 A procession of mourners en route to the home of the deceased. The performers for this event are customarily women who play the gourd rattle, *sásáa*. Photograph by Lester P. Monts, Bulumi, 1988.

After death, the body of a high-ranking chief continued to be a symbol of authority and power. For this reason alone, the death of a chief was kept secret. Great chiefs controlled war medicines called *kèlé kóndó*, which remained manifest in his body after death. Hence, it was believed that various body parts were endowed with special powers, powers that could be filched and used by his adversaries to increase their prowess. During periods of warfare, burial parties took extreme measures to conceal the location of the chief's grave. One practice called for burial in a creek bed. A flowing stream was diverted temporarily while the grave was dug, the body was interred, and the flow of water was rechanneled to its original course. Moreover, reverence and respect were accorded high-ranking individuals by burying them in graves within their family compounds. The grave of an important person though not a permanent effigy, was a sociopolitical symbol. Though the chief was dead, his grave continued to symbolize power and well-being. The final burial in the town among the living symbolized a continuity of permanence and high authority. Whether in the family compound or the village cemetery, graves continued to provide a site for prayer, sacrifice, and consultation.

Conclusion

Apparently the music, mythology, and ritual structure of present-day Islamic funerary rites cannot be fully understood without a basic understanding of pre-Islamic practices. Once the Vai adopted a new eschatology based on Islamic teachings, many of their funerary procedures changed. While some practices have endured, such as preparation of sacrificial rice, ritual washing of widows, and "house visits," each procedure has been carefully scrutinized and adapted to conform to Muslim interpretations (fig. 4.9).

Pre-Islamic funerary ritual was full of variation. The attempt here has been to establish a paradigm based on the careful analysis of data gathered from a variety of oral and written sources. The parameters of a given paradigm and its theoretical success depend on the amount of flexibility one lends to it. For example, the funeral rites held for "a king" were much grander than those held for a commoner, as was the level of music making, yet the basic ritual procedures and roles of music therein were the same. Moreover, the level of emotional stress induced by death may seem more intense in descriptions of fifteen wives wailing for a dead chief than those of two wives mourning a man of lower sociopolitical status. In both instances, elements of the established model (ritual content and mourning) hold, despite the deceased's sociopolitical status or the magnitude and resources devoted to a given celebration.

Overall, one should conclude that celebrations of death during the latter nineteenth and early twentieth centuries remained outside the direct influence of Islam. Though the traditional rituals and ceremonies surrounding death were later abolished or absorbed by Islam, the examination of the traditional beliefs and practices provides rich data for comparative analyses. Such an analysis poses several questions about the fundamental changes in the belief system and how they affected one's concept of self, family, society, and worldview. The beliefs and practices that did not conform gave way to Islamic dogma, causing the transformation or decline of traditional institutions such as Póró and Sàndè.

After many years of reorientation and modification, Islamic funerary practices have become the norm. Today, the Vai direct their funerary song and prayers to Allah, not to intermediary ancestor spirits, and the language of songs and prayers is not in the vernacular in Vai, but in Arabic. The dead begin a journey to heaven, not "[a]cross the river" into the world of ancestor spirits. A person's soul is still subjected to scrutiny—not by ancestor spirits, but by the angels and the prophets, Adama (Adam), Musa (Moses), and Isa (Jesus). Hence, a juxtaposition of pre-Islamic and present-day funerary procedures provides an important link to the Vai past and adds coherence to their complex cultural history.

4.9 The creek-side washing of widows, another pre-Islamic ritual that continues as an important part of the modern funerary sequence. Photograph by Boakai Zoludua, Sinje, 1990.

5. Ingolole: Then We Shall See

JEAN NGOYA KIDULA

5.1 Tiriki initiates. Photograph by Onni Rauha (Sangree 1966, pl. 7)

Ingolole is the name of the helmetlike mask worn by male initiates among the Tiriki people of western Kenya. Initiaion begins with the circumcision of boys, who are subsequently isolated from the community during the period of healing. Physically and symbolically, circumcision is the most important rite of passage for males; and it clearly signifies the transformation from boy to man. After this rite, it is said that the initiated can "truly see." In the past the period of seclusion following circumcision lasted at least six months, during which the boys lived in isolated dwellings (*irumbi*) and were educated regarding male activities and responsibilities to the family and community at large. They collectively herded cattle for their village and learned skills related to animal husbandry, hunting, and war. Initiates wore the *ingolole* whenever they left their secluded dwellings and might be seen by others. To indicate the end of the period of seclusion, the "men," also referred to as "newlyweds," removed the masks at a formal public appearance known as graduation.

Today, the period of seclusion has been reduced to five to seven weeks. With changes in economic and political systems, some of the education in male responsibilities has been replaced by modern national schooling. The age of initiates has also become increasingly younger. Whereas formerly, only adolescent and older boys were initiated, today circumcision can even take place at birth. The psychological preparation for the physical changes and for the responsibilities assumed by "adult" male Tiriki is perhaps weakened for some, but the definitive symbolism of the rite remains evident for all.

Following a description of the many initiation customs (*itumi*), I will describe my observations of this event as an outsider both ethnically (as a member of the Logooli ethnic group) and in terms of gender. As a child spectator, I witnessed ways in which this event defined linguistic and cultural boundaries. As I grew older, the masking process signaled the beginning of the separation that was to occur between me and my neighbors, classmates, and playmates. It was also the period at which I became aware of my uniqueness as a female and began to glory in it.

Of *Itumi* and *Vukhulu*

The Tiriki initiation rites are normally held every four to six years in July after the harvest season. At this time of year there is little gardening to do, and there is enough food and free time to feed the candidates (*vakhulu*). The rites not only make men of boys, they also demarcate the various ethnicities in Goibei, my birthplace, and the surrounding villages. Goibei is a part of the administrative unit known as Banja Location, which comprises eight different villages. Historically, the area has been inhabited by two different language groups, the Nandi and the Luyia. The Luyia groups are further subdivided into two main dialects, the Logooli and the Tiriki. While Nandi and Tiriki people originally lived in this area, Logooli immigrants were invited to the region in the 1930s. Most Logooli migrated from the neighboring overpopulated Maragoli locations. They settled wherever they could buy land. While most of them settled among the Tiriki, a few bought land among the Nandi. As a result three different groups live together. Goibei village is on the border between Banja and Tiriki Locations; Logooli and Tiriki people live in both of these administrative units. The members of yet another language group called Luo pass through the village twice a week on market days. As the Luo do not practice circumcision, Luo boys and men avoid doing business in our area during the time that initiation rites are held. If they were discovered, they would be circumcised.

While the Nandi, Logooli, and Tiriki all practice circumcision, they do not collaborate with each other except to procure a government license to hold the rites. During the initiation period, each boy must associate with his ethnic group and paternal relatives, irrespective of where he lives. This is illuminating for some boys who until the time of circumcision may have been unsure of their paternity; they are sent to their fathers' homesteads for sanction and care during the rites. Other boys who had previously associated with a particular ethnic group come to realize that a distinction is now being drawn: no matter how well they might speak another language, this ceremony aligns them patrilineally.

Among all the ethnic groups that live together in and around Goibei, the tendency is for everyone to speak his or her own language or dialect even when conversing with speakers of other languages. Tiriki and Logooli are mutually intelligible so that I can converse in Logooli to my Tiriki neighbors. But I always know when a Tiriki tries to speak Logooli from the speaker's accentuation of words. We even pronounce songs that we have in common in our individual dialects when we perform them, unless we are in a school or religious context where we have learned the songs in a specific dialect. Logooli and Tiriki languages are not at all related to Nandi and Luo; neither is Luo related to Nandi. Communication on market days, however, does not require great knowledge of another language, so despite the differences, one can always get by. It is during rites of passage like circumcision, however, that cultural and linguistic boundaries come to be defined and reinforced. Age-group demarcations are also clearly perceived.

The Logooli and Tiriki conduct male initiation ceremonies very differently. There is no way a Logooli would ever consider undergoing the Tiriki ritual, or vice versa; this will be discussed more fully below. The Tiriki ceremony has borrowed several elements (ritual and musical) from the Nandi group. The Logooli abhor these elements, and the Tiriki in turn despise the Logooli for not practicing them. Due to historical links, a Tiriki could possibly be circumcised together with the Nandi. In fact, the names given to the age groups of the Tiriki are the same as those of the Nandi because the Tiriki directly borrowed the masking and other practices for this ceremony from the Nandi (Sangree 1966, 67–82). Many Tiriki songs, musical forms, and instrumentation are also easily associated with the Nandi ceremony. Linguistically, however, Tiriki is in the same family group as Logooli, and in other ceremonies this relationship is overt.

While the Logooli have only one circumcision option, the Tiriki initiates now have two: one for those who wear the *ingolole* and the other for those who have chosen not to wear it. Those wearing the *ingolole* call themselves *vadirichi*, signifying that they are the true and fundamental Tiriki stock, while those who have forsaken the mask refer to themselves as *vasoomi* (those who have "read," i.e., have been to mission schools or adopted Christian beliefs). This choice was instituted in 1940 as a viable alternative for those Tiriki who, although Christianized, wanted to affirm their ethnic identity through this rite. Missionaries could not tolerate the wearing of masks or the entire behavior that accompanied the ceremony. For a time, the Christianized Tiriki were disconcerted. Some of them sent their sons to the traditional ceremony because it was definitive of manhood and then later "repented" and were "disciplined" by the church. Others had their sons circumcised at the mission hospital, only to have the boys suffer social ostracism because they had not been "schooled" in the ways of their people and so were not officially men. The institution of a separate ceremony conducted by Tiriki Christians provided a safe alternative; the boys could now participate in the ceremony surrounded by their people in a manner that the church deemed legitimate (Sangree 1966, 88). The *vasoomi* did not wear *ingolole*; they sang mainly Christian and social songs; and they did not go through some of the ritual phases that were deemed "pagan" or were associated with the drinking of traditional beer. These distinctions persist.

Although the Logooli and the Tiriki engage in circumcision rituals at the same time of year, it is the *vadirichi* who provide the most entertainment and spectacle. They make us aware of themselves as different and as proud of their heritage. They also reinforce our desire to be different from them. The Nandi are not a factor. In fact, during this period, we ignore them altogether and concentrate on the differences that demarcate the Luyia groups.

The Tiriki male goes through several stages in this rite. First he is a boy; then a potential candidate; an initiate; and ultimately an "ancient one," a graduate, and a "newlywed." Every stage is marked by music (*vukhulu*), primarily song. These "markers" serve to indicate to outsiders the onset, the progress, and the end of events. Different song subjects and texts further specify the events and their proceedings to the listeners and participants. The musicians are mostly male. Only at certain stages do women and children sing or even dance;

and only those with relatives undergoing or having undergone this ritual can actively participate. The rest of the time, only the initiates, those attending to them (*vadiri*), and those who have already undergone the ritual in the Tiriki manner are allowed to sing or even imitate the dance movements. For music performances in public arenas, the initiates wear the *ingolole*. These masks are individually woven by the initiates during the first weeks of healing.

The main musical activity is song, reinforced and reiterated by dance spectacle in public arenas. There is always a specialist singer recognized by the community as the musician-leader. The singing is sometimes unaccompanied. Otherwise hand clapping and flat wooden beaters called *virangasia* form the primary instrumentation when the candidates begin their journey. V*adiri* who have a proper understanding of the musical genres provide the accompaniment and lead the choral responses in public appearances. Other accompaniment is derived from the palm leaf attached to the top of the *ingolole* and flat sticks, spoons, or jewelry hung around the waist of the mask when the initiates dance. The movement of the feet is light and inaudible, resulting in graceful rhythmic movements initiated through a springing motion. In private and in special public appearances, the pulse is maintained on *virangasia* or by beating on *mulinga*, a manger. *Mulinga* symbolizes the male activity of animal husbandry, and there must be one in every hut where the initiates reside. Originally, food was served on *mulinga*, but in recent times alternatives have been used. The *ingolole* cannot be separated from its ritual and musical accompaniment. Together, they are used to create a spectacle of physical and symbolic transformation, a drama performed by a select group and observed by the community.

First Encounter

I first became aware of the Tiriki initiation ceremony at about age four. At that time initiation was still restricted to adolescent boys. As previously noted, although my family is not Tiriki, my ethnic group, the Logooli, also practices male circumcision. The Tiriki continue to have many taboos regarding observation of the unmasked initiates by non-Tiriki and females. When the initiates emerged from the grove after circumcision, we had to run into our house, close and lock all the doors and windows, and hide. We were warned of their impending arrival by their singing and also by scouts who were sent ahead to make sure there were no hidden and unwanted observers. Since the initiates were not wearing masks at this time, we hid to protect ourselves from possible repercussions but also to show respect for their ritual space. Officially, the period of separation and seclusion had commenced.

I heard at this time a song composed about my grandfather Zakayo. The Tiriki were unhappy with him because he had not hidden himself when a group of initiates and older males had emerged from the grove. Subsequently, when another group received the same treatment, they felt they should make an example of Zakayo. There was no physical confrontation. Zakayo simply continued cutting timber while the initiates urged him to go and hide, threatening to "spoil" him if he didn't comply. My grandfather's actions, however, only served to encourage other Logooli men to continue the outdoor activities that they had abandoned. By "spoiling," the Tiriki had meant circumcision on the spot. As my grandfather was already circumcised, however, they really had no other choice than to criticize him in song. The song consisted of one line that was heavily laden with meaning. The basic text stated

Zakayo Woi ndadunya
mm mm mm mm
Zakayo woi khuBanja
mm mm mm mm

Oh Zakayo, I am distressed/unhappy/sad
mm mm mm mm
Oh Zakayo, in Banja (marketplace)
mm mm mm mm

Everybody "understood" the song as expressing disapproval and possibly even containing a curse. A second stanza mentioned female genitalia. Since my grandfather had many female grandchildren, the implicit warning was that if we were found, we would be raped—another means of "spoiling." The song was sung nearly every time the initiates passed by my grandfather's house and in the evening it could be heard emanating from the initiates' secluded dwellings. Gradually it spread to other villages. To this day, the song remains part of Tiriki *vukhulu* repertoire. New stanzas mentioning other defiant people have been added over the years. Before I understood its significance, I used to sing the song with my friends when we played "circumcision." After my parents explained the implication of the song to us, however, we were forbidden to sing it.

Redefined and Transformed

My next chance to observe *itumi* occurred when I was in fifth grade, and it changed and redefined my relationships with my schoolmates. It was on a Friday, the week before school should have been officially out, that all the boys in my fifth-grade class disappeared. Although we had been expecting this, the effect was nonetheless paralyzing. It was not, after all, only the boys in my class who had vanished but virtually every boy aged nine to fifteen. It was time for the male initiation ceremonies. Physically and symbolically the boys were being initiated into manhood. Their distinctive role as males would be outlined during the time of their seclusion. Our relationships would never be the same again.

The following Monday, the teachers tried in vain to maintain a semblance of order at school. Since my village of Goibei and its environs were fully involved in the initiation ceremony, there was an air of restlessness everywhere. The next day, school was officially closed, three days earlier than specified by the government. Now the rest of us could observe the drama. The day after school closed, the first group of boys was circumcised. This explained why they had needed to leave school early. They required time to prepare for the event. While the period of preparation had been shortened due to the school calendar and other factors, the school administrators, who were themselves from the area, were aware of this need. We had done our finals earlier than usual so the boys could be graded with the rest of the school.

Prior to the boys' departure, male family members and clan elders had convened, performed the necessary pre-rituals, decided on dates and applied to the government for a license to perform the rites. The Logooli and the two Tiriki groups (*vasoomi* and *vadirichi*) did not circumcise in one day. This would have made it difficult for those who had relatives in all groups to participate. The elders decided who would circumcise when and which group of villages would perform the rite together. Most people in a given village in the same language group were related by clan or marriage. It was possible, however, to have relatives in another village, and this fact was taken into consideration.

The year my classmates were circumcised, the three groups went to the forest on different days. The Logooli boys were taken from their homes at around four o'clock on the morning of their ceremony for briefing. Then, since many Christian elements had been incorporated, prayers were said on their behalf. At around nine o'clock, they were escorted to the forest with singing by other members of the community, including women and children.

After all the boys had been circumcised, they emerged from the forest surrounded by their male relatives and were escorted to various dwellings (*irumbi*) for the six weeks it would take for them to heal adequately. We (the women and children) did not see them again until graduation. But we heard them singing every evening. The same thing happened with the Tiriki *vasoomi* group. Relatives now made sure that the boys were cared for, fed, and educated.

The day before the *vadirichi* were circumcised, however, the boys sang and danced naked for several hours on a stage called *khungusa* located on a hill. Anyone from the village was allowed to attend this dance. The boys wore crowns on their heads that had been made from a creeper. Attached to the crowns were vines that trailed down their backs. This covering, called *isenende*, was worn only until they arrived in the circumcision grove the next day. The dancing was the last time anyone would voluntarily see the boys naked and verified the sex of all those going to the forest. The boys had been taught the basic *vukhulu* dance, which involved a rhythmic movement of the head to the accompaniment of song and special patterns beaten on *virangasia*. The characteristic leg movements and body twists that form a part of this dance were also taught and reinforced to the entertainment of all present. The songs contained vocable responses to the rhythm of the *virangasia*. The vocables, the most prominent being "*hoiyohe*," were those used in the Nandi language as a signal. Other types of vocable "calls" would be improvised by the lead singer with a choral response. The feel was in compound quadruple time. The underlying meter being a four-feel while the subdivisions were in triple time. The feet would feel the four time while the head and neck would pulsate rhythmically as a short-long in triple time. For example, in one piece based around a two-phrase *hoiyohe* response, the *virangasia* provided the "call" by continuing to play the strong pulses in between the response. Or a leader could decide to incorporate a text made up of vocables, grunts, praise or reprimand of a candidate-dancer, or general commentary related to the ceremony during the silences.

X x x X x x X x x X x x X x x X x x X x x X x x :II
Hoi yohe *hoi yo he*

The lyrics of other songs performed at this event ridiculed boys who were deemed afraid to attend the ceremonies. A male relative, usually the father or a paternal uncle, had to sanction participation, and some boys had been frustrated because their parents as Christians wanted them to participate in the *vasoomi* ritual. This decision was generally ridiculed in song. As a result of these taunts, some potential *vasoomi* boys joined the *vadirichi*.

At dusk, the boys were taken to the home of the oldest elder of the *itumi* council. According to Musambi (1994, 22), a Tiriki initiate and scholar, and Sangree (1966, 90), a researcher on Tiriki age groups and politics, it was at the house of the elder, surrounded by older men, that boys had to meditate preparatory to confessing any forbidden acts they may have committed. They were questioned in various ways, and if they were found guilty, they would pay an agreed upon fine. If something unusual happened to a boy in the course of the circumcision or healing period, one possible explanation was that he had not been honest about his misdeeds. In order to make sure that the boys understood what they were required to do, older men would give examples or implore them in song. Sometimes after a boy confessed, a song would report what had happened. For the most part, this would consist of a solo singer using a known melodic formula with a vocable choral response. Then the rest of the group would take up the text to report the action. Typical lyrics went as follows:

Solo: *Mundu muchwanachi wonyene mu vandu*
Response: *Ha Ha Ha*
Response and solo: *Mundu muchwanachi wonyene mu vandu Ha Ha Ha*

Refrain
Solo: *Hiyo hoo, laleyio haa hee*
Response: *Ha Ha Ha*

The solo may be translated as: A single (lone) sly person is among the people. As a female, I had no idea who was being discussed nor what else had transpired; the boys were sworn to secrecy, and the matter was put to rest at that meeting. It was also at this time that the council decided on the order in which the circumcisions would be performed. It was an honor to be first but a challenge to be last. These two boys eventually became the leaders of their group. Just before dawn, the boys returned to their homes to eat and be "blessed" before being led to the circumcision grove. All the while, they wore the *isenende*.

At around nine o'clock, the boys danced through the villages en route to the grove. Most of the songs sung at this time were the same as those performed on the hill the previous night. Anyone could follow along, sing, and dance behind the initiates as they went to the grove. Given our various identities and demarcations, however, only those who belonged to the Tiriki language group and the *vadirichi* joined in. The rest of the village became spectators and evaluators of the performance. The singing and the sticks alerted us to the arrival of the procession in the grove; they continued until the circumcision ceremony ended. The singing changed once all the boys had been circumcised. We no longer heard women and children's voices. It was time for us to get into the house and shut and lock all the doors as we awaited the procession's return to the *irumbi*. It was also a signal for the females to start preparing food for their respective camps. Not all the initiates stayed in one *irumbi*. They were divided up according to family or clan to facilitate control and education. By the time the boys emerged from the forest to go to *irumbi*, we had already heard through the grapevine who had been brave and who had flinched and in so doing disgraced their parents. This was confirmed through the action of the various counselors and guardians of the boys. The *isenende*, the "vine dress," worn before circumcision was given to each boy's mother. If the counselor threw grass on the mother as he handed over the *isenende*, her son had been brave. If on the other hand a bit of the vine dress was cut off before it was handed over, it was a sign of shame. The vine dresses were then carried to the homes of the initiates and hung from the roof above the cooking hearth in anticipation of the day when they would be ritually burned. Meanwhile the boys were provided with short leather skirts. A few weeks later, after the initiates had sufficiently healed, the skirts would be exchanged for cloaks. Traditionally, this cloak was a Tiriki elder's garment. It was worn draped from the shoulder like a toga during the day, and it was slept on at night. Nandi elders wore this type of clothing as well. This clothing exchange was marked by the drinking of beer, singing, and dancing.

For a few days after the period of seclusion began, all we heard was occasional chanting in the mornings. The songs were mostly nonverbal involving a solo with a response by the initiates, the basic text being "*wo*." After a week, we began to hear songs in the evening from the *irumbi*. The sounds were accompanied by *virangasia* with additional rhythm from the manger (as previously noted, an essential requirement in the *irumbi*). It was as if boys from the different *irumbi* competed against each other every evening. The nights were clear so the sound carried far. It was not just *vadirichi* boys but all the other initiates from other events. Of course the lyrics of *vadirichi* were the most provocative and entertaining for us at that age, and there was nothing our parents could do about this. There were texts that praised people and happenings surrounding the rituals as well as lyrics that expressed disapproval and ridicule. A complete song was sometimes composed of only one or two lines, but the depth and implications were often far-reaching. The songs were not only about famous people or historical accounts of the preceding age groups but also about girls and relationships. There was a license to utter words and phrases that one did not dare say in public at any other time. The boys could discuss intimate body parts and physical desires. In essence they were learning in a public space how to privately approach a woman.

The boys also learned, recited, and composed songs outlining the Tiriki "age sets" and various "age groups." An "age set" lasts between eight and twelve years and consists of several "age groups," which are composed of boys who undergo initiation in the same year. From these songs it was therefore possible to determine when the Tiriki adopted this ritual from the Nandi groups. Because the ceremony is held only once every four to six years, boys who might chronologically fit into an age group but have not met all the requirements for inclusion might be held back until the next occurrence. If there was a particularly large number of boys, it was possible to have another "age group" within the same "age set" that was initiated eight to twelve years later.

One of the songs I learned was composed by a man who was initiated with the age set preceding that of my classmates. My classmates were of the second age group of the Kolongolo age set. The age set preceding Kolongolo was the Sawe age set, which was divided into two age groups. In this song the singer suggests that he could even have been initiated in the earlier Chuma age set. The song was used as a starting point to teach about the other age groups. Some of the lyrics of this song were:

Lead/ solo	Response/ chorus
Likhula lia Sawe	*Sawe woi ye yeha*
The age group of Sawe	Sawe (Luyia vocables suggesting sadness)
Khaviri lia Saw	*Sawe Woi ye yeha*
The second age group of Sawe	Sawe (vocables)
Likhula lia Chuma	*Chuma woi ye ye aha iyoho, shio*
The age group of Chuma	Chuma (vocables suggest curse)
Shio vashiele vandindiranga	*iyoho, shio*
The women are ridiculing me	(vocable curse)
Shio ngonanga ilwanyi vava	*iyoho shio*
I truly sleep outside	(vocable curse)
Chuma wa khaviri	*Chuma woi ye yeha*
Second age group of Chuma	Chuma (vocables)
Likhula lia Maina	*Maina woi ye yeh*
The age group of Maina	Maina (vocables) etc.

It is possible to sing such songs going back to the first remembered age set Kaplelachi. But historically the earliest set that can be ascertained is Kimnyikei, which has been given a date of 1900 (Khadambi 1994, 16; Sangree 1966, 65); the Kaplelachi, supposedly, was earlier than this. As the boys sang, we learned along with them the names of the age sets and important historical figures or events that bounded a particular group or time. New songs were also composed to reinforce the learning of this historical data.

According to Sangree (1966, 92) and Musambi (1994, 27), from about the second week of seculsion, the boys begin to weave their individual *ingolole*, learn new songs, and practice dances. We knew they were engaging in this process from the lyrics of their songs. One of the songs was in praise of the fact that only *vadirichi* know how to weave. The lyrics further stated that some of the boys who did not want to go through their type of ritual avoided it because of their inability to make beautiful *ingolole*. They used Christianity merely as a cover for their lack of skill. *Vadirichi* ridiculed such people, sometimes by name. Occasionally all we could hear were the rhythms of the *virangasia* and *mulinga* accompanied by a few lower voices grunting or singing vocables. We knew then that the boys were being taught how to dance gracefully.

Before Kenyan independence in 1963, the seclusion period was long, and boys learned skills necessary for hunting as well as being counseled in various ways intended to make them profitable members of society. After the period was shortened, new skills were needed for survival in modern times, and the instructions focused on the role and behavior of the male in a home. One common prohibition irrespective of how one underwent the initiation ritual involved going into a parent's bedroom. We learned this not only from the initiates' later behavior but from the songs. Years later when my Logooli nephew was initiated at the tender age of four, it was quite amusing and painful to watch him struggle with that dilemma in his grandmother's house. He needed some goodies and no longer had the freedom to play hide-and-seek in my mother's room. We had to find ways to help him out.

When the initiates were sufficiently healed, word went around the village that they would soon make their first public appearance since circumcision. Their parents were required to brew a ceremonial beer for this occasion. On the morning of this event the initiates appeared wearing *ingolole*, cloaks, and sisal leggings. They also wore a calabash and two sticks tied to the waist of the mask. The calabash was a plate and the sticks, cutlery. To lend spectacle and beauty to the costume and subsequent dance, a palm leaf (*lishindu*) was attached to the top of the mask. The leaf emphasized and exaggerated head and neck movements and lent a dimension of gracefulness. It also provided percussive accompaniment to the music in addition to that of the *virangasia*. This was the *lishindu* dance. The sisal leggings accentuated the springing motion. There were four groups of people involved, the initiates, male dancers, women and children related to the initiates, and the rest of us. The first three groups would participate in certain formations. *Mulinga* would be brought from some of the initiate's huts. The instrumentalists who included *mulinga* and *virangasia* players and a lead singer would be to the right, and the other participants would form a semicircle around them. The women and children who wanted to dance and were allowed to do so would be on the inside next to the accompanists; *vadirichi* men were on the outside of the semicircle formation with the initiates in between the two groups. The rest of us could either stand to the right of the musicians or outside the male dancers.

We had no idea of the identity of the initiates unless they had some idiosyncratic movement that we could recognize. Mothers had to have their sons pointed out to them while the initiates danced the characteristic graceful *vukhulu* movements. A lead singer, instrumentalists, men, women, and children did the singing; the *vakhulu* themselves did not sing. The spectacle lay in the movement of the *vakhulu* accompanied by the groove created by the music. The speed of the music was never hurried. The dancing went on for about three hours, then we disbanded. It was on this day that *isenende*, which had been hung over the hearth, was burned. From then on, the initiates danced every afternoon in the village square or market. They sometimes smeared themselves with ash. This made it even more difficult for us to identify them. The dance had a competitive edge, and the initiates would try to outdo each other in showing how skillful they had become. While there was group dancing, an initiate could break formation, go into the center next to the musicians, and dance with vigor. A second initiate could challenge the first and the two of them would put on a show. We demonstrated our pleasure at the entertainment and applauded the skill of the dancers by ululating and joining in the choral response. It was appropriate for outsiders to sing some of the responses in this context.

During the dancing, the initiates used the utensils that they had appended to the waists of their masks to their advantage. An initiate could break formation and approach a specific member of the crowd while extending the two sticks. Essentially, we were supposed to put some money or a trinket on the sticks. Sometimes it was a way for a boy to let you know his identity and that he was interested in you. But we always ran away. The boys were allowed to follow us, but only to a point; pursuing us further would have been deemed unseemly. Meanwhile, in the evenings the singing competitions continued, growing stronger and louder every day. Though we soon learned all the songs, there were taboos relating to child bearing that prohibited girls and non-initiates from singing *vukhulu* pieces or, even worse, performing the type of dance associated with the initiation.

About four to five weeks after circumcision, parents of the initiates were advised to prepare a ceremonial beer in preparation for the confirmation ceremony (*shigong'o*). In the past this ceremony had taken place at least two weeks before the initiates came out of seclusion, but by this time it was done a week or less before they graduated. For this event, the initiates were taken back to the circumcision grove in the late afternoon or early evening to be confirmed into manhood. On the morning before the confirmation, there would be a vigorous dance session in the village or in the market. Soon after dusk, a ceremony was held where the initiates were sworn to secrecy regarding the rites. What we heard on the outside was the accompanying singing: choral responses by the men that sounded like deep grunting and the sound of hitting. We knew from the hitting sound that one of the boys had been confirmed. Officially, this was also the first time the boys drank local beer. Whether they drank it or not, they emerged from the forest the following morning staggering as if they were truly drunk. We knew that it was only a matter of days before they officially graduated and unmasked themselves. The lyrics of the songs changed to a more coherent text; the musical structure was more like that of other Luyia people but still accompanied only by sticks.

To signal to the village the impending graduation (*shialukhu*), songs incorporated lyrics suggesting completed requirements. The lyrics of one of the standard songs follow:

Lead	Response
Sevule O sevule	*O o o*
It is finished/ complete, oh it is finished	
A a a	*A A A A sevule*
Itumi ni ya va shisenya	*A A A A sevule*
This rite of the Shisenya (family group)	

Family names were mentioned in the songs to let us know who had participated. This particular song was still in slow tempo, and it was accompanied by instruments but had Tiriki text and vocables. On the morning of *shialukhu*, new types of songs were heard. These were called *kwikweya*. The graduates issued forth from the grove unmasked and singing as they went to the house where they had first slept after their dancing with the *isenende*. The lyrics of one standard song are "*Undevanga, alandola* " (Whoever has been asking for me can now see me). The tempo was much faster than at any other time of public appearance. The young adults changed into regular clothes and were then led to their respective homes followed by a procession of villagers who sang with them and danced along. This time the dance was unaccompanied by any instrument. There was feasting; the new "age-mates" visited various homesteads and relatives for several weeks to come, but now they had officially become adult males in Tiriki culture.

The day the boys "graduated," regular school had already resumed for the rest of us. The "men" were supposed to come to school, but for a while, the administrators "allowed" them to stay away in order to rehabilitate themselves to their new status in their cultural space. It was at least a week later before the first batch came back to school. I knew my relationship with them would be different when they returned. We could not play or even talk on the same terms. They looked at us with different eyes. For many of my older schoolmates, this was the beginning of a new awareness of themselves as female. A period of male/female relationships began to be visibly manifested even in the classroom. By defining ethnic and gender space, the ceremony outlined possible spouses for us, since we now knew which boys were unsuitable partners by virtue of their close filial and clan relationships. At the end of that school year in December, my parents decided I should go to boarding school. Two years later, most of my female classmates who had remained were married, some to our male classmates.

Though it was the boys who were circumcised, the ceremony signaled the maturity of girls the same age, who were also going through puberty. All of us were transformed and thereby redefined.

Interpreting the Ritual

The *vadirichi* format was despised by the Logooli not just because it entailed the wearing of masks and its subsequent symbolisms, but also because of the music used. The drinking of beer and other Luyia social and symbolic traditions were the norm for non-Christians in any of the groups. What was especially questionable was the adoption of Nandi age-group names and their musical styles. As I observed and analyzed the process and its repertoire, the vocables used when the boys were dancing on the hill, going to the forest for circumcision, coming out of the forest, and any other time they appeared in public during the seclusion period were of Nandi origin: words like *hoiyohe* or *laleyio*. Luyia texts were sung at these times by those who had already graduated from this ceremony—caretakers, song leaders, and other men. Whenever the initiates made up songs in the evenings or learned historical texts at the approach of the graduation day, almost any time the initiates were unmasked, most of the lyrics were in Tiriki language. Tiriki vocables had greater affinity with Tiriki musical structures. The suggestion here was that the initiates could not be transformed unless they had been in some other state. Before circumcision, during the time of introspection, the boys emptied themselves verbally, spiritually, symbolically. The circumcision itself signified the beginning of a process of being re-created. From this point until graduation, they were no longer "people." They were referred to as *vakhulu*, literally "the ancient ones." The process of reincarnation and reinterpretation was reinforced visually by the mask and aurally by the adoption of "foreign" sounds. The use of vocables is especially interesting; unintelligible words, the language of the ancient ones, the depth and meaning of which we were not required to know. The gradual use of Tiriki language lyrics and musical structures aurally prepared us for the ultimate visual unmasking at graduation when the "ancient ones" became "newlyweds." The Tiriki word for newlyweds is *viha*, the etymology of which suggests uprooting or bringing out of the earth. This concept also suggests a new relationship in the sense of marriage accompanied by the expectation of procreation. Interestingly the word is often used to refer to female newlyweds, or brides. Marriage is the most important rite for a woman. In this patrilineal, patrilocal society, she is reinvented by changing her physical space and attaching herself to her husband's household. The use of the same word for males at initiation provides a paradoxical reversal of gender terms. The word also foreshadows the next major rite of passage that these males have been initiated for, that of marriage. It is "newlyweds" who continue the process of making people. Thus the initiates are symbolically licensed to procreate. This is a Luyia conception. The Nandi from whom the masking process was borrowed never use Tiriki or other Luyia words or music in their ritual; nor do other Luyia groups adopt Nandi behavior.

Reencounter with a View

I witnessed a change in the presentation of the *vukhulu* repertoire when I judged contestants at a national music festival in 1989. When I was growing up, it was taboo to perform these songs anywhere except in the village. Some boys who had gone to boarding school in other parts of Luyialand, however, now shared this musical experience with the rest of the country by presenting selections of the songs on a stage in an auditorium. Of course the venue seriously compromised the presentation.

In one school performance, some of the participants came from my village. They had to have permission from the village to perform a staged version of the repertoire. The criterion used to select the participants was that they had to be circumcised. Although the school is ethnically diverse, only boys of the Luyia ethnic group participated. Boys who had actually gone through *vadirichi* ritual demonstrated the *vukhulu* dance. The sonic effect in a closed space was different. But the performance was electrifying and educational for many Kenyans who had not previously been aware of this masquerade tradition in their country. Because of the spectacular aspect of the genre, it was not strange to have a nonparticipating audience. The type of music was different from other Luyia music not just by virtue of its presentation but in the instrumentation. Some Luyia people of other dialects had never even heard of this mask and its accompanying music. That is how secret the event was. Once again *Ingolole* had defined a specific ethnic space.

Circumcision continues to be practiced in Goibei and in the surrounding areas every four to six years. To date, I have observed seven such events, the last one occuring in 1995. It still takes place after the harvest season at the end of July continuing into August. The demarcation by ethnicity, language group, and religious affiliation is still evident in the manner in which the rites are performed. *Ingolole* is still worn by *vadirichi*, while the other groups avoid and despise these masks. Because of the younger ages of the boys, some of the traditional educational elements have been compromised, since the initiates are not mature enough to appreciate or apply them. Still, by the time they reach puberty, they are aware of the transformation that will take place in their bodies and their response to it. Despite their young age, some of them begin to relate to their mothers and sisters differently after this period because of prohibitions they have been advised about during seclusion. The period of confinement remains four to six weeks to accommodate the modern national education system. Because of modern medical practices, some cases of excessive physical reaction to the process are treated in hospitals and not necessarily ascribed to ritual impurity and sexual misconduct. The government has also prohibited the Tiriki from circumcising Luo men found along the road or in any other improper venue during this period. But the Luo know better than to place themselves in such situations. Some of the ritual ceremonies involving consumption of beer have also been interfered with by the government for health, religious, and political reasons. While there is a classic *vukhulu* repertoire, new songs are also composed with each age group, relating to the acknowledgment of the time and the society.

Although many aspects have changed, *ingolole* continues to be definitive, indicative, and symbolic of a particular expression of Tiriki rites of passage and to define dialectic, ethnic, linguistic, and religious borders.

5.2 *Ingolole*, the mask worn by Tiriki males during intiation ceremonies. Plant fiber and animal hide. Height 42 cm. Private Collection. Photograph by Don Cole.

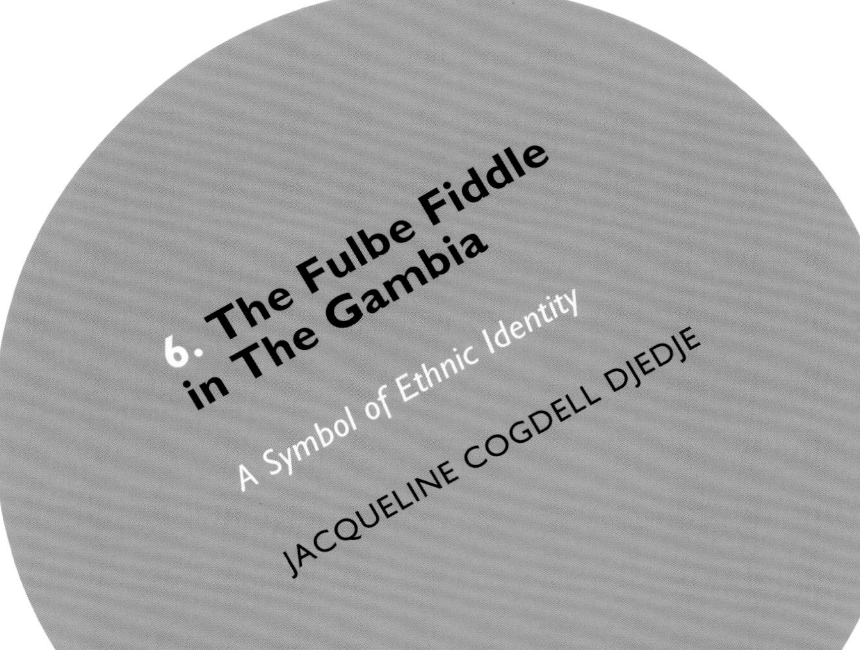

6. The Fulbe Fiddle in The Gambia

A Symbol of Ethnic Identity

JACQUELINE COGDELL DJEDJE

6.1. Tamba Kandeh playing a *nyanyeru* (Fulbe fiddle) in his compound. Photograph by Jacqueline Cogdell DjeDje, Lamin, The Gambia, August 19, 1990.

In The Gambia,[1] the fiddle is most often associated with the Fulbe people even though other groups in the country perform and have their own terminology for the instrument. In spite of the fact that the fiddle may be used by several ethnicities, I argue that the instrument has become a symbol of identity for the Fulbe because of their unique culture history and intercultural contacts with others in the area. This argument raises several questions that will be addressed in this article. Who are the Fulbe, what is their history, and how are they distinct from other groups in The Gambia? What are the central markers of Fulbe identity? In what way do features of the fiddle tradition (instrument, fiddler, and performance) serve as signifiers of Fulbe identity? How has Fulbe identity and the role of the fiddle changed as a result of urbanization and modernization? Using oral interviews, personal observations, musical analysis, as well as secondary sources on history, music, and other topics, I present a general discussion of Fulbe culture history, identity, and Gambian history. After a brief description of the fiddle in performance, I discuss Fulbe music in The Gambia generally, before focusing more specifically on the fiddle tradition.

History and Identity

Fulbe Culture History

The Fulbe people (also known as Fula, Foulah, Fulani, Ful, Foulbe, Fellani, Filani, Fellata, Peul, Pullo)[2] are found throughout the savanna belt region of Africa. From Senegal to Ethiopia, the Fulbe live in the midst of other populations and rarely constitute a majority in any area.[3] Fulfulde, the Fulbe language, belongs to the West Atlantic subfamily of the Niger-Congo linguistic family and is closely related to the Serer-Sin and Wolof languages of the Senegal area (Greenberg 1970, 25). Spoken widely throughout the grassland areas of West Africa,[4] Fulfulde can be divided into several dialects that correspond with the location of the speakers (Swift et al. 1965, ix). Charlotte Quinn (1971, 430) states, "Although the Fulbe are often referred to as a homogeneous ethnic and cultural unit, in fact there were wide diversities existing between them arising from differences in origin, period of arrival in the area, and cultural contacts. Fulbe in the Gambia region spoke at least nine dialects within the West Atlantic group of languages."[5]

While there is much controversy surrounding the history of the Fulbe,[6] oral tradition and most scholars suggest that they originated in Takrur, an eleventh-century Sudanic state located in the middle Senegal valley near present-day Mauritania. It is believed that interactions between the Serer, Wolof, and northern Saharan Berbers gave rise to the Tukulor people (Hiskett 1984, 28).[7] The pastoral and sedentary Fulbe are thought to be the product of an intermixture between the Tukulor and Berbers (Mabogunje 1976, 26).

Takrur's role in the history of West Africa sheds light on historical developments among the Fulbe. When the ancient kingdom of Ghana declined, Takrur became an important power in the Western Sudan. Not only did it take over Ghana's western territories, it also gained control of the trans-Saharan caravan trade and became a flourishing market. A number of people from Takrur even traveled to the Middle East and took up residence (Al-Naqar 1969, 370). Takrur's power and influence waned when the Mali Empire rose to power in the thirteenth century. The Mande[8] eventually dominated Takrur, but as Mali declined between the fifteenth and seventeenth centuries, Takrur broke up into three kingdoms. First, the Wolof Kingdoms in the western half of the area enclosed by the Senegal and Gambia Rivers were dominated by the central kingdom of Jolof.[9] Second, north of Jolof on the south bank of the Senegal River arose the Denianke Kingdom of Futa Toro, which was ruled by a Fulbe dynasty. Finally, further south, in the hilly country where the Gambia and Bafing Rivers have their source, was Futa Jalon, ruled by the Jalonke kings of Mande origin (Hiskett 1984, 138–39).

The spread of towns and cities during the formation of the Takrur state caused some Fulbe to leave. The migration of the pastoral Fulbe into the savanna dates from the twelfth and thirteenth centuries when they spread eastward across Sudanic Africa, taking over at first only lands ill-suited to agriculture. For this reason their expansion caused no alarm to their neighbors who, in fact, welcomed them for the manure their cattle provided on the fields and for the milk and butter that could be exchanged for agricultural products. Few of the pastoral Fulbe were Muslim so that religion was not a point of sharp difference with their neighbors. Even when they were Muslim, the pastoral Fulbe were generally of a tolerant disposition. They were, however, invariably accompanied in their migration by some of their sedentary kinsmen, who were usually better educated, more sophisticated in political matters, and less tolerant of non-Muslims. It was the sedentary Fulbe who fostered the political interests of the whole group by military aggression often in the form of a jihad, or holy war. In this way the Fulbe became politically dominant in areas such as the Futa Jalon, Masina, the Hausa country, and the Nupe country (Mabogunje 1976, 26–27).

During the fourteenth century, one wave of Fulbe migrants arrived in Mali and established communities in Masina near the Niger Bend. By the mid-fifteenth century, some Fulbe had reached Hausaland, beginning an infiltration into Hausa country that continued through the sixteenth century. Also, in the sixteenth century, a group of Fulbe moved southward from Senegal into Futa Jalon (present-day Guinea). The Fulbe began to arrive in Adamawa and other parts of the Cameroon during the eighteenth and nineteenth centuries (Hiskett 1984, 52–53; Adamu 1986, 55; Murdock 1959, 417; Greenberg 1960, 479–80). Fulbe who did not migrate eastward stayed in Senegambia and lived among the Wolof, Serer, and other groups.

The Fulbe who settled in Masina are important to the history of those in The Gambia, for some later returned to Senegambia. Under their clan leaders in Masina, the Fulbe formed a rigid social structure—serfs, traders and aristocrats—and an economy based on cattle rearing and agriculture. Originally, they followed their traditional religion but became influenced by Islam through contact with the Mande and the Tuareg who settled alongside them in and around Masina (Hiskett 1984, 151). Their interaction with the Songhai led to tensions. Sonni Ali, the Songhai leader who attacked them constantly, was their bitter enemy. After the fall of Songhai, the Fulbe began to have conflicts with the Tuareg. As a result of this pressure, many Fulbe returned to Senegambia during the sixteenth and early seventeenth centuries. Despite their departure, Masina remained an important Fulbe center (Hiskett 1984, 152).

While many of the Fulbe immigrants who returned to Senegambia had embraced Islam, their Mande landlords[10] in Futa Jalon and surrounding areas continued traditional religious practices even though many considered themselves to be Muslims. Upon arrival in Senegambia, certain Fulbe groups gave up the purely nomadic life for a relatively regular change of pasturage and settled in one region where they established relations with the non-nomadic farmers on whose lands they settled during the dry season. By the early eighteenth century, the Fulbe were found in every kingdom along the Gambia River. While the exact size of such a mobile population centuries ago is difficult to assess, scholars know that Fulbe settlements were scattered throughout the

Mande states, ranging in size from a cluster of a few huts to villages of one or two thousand (Quinn 1972, 19).

Although tensions existed, groups in this pluralistic environment learned to tolerate each other. The Fulbe normally bartered their dairy products for rice or millet. The Mande farmers willingly agreed to let the skilled herdsman take charge of the cattle that represented their life's savings and promised to give them protection from slave raids in return for services, taxes, or gifts. Not only were the Fulbe the acknowledged experts in the care of cattle, the accepted wealth in the country, they were also in sole charge of this desirable commodity. Although both sides profited from this association, over a period of time the Fulbe were less willing to be treated as vassals, harried and oppressed as though they were slaves. Tensions eventually arose, which led to several Islamic reform movements between the mid-1600s and the late 1800s (Quinn 1971, 428; Suret-Canale and Barry 1976, 489).[11] Those revolts that took place during the seventeenth and eighteenth centuries were small-scale and did not have as significant an impact as those that came later in the nineteenth century. Because jihad leaders in the seventeenth and eighteenth centuries lacked support of powerful clan and family networks, no large empires emerged. Mande rule continued until the second half of the nineteenth century before it came under Fulbe attack and was swept entirely away.

The two jihads that most affected Gambian culture took place in the nineteenth century and were led by Maba Diakhou Ba (a Fulbe whose family migrated to the Gambian region from Futa Toro) as well as Alfa Molo and his son, Musa Molo (both were Fulbe from Kabu near Futa Jalon). Maba's greatest achievements were the spread of Islam and the unification, however brief, of Mande, Fulbe, and Wolof peoples behind a single cause. Statistics collected in the middle of the twentieth century show that by then 80 percent of the Gambian population was Muslim, which can be attributed largely to the influence of Maba and the effects of his movement (Quinn 1968, 1–12; 1979, 233–58; Hiskett 1984, 232–33).[12]

Under Alfa Molo's leadership, Fulbe groups in other areas of Gambia and Futa Jalon as well as Serahuli[13] and Mande who were disenchanted with the old Mande aristocracy combined forces and successfully conquered the Mande landlords; the cluster of surrounding chiefdoms together became the new Fulbe state of Fuladu. Alfa's son, Musa Molo, continued the reforms and carried the Fulbe conquest over much of Gambia's south bank, which included some 5,000 square miles near the Gambia River. By the 1870s, the Fulbe state of Fuladu in the east possessed the richest economy along the Gambia River. The state was divided into approximately forty districts administered by Musa's principal followers, who included Fulbe, Mande, Serahuli, and even Wolof from the north banks of the river. Thus, Musa developed a state structure that replaced the pluralistic local institutions that had survived more or less intact from the days of Mande rule. Although both Fuladu and its Muslim neighbor states were superseded by European colonial rule at the beginning of the twentieth century, Musa Molo is considered to be one of Senegambia's strongest leaders because of his attempt to unify the Gambia valley (Quinn 1971, 427–40). Though he was not regarded as a religious man, his closest advisors were Muslims, and he entrusted his courts to Muslim jurists (Klein 1972, 433).

During the nineteenth century, the pastoral Fulbe were egalitarian except for wealth distinctions and slavery. Sedentary groups, however, were commonly stratified into free men or nobles and commoners (Fulbe Foro); slaves (Fulbe Diado); endogamous classes of *griots* (praise singers); artisans; and fishermen. Normally, the slaves were not Fulbe in origin but were acquired through capture or purchase. Cultural indicators, such as surnames, first names, body adornment, and scarification served as a means of identifying a person as freeborn, artisan, or of servile descent. Also, members of the different groups spoke different dialects just as they do now (Clark 1992, 2, 18; Quinn 1971, 431; Murdock 1959, 419–20).

Fulbe Identity

The Fulbe favor a cultural approach to ethnic identity rather than basing it on historical origins or lineage (Azarya, Eguchi, and VerEecke 1993, 3). The two elements that serve as the central markers of Fulbe identity include *pulaaku* or *pulaagu*[14] (code of behavior or way of life) and Fulfulde (Fulbe language).

> These aspects not only distinguish the Fulbe from other ethnic groups, but also color Fulbe perceptions of themselves and their world and prescribe the way the Fulbe should present themselves, as a sort of moral code. In particular, pulaaku prescribes how a *Pullo*... should act vis-à-vis specific types of people, such as affines, agnates and elders, as well as the public in general, in terms of behavior and appearance. Foremost of the many components of pulaaku is *semteende*, which may be defined as a kind of shyness, reserve, and even embarrassment when in the presence of relative "others." Other components may include *munyal* (endurance), *hakkiilo* (common sense, care), and a host of others. These values and behavior prescriptions have aided the Fulbe in their mastery of their precarious physical environment and in their quest to remain distinct from other peoples.... During the Fulbe jihads...pulaaku described behavior associated with militarism, such as bravery and courage (*cuusal, ngorgu*) as well as religious qualities such as piety (*njuuldamku*). [Azarya, Eguchi, and VerEecke 1993, 3–4]

Ryo Ogawa (1993, 129–30) believes that the most "important aspect of pulaaku is...not as a value system by itself but the fact that it is always defined in relation to other peoples or cultures.... When a Pullo thinks or speaks about pulaagu, he necessarily has in mind an image of some other people. Pulaagu is always defined in contrast with others, and this 'otherness' is of absolute necessity. It is a system of ideas or symbols which makes the Fulbe distinct from others." Most important, "Fulbe society and culture is and has always been dynamic" (VerEecke 1993, 146). Fulbe identity is also affected by the demographic balance between the Fulbe and other populations in a given location. In such instances, the Fulbe tend to absorb and integrate other societies into their culture and identity (Azarya, Eguchi, and VerEecke 1993, 6–7). Galina Zubko (1993, 203) believes that an important component of Fulbe behavior is the relative openness toward contacts with and borrowings from other cultures. As a result, much diversity exists within Fulbe culture. "It may be stated, with certain limitations, that heterogeneity is one of their most essential ethnic characteristics" (Zubko 1993, 207). Henri Gaden (1931, 313) speaks of two categories of Fulbe—the martial ones and the peaceful herdsmen. Whereas the first category managed to keep their independence with regard to former rulers, the second category infiltrated West African countries in small, mostly family groups, attempting by all means to minimize the information available on actual cattle possessions. Zubko explains further:

> Among the characteristics of the first model are social and political activity, openness for contacts and outside influence (specifically materialized in active Islamization), formation of feudal theocratic states, sedentarization and intermarriage with neighbouring

> peoples (this could only bring about considerable changes in the anthropological type of the Fulbe). In the second case, the tendency is to preserve their isolation, to adhere to ancient social and religious institutions, and to maintain comparative closeness, avoiding outside influence. Between the first and the second categories of Fulbe there exist complex hierarchical relations: the nomadic Fulbe admit their dependence on certain families of the sedentarized Fulbe. [Zubko 1993, 207–8]

During the precolonial period, militarism was an important marker of Fulbe identity in the Senegambian region. As a result of their success in the jihads, the Fulbe enjoyed an aristocratic position. After the arrival of the Europeans in the late nineteenth and early twentieth centuries, Fulbe leaders in several regions of West Africa were able to retain their Islamic titles and political offices as long as they assisted the European governors in administering the local (Fulbe and non-Fulbe) population. In The Gambia, however, this did not occur. Rather, the Islamic states and traditional political structure were disestablished with European colonialization. Some local village chiefs exist, but they have little political power (Mohammed Sissokho, personal communication with the author, August 1990). Thus, it was very early in the twentieth century that Gambian Fulbe began to lose their influence in national and regional political affairs, which led to competition and an ongoing negotiation with non-Fulbe for economic and political power (Azarya, Eguchi, and VerEecke 1993, 4). Fulbe ethnicity, then, is most noticeable when Fulbe interact with non-Fulbe, and characteristics that differentiate the Fulbe from other groups are highlighted and emphasized.

A History of The Gambia

It was not until 1888 that Gambia was administratively separated from Sierra Leone and a Gambia legislature was established. In the following year, negotiations with France delimited the boundaries between Senegal and Gambia. By 1901, the British had extended the protectorate over all of the major cheiftaincies along the river but did not initiate social and economic changes until after World War II. Although Gambians were given limited representation in the colony's legislative council in 1932, it was only between 1948 and 1963 that the local populace was allowed greater participation in the political process. The Protectorate People's Party, founded in 1959 and led by Dawda Jawara, sought to integrate all of the ethnic groups; in fact, the party changed its name to the People's Progressive Party (PPP) to ensure that political offices were distributed on an intercommunal basis. The PPP won the 1962 elections that initiated self-government with Jawara as prime minister. In 1965, the PPP led the country to independence as a constitutional monarchy. In 1970, The Gambia became a republic with Jawara as its first president. In 1982, The Gambia and the Republic of Senegal—after a failed military takeover in The Gambia—signed an agreement to bring the Confederation of Senegambia into existence, but the confederation was dissolved in 1989 (Hughes 1994, 392). In July 1994, the civilian government of Jawara was overthrown and a military regime came into power with Yahya Jammeh as leader.

The Republic of the Gambia comprises the valley of the navigable Gambia River. Except for the sea coast, the country is surrounded by Senegal and extends inland for about 200 miles. At the mouth of the river in the west, the country is 30 miles wide and narrows to 15 miles at its eastern border. Although The Gambia is one of the smallest countries in Africa, it is extremely diverse in population. The principal ethnic groups include the Mande (42%), Fulbe (18%), Wolof (16%), Jola (10%), and Serahuli (9%), with small numbers of the Serer (2%), Aku (1%), and Manjago (1%) (Church 1994, 392; Elmer 1983, 3). The Jolas are considered to be the longest residents in The Gambia, while the Mande, Wolof, and Fulbe migrated from further east (Gray 1940, 326–27).

In 1983, the country's population was 698,817; the 1998 estimate was 1,205,000. Although large numbers of Gambians have moved to cities since the end of World War II, more than 80 percent still live in rural areas outside the urban communities of Banjul (the capital city), Bakau, and Serrekunda. The Gambia is a country of small peasant farmers with few major industries or mineral resources, although reserves of petroleum have been identified. Groundnuts, millet, and sorghum are the important cash and food crops, but swamp rice is also cultivated. In recent years the Gambian government has attempted to diversify its economy through the development of fishing and tourist industries (Elmer 1983, 1–2; Gamble 1949, 5–35). At present, The Gambia's residents are believed to be 85–90% Muslim; the remainder are Christians and, to a lesser extent, followers of traditional religious beliefs and practices. Like groups in other areas of Sudanic Africa, children attend both Koranic and Western schools. Since 1965, there has been more than a 40 percent increase in the enrollment of primary school students (Costa 1990, 361).

English is the official language of Gambian schools, courts of law, and public offices, but various African languages are widely spoken. Wolof serves as the language of commerce in urban areas, while Mande and other local languages predominate in rural areas. Aku (a Creole language that is a mixture of English with various local languages) can also be heard in urban areas (Elmer 1983, 4). In addition, words of French, Portuguese, and Arabic origin have been incorporated into the lingua franca of the area (Gamble and Baldeh 1981, i–iv).

The Fiddle in Performance

A Fulbe Wedding

The Fulbe fiddle is most often used at naming, circumcision, and wedding ceremonies. My first opportunity to hear the fiddle in performance took place on Sunday, August 19, 1990, when Tamba Kandeh,[15] a Fulbe fiddler who lives in Lamin, The Gambia, invited me to the wedding (*bangal*) of one of his relatives. Tamba had been asked to provide the musical entertainment for the wedding (fig. 6.1).

Before going to the wedding, Tamba requested that I visit his compound so that he could record and hear his fiddle playing on tape. For about six minutes, he performed four praise songs, although one was played twice. The first two songs—"Supere Demba" and "Mamareh ko bengel Kaddy Jakou"—were in praise of two of Tamba's patrons; the songs consisted of several repetitive melodic phrases played on the fiddle without vocal or instrumental accompaniment. Short, intricate ornaments on various notes of the melody helped to embellish the melodic phrases. On the third song, "Jawara" (a praise song in honor of The Gambia's former president), Tamba sang and accompanied himself on the fiddle; the fiddle playing in "Jawara" was noticeably less intricate, and Tamba sometimes stopped playing briefly whenever he sang the text. The final song was a repeat of "Mamareh ko bengel Kaddy Jakou," but this time he sang. After listening to the playback with earphones, he was pleased with the sound but disappointed that there were no speakers so that the music could be heard aloud.

We departed for the wedding around two o'clock in the afternoon and arrived at the home of Ngeya Kandeh (the groom)[16] around three o'clock. Ngeya lived in a town called Nema Kundu Combo North, a suburb of Serrekunda. Upon arrival, I learned[17] that the wedding celebration would not be extensive because Ngeya, who was in his fifties, felt that an elaborate celebration was not necessary. Although this was going to be his second wife, it was the bride's first marriage. Around four o'clock, guests began to arrive. Most were Fulbe men who had come for an Upper River Division (URD) committee meeting.[18] While the men conducted their meeting in one area of Ngeya's courtyard, about four or five women cooked and did other chores in another area in preparation for the wedding. Around 6:30 p.m., some of Ngeya's friends and family members left in a van to pick up the bride from her home even though she was not expected to leave for the groom's residence until late in the night.

Although members of the wedding party were in two locations (both the bride's and groom's residence), all of the music making took place at the Ngeya's compound. Intermittently, throughout the two-day event,[19] Tamba provided entertainment as wedding guests ate, danced, and listened to music. Interestingly, few of the songs were concerned with people in attendance at the wedding. In addition to songs that he had performed at his compound earlier that day, he played a variety of songs on all sorts of topics and themes. While a few were praise or social comment songs that he had personally composed or arranged, most were compositions that he had adapted from other Fulbe fiddlers.[20]

In most instances, Tamba performed alone. As he played various melodies on the fiddle, he also sang the vocal response. On occasion, he was accompanied by a chorus. At the evening performance on the first day of the wedding, a chorus (a group of five to six girls, ten to sixteen years of age) sang the response to the fiddle and provided rhythmic accompaniment with handclapping. As Tamba stood and played, he shifted his weight from one foot to the other, moving back and forth slightly to the rhythm of the music. Although Tamba and the singers did not dance, those looking on joined in by dancing. There did not appear to be any set pattern to their movements; rather, the dancing was free and improvisatory.

When the girls left that evening, Tamba played alone and sang by himself. After the girls' departure on that first evening, a few people at the wedding commented that the girls' singing was not the best. Some guests felt that the girls did not know the music that well because they had lived in the city too long. It was believed that if the wedding had taken place in the provinces, or if the females had been older, the music would have been livelier (DjeDje 1990, 57–64).

Fulbe Music in The Gambia

Little scholarly work has been done on Fulbe music in Senegambia. Rather, brief comments about music of the Fulbe can be found in general works on The Gambia as a country (e.g., Elmer 1983, 15–18) or publications that include discussion of other ethnic groups who reside in or near Senegambia—see Knight (1980; 1983); Gamble (1967); Gamble et al. (1985); Coolen (1982; 1983; 1984; 1991); Nikiprowetzky (1963; 1980); Rouget (1980); and Oven (1981). A few scholars in related disciplines have devoted some attention to the Fulbe in Mali (Bâ 1966), Burkina Faso (Riesman 1977), and Senegal (Sow 1993), but their discussion of music is limited. Even Arnott's (1980) article on "Fulani Music" in *The New Grove's Dictionary of Music* contains minimal discussion of traditions in Senegambia. Some discussion of Fulbe music in Senegambia is included in *The Garland Encyclopedia of World Music* (see DjeDje 1998); the information, however, is not extensive because the focus is on the West African region and not the music of specific ethnic groups. Two of the most valuable studies are by Gaden (1931) and Seydou (1972). Although these works do not contain information specifically on Fulbe in The Gambia, their discussion of Fulbe in other areas—Futa Jalon, Futa Toro, and the Nigerian complex—provide valuable insight about Fulbe traditions in West Africa.

Commercial sound recordings present a more balanced picture of Fulbe music in various culture clusters, with representative samples from the Western Sudan, the Voltaic area, and the Central Sudan. While little research has been done on the music of the Fulbe in Senegambia,[21] a substantial amount of information is available on the Mandinka and Wolof.[22] Also, Fulbe groups in other parts of West Africa, particularly the Central Sudan, have been the subject of scholarly publications.[23]

There are several reasons for the lack of information on the Fulbe in Senegambia. First, as noted in the culture history, Fulbe culture is not a single entity. Not only are the Fulbe dispersed throughout West Africa, their migration into The Gambia spans several centuries with different waves of people arriving from the north, east, and south. Upon arrival, rarely did they form themselves into a unified group. Rather, they were divided into a variety of linguistic, occupational, and class groupings—a diversity that probably dissipated the political impact of their considerable numbers. Quinn (1972, 21) states, "There is little evidence of intergroup cooperation, and a pattern of reserve, if not hostility, between them [the Fulbe] was characteristic.... As a result, their relationships with other ethnic groups along the river were highly particularized."

Second, similar to investigations in history and other disciplines, scholars who have done music research in West Africa have focused on the politically powerful and those who were the most visible within a society.[24] Of course, there are exceptions, and this trend has changed in recent decades. Nevertheless, the political dominance of the Fulani in Hausaland and their large numbers in northern Cameroon and other parts of the Central Sudan have made them prime subjects for investigation. Fulbe leadership in the Senegambian region did not have a significant and long impact on society when compared to the empires, kingdoms, and states established by the Mandinka and Wolof in earlier years. Also, the Fulbe do not constitute a majority in Senegambia. While the Mandinka are the largest group in The Gambia, the Wolof are in greater numbers in Senegal. In both areas, the Fulbe rank second in population.[25]

Finally, because of the extensive amount of intercultural contacts among groups in Senegambia, some investigators discuss Senegambian music generally without specifying or delineating what is unique among the different ethnic groups. Knight (1983, 45) states, "it is clear that Fula-Mandinka relations have encompassed a wide range of situations.... The most fruitful situation for both parties concerned, that of intermarriage, doubtless went hand in hand with most of the others, and continues to this day, making clear-cut distinctions between the two peoples less and less meaningful." In Njie's (1970a; 1970b; 1970c) three-part series on music in The Gambia, rarely does he mention differences among the various societies. Rather, he discusses aspects of music making as if all groups participated similarly.[26] A few scholars suggest that what is found among one group may be applicable for another. Commenting on Wolof culture, Gamble et al. (1985, 2) state that when one analyzes the details of Wolof culture, one finds little that is not to some degree shared with other peoples. Not only have the Wolof adopted Islam from the Tukulor and been greatly influenced by Fulbe religious scholars, but their naming, circumcision, and marriage ceremonies show parallels to Mandinka and Fulbe customs.

The few scholars who have examined Fulbe music provide information that not only helps us to understand the features that are unique to the culture but also gives some insight about the meaning and value of music to the people. Arnott (1980, 24) states, "it is difficult to generalize about [Fulbe] music. Nevertheless two important general distinctions must be made: firstly between the music in which the Fulani themselves take part and that of the professional musicians who sing and play for them; and secondly between the hymns and songs (both religious and secular) which have developed from the Arabic Islamic tradition and the everyday songs which are integral to the tradition of Fulani herdsmen."

In Fulbe culture, several categories of musicians exist, but they are organized differently in various areas of West Africa. Writing about traditions of the early twentieth century, Gaden (1931)[27] states that Fulbe and Tukulor musicians in Futa Toro (Senegal) were divided into three groups: *maabu'be* (pl. of *maabo*), who were weavers as well as singers; *wammbaa'be* (pl. of *bammbaa'do*), musicians whose instruments were the *hoddu*, a sort of guitar, and the *nanoru*, an instrument played with a bow; and *awlu'be* (pl. of *gawlo*), singers who beat drums.[28] The *wammbaa'be* were the ones "à être venus avec les Peuls, les autres sont d'origine sarakollé, mandingue ou ouolof" (who came with the Fulbe or are derived from Fulbe culture, while the others were of Sarokolle [Serahuli], Mandinka, or Wolof origin; Gaden 1931, 12). To support the common origin and close association of the *wammbaa'be* with the Fulbe, Gaden (1931, 321) relates the following myth:

> There were three brothers who were forced by famine to disperse or separate from each other. The eldest brother took a hatchet, cut trees and obtained an income by making wooden objects. The second brother became a cattle herder. The third brother, supplied with his *hoddu*, became a singer and received gifts and profit for his activity. After the death of their parents and the famine had passed, the three brothers continued to follow their respective activities.
>
> The eldest was a wood worker (*labbo*), the junior was a cattle herder (*poullo*), the third was a musician (*bambâdo*). The Peul, after finding that his two brothers were spending their life in a degrading way, did not want his children to have an alliance with their children. Thus, the Laobé and the Wambâbé form today the inferior castes with which the Peuls do not marry or mix. [Translation mine]

Arnott (1980, 24) states that the French term *griot* refers to singers in any of the three categories described by Gaden (1931). Both *wammbaa'be* and *maabu'be* were, and to some extent still are, basically court musicians. Not only do they sing praises and genealogies of chiefs and other wealthy patrons, they also sing about the exploits of their ancestors and epics of the Fulbe past. While some may be attached to individual patrons, others move from one chief's court to another.

The music culture of Fulbe musicians in The Gambia[29] is slightly different from that of their neighbors and kin in other parts of West Africa. The Gambian Fulbe whom I interviewed categorize musicians into two groups: *awlu'be* (pl. of *gawlo*) and *jalibeh* or *jali* (pl. of *jalijo*).[30] The *gawlo* specializes in praising or promoting important people through song without instrumental accompaniment.[31] The term *jalibeh* refers to individuals who play musical instruments (strings, drums, etc.) as well as those who sing to the accompaniment of musical instruments. While the Gambian Fulbe musicians whom I interviewed are familiar with the terms *wammbaa'be* and *maabu'be*, these words are rarely used in conversation.[32] More importantly, Fulbe musicians in The Gambia associate the *maabu'be* solely with weaving and not music making.

Similar to their neighbors, the music profession among the Fulbe is hereditary and organized around family groups that perform certain musical instruments. If a person is born into a family that specializes in the playing of the *hoddu*, that individual is expected to learn to perform the instrument either from a kinsman or an established musician and continue in the profession as an adult. Some families specialize in several instruments, particularly if the music that they play includes several instruments in the ensemble. For example, those raised in a family of fiddlers not only learn how to play the fiddle; they are also taught how to play the *tama* (*tema*) and in some cases how to sing (see further discussion below). With westernization and particularly since independence, these rules have changed and are not rigidly upheld. There is no evidence that distinctions are made between Fulbe and non-Fulbe musicians wherein the role of non-Fulbe musicians is different from those who are Fulbe. Yet, it should be noted that many of the musicians that I interviewed belong to the Fulbe Firdu[33] dialect group and trace their heritage to Futa Jalon. Interestingly, during the nineteenth century, the so-called "purer" nomadic Fulbe believed the Fulbe Firdu to be of slave origin.

The only evidence that Fulbe in The Gambia served as court musicians is when they performed for the nineteenth-century leader, Musa Molo.[34] Because the Fulbe lived in a pluralistic society, with leaders (warriors) who ruled a heterogeneous population, they were not the only individuals that served as court musicians.[35] This was a profession and status they shared with other musicians in the region; thus, their role as court musicians was somewhat limited because when Fulbe rulers came to power during the mid-nineteenth century, they maintained many of the court traditions that had existed under Mandinka rule, which included the use of Mandinka *jalolu* as court musicians.[36] Thus, even though the rulers were Fulbe, it was Mandinka, Fulbe, and perhaps Wolof performers who sang the praises, recited the genealogy, and recorded historical accounts (Innes 1974, 7; 1976; Ngansumana Jobateh, interview with the author, December 10, 1994). While some Fulbe musicians were attached to royalty and important personages, many were also itinerant musicians, performing for different patrons in various contexts. Therefore, in addition to a core repertory or body of material that served as a historical or permanent record for the Fulbe ruler, Fulbe musicians also had to learn praise songs for commoners.

The Fulbe Fiddle Tradition in The Gambia

The one-stringed fiddle or bowed lute is classified as a spike bowl lute, sounding by bowing with a bow. Like other West African fiddles, the body resonator of the Fulbe fiddle in The Gambia is covered with the skin of a reptile (lizard) and the resonator hole is placed in the sound box.[37] The term for the fiddle among Gambian Fulbe is *nyanyeru* (*nyaanyooru*, *nyanyaru*, *nyanyur*, *nanoru*). However, the Wolof term, *riti*, is also used by groups in Senegal and The Gambia, even by the Fulbe.[38] Because Wolof is the lingua franca in cities and towns in Senegambia, the use of the term *riti* is not surprising. Although the Mandinka use the term *susaa* for the fiddle, rarely do they actually perform the instrument. Rather, *susaa*, like *riti* and *nyanyeru*, refers to the scratching or rubbing of two objects together, which is

6.2 A *nyanyeru* (Fulbe fiddle). Photograph by Jacqueline Cogdell DjeDje, Lamin, The Gambia, August 19, 1990.

6. 3 Side view of a *nyanyeru*. Photograph by Jacqueline Cogdell DjeDje, Lamin, The Gambia, August 19, 1990.

6.4 Front view of a *nyanyeru*. Photograph by Jacqueline Cogdell DjeDje, Lamin, The Gambia, August 19, 1990.

6.5 Resonator hole of a *nyanyeru*. Photograph by Jacqueline Cogdell DjeDje, Lamin, The Gambia, August 19, 1990.

the action used to produce a sound on the fiddle (Tamba Kandeh, interviews with the author, August 19–25, 1990, and December 8–11, 1994; Ngansumana Jobateh, interview with the author, December 10, 1994; Knight 1995). See figures 6.2–6.5.

History

No information has been written on the history of the fiddle tradition among the Fulbe in The Gambia. In fact, the majority of Senegambian fiddlers whom I interviewed stated that they knew nothing about the history of the fiddle. Samba Juma Bah,[39] a Pullo fiddler from Guinea (fig. 6.8), stated, "I did not bother to ask my teacher where the fiddle came from and I don't know where the fiddle comes from." However, Majaw Bai,[40] a Tukulor fiddler from Senegal, stated that he believed the fiddle and plucked lute were introduced into Africa by cattle herders.

In my opinion, the history of the fiddle in Fulbe culture is directly related to earlier contacts that the Fulbe had with Arabs, Berbers, and Tukulors. One of the characteristic features of Arab music is the performance of melodic instruments, particularly bowed and plucked lutes. For centuries, Arab Bedouins have used the fiddle to accompany epic poems in praise of warriors and other heroic figures.[41] Similarly the Berber and Tuareg also perform the fiddle (Dalby 1980).[42]

Therefore, it is possible that just as the Tukulor were one of the first groups in West Africa to convert to Islam, because of their interaction with Berbers and Arabs, the Tukulor and by extension the Fulbe were two of the first groups to adopt the fiddle. If this hypothesis is correct, then the Fulbe would have been introduced to the fiddle sometime between the eleventh and thirteenth centuries. After the initial introduction, the use of the fiddle may have been reinforced through repeated and continuous interactions with North Africans. During their migrations eastward, some Fulbe came in contact and intermarried Berber pastoralists who were moving south from the Sahara. Also, there were centuries of contact with the Tuareg in Masina (Mali) before some Fulbe migrated west and settled in Senegambia. In fact, either the Fulbe or the Tuareg may have been responsible for the introduction of the fiddle in Songhai culture, because both groups had numerous interactions with the Songhai.

If the distribution of the fiddle in West Africa is closely intertwined with Fulbe migration patterns, this would mean that the fiddle was introduced into Senegambia with Fulbe migrations into the area some time during the seventeenth century and later. As a result of interaction with the Fulbe, other groups in the Western Sudan (the Wolof, Serer, Balante, Koniagi, and other neighboring groups) began to use the fiddle.[43] For example, in Sierra Leone the Temne have also adopted the instrument, but the fiddle is played mainly by Fulbe musicians (Oven 1980, 302; 1981, 10). Yet the possibility that these groups were introduced to the instrument earlier as a result of contacts with the Tukulor should not be ruled out.

Regardless of the date or time period, it is significant that when a close examination is made of the various groups that use the fiddle, many of these people have either had direct or indirect contact with the Fulbe (fig. 6.6). In some instances, descendants or people who have intermarried with the Fulbe become the performers and/or propagators of Fulbe culture. Gamble (1967, 77) acknowledges that the Wolof use of the fiddle is derived from the Fulbe when he states: "As they [Wolof] are living in close association with the Fulbe, they are also familiar with the one stringed fiddle (*riti*)." It is also noteworthy that most Wolof *xalamkats* credit the Khassonke (a people of Fulbe origin) of Mali and Eastern Senegal with being the source of their expertise on the *xalam* (Coolen 1982, 74). In so doing, the Wolof are acknowledging the influence of the Fulbe even though these particular Fulbe have assimilated some Mande customs and language (Dalby 1980, 573; Murdock 1959, 72). In fact, Coolen (1983, 481) suggests that the Fulbe's "diasporatic movements have undoubtedly been partly responsible for the diffusion of the plucked-lute in this region."

In discussing the development of the *griot* tradition in The Gambia, Elmer (1983, 16) states, "Griots of the Mandinka, Fula, Wolof, and Serahule traditions used string instruments to accompany their historical narratives. While all played a type of lute with a wooden resonating chamber and a varying number of strings, the *kora* has become the hall-mark of Mandinka musicians...the Wolof play the *xalam*... the Fulas are known for their fiddles." The media in The Gambia also associate the fiddle with the Fulbe.[44] Fiddle music is used to announce the beginning and end of Fulbe news on the radio, while the *kora* is heard when Mandinka news is announced.

Social Organization

The few accounts in the literature about Fulbe fiddlers provide little information about social organization, role, and status. Fulbe oral traditions in The Gambia include mention of two Fulbe musicians who performed for Musa Molo: Mamadou Patah Gawlo (a praise singer) and Yorro Buka

6.6 Ousainou Chaw, a Serer, performing a *riti* (Wolof term for fiddle) in his compound. The resonator of the *riti* is made from a round tin can. Photograph by Jacqueline Cogdell DjeDje, Dakar, Senegal, August 30, 1990.

(a fiddler). According to Maulday Baldeh,[45] Fulbe musicians did not stay in the village (Kesserkunda) with Musa Molo but lived in a nearby town. When Musa Molo needed musicians to play for him, he sent his servants for them. The servant would ride one horse and travel with empty horses to collect the musicians. When Musa Molo prepared for war, musicians went with him and sang praises and genealogy songs to get him mentally fit to go and fight. After the battle, musicians returned to Kesserkunda where Molo slaughtered bulls for their dinner. Along with other musicians, the fiddler would sing songs to promote Musa Molo. Special historical songs have been composed in honor of Musa Molo, but Baldeh stated that he only knew two "old" songs ("Balla" and "Sorronna") and one "new" song ("Sodahnam Padeh Jelleh").[46] Fulbe fiddlers in the provinces knew other songs in praise of Musa Molo and still performed them for local chiefs and at rallies for political leaders in the modern government.[47]

Baldeh and other Gambian fiddlers who have inherited the fiddle tradition from kin trace their heritage to Yorro Buka, which suggests that fiddling among Fulbe in The Gambia dates back to the precolonial period. However, the fact that fiddlers are not aware of court musicians who lived before the time of Musa Molo suggests that their role as court musicians probably evolved during the late nineteenth century with the rise to power of Fulbe kings in the Gambian region. Prior to that time, the position of Fulbe fiddlers in this area was probably comparable to what Leymarie-Ortiz (1979) describes for common *griots* among the Wolof. Although some were attached to families and individuals, most had to move from place to place to find performances; a large number probably had to supplement their income through farming and other occupations.

Like other Fulbe musicians, many of the Fulbe fiddlers whom I interviewed in The Gambia refer to themselves as *jali*,[48] demonstrating the influence of Mandinka culture on Fulbe in this area. The identity of musicians is associated with the instruments that they play. The fiddler as well as the musicians who accompany him in performance are given specific names: *jali nyanyeru* (fiddler), *jali jeymowoh* (singer), *jali tamaaru* (*tama* player), *jali mbahgu*/*jalibeh bawdi* (drum player, sing. and pl., respectively). Gambian fiddlers distinguish between musicians who inherit the profession from family members and those who achieve the profession by learning on their own or from an established musician. While those who inherit the fiddling profession from kinsmen state that they trace their heritage to Buka, other Fulbe fiddlers know little about Buka and the fiddler's association with Musa Molo.[49] In spite of the connection with Buka, there does not appear to be a formal social structure wherein all fiddlers believe they are related to each other or pay homage to one fiddle leader similar to the situation among Dagbamba fiddlers in Ghana (DjeDje 1978; 1992). For example, in discussing the fiddlers in the Upper River Division, Tamba Kandeh states, "The fiddlers in Basse, they are in groups. You sometimes find one group here, and you go to the next compound and you find another group. There are small villages near Basse. They have many fiddlers in those villages. These fiddlers, they sometimes meet at Basse. Each is with his own group. They don't mix together" (interview with the author, August 19–25, 1990).

Patrons who support fiddle music can be categorized into two groups. On the one hand, there are persons who maintain a long and continuous relationship with the fiddler and call on him at any time for services because a prearranged contract or agreement between the two parties has been established. On the other hand, clients for whom the fiddler provides services for a short moment or period, such as when he plays a praise song for a person whom he may or may not know at a public gathering, would have to be placed in an entirely different category. The decision to enter into these contracts may be initiated by either party—musician or patron (DjeDje 1982).

In modern times, Fulbe fiddlers are not attached to one patron but perform services to several people at one time. It is not uncommon for the names of a number of patrons or promoters to be mentioned in one song. For example, in a performance by Juldeh Camara (fig. 6.7), the names of at least four of his patrons were included. On occasion, the praise song for one patron becomes the fiddler's favorite. Tamba Kandeh states that he always begins his performances with a song that he composed in honor of a friend who was a well-known wrestler. Even though Kandeh, in 1990, had not seen the wrestler for four years because the wrestler moved to Senegal, Kandeh continues to play this song to remember his friend. "If somebody tells or asks me to start with another music rather than 'Supere Demba,' I would do that. But if I am to suggest, I always need to start with the song 'Supere Demba' " (interview with the author, August 19–25, 1990).

Because a fiddler's services are crucial to those in politics, long-term agreements are often established between politicians and fiddlers. In the mid-1960s, Tamba and Ngeya Kandeh decided to form a group as a result of their working with Mohammed Cherno Jallowe, one of the first politicians from the Upper River Division to serve in the modern government's cabinet. When Jallowe moved to Banjul to serve his term of office, he felt that he needed musicians in his home district to sing his praises both in his absence and when he returned to his district on visits.[50] Juldeh Camara states that when he was performing in the provinces, a politician heard him playing with his troupe and liked what he was doing. So the politician asked him to travel around the Upper River Division area so that they could campaign together. After the elections, the politician asked Camara to follow him to Banjul where both stayed. In Banjul, the politician is responsible for Camara and helps by taking him to hotels and other places to perform.

Most Fulbe fiddlers believe that their profession is a good one. Ngeya Kandeh, who at one time was considered to be the champion fiddler for The Gambia,[51] states, "Fiddling is something very high in the country because it's a culture and it's a remembrance and it makes the Gambians happy." Commenting on the meaning or significance of fiddling, Tamba Kandeh states,"Muslims say fiddling is good. Fiddling is good to Allah. Fulbe fiddlers believe that the fiddle is a music of heavens. If the person did good things here, then he's going to find good things there [in the heavens]. If he did bad things here, then he is going to find bad things there. For those who did good things, there are doors. When opening the doors, the sound it gives, it's the same sound the fiddles are giving. The sound of the fiddle is similar or is the same as when the doors of heavens are opening or closing" (interview with the author, August 19–25, 1990).

In Senegambia, performing the fiddle is a male profession. Prior to The Gambia's independence in 1965, the majority, if not all of the individuals who played the instrument, had been born into a family of fiddlers and begun their training when they were between the ages of seven and ten. In most instances, fiddlers were taught by their fathers. But if the father had reached an age at which he no longer wanted to fiddle, the child was sent to a family member or a professional fiddler for training. It is also noteworthy that before the mid-1960s, Fulbe fiddlers specialized in certain aspects of the fiddling profession.

Those who learned how to play the *nyanyeru* and *tama* were not always taught how to sing, and those who sang were not able to perform an instrument.

For the most part, the tradition still exists in this way. Fiddlers who have inherited the fiddling profession still follow the same rules that were in place before the mid-1960s. Maulday Baldeh, who was born in the 1960s, stated that he began his training when he was nine years old and his father taught him and his brothers about the fiddle profession. Because Mamadou Baldeh's father had stopped fiddling by the time Mamadou was born, Mamadou did not learn to fiddle until he was fifteen years old. He learned through an apprenticeship with a professional who lived about ten to fifteen miles from his home. During the dry season, Mamadou stayed with his teacher and returned home during the rainy season in time for farming. Both Maulday (who plays the *tama* and fiddle but does not sing) and Mamadou (who performs only the fiddle and does not sing) stated that it took them at least four years before their teachers felt they had learned enough to be recognized as professional musicians.[52]

Juldeh Camara,[53] who had lived in The Gambia since the mid-1980s, also inherited the profession from kin. He began his fiddle training when he was seven years old and was taught by his father, who allowed Camara, as a young child, to travel and perform with him. All of Camara's brothers, who still lived in Casamance, played the fiddle. In addition to the fiddle, Camara was able to perform the *tama*, the *djembe* (*djimbe*, *jimbeng*) and the *lala* (see discussion of these instruments below).

Camara states that his older sister used to play the fiddle but stopped when he was born. She did not continue in the profession because, by tradition, females do not perform the fiddle. Camara (1990) states :

> For a girl to fiddle and go around the village, I have never seen it. She can sing with women, but not fiddle. I have never seen a girl or women going to a village fiddling. I don't do things I have never seen. It's not good for a woman to travel as I am traveling four or five years without going back to their homeland. A woman is to be married. If she has a very good experience on this fiddle, maybe she won't accept to be married. Or the husband wouldn't allow her to go. Maybe there may be a problem between her and her husband. If she is stopped, then there is problem. Everybody wants a woman. If she became famous, many, many, many people would like to have connections with her. If she became a fiddler and is maybe a pretty girl or woman, looking so attractive to many people, she may be loved by many people. For a woman to travel like that for years on fiddling is not done. [Juldeh Camara, interview with the author, September 1, 1990]

Although he did not inherit the profession, Samba Jumba Bah started fiddling when he was seven years old while tending herds. He says, "Small boys sometimes play drums, *koras*, and fiddles. I kept on playing this fiddle until I got interested. So I continued playing." He says that he learned from an old man who lived in Kindia, his hometown. "I went to Maro Tembo for him to teach me because I see what Maro Tembo was playing in town and how he plays. So I liked it. So I tell Maro Tembo to make one fiddle for me. And Maro Tembo asked whether my father would make any problem or not. I said, 'No there would be no problem.' Maro Tembo made a fiddle for me and I started to train and learn how to fiddle" (interview with the author, August 23, 1990). After two years of instruction, Bah began to travel to various towns and cities in Guinea. Later he visited Bamako [Mali] and Senegal before settling in The Gambia where, in 1990, he had lived for nine years.

By the mid-1960s, it was not uncommon for individuals in The Gambia to leave the profession of their family and choose another. Also, musicians whom I interviewed stated that the low status or stigma that had been associated with the music profession in earlier years had almost been abolished. Tamba Kandeh states, "we have started in a new generation whereby everything was accepted" (interview with the author, December 8–11, 1994). Fiddlers, however, born into the profession are not entirely pleased with newcomers because it causes them to lose some of their clientele; as a result, they have to spend more time pursuing occupations unrelated to music making. Maulday Baldeh states: "I do not like somebody who is not born in the fiddle profession to come and fiddle. This bothers me because that means I got to farm" (interview with the author December 9, 1994).

In spite of these objections, which some fiddlers are probably not aware of, many persons in recent years have decided to become fiddlers because they believe it is part of their heritage as Fulbe. For example, although they were born into the cattle herding family group (Rorobe), several members of the Kandeh family have chosen the fiddling profession; most began their training in their late teens or twenties. Although some received instruction from an established musician, a few learned from

6.7 Juldeh Camara, a Fulbe fiddler from Casamance, Senegal, performing a *nyanyeru* at the home of Tamba Kandeh. Photograph by Jacqueline Cogdell DjeDje, Lamin, The Gambia, September 1, 1990.

6.8 Samba Jumba Bah, a Fulbe fiddler from Guinea, performing a *nyanyeru* at the home of Tamba Kandeh. Photograph by Jacqueline Cogdell DjeDje, Lamin, The Gambia, August 23, 1990.

kinsmen. Ngeya Kandeh, who learned to fiddle when he was twenty-seven years old from an established fiddler in his hometown,[54] explains: "I learned fiddling because it's what I met. I found that my relatives and other Gambians are fiddling so I joined them. Fiddling makes Gambians happy. I met many people fiddling when I learned how to fiddle. These people fiddled to make old men remember the culture. So I find that I also should learn to fiddle so I can make those people remember also." Ngeya Kandeh gave up the fiddling profession in the late 1970s. "I left fiddling because I had three sons and one daughter. I found that we are in a poor country and I have nothing. I have no other technical abilities. So I find that I must leave the fiddling and follow the farm. In the farm, there is where I can get money to survive with my family and some of my relatives" (interview with the author August 19, 1990).

Tamba Kandeh states that he was eighteen years old and living in his home village of Sarekokeh when he taught himself how to play the fiddle. After three months, he states that he was able to play the instrument: "I heard how people fiddle. So I made a small one for myself until I started learning how to form my fingers. Then I went to my brother [Ngeya Kandeh]. When my brother was fiddling, I would also come and sit beside him and look [at] how he did the fingers. Then I started to follow him. The first song that my brother taught [me] was 'Tapa Tura.' At that time, people were fiddling 'Tapa Tura.' Everyone was happy with that song. 'Tapa Tura' is a type of bicycle. My brother wrote the song."[55] When learning to fiddle, Kandeh states that the bowing was the easiest. "Forming the fingers is difficult because the fingers play everything. The fingers give different sounds." Before leaving his hometown, Tamba Kandeh states that he also taught his younger brother how to play. Commenting on his children's fiddle training, Tamba states, "They [my children] are going to school. If they complete their schooling, then I'll teach them how to fiddle because it's a part of our culture."[56]

Although many fiddlers state that fiddling is highly regarded, there is some ambivalence about teaching their children how to fiddle. Samba Juma Bah states, "I don't want them [my children] to be frivolous. I want them to go to school, for them to learn and get very good jobs. Fiddling is good but since I fiddle, I don't want all of them to be fiddlers. Some of them must get other technical training than fiddling. It was not the aim of my father for me to learn fiddling. My father did not want me to fiddle. So when I learned fiddling, I had to go away from him" (interview with the author, August 23, 1990). In spite of the obstacles facing fiddlers, Camara encourages young people to continue as musicians:

> Despite the difficulties they are facing, they should continue to develop their talent. Whenever one has time, one should try to compose new songs and new tunes. Whenever one sits down to compose a new tune, even if one is not successful immediately, one is in the process of developing one's talent. One should continue to meet the challenge and sooner or later one would come up with something new. One has to enjoy what one is doing before one can develop it. Everyone of us should work hard and try to encourage each other to develop our talent for the common good. Music gives joy to people. It is needed in society. If we continue to develop our talent, sooner or later we will come to enjoy the fruits of our labor. As for me, my major ambition is to develop the *riti* (violin) so that it will not be limited to our subregion. I want it to be appreciated everywhere in the world. [Interview conducted by Mamma Kandeh, April 29, 1991]

The attributes of a good fiddler in Fulbe society vary. Camara, who has made a professional commercial recording and become well known both in the Banjul area and the Upper River Division, states that he is not sure how he gained fame: "As a small boy, I used to play with my father. I learned some of these songs from my father. I don't know how I got my own group. Maybe it is because people invited me. And I'm famous for that. There are many, many fiddlers who are older than me who used to come to me to ask many questions about fiddling. They would ask about the titles of songs and want to learn songs that I have written" (interview with the author, September 1, 1990). In addition to being able to create new songs, technical virtuosity on the fiddle is an attribute that gives distinction to a fiddler. Fiddle melodies are not simple but tend to be long, florid and melodically complex.

Performance Contexts

Fulbe fiddlers have always performed in a variety of contexts: birth, circumcision, and marriage ceremonies, as well as at work, festivals, and other public gatherings. Fiddlers also privately entertain clients in the client's home. Camara states, "If I am in the house with a few men, without any noise, I can play the fiddle gently and explain about Fulbe warriors" (interview with the author, September 1, 1990). Since The Gambia regained its independence, fiddle performances at political activities have become commonplace. Many of Camara's performances take place at luxury hotels, where he plays for tourists and guests, most of whom are from European countries. Even though these new performance contexts provide income, he believes entertaining tourists at hotels affects his playing: "One has to play the song the audience seems to appreciate. That is the difficulty in playing music for commercial purposes. One must satisfy the audience. The financial dimension is therefore very important. If one is not financially secure one would find it very difficult to have enough spare time to develop one's talent" (interview conducted by Mamma Kandeh, April 29, 1991).

Tamba Kandeh says, he plays after dinner when he is happy, and when he is invited to special occasions: "I play when children go to circumcision in the bush. When they are going, I use the fiddle. When they are coming back, I use the fiddle. When I collect people to go to the farm, I play the fiddle as they work. The fiddler follows them, and they are happy. I play at festivals [Ramadan, Tobaski, and Haran Deseh]. As Muslims walked to the mosque to pray, I would move with them. I would not play at the prayers, but just when they go to and from the prayers. When we had festivals to celebrate groundnut harvests, I would be invited."

Organization of the Ensemble and Performance Style

Prior to the 1960s, most fiddle ensembles consisted of a fiddler, a *tama* (an hourglass-shaped pressure drum played with a curved stick and hands) player, and a singer.[57] At present, the organization of a fiddle ensemble among the Fulbe in The Gambia is not set. A fiddler may play alone or be accompanied by calabash (*horde*), sistrum rattle (*lala*), or drums—the *tama*; the *djembe* (*djimbe, jimbeng*) a goblet-shaped drum played with hands; the *bawdi* (also referred to as *baudi*, pl. of *mbahgu*), a set of four cylindrical-shaped drums played with hands; or the *gedundung* (a water drum), a hemispherical calabash placed upside down in a large gourd filled with water.[58] Sometimes melodic and rhythmic instruments—e.g., fiddle, flute, calabash, sistrum, one or more drums—are combined in one ensemble. When women are included in the ensemble, they sing and provide rhythmic accompaniment with handclapping. If women are not used, men sing and play instruments. (See figs. 6.9–6.17.)

Many instruments included in a Gambian Fulbe fiddle ensemble are ones used by Fulbe throughout Sudanic Africa. In discussing Fulbe music in The Gambia, Knight (1980, 140–41) states:

> The instruments of the *awlu'be* are the *nyaanyooru*, a monochord bowed lute with a horsehair string on both the instrument and its bow; the *hoddu*, a three-string plucked lute similar to the Mandinka *konting* [and Wolof *halam* (*xalam*)]; the *bolon*, identical to the Mandinka *bolon* [arched harp]; and the *serndu*, a transverse flute. The instruments are played alone or in various combinations, with singing. One or two percussive instruments are generally included, the most common of which is the *horde*, a half-gourd percussion vessel with a metal rattling-plaque attached inside. The player holds the opening towards his chest and beats the outside with his palms and with rings on some of his fingers. Another percussive instrument is the *lala*, a pair of L-shaped stick-rattles, each with a sistrum with discs of calabash loosely skewered on one arm, while the other forms a handle.

Several Fulbe terms are used for the flute, which is usually made of bamboo with four to six holes. In addition to *serndu* (*sereendu*, *serendou*, *serdu*), other terms include *forrdu*, *chorumbal* (*tiorumba*), *tambing*,[59] *neffara*, *fulannu*, *poopiliwal*, and *wombere* (see fig. 6.19). While many researchers give no African term, most indicate that the flute is associated with herdsmen. In some societies, the flute is used as a court instrument.

Two types of plucked lutes[60] are associated with the Fulbe. The *hoddu* (*hodu*, *hordu*, *kerona*) has anywhere from one to five strings and is found among most Fulbe groups in Sudanic Africa.[61] The *molo* (*mpolaaru*, *gambra*, *jirkil*)[62] is always constructed with one string and more commonly associated with Fulbe in the Western Sudan and Voltaic clusters (DjeDje 1998). Yet in many parts of Senegambia, it is the Wolof who are associated with plucked lutes. Coolen (1982, 74) suggests that the Wolof may have adopted the lute from Fulbe groups (in Mali) that intermarried with the Mande (see discussion above). The Hausa in northern Nigeria and northern Cameroon are generally identified with lutes (several varieties are used). Erlmann (1983a, 23) states, "As for the three-stringed lute *moolooru*...its adoption by the Fulani is certainly as old as that of the horn *buusawru*."[63]

Most calabashes and rattles used by Fulbe groups in Sudanic Africa are similar

6.9 Ousman Barry performing the *horde*, a half-gourd percussion vessel, at the home of Tamba Kandeh. The *horde* is held near the chest. Photograph by Jacqueline Cogdell DjeDje, Lamin, The Gambia, August 23, 1990.

6.10 Ousman Barry performs acrobatic stunts as he also plays the *horde* at the home of Tamba Kandeh. Photograph by Jacqueline Cogdell DjeDje, Lamin, The Gambia, August 23, 1990.

6.11 Ebrima Barry performing a *lala* (sistrum rattle) at the home of Tamba Kandeh. Photograph by Jacqueline Cogdell DjeDje, Lamin, The Gambia, August 23, 1990.

6.12 Salif Badjie performing the *tama* at the home of Tamba Kandeh. Photograph by Jacqueline Cogdell DjeDje, Lamin, The Gambia, September 1, 1990.

6.13 A set of *bawdi*. Photograph by Jacqueline Cogdell DjeDje, Serrekunda, The Gambia, August 25, 1990.

6.14 Felli Jallow holding a *djembe* (*djimbe*) (Mande drum) in a side-view position. Photograph by Jacqueline Cogdell DjeDje, Lamin, The Gambia, August 23, 1990.

6.15 Felli Jallow performing a *djembe* (*djimbe*) Photograph by Jacqueline Cogdell DjeDje, Lamin, The Gambia, August 23, 1990.

6.16 Tamba's wife performing the *gedundung* (water drum). Photograph by Jacqueline Cogdell DjeDje, Lamin, The Gambia, August 23, 1990.

6.17 Juldeh Camara (*nyanyeru* player) and Salif Badjie (*tama* player) in performance at the home of Tamba Kandeh. Photograph by Jacqueline Cogdell DjeDje, Lamin, The Gambia, September 1, 1990.

to those described by Knight (1980, 140–41) in The Gambia. However, in some societies, the *horde* is not held near the chest (see fig. 6.9); rather, the *horde* player sits on the ground, places the inverted calabash between his legs and strikes it either with hands or sticks. Other instruments (e.g., musical bow, Jew's harp)[64] performed by the Fulbe are widespread among various ethnic groups throughout the continent (Arnott 1980, 25).

There have been significant changes in the performance of Fulbe fiddle music since the 1960s. Prior to The Gambia's independence, a fiddle ensemble was composed of at least two or three people who performed different roles. The fiddler, the leader of the ensemble, was responsible for performing only the fiddle melodies, while another person responded by singing. Generally, the person(s) who sang did not play a musical instrument. The *tama* player provided rhythmic accompaniment and, in some instances, joined in the choral response with the singers. Fiddlers who inherited the profession from kin were rarely taught how to fiddle and sing simultaneously. Mamadou Baldeh states, "Those who learn how to fiddle do not learn how to sing. When we are fiddling in groups, we have the women singing. Those who sing, normally those people cannot fiddle. The group goes like that."[65]

Since the mid-1960s, many *nyanyeru* players sing and perform the fiddle at the same time in performance. Most Gambians credit Ngeya's group and their performance at the country's independence celebration in February 1966 for the change in performance style. In addition to the fact that his group wore traditional Fulbe attire, Ngeya believes his group won the competition because of innovation; they decided to perform differently from other musicians in their area. In explaining the uniqueness of his group, Ngeya states:

> They [members of his group] all performed the same song at the same time. They all possessed the same sound in the fiddles. Secondly, whenever they moved backward or forward, their steps always came at the same time, like soldiers marching or policemen marching. When they were fiddling, they moved the stick [bow], they moved it forward always equal. When they sang and fiddled, their fiddle sound and song matched. No one led the other. Fourthly, when they were fiddling and when they sang, the ladies who sang after them, when the women started singing, they started and they stopped the same. Nobody led the other. So that's why we were picked as the traditional, we were picked to be the first champions. [Interview with the author, August 19, 1994]

Since making this innovation, Ngeya states that many fiddlers have begun to sing and fiddle simultaneously: "The population came to be high and they came to be champion over me." When asked why he decided to make changes, Ngeya gave the following response:

> The one who taught me, when he is fiddling, there was somebody singing. I learned how to fiddle while this man [my teacher] is fiddling. And secondly, I learned what the person is singing. I said to myself. "Look at this man singing. He cannot sing and fiddle at the same time." In my mind, I said, "This man can fiddle but cannot sing." Then I decide to take both to make myself popular and famous. I don't know about these places outside. But in The Gambia, I am the first person to sing and fiddle at the same time. I am the first person who learned that. [Interview with the author, August 19, 1994]

In modern times, the fiddle can be the lead or accompanying instrument in the ensemble because groups now include other melodic and rhythmic instruments. When a fiddler functions in the primary role, not only is he responsible for the sound, he plays an active role in all aspects of the performance event. As leader of the group and sole fiddler, he sings the lead vocal, plays the lead fiddle part and fiddle response, and is involved in movement. In instances when a fiddler in the primary role sits and performs with no accompaniment, his physical involvement in the performance is limited, except for the slight movement of the head, shoulders, and feet to the rhythm of the music. On occasions when a fiddler stands during a performance, he tends to shift the weight of his body from one foot to the other as he moves to the rhythm of the music. The sound from this movement and the movement itself help the fiddler to maintain the tempo as he improvises and develops his material, particularly when no accompanying percussion instruments are used.[66] In some cases, a fiddler may dance as he plays the fiddle, turning around to the rhythm of the music or performing small intricate steps with his feet. A fiddler's clothing is generally simple and not different from that of members of the audience. However, some fiddlers wear special costumes (see Camara in fig. 6.7).[67]

The fiddler who performs in a secondary role generally is an accompanying instrumentalist in the ensemble. Although the music that he performs tends to be less improvisatory when compared to that of the lead performer, there are moments during the performance when he may vary his fiddle part and performance style. Nevertheless, he is expected to complement and not overshadow the performance of the lead performer. For example, when Samba Bah performed for me, he was the sole fiddler but not the primary or master artist. The ensemble in which he performed included two melodic instruments (*chorumbal* and *nyanyeru*) and several rhythmic instruments (one *djembe*, one *lala*, and two *hordes*; see fig. 6.18).[68] The flute player performed the lead melodic parts and was the primary improviser. The fiddler and four percussionists all performed ostinato patterns with some variations. It is also noteworthy that the *lala* player served as vocalist (there was no choral response), and the administrative leader of the group was one of the *horde* players. Thus, the accompanying instrumentalists in a Fulbe fiddle ensemble not only help to establish the time line, but the interplay of parts with different timbres at various pitch levels provide rhythmic interest and a foundation upon which the lead performer improvises.

Since the 1960s when the Gambian government began to place greater emphasis on developing the tourist industry, more and more musicians have begun to perform at luxury hotels. As a result, a different performance style has evolved; performers feel they must do whatever necessary to entertain this "new" audience because a major part of their income comes from European tourists. At many hotel performances three or more songs (with each song extending anywhere from ten to twenty minutes) may be played at one event. While a few of the songs include text, several are entirely instrumental. One of the most interesting features of hotel performances is that considerably less emphasis is placed on singing, probably because the audience does not understand Fulfulde, but also because musicians know little about members of the audience to create praise songs. In addition, less singing allows each person in the group to showcase his other talents, which musicians believe are more appealing to this "new" audience. However, the movement and drama are not innovations. Fiddlers state that "magic" (acrobatics and fire-eating) has always been apart of their performances, even in the provinces. Mamadou Baldeh explains, "That [magic] even comes before fiddling. That's our magical systems. You did fire.

You cut your tongue with a blade, everything such like that. They come even before fiddling and before the tourists come in Africa. You can invite those people who do magic without the fiddle. Sometimes you can do the fiddling without those magics. Some people, if they are fiddling, would like to call these magicians to come to do some magic just to make the thing 'groovy.'"[69] Although fiddlers have always accompanied acrobats and fire-eaters, at present, the singing, which was an important feature of the fiddle tradition in earlier times because the singer responded to the fiddle, has given way to greater emphasis on movement and theater in this new context and environment (see fig. 6.18).

Similar to other aspects of Fulbe culture, the form of fiddle songs is not set. The feature that seems to be constant is the fiddle ostinato melody. Also, there is call and response between: (1) the fiddler and vocal chorus, (2) the vocal leader and vocal chorus, and (3) the lead fiddle part and fiddle response. Most of the music can be categorized as praise songs, but a variety of topics and themes may be used. Also, proverbs, social commentary, and historical events are often inserted with praises. Although fiddlers perform historical songs in honor of kings, warriors, and heroes,[70] there is no indication that there is a set, standard repertoire of melodies or texts for songs. Rather, fiddlers create their own compositions for various kings and heroes. Furthermore, when fiddlers perform songs that have been written and made popular by others, most indicate that they change the song and make it their own. For example, after Ngeya taught Tamba how to play "Tapa Tura" (a song that Ngeya composed during the mid-1960s and was popular during that period), Tamba states that he always changed the song whenever he performed it (interview with the author, August 19–20, 1999).

Most Fulbe fiddlers pride themselves on being able to compose their own songs, most of which are praise songs that include some social commentary. Camara states, "I compose my own songs. This is more creative and inspiring. To repeat what others have composed over and over again is not a demonstration of talent. The true musician must be able to compose his or her own songs." When asked what inspires him to compose, Camara (1991) indicates, "My mind is always in touch with my environment. 'Chemedo,' for example, was composed as I contemplated on the life of young women and their babies. Another composition was an appeal to the whole of Africa to stand firm and struggle for the betterment of the generation. My music talks about marriage, respect for others and other values which promote good human relation. I also have a song dedicated to the African youth. In that song I called on the youth to accept the responsibility of working for a better future" (interview conducted by Mamma Kandeh, April 29, 1991).

Conclusion

The fiddle tradition serves as a signifier of Fulbe identity in several ways. First of all, the Fulbe take great pride in distinguishing themselves from others; an important aspect of *pulaaku* is for the Fulbe to define their identity in relation to other peoples. In Gambian music culture, the fiddle is the primary instrument used to differentiate the Fulbe from other groups in the country,

6.18 Fulbe musicians in performance at the home of Tamba Kandeh. From left to right: Samba Jumba Bah (*nyanyeru*), Jangsawo Jallow (*horde* player and leader of the group), Ousman Barry (*horde*), Felli Jallow (*djembe, djimbe*), and Galleh Sanneh (*chorumbal*) at front center performing the flute while executing an acrobatic stunt. Photograph by Jacqueline Cogdell DjeDje, Lamin, The Gambia. August 23, 1990.

6.19 Galleh Sanneh performing a *chorumbal* (Fulbe flute) at the home of Tamba Kandeh. Photograph by Jacqueline Cogdell DjeDje, Lamin, The Gambia, August 23, 1990.

particularly the Mande and Wolof. Second, throughout their history, the Fulbe have absorbed other societies into their culture because of the delicate demographic balance that has existed in the areas where they have lived. In modern times, not only do Fulbe fiddlers refer to themselves as *jali nyanyeru* (combining the Mande term for musician with Fulfulde for fiddle), the Fulbe often use the Wolof term *riti* for the fiddle. Third, heterogeneity is one of the most essential characteristics of Fulbe identity. And fourth, Fulbe culture is and has always been dynamic. Not only are the third and fourth reasons interrelated, but these are the factors that have helped the Fulbe fiddle to survive in a modern and urban environment. A Fulbe fiddler's attempt to mold an identity that is distinct from other fiddlers results in change and re-creations. Historically, there has been very little standardization within the fiddle tradition. But even the little that has existed is giving way to more adaptation and flexibility. Not only is there not a set song repertoire that all fiddlers know or refer to, there is much variation in how they teach their craft. With modernization, anyone can learn to perform the fiddle for the profession is not limited to a particular family. The organization of a fiddle ensemble is not set; all types of instruments may be used. Also, there is great diversity in the way the music is performed. While some are able to sing and perform the fiddle simultaneously, many are not able to do both at the same time. The emphasis on individuality is seen in the creation of new compositions and performance practices. Also, new contexts and patrons have begun to be associated with the tradition, which allow for even greater creativity. The fact that themes related to the courage and bravery of warriors are included in song texts and sounds from the fiddle are identified with the heavens also provide evidence that the fiddle is associated with qualities (religion and militarism) that are important to the Fulbe.

Not only has this study on the Fulbe fiddle helped us to understand more clearly how intercultural and intracultural relations affect music making in The Gambia, it serves as a model for what occurs in other African societies. The fiddle represents the old and new; it signifies a tradition and people who are proud of their cultural heritage but also eager to adapt to modernity. The fiddle tradition continues to be dynamic as performance practices in modern urban areas inspire and lead to new innovations and creations. As most fiddlers indicate, the fiddle is a symbol of culture that makes the Fulbe happy.

Discography

Central Sudan

1951	*Fulahs: Territoires du Niger*. UNESCO-Al 55/70.
1956	*Musique du Nord-Cameroun: Peuples Kirdi et Foulbé*. Boîte à Musique-LD 331.
1961	*Music of the Cameroons*. Folkways-FE 4372.
1967	*Nomades du Niger: Musique des Touareg et des Bororo*. OCORA-OCR 29.
1976	*Music of the Peuls*. EMI-Odeon C064-18121 (UNESCO Collection Musical Atlas).
198?	*Music of the Cameroons: The Fulani of the North*. Lyrichord-LLST 7334.
n.d.	*Niger*. OCORA-SOR 5.

Voltaic

195?	*Au coeur du Soudan*. Chant du Monde-LD-S 8246.
1962	*Haute-Volta*. OCORA-SOR 10.
1965	*Afrique Noire. Panorama de la musique instrumentale*. Boîte à Musique-LD 409A.
1981	*Savannah Rhythms: Music of Upper Volta*. Nonesuch-H 72087.
1983	*Rhythms of the Grasslands: Music of Upper Volta, Volume II*. Nonesuch-H 72090.

Western Sudan

1961	*Sons nouveaux d'une nation nouvelle: La Republique de Guinée. Presentation Haute-Fidélité Les Rhythmes de l'Ouest Africain*. Tempo 7008.
1969	*African Rhythms and Instruments, Volume 1: Mali, Niger, Ghana, Nigeria, Volta, Senegal, Liberia*. Lyrichord-LLST 7328.
1971	*Le Mali du fleuve: Les Peuls*. Baerenreiter Musicaphon-BM 30 L 2502.
1975	*The Griots: Ministers of the Spoken Word*. Folkways-FE 4178.
1978	*African Flutes*. Folkways-FE 4230.
1979	*Sierra Leone: Traditional Music*. OCORA 558549.
1990	*Ancient Hearts: Mandinka and Fulani Music of The Gambia*. Axiom-Island Records 314-510 148-2.
1993	*Blues Masters. Vol. 10: Blues Roots*. Rhino-R2 71135.
n.d	*Chants et musique Peul: Chants et musique Maures*. Institut Francais d'Afrique Noire-IFAN 3-4.
n.d.	*Djungdjung* [Field Recordings from Mali]. Love Records-LRLP 12.

7. The *Luŋa* Drum as Social Mediator among the Dagbamba of Ghana

LEIGH CREIGHTON

In the study of musical texts, ethnomusicologists have chosen to focus primarily on song texts, since they are readily intelligible as language. Scholars frequently study the words and structures of these texts to illuminate both the musical tradition from which a song came and any cultural practices that are described or demonstrated in the song. In his landmark work *The Anthropology of Music*, Alan Merriam devotes an entire chapter to the study of song texts, analyzing them specifically as forms of "language behavior" (1964, 187). Discussing this emphasis on language rather than musical sound, Merriam states:

> We can say, then, that not only are music and language interrelated in the formation of song texts, but also that the language of texts tends to take special forms. Therefore we should expect that the language of texts would have special significance and would function in special ways.... One of the most striking examples is shown by the fact that in song the individual or the group can apparently express deep-seated feelings not permissibly verbalized in other contexts. [1964, 190]

Among the Dagbamba people of Ghana, musical texts often operate as Merriam describes—they enable communication that would not normally take place in verbal discussions. However, this phenomenon does not occur solely in song texts. Within the Dagbamba music culture, a wealth of cultural, historical, linguistic, and musical information is found in the texts performed by musical instruments such as drums, fiddles, and bells. Through direct imitations of the Dagbamba language (Dagbani), these instruments convey the same wide range of emotions and meanings in their texts as vocalists do in their songs. In this essay I will discuss the role of the Dagbamba *luŋa* drum as a social mediator that facilitates both the conveyance of cultural information to the community and the direct communication between musicians and Dagbamba chiefs—communication that does not occur in other social settings. An examination of *luŋa* texts reveals musical and linguistic techniques that make this type of communication preferable to the use of spoken words within the context of Dagbamba culture.

The Dagbamba, or Dagomba, people live in the savanna grasslands of northern Ghana. Like other cultures in the West African savanna belt, they are Islamic, although their adherence to strict Islamic practices is less rigorous than that of other regional groups such as the Hausa of Nigeria (DjeDje 1998, 451). In this area Islam has blended with Dagbamba traditional religion, resulting in a heterogeneous system of religious beliefs and practices. The Dagbamba maintain a traditional state within Ghana called Dagbon, which is governed by a hierarchical system of chiefs. The leader of Dagbon is the Paramount Chief (Yaa Naa), and senior members of the Yaa Naa's family serve as regional chiefs, each with their own delineated territories.

7.1. Alhaji Yakuba Alhassan, the now-deceased Tolon Naa, with his entourage at the Damba festival. He is flanked by one of his wives who acts as water bearer, protective riflemen, and a fan bearer. He is protected from the sun by the special umbrella used specifically for the Tolon Naa. In the left foreground, a quickly moving *luŋa* stick shows the proximity of drummers to the chief during this procession. Photograph by Leigh Creighton, Tolon, Ghana, September 6, 1993.

7.2. The Tolon Naa is seated with his entourage, including several of his wives, at another event during the Damba festival. Although not shown in this photograph, fiddlers and drummers are nearby. Photograph by Leigh Creighton, Tolon, Ghana, September 6, 1993.

In a treelike system of governmental branches, the regional chiefs preside over sub-chiefs who oversee smaller areas within each region. This traditional hierarchy ranges from the Yaa Naa himself to the local chiefs whose jurisdiction may only include one town or grouping of villages (Locke 1990, 10; Oppong 1973, 20–21).

Music in Dagbon is integrally connected to the traditional hierarchy of chiefs (figs. 7.1, 7.2). Two musical instruments in particular, the fiddle (*gondze*) and the *luŋa,* have long-standing historical ties with the chieftaincy. Although the *gondze* was adopted by the Dagbamba in the eighteenth century, Dagbamba oral history states that the *gondze* originated among the Gurma people of present-day Burkina Faso (DjeDje 1982, 121; DjeDje 1978, 113). As related by one informant, a Gurma man named Yantsebli was the first to play the *gondze*. During his musical training, he was also taught to cure madness. This ability eventually brought Yantsebli in contact with the chief of Gurma who had become insane. By providing the chief with medicines and playing the *gondze* for him, Yantsebli cured the chief. In gratitude the chief decided that *gondze* players would be granted a special status and would have the privilege of regularly waking the chief of Gurma from sleep by playing the *gondze*. During a visit to Gurma, the Yaa Naa of Dagbon, Naa Sigli, heard the music of the *gondze* being played for the chief. Enjoying the performance, Naa Sigli decided to bring a *gondze* player with him back to Dagbon to play for the Dagbamba chiefs (fig. 7.3), a musical practice that became tradition with the hereditary transmission of the *gondze* players' knowledge and duties from generation to generation (DjeDje 1978, 112–15).

The history of the *luŋa* in Dagbon has certain elements in common with the history of the *gondze*—both stories link the musical instruments to the traditional hierarchy at the inception of their use in Dagbon, and they also describe the hereditary nature of *luŋa* and *gondze* playing. Abubakari Lunna, the master Dagbamba musician with whom both David Locke and I have worked, has recounted the history of the *luŋa* to both of us (see fig. 7.5). This history is also the story of his own lineage, since *luŋa* players, or *lunsi*, "all trace their genealogy to Bizum, the first *luŋa* player in Dagbon and founder of the drummers' lineage" (Locke 1990, 11).[1]

Bizum was the son of Naa Nyaɣlsi, a Yaa Naa of Dagbon who reigned circa 1353. Since Bizum's mother was a lesser wife of Naa Nyaɣlsi, he was neglected within the Yaa Naa's household. In order to voice his unhappiness, Bizum began playing loud and entertaining rhythms on a calabash. This sound drew attention to the boy's needs and to his musical talents. Noticing Bizum's abilities, Naa Nyaɣlsi began taking considerable care of him, and in the process, he taught Bizum the history of the Dagbamba people and their chiefs. Upon reaching adulthood, Bizum was offered the position of Yaa Naa but refused it in order to continue gathering and preserving the history of the Dagbamba. This information, in the form of stories and genealogies, was later passed from Bizum to his son Lun'ʒheɣu who set the texts to music, eventually settling on the *luŋa* as the instrument of choice. Continuing the tradition, all *lunsi* since have passed these texts down to each new generation of drummers (Locke 1990, 11–12).[2]

Lunsi today have retained their important position as the cultural historians

and musicians to the chiefs of Dagbon. As they have for hundreds of years, "*lunsi* perform indispensable services for the chief on all state and politically significant occasions, as well as providing music for funerals and naming ceremonies" (Oppong 1973, 25). As I will elaborate below, the music of the *lunsi* functions in many ways; it is used in part to inform the community of historical facts and cultural morals as well as to entertain and to advise the chiefs regarding political policies.

The main reason why the *luŋa* as a musical instrument is so successful at fulfilling these social functions is its ability to closely represent language. In the story of Bizum, it is noted that his son set the historical texts he had gathered to music. Lun'ʒheɣu, however, did not immediately use the *luŋa*. As related by Abubakari Lunna, he originally played rhythms on a calabash, which did not generate the range of sounds necessary for this music. In trying to develop an instrument that would produce languagelike sounds, he tried to re-create the wooden hourglass-shaped drum he knew existed in Nigeria.

> In northern Nigeria [the people] had music, they had drums. Bizum's son had heard of them and he knew the style, but he didn't know how to carve the drum. So they used clay. When they used clay, the clay sounded, but it didn't give vibrations and dialogue.... If you see our *luŋa*s, the carving is different than in Nigeria, you see. So they used their own techniques to carve the *luŋa*.... When they carved it, they used skins to cover it. Before they used skins, they tried different animal skins, and it didn't sound good. So they used goatskin. And then they felt that goatskin was thicker and tight enough so that when you hit it, it wouldn't tear and that it could also make the correct sound. Then, they were able to talk with the drum, and when they got to that point, they started putting the talk into the music.[3]

The instrument they developed, the *luŋa* (fig. 7.4), is termed an hourglass-shaped tension drum by scholars, but it is commonly referred to as a "talking drum." This more popular term brings with it many misconceptions about both this type of instrument and the nature of various African musical traditions. First of all, many cultures in West Africa and

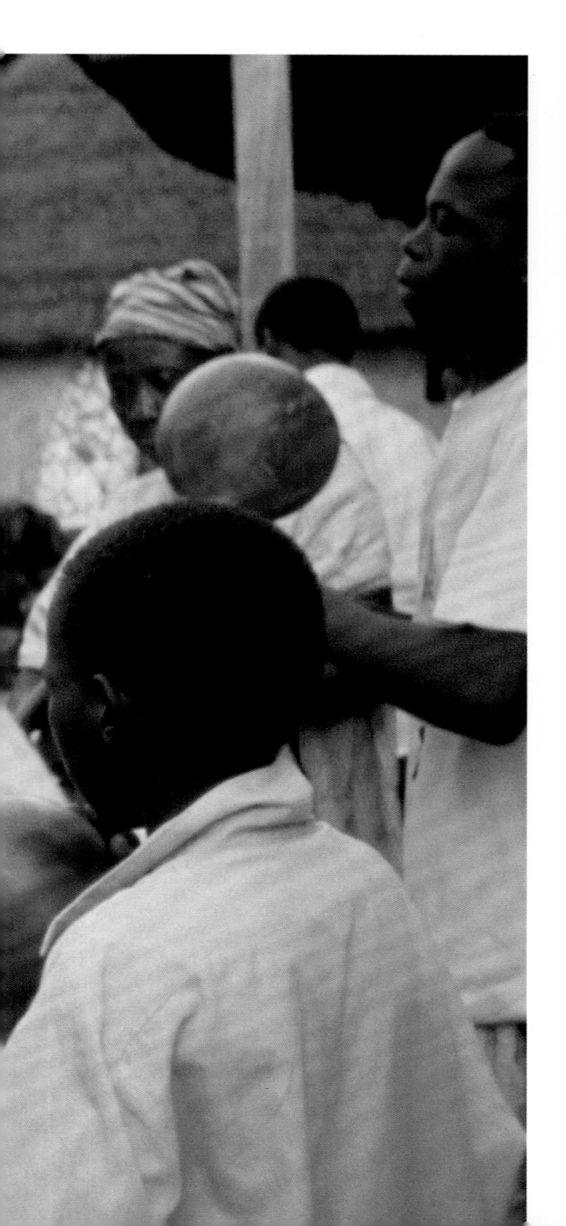

7.3. Well-dressed for the Damba festival celebration, a Dagbamba man dances as a *gondze* ensemble plays for him. The round calabashes have seeds inside and are used as rattles. The bow of the *gondze* itself can be seen to the left. Photograph by Leigh Creighton, Tolon, Ghana, September 6, 1993.

7.4. Carved wooden *luŋa* shells drying in the sun after being treated for insects by Abubakari Lunna. Photograph by Leigh Creighton, Tamale, Ghana, October, 1993.

elsewhere utilize very different hourglass-shaped tension drums. Due to their common hourglass shape, these drums are all lumped into the category of "talking drums." The construction of these drums in different cultures varies widely, however, and as a result, each type of so-called "talking drum" reproduces speech very differently, if at all. A second, but related, point is that among the Dagbamba and other cultures, many different types of instruments "speak." As mentioned above, the Dagbamba have bells, fiddles, and multiple drums that can produce language through their musical sounds. Among the different types of "talking drums" and among the various types of "talking" instruments, therefore, many types of speech representation exist. Having established this, I will focus solely on the specific manner in which the *luŋa* imitates spoken language and how that method enables types of communication unheard of in other contexts (fig. 7.5).

The construction of the *luŋa* itself is crucial to the drum's ability to imitate language. The carved shell of the drum (see fig. 7.4) is fitted with goatskin on both ends, and ropes, often made of bush antelope skin, run between the drum skins to keep them attached and to produce tension between them. Interestingly the Dagbamba call the two *luŋa* skins the "faces" of the drum in part because the drum speaks. As a result, it is forbidden to place the drum with the skin side on the ground—putting the *luŋa* on its "face" would be an insult to the drum itself. Instead, the *luŋa* is always placed on its side, resting on the rims so that the wooden shell is parallel to the ground. The drum is worn under the arm, allowing the musician to squeeze or release the ropes, resulting in the production of a higher or lower pitch, respectively. This ingenious construction allows musicians to play a wide range of pitches and nuanced inflections on the *luŋa* through the subtle tightening and loosening of the ropes. The sounding of the *luŋa* comes from the musician beating or stroking the drum with a curved wooden stick (see figs. 7.5, 7.6). When they are initially carved, these sticks are straight. They are later boiled to soften the wood and are bent at a sharp angle. A string is then attached to maintain the correct shape of the stick. Special techniques of hitting the *luŋa* with the curved stick expand the expressiveness of the instrument. Drum rolls can be played on the *luŋa* by bouncing the stick against the drum head to make a buzzing sound. Grace notes are produced by lightly hitting the drum head shortly before playing a louder note. Press strokes on the *luŋa* are played by pressing the stick at an angle on the drum head (Locke 1990, 40). These techniques are all very complex and difficult. Only extremely skillful players can successfully tap the potential of the *luŋa* for expressively reproducing language (fig. 7.6).

Musicians do not play random pitches on the *luŋa*. If they want to correctly speak Dagbani or other languages on the drum, they are required to follow the tonal patterns defined by the languages themselves. Most *luŋa* texts are a mixture of regional languages, primarily containing Dagbani and Hausa, a language spoken by the Hausa people of northern Nigeria. Both of these languages are tonal, meaning that words are identified not only by spelling and pronunciation but also by the specific tones associated with each one. The *luŋa* is conducive for playing tonal languages since it is built to produce a very fluid range of tones. Three main tones—a low-pitched, mid-pitched, and a high-pitched tone—are

played on the *luŋa*, however, thus narrowing the flexibility a musician has when playing musical texts (Locke 1990, 39). The *luŋa*'s potential for fluidity is utilized not in playing different tones with each drum stroke but in the types of pitch bending and glissandi (sliding between pitches) that occur between strokes, making the drumming sound more like speech. No studies have yet been conducted examining the exact relationship between *luŋa* texts and the languages they reproduce. This type of study would be useful for understanding the linguistic similarities and differences between these spoken and drummed languages.

Turning from issues of linguistics to musical organization, the settings in which the *luŋa* performs vary. In some cases the *luŋa* is played by itself to communicate a single line of text. For example, when his daughter Aliatou was born, Abubakari Lunna announced the good news to the community on his *luŋa*. The sound of the drum carried far enough so that when he later went to the nearby city of Tamale, everyone had already heard about the birth. The *luŋa*, however, is more commonly played in an ensemble setting. Within an ensemble, two instruments are used: the *luŋa* and the *guŋ goŋ* (figs. 7.5, 7.7).

The *guŋ goŋ* is a drum that has a hollowed-out tree trunk for its shell. Skins are attached to the shell on either side, and a single snare (*chahira*) runs along the top portion of both skins. An ensemble of these two instruments is often broken into four parts: the lead *luŋa*, the supporting *lunsi*, the lead *guŋ goŋ*, and the supporting *guŋ goŋ*s. Unlike the lead parts, both supporting parts are collectively played by multiple musicians. Therefore, most members of any ensemble play supporting parts (see fig. 7.6). Importantly, it is not only the *luŋa* that reproduces language through music; the music played by the *guŋ goŋ* is also imitative of speech. Of the four parts in the ensemble, that of the lead *luŋa* is most important since the musician playing this part is the one who chooses which music will be played and when. The lead *luŋa* player directs the program of a performance and, in turn, the information that is communicated through the music. Additionally, the lead *luŋa* part is arranged in order to leave the musician space for personal expression within the theme of the music and the text being played. This

7.5. Abubakari Lunna, shown here wearing blue in the foreground, and another musician play the *luŋa* accompanied by a *guŋ goŋ* player. Photograph by Chris Provenzano, Tolon, Ghana, July, 1994.

7.6. *Lunsi* of all ages gather to play for the Damba festival celebration. Photograph by Chris Provenzano, Tolon, Ghana, July, 1994.

freedom of the lead *luŋa* player facilitates the type of communication that I will discuss below: the expression of sentiments that are not orally conveyed from musician to chief in the course of normal daily life.

Many of the photographs illustrating this essay show musicians playing at an event called the Damba festival. This event provides a good example of the type of setting in which a *luŋa* and *guŋ goŋ* ensemble would play, the arrangement of their performance, and the functions of their music. The Damba festival is a yearly event held both in commemoration of the birth of the prophet Muhammad and in celebration of the Dagbamba traditional hierarchy of chiefs. In Dagbon, celebrations of this event occur separately in each village and town with the entire population from the area gathering to honor their regional chief. Music is an essential element of the Damba festival since it entertains the crowd, provides a setting for dancing, and imparts important information through the drummed texts, such as cultural history and praise for the chief (fig. 7.8).

The physical organization of a public musical event at the Damba festival facilitates both the entertainment and the educational elements of the music. The *luŋa* and *guŋ goŋ* players gather loosely in an open space designated for the event. Adjacent to this space is the seating area designated for the chief, his entourage, and other important community members, such as sub-chiefs. The majority of the crowd forms a ring around the perimeter of the open space. As music is played, one observer at a time enters the open space to dance (see fig. 7.8). At times, the lead *luŋa* player invites a particular person to dance by gesturing and by playing music specifically appropriate to the person, such as a genealogical history of his or her family. Inviting the chief to dance, the lead *luŋa* player might play a rhythm in praise of him or in praise of his ancestors. Among those gathered for the festival, not all will understand the entirety of the texts played on the *luŋa* and *guŋ goŋ* or appreciate their full complexity. Most observers, however, will be able at least to recognize the general topics of each musical piece. It is evident that chiefs and possibly other people of high status in Dagbon have a greater knowledge of the drum language played on the *luŋa*, in particular, and would thus absorb more detailed information from a musical performance than would others. For those with political power, such as the chiefs, this understanding is crucial since it is often to them that musicians will address their music, playing topical themes relevant to the chief's success or failure. Through this musical channel, chiefs can gain feedback from musicians regarding their political position and activities. The fact that this type of feedback is communicated not orally but musically from musician to chief during an event like the Damba festival actually increases its potential as effective advice. By using specific linguistic devices and patterns of speech that are played on the *luŋa*, a musician can make his opinions known in a way that is culturally appropriate and palatable to the chief.

A common genre of texted music played by the *luŋa* and *guŋ goŋ* ensemble is called "praise name music," or "praise name dances" (*salima*). Within a specific musical piece, the lead *luŋa* player will vary his playing to include a range of texts that fit that music; these include praise names. The texts played in praise name

music honor particular figures of Dagbamba history such as chiefs and warriors and contain a great deal of cultural information. For example, the text of a praise name will sometimes include a historical account of the exploits of the person being praised and will discuss the moral outcome of events. Within the musical piece *Damba Sochandi*, played specifically during the Damba festival, musicians often include praise name music to honor certain chiefs. The praise for Yaa Naa Abudulai (r. 1845–1866) played on the *luŋa* relates that: "the millet grain spread on the floor for threshing can never be completely gathered up, some will remain for the ants" (Locke 1990, 12, 129). As interpreted by Abubakari Lunna, who played the passage during a performance in 1976, this statement explains that "if a person dies, his family will inherit his possessions," probably referring to an event in Yaa Naa Abudulai's life (Locke 1990, 129). Some chiefs have special pieces of music that are solely intended as their praise name music. The piece called *Zim Taai Kulga* is a praise name for the chief Naa Alhassan (r. 1899–1918). A part of the text states "'There are many fish in the river, yet they cannot be caught,' [meaning] 'Jealous rivals cannot defeat you' " (Locke 1990, 52). This may refer to the power of Naa Alhassan in overcoming his enemies.

The musical texts of these two praise names contain many levels of Dagbamba cultural information. Historically the texts both refer to particular events and describe important chiefs. Morally they can be interpreted as advice for those listening—especially since their somewhat vague nature allows for multiple interpretations. The text of Yaa Naa Abudulai's praise name music could be interpreted as "one cannot horde his possessions forever, they will eventually go to his descendants"; this could be understood as a message of warning to the possessor, or a message of hope to his family. Similarly the praise for Naa Alhassan, seemingly more straightforward, may be advice to either an undefeated and powerful person or to the jealous rivals who cannot succeed. In both of these cases, a particularly important type of linguistic device has been employed to express information: the proverb. Describing the use of proverbs

7.7. A portion of a *luŋa* and *guŋ goŋ* ensemble with friends. Photograph by Leigh Creighton, Tamale, Ghana, October, 1993.

7.8. *Lunsi* of all ages play for a twirling dancer at the Damba festival. Photograph by Doran Ross, Yende, Ghana, 1976.

among the Akan people of Ghana, Kwesi Yankah notes that these figures of speech "embrace moral-embedded extended metaphors, illustrative anecdotes, and parables, when these are used to drive home a moral in an on-going interaction" (Yankah 1989, 88). This statement applies equally well to Dagbamba proverbs, as they use stories drawn from the past to provide guidelines for moral behavior in modern Dagbon.

Placing these proverbs back into the cultural context of a musical performance, it is possible to examine how musical instruments are used to facilitate communication. The two praise name texts related above could be performed in the context of an event such as the Damba festival. In this setting, the lead *luŋa* player could deliberately choose to play one of these praise names in order to give a piece of advice to the chief. If the chief was very wealthy but governed over a poor region, the *luŋa* player could play the praise name music for Yaa Naa Abudulai to express the concept that greed is bad and to urge the chief to share his wealth. This moral judgment could never be expressed orally by a musician to a chief during a public festival, but with the *luŋa* player's choice of praise name music, he has the ability to advise the chief on potentially sensitive matters.

Since moral advice that is communicated orally and that played by the *luŋa* are both forms of language, one may wonder why the musical version is acceptable to Dagbamba chiefs and to the musicians who advise them. At a very basic level, communication of this musical type is the accepted cultural practice in Dagbon. In addition, however, there are elements of expression embedded in this communication that make it logically appropriate within this context. In the hypothetical example of the greedy chief, the original proverb in the praise name music could be played to suggest wrongdoing obliquely. As in Akan proverbs, this type of *luŋa* text sometimes contains political innuendo, which implies but does not specify the negative activity being undertaken (Yankah 1989, 94–95). As Yankah notes: "Such devices…touch on themes of sociocultural delicacy that may otherwise offend dignified audiences in a public forum. In this case, it is the trope's obliqueness that the speaker [here, the drummer] may count on" (Yankah 1995, 56–57). The use of innuendo couched within a proverb produces a double layer of protection against the harsh nature of the criticism.

The use of proverbs in praise name music not only softens potentially sensitive topics for the chief's ears, it also gives musicians—*luŋa* players in particular—greater freedom of expression by protecting them from possible negative repercussions. As Yankah explains, "such uses of proverb… agree with the general tendency to protect the vulnerability of face in formal discourse. In this case…the [drummer] avoids responsibility for any potentially damaging interpretation, since he may plausibly disclaim an offensive intent (Yankah 1995, 57). Termed "facework" by Erving Goffman, this type of self-protection through the use of oblique proverbs is effective in freeing the musician to function as chiefly advisor without feeling personally at risk of retaliation for any negative comments made (Goffman 1967, 12).

The methods described above for facilitating smooth communication between advisor (*luŋa* player) and advisee (chief) utilize language effectively toward this end. However, within the context of Dagbamba music culture, the most important method of facilitation remains: it is the *luŋa* that "speaks" advice to the chief, not a person.

7.9, 7.10. *Gondze* players at the Damba festival. Photographs by Doran H. Ross, Yende, Ghana, 1976.

When the *luŋa* player chooses which general piece of music to play and the individual praise names within that piece, it is he who develops the nature of the advice for the chief, but it is the *luŋa* that articulates it. In this case, the indirection of speech—similar to the obliqueness of proverbs—is made possible by the *luŋa*, which mediates the communication between the musician and the chief (Yankah 1995, 52). The role of the *luŋa* as social and verbal mediator has certain interesting parallels with the position of the linguist found in Akan and Dagbamba cultures, among others. The inadequate term "linguist" (see Yankah 1989, 83–84) has been used to describe the "liaison between the chief and the chief's addressees" (Yankah 1989, 84). At least among the Akan, the position of linguist (*ɔkyeame*) is extremely multifaceted. As a high-ranking social mediator, the *ɔkyeame* needs to be well versed in the politics of the region, cultural etiquette, and most importantly, in skills of oratory (Yankah 1995). Similarly, the *luŋa* itself "translates" the advisory words of the drummer into a culturally acceptable medium through the creative use of words and musical sound.

Both the linguist and the *luŋa* are intermediaries between people, and as such they provide a barrier of protection for each party against the other's harsh words or actions. Additionally, the types of language utilized by the linguist and the *luŋa* are special. The job of the linguist is to embellish the words spoken to the chief in order to make them more pleasing and palatable when he eventually hears them (Yankah 1989, 84). Similarly the *luna* has its own vocabulary, which has accumulated during the hundreds of years of its use. Therefore, it functions by taking the advisory ideas of the musician and placing them into words having a historical and cultural relevance, making them even more applicable and interesting to the chief. Both examples of speech—that crafted by the linguist and by the *luŋa*—are forms of art; the linguist embellishes words with other words, and the *luŋa* utilizes both the embellishments of words and music to create a socially acceptable and pleasing form of communication.

Musical instruments in Dagbon, the *luŋa* in particular, function as mediators on many levels. When they are played, these instruments facilitate the connections made between language and music, drummers and chiefs, and between all members of Dagbamba culture. By constructing their music culture in this way—designing and using instruments that can successfully represent language—the Dagbamba have developed a type of musically-mediated communication that fits the social and aesthetic needs of the community. Socially, the *luŋa* player fulfills his role as advisor to the chief through musically and linguistically indirect interaction. Aesthetically, the stories of historical figures, events, and cultural morality played primarily on the *luŋa* make the underlying advice and social commentary interesting. Equally important, however, is the musical aesthetic that is expressed in this context. Music facilitates communication through entertainment—not only between the drummers and chiefs, but among all members of the culture. By providing a context of entertainment meeting the aesthetic criteria of the culture, this music brings people together and gives them an opportunity for interaction. In the midst of this discussion on the *luŋa* as social mediator, it is important not to forget the power of the music itself as part of this mediation process and as a meaningful part of the Dagbamba aesthetic.

7.11. A *luŋa* constructed by Abubakari Lunna from one of the shells shown in figure 7.4. The green scarf shown here, which is used to fasten the drum around a drummer's shoulder, is a winter scarf as might be worn in the United States. Private Collection.

8. Make Army Tanks for War into Church Bells for Peace:

Observations on Musical Change and Other Adaptations in Ethiopia during the 1990s

CYNTHIA TSE KIMBERLIN

Background

Economic and sociopolitical upheaval occurring in Ethiopia beginning in the 1960s and continuing until the early 1990s, profoundly affected music along with its performance, marketing, and distribution. At the same time, scholars conducting field research planned their research strategies to accommodate governmental restrictions on travel; and their plans were often further complicated by uncertainties associated with political instability. My research for this article is based on material gathered in Addis Ababa and environs and in northern Ethiopia in 1972 and during two subsequent field trips: to Addis Ababa nineteen years later in May 1991, just before the abdication of Mengistu Haile Mariam in May, and to Regions One, Two, Three and Fourteen[1] during Ethiopia's first democratic local and regional elections in June 1992. In contrast to my earlier trip, the last two were not the result of long-term planning but of serendipitous invitations.

The changes that have taken place in Ethiopia are perhaps best understood by beginning with a brief overview of its gradual transformation from a dictatorship to a more democratic form of governance. In the 1960s university students witnessed the appalling living conditions of peasants residing in rural areas. Their subsequent protest of this inequity set the stage for the Ethiopian Revolution (1974–1991) beginning with the overthrow of Emperor Haile Selassie who had reigned for forty years. A provisional military government took over, and Lieutenant Colonel Mengistu Haile Mariam assumed full power as the military dictator of Ethiopia in 1977. In 1984 a Marxist-Leninist regime was established with Mengistu at the helm. Ultimately, however, withdrawal of support due to the collapse of communism in Eastern Europe and the Soviet Union led to his downfall. A rebel offensive began to grow and forced Mengistu to flee in 1991. Today, Ethiopia's government is undergoing reorganization and laying the foundation for a more democratic system. Some observations on the impact that war and political unrest have had on music in Ethiopia from approximately 1972 to 1992 form the basis of this essay.

Although Mengistu was technically still in power in May 1991, he had already lost the confidence of the people and was referred to by individual citizens not by his name but disparagingly as "that man." Before June 1991 travel within Ethiopia was severely restricted due to political uncertainty. But my trip to Ethiopia a year later in 1992 proved quite different coming as it did during the first local and regional democratic election proceedings. Two hundred and fifty observers from twenty-three countries and ten international organizations were invited to witness this historic event (National Democratic Institute for International Affairs 1992,100).

Since travel was relatively easy for election observers, some, including myself, chose to conduct research that related to their own interests in conjunction with their official responsibilities. In many cases, this research provided valuable background material relating to the election process itself. Visiting a number of locales over a one-month period helped me to understand the circumstances that had engendered the many changes that had occurred since my field trip of 1972. The locations I elected to visit with a Dutch colleague included Addis Ababa, Dessie, Debra Berhan, Makelle, Wokro, Adi Grat, Zala Ambassa, Inticho, Adua, Axum, Ende Selassie, Shilaro, Seleklaka, Hawzien, Abiy Adi, Maychew, Korem, Alamata, Waja, and Kobe.

Because of the long-imposed travel restrictions (1974–May 1991) Ethiopians had come to regard anyone from outside their own region as a foreigner. In the small towns of Region One where most Ethiopians only saw individuals from other countries via the media, their perception of outsiders was shaped by movies, videos, and posters, as well as by hearsay. As an American of Asian descent traveling with a Dutch male colleague, I was therefore to experience some unusual reactions. We were thought to be at various times English, Italian, German, Russian, Japanese, and Chinese. We were even given the names of popular stars of martial arts films. My colleague was referred to as "Chuck Norris," and I was addressed as "Bruce Lee" (Norris and Hyams 1988; Lee 1991).[2] Because I am female, Bruce Lee (pronounced "Bru-sah Lee" by Ethiopians) was sometimes altered to Rosa Lee (pronounced "Ro-sah Lee").

Music and the Collective Spirit

The political and cultural environment during Mengistu's regime created a situation whereby individuals and groups learned to respond to certain questions using formulas or sloganistic jargon. Often these slogans were sung rather than spoken, as I was to witness in Shilaro, a town with a population of over four thousand inhabitants. Group singing with accompanying musical instruments could be more easily heard in a crowd, and more easily recalled than speech. Shilaro has a very active and vocal women's association. At one of their meetings in response to a question concerning prospects for the future of Ethiopian women, about fifty members responded simultaneously by bursting into song. It was as if the question itself gave them the cue for the appropriate response. Although it was often frustrating as an observer to receive a response in the form of a sung slogan, it was interesting to note that through the medium of song, older women advised their younger female counterparts on the best way "to fight against the reactionary period of Mengistu and Haile Selassie and to avoid a return to the Dark Ages." It was only in the more remote town of Abiy Adi that I observed an administrator who did not answer questions with prepared slogans (National Democratic Institute for International Affairs 1992, 140). When I visited Ethiopia in 1972, solo musical performance was prevalent. In my more recent visits, however, group rather than solo music performance was normal practice throughout northern and central Ethiopia. These musical performances seemed to symbolize Ethiopia's collective spirit in supporting political reforms between 1974 and 1991. In fact, when questions were posed to special interest groups regarding the upcoming elections, they often responded en masse with slogans in song using a "call-and-response" format.[3]

Music was used to support the entire election process in 1992, although not to endorse particular candidates, according to a candidate whom I interviewed in Axum. In Ende Selassie, the chair of the election committee, who had been a freedom fighter for fourteen years up until 1989, told me that general election slogans were presented in song and dance. On election day in Makelle, there was drumming with lyre accompaniment and singing throughout the evening of the day before the elections and continuing throughout election day; it was used as a way of mobilizing people to vote. Candidate lists along with their respective symbols were posted on the sides of the truck transporting the musicians.

Despite emphasis on group musical performance, one could occasionally witness a solo performance. I saw a lone musician carrying an Amhara-style bowed lute, or *masinqo*, walking on the road from Shilaro toward Adi Daro. I also saw a Tigre lyre, or *krar*, player performing in a bar in Maychew. I suspect the solo tradition of reporting the daily news via song with instrumental accompaniment never completely died out. With the new government, solo music is regaining its former prominence.

Visual images and words printed on clothing served as another means of reinforcing group identity. It was relatively easy to spot members of the Tigrayan People's Liberation Front (TPLF)[4] because they all wore the same genre of T-shirt. The T-shirts seen in 1992 in Tigre-speaking areas such as Axum, Shilaro, Seleklaka, and Kobe incorporated images and logos associated with American and European rock and heavy metal bands including Guns N' Roses, Metallica, U2, Poison, Alice Cooper, Boss, Iron Maiden, Bon Jovi, Dread, Rolling Stones, and Fido Dido Dancing. To my knowledge no member of another political party in Tigray wore this type of T-shirt (fig. 8.1).[5] I questioned an Ethiopian restaurant owner—a man in his fifties who travels between Ethiopia and the United States—about this phenomenon. He stated that a shipment of T-shirts was probably sent from the United States by TPLF contacts and sympathizers as a show of solidarity. Interestingly, the majority of those wearing these T-shirts could not identify the symbols and images printed on them.

8.1 Three members of the Tigrayan People's Liberation Front (TPLF) wearing the music T-shirts that are used to indicate their political party affiliation. The T-shirts feature the groups U-2, Bon Jovi, and Guns N' Roses. The woman on the far right wears the Guns N' Roses T-shirt with slacks. She also wears her hair in an Afro, a hairstyle characteristic of women freedom fighters. Photograph by Cynthia Tse Kimberlin, Axum, 1991.

Censorship and the Distribution of Music

Under Mengistu, censorship of speech and music was imposed as part of overall repressive policies. Some types of traditional Ethiopian music were banned in public, such as traditional love songs. Songs singing the praises of the former Emperor Haile Selassie were forbidden in public as well as on radio and television. Also forbidden was a well-known symbol of Ethiopia that has long been associated with religious worship and meditation: the *bägänna* (also *bagana*), the ten-string plucked lyre reputed to be descended from the biblical David's harp. The *bägänna* is linked with biblical and religious songs although the instrument itself is never played inside the church (Kimberlin 1978, 20). Between 1974 and April of 1991, religious worship and the performance of songs by solo vocalists accompanied by a *bägänna* were forbidden in public and in the media. Around 1978 *bägänna* music and songs associated with this instrument were dropped from the curriculum of the Yared Music School, at that time the only officially recognized music school in the country. The Ethiopian Orthodox Christian Church and *bägänna* music never actually disappeared, however; they just went underground. The ban on religious worship was finally lifted in April 1991 the day before Easter Sunday. Now the *bägänna* and religious music including ritual dances and chanting are again performed in public as witnessed by overflowing attendance at churches throughout Ethiopia on Easter Sunday.

Despite censorship Ethiopian musicians were often able to broach sensitive and forbidden subjects through cleverly and skillfully concealing the true meanings of words and phrases. For instance, *bägänna* players may compose their own texts using the *qəne*-form which consists of couplets containing a surface meaning, known as "wax," and a deeper, or concealed, meaning known as "gold." For example, the "gold," or concealed meaning of the words "We thought Death will learn how to read. Let alone reading, he is still studying the alphabet" is: "He is killing and carrying everybody to the grave" (*Amariñña Qəne* 1958, 119, no. 167). Throughout history, musicians in their capacity as "entertainers" and "performers" have often been spared from close scrutiny. Using the medium of music and song, a performer is often able to "discuss" personal, familial, community, and national concerns more freely than with speech.

During the period of censorship between 1974 and 1991, successful black market and counterfeit tape industries sprung up and thrived. In Addis Ababa alone there were hundreds of "shops" in the commercial sector specializing in these counterfeit and black-market tapes. An even greater number were concentrated in the Marcato, believed to be the largest open-air market in East Africa. Further north in Makelle, one could also purchase a wide selection of pirated tapes. For between three and four U.S. dollars, customers could obtain a dubbed copy of a tape in about five minutes with the title and artist's name handwritten on the cover (fig. 8.2). However, the original cover with a photograph of the artist and the liner notes was usually only to be had when purchasing an authentic tape (fig. 8.3a,b).[6] Dubbed and pirated tapes with no consideration for copyright regulations appeared to be the norm rather than the exception.

In Makelle, I was to find the very popular Mozart Music Shop. Other than his name, however, there was no further reference to Wolfgang Amadeus Mozart or his music in any guise or form. Proprietor Daniel Berhane's calling card bears his name, phone number, and telex address in Amharic and in English. Daniel relates that to him "Mozart" means "good music," and he enthusiastically employed this concept with the intention of increasing sales despite the fact that most Ethiopians are unaware of who Mozart actually was. In the Mozart Music Shop, Ethiopian popular music was well represented, especially music performed by highly regarded vocalists accompanied for the most part by Western instruments and synthesizer. Popular solo vocalists who accompanied themselves on Ethiopian traditional instruments were also present to an extent. If customers specifically requested artists known for their renderings of traditional songs, particularly love songs, or if a customer requested a recording of a religious chant of the Ethiopian Orthodox Christian Church, a music store owner might keep these musics in stock, but up until 1991 they would not be openly displayed at the front of the store or placed in any of the display cases.

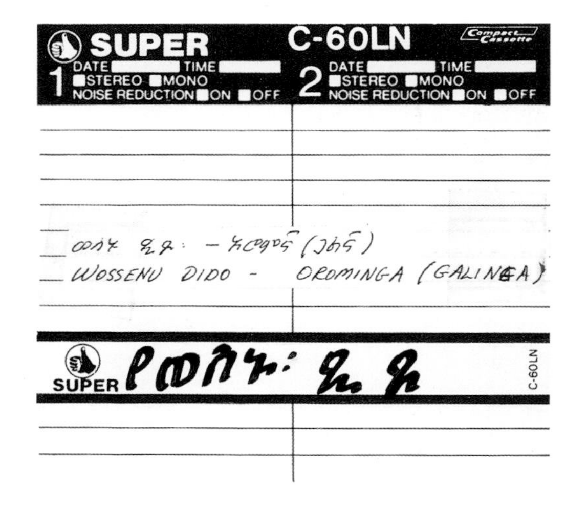

8.2 This paper cover belongs to a dubbed cassette tape purchased at the Marcato. The title and the artist's name have been handwritten.

አጃቢ ዝነኛው ሮሃ ባንድ በጅቡቲ

የአዲዲስ ዘፈኖች ግጥምና ዜማ ደራሲ አበበ መለሰ

-ሀ-	-ለ-
1 እንደምነሽ የሀገር ልጅ	1 ጣል ጣል አታርጊኝ
2 እረ እንደምን አለሽ ?	2 ሰበቤ ነሽ
3 ሞት አይላድሉኝ	3 የስላሴዋ
4 ካላጣሽው አካል	4 ፍቅር ያለበት
5 ጋራ ሥር ነው ቤትሽ	5 እያዩ ነው ሸጋ
	6 ስንብት

Graphic Printers

8.3a,b This paper cover accompanied an original (legally manufactured) tape purchased from a music shop in Makelle. It includes a color photograph of the artist, the artist's name, and a list of featured songs on the reverse side.

Recycling and Musical Instrument Construction: From Army Tank to Church Bell

Throughout the war years, the Ethiopian penchant for not throwing anything away was given full reign. Out of necessity, individuals appropriated discarded objects often for uses other than they were intended. Thus, ammunition boxes were converted to book satchels, artillery shells made into pots and pans, and other military equipment used as furniture. At present Ethiopia does not have the money, equipment, or industrial base to "recycle" abandoned tanks and other weapons of war into peacetime use on a large scale. On a small scale, however, I found one very interesting example of reuse in the town of Wokro. Here a traditional musical instrument associated with the Ethiopian Orthodox Christian Church was made from abandoned army tank components (a T-34, T-54 or T-55 model produced in the former Soviet Union). Six hundred of these tanks were used in Ethiopia during the 1970s and 1980s (Nelson and Kaplan 1981, 265–66, 312). Components from one or more of these tanks were adapted and reused to form the three-piece gong ensemble employed by the Ethiopian Orthodox Christian Church to function as church bells marking the beginning of the service and other notable events (fig. 8.4). In addition to church bells made from Russian tank parts, a church in the town of Seleklaka also possessed a traditional lithophone set of three church bells made out of smooth, thin, shaped stones. Like the army tank components, this stone ensemble was placed outside near the church itself (fig. 8.5). Both the metal and stone sets of "bells" were struck by the acolyte in the appropriate place using a round stone the size of a small potato.[7]

8.4 Ethiopian Orthodox Christian Church bells made from Soviet tank components. Photograph by Cynthia Tse Kimberlin, Wokro, 1991.

8.5 Lithophone set consisting of three church bells made out of the traditional, thin, shaped stones. Photograph by Cynthia Tse Kimberlin, Seleklaka, 1991.

Musical Instruments as Ballot Symbols

If a nonmusical object such as an army tank could be adapted and used in a musical context, might musical objects also be adapted for nonmusical use? On the occasion of the first democratic elections held throughout Ethiopia on June 21, 1992, the election ballots included a set of pictorial symbols intended to help nonliterate voters identify specific candidates. If voters were unable to read the candidate's signature, they were given two other options: a photograph of the candidate or a pictorial symbol chosen by the candidate from an approved list.[8] The photograph was not placed on the voting ballot itself but affixed to a poster bearing an enlarged version of the ballot together with the facsimile of the candidate's signature and symbol. The ballot posters were placed on bulletin boards or building facades. In many cases, black-and-white photographs proved too expensive to produce and the pictorial symbols were used alone.

Out of forty pictorial symbols available to the candidates—twenty at the *wärada*, or county, level and another twenty at the *kəlɘl*, or regional, level—there were four musical instruments. They were the *krar* a six-string plucked lyre (no. 3), *masinqo* a single-string bowed lute (no. 1), and *käbäro* a two-headed conical shaped drum (no. 19) on the *wärada* ballot; and the *huldudwa* a curved zebu horn with an inserted bamboo tube and mouthpiece on the *kəlɘl* ballot (no. 13; figs. 8.6, 8.7). These instruments are all traditionally played by men, although women also now play the *krar*. Generally speaking, each ethnic group possesses its own instruments, although instruments of one ethnic group may include instruments similar to those found among other groups, e.g., morphological variations of the *masinqo* are found among the Amhara, Oromo, Tigre, and Tigrinya, and likewise variations of the *krar* are found among the Amhara, Dorze, Tigre, and Tigrinya. The Tigre prefer metal *krar* strings, while many Amhara prefer gut strings. Among the Dorze, the *krar* strings are wound around the crossbar, which also acts as a friction bar. The Tigre prefer strings wound around the friction pegs, which are then pushed through the crossbar and rotated to adjust the pitch. Thus, certain instruments can be identified as belonging to one or to several groups.

In seventeen of the twenty towns I visited where I was able to study the actual ballots, not one candidate appeared to select a musical instrument. Three reasons for this suggest themselves. First, immediate needs were foremost in people's minds. The town of Hawzien, for example, appeared to be the most devastated by war and famine in Region One. It had suffered the greatest number of civilian casualties due to bombings, gunfire, and famine. Buildings, farms, and roads had also been destroyed. These misfortunes were reflected in the symbols the candidates selected: *masob* (a traditional table at which meals are eaten), corn, maize, house, and lock and a key. These symbols are clearly associated with food, shelter and security (fig. 8.8).

A second reason may be that ethnic origin, as well as some degree of familiarity with the symbol, influenced who might select it. The *huldudwa* for example is found in southern Ethiopia among the

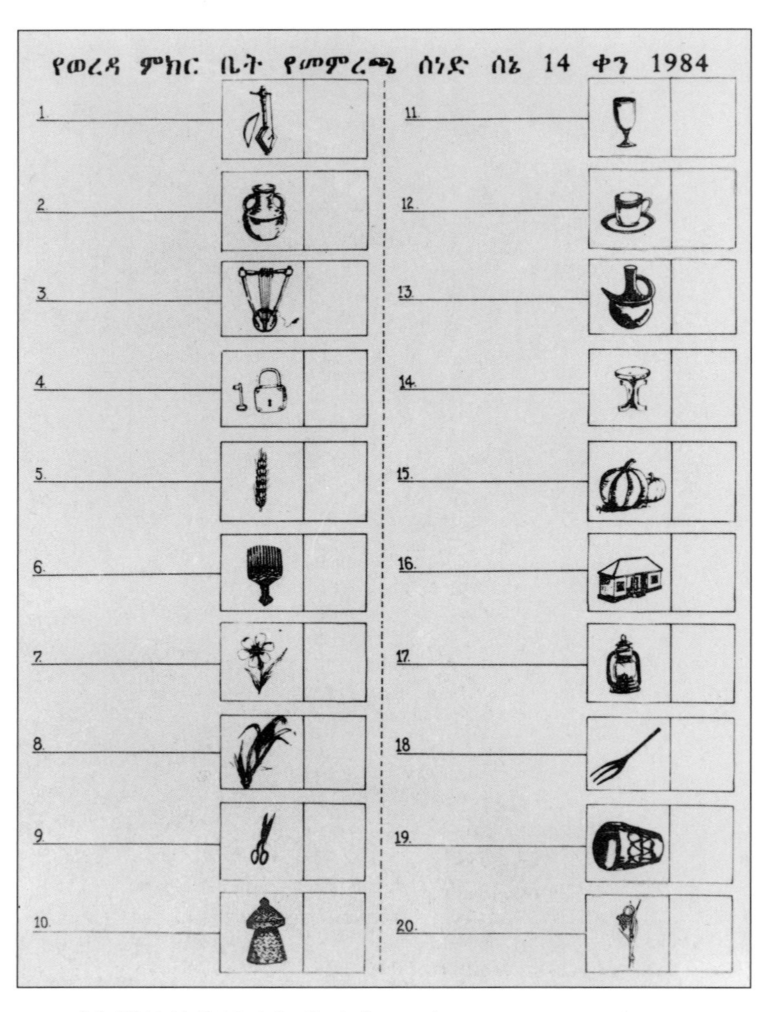

8.6 District ballot depicting the Amhara *masinqo*, or single-string bowed lute listed as no. 1; *krar*, or six-string plucked lyre, listed as no. 3; and a *käbäro*, or two-sided conical drum, listed as no. 19.

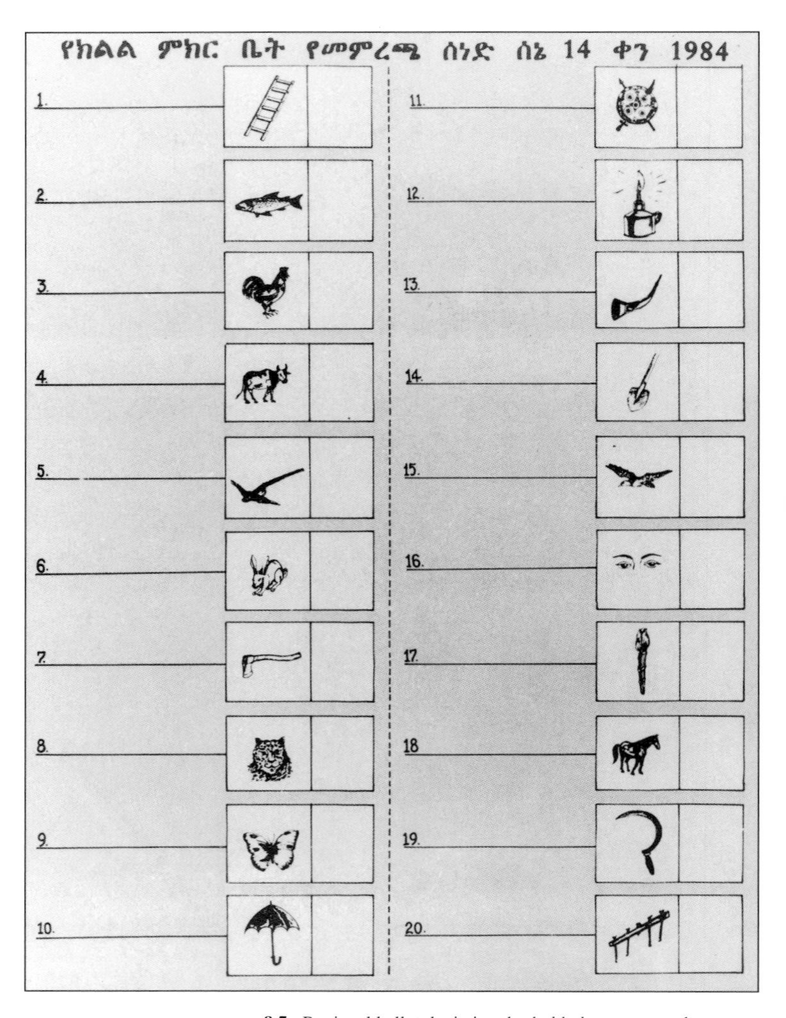

8.7 Regional ballot depicting the *huldudwa*, or curved zebu horn with an inserted bamboo tube mouthpiece, listed as no. 13.

Sidamo where it is used to announce a death or funeral (Tsefaye 1975, 23). The deceased may be an ordinary person or a leader of the community. Non-Sidamo candidates would probably not select this instrument. The six-string *krar* is found in central Ethiopia among the Amhara; the five-string *krar*, however, is found in the north among the Tigre and in the south among the Dorze. Furthermore Amhara- and Tigre-style *krar* pillars form a slight V-shape while the Dorze pillars are perpendicular to the crossbar (Kimberlin 1983, 248). The *krar* appearing on the ballot and poster was clearly that of the Amhara. Similarly, shape is an important criterion for determining drum type, function, and, to some extent, ethnic affiliation. The oval-shaped *käbäro* with two heads of unequal size was found on the poster and ballot as number 19; it is associated with the Ethiopian Orthodox Christian Church of northern and central Ethiopia. *Däbtära,* or lay priests, play the *käbäro* to accompany ritual dances and chants (Tsefaye 1975, 26 Kimberlin 1983, 237). The Tigre and Amhara are by and large orthodox Christian. A Moslem candidate would never select this *käbäro* as his or her ballot symbol. With the church music being banned for so long, Christian candidates may also have been unsure as to whether they had the freedom to select the *käbäro* symbol.

A third reason is perhaps the result of discrepancies in the voting materials. It was assumed that only one official version of the two slates of symbols was reproduced for the entire country so that the enlarged poster version of the actual ballot would be identical to the ballot itself. In examining the four musical instruments and comparing the ballot and the poster versions, however, I found that there were actually minor differences between them. These would have been important enough to influence the candidate's decision whether or not to use a particular symbol. As an example, *masinqo* distribution closely follows the areas occupied by the Amhara, Tigre, and Oromo ethnic groups found in northern and central Ethiopia (Kimberlin 1976, 12). The size of the *masinqo*'s diamond-shaped sound box is determined by ethnic group preference and performance context; for example, the audience at a *täg bet* (a house where honey wine is sold) would be much smaller than at an outdoor wedding celebration, and the instrument would not require a very large sound box (Kimberlin and Kimberlin 1984, 258). In general, a small *masinqo* sound box is known as the Oromo style and a large *masinqo* sound box as the Tigre style. Amhara *masinqo* have a box volume somewhere in the middle. While larger sound boxes produce a fuller and louder sound, no reasons can be found why the Oromo prefer sound boxes half the size of the Tigre except that the Tigre prefer a louder sound that may be related to the size of the venue where musicians perform. The ballot depicted an Amhara *masinqo*, and the poster version depicted a Tigre *masinqo* (fig. 8.9). This was determined by examining the spike size and bow contour and size in relation to the sound box. These differences may have confused the candidates and perhaps as a result this instrument symbol was not selected.

8.8 Four local candidates holding up their respective ballot symbols, from left to right: maize, lock and key, *masob,* and corn. Photograph by Cynthia Tse Kimberlin, Hawzien, 1991.

Historical Update and Recent Trends

After transitional government rule from 1991 to 1994, the country was renamed the Federal Democratic Republic of Ethiopia in 1994. The new government granted Eritrea independence in 1993, ratified a new constitution, and realigned political administrative divisions. Ethiopia has witnessed an increase in the number of political parties and newspapers and has encouraged investment and tourism, but to this day it remains cautious in the area of communication technology and the media. Restrictions affecting music and musicians were relaxed after 1991. The nighttime curfew was lifted. Love songs, *bägänna* music, and religious worship reentered the public domain. Solo performing artists have regained their popularity. Musicians are able to travel more freely. There is growing interest in intercultural and cross-cultural music collaborations. Musical instruments are adapting to accommodate the needs of contemporary musicians, and new strategies are being developed to market Ethiopian music. In this context, I would like to offer some final observations on the state of music in the wake of years of censorship and other repressive policies.

Although the history of Ethiopian music can be documented via recordings on glass and vinyl discs, cassette tapes, DAT tapes, videos, and the Internet, the government still monitors music, especially lyrics that are critical of it. The restrictions are less overt than was formerly the case, but the government still exerts control over the Internet and music recordings and publications produced within Ethiopia. As a result, black market cassette shops continue to thrive. Censorship in Ethiopia in general has been exposed by the news media and international human rights organizations, which have documented the number of Ethiopian journalists detained or incarcerated for expressing their views.

During the Revolution, imposition of a curfew and travel restrictions eliminated nighttime employment in public venues for musicians and forced them to seek alternative means of employment. Lack of mobility eliminated a major incentive for pursuing a career as a professional musician—freedom to travel. Restrictions on movement resulted in less public access and exposure to current news and gossip, eliminating a primary pipeline for obtaining new and timely song texts (Kimberlin 1995, 140–41). When the curfew was eliminated, nightclubs (*azmaribet*) with a cabaret atmosphere sprang up throughout the country, providing places for people to drink, to relax, and to be entertained by musicians playing popular and traditional Ethiopian music. Increased mobility has meant that music and musical performances are no longer limited to specific locales and groups. Collaborative efforts in live performance and on recordings now often include individuals from different ethnic groups, regions, and countries, such as the recordings of the internationally known vocalist Aster Aweke and composer/performer Mulatu Astatqé. In fact, defining Ethiopian music within geographical boundaries is now problematic, as many musicians live a mobile existence. They may have multiple residences, and their profession may obligate them to work the international circuit. Collaborative efforts are particularly evident in the areas of technical assistance, marketing strategies, and arrangement and orchestration.

Love songs have returned to the public arena with a vengeance. One type of music commonly heard is *tizita* (reminiscence), a melodic style based on the traditional Amharic song titled "Tizita." The song expresses the agonies of unrequited love and of longing, loss, and despair and has special appeal to virtually all Ethiopians. Its numerous renditions and musical permutations are disseminated worldwide.

Bägänna music is now heard on the radio and television particularly during Lent and at New Year's celebrations and has been reintroduced into the Yared Music School curriculum. Ethiopia's foremost *bägänna* player, Alemu Aga, is heard on

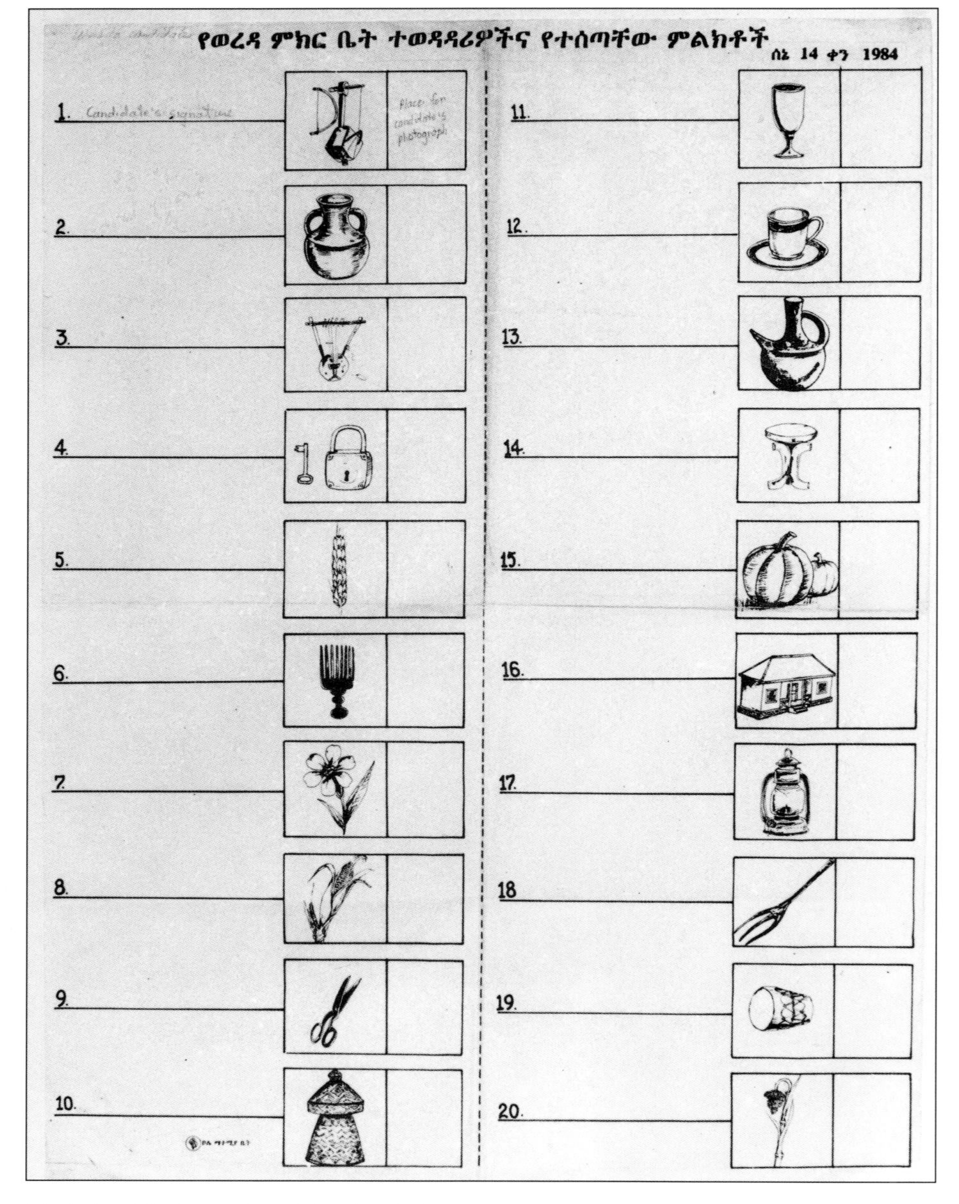

8.9 Portion of the large poster depicting the *wärada* (district) ballot showing the Tigre *masinqo*, or single-string bowed lute listed as no. 1.

numerous domestic and foreign recordings. He performs not only in Ethiopia but has been invited regularly to perform in Europe, notably in France, Germany, Italy, and England.

Religious worship is much in evidence. One manifestation that has received little outside attention is the growth of the Protestant evangelical church. Unlike the Ethiopian Orthodox Christian Church, these evangelical churches allow women to sing, dance, and play musical instruments—including the *käbäro*, *tsenatsil* (sistrum), and *maqwamya* (staff)—with the men. The Western six-string guitar is now a familiar fixture in services along with the *krar*. Musical groups such as the famous *Shibsheba* choir of Addis Ababa perform at Protestant churches throughout the city and have received invitations to perform in other towns including Addis Alem, Kombolcha, and Debra Berhan (Liyounet 1996, 2).

In the past, traditional Ethiopian musical instruments were made to order by an instrument maker. This tradition continues but to a lesser extant. Some *masinqo* are now produced in a factory in three "standard" sizes. With greater access to exports and outside resources, instruments have undergone structural modifications to produce a fuller sound. Electronic amplification devices are attached to the resonators of *krar* and *bägänna*. *Krar* have nylon and wire strings instead of the traditional gut, resulting in a less mellow sound. Because of these modifications, instrumental music groups produce massive sound volume in large venues, e.g., sports stadiums, to show off their knowledge and use of sound enhancement equipment, which has generally been embraced by the younger generation of urbanites. Change is apparent in the attitude of the public toward the cultural symbolism of these instruments. For example, the *krar* was traditionally associated with the ox and the *masinqo* with the horse (Ashenafi 1995, 114). Today, these and other similar symbolic attributes are no longer considered relevant.

The movement of some music toward a global orientation has led to a new phenomenon in the 1990s. Although many applaud the fact that Ethiopian music has been taken out of the local environment and placed in the international arena, this has entailed an ethical dilemma. There has been a marked increase in the number of domestic and foreign music agents (often business people rather than musicians) who will gladly pay generous fees for new talent whose songs they can purchase. Conglomerates such as Sony, guided by multinational tastes and marketing acumen, sponsor local music contests in hopes of discovering the next "super star." This environment tends to measure a musician's worth in terms of cassettes and compact discs produced and sold rather than the merit of the music. As a result, tapes of inferior quality featuring similar sounding music (usually with over-amplified keyboard synthesizers and drum boxes) are produced and marketed. This trend is lamented by the older generation, which acutely feels the lack of inspired lyrics and the creative integrity of earlier times. There will always be, however, a coterie of serious musicians who are compelled to compose and perform traditional, popular, and intercultural music for its own sake. It is this group that will be interesting to watch for the emergence of new forms, styles, and artists.

Epilogue

Since February 7, 1999, a state of war has existed between Ethiopia and Eritrea. Conflicts and negotiations continue. The source of the dispute is the exact location of borders between these two nations. While there is tension along the entire border, its focus is an area referred to as "Badme" (also the name of a village). Underlying this dispute are economic and political issues that are even more difficult to resolve than the demarcation of a border. It will be interesting to observe how these and other unforeseen forces impact Ethiopia's future and its music.

NIEVES

PART TWO:

Africa and the Diaspora: Cross-Cultural Influences

Trio Electrico of Bloco da Aurora during Carnaval. Photograph by Doran H. Ross, Salvador da Bahia, March 1981.

9. The Lyre of the Arab Gulf:

Historical Roots, Geographical Links, and the Local Context

ALI JIHAD RACY

Musical instruments often seem enigmatic in terms of their construction, history, and symbolic significance.[1] Like other artifacts, they may be borrowed, retained, modified, and even discarded. Furthermore, like living organisms, instruments adapt to different cultural settings, thus dropping or maintaining some of their older connotations and acquiring new functions and meanings. Consequently, the study of musical instruments may necessitate applying a combination of historical, anthropological, musicological, and organological approaches. In the music cultures of the Arab Gulf region, the lyre, known by the name *tanbūrah,* appears strikingly distinct in terms of its physical features, social function, and playing technique, but it also has close parallels in other world communities both ancient and modern. Thus, its current position poses a number of fundamental questions: How does the Gulf *tanbūrah* relate to other lyre types from previous epochs and from other world communities? And to what extent do the various lyre examples, including the *tanbūrah,* exhibit individual characteristics and represent the cultural settings they belong to?

Cross-cultural studies on instruments have addressed both aspects of continuity and change. In the case of the lyre, broad patterns of historical consistency and variation have been discussed (e.g., Marcuse 1975; Rashīd 1989). Many studies have linked the origins of the modern lyre with earlier cultural and demographic contacts (e.g., Olsen 1967). Meanwhile, the adaptability of instruments to various cultural settings and their transformation in form and meaning have been dealt with in various general studies (e.g., Racy 1986a). Ethnomusicologists have generally maintained that individual cultures are highly selective in their borrowing of outside musical elements (Blacking 1977) and that ultimately, borrowed musical phenomena derive their meaning and relevance from the human contexts of which they become a part.

In terms of structure, the lyre is defined as a string instrument, the strings of which are attached to a yoke that lies in the same plane as the sound table and consists of two arms and a crossbar (Wachsman 1980, 397). Historians generally believe that the lyre, or *kinnarah,* originated in Mesopotamia and that a lyre with a box resonator first appeared in Sumeria around the year 2700 B.C.E. (see Rimmer 1969, 13; Marcuse 1975, 358; and Rashīd 1975, 196). Information about the structure and playing technique comes from a variety of sources including

9.2 Eucharides Painter, Attic Red-Figure Lekythos, circa 480 B.C.E., terra-cotta, Height 33.8 cm. The J. Paul Getty Museum, Malibu, California, 73.AE.23.

9.1 Performer playing the *tanbūrah* of the Arab gulf. Photograph by Barbara Racy, Dubai, United Arab Emirates, 1988.

extant specimens. As illustrated by a sample now at the University Museum in Philadelphia, the Sumerian lyre, in some ways, resembled the lyres now found in Ethiopia, for example, in the manner in which the strings are tightened, rolled around the crossbar, and knotted (Sachs 1940, 77). Also cited is a later Sumerian lyre, thought to have been played in a manner, reminiscent of certain types of lyres now played in Africa. Carried obliquely by the player, the instrument had strings that were struck with a plectrum "scratching over all strings at once while the fingers of the left hand plucked or deadened those which should not be heard" (Sachs 1940, 79). This method has been shown to have existed in ancient Greece as well, where the lyre figured prominently as a musical instrument and a ritualistic symbol (fig. 9.2).

Historians have studied the geographical diffusion of this instrument and its proliferation into ancient Egypt, Greece, and the eastern Mediterranean. Appearing in Egypt during the Hyksos migration (approximately 1700–1580 B.C.E.), the lyre also moved to Europe, where one ninth-century picture showed King David holding a lyre with an added fingerboard. The instrument was also known to the Arabs in the Middle Ages. In the tenth century, it was recognized by al-Fārābī, although he reportedly mentioned that in Baghdad the lyre was laughed at as a rattrap (Wachsman 1980, 398).

In Africa, however, lyres and harps with strings set in a plane vertical to the soundboards are very common, particularly in the Sudanic desert region and parts of the East Coast. It is generally thought that by the end of the Pharaonic era, these instruments spread out of Egypt into neighboring areas to the west and south (see Powne 1968). This process appears to illustrate what is commonly referred to among musicologists as "marginal survival," that is, traditions or artifacts surviving primarily in the geographical peripheries of their places of origin. In the area of their concentration in Africa, however, lyres are believed to have spread from Ethiopia southwest into what is now Kenya, Uganda, Sudan, and the Democratic Republic of the Congo (formerly Zaire), a migration that may have taken place as late as the second half of the nineteenth century (Wachsman 1980, 398).

Throughout history, lyres have been used in a wide variety of contexts, especially ritual services and worship. One modern scholar, Gilbert Rouget, described the biblical use of the lyre and the harp as being closely connected with prophetic trance. Accordingly David played his lyre, or *kinnor*, to calm a violently agitated Saul or, as explained by Rouget, in order to reverse Saul's obsession with the evil spirit and to reestablish God's presence within him (Rouget 1985, 77, 158). Similar efficacy was attached to the lyre among the ancient Greeks who correlated it and other instruments with possession and trance. Some Greek vase paintings even depicted gods playing the instrument (Rouget 1985, 76–77). According to Greek legend, Orpheus was taught to play the lyre by Apollo and was so accomplished that when he sang and accompanied himself on the instrument, he could charm even savage beasts.

Today, lyres exist in a variety of shapes and sizes, and they feature different tunings, playing techniques, and symbolic connotations. In Africa the lyre, which is most often played as a solo instrument to accompany the voice, is an adjunct to entertainment and formal rituals. In modern Ethiopia, the *bagana*, sometimes also referred to as "David's harp," has a square sound box, produces a very low pitch with a distinctive buzzing effect, and is considered a semisacred instrument used to accompany Ethiopian church hymns. In contrast, the *krar*, a much smaller instrument equipped with a round bowl-shaped sound resonator, is a secular instrument used by the *azmari*, or the semiprofessional village musician (Kebede 1977, 381). Traditionally, the *krar* is played either using the strumming technique described above or by plucking each string separately, a method commonly encountered among East Africans, including Ugandan lyre players (figs. 9.3, 9.4). In other areas of Africa we also encounter types of lyres that are used for festivities as well as for healing connected with spirit possession. In western Kenya, for example, where the lyre is considered a ritualistic

9.3 James Makubuya performing on the Ugandan lyre. Photograph by Barbara Racy, 1993.

9.4 Frontal view of the Ugandan lyre. Photograph by Barbara Racy, 1993.

9.5 Lyre and other instruments as illustrated in M. Villoteau's "Description historique, technique et littéraire, des instruments de musique des Orientaux," which appeared in the *Description de l'Egypt* prepared by the Napoleonic scientific mission.

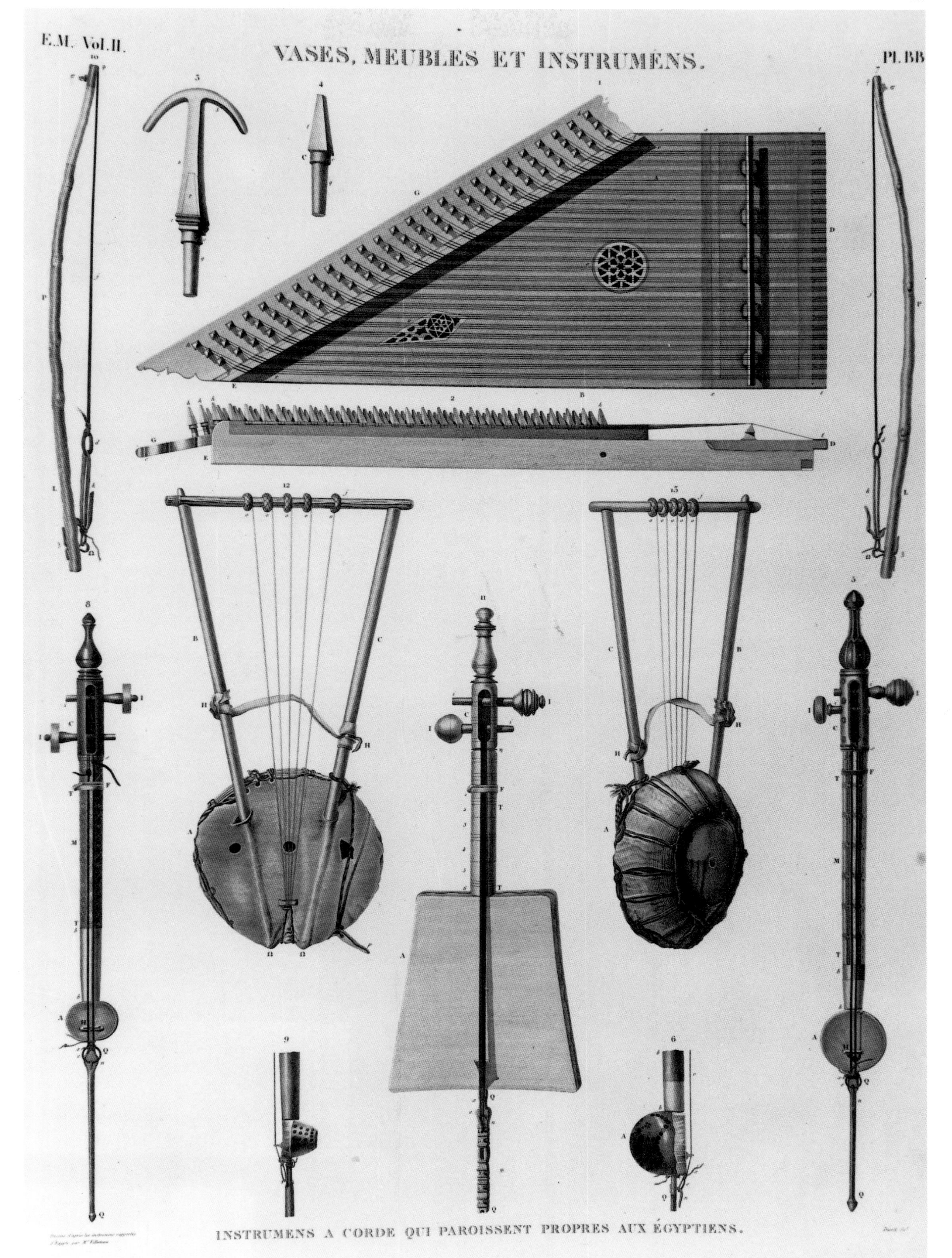

INSTRUMENS A CORDE QUI PAROISSENT PROPRES AUX ÉGYPTIENS.

healing object, it is played at weddings where it both provides entertainment and is linked with spirituality (Wachsman 1980, 399). In the traditional culture of Sudan, the lyre is the most commonly used string instrument—employed by many ethnic groups who give it various names. It is known as the *tanbūr* by the Nubians, Mahas, and Shakia in the north; *brimbiri* by the Nuba of the west; *bangia* among the Berta and *shangar* by the Ingassana, both from the southeast; and *rabābah* by the Bija in eastern Sudan. Here too, as Mahi Ismail writes, the lyre is used in healing rituals, as well as for entertainment. For example, a *bangia* and four gourd trumpets perform the *moshembe da*, a southeastern Sudanese dance ritual for treating individuals possessed by spirits (Ismail 1980, 328). Such usage is also encountered in Egypt (see Dūkhī 1984, 345), where the *tanbūrah* appears in one type of healing ritual. In fact, the lyre, specifically the *kissar*, was among those instruments depicted around the turn of the nineteenth century by the Napoleonic scientific mission to Egypt (figs. 9.5, 9.6), specifically in a volume on musical instruments (Villoteau 1923, 365). Meanwhile in Sinai and on the Red Sea coast, one type of lyre appears to possess a contrasting profile. The *simsimiyyah*, a small lyre, which usually has metal strings and a sound box made from a gallon-size tin can, basically shares the secular standing of the Ethiopian *krar* and is used in parallel contexts of social entertainment.

In Kuwait, southern Iraq, Bahrain, Qatar, the United Arab Emirates, and Oman, *tanbūrah* refers to both the lyre and the ritual connected with it. Its music and dance manifestations are by and large associated with spirit possession and therapeutic healing. As a ritual, the *tanbūrah* is associated with specific paraphernalia, including the lyre itself; a social structure; and a set of beliefs. Its practitioners (musicians, dancers, spiritual leaders, and other local group members) are basically Gulf Arabs, whose ethnic and racial background is African, but who today constitute an integral part of the communities they live in (see Olsen 1980, 513; Hassan 1980, 144).

As an instrument, the Gulf *tanbūrah* bears the closest resemblance to the *tanbūrah* of Nuba and Sudan. It has six gut strings mounted on a wood bridge, a skin-covered sound box consisting of a round wood-bowl, and two symmetrical side posts connected to a straight crossbar. The strings, which are plucked by a solid piece of cow horn, are fastened to the crossbar and tuned through round friction-thongs made typically from braided cloth. Customarily the right hand strums all the strings with single plectrum strokes, while fingers of the left hand stop those strings not intended to be sounded and release those intended to be played. Producing low pitches with a distinctive percussive quality, the instrument is, with some exceptions, tuned to a five-note (pentatonic) scale.[2] In the Gulf and in Egypt, too, the *tanbūrah* is accompanied by a *manjūr*, or a wide cloth belt to which a large number of hollow animal hooves are attached (fig. 9.7). When the *manjūr* player wears the instrument around his lower torso and moves his body rhythmically, he is able to produce a regular metric pattern through the rattling sound of the hooves. Occasionally several *manjūr* players perform simultaneously. Most often, the performances feature three or more upright cylindrical drums, the single heads of which are played by single rubber-hose or palm-stem beaters in addition to being softly tapped with the palm of one hand. As typical in the United Arab Emirates, however, bottomless drums are partly buried in the sand floor of the *tanbūrah*-house courtyard when they are played.

From all this it appears that the lyre has existed for at least three millennia during which it has enjoyed considerable proliferation and has served a vast number of functions: secular, sacred, therapeutic, and supernatural. In some cases, it seems to have enjoyed special significance, as suggested by the adjunct symbolic ornamentation, for instance, the bull's head on a lyre from Ur, the duck heads carved at the end of the yoke on lyres from ancient Egypt, and the decorative tassels attached to the yokes of East African lyres (Wachsman 1980, 399). Also, although some examples (particularly smaller ones, such as the *krar* and *simsimiyyah*) are used purely for recreational purposes, it is clear that lyres occupy a special position in the domain of spirit possession, a phenonmenon that can be observed in the case of the *tanbūrah* tradition of the Arab Gulf.

The life story of the lyre from its ancient manifestations to its modern forms can provide music historians and ethnomusicologists with a variety of insights. Lyre studies attest to relative historical consistency in matters of construction and playing technique. Thus, features such as the strumming method and the way strings are connected to tuning rings around the crossbar appear to be serveral millennia old. With such consistency in mind, the distribution of the

9.6 Egyptian musician playing the *tanbūrah*. Photograph by Barbara Racy, 1989.

9.7 *Tanbūrah* ritual performed with drums and *manjūr* belt-rattles. Photograph by Barbara Racy, Dubai, United Arab Emirates, 1988.

lyre can shed light over the various ethnic, political, and artistic contacts between Southwest Asia and East Africa. Indeed, the return of the ancient lyre to the Arab Gulf and southern Iraq in the form of the *tanbūrah* (see Rashīd 1989) can be viewed as the completion of an old geographical and historical cycle.

As the study demonstrates, the *tanbūrah* essentially belongs to a Nubian-Sudanese variety, which can also be found in some areas of Egypt. This variety may be contrasted with instruments existing in East Africa to the south of the African horn. These instruments, for example, possess a relatively large number of strings that are plucked by the fingers directly to produce interlocking texture; they are also mounted on rather shallow bridges, thus rendering characteristically African buzzing effects. The Gulf type, which attests to historical, cultural, and demographic links with Nubia, shares with Nubian lyre types a number of essential features. Among the shared features are: the general symmetrical shape of the yoke; the bulge tuning-devices; the bowl sound box; the typical number of strings, which pass over a relatively higher bridge and connect with the bulges from behind the crossbar thus forming a sharper angle; and added tension over the bridge, a phenomenon that increases the resonance and clarity of the strings, unlike the case of some East African lyres. Other shared features include: the manner in which the instrument is held, the strumming and muting technique, the prevalence of pentatonic tunings, the use of a horn plectrum, the inclusion of elaborate decorative designs, and the close connections between the instrument and spirit possession.

Here, for example, we may refer to S. Zenkovsky's accounts of the *tanbūrah* ritual in Sudan (1950) or examine the *zār Sūdanī* music that was recorded at the Congress of Arab Music held in Cairo in 1932, which featured pentatonic music on the *tanbūrah*.[3] Pentatonicism was amply discussed by Juma'ah Jabir in his book (n.d) on Sudanese music. The Nubian link with the Gulf *tanbūrah* and the related *tanbūrah* ritual, also called *nūbān*, was made by Poul Olsen, who speculated that the instrument may have entered Arabia through the Somali coast and maintained that its music was Sudanese (1967, 28, 36).

Cross-cultural studies of the lyre also make us more conscious of the individuality of musical cultures. As instruments are transmitted from one community to another or from one period to another, they obviously undergo important modifications not only in matters of construction but also in repertoire, symbolic meaning, and social function. This study has pointed to a general correlation between the instrument and spiritual powers. However, the numerous exceptions to this correlation testify to the flexible and varied roles played by musical instruments and provide fascinating clues to the rich diversity within the cultures of East Africa and the Near East. In this sense the Gulf *tanbūrah* cannot be divorced from Arabian history and culture within which the instrument represents a basic ethnic symbol and a highly revered ritual object. Like other artistic forms of the area, the Gulf *tanbūrah* is intimately linked with its social and spiritual ambiance (Racy 1986b, 27). As fieldwork clearly demonstrates, in the minds of those who perform the *tanbūrah* as a ritual, the instrument and the songs and dances it accompanies are connected symbolically with Arabian and Islamic history and are part of the people's shared spiritual and artistic lore.

10. "Turn Up the Volume!"

The African Aesthetic in Trinidad's Carnival Music

ERNEST D. BROWN JR.

10.1 Band on a truck at the Toronto Caribana festival. Photograph by John Nunley, 1986.

The emancipation of African slaves in the 1830s introduced an African aesthetic to Carnival that still informs the Trinidadian approach to making music, dancing, and creating an atmosphere of celebration. This African sensibility transformed Carnival from a series of exclusive private parties held in the homes of the plantocracy to a raucous street parade in which anyone could participate. The size of the festival and number of voices represented in it increased. Africans democratized Carnival and turned it into a people's art form, one in which all of the peoples of Trinidad would eventually find their place. This Africanized Carnival differed from its more European predecessors in featuring loud percussive music, more colorful costumes, more social satire and commentary, more African dance movements, and new masquerade characters. Africans "turned up the volume" at Carnival in a process that involved all of these contributions, not just increasing the sound level.

This Africanized Carnival still exists, and within it there is room for many points of view, styles of music, and ways of masquerading. Unlike the Carnivals that are held in the Catholic areas of Europe, many of which have become preservationist museum pieces, Carnival in Trinidad looks toward the past and toward the future. It is conscious of tradition, but it is in touch with a changing society and is constantly being augmented in unpredictable ways. This is particularly true of music and *mas* (masquerading), the two art forms that are most central to Carnival. New costumes are made each year, and they incorporate new technology in their construction. Masquerade characters change with fashion and the times, although there are many classic personae. Similarly, Carnival music has changed greatly since the time of the initial African involvement.

Attempts by those in authority to channel Carnival in a particular direction have often succeeded in the short run, only to fail in the long run. Throughout its history, this festival has been consistently loud, unruly, eclectic, and multidirectional. Africans have continued to expand the expressive range of Carnival in a variety of ways, and a strong anti-authoritarian emphasis is a part of the process. This high-volume approach was much in evidence during Carnival '96,[1] which I had the privilege of attending with a group of scholars who were studying Carnival under the auspices of Trinidad's National Carnival Commission, a government agency charged with organizing various official Carnival activities, and Trinity College, an American liberal arts college, which is in the process of instituting a Trinidadian-style Carnival in its hometown of Hartford, Connecticut. Carnival '96 was my first Trinidad Carnival. I thought I had some experience to draw upon, having written about Trinidadian music (Brown 1987, 229–49) and having witnessed a number of Brooklyn Carnivals (officially the West Indian American Day Parade), one of several overseas Trinidadian-inspired Carnivals (fig. 10.1). However, some Trinidadian friends pointed out that these are "like chalk and cheese," meaning that there is no comparison to the real thing.[2]

What is the real thing? I cannot provide the definitive answer, but at Carnival '96, I was struck by the festival's volume, especially whenever I came within a few blocks of a sound system, a massive sound amplification system mounted on a tractor-trailer truck. I was also struck by the profusion of people, color, meaning, movement, and spectacle I observed. Carnival seemed to be a multidirectional collage of contradictory elements (figs. 10.2–10.5). I wondered what held it all together and what all this had to do with the Africans who took over Carnival in 1838.

Collage and multidirectionality seem to be fundamental to the Carnival aesthetic. I believe that strong precedents for these qualities exist in African cultures, for example, wearing "loud" clothing with bright colors and different patterns juxtaposed, combining elements of more than one religion in worship, treating illness with both European and African medicines, and interlocking conflicting rhythms in music to create loud, dense sonic textures. Carnival is an inclusive, nonlinear assemblage that has clear parallels to African sensibilities and ways of acting in a number of social arenas.

Carnival is a celebration of excess that is set loose once a year. As a friend once put it, "At Carnival, some is good, more is better, and too much is just about right!"[3] What is the purpose of this celebration of excess? Carnival seems to involve overloading the senses as a means of creating a ritual space that is outside of everyday life, a space where personal expression can roam free and where people can escape from, reverse, and comment upon social realities and restrictions. This ritual space is public and social, but it is accompanied by the creation of a private, psychological space. This altered state of mind is, I believe, what Trinidadians call "Carnival fever." It is a state of ecstasy and enthusiasm for Carnival that is a by-product of its sensory overload or even the anticipation of such overload. Such private psychological spaces, which are free from external authority, are important resources for oppressed peoples. They are in fact another kind of ritual space or sanctuary in which stifled voices can be heard and wounded psyches can heal. Turning up the volume in music and *mas* is an essential part of creating these public and psychological ritual spaces.

Below, I will concentrate on ways in which music has "turned up the volume" at Carnival, based on my experiences and reflections on Carnival '96. I will comment to a lesser degree on the role of masquerade bands in turning up Carnival's volume, but *mas* is clearly a related form of cultural expression that uses the visual arts and theater to convey concepts similar to those expressed through music.

At Carnival '96, four different kinds of musical ensembles were in prominent use. As we shall see, each of these ensembles is a layer of Carnival tradition, and each has turned up the volume at Carnival in its own way. The ensembles included:

1. Percussion bands consisting of drums and metal cans or other objects that were struck
2. Steelbands consisting of between a dozen and a hundred steeldrums, or pans[4]
3. Brass bands consisting of vocals, electronically amplified instruments (guitars, keyboards, horns), and electronic sound generators (for example, synthesizers and drum machines)[5]
4. Sound systems in which a disc jockey plays prerecorded music of any type (usually *soca*[6] or reggae)

African Drumming at Carnival

Percussion bands represent the earliest layer of Africanized Carnival music that remains in current use. Consisting of vocals, drums, rattles, and various struck metal objects that produce bell-like sounds, these bands first entered Carnival when newly freed Africans took over and transformed the festival after 1838. These ensembles are very close in composition and playing style to the West African drum, bell, and rattle groups that dominate the music of the coastal forest region, an area of tropical rain forest along the African coast from Côte d'Ivoire to Gabon. The percussiveness, rhythmic drive, dense polyrhythms, call and response, improvisation, and energy of Trinidadian percussion ensembles also resemble these West African ensembles.

10.2–10.5 Costumes reflecting the diverse and often contradictory influences that inspire Carnival in Trinidad. Photographs by Robert Jerome, Port of Spain, 1984.

10.6 East Indian drum ensemble on Jouvay, the first day of Carnival. Photograph by John Nunley, Port of Spain, 1987.
10.7 Mud masqueraders on Jouvay morning. Photograph by Ernest D. Brown Jr., Port of Spain, 1999.
10.8 Truck carrying the San Juan Rhythm section. A female mud masquerader rides on the back of the truck. Photograph by Ernest D. Brown Jr., Port of Spain, 1999.

In the preindustrial world, loud, intense musical ensembles of this type played outdoors at major public events where they could be heard for miles around. They were acoustic broadcast media that announced important social occasions and told people what to expect when they attended. African percussion bands were intimately involved in communicating meaning at public events. At Carnival percussion bands not only display their African origins in their musical style, they also continue African traditions of social commentary and irreverence toward those in authority, especially at Jouvay,[7] the first day of Carnival, which begins early on the Monday morning before Ash Wednesday when the mud masqueraders take over the streets from two o'clock in the morning until dawn.

On Jouvay morning of Carnival '96, I followed one of these percussion bands through the streets of Port of Spain (fig. 10.6). The band was known as the Merry Darceuils and hailed from Belmont, an African working-class neighborhood. I arrived at the band leader's house at two o'clock in the morning on Carnival Monday after having attended a Dimanche Gras (Fat Sunday) *soca* show the night before. People were milling about, putting on their costumes, and making last-minute preparations before getting on the road.

The band had selected as its theme "What are you a slave to?" The band leader had made costumes out of cardboard boxes and other found objects that related to the theme. For example, if you were a slave to food, then your costume might feature a hat with a Kentucky Fried Chicken box on top (complete with bone). The band's costumes provided a striking visual example of an African-derived, improvisational, make-something-from-nothing aesthetic that is so prominent in Trinidadian musical contexts, where people commonly turn everyday objects (such as cans and bottles) into impromptu musical instruments.

The Merry Darceuils' choice of theme and costumes also exemplifies an African-derived tradition of social commentary,[8] for despite the humorous, personal, and contemporary references in the costumes, there were other, more serious references to slavery in Trinidad. On the road, the band was led by a pickup truck carrying a group of drummers and hauling a large cardboard boat on a trailer. The boat was entitled the ss (for Slave Ship) Middle Passage. In addition, the Kentucky Fried Chicken box could be interpreted as a criticism of the growth of United States cultural and corporate influence in Trinidad. Such social commentary is a prominent part of Jouvay, and percussion bands are closely associated with it. The loud sound of the bands and the multiplicity of meanings communicated in Jouvay *mas* help raise its figurative volume. It is as if there are many voices speaking, if only you are sensitive enough to hear them.

Aside from cardboard hats, the rest of the Merry Darceuils' costume consisted of mud, liberally applied over all their skin and clothing. It was quite an effective form of costuming. A coating of mud conceals the social markers of class, gender, religion, and ethnicity by which people commonly classify each other and transforms people into fantastic creatures that stand outside these categories (figs. 10.7, 10.8). Mud *mas* allows people to become actors in the public and private ritual spaces described above. In addition, mud-masking can be seen as a liminal, transitional stage between everyday life and Carnival Tuesday, when masqueraders appear fully costumed in all their finery, like butterflies that have emerged from their cocoons.

The practice of mud-masking may be derived from African ritual practices where kaolin or ocher is applied to the skin or it may have been another make-something-from-nothing improvisation introduced by the newly freed slaves in the 1830s, because they had nothing else with which to costume themselves for Carnival. In any case, it is a simple yet very powerful form of expression and one that is associated with percussion bands.

The members of the Merry Darceuils, about forty of us including neighborhood residents and visiting scholars, danced and paraded behind the truck carrying our drums, which played constantly. The drums not only kept the group energized and dancing for several hours, but they provided a sonic identity for the masqueraders who moved en masse through the streets to their music. This sonic identity was just as powerful as the visual identity provided by a band's costumes. The music transformed people just as their costumes did.

Unlike the organized parades that occur on Carnival Tuesdays, many Jouvay bands follow no prescribed routes. These bands simply come out of their neighborhoods in the middle of the night, take over the streets, stop traffic, and make their way to the center of town to join hundreds of other bands jamming the streets of downtown Port of Spain. Jouvay bands embody a spirit of anti-authoritarian rebellion. This too has its roots in the street parades of the first Africans. Freed from slavery, they took every opportunity to show disrespect for and parody their former masters.

This tension between moral or legal authority and the spontaneous impulse of the people is also present in devil bands which play *mas* on Jouvay. Again, percussion bands are closely associated with social commentary. The members of devil bands accompany themselves by beating out one or two rhythms with sticks on biscuit tins. These are five-gallon rectangular metal boxes used to hold cookies (biscuits in Trinidadian English). Members of devil bands typically carry pitchforks and wear horns and tails and little else. In addition, they cover themselves with thick black grease or blue dye and behave in ways calculated to upset spectators—by rubbing against them, spitting up a red liquid that looks like blood, acting aggressively, etc. In other words, devil bands display an in-your-face, punk sensibility. They appeal especially to young males, although older men also participate. Women generally do not participate.

> Devil bands go back to the masquerades of the newly freed slaves.
> The first notice of a masquerade band enacting scenes from slavery is that recounted by Charles Day of the 1848 carnival. He described a gang of almost naked primitives bedaubed with black varnish, pulling at a chain attached by padlock to one of their number who was occasionally knocked down and "treated with a mock [beating]." [Cited in Hill 1972, 24]

A similar masquerade was observed in Martinique in 1888 by Lafacadio Hearn who wrote: "[This character] wore nothing but a cloth about his loins; his whole body and face being smeared with an atrocious mixture of soot and molasses. He is supposed to represent the original African ancestor" (cited in Hill 1972, 25). This observation is relevant to Trinidad since many Trinidadian slaves had roots in Martinique, their masters having immigrated with them from there or from other French islands in response to the chaos the Napoleonic Wars caused in the colonies and the invitation made by Spain in 1783 for Catholics to populate its colony.

Because of their dirty costumes and obnoxious behavior, devil bands have a powerful voice and people give them a wide berth. At Carnival '96, I saw a devil walk through a crowd of several hundred spectators, which parted for him like the Red Sea for Moses. Nobody who is not a devil wants to be touched by one, just as White racists never wanted to come in

contact with African skin. Such a masquerade must have been very appealing to newly freed African men, their Black skin stigmatized in slavery, now transformed into a powerful weapon.

A young *mas* man, Wendell Manwarren, who brought out a blue devil band for Carnival '97, commented, "Jouvay... is the one time when the more dirty you are, the more you are held in high regard" (Sandy 1977, 16). Devil bands gave African men a voice, which did not need to speak in order to be heard.

Turn It Down! Turn It Up!

In the late nineteenth century, African efforts to turn up Carnival's volume met with reactionary efforts to turn it back down. Percussion bands composed of drums, bells, and rattles dominated Trinidad Carnival until they were banned in the 1880s by British colonial authorities who found their sound to be too loud and the behavior of the masqueraders they accompanied to be too uncouth. These reactionary efforts were always cloaked in appeals for law and order and morality, but in reality British colonial authorities merely wanted to turn down the volume of Carnival music and force their own cultural biases and sensibilities onto the Trinidadian people whose culture was African (fig. 10.9), Spanish, and French Creole, not British.

> African percussion in Trinidad, and elsewhere in the plantation regions of the Americas, was generally associated with celebration, power, resistance, and identity. . . . At the same time, public condemnation of the steelband [and other forms of percussion] derived from a well-established discourse on the immorality and disruptiveness of African percussion and related festive expression. [Stuempfle 1995, 14]

One late nineteenth-century calypso captured the essence of this conflict of national sensibilities quite effectively.

> Can't beat we drum,
> In my own, my native land.
> Can't have we Carnival,
> In my own, my native land.
> Can't have we bacchanal,
> In my own, my native land,
> In my own, my native land,
> In my own land. [Cited in Samnadda 1970, 11]

The decision to prefer one or another musical ensemble at Carnival has often had to do with conflicting attitudes toward the volume level—the amount of sound, the kinds of spectacle, and the meanings in the broadest sense of Carnival itself. It is a debate that continues today, with some trying to turn the volume up and others trying to turn it down, for various reasons. For example, before Carnival '97, there was an intense debate over restricting sound trucks to certain areas so that they would not overpower acoustic ensembles.[9]

In the 1880s, the vacuum in Carnival music was filled by two types of ensemble distinguished along class and color lines. The African poor began to parade to the music of *tamboo bamboo* bands consisting of lengths of bamboo three to four feet long, which are stamped on the ground and produce a sound very much like drumming, but quieter. Similar instruments are also found in parts of Africa. In Venezuela, which is only ten miles across the sea from Trinidad, they are known as *quitiplas* (Sadie 1980, 19: 612). These African-derived musical instruments satisfied the need for polyrhythmic, percussive music for public processions for many years.

As in many African drum ensembles, the sound of the *tamboo bamboo* band is stratified, and the instruments are tuned in three pitch ranges. The boom is a bamboo tube four-and-a-half feet long, five-and-a-half inches in diameter, which produces a bass sound. The cutter is a bamboo tube twenty-five inches long and three-and-a-

half inches in diameter, which is hit with a stick on its side as well as being tapped on the ground. The tapping of secondary rhythms on the sides of an instrument is an Africanism found in many Central African (Bantu) music cultures. Finally, the highest-pitched instrument is the *foulé*, a bamboo tube a foot long and three inches in diameter (Gonzalez 1978, 4).

At the same time, Venezuelan-derived string and wind ensembles, consisting of flutes, guitars, *cuatros*,[10] violins, and maracas became more prominent in Carnival, being performed by lighter-skinned people of African and European heritage, the so-called colored middle class (figs. 10.10, 10.11). This ensemble produces music that is polyrhythmic, and the *cuatro*, in particular, is strummed percussively; but overall this music is more melodic than drumming, and it lacks the loud heavy sound of drumming. More European in their aesthetic, these string and wind bands became social markers of upward mobility and middle-class status. Similar ensembles are still used today to play *parang*, a genre of Hispanic Christmas carols popular in certain parts of Trinidad. Spain ruled Trinidad from 1498 to 1797 when Britain conquered the island. *Parang* may be a survival of Trinidad's early Spanish colonial past, or it may have been introduced through the free movement of peoples between Trinidad and Venezuela, which began in Spanish colonial days and continued well into the twentieth century.

Each of these ensembles added a new and quieter voice to the Carnival mix and subtly turned up the volume by increasing the range of expression and meaning. However, what was essential to the British was that these ensembles were quieter than drums. The volume of actual sound produced at Carnival was reduced by law, and legal restrictions on the bawdiness of the festival muted its voice in terms of costumes, behavior, and dance movement.

In the 1930s, a louder and more unruly African aesthetic reasserted itself through the medium of the steelband (figs. 10.12–10.17). Although not directly derived from a specific African musical ensemble, the steeldrum, most commonly called the "pan" in Trinidad, is a development out of *tamboo bamboo* and the percussion bands that today accompany the Jouvay mud *mas* and the devil bands. Pan developed from a process of experimentation carried out by a number of people who gradually discovered that metal containers could be shaped to produce more than one musical note.

The connection with percussion bands is further emphasized by the fact that all steelbands contain within them a percussion

10.9 Drummers and participants in a Yorùbá ceremony honoring the deity Ṣàngó. Photograph by Ernest D. Brown Jr., Port of Spain, 1985.
10.10 The San Jose Seranaders, a *parang* band. The musician in the blue shirt plays a *cuatro*. Photograph by Ernest D. Brown Jr., Port of Spain, 1985.
10.11 The bass-box used in *parang* bands. Photograph by Ernest D. Brown Jr., Port of Spain, 1985.

10.12 A member of the Renegades Steelband. Photograph by Ernest D. Brown Jr., Port of Spain, 1999.
10.13 Tractor pulling a steelband. Photograph by Ernest D. Brown Jr., Port of Spain, 1999.
10.14 The Exodus Steelband. Photograph by John Nunley, Port of Spain, 1994.
10.15 Steeldrums from the Renegades Steelband. Photograph by Ernest D. Brown Jr., Port of Spain, 1999.
10.16, 10.17 Steelbands on the road. Photographs by John Nunley, Port of Spain, 1994.

Six Flags
COURTS
LAVENTILLE SOUNDS SPECIALISTS
ARRANGER: TREVOR "INCH HIGH" VALENTINE
BACARDI
and Friends

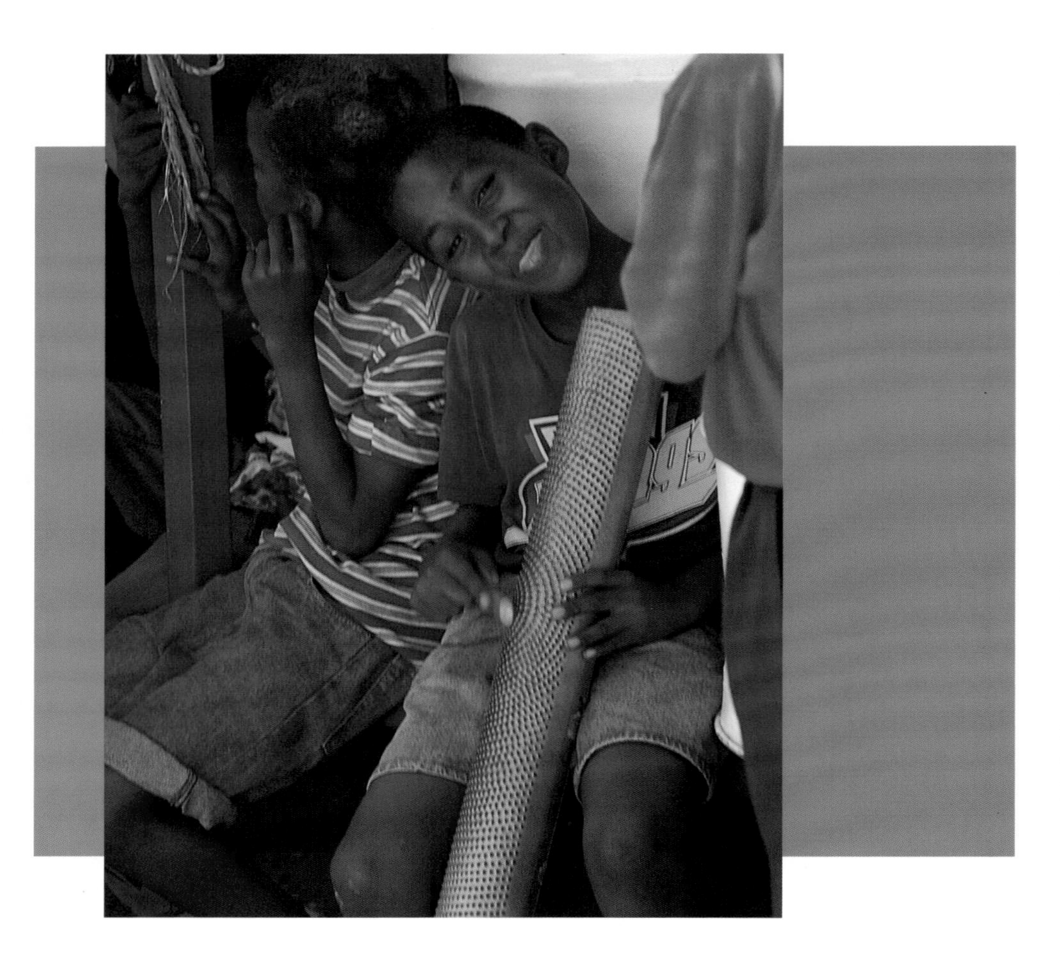

band known as the "engine room," where drums, tambourines, bells, brake drums, rattles, and other percussion instruments prevail (fig. 10.18). Like the engine room of a ship, the engine room of a steelband provides the rhythmic drive for the much larger number of melodic instruments (the pans) in the ensemble. The engine room is also the heir of the *tamboo bamboo* band in that it contains several relatively fixed supporting parts (played on an assortment of brake drums, rattles, scrapers, and congas) and a lead part known as a "cutter" (played on a brake drum), which cuts across the rhythm of the supporting parts and improvises more freely.

In creating the steeldrum, Trinidadians were not simply reviving African traditions from their distant past. Instead they were finding a way to extend those traditions by creating a variation upon them that resonated with the social realities of the 1930s and 1940s. This is a prime example of the way in which Trinidad Carnival differs from European Carnivals by expanding in unpredictable ways. It incorporates innovation, yet does not abandon older traditions.

Steelbands were a twentieth-century response to the development of an urban African industrial working class in Trinidad. This new working class flexed its muscle in the social sphere through political action, strikes, and labor union organizing. This Black industrial working class wanted Carnival music that gave voice to its life and social reality, and it did not care if British colonial authorities disapproved. Africans in Trinidad turned up the volume at Carnival once again.

By the 1950s this effort had gained widespread acceptance. Steeldrums became *the* music of Carnival and a symbol of the Trinidadian nation, a symbol of which all ethnic groups and social classes were proud. The era of steelband dominance lasted until the mid-1970s when sound systems began to dominate Carnival, raising the volume yet another notch. Like the rise of African percussion bands in the 1830s and the steelbands a century later, the rise of the sound systems in the 1970s is linked to rising social aspirations and the need of a new generation to find a way to add its voice to Carnival through music that is loud, percussive, and African in inspiration.

Turning Up the Volume Electronically: Part 1

At Carnival '96, it was evident that today sound systems provide *the* music of Carnival. A sound system is an electronic amplification system that may either be mounted on a truck to provide music for masquerade bands as they move through the streets (fig. 10.19) or may be set up outside a bar or at a private party (a fete). The sound source for these systems may be prerecorded music or a live band.

The most noticeable feature of sound systems is their raw power. The bass notes are so loud you can feel them in your chest. Sound systems provide an intense listening experience. They make you feel like you are inside the music, and it is inside of you. Sound systems are a powerful force that transforms people, allowing them to step outside of everyday life. Through electronic technology, sound systems (like *mas* costumes, dancing, steelbands, or drumming) create a ritual space that has both public and private dimensions.

One Internet newsgroup answers the frequently asked question, "What is a sound system?" as follows:

> A sound system, well consider it to be a glorified stereo system. Basically it is usually lots of bass boxes, lots of mid-range boxes, and lots of high end boxes (what I mean by boxes is large speaker cabinets). All this is driven by lots of amps to make it so loud that the bass makes the hair on your neck move to the beat. You really haven't experienced true dancehall until you've been to a true yard dance like Stone Love at House of Leo [a sound system in Jamaica]. [rec.music.reggae 1999]

At Carnival, sound systems have a similar effect. They are so loud that they totally dominate the sonic environment within a radius of a few blocks. In their presence, it is impossible to talk or to hear anything else. Thousands of people, masqueraders and spectators, gather around sound trucks and travel with them as they move through the streets, transformed into a sonic juggernaut that is itself a Carnival character.[11]

In the 1980s sound systems began to push the steelbands and percussion ensembles off the streets, especially on Carnival Tuesday when the main street procession happens. Steelbands and percussion ensembles still occupy particular niches during Carnival, Jouvay morning or Panorama, but today on the streets on Carnival Tuesday, sound systems rule. No other sound source can compete.

Where did sound systems come from and what do they have to do with the aesthetic of the African slaves who took over Carnival one hundred and sixty years ago? Is this legacy dead? Is it an archaic museum piece in need of preservation or revitalization? Or is the African aesthetic not only alive but still a motivating force in Carnival music, including sound systems, today?

Sound systems originated in Jamaica in the late 1940s when people there developed a taste for Black American music (Louis Jordan's jump blues, Count Basie's big band swing, and boogie woogie), which they heard via radio broadcasts from Miami and New Orleans when the weather was clear.

> Yet the weather wasn't clear often enough and Jamaicans couldn't get enough of the R&B they wanted to hear, so to fill this gap, the sound system was born. Sound systems are mobile amplification setups controlled by a disc jockey. They include turntables, records, amps, and speakers large enough to blast an open-air dance space yet small enough to fit in a truck. The United States and Britain had many sound systems during the late seventies disco craze, but this kind of operation originated in the late forties in Jamaica. The Jamaicans responded to the growling bass lines resounding from the giant woofers and subwoofers, and they could finally play the hard-to-get black American music they were so hungry to hear. [Bergman et al. n.d., 21–22]

Especially appealing to Jamaicans was the syncopated sound of New Orleans rhythm and blues, which itself is Caribbean-influenced and among the most African sounding of twentieth-century Black American social dance music genres. The musics of Africa and the African Diaspora in North and South America and Europe comprise a cultural system whose diverse parts have long been in dialogue with each other. The Jamaican interest in New Orleans rhythm and blues is only one example of this.

What is instructive about this example is that this dialogue was facilitated by radio, an electronic medium. In the twentieth century, electronic media, especially radio, recordings, sound systems, TV, and the Internet, have accelerated the Pan African dialogue, along with advances in transportation, which have made it easier for people to travel. Today, most African peoples around the world will first come in musical contact with each other through some nonacoustic, electronic medium.

But, there is more to this Pan African dialogue than sharing musical ideas. The Black peoples within this transatlantic cultural system have often taken inspiration from the struggles of other Black peoples, celebrating a positive identity and bolstering resistance to oppression. Today, electronic media are the most important means by which the urbanized Black cultures of Africa and its Diaspora communicate with and learn from each other. This explains, at least in part, the interest of Black Trinidadians, Jamaicans, and Americans in one another's musics.

When sound systems entered Trinidad, they brought with them all of these associations. Although sound systems today are employed by both live bands and disc jockeys (DJs), the latter played the major role in gaining acceptance for these systems in the 1960s by spinning discs at parties for young people. For example, Earl Crosby, who is today an important record producer and record shop owner in Trinidad, began his career in the 1960s as a DJ playing records at secondary school parties with a homemade sound system. Crosby was like many local Trinidadian DJs who were working parties and spreading a taste for the latest Black American hits by James Brown, Aretha Franklin, Otis Redding, and other soul artists.[12]

The music was hip, modern, urban, and identifiably Black (that is, associated with Africa or the African Diaspora). In the

10.18 Young percussionist in the engine room of the Renegades Steelband. Photograph by Ernest D. Brown Jr., Port of Spain, 1999.
10.19 One of the many sound trucks that are now a major feature of Carnival in Trinidad. Photograph by Ernest D. Brown Jr., Port of Spain, 1999.

United States in the 1960s, soul music articulated the hopes, aspirations, and determination of Black Americans. This music was the voice of the Civil Rights and Black Power movements expressed through social dance music. This music provided a new and appealing voice with a powerful message for the Trinidadian people who, like the Jamaicans, only gained their independence in 1962. For the same reasons, this Black American voice had a similar impact in Africa at the time.

In the 1960s sound systems were not yet used in Carnival celebrations. Steelbands still ruled but not for long. Whether they knew it or not, Trinidadian DJs were sowing the seeds of an electronic revolution in music. DJs began to develop into entertainers who interacted with the crowd and geared their music to the mood of their audience, as they had in Jamaica and the United States. Trinidadians, like Jamaicans and Black Americans, began to accept the DJ and his sound system as the equivalent of hearing a live band. In each of these countries, sound systems developed into a new and very important electronically mediated listening experience that constituted an alternative to hearing music performed by live musicians on stage.

At first a DJ operating a sound system might seem to be the antithesis of African-derived performance practice in which improvisation and interaction among musicians and the audience are key qualities. Some believe, and I must confess I am among them, that something is missing in music without these qualities. DJs have tried to compensate for these drawbacks by choosing music according to the mood of the audience and by becoming performers themselves, working the mike, manipulating the music, and interacting with the crowd.

Similarly, today the musicians who record the music DJs play compensate for this lack of live interaction by including dance instructions in their recordings. A good example of this is Nigel Lewis's "Movin'," which won him the title of Road March King for Carnival '96. The Road March is the people's choice as to the most popular tune actually used on the road in Carnival processions. "Movin' " includes instructional lyrics such as "movin' to the left, movin' to the right... on four, on four, on one, two, three, four." Including dance instructions in a song's lyrics is an important element in the African aesthetic, and parallels can be found in much Black American popular music.

At Carnival '96 it was truly striking to see large crowds of people moving in a coordinated fashion. These audiences took an active role in structuring their own interactions with machine-made music, dancing and improvising their own movements freely. Thus, even in situations where the music is "canned," strong elements of audience participation, dance improvisation, and self-expression are preserved. These elements provide continuity with African traditions of music and dance at Carnival. By providing numerous opportunities for audience participation involving the coordinated movement of large numbers of people, DJs and musicians re-create the excited atmosphere of the fete in the streets and connect contemporary performances of prerecorded music with Trinidad's African-derived traditions of music and dance.

Since their introduction, Trinidadians have discovered that there are many advantages to the DJ and his electronically mediated listening and dancing experience. First, it is cheap and accessible. People who cannot afford to attend concerts, or who live in countries where their favorite artists rarely tour, can attend sound-system parties where the current hits are played. Second,

DJs have a better selection of music than do most individuals, so those attending will be sure to hear the latest hits at their parties. Third, people have developed a taste for the loud bass sounds and high-quality, high-volume sound reproduction that sound systems make possible. Home stereos and radios cannot compare. Sound systems make urban, contemporary, African-derived dance music sound the way it was designed to sound, the way it sounds in a recording studio, concert, or fete.

In the 1960s, DJs and sound systems brought this new listening and dancing experience to large numbers of people in Trinidad. In exchange many were willing to overlook the absence of live musicians on stage at sound-system parties. In the 1970s, Trinidadians began to prefer sound systems to steelbands at fetes because of their sound quality. This change in the way in which music was delivered was only the first step in an electronic music revolution that would eventually affect the sound of Trinidadian music itself, leading to the creation of *soca*. As in the introduction of sound systems, the influence of Jamaican and Black American musics was key.

Turning Up the Volume Electronically: Part 2

Technological innovations began to change the sound of Black American dance music in the late 1960s and 1970s, and this music (first soul, then funk, and disco) began to dominate the airwaves in Trinidad. American and British rock also became important influences, particularly for young people. More and better quality electronic instruments—electric basses, electric guitars, etc.—had become available and were being used. Synthesizers, which allow musicians to electronically generate a wide range of sounds, began to be used with increasing frequency. In addition, various electronic devices that allowed musicians to manipulate the sound of their instruments either in the recording studio or in live performance entered common usage through the efforts of Jimi Hendrix and others.

Finally, the way in which recording studios operated changed as a result of multitrack recording, which allowed more instruments to be recorded more clearly, and postproduction technology, which allowed greater manipulation of recorded sound. As a result, the production values of Black American music went up. From soul to disco, electronically generated or manipulated sounds became an increasingly important part of American popular music in the 1970s.

The same was happening in Jamaica. Bob Marley was busy spreading reggae's new electronic sound around the world in the 1970s. The high production values of Black American and Jamaican musics made them popular in Trinidad and raised the level of expectation of the Trinidadian audiences. In addition the message of Rastafarianism began to strike a responsive chord among Trinidadians, especially among those whose economic status and prospects had not changed with the coming of independence.

By comparison, calypso was behind the times. The Mighty Sparrow and Lord Kitchener, whose musics were revolutionary when they first gained prominence as part of the Young Brigade in the 1940s and 1950s, dominated the field. But what was once groundbreaking had become status quo twenty years later. Sparrow and Kitchener's musics were no longer the music of youth. Furthermore calypso's production values and sound quality reflected the recording technology of an earlier era. Black American and Jamaican musics seemed to be of higher quality and to be more contemporary to many in Trinidad.

Trinidadian newspapers of the 1970s were filled with laments over the sorry state of calypso, and all sorts of reasons were offered for what seemed to be the music's imminent demise. One top radio DJ was quoted in an editorial as having said that in calypso there had been

> "no progression" in the art form, the recordings are of a poor standard and youth was identifying more with "soul" and "hard rock." Probably unfairly, he added that "it is the calypsonians themselves who are killing calypso: the youth are only burying it." [*Sunday Express* 1972, 4]

In another newspaper article, Sparrow argued against those who considered calypso recordings to be substandard.

> What many people do is compare our music with American music. And they flock to whichever one they find more attractive. That's wrong. Culture is not a thing to be compared. It is like a person's face. It might not be as pretty as another's, but it is yours, in that way our local artistes are being denied an opportunity. They are being told indirectly that they are sub-standard. [Pitman 1972, 16–17]

In the early 1970s calypso was in trouble for a variety of reasons. Stylistic stagnation was only one problem. Other problems were structural in nature, having to do with the belief system of Trinidad's music culture and with the way in which it is organized. Since calypso is associated with the excesses of Carnival, many Trinidadians consider it to be inappropriate to listen to calypso outside of the Carnival season, the period between New Year's Eve and Ash Wednesday. The word *Carnival* means "farewell to the flesh." Once Lent arrives, many Trinidadians believe that they should abstain from calypso, just as they abstain from eating meat and from enjoying other earthly pleasures. This belief has been eroded by the mass media, which distribute American and other music and TV programming, which are dominant in Trinidad and do not observe Lent.

Finally, within Carnival, calypso's role has been reduced over the years. In the nineteenth century, the forerunners of the calypsonians played a central role in Carnival, singing with masquerade bands that paraded through the streets, but in the 1920s calypsonians turned professional, abandoning the masquerade bands in the streets to perform in tents, indoor venues where people paid money to hear them. Except for going to calypso tents during the Carnival season, many Trinidadians had in turn abandoned calypso by 1974.

The situation was critical. Calypsonians had to change or face extinction. To compete with American and Jamaican music, Trinidad's calypsonians needed their own electronic music with higher production values, and they began to create it through the efforts of The Mighty Shadow, Maestro, and Lord Shorty (now Ras Shorty I). They called it *soca*, or the soul of calypso. It was a music that used multitrack recording technology and electronic instruments, such as drum machines and synthesizers, to produce music that satisfied the Trinidadian audience's demand for high quality, electronic sound. These developments have defined the sound of the contemporary brass band in Trinidad.

Soca was an effective response to the technological challenge presented by Jamaican and Black American musics. It gave the calypsonian an electronic voice that was suitable for modern times, one that appealed to young people and resonated with hopes for social progress and prosperity. It placed the voice of the calypsonian within a new context, that of an Africanized electronic big band with riffing horn lines, heavy bass, and driving percussion. As they say in Trinidad, "heavy jammin' comin' down de road."[13]

At the same time that technology was revolutionizing the sound of calypso,

10.20 A truck carrying the very popular Trinidadian band Charlie's Roots. Photograph by John Nunley, Port of Spain, 1984.

turning it into *soca*, Carnival bands were growing in size and needed new means of delivering music to larger and larger crowds in the streets at Carnival. This new need would also affect the sound of Trinidadian music. The change in *mas* band size was itself an important reflection of changing social realities in Trinidad. Trinidad was newly independent and relatively prosperous. The middle class was growing and was in control of the new nation, and after many years and much persuasion, it had accepted calypso, Carnival, and steelband as symbols of national pride and an emergent Trinidadian national culture. The middle class began to participate in Carnival in larger numbers and to promote Carnival as an international tourist attraction. As a result, more and more people wanted to play *mas*.

A whole new style of pretty *mas* became dominant on Carnival Tuesday. Many more women began to play *mas* and play in steelbands. A few even began to sing calypso, as a result of the women's liberation movement and the removal of the social stigma attached to these art forms. At the same time, King and Queen costumes became more spectacular and larger than life size. Each masquerade band has a designated character who is the King and another who is the Queen of that particular band. These Kings and Queens then compete against each other for the titles, King or Queen of the Bands. As masquerading grew more spectacular and more people participated in it, bands grew from being neighborhood outfits with fifty or one hundred participants to being middle-class business enterprises involving several thousand masqueraders.

Steelbands could not provide loud enough sound for such large groups. Some had tried to amplify pan, but without success. Steelbands increased their size, doubling and redoubling the number of players playing particular parts, but ultimately the whole effort became increasingly unwieldy and expensive. No acoustic ensemble can compete with an electronic sound source in volume, consistency, and endurance. Machines never get tired.

In 1975 Maestro, one of the founders of *soca*, expressed the frustrations of many:

> Masqueraders bawling
> I hear them complaining,
> Steelbands playing too slow.
> They say they want tempo.
> Playing too much classic.
> Too much Yankee music.
> Straying from the beat,
> And they leaving we in heat.

Clearly steelbands were not responding to the needs of their audiences. Furthermore, neither steelbands nor percussion ensembles had the instrumentation to make the latest brass band hits sound like they are supposed to, the way they sound in concert, at a fete, or on a good sound reproduction system. There was a need for another sound source that could provide urban, contemporary, electronic dance music and keep a crowd of thousands dancing and energized. Sound systems controlled by DJs and sound systems amplifying the music of brass bands filled this gap. The vocalists in these brass bands were either calypsonians or band singers.[14] In 1996, for example, Charlie's Roots and Byron Lee and the Dragonaires were just a few of the brass bands that rode sound trucks to play music for masquerade bands (fig. 10.20).

The popularity of these bands and DJs has forced steelbands to the margins of Carnival street parades. At Carnival '96, I found a number of small steelbands with an equally small but loyal following parading in the side streets of Port of Spain, well away from the main Carnival parade route. As I followed one steelband, it entered an intersection where a sound system was installed outside a bar. The steelband could not compete with the volume of sound and stopped playing. The DJ kindly turned off his sound system and invited the steelband to strike up a tune and move through the intersection. Some DJs are not so considerate.

As a result, steelbands focus more on Panorama, a national steelband competition held on the Saturday before Carnival begins. By 1996 steelbands had become so nonessential to Carnival parades that the Trinidadian government provided a large monetary prize to induce them to accompany masquerade bands through the streets as they once did. In 1996, Desperadoes, one of the top Trinidadian steelbands, paraded through the streets at Carnival with a masquerade band composed of sailors, a costume rooted in the World War II era when American GIs were stationed in Trinidad and steelbands were in their glory days. For Carnival '97 prizes were offered again to encourage more steelbands to parade with a *mas* band. By Carnival '99 several steelbands were organizing masquerade bands of sailors to parade through the streets on Carnival Tuesday (figs. 10.21, 10.22).

These revivalist efforts may have been successful in the short run in restoring a piece of tradition that many Trinidadians feared was slipping away. However, in the long run, Carnival may not be so easily channeled. Unless steelbands begin to fulfill a more essential role in Carnival processions, the government carrot will not be enough to make steelbands a vital part of the music for Carnival processions. Perhaps, rather than lament the passing of this aspect of Carnival, we should recognize the transformation of Carnival music traditions that has occurred and try to understand a new manifestation of the African aesthetic that has guided Carnival for the past 160 years.

Sound systems have many positive features and fulfill important functions. Sound systems with DJs or live bands provide dance music for larger groups than acoustic ensembles can. Sound systems more effectively provide dance music for people in large spaces, such as the stage of the Queens Park Savanna where the King and Queen of the Bands competitions take place. *Soca* music delivered via sound systems certainly has turned up the volume of Carnival music and made the current form of middle-class participation in Carnival possible.

Amplified brass bands and DJ-controlled sound systems also have a strong appeal for young Trinidadians. In the 1990s brass bands like Atlantik and Xtatik speak for the younger generation in a way that steelbands never could, just as in the 1970s and 1980s, the pioneers of *soca* spoke for young people. In the 1990s young Trinidadians like Brother Resistance have developed their own form of rap, much as Black American teenagers did in the 1980s. Called *rapso* (rap/*soca*), this music employs rap vocals, Trinidadian rhythms, and various electronic devices (sound systems, turntables, mixers, electronic sound generators, and sampling devices).

Today, sound systems, radio, TV, and other electronically mediated forms of musical reproduction are everywhere in Trinidad. They are in the taxis and the restaurants. You hear electronically reproduced music spilling out of shops as you walk along the road. Sound systems have made music a part of everyday life to an extent that live music could never be. Especially at Carnival, sound systems are immersed in life, and sometimes it seems that life is immersed in them. This parallels the way in which music forms part of everyday existence in many traditional African societies. Sound systems have updated this phenomenon for urban, late twentieth-century Black societies that are in contact with modern electronic technology.

The ubiquitousness of electronically reproduced dance music is a comment upon modern society in Trinidad. *Soca* and *rapso*

10.21 The Exodus Steelband in "Sailor Fantasea." Photograph by Ernest D. Brown Jr., Port of Spain, 1999.

musics reflect the interaction of young people with the world around them. Their fascination with electronic technology and progress is obvious. The preference of young Trinidadians for music in which technology plays a major role parallels their interest in computers, video games, the Internet, satellite television, and other contemporary technological developments. This music is in tune with the spirit of the times for many young people. They are aware of and are growing up with various forms of electronic technology, and they are comfortable with it. It is as part of their experience. The middle class also accepts technological innovation, since they encounter it in their jobs and in their private lives, where, for example, many subscribe to the services of American satellite and cable TV companies. The poor, however, often do not have the money, education, or inclination to take advantage of new technology.

Young people have also encouraged an increase in *soca*'s tempo. This may reflect the influence of rap and techno-funk, two Black American dance music genres known for their rapid tempos, or it may be part of a general trend toward an increase in tempo that is evident in post-World War II Black music in the United States and in Trinidad. In any case, the tempo of much *soca* is now very fast. The older generation may not have the energy to dance to a fast *soca* beat for miles at Carnival, but the kids are up for it.[15]

The speed of the music has restricted the content of its lyrics.[16] In fast *soca*, there is little time to tell a story, little time for social commentary, an important African feature of the music. Fast *soca* is "jam and wine"[17] party music. While the older generation may miss the humor and storytelling of calpyso, the younger generation finds these things in *rapso*, which, like rap, contains many more words than does music that is sung.

Fast *soca* party music also appeals to those with middle-class status or aspirations. Many in this market segment do not want to hear complaints about injustice and inequality at Carnival. They want to party. In this sense, "jam and wine" *soca* songs complement the middle-class tradition of large bands and pretty *mas*. Pretty *mas* and fast party songs are manifestations in different art forms of the same basic sensibility.

Thus, the middle class and the young are the two most important groups of consumers in the *soca* marketplace and have a powerful effect upon the kinds of songs that are recorded. The middle class hires more bands and buys more recordings than do the poor, and young people spend more on music than do the middle-aged or the elderly. Until the tastes of these two groups change, the letters to the editor (which appear repeatedly in Trinidadian newspapers), bemoaning the loss of social commentary and decrying the emphasis on sex in *soca*, will fall on deaf ears. These two demographic groups have turned up the volume at Carnival in a way that is to their liking.

Jammin' with Electric Africa

Sound systems and electronic dance music are here to stay for the foreseeable future. It is pointless to wish that they were not, and the gallant efforts to revitalize older forms of music and *mas* will continue to swim against the current of middle-class and youthful taste. These demographic groups are jammin' with electronic drums at Carnival.

Soca and *rapso* are extensions of an African-inspired, Carnival music tradition. There are strong elements of continuity with traditional African music, even within these contemporary electronic dance musics. Electronic drums are not so different from acoustic drums, same sensibility, different medium. Musically, the general principles underlying the

10.22 The Exodus Steelband in "Sailor Fantasea." Photograph by Ernest D. Brown Jr., Port of Spain, 1999.

production of *soca* and *rapso* are the same as those underlying the formerly dominant acoustic Carnival musics, even though the specific features of these musics (rhythms, melodies, harmonies, tone colors, and song forms) differ radically from each other. The relationship of these diverse genres consists in their being successive applications of general principles for organizing musical sound that are derived from African musical cultures. In other words, there is an African aesthetic at work in all of these ensembles despite their differences in specific musical features.

A short list of these general African-inspired principles include creating music that is repetitive and has a strong beat or sense of rhythmic drive that is good for dancing. Musics inspired by an African sensibility are highly syncopated and percussive with dense polyrhythms, even when the musical instruments being played are strings, winds, or keyboards, as opposed to drums. Melodically these musics include solo-chorus melodic structures, prominent bass melodies, riffs (short, repeated melodic phrases) especially in horn lines and vocal choruses, and polyphony (more than one melody occurring at a time). These music and dance styles often emphasize improvisation and encourage audience participation by providing opportunities for the audience to sing, move, or comment upon a performance as it is occurring. This approach makes the audience an active participant in a music-making situation and reduces to a minimum the gap between performer and audience. Finally, this music is loud enough to dominate its immediate environment, announcing Carnival as a social occasion, drawing everyone in its vicinity into its spirit, keeping people focused on the occasion at hand, and providing them with the psychic energy to keep dancing over long periods of time and under difficult conditions (heat, crowds, heavy costumes).

Several times at Carnival '96, I could have sworn that I heard drumming somewhere in the distance. Every time I followed the sound, however, I realized as I got closer that I was hearing a sound system (or more precisely, the bass and drums of a live or prerecorded brass band). In a recording studio or in live performance, *soca*, reggae, and *rapso* are usually mixed so that the bass, drums, and other percussion are very prominent. The bass and drums throb and pulse through your body in much the same way that acoustic drums or steeldrums do, when you are close to them. Sound systems can accomplish this effect from further away. I began to think of these musics as electronic drum musics.

Soca, reggae, and *rapso* are only a few of many electronic drum musics from Africa and the African Diaspora. The electronic media are the appropriate means through which these drumming and dance musics should be experienced. These electronic Black popular music genres from Africa and the African Diaspora are the drumming of today for urbanized Black populations. They are part of an electrified African sensibility that affects popular music and pop culture around the world. *Soca* and *rapso* are part of this wider contemporary Pan African context.

This electrified African sensibility does not fit the romantic stereotype that some hold dear, wherein Africa functions as a simple, natural, nontechnological, and (ultimately) primitive counterbalance to the stress, technology, urbanization, and problems of late twentieth-century life. This stereotype takes many forms. Sometimes, Africa is feeling and poetry, while Europe is rationality and science. This false dichotomy pretends that electronic technology is somehow "un-African." There is, however, a real electrified African music sensibility that does exist in the world and does express the urban, technological, industrial, or postindustrial social realities with which increasing numbers of African peoples around the world must cope.

Like the drumming of earlier times, these electronically mediated Black music genres continue the association of percussive music with the themes of power, resistance, identity, and celebration discussed above. They accomplish this by being in touch with the people and in tune with the times. In African and African-derived cultures, there seems to be a recurrent demand for music that expresses the spirit of the age, whether it is reggae, soul, jazz, rap, *soca*, steelband, *tamboo bamboo*, or African drumming. Each of these musics, in its day, was hip, modern, and up-to-date. The music of Carnival is no exception to this pattern. Each of the diverse genres of Carnival music became part of the festival at a particular time and was adopted for particular reasons, relating to social pressures, new technology, shifts in musical taste, rising social aspirations, and a variety of other factors. *Soca* and *rapso* continue this tradition.

Carnival continues to preserve voices from the past and make room for new voices and means of expression that reflect contemporary concerns and attitudes. Over the years, its music has changed greatly, musical instruments and genres have come and gone. This process of musical change is a basic part of the festival. Revivalist efforts cannot stop this.

Regardless of changes in musical instruments and styles, a flexible and adaptable African sensibility has been at work in Carnival's musical traditions. This sensibility is at once radical and conservative. It finds ways to keep past traditions alive by adapting them to present needs and realities. Carnival is thus a mosaic of music and masquerades that retains associations from a variety of eras. As each successive voice is added to the

Carnival mix, the collective voice of the festival grows richer and louder. In this way, an African sensibility has repeatedly turned up the volume at Carnival over the years. It promises to do so in innovative ways for many more years to come.

Today Electric Africa rules the Carnival street. He's ready to pump up the jam and make you move your feet. He's gonna bust a move and get you in the groove. He's ready to shout it out loud and clear. He is the jam master blaster, the inhuman stratocaster. His bass so low, you can't get under it. His volume so high, you can't get over it. He jams so hard, he cuts diamonds. Have amp will travel. He rules the world. His father was RCA Victor, and his great grandfather an African drum. Listen carefully and you will know from where he come. He wakes up the sun and serenades the moon. Before you know it, he is in your room. He will dance you in your dreams. He is not just what he seems. He's come to mash up the party. He's come to free your mind.

Electric Africa is the Midnight Robber[18] for the twenty first century—ready to steal your misconceptions, all the while taking no prisoners (*sans humanité*). If you don't like his music, tough. To paraphrase an old Black power slogan, "Move over, or he will move over on you." This is the message that Electric Africa brings to Carnival. It is a new version of the message carried by the steelbands in the 1930s and the African drummers in the 1830s. It is a message in tune with today's reality and tomorrow's technology. Electric Africa is in the house. So pop in a CD, turn up the volume, and join the jam. He's coming through your nearest sound system, right about now!

11. The Voice of Ginen:

Drums in Haitian Religion, History, and Identity

VICTORIA SIMMONS

11.1 Mural of drums in the peristyle of a temple. Photograph by Victoria Simmons, Port-au-Prince, 1999.

In its native setting a musical instrument becomes inscribed—both as an object and as an instrument—with multiple and varied meanings. If transferred across time and space to another home, it becomes all the more a vessel of signification, gaining layers of additional meanings. Such an object, such an instrument, is the sacred drum of Haitian Vodou.

Vodou is a religion deriving from the West African traditions that took root in Haiti with slavery and flourished in the subsequent history of the world's first Black republic. Long opposed by the Europhile Haitian elite and vilified by outsiders who were as eager to despise the only republic ever to have been established by slave revolt as they were fearful of "tribal" religion, Vodou has survived numerous persecutions. As the Haitian painter Ernst Prophète has suggested in his work, Vodou has endured in the very trees of Haiti and in the colors of the people's clothing. It has persisted to the point that it is currently embraced by many of the elite as Haiti's indigenous religion.

Haiti has often been described as 90-odd percent Roman Catholic and 100 percent Vodou. While this may be an exaggeration, it is difficult to overestimate the importance of Vodou in Haitian culture. Most expressive arts in Haiti have long been religious or imported from religion, so that, for example, a taxi driver may pass his time while stalled in traffic by singing about the *lwa* (spirit) Ogou. In Haiti's poverty, and in the nation's long history of political and cultural upheaval, Vodou has been both the cement of ordinary society and the conservator of expressive traditions. It provides a historical and conceptual connection to Ginen—Africa. Therefore, the drum used in Vodou ritual is not only the means by which the spirits are called down into communion with their *sèvitè* (servitors) but also an object of art, history, and identity.

11.2 The Vodou drum infiltrates art even in an Episcopal cathedral. Wilson Bigaud's version of the Wedding at Cana in the Cathédrale Ste.-Trinité includes details of Vodou ritual. Photograph by Victoria Simmons, Port-au-Prince, 1999.

African Origins

The African peoples listed by slaveholders as contributing to the population of Haiti included Senegalese, Wolofs, Fulbe, Bambara, Quiambas, Aradas, Minas, Caplaus, Mahi, Nago, Mayombe, Mondongues, Angolese, and Kongolese. However, the vast majority of the African population of Haiti has always been understood to be of Fon origin, brought from the densely populated shores of the Gulf of Guinea (Métraux 1972, 25f). The lexicon of Haitian Kreyòl and many of the names of Vodou deities appear to bear this out.

James G. Leyburn (1941) sees four stages in the creation of the religion of Vodou. From 1730 to 1790, when great numbers of slaves were being brought from the Gulf of Guinea and elsewhere, the practices of the Fon and other peoples underwent a gestation period in the new environment. From 1790 to 1800, the revolutionary period, the separate peoples finished fusing under Vodou. The next fifteen years saw a period of persecution by Haitian rulers fearing Vodou's power for unification against authority. Then, from 1815 to 1850, the religion diffused and unobtrusively settled into its present form (Barrett 1977, 199).

From the revolution's end in 1804 until the signing of the Concordat between Haiti and the Vatican in 1860, the republic was almost completely isolated, with little or no contact with Europe, the Americas, or Africa. The schools were Roman Catholic and usually French staffed, but the reality was that the religious establishment had been abandoned by Rome, so that for half a century Haitian religion—Christian or Vodou—existed with little official hierarchy (Nicholls 1979, 84).

Vodou

The word *Vodou* comes from an Ewe word meaning "spirit" (Barrett 1977, 199). Practitioners of Vodou believe that there is a single god, the Bondye (or Bon Dieu), but he resides at a great distance and does not involve himself in the day-to-day life of his people. The *lwa*, who are ancestral spirits that have been deified, do involve themselves in the lives of ordinary people and, on occasion, even intervene with the Bondye.

A *sèvitè*, who must also be a practicing Roman Catholic, will belong to a religious house, or *ounfò*, which is led by a priest, an *oungan* (male) or *manbo* (female). Although there are private altars in the religion and many types of devotion are possible, the standard Vodou *sèvis* (service) uses singing, chanting, movement, and usually drumming to call down one or more of the *lwa* into communion with the *sèvitè*. The *ounfò*, the priests, the initiates, and the ritual objects all have their own patron spirits.

Especially in urban areas, there are two primary *nanchon* (nations of *lwa*). The Rada are named for the town of Allada in Benin (formerly Dahomey). They are held to be more purely African, the "root" *lwa* associated with family, healing, and "coolness." The Petwo spirits are fierce,

"hot," and uncompromising. They are associated with outsiders and foreigners, including non-Dahomean Africans (especially the Kongolese) as well as with the original Native American population of Haiti. The Petwo rite is also associated with the anger or power of slaveholding, attempting, according to Karen McCarthy Brown, to appropriate that power to itself. The Petwo spirits are worshipped with sharp tastes and loud noises, such as the crack of whips and the pop of gunpowder (Brown 1989, 67).

In a *sèvis* the ritual singers and dancers are called *ounsi*. They are led by an *ounjenikon*, who is usually a woman. The *ounsi* dress all in white, except sometimes in the case of the Petwo rites, where they may wear red. The prefix *oun-* in these terms, as well as in *ounfò* and *oungan*, means "drums," or, more generally, any instrument of sacred music. The drummers, usually called *tanbouyè,* may also be called *ountorgye* (Rigaud 1969, 114f). The trees in the yard of the *ounfò* are *reposwa*, sanctuaries for the *lwa*. Services may be held among them, with the drums brought out for the occasion (Rigaud 1969, 18).

A typical service is preceded by the blessing of the precincts. The drums are the second thing to be ritually saluted, right after the *poto mitan*, the post of the central altar along which the *lwa* will enter (Deren 1953, 184). The service begins with Catholic prayers and invocations of the saints (Rigaud 1969, 120). The beginnings of *langay*—a rising mixture of African words, Kreyòl phrases, and Roman Catholic litany—is the signal for the drumming to begin (Brown 1991, 280). The *ogan*, a flat, tongueless bell, is struck by a small iron rod. It directs the ensemble, setting a rhythm for the drummers. A triangle is played to add an opposing beat and to open the path of the air for the *lwa* (Rigaud 1969, 111f). The drumming adds intensity, yet at the same time provides order to what otherwise would be a chaos of strolling, dancing, chatting, singing, chanting, eating and drinking, offering, and so on. The drumming and the chants together are said to magnetize and draw down the *lwa* (Rigaud 1969, 121). A switch in the fixed rhythm of the lead drum to a brief, highly syncopated counterpoint (Deren 1953, 239) is the point where possession most often begins. Every rite has its own rhythm. There are chants and songs for every *lwa* and every occasion. There is also extreme local variation in songs (Rigaud 1969, 122f). The correct song and rhythm must be used to attract the desired *lwa*.

11.3 A ritual flag by Simeon shows the *lwa* Aida and Damballah uniting around a sacred drum. Photograph by Victoria Simmons, 1999.

11.4 Mural on the wall of an altar room in a temple. Photograph by Victoria Simmons, Port-au-Prince, 1999.

As one *sèvitè* after another is "ridden" by the *lwa*, he or she is dressed in the clothing associated with that spirit. The *lwa* then proceeds to join the party, eating, drinking, and offering advice to the remaining *sèvitè*. Sacrifices of chickens, or sometimes other livestock, are made to the *lwa* during this "party" period. Later, when the *lwa* has departed, its "horse" will have no memory of the possession. In Vodou, unlike, for example, Pentecostalism, children and outsiders are almost never ridden. An experienced *sèvitè* can call down a *lwa* almost at will or reject being ridden once the possession has begun.

Although some writers, such as the European Milo Rigaud and the Haitian Rachel Beauvoir-Dominique (1995), lay great emphasis on the mystical aspects of Vodou, especially the quite genuine influence of Freemasonry (Rigaud 1969, 112f), in general Vodou is a religion that emphasizes praxis over theory. However, one of the purposes of Vodou ritual is to achieve connection with Ginen, Mother Africa, where all *sèvitè* go after death.

The Drummer in Vodou

Drummers occupy an ambiguous position in Vodou. "Beating the drum" has long been a synonym for performing a *sèvis* that calls the spirits (Métraux 1972, 177). The drummer himself, however, is usually not a member of the *ounfò*, but a highly trained professional—in fact, the only participant in Vodou whose skills require extensive craft training (Deren 1953, 233). When an initiate does play, he has his own *lwa* (Rigaud 1969, 114). Initiates rarely play, though, for the possibility of possession is unwelcome in a drummer, who must be attentive to everything that is happening in the *sèvis*.

A great deal is demanded of the drummer. He must learn a huge variety of songs and chants for different types of ceremonies and different *nanchon* of *lwa* (Deren 1953, 234). He must have a great deal of stamina, for Vodou ceremonies go on for many hours. He must follow the actions of the *oungan* or *manbo* in order to deduce their wishes and watch the *sèvitè* carefully so as to help or delay their possession. Drummers must serve a long apprenticeship, the younger players acquiring their skills by taking over the drumming very late at night and continuing until the end of the *sèvis* at dawn. Because they must serve the *lwa* and the needs of the ritual, drummers cannot express their individuality in the *sèvis*. Nevertheless, professional drummers can achieve money, fame, and honor (Métraux 1972, 179).

11.5 Drummers at a Flag Day service for Papa Zaka held by the Societé Reine de Saut D'eau, a Vodou society in Port-au-Prince. Photograph by Victoria Simmons, May 18, 1999.

11.6 A Rada drum battery used for a service for Papa Zaka held by the Societé Reine de Saut D'eau, a Vodou society in Port-au-Prince. Photograph by Victoria Simmon, 1999.

The Batteries of Drums

Each type of rite, each *nanchon*, has its own characteristic drums, chants, and dances. The most common set is for the Rada *sèvis*. Described by Rigaud as the most "brillant" battery (1969, 115), the drums are typical of those of Benin. They are constructed of a conical tree-trunk shell, with a head made of bullock-skin or goatskin that is stretched with cord-braced pegs, usually inserted at an angle. The drums are painted in bright colors that symbolize the patron *lwa* of the sanctuary or of the particular drum set (Métraux 1972, 179). Identical in shape, the drums differ in size. The *manman* is over three feet tall, the *seconde* around two feet tall, and the *bula* about a foot and a half tall. Each is beaten in a different way. The *manman* is struck with the hand or with a small wooden hammer on the rim or the membrane. The player stands or sits behind the drum, which is bound to him or his chair with rope and held away from him at a wide angle. The *seconde* player sits with the drum held between his legs. He strikes it with one hand, while with the other he uses a bent stick or a strung bow called an *agida*. The *bula* is held vertically and struck with two sticks.

Two drums are played in the Petwo rites. They are smaller than the instruments used in the Rada *sèvis*, and the cords that attach the heads have a characteristic Y-shaped arrangement. The larger drum is called the *manman* or *gros baka*, while the smaller, which dominates the set, is called the *ti baka* and is struck with the flat of the hand (Métraux 1972, 179f). As with other ritual objects, drums can be overendowed with meaning: Rigaud associates the *manman* with the thunderbolt and the southern sky, while the *ti baka* represents the earth, Ginen, and the northern sky. The Petwo drums are not only "hot," they are "demonic" and "cannibalistic" (1969, 115f). (Although Rigaud is a sympathetic student of Vodou, even he is willing to attribute to Petwo the sort of inflammatory ritual details attributed by more hostile observers to the religion as a whole.)

Kongo sets include three different drums that are cylindrical and double-headed. They are called the *manman*, *timbal*, and *ti-kongo*, or *Katabou*. The first and last are held vertically or tilted and played with the hands, while the dominant *timbal* is held horizontally and played with sticks. The head is attached with two wooden rings, "like European drums" (Rigaud 1969, 116). The *timbal* is sometimes called the *Gwonde*—"thunder"—according to Rigaud (1969, 116), or "the growler" (Valdman 1981, 240).

Igbo drums are cylindrical, like Petwo drums, but the sheepskin heads are attached with strings run through holes in the wood and laced through the base. The *djuba*, or *martinique*, drum is used only for the peasant *lwa*, Papa Zaka, when he wants the *djuba* dance performed. It consists of a cask drum with one cord-attached head. It is played by two musicians, one of whom strikes the head with his hands while the other hits the casing with sticks (Métraux 1972, 180f). Both Kongo and Igbo drums are played as Petwo batteries when their rites are not differentiated.

More unusual sets, more often found in the countryside, are the Mahi, Nago, Dahomée, Asson-Rou, Banda, and the set variously known as Crabignin, Nago, or Kongo. Each of these has three drums and its own associated dances (Rigaud 1969, 136f).

The *assoto*, an especially rare drum, is six or seven feet high and used only on very solemn occasions. Most examples disappeared in the Anti-Superstition Campaigns that began in 1915. In his fieldwork in the late 1950s, Alfred Métraux only saw one, which he described as over six feet tall, ritually dressed in white, and kept in its own room (1972, 183). In 1998, Port-au-Prince's Museum of the Haitian People had on exhibit a drum that was labeled an *assoto* but that was much smaller than has been claimed of the *assoto* of the past.

According to Jacques Roumain, the founder of the Haitian Communist Party and director of the Bureau of Ethnology, prior to 1915 the *assoto* drum had an especially elaborate construction ritual. It could only be made out of a few special kinds of wood, in particular the *mawodenm* (*Ochroma pyramidale*, or balsa)—wood that "has much blood." It had to be cut on the full moon, and the drumhead was laid at the stroke of noon. The drum was baptized in the presence of seven or thrice seven godparents. Then services for various *lwa* were performed, and a black or white goat was sacrificed (or better still, a red ox). Unusually, the drum was beaten only by *sèvitè* being ridden by *lwa* (Rigaud 1969, 117).

After the services were completed, the *lwa* of the drum was sent away. A basket was filled with cooked food, raw food, needles, cotton, linen, a pipe, tobacco, matches, eating utensils, small change, and a paper on which everyone present witnessed that they had contributed something. An especially strong man was anointed and protected with assorted charms against the spirit. A sad song was sung as he lifted the basket onto his head. As a whip was cracked three times behind him, he went to throw the basket into the

11.7 Vodou drums for sale across from the Baptist mission on Mount Kenscoff, above Port-au-Prince. Photograph by Victoria Simmons, 1999.

sea (or to leave it in the woods). The services continued, with possessions occurring and the drum being played alternately by the *ounsi*, who, using a stick with a nail in one end, beat it until the membrane burst. The drum was then retired, presumably having to be reconsecrated before being used again (Métraux 1972, 183f).

The Drum As Sacred Object

The treatment of the *assoto*, and the fact that the drums are saluted second in the order of standard ritual, suggest their importance as ritual objects. The drum, in fact, is not merely an object; it is held to be endowed with a soul or a spirit (Métraux 1972, 182). It has a parallel life as a mythical object: the membrane is said to be the ear of the patriarchal *lwa* Damballah, and the copper hoops on drums of earlier times were said to represent the sun and the *lwa* Ezuli (Rigaud 1969, 117).

Haitians say that the construction methods of the sacred drums were revealed by the same means as the construction of the tabernacle was revealed to Moses. Rada drum construction is based on geometric principles representing the specific rite and *nanchon* for which the drum is intended (Rigaud 1969, 117). Before the tree is cut down, the *oungan* performs a ceremony to the *lwa* who will be patron of the drum. When the drum is hollowed out, rum is burned inside. The first peg hole made is called the *manman* and has a privileged position: the fastening of the drumhead uses a ritual formula and movements, all beginning on the first peg hole. When the drum is baptized, it is dressed in the robes of the *lwa*. With godparents present, it is given its names first by a *père-savane* (an unordained bush-priest) in a pseudo-Catholic rite, then by an *oungan* in a Vodou *sèvis* (Métraux 1972, 183).

The sacredness of the drums is expressed again in their treatment. They are kept apart from other instruments and from ordinary music. If, as rarely happens, a Rada drum set is used in *rara* parading bands or in Carnival, it is held to be ritually unclean and must be rebaptized. The drums are housed in the *ounfò*, never in the open (Dunham 1983, 13–14). They are often hung from the ceiling, along with calabashes, baskets, trays, and ritual flags (Rigaud 1969, 16). They may share the *ounfò* with sleeping pallets, bicycles, or household laundry (see fig. 11.9). However, the drums of different cults are housed separately. It is especially important to keep the drums of the "cool" Rada rites separate

11.8 A street mural incorporating Vodou drums promotes a local *rara* band. Photograph by Victoria Simmons, Bel-Air district, Port-au-Prince, 1999.

11.9 Vodou drums stored in the peristyle of a temple. The peristyle, or main room of the temple, doubles as a living space—note the laundry basket and clothesline. Photograph by Victoria Simmons, Port-au-Prince, 1999.

from those of the "hot" Petwo rites. Women are not allowed to touch the drums, and in Haiti the drummers are invariably male (Dunham 1983, 14).

The drums are sometimes ritually fed (*baye-tanbou-manje*) and put to bed (*kouche-tanbou*). To put the drums to bed, the *sèvitè* lay them on their sides on a bed of banana leaves representing Ginen. A candle is lit and placed on each of them, and food and libations are sprinkled over them. Some of this food is fed to the chickens that are later to be sacrificed to the drums. When the candles are put out and the instruments covered with white sheets, they are said to have "gone to Ifé" in Ginen. A machete is plunged into the ground before them, and ritual flags cover them while the *sèvitè* sing funeral chants (Rigaud 1969, 117f).

A Note on Dance

As with the songs, there is great local variation in dances, with the names of the more ritual ones indicating which drum sets are to be used. The *kitha* dance, for instance, is only performed to Petwo drums, while the *Kongo payèt* is only danced to a Kongo set. The *fla voudoun* is a Rada dance. The *Dahomée zepole* is danced to *Dahomée* drums, but where that set is not used, it is danced to Petwo drums. Even non-Haitian dances are adapted to this system of specialization, so that when the *mascaron* or the *méringue* are performed at Carnival, the latter may be danced to Rada or Petwo drums, but the former can only be performed to a Petwo set (Rigaud 1969, 136f). As this suggests, there is a wide variety of dances that may be performed at a *sèvis*, not all of them sacred, although the bawdiest of them, the *lwa* Gede's *bonda*, is sacred (Métraux 1972, 192).

Vodou and Its Music in History

During the period of slavery in Haiti, slaves who were found with ritual objects were punished savagely, with lashing, imprisonment, hanging, or flaying. According to Rigaud, this treatment "succeeded in destroying...the feeling and taste for making sculptures of clay or wood," so that sculpture became uncharacteristically rare by the standards of the Diaspora as a whole (1969, 13). Nevertheless, persecution of Vodou in colonial days seems to have been haphazard and opportunistic, with little actual effort made to root out the religion. As they would continue to do until the late nineteenth century, Europeans overlooked Vodou as a religion, seeing only a congeries of practices held to be dimly remembered customs from Africa. When *sèvitè* were punished or their objects destroyed, the motivation seems to have been that of isolating and alienating the slave from the homeland rather than fear of the practices themselves, even though slaves were thought to use their ceremonies to communicate through "talking drums" (Leyburn 1941, 137). (Haiti seems, in actuality, never to have had true talking drums.)

In fact, Vodou was invisible to non-Haitians throughout most of the nineteenth century. The Englishmen James Franklin (1828) and John Candler (1842) wrote largely sympathetic traveler's accounts of the republic. In discussing religion in Haiti, they made no mention of Vodou, or even of "superstitions" or such euphemisms, confining their remarks to the state of the Roman Catholic and Protestant establishments (Franklin 1828, 390f; Candler 1842, 94f). Franklin, however, was the first of a number of foreigners to be confused by the fact that this Roman Catholic country professed religious toleration while exhibiting hostility to Protestantism (1828, 392), obviously not understanding that the government did not have Protestantism in mind when it spoke of "toleration." However, Franklin did note that there was little sincerity or genuine faith among the Roman Catholics he witnessed (1828, 394), even though the elite he would have been more likely to observe were supposedly not influenced by Vodou during this period.

In 1830, Charles MacKenzie, England's former consul general in Haiti, wrote a two-volume account of the country. He described the chaos of the ecclesiastical establishment, with monastic institutions in ruins and church authorities isolated from the Vatican, but again no mention was made of Vodou. He, too, noted that hostility to Protestantism existed alongside an unwillingness to inquire too closely about someone's religious beliefs for the purposes of burial, etc. (1830, 128f). Significantly, none of these accounts are by Americans, who during most of the century assiduously ignored the existence of the "Black Republic" on their doorstep.

When Sir Spenser St. John wrote an account of Haiti called *Hayti; or, The Black Republic* (1889), Vodou was finally brought to the fore: "'Who is tainted by Vaudoux-worship?' I fear the answer must be, 'Who is not?'" St. John associated the religion with serpent-worship and cannibalism, practices that the government, of course, was at pains to deny (or conceal, according to St. John and his ilk [1889, 187f]).

By 1900, Hesketh Prichard could write an exposé of the religion, in which "Vaudoux" is described as an all-powerful deity. Rada and Petwo become two cults: the former characterized by the color white (using white chickens in sacrifice and so on), the other, by red or black. According to Prichard, Rada is merely "superstitious," while Petwo is characterized by rites in which children are dismembered, cooked, and eaten (1971, 76, 79). Puzzled by the existence of such debased cruelty ("leavened with the horrors of serpent-worship") among such a kindly people, Prichard attributes the existence of the religion to the corruption and cruelty of the government (1971, 81, 232). Since he finds no direct evidence of cannibalism, he allows himself to hope that such practices are on the wane (1971, 79). Here, at last, we have mention of the drums, which Prichard makes marvels of physics, able to be heard loudly at a distance of a mile, but barely audible from nearby. This, he says, makes it possible for the cultists to conceal their gatherings, while at the same time announcing themselves over long distances to initiates (1971, 80).

It was left only for the American W. B. Seabrook, in his 1929 travelogue *The Magic Island*, to take a view of Vodou that was romantic rather than demonizing. However, the pounding drums, voodoo dolls, and zombies of his account provided images that have since become staples in the portrayal of a demonic Haiti (Seabrook 1929).

Meanwhile, in Haiti itself, the early leaders, such as Toussaint L'ouverture (1746–1803), were well aware of Vodou's power to unite, thus forbidding Vodou assemblies and all dances (Leyburn 1941, 139). Later in the century, the Church and the state opposed Vodou officially but tolerated it in practice, persecuting it intermittently after key events, such as the Concordat with the Vatican in 1860 and the occupation by United States Marines in 1915. Haiti's relationship to its own origins was ambivalent and fraught with conflict. On the one hand, educated Haitians had an elevated idea of the African past, yet on the other hand, they viewed contemporary Africans as primitive and debased and wished to associate themselves instead with Europe. Vodou, when it was acknowledged at all, became a victim of this ambivalence. The writer Léon Audin, for instance, tried to portray Vodou as entertainment rather than religion: the function of a Vodou gathering was singing, dancing, and feasting, and its tone could easily be changed from sensual and primitive to "a simple popular dance, joyful and decent" (Nicholls 1979, 131f).

Such a project would have a natural tendency to suppress the use of drums.

But this was nothing, however, compared to the fate of drums in the series of Anti-Superstition Campaigns that seared themselves into the public's memory. Many drums were burned during the 1915–1934 occupation by the Marines. The dancer Katherine Dunham owns a set of Rada drums in unvarnished wood that are one of the few pre-1915 sets ever found (Dunham 1983, 13).

During the American occupation, a great split occurred among the elite. Most denied their African heritage and wished to identify with France, so that even the Mulatto Colonel D. P. Calixte could write in 1939 that "the only difference existing between the French and Haitian *élite* is the color of their skin" (1939, 22). Intellectuals—usually Mulatto and socialist—tended to be pro-French only because they were anti-American (Nicholls 1979, 159). But, beginning around World War I, Jean Price Mars (1876–1969), who had studied in Paris, initiated the "ethnological" school, which argued that Haiti was not French but mixed, and predominately African (Nicholls 1979, 156). Vodou itself, long denigrated or denied, began to be rehabilitated by this movement in the 1930s. Although most of the "ethnologists" were socialists and had little sympathy with Vodou as a religion, they supported it as a bearer of African culture and in their own opposition to the Roman Catholic Church, which they saw as a prop of the Mulatto elite (Nicholls 1979, 180f).

On the eve of World War II elite Haitians were still pretending to the world that Vodou did not exist, and the exiled Colonel Calixte, writing to solicit American support for his cause in 1939, mentions "voodoo" only once, in his description of the beginnings of the revolution (Calixte 1939, 18). In his "True Picture of Haiti," a long chapter describing Haitian life and religion, he never mentions it at all.

Although President Sténio Vincent in the 1930s made an effort to unite the interests of the Mulatto elite, the Black middle class, and the intellectuals, he was succeeded by Elie Lescot, who alienated special interest groups in various ways, including his willing support of the Church's Anti-Superstition Campaign of 1941–1942 (Nicholls 1979, 166f). This campaign was begun in April of 1941 by Monseigneur Paul Robert, the bishop of Gonaïves and, like many clerics in Haiti, a French Breton. (The fact that Haiti was still being missionized in the 1940s says a great deal in itself.) In a pastoral letter he stressed the complete incompatibility between Christianity and superstition, with the latter defined as "the collection of religious beliefs and practices which came from Africa." The campaign became a lightning rod for an assortment of conflicts, including elitism vs. democracy, Blacks vs. Mulattos, and Francophiles vs. Africanists. Although Vodou had long been officially illegal and the penalties for practicing it made more severe in 1935, the laws had rarely been enforced. Now they were, in support of the Church, which held congresses to oppose Vodou, persuaded over a hundred thousand Haitians to renounce the religion, instituted a special catechism equating the *oungan* with a slave of Satan and the *lwa* with demons, and in other ways conducted what the missionaries liked to call a "spiritual blitzkrieg." The campaign ended suddenly in February 1942 when a mission service was fired upon. This incident brought about a sudden storm of opposition in which those previously silent began to speak out. Others, such as Jacques Roumain, had always vigorously opposed the campaign and continued to insist that what Haiti needed was not an anti-superstition campaign, but an anti-poverty campaign. The persecutions of Vodou, he said, only abused the peasants and confirmed them in their wrong ideas (Nicholls 1979, 181f).

The results of the campaign on the material objects of Vodou, as well as the spiritual life of the people, may be gauged from Alfred Métraux's vivid description of a local manifestation of the movement in the Marbiel Valley, where in the 1940s Vodou was almost exterminated. The crusade was led by a French curé (who became known as Lavalas, the "torrent") and a Haitian curé who had been brought up in Vodou and hated it with all the passion of a convert.

Lavalas would lead a band of fanatical anti-Vodouistes on an *ounfò*, demanding that every object be handed over. Actual violence was almost unknown, but there was much noise and intimidation. The local police were made to help. Information passed on by informers helped in the location of objects that had been secreted, and the *sèvitè* then attributed their inability to keep anything hidden to the supernatural talents of their persecutors. Sacred trees were cut down, fanatics threw stones at objects and cursed them, and drums, flags, and other objects were piled in heaps and burned.

The *sèvitè* were so traumatized by this that some went into trances, the *lwa* crying out things such as "I'm not going. I don't want to go." The "horses" would run off into the forest and then be dragged back by the priest's helpers so that they might be exorcised. The crosses in graveyards were seen as emblems of Gede; they were uprooted, heaped in piles, and burned. Gedes appeared and are said to have shouted, "All you are burning is wood. Us you will never burn" (Métraux 1972, 345–47).

Some peasants who had no real objection to Vodou used the campaign as an opportunity to settle old scores with neighbors or to rid the countryside of the entities they did fear: the witches who could become werewolves. Some converted quite willingly without malice, seeing Vodou as bondage to savagery or ignorant peasant behavior, or as too expensive in its ritual demands. Some converted to curry favor with those in authority.

Many converts continued in their practice of Vodou, though, hoping that the *lwa* would forgive them for their defection. One *lwa* whose residence, a pot, was destroyed appeared in a *sèvis* to reassure his *sèvitè* that he was all right and could live anywhere. Another *lwa*, whose tree was cut down, simply moved to another tree. One *sèvitè* replaced his "fetishes" with chromolithographs of the saints and went on serving the *lwa*. "That's how we fix things," he said, "so the curé serves the *lwa*." Subsequent drought in the valley was blamed on the Church (Métraux 1972, 344f).

After World War II, the picture changed. The government, the Roman Catholic Church, and foreigners seemed each to find their own accommodations with Vodou. (Protestantism, however, has remained extremely hostile to the religion, especially to its music [Métraux 1972, 351].) Ceremonies and dances held for the benefit of tourists became quite common, with costumes more vivid (and more sinister) than the real thing. The government-sponsored Troupe Folklorique gave a wide variety of performances, rooted solidly in African traditions, but slanted to the art audiences and tourists. Although decried by anthropologists as theatrical, the Troupe was very popular with Haitians as well as with tourists. The Troupe's star drummer, Ti-Boro, became internationally known, although the music of composers such as Justin Elie was described as "more serious" (Wilson 1957, 45). Harold Courlander and the Haitians Werner Jaegerhuber and Lina Mathon-Blanchet have been among those recording and popularizing more "authentic" Haitian folk music since the 1930s (Weil 1973, 99).

Publications show that Vodou made its entrance into the beginnings of respectability through the door of music. In a Pan-American Union survey of Haiti, published in 1947 and aimed mainly at American business interests, there was no mention of Vodou or its music anywhere, although some space was devoted to Haiti's folk-influenced contributions to Western classical music. Attention was focused on individual composers such as Elie and Occide Joanty (Pan-American Union 1947, 27). When the Haiti Government Tourist Bureau published a brief guide in 1954, the 150th anniversary of the republic, no mention was made of Vodou in the chapter on religion, but it appeared under the heading of "Music and Dance," where misconceptions concerning the religion were briefly acknowledged and dismissed (Haiti Government Tourist Bureau 1954, 25). Katherine Dunham adapted Vodou dances to her modern style and also published books on the religion (Weil 1973, 99).

The Duvalier regime was openly pro-Africanist and widely considered pro-Vodou, although it often used popular belief to terrorize the people. Both Duvaliers dressed so as to cultivate an association with the sinister *lwa* Bawon Samdi. The Ton Ton Macoute were named for the peasant *lwa* Papa Zaka. In contrast to the Anti-Superstition Campaigns of the past, in November 1962 Monseigneur Paul Robert was expelled from the country on the grounds that he had used the campaign of 1941–1942 to pillage the "archeological and folklore" heritage of the people (Nicholls 1979, 224). (However, another wave of anti-Vodouism occurred in 1986, after the Duvaliers were deposed.)

The United States *Area Handbook for Haiti*, published in 1973, gave an accurate and sympathetic description of the religion, and fully credited its influence upon even secular music. Dances other than the *méringue* were described as uniquely Haitian, and the importance of drumming was emphasized (Weil 1973, 82, 98).

For those emigrating from Haiti to New York, the United States offered another challenge beyond that of prejudice: apartment living. The *manbo* about whom Karen McCarthy Brown wrote *Mama Lola* stopped initiating *sèvitè*, as she no longer had access to the soil of Haiti. Drums usually could not be used unless a house with a basement could be found. But Mama Lola and her fellow *sèvitè* learned to make do with singing and the rattle of the *asson* (sacred gourd). Libations which could not be poured onto linoleum were poured into a basin and then used for a ritual bath—the skin now absorbing what in Haiti is absorbed by the earth (Brown 1991, 377).

11.10 The Vodou drum as tourist art. Statue of a female drummer suckling a snake at the Hotel Oloffson. Photograph by Victoria Simmons, Port-au-Prince, 1999.

Where drumming was possible, the drums were reinstated, but usually in *ounfò* with a mixed Caribbean congregation and little attention paid to the traditional means of construction or the highly elaborate categories of song (Kramer 1986).

Mother Ginen

It is easier to trace Vodou drums forward to New York than backward to Africa. Scholars have rarely addressed the specific ethnic origins of the various Haitian drum styles. Most often, connections have had to be inferred from very general descriptions of the drums and their use and from descriptions of religious systems.

These clues confirm that the dominant streams of culture flow from the Fon people of Benin, while Yorùbá influence, so important in Brazil and Cuba, is comparatively slight. Where Yorùbá deities such as Ogun or Éshu-Élégba are found in Haiti, they had already colonized Fon religion before the passage across the Atlantic (see Barnes 1989). Other important Yorùbá deities, such as Oshun and Yémanya, do not appear in Vodou, although some of their characteristics may be found in Haitian *lwa*. Contributions from Igbo culture or the Kongo are fragmentary, although still recognized by Haitians.

Fon religion, however, has by no means been simply transplanted. Many of the more mystical subtleties, such as the Fa divinatory system, did not make it across the Middle Passage. Deities who are central to Fon religion, such as Mawú-Lísa and Hevioso, are remembered in Haiti only in a few lines of *langay* and a song or two (Brown 1991, 280).

Haitian musical styles, however, are West African, rather than uniquely Fon. Although Melville J. Herskovits describes Dahomean music as primarily vocal, he stresses that the use of drums and rhythm is so integrated in the music that a person singing a cappella will accompany himself by clicking his fingers. Idiophones (such as the triangle) and stringed instruments are rather rare, flutes less so. There are many different kinds of drums alluded to, although Herskovits describes only a few. As in Haiti, each use, secular or religious, ancestral or fertility related, and so on, has its own special drum set. The drums are usually played in ensembles of three or five. The drums are constructed as has been described for the drums of Vodou, with a peg attachment usually anchored with strips of the membrane rather than cords (Herskovits 1938, 2:316f).

As for particular drums and particular rites, Herskovits discusses the *zokwete*—"long drums fastened with cords around the waist of the player and used only in the [Fon] ancestral cult" (1938, 2:114f). The Fon deity Hevioso has special rhythms played for him by a set of three drummers (1938, 2:163). In a ceremony for the deity Mawú-Lísa a single pair of drums is used, both played by one drummer, as this particular rite requires. One drum, about three feet high, is a tenor; the other, smaller drum is deeper in tone. The drums are painted red, black, and white, and patterned with a horizontal zigzag design. Once consecrated for this ritual, they cannot be used for any other purpose until they are replaced and destroyed (Herskovits 1938, 2:114f). Here can be seen similarities with Haitian practice in the treatment of the drums, but there are also obvious differences.

Again, Yorùbá practice seems rather alien in the Haitian context. J. H. Kwabena Nketia describes an important Yorùbá drum, the *iye ilu*, to whose rim are added

11.11 A street mural shows the mermaid *lwa* La Sirenne, a drum, and dancers. Photograph by Victoria Simmons, Jacmel, 1999.

little bells to make a metallic jingling sound (1974, 89). This is not a Haitian practice, and Yorùbá pressure drums are also unknown. Somewhat more familiar are the traditional palace rites for Ogun, in which special drums are played as the king dances, sword in hand (Pemberton 1989, 110f). The behavior of the dancer here is characteristic of Ogun. But we are also told by the Yorùbá that Ogun is said to have learned to chant from a human hunter, and in turn taught him how to make drums and to play and dance (Babalola 1989, 149). Haitians do not tell this story.

One issue of concern, whether dealing with Fon or Yorùbá tradition (or Ewe or any of the other peoples), is that in Haiti drumming became detached from court traditions, which among the Fon and the Yorùbá were and are quite elaborate. Andrew Apter (1992) has written a monograph concerned largely with how the Yorùbá use talking-drum texts in the negotiation of power between king and people. The Fon have a similarly rich tradition of court music. All of that has been lost.

One could argue that nothing "survives" the transition from old to new. A symbol must find a new meaning in its new setting or it does not survive at all. (However, the meanings may be very close to their old form.) Many observers, including Herskovits, Métraux, and Robert Ferris Thompson (1995), have seen specific connections between West African drum traditions and those of Haiti. What is important, though, are the new meanings acquired in a Haitian context. Contemporary Haitians are as likely to look to Native America and even Europe as they are to the "shattered jewel" of ancient African religion (see Beauvoir-Dominique 1995), although what they find may be reanalyzed as African.

Conclusion

Many African forms, including material art as well as music and dance, were channeled through and maintained by Vodou when they were opposed elsewhere. The objects of Vodou, most particularly the drums, became not only sacred objects but also emblems of personal identity, class rebellion, and national pride. Vodou drums have been painted with the flag of Haiti as well as with the emblems of the *lwa* (Thompson 1995, 95). They have been used in public art, advertising, and the decoration of tourist hotels. The value of the drums has spread beyond the realms of religion or music. Philippe Thoby-Marcelin has argued that painting in Haiti survived only on the barrels of drums during long periods of persecution, and that it was only from the mid-twentieth century on that painting has been transferred from drum to mural to canvas (Thompson 1995, 95). Even in New York apartments, the drum is brought back to the *sèvis* as soon as it can be.

In Haiti, where French culture dominates to a surprising degree, African identity has remained most powerful in the practice of Vodou. Africa endures physically in the bodies of the people, an African people, and in a material object, the drum. Both Black skins and drums have been lifted above mere issues of African descent and reified as emblems of Africanness. The African drum in Haiti was from the beginnings of slavery a link with the Motherland—a way of reaching across the Middle Passage to the art, the craftsmanship, and the beliefs of Ginen. But the drum, already susceptible to being dressed, fed, and treated as a living being, became itself a character in the largely tragic drama of Haitian history. The Vodou drum, like the people of Haiti, has suffered physical persecution, but without losing the (literally) polyvocalic spirit from which its true power derives. What had been a sacred symbol in Africa became a sacred symbol of Africa, and a sacred symbol of Haiti.

11.12 Vodou flag by Yves Telemak showing a ritual drum. Photograph by Victoria Simmons, Port-au-Prince, 1999.

DAMBALAHWOUEDO
ART Y.T 1999

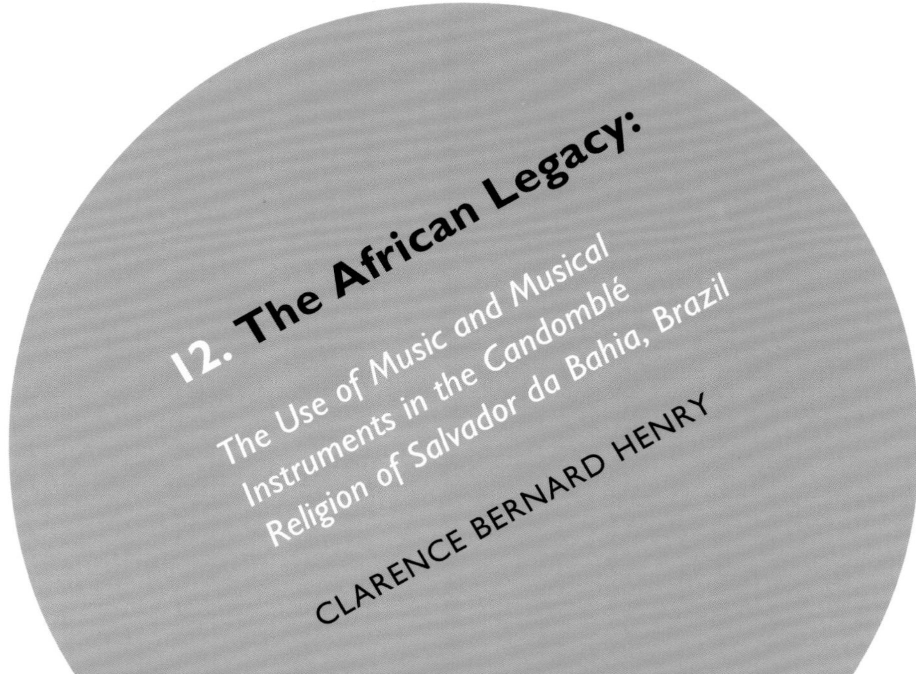

12. The African Legacy: The Use of Music and Musical Instruments in the Candomblé Religion of Salvador da Bahia, Brazil

CLARENCE BERNARD HENRY

12.1 Woman with basket of flowers on her head. Photograph by Clarence Bernard Henry, Salvador da Bahia, 1999.

Music is one of the most important expressions of a society or culture. According to the scholar Bayo Martins, "[a] society without music is said to be without a soul and may be regarded as dead" (1983, 17). Through music, people express love, hate, pride, hope, and religiosity. As Clifford Geertz has observed, music and religion are closely related in all cultures (1966, 103–28).[1] Also, in many societies, musical instruments (drums, bells, gongs, flutes, etc.) are considered to be symbolic, mystical, and sacred because they are the means (other than the human voice) through which music is expressed and produced. For example, in sacred rituals of various areas of the world, musical instruments are crucial in summoning deities, evoking trance and other possessive states, and controlling expressions of dance. There may also be musical instruments used in secular events, such as festivals, concerts, and other communal activities. Because of this, many scholars have distinguished musical instruments as "sacred" or "profane" (Nodal 1983, 162–63).

In some societies musical instruments are constructed by trained craftsmen who are required to use certain materials—animal skins, wood from special trees, etc.—that are considered sacred (Dagan 1993). The instruments may be built to resemble humans or animals. Occasionally they are given male or female names, birth dates (which are celebrated in the community), godparents, christenings and baptisms, food, and clothing. In Salvador da Bahia, Brazil, many of these activities and rituals are important aspects of the instruments used for the Candomblé religion. This paper will examine the use of music and musical instruments in Candomblé and show how the religion has become an important source for music making in Bahia as a whole.

Salvador da Bahia, Brazil

Salvador da Bahia, Brazil, is unlike any other city that I have visited. It is a mixture of European, African, and Native American influences all merged into a metropolis of approximately one and a half million people. Many individuals wear typical African clothing; some even carry large packages or baskets of fruit and flowers on their heads (fig. 12.1). Women called Bahianas, dressed in white lace skirts, wearing long beads and colorful head scarves, and selling a traditional delicacy called *acarajé,* are a major symbol of Bahia. Because of the mixture of races, the people range in color from white to tan to brown to black, with many Mulattoes.[2] This ethnic diversity contributes to Salvador's uniqueness.

The city is divided into two parts: *cidade alta* (upper city) and *cidade baixa* (lower city). The neighborhoods in the winding cobblestone streets of the Pelourinho[3] area are filled with colonial-style buildings constructed with beautiful ironwork and painted in bright colors such as yellow, green, white, and blue. Many of the buildings bear Candomblé symbols, such as the bow and arrow of Oxóssi (fig. 12.2). Also in the Pelourinho are numerous old churches that blend in with the European architecture (fig. 12.3). These seventeenth-century churches are filled with beautiful gold-trimmed altars, sculptures, and paintings by famous artisans.

One of the major attractions in Salvador is a lagoon where statues of the *orixás* (African deities) are erected (fig. 12.4). In the background are high-rise office buildings, condominiums, parks and recreational areas, and crowds of people in daily interaction. The statues seem to guard the city from all evil forces. They also give Salvador a special kind of ambiance, because most people understand and relate to the Bahian culture through the eyes and mythology of the *orixá* legacy. The importance of these images is similar to that of the Statue of Liberty in New York and the Hollywood sign in Los Angeles in that they have the power to attract people from many areas of the world.

The Africanization of Salvador

Salvador was the first city established by the Portuguese when they began to colonize Brazil in the early part of the sixteenth century (Burns 1993; 1994). The land was already populated with indigenous peoples, but because of its wealth and the need for

12.2 Building with Candomblé symbol. Photograph by Clarence Bernard Henry, Salvador da Bahia, 1999.

12.3 View of historic Salvador. Photograph by Clarence Bernard Henry, Salvador da Bahia, 1999.

labor, Africans were imported. Because official documents concerning the slave trade in Brazil were destroyed after the suppression of slavery, there is much speculation about the number of Africans taken to Brazil. Scholars estimate that from the sixteenth to the nineteenth centuries (1530–1855) approximately 3,600,000 Africans were transported to Brazil as slaves (Bastide 1978, 34). Thus, for approximately three centuries certain parts of Africa and Brazil were intimately linked together as Portuguese colonies. With the large supply of slaves, Brazil became a more profitable colony. This is the beginning of what many scholars refer to as the "Africanization" of Brazil (Alexander 1922; Conniff and Davis 1994, 106; Rodrigues 1988, 13–37).[4]

Slaves in Salvador are believed to have originated from several areas of Africa, including the Bight of Biafra, the Bight of Benin, Congo, Angola, Gabon, Mozambique, Madagascar, etc. (Curtin 1969, 24–41; 1976; Miller 1992).[5] In terms of ethnic affiliation, the following were represented in Brazil:

1. Sudanese civilizations: Yorùbá (Nagô, Ijesha, Egba, and Ketu), Dahomans of the Gêgê group (Ewe and Fon), Fante-Asante (known during the colonial era of Brazil as Mina), and smaller groups (Krumano, Ani, Zema, and Timini).
2. Islamized civilizations: Peul, Mandingo, Hausa, Tape, Bornú, and Gurunsi.
3. Bantu civilizations of the West Coast: Congo-Angola (Abunda, Caçanje, Bengala, Umbengala, and Dembo), Cabinda, and Benguela.
4. Bantu civilization of the East Coast: Mozambique (Macua and Angico). [Bastide 1978, 46; Ramos 1939, 11–14][6]

Since a large number of Africans who were taken to Bahia came from contiguous territories in Africa, it is believed that they shared closely related languages and could easily communicate among themselves. Slaves in Brazil came to gradually use an African language known as Nagô, a term that has several grammatical forms—Nagot (French) and Nagote (feminine; Parrinder 1947; Garcia 1935). The use of Nagô intensified the slaves' isolation from the White world and retarded the process of acculturation. It was also one of the major reasons for the retention and preservation of African culture in Bahia.

The manner in which the Portuguese attempted to maintain social control also contributed to the preservation of African cultural traditions. Slaves were organized into *nações* (nations) based on similarities of origin, language, and culture (Brown and Bick 1987). At first the designation of *nações* was only used (by government officials, slave owners, and overlords) as an indication of "ethnic affiliation," but later it was employed as a "symbolic reference" for the gamut of cultural, social, and religious similarities of African groups in Salvador. These ethnic groups were important, because this is how many Africans found spouses. Furthermore, as a point of identity, Africans eventually began to use the Portuguese word *parente* (relative) when they spoke of someone of their own ethnic group (Póvoas 1989; Mattoso 1988). The *nações de* Candomblés

12.4 Images of the African deities in Salvador. Photograph by Clarence Bernard Henry, Salvador da Bahia, 1999.

are Gêgê, Ketu, Ijesha, and Congo-Angola. Two of the groups (Ketu and Ijesha) show a close cultural resemblance to the Yorùbá of southwest Nigeria and southeast Dahomey (now known as Benin). These groups are known as Nagô (or as Ketu-Nagô). The other two *nações* show a resemblance to the Ewe of West Africa (Gêgê) and Central Africa (Congo-Angola). Each of the various *nações* are also identified by their special deities: *orixás* (Ketu, Ijesha), *voduns* (Gêgê), and *inkisses* (Congo-Angola; Pinto 1991). Another important group is the Candomblé *de caboclo*, whose deities and religious worship are based on a combination of African and Indian mythology.

The Emergence of African Religions in Salvador

Many slaveholders allowed Africans to participate in special religious activities as a way to help them adjust to a new environment (Bastide 1978, 128). However, there were some slave owners who would not allow their slaves to practice their own traditional religion. As a result, a large number of slaves converted to Christianity and attended the Roman Catholic Church on a regular basis. Although these Africans converted to Catholicism, many used the White saints of the church as camouflage for worshipping their own spiritual guardians, concealing African deities and rituals behind the masks of Catholic saints. The Catholic saints were given African names, their images were painted black and dressed in traditional African clothing, and a specific African mythological attribute (i.e., god of thunder, water, fire) was assigned to each (fig. 12.5). All of this resulted in the syncretism of African culture and Catholicism (Omari 1984, 14).[7] For the Africans in Salvador, the Catholic saints became known as *orixás*. These were responsible for particular areas of life and acted as intermediaries between humans and the supernatural world (Walker 1990, 108–11). The following chart shows the names of the African *orixás* and their syncretized Christian names:

Orixá	*Syncretized name*	*Special foods*
1. Ogun	São Antonio	*feijoada*[8]
2. Omolú[9]	São Lazaro, São Roque/São Bento	popcorn, meats, palm oil (*ebo*)
3. Nanan[10]	Santa Anna	cooked black-eyed peas
4. Oxun-maré	São Bartolomeu	white corn, coconut
5. Oxóssi	São Jorge	yellow corn, yams, black beans
6. Longunede	São Miguel	black-eyed peas, eggs
7. Ossaim	São Benedito	black beans, manioc flour
8. Xangô	São Jeronimo	okra, beef, yams
9. Yansan[11]	Santa Barbara	black-eyed peas, okra
10. Obá	Santa Catarina	black-eyed peas, banana leaves
11. Oxum[12]	Nossa Senhora das Candeias	onion, shrimp, honey, peas
12. Ewa	Joan of Arc	sweet potatoes, bananas, corn
13. Yemanjá	Virgin Mary (Nossa Senhora da Conceição)	white corn, onion, palm oil
14. Oxalá[13]	Jesus Christ	yams, white corn
15. Exú[14]	Satan	palm oil, manioc flour, rum
16. Onile	(no designation)	palm oil

12.5 The *orixá* Omolú, also known as São Lazaro. Photograph by Lazaro Roberto, Salvador da Bahia, 1999.

African Music and Dance

In Salvador one of the greatest traditions is that of African-influenced music and dance. In Africa, musical activity had always been an integral part of society. Music, dance, and the other performing arts were not separated or segmented as they are in Western society (Rower and Schelling 1991). Moreover, performance was not relegated to a few professionals who performed for the masses; rather, large numbers of people participated in music making. In most African societies music was an important part of life cycles and often performed at births, deaths, harvesting, etc. (Vassberg 1976; Stevenson 1968, 68). Also, in traditional African cultures, religion did not exist as an autonomous practice separated from other aspects of the community. In religious worship, dance and music served as the basic means of communication between humans and with the natural and supernatural world. In some areas of Africa the drum was the musical instrument that symbolized the community. It linked men and women to the gods and living spirits of ancestors. More than any other instrument, it represented a living being that was to be fed with proper sacrifices and surrounded by complex ceremonies. The well-being of the community was intimately connected to the drum, and its loss or destruction was thought to bring about misfortune and even death (Nodal 1983, 162).

When Africans arrived in Salvador, they continued to perform music in both secular and sacred activities. Music served as a means for adjustment into the new society, an emotional release, and as a mechanism for maintaining African traditions. For Africans in Salvador, one of the most important aspects of music making was the use of African and African-derived musical instruments such as drums, bells, gongs, rattles, etc. Africans introduced not only their native instruments to Salvador but also distinct playing styles and specific attitudes toward music and musicians. Another major tradition that was maintained in Salvador was the virtual male domination in playing the drum, feeding the musical instruments, and participating in complex religious ceremonies (Vassberg 1976; Stevenson 1968, 30). Similar to women's roles in Africa, in Salvador women became responsible for cooking the sacred foods, caring for the altars, ornamenting the Candomblé house on special holidays, and taking charge of the religious instruction of the women and children (Browning 1995; Galembo 1993; Landes 1940 and 1947; Carneiro 1940, 271).

Candomblé

Gerard Béhague states that various etymologies have been proposed for the term Candomblé (1984, 254). He also notes the term first appeared in the literature only in the latter part of the nineteenth century and is most likely derived from the contraction of *candombe* (a dance of African origin in Brazil and the Río de la Plata) and *ilê* (from the Yorùbá meaning house). Mikelle Smith Omari states that Candomblé is a Portuguese term believed to stem from a Bantu term, *kandombele*, which literally means "to pray" (Omari 1985, 52).[15] In Salvador and in other regions of northeast Brazil Candomblé is used to designate the various religious groups that exhibit varying degrees of West African religious beliefs and practices (Béhague 1984, 222). Lorenzo D. Turner acknowledged this influence when he stated that:

> Those Brazilians...not only speak Yoruba fluently, but, as leaders in the fetish cults, they use their influence to keep the form of worship as genuinely African as possible....In Bahia, every garment that is worn, every variety of food that is eaten—in short, every article in the household has its Yoruba name as well as its Portuguese one.... [Moreover, the] Negro musicians... have...[an] extensive repertory of Yoruba songs as of Portuguese ones.... To most of them the more a thing savors Africa, the more the value is to be attached to it....[T]herefore, who undertakes to explain the nature of the African influence on the culture of Brazil would do well to acquaint himself with the customs and language of these people and to realize the significant role they have played and are still playing in Brazilian life. [Turner 1942, 58–67]

In singular form the term Candomblé denotes the large body of ritual practices brought to Brazil by enslaved Africans. The plural term Candomblés refers to the sects (*seitas*) or temples (*terreiros* or *barraçaos*) of the religion as well as the huge festivals and parties held on the slaves' free days, which provided opportunities for honoring Afro-Brazilian deities (Omari 1984, 16). Candomblé is a monotheistic religion based on the worship of a supreme being (Olorun/ Olódùmarè) who rules through several lesser deities known as *orixás* (Santos 1993, 33–59). In Yorùbá mythology, Olódùmarè is a male being who is viewed as the foundation of all benefits. He is the author and giver of all good things that a person can possess, including material possessions, good living, good character, etc. The Portuguese term *orixá* stems from the Yorùbá term *orìsà*, which has several meanings: deity, the family of deities, ancestors, forces in nature, and divine spirits.[16] In the Yorùbá religion, each *orìsà* has its own priest or priestess (the *àwòrò*) whose basic function and status is to be a mediator, to offer up a person's prayers and rituals, and to bless people in the name of the *orìsà*. The power of the priest or priestess to act as a genuine arbiter between humans and the *orìsà* is essentially due to his or her discipline and training, which equips them with the *àse* (a spiritual force; Opefeyitimi 1975). In Candomblé (in Salvador) there are also priests and priestesses who function in similar roles, and each Candomblé house is said to have a spiritual force known as *axé*.

Communication with the *orixás* is reached through a trancelike state of possession. This state of possession represents the incarnation of an *orixá*, whose presence brings the community joy. Possessive states in Candomblé are referred to as "being possessed" or "state of the saint" (*estado de santo*; Pinto 1991). Each *orixá* is said to manifest itself in human form and speak at will. Such a manifestation is accomplished by "arriving in the head" of an individual who is dedicated to the *orixá*. During the state of trance, the legendary past of an *orixá* is enacted through the sons or daughters (*initiates*) of the Candomblé house taking on the personality of the *orixá* (Pierson 1942, 281). Through trance it is possible for a man to be possessed by a feminine *orixá* or vice versa; frequently an *orixá's* personality may be in conflict with the individual's social role (Rower and Schelling 1991).

Dance is a very important aspect of communication with the *orixás*. Through dance the initiates (while in a trance) are said to be the manifestation of the *orixás* in human form. The possessed individuals display the *orixás'* individual personalities. Thus, choreographic movements may be fast, slow, contorted, or a combination of all three. Other patterns may include shuffles, twirling, and circular motions. The initiate's body may also be positioned like someone shooting a bow and arrow, galloping, sweeping, or holding sacred objects (i.e., mirrors, amulets, whips, etc.).

The first Candomblé house is believed to have been founded in the 1830s in Salvador by three African women. The African title of the house was Ilê Iyá Nassô (House of the Priestess Nassô). From this *Ketu* affiliation originated the largest and best-known Candomblé *terreiros* in Salvador: Engenho Velho (also known as Casa Branca), the Gantois, the Axé Opô Afonjá, and the Alaketo (Ilê Maroialaje; (dos Santos 1994; Béhague 1975). Candomblés are similar to independent churches; each is led by a priestess or priest known as "saint mother" (*iyalorixá/mãe de santa*) or "saint father" (*babalorixá/pãi de santo*). The term *caretaker* is also used to identify the cult leaders. The meaning of saint mother and saint father centers around the idea that the father and mother take sons and daughters and train them as initiates for the devotion to the *orixás*. After these initiates undergo the required training and are accepted into the Candomblé community, they are considered to be spiritual children (Pierson 1942, 3–25). As caretakers, the leaders must perform several major functions (consult *orixás*, transmit messages, organize ceremonies, etc.) for the spiritual well-being of the initiates and the Candomblé community as a whole. In addition leaders serve as musical repositories. They lead the singing on most occasions and decide on the sequence of songs (*orô*). In a given ceremony leaders are also expected to have a vast knowledge of the musical repertoire of all the *orixás*, a familiarity with specific songs, and particular knowledge of various rituals. This is because the leader's position of teaching the new initiates of the houses and presiding over the ceremonies is considered to be crucial. However, the leaders rely on assistance from drummers, civil protectors of the house (*ogans*), and others, such as the *pãi pequenos/babakekerês* (little fathers) and *mãe pequenas/iakekerês* (little mothers).[17]

The little mother serves as the immediate substitute for the *iyalorixá*. If the *terreiro* has a *babalorixá*, the second in command will be the little father. Normally the little mother and the little father are the initiates (*iaôs*) who have served for the longest period of time.[18] The *mãe pequena* or the *pãi pequeno*, who is rarely a friend or blood relative of the leader, exhibits as much knowledge of the rituals as any leader. Although leaders preside over the ceremonies, it is the *mãe pequena* or *pãi pequeno* that most often executes the appropriate ritual gestures and acts as the organizer of the choral responses to the singing. It is only upon the death of a leader that the little mother or little father becomes the new leader. The *mãe pequena* or *pãi pequeno* also directs activities of the initiates (i.e., teaching and supervising), leads special songs for each daily activity, and prepares for certain stages of initiation rites (i.e., *abô*, *kelê*, and *contregun*; Béhague 1984, 226–27).[19] In return, an initiate has to learn the drum rhythms and special canticles of the *orixás* who rule the *terreiro* with which he/she is associated. The initiate not only has to be familiar with the specific repertory of his/her own *orixá*, but also the repertoire of other *terreiros* (Béhague 1975, 68–69).

As mentioned earlier, Africans in Salvador practiced their religions under the cover of Catholicism. The same custom has continued with Candomblé. One of the many churches in Salvador that has maintained African traditions is Nossa Senhora do Rosário dos Pretos (Our Lady of the Rosary of Black People; fig. 12.6), which was built by slaves. Many members are Catholic but also practice the Candomblé religion. In this church there are images of Black saints who are celebrated annually. Also, the music is unlike traditional music of the Catholic Church. Instead it is highly rhythmic, with musical instruments that include bells, drums, tambourines, guitars, etc. In addition, many of the songs pay homage to the Black saints and make reference to the spiritual force that is said to exist in Candomblé (*axé*) as in the following:

> *Oh! que coisa bonita...*
> (Oh! what a wonderful thing)...
>
> Deus, Pãi, Libertador,
> (God, Father, Liberating)
>
> *Negro de Santos...espírito, o fe', o axé*
> (Black Saints...Spirit, faith, power)
>
> *Deus, Pãi...Amém...*
> (God, Father...Amen)...

12.6 Nossa Senhora do Rosário dos Pretos. Photograph by Clarence Bernard Henry, Salvador da Bahia, 1999.

Musical Expressions in Candomblé

In Candomblé, music not only serves as a mediation between the spiritual and physical worlds, it also has a transcendental importance. No worship would be possible without it. Its basic function is to "call and summon" the *orixás* in purification, initiation, communion, social, or funeral ceremonies. Every aspect of the Candomblé liturgy is accompanied by ritual songs, drum rhythms, and dance (Carvalho 1948; Béhague 1975; Pinto 1991; Lavergne and de Barros 1986).

The musical instruments of Candomblé include drums (*atabaques*) and a double bell (*agôgô*) (figs. 12.7, 12.9). Other instruments include basket rattles (*caxixi*), scrapers (*canzá* or *ganzá*), the *aguê* (also known as *cabaça*, or *piano-de-cuica*), other bells (*adjá*, *ázà*, *gan*, and *chocalho*), and occasionally the gourd rattle (*xaque-xaque*). The drums are indispensable in every ceremony. Depending on a particular ethnic group (*nações de* Candomblé), they can either be played with the hands (open palms) or sticks (*agidavis*) (fig. 12.8).[20] A drum ensemble normally consists of three male drummers playing on different sizes of drums called *rum*, *rumpi*, and *lê* (fig. 12.9). The large drum (*rum*) is considered to be the "talking and mother" (*íyà 'lù*) of the instruments. Together, the drums and other instruments create a dialogue that is understood by the *orixás*. In a performance there is much polyrhythmic interplay between the drummers and other instruments. The rhythms have distinct tones and patterns that vary as each *orixá* is evoked. The heavy sound from the *rum*, which has the predominant role, is intersected by higher tones of the *rumpi* and the *lê*. For the occasions on which an evoked *orixá* delays in manifesting itself, a special vibrant and rapid rhythm known as *adarrum* is used to summon all the *orixás* simultaneously and evoke possessive states (Pierson 1942, 289–90).

The songs are ordinarily composed of simple sentences based on five (pentatonic) to seven (heptatonic) tone scales imported from Africa. The invocation (*oríkì*) often sung to various *orixás* is the following:

> Egbêji mori ô ri, okorin-kam
> Orolu mori ô ri okorin-kam
> (Powerful One, I know thee as the first man)
>
> Ôkum-kum biri-biri
> Ajá lê mori ô korin-kam
> (Even in the dark I can see thou art powerful)
>
> *A orêrê aiê, orixa loman,*
> Iá, ochê Egbêji orêrê, aiê
> (In the whole world, nothing is hidden from the Great-One)
> [Pierson 1942, 289–90; Querino 1938, 108]

Musical instruments are considered to be sacred/living beings (Lindon 1990; Adegbite 1988; Ramos 1954; 1988; Thieme 1970; Verger 1957; Medeiros 1957). Ritual drums are normally clothed with an *ojá*, a cloth of the colors of the *orixá* that is being celebrated (fig. 12.10); when they are not used, they are covered and protected from outside forces (fig 12.11). The power of an instrument is bestowed through such processes as baptism, preparation of sacred foods, or animal sacrifice (e.g., chickens, goats). In many *terreiros* a ritual of bestowing power to an instrument may be similar to what the anthropologist Melville J. Herskovits has described. Sacrificial offerings to the drums normally consist of blood, palm oil, honey, and holy water (Herskovits 1944, 485).[21] In bestowing power, an *atabaque* may be held in a slanted position where great care is taken not to allow the animal blood to fall on the drum heads. This is because the oil, honey, and water are poured over the heads and the blood is allowed to flow over the "body" of the drums.[22] The drums are then left in a special place until the following day when the first ceremony takes place. During the sacrifice the leader (*babalorixá* or *iyalorixá*) may state, "the drums will eat today." After the sacrifice, certain parts of the animal (the head, intestines, wings, and feet) are cooked with palm oil, shrimp, and onions and placed on a dish near the drums for an entire day. A candle lit and placed with the food is allowed to burn out.

In every house there is a master or divine drummer known as the *alabê*. He has a high social status in the house and is assigned the task of overseeing drum construction. The *alabê* is also responsible for constructing the drums used for ceremonies (Herskovits 1944). An *alabê* who cannot construct a drum or take it apart when it needs to be repaired is not worthy of being a drummer. To make the drum sound more vibrant, in Salvador drums are often taken to a professional cabinetmaker for varnishing. Pegs for the drum are also constructed by a professional cabinetmaker; the largest drum may have as many as seven pegs. *Atabaques* are held together with a special type of rope called *corda de linha* (fig. 12.12). The drum sticks are ordinarily made of hardwood (*pitanga* or *ingá*) or softer wood (*arassa*) and rubbed with fat. They are then left in the sun for several days, smoked in a fire, placed in a shrine "at the feet of the *orixás*" (where they remain until the next ceremony requiring drums), and eventually given to the *alabê*.[23] Sticks are provided by each Candomblé house, and a visiting drummer who brings his own sticks to a Candomblé house is at once under suspicion (Herskovits 1944, 486–89).

Young boys from many neighborhoods in Salvador often take an interest in becoming musicians in the Candomblé religion. Many of the houses recruit these boys early on for musical training. During ceremonies many boys (who range in age from eleven through thirteen years of age) in the community bring with them sticks (or what seem to be cardboard rolls taken from paper towels). With these devices they mimic the rhythmic patterns of the Candomblé musicians, beating the rhythms perfectly. This is one way many of the master musicians of Candomblé are able to find and recruit the boys as musicians and bring them into the religion. In addition, many young girls who attend the ceremonies often practice dance movements of the *orixás* and they are recruited as initates or singers.

Salvador prides itself on the variety of popular music that is heard twenty-four hours a day in streets, homes, shops, etc. Daily, one often hears African rhythms meshed with popular music from the United States (i.e., jazz, rock, rap), reggae, samba, and other types of Brazilian popular music (*forró* and *axé*).[24] The dynamic quality of the music is expressed in the following statement:

> Salvador da Bahia [is] one of the handful of truly great and historic cities in the Western hemisphere...Cross a graceful plaza ringed by majestic churches and hear the one-note twang of the *berimbau*[25].... Stroll along one of the perfect beaches and hear an impromptu jam session of drumming and singing, a knot of musicians surrounded by a crowd.... [Salvador is the] place they call the Black Rome [Roma Negro].... There is music everywhere,...music that is a defining part of the cityscape as any church or square. [Robinson 1997, 11]

Although Salvador has a special appeal (in terms of religion, music and culture), it is similar to other urban areas. There are large segments of the population who are very poor and live in small *favelas*,[26] but there is also the opulence]and wealth of the elite. One can think of the poor and the elite as living in two different worlds. It is the Candomblé religion that is the mediation between these two worlds.

12.7 *Agôgôs* (bells). Photograph by Clarence Bernard Henry, Salvador da Bahia, 1999.

12.9 Candomblé musicians playing *atabaques* (drums). Photograph by Clarence Bernard Henry, Salvador da Bahia, 1999.

12.8 *Agidavis* (sticks). Photograph by Clarence Bernard Henry, Salvador da Bahia, 1999.

12.10 *Atabaques* (drums) encircled with a white *ojá* (cloth). Photograph by Clarence Bernard Henry, Salvador da Bahia, 1999.

12.11 *Atabaques* (drums) protected from outside forces. Photograph by Clarence Bernard Henry, 1999.

On many nights the poor and rich often attend the same Candomblé ceremonies. During a ceremony people seem to forget about their social status and become part of a unified community. Besides ceremonies, people in the community (including government officials) often seek consultation (i.e., advice about financial and family problems, elections, love, illness) through Candomblé rituals such as *jogo dos búzios* (casting of shells; fig. 12.13).[27]

Thus, for many, Candomblé determines the very details of daily existence. Each day of the week is associated with a specific *orixá,* whose colors are apparent in the clothes people wear or foods they eat. The association of days with particular *orixás* may even determine whether people have intimate relations, in that individuals must abstain from sex on the day their guardian *orixá* is celebrated so as not to provoke the deity's wrath. Also, individual behaviors and social relations are understood in terms of the *orixáś* and their interrelationships with other gods as recounted in Yorùbá history. In many ways, this is similar to the way some people interpret the zodiac (Walker 1990).[28]

The *Candomblé* House *(Terreiro)*

Candomblé houses are located in a variety of neighborhoods in Salvador. They can be found in private homes, apartment buildings, or secluded areas of a community. An indication that a house is in the vicinity is a white flag (or scarf) hanging from a pole or encircled around a tree. Many houses have special foods (manioc flour, eggs, beer, etc.) of the *orixá* that is being celebrated on a given day at the entrance. In the doors and windows dried coconut leaves (used to ward off evil forces) are normally hung. The room where the ceremony is held is normally painted white. Strips of crepe paper (of two varieties: red and white) are hung on the ceiling so that as the wind blows through the windows (which sometimes have no panes), a rustling sound is produced, inspiring feelings of awe and mysticism (fig. 12.14).

Candomblé houses are often one of the major repositories of history for surrounding communities. Members take pride in hanging on the walls a chronological display of photos of all past officials (i.e., *mãe de santas, pãi de santos*) along with different types of items such as animal horns and skins, religious pictures, crucifixes, etc. In addition, houses may have special altars (fig. 12.15). In many houses a stone marker shaped like a square or star is constructed in the middle of the floor. Many people believe that this is the place where positive energy and force are found. This area is mainly where devotees dance, go into trance, and kneel in reverence in order to ask for blessings from the *orixás*, leaders, and musicians. It is also where vases of sacred liquids and bowls of manioc flour (the *padê*) are left during Candomblé ceremonies (as an offering to Exú). At various intervals in a ceremony purified water from the vases is sprinkled on the floor in this area.

The musicians also have a special seating area. They normally sit in a space that is close to the center of the room (the sacred area). Their seating is oftentimes elevated and resembles a bandstand (fig. 12.16). Before a ceremony begins, leaders purify the area with holy water or with a powdery substance that is blown on the musical instruments as well. As a symbol of good fortune and prosperity, in various ceremonies a straw basket is left near the musicians for depositing money. Part of the money is used for the house and for the musicians. Initiates dance close to where the musicians are located. They may also kneel or lay face down with their hands stretched outward. By doing this, they are acknowledging the musicians and the power of the "living drums." During trance, the initiates seem to gravitate to this area where the musicians are located.

People in trance often shiver, moan, scream, and make contorted movements. Although they move about rapidly, they never seem to bump into or touch any other person. In some houses (Congo-Angola), while in trance the initiates normally place both hands on the right side of the body as they sway back and forth. In other houses (Ketu) the hands are placed in a cupped position behind the back. Other gestures that are common to all houses may include kneeling three times at the entrance of the house to ask Exú for permission to begin the ceremony.[29]

In trance, initiates are often assisted by a person known as an *ekede*. He or she is also a kind of initiate but is not expected to reach a possessive state. When a woman (*filha de santa*) goes into a trance, her scarf is removed and rewrapped around her head by the *ekede*. A special white garment is then placed around her waist. When a man (*filho de santo*) goes into trance, his shirt is removed and a white scarf is wrapped tightly around his upper torso. While in a trance, a person's jewlery and shoes may also be removed. This is all done to ensure that the initiates will remain poised throughout the rituals and trance state.

Candomblé ceremonies often begin at night between the hours 7and 9 p.m., although many are known to start much later. This is because much preparation is done beforehand, including animal sacrifice, the fixing of special foods, dressing the participants, rehearsing the musicians, etc. When the ceremony does begin, however, with the musicians beating the Candomblé rhythms, the house immediately becomes filled with members and visitors. The ceremony may last until the next morning, for many Candomblé worshippers believe that from midnight to early morning, Exú is most active (at the crossroads of good and evil), therefore making it dangerous for anyone to leave the protection of the Candomblé house. Furthermore, during these hours, outside of the house are various types of problems to which people would be exposed (i.e., robbery, fights, police brutality, drugs). But, it is also believed that the *orixá* Ogun has the power to control Exú's trickery by dispatching two types of spirits who act as policemen: Da Roda and Xorokquê.

Participants in the Candomblé ceremony itself are not only the *orixás*, initiates, and musicians but also the members of the audience, who are encouraged to participate through singing and clapping. They may also respond by lifting their hands in reverence to the *orixá* that is being celebrated or by going into trance themselves. However, this is rare and not encouraged by the house. People also participate by eating the sacred foods of the *orixás* at certain parts in the ceremony. This is another way children begin attending the ceremonies.

12.12 Drum constructed with pegs, rope, and special animal skin. Photograph by Clarence Bernard Henry, Salvador da Bahia, 1999.

12.13 *Búzios* (shells). Photograph by Lazaro Roberto, Salvador da Bahia, 1999.

12.14 The inside of a Candomblé house. Photograph by Clarence Bernard Henry, Salvador da Bahia, 1999.

12.15 Candomblé house with special altars, prayer beads, and crucifix. Photograph by Clarence Bernard Henry, Salvador da Bahia, 1999.

12.16 Seating area for the Candomblé musicians. Photograph by Clarence Bernard Henry, 1999.

Candomblé at Ilê Axé Opô Afonjá

One of the major houses I had an opportunity to visit in Salvador is the Ilê Axé Opô Afonjá, which was established in 1910. This house sits on land that was previously a ranch. It has special houses for the *orixás*, a school (Eugênia Anna dos Santos), museum, bookstore, library, and living quarters for the *mãe de santa* and her staff.[30] Ceremonies at this particular house attract many famous musicians and members from the community. One of the most exciting celebrations that I attended was for the *orixá* Shango. The entire floor was covered with sacred leaves. In the front portion of the room were several chairs, one of which resembled a throne. This was the *mãe de santa's* chair. Also, on opposite sides of the room were special seating for other officials (i.e., *ogans*, senior women of the house). For ceremonial purposes the men and women in the audience are not allowed to sit in the same areas.

The first part of the ceremony began with a procession of initiates, which lasted approximately forty minutes. After this, there was a great barrage of fireworks for the entrance of approximately twenty women, led by the *mãe de santa*, all carrying a large wooden bowl. This was in honor of Shango, the *orixá* of thunder and lightning. As the women entered the room, they placed the bowl in the sacred area and all knelt in honor of Shango. The *mãe de santa* was then seated and people from the audience were allowed to assemble in the area to eat from the contents of the bowl, which was filled with okra (one of Shango's favorite dishes). While all of this was going on, many of the initiates were going into trance. Also, at this time songs were being sung in honor of the different *orixá*. The drums were vibrant with complex and virtuosic rhythmic patterns.

The ceremony climaxed when the initiates entered the room a third time carrying a long red cloth called the *ojá abalá*. People in the audience again were allowed to gather in the sacred area, this time to encircle themselves with the cloth. This was a ritual for becoming empowered by Shango. This was followed by the initiates dressed in the garments and holding items (mirrors, swords, amulets, bow and arrows, etc.) of their particular *orixás*. Bouquets of flowers were given to the initiates as they danced. Trance at this time was particularly evoked through the use of an unusual instrument constructed of two triangular-shaped pieces. It seemed to be made out of a very thin metal. The instrument was played by clapping the two pieces together, producing a sound similar to very thin brass cymbals. As the music and dance became more intense, so did the tempo of the musician who was playing the instrument. He then moved into the area where the initiates were located, continually playing the instrument as trances were evoked.[31]

Modern Salvador and the Candomblé Experience

Today in Salvador Candomblé has become a major part of the culture, one of Bahia's money-making commodities. This is partly due to the government's role in making it a sort of national religion of Brazil as well as a tourist attraction. Images of the *orixás* are glamorized in music, the media, and in shopping malls (figs. 12.17, 12.18). Many annual festivals combine aspects of Candomblé, Catholicism, and popular music. These festivals attract large crowds of people from all over the world. At one of these festivals it is not unusual to see a procession beginning from the Rosário dos Pretos, led by *mãe de santas*. These processions are followed by drumming and music of the *trios elétrios* (bands that play on flatbed trucks and provide music for dancing in the streets).

In many of the festivals that I attended, I was able to experience firsthand how the Candomblé religion has had a great impact on the lives of the people in Salvador. The French sociologist Roger Bastide notes that the Afro-Brazilian religions can be understood only by examining them in a dual perspective (Bastide 1978, 160–67). After personal observation, I tend to agree with this statement. I witnessed firsthand the *mãe de santas* and Catholic priests leading the processions. These processions often consisted of someone carrying a crucifix followed by people of the Candomblé religion. Since many of the festivals celebrated a Catholic saint as well as an *orixá* of Candomblé (such as the celebration for Santa Barbara, who is syncretized with *Yansan*), it was not unsual for a member of Candomblé to go into trance during these activities (fig. 12.19).

Some of the major festivals include the *Lavagem do Bonfim* (Washing of the Bonfim Church), which occurs on the second Thursday in January of each year. This festival involves the ritual washing of the Bonfim church by the *mãe de santas* and *filha de santas*.[32] The *Festa de São Lázaro* is dedicated to the *orixá* Omolú and culminates on the last Sunday in January with a mass, procession, and ritual cleansing of the church. The *Festa de Yemanjá* is a maritime procession celebrated on February 2nd of each year that takes flowers and presents them to the *orixá* Yemanjá, the "mother and Queen of the waters." This is Candomblé's most important festival. *Santa Barbara* is the Candomblé festival of the markets and occurs from December 4th through the 6th in Rio Vermelho, at the Fish Market (*Mercado do Peixe*).

Conclusion

The African legacy has played a great role in Brazilian society as a whole. Because of Candomblé worship in Salvador da Bahia, African influence is strongly felt. This began during slavery when many Africans were imported into Brazil. Thus, in spite of their exposure to Christianity (in the small chapels of the sugar plantations), many Africans continued their own forms of worship in the Candomblé houses. Although they appropriated many Western traditions in their forms of worship—such as godparenting, christening, and baptisms—Africans were able to maintain their identity. This identity is based on the worship of several African deities (*orixás*) who are manifested through trance, dance, and music. The music and the use of special musical instruments are a crucial element in Candomblé worship. No ritual of Candomblé is complete without music. Music and the use of musical instruments (drums, bells) serve as a type of "language" spoken and communicated directly to the *orixás*.

It should also be noted that a major part of the African experience in Salvador seems to be based on dualism (e.g., Catholic saint-Candomblé *orixá*, chapel-Candomblé house, sacred-secular). This duality stems from the Africans' innovativeness in finding ways to accommodate and maintain many of their traditions in Brazilian society. But, what resulted was that the Brazilian society appropriated much from the African experience—food, cuisine, music, musical instruments, song genres, dance, and religion. Because of this, there is richness in terms of folklore, religion, music, and dance.

Today not only has Candomblé become a major aspect of the popular culture but it has become a sort of national religion in Brazil. The discourse on

Candomblé has attracted many scholars from around the world, and exhibitions of this religion have appeared in museums, universities, churches, etc. Moreover, many musicians come to Salvador to learn how to play the drums (*atabaques*) and rhythms of Candomblé. Also, in Salvador there are contemporary musical groups such as *Olodum* (founded in 1979, the group took its name from the Yorùbá deity Olódùmarè) that use various aspects of Candomblé by mixing samba beats, salsa, merengue, and reggae with Candomblé rhythms. In addition, many of their songs are dedicated to the *orixás*.

A great number of Candomblé houses have been modified and become "Brazilianized" in that many of the ritual activities do not seem to be authentic but are shortened and altered for tourist spectators. Also, on numerous occasions songs traditionally sung in Yorùbá are now performed in Portuguese. Most people in Salvador consider themselves to be simply Brazilians; their "African cultural memory" has decreased as a result of generational and cultural change. Candomblé themes have become central features in the shows of many Bahian folkloric groups that perform in theaters, restaurants, and nightclubs (in Salvador as well as abroad).

In recent years a substantial number of people from Salvador have migrated to the United States, particularly to New York City and Los Angeles. Many have continued the Candomblé traditions. In Los Angeles some Salvadorians practice Candomblé in their homes, and a lot of music performed in Brazilian clubs throughout the city is a "new sound" that may include aspects of Candomblé fused with elements and fragments of samba, *baião*, reggae, jazz, rap, hip-hop, and bossa nova. Again there is dualism in terms of the sacred practice of Candomblé held in homes and the secularization in club performances. In New York City there are a few Candomblé houses and an area of the city is known as "Little Brazil." The history of Salvador is rich with cultural, social, and ethnic influences. The African presence and influence in Brazil will continue because it has permeated the entire society. No one can fully comprehend the heritage of Salvador da Bahia, Brazil, without considering the legacy of Africans. This legacy continues to be realized through the use of music and musical instruments in the Candomblé religion.

12.17 Image of the *orixá* Yemanjá in a shopping mall. Photograph by Clarence Bernard Henry, Salvador da Bahia, 1999.

12.18 Music group influenced by the music of Candomblé. Photograph by Clarence Bernard Henry, Salvador da Bahia, 1999.

12.19 Woman in a trance during the festival held in honor of the *orixá*, Yemanjá. Photograph by Clarence Bernard Henry, Salvador da Bahia, 1999.

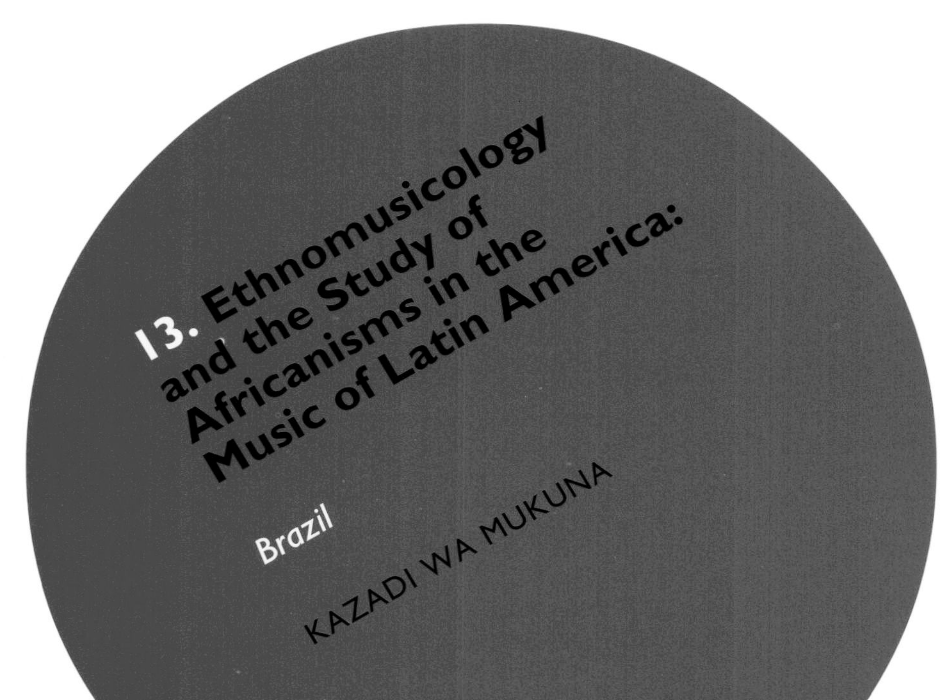

The fascination with African cultural materials and practices in Latin America began to be recorded in the eighteenth century by European travelers in search of the exotic. At the turn of the nineteenth century, however, it became the subject of concern for humanists and social scientists who explored it from their respective focal points, but with a common objective to shed light on the contribution made by the African to the formation of the emerging societies in the Americas and to their cultural fabric. Reports, formal or informal as they may have been, began to appear in local chronicles, diaries, and sketchbooks of the early travelers.[1] Although Africans began to be enslaved in Brazil in the sixteenth century, their cultural materials were not documented on a large scale until the second half of the eighteenth century. An examination of documents that have appeared in print between the eighteenth century and the present reveals three overlapping but distinct trends in the quest for Africanisms in Latin American music in general and that of Brazil in particular. These overlapping trends are distinguishable in their focus. I have chosen to refer to them as: (1) awakening interest; (2) identification and description; and (3) conceptual and contextual analysis.

Awakening Interest

This trend is characterized by the publication of eyewitness accounts by European travelers who visited Latin American regions. These reports about African musical materials and dances in Latin America are often set against geographic backdrops of the regions, plantations, etc., and are void of analysis and interpretation. Where interpretation was attempted, Europe was often taken as a point of reference. For example, Alexandre Rodrigues Ferreira (1971–1974), referring to a drawing of a *chihumba*, a southwestern Angolan pluriarc, or bow-lute, that he observed in northern Brazil in the late eighteenth century, labels it as "Viola q. tocão os Prétos" (guitar that the Blacks play; fig. 13.1). Referring to a *mbira*, or lamellophone, in the same source, the author identifies it in his drawing as "Marimba, Instrumento q. uzão os Prétos" (marimba, instrument that the Blacks use; see fig. 1.11 and Gerhard Kubik's analysis of this image in chapter 1 of this volume). The same error is also found in the nineteenth-century painting of a street scene in Rio de Janeiro by Jean-Baptiste Debret, in which a group of Blacks are shown walking and playing a *mbira* and a *recoreco* (scraper; fig. 13.2).

As such, these records were not studies but eyewitness accounts reported in various formats. In Brazil, however, information provided by Alexandre Rodrigues Ferreira (1971-1974), Henry Koster (1966), Carl Friedrich Phillip von Martius and Johann Baptist von Spix (1966–1967), Jean-Baptiste Debret (1834), Johann Moritz Rugendas (1835), and James Wetherell (1860), to name just a few, yields concrete evidence pertinent to the issues of the resilience and transformation of African musical elements and the process of their assimilation in Latin America. Brief as they are, the sketches and drawings contained in these documents are historically valuable, as they recorded the use of certain musical instruments and the practice of certain dances of African origin prior to their demise.

Identification and Description

This trend reflects a phase in the evolution of the field of ethnomusicology, a period when it was on the defensive, struggling to justify its existence with reports of diverse musical cultures and seeking recognition in academic circles as a field of scientific investigation. It reflects also a phase in anthropological studies when musical elements were discussed to corroborate the presence of different racial groups in the cultural fabric of Latin America. At this embryonic stage, ethnomusicology, defined as a "comparative study of non-Western music," derived its analytical concept (and the prefix *ethno*) from a discipline within cultural anthropology—ethnology.[2] With this definition, ethnomusicology was placed in the category of systematic musicology, together with music theory, aesthetics, and pedagogy.

As a field of scientific investigation, ethnomusicology found support in a publication of 1884 by Alexander John Ellis entitled "Tonometric Observations on Some Existing Non-Harmonic Scales," which was revised and republished as "On the Musical Scales of Various Nations" in the *Journal of the Society of Arts* (Ellis 1885). The conclusion of this study—that

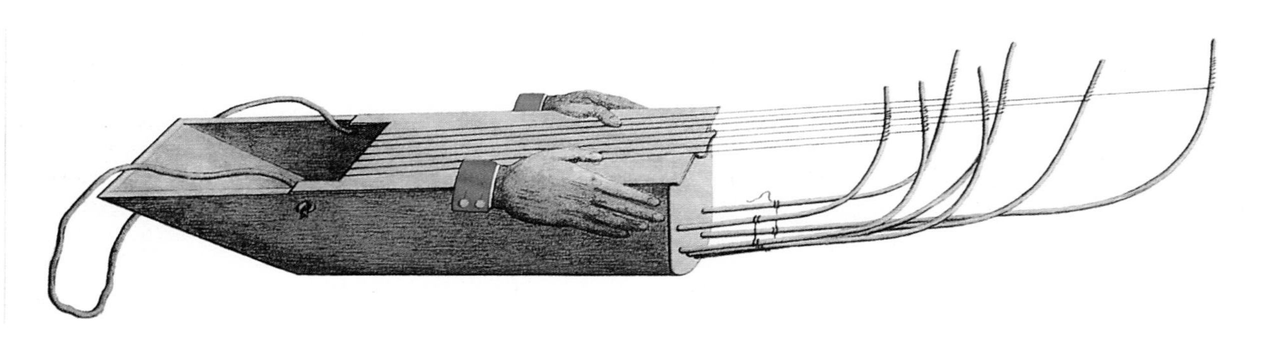

13.1 "Viola q. tocão os Prétos" Alexandre Rodrigues Ferreira

13.2. Jean-Baptiste Debret, *La promenade du Dimanche Midi* (Sunday Afternoon Walk).

the basis of the scale was not one and "natural" as Europeans had hitherto thought, but that other races had scales based on quite different principles—legitimized the existence of other musical cultures outside of Europe and provided an impetus to ethnomusicological activities geared toward proving the diversity of music cultures around the world. Armed with Ellis's conclusion, travelers, colonial administrators, and adventurers began to include reports of music and dance activities from around the world in their eyewitness accounts. Studies in this trend can be divided into two categories: (a) identification of African musical materials in the Latin American regions and their respective functions therein, and (b) identification of the African regions of origin of musical materials found in the Americas, the function of these materials on the African continent, and the process of reinterpretation and transformation in the "New World" societies.

In Cuba, the works of the anthropologist Fernando Ortiz are characteristic of the first category. In his *Los instrumentos de la musica afrocubana* (1952), for example, he identifies and describes musical instruments used in Afro-Cuban communities, without necessarily identifying their countries of origin in Africa. In *La Africania de la musica folklorica de Cuba* (1950), however, Ortiz approaches the social history of Cuba by focusing on the history and ethnography of Afro-Cuban music. Similar studies are also found in Brazil, where contributions by Arthur Ramos (1937), Edison Carneiro (1961), and Mario de Andrade (1959) identify musical instruments as coming from Africa and discuss them in conjunction with religious and secular cultural manifestations with which they are associated and which ensure their survival in the Americas.

Whereas studies in the first category approached musical materials anthropologically to formulate theories and define new methodologies for the study of African cultural elements in the Americas, those in the second category are predominantly in the field of ethnomusicology. The number of published case studies of Latin American musical styles, complete with the organological study of their musical instruments and melodic analysis, not only increased in the last decades but also affirmed the rise of a new focus in ethnomusicological studies. This trend reached its apogee with the publication of the present author's *Contribuicao bantu na musica popular brasileira* (1979) and Gerhard Kubik's *Angolan Traits in Black Music, Games, and Dances of Brazil: A Study of African Cultural Extensions Overseas* (1979). In these studies, musical materials found in Brazil are identified with their African regions of origin. Discussing their roles in these regions and comparing these roles with those that they fulfill in the Americas corroborates the assertion that conceptual mutation in the minds of Africans in the "New World" resulted from a cultural rupture caused by slavery. This approach became the basis of ethnomusicological studies in the third trend, where the contextual dimension is added to define its peculiarity.

In his *Los instrumentos de la musica afrocubana* (1952, 1), Fernando Ortiz defines music as:

> Un acto humano inequivocamente integral, es decir emocional, intelectual, volitivo, psiquico, fisiologico, individual, social y ecologico; es un acto en la plenitud humana, que asi fluye del cerebro como del vientre, de la sangre como de las hormonas, de la tierra como de la atmosfera, de todo el "yo" y de todo "lo demas."
>
> An unequivocally integral human behavior, like the emotional, intellectual, volatile, psychic, philosophic, individual, social, and ecological; it is a human behavior that flows from the mind as from the stomach, from the blood as from the hormones, from the earth as from the atmosphere, from all of me and everyone else. [Translation mine]

The essence of this definition was captured and expanded upon by Alan P. Merriam (1964, 7) in his discussion of the field of ethnomusicology:

> Music is a product of human behavior and has structure, but its structure cannot have an existence of its own divorced from the behavior which produces it. In order to understand why a music structure exists as it does, we must also understand how and why the behavior which produces it is as it is, and how and why the concepts which underlie that behavior are ordered in such a way as to produce the particularly desired form of organized sound.

This anthropological definition of music helped to broaden the scope of ethnomusicology beyond the mere "study of music in its culture" (Merriam 1964, 6) and to dismiss the view once held by many that the "ethnomusicologist is a research scholar, and he aims primarily at knowledge about music" (Hood 1957, 2). With this definition, the interdisciplinary nature of the methodology of the field of ethnomusicology was delineated. Whereas the analysis of the rudiments of music and the understanding of their quantitative values is vital to ethnomusicology, the ultimate objective of the latter, as a discipline of the humanities, is the quest for the understanding of the maker of music in his/ her social context. The following chart illustrates this concept (fig. 13.3). To properly solve this equation, one must begin with the known—music—and proceed backward, asking the question, "Why is this music the way it is?" at the end of each analytical phase.

Starting with the premise that the unknown in this equation is the human, whose concept reflects the effect of the sum of a variety of phenomena that have impacted his/her thought formation, it is safe to assert that an individual's behavior is the manifestation of the concept. Therefore, as a result of a conceptualized behavior, music reflects the ethos of its makers and their worldview, and its study can only be properly accomplished in light of the social, political, economic, cultural, intrinsic, and extrinsic phenomena that have molded the process of conceptualization of its makers. Briefly, music mirrors the conditions, social and otherwise, to which its maker is subjected. With this conceptual framework, the goal of ethnomusicology in the study of the "Africanisms" in the music of Latin America, then, is not to identify and describe those musical elements of African origin for the sake of understanding musical practices. Its goal is twofold: (1) to capture the plight of the population of African descent in Latin America through the understanding of the various processes of transculturation, retention, resilience, extension, innovation, and creation of these musical elements and expressions, and (2) to shed light on the interaction of the network of social relations in their respective societies. This concept underlines the methodological guidelines of our third analytical trend.

Conceptual and Contextual Analysis

Identification of the ethnic origins of musical materials from Africa and the process of their incorporation into musical expressions in the "New World" constituted the essence of studies in the second trend. However, with the development of new research perspectives focusing on the process of assimilation and rejection of African musical elements in Latin America, ethnomusicologists began to consider the role of both psychological and social phenomena in their studies. This level of consideration is best understood when seen in terms of the resilience of musical elements, which are often strengthened by the renewal of cultural contacts from both sides of the Atlantic (discussed in Mason 1992). It is in this light that scholars have formulated new theories and suggested new methodological guidelines to implement them.

More recently, the "Grupo de Trabajo"[3] proposed the following research guideline:

> The identification of African elements in the musical fabric of Latin America should . . . take into consideration the historical aspect which includes the impact of all phenomena, social and economic, on the carriers of the cultural material. This sustains the fact that a musical expression is indeed a product of the influence of these phenomena on the conceptual level of its makers. To the latter, music is not conceived as mere organization of sounds, but rather as integral parts of a total expression, which include languages, dances, movements, games, and special behaviors, pertaining to a dynamic society. [Kazadi wa Mukuna and Pinto 1990–1991, 47]

Significant works in this conceptual framework include John Mason's *Orin Orisa: Songs for Selected Heads* (1992), Gerhard Kubik's *Extensionen Afrikanischer Kulturen in Brasilien* (1991), Tiago de Oliveira Pinto's *Capoeira, Samba, Candomble: Afro-Brasilianische Musik im Reconcavo, Bahia* (1991), and the present author's "Resilience and Transformation in Varieties of African Musical Elements in Latin America" (1994), "Rise of Bumba-meu-Boi in Maranhao: Resilience of African-Brazilian Cultural Identity" (forthcoming), and "Sotaques: Style and Ethnicity in a Brazilian Folk Drama" (1994). Embracing Fernando Ortiz's concept of "transculturation," but dismissing that of "acculturation" and its application in the study of African cultural material in Latin America, Kubik finds the concepts of "survival" and "rentention" obsolete because it is as if traces of African culture have survived in Brazil "so por clemencia de uma outra cultura percebendo-se como dominante." "De fato," asserts Kubik, "o que se passou no Brasil nao se reduz a retencoes e sobrevivencias, mas, pode ser definido como extensoes de culturas africanas" ("only by the mercy of one culture considering iteself as dominant. In fact what occurred in Brazil cannot be reduced to retention and survivals, but can be defined as an extension of African cultures [Kubik 1991, 226; translation mine]).

Kubik's objection to the use of these concepts is well taken. However, it can also be argued that cultural elements do resist and survive, that they undergo transformation to ensure their compatibility with and use in changing times. This phenomenon is an integral part of any dynamic society and does not require the polarization or the hierachy of cultures. In Brazil, for example, not all musical materials that were reconstructed by the African slave continue in use today. Some, such as the Angolan pluriarc (*chihumba*) and the *mbira*, which were once prominent among slaves, are found today only in museums. On the contrary, the friction drum *puita, kinfwiti*, and the musical bow, or *mbulumbumba (berimbau)* are still being used because they were reinterpreted and given new functions in cultural manifestations different from those of their origin. In Cuba, Fernando Ortiz (1952, 1: 21) sustains this argument with this passage:

> El balafon o marimba requeria, aun en Africa, una funcion social jerarquica, de cortesano ceremonial, que en el ambiente de Cuba no tuvo equivalentes ni valiosos sustitutos. Los ritos religiosos tuvienron aqui su especiales instrumentos sacros y no admitian la marimba. Esta no tuvo aqui una religion establecida que la mantuviera, y como instrumento "melodico" fue sustituyendose para la bandola, la guitarra y otros instruments de cuera, que daban un satisfactorio rendimiento artistico, aparte de rango social, porque eran instrumentos de blancos.
>
> The *balafon* or *marimba* had, while in Africa, a hierarchic social function, of court ceremony, which did not have an equivalent or viable substitute in Cuba. The religious rites had here their special sacred instruments and did not admit the *marimba*. It [the *balafon*] did not have here an established religion to maintain it, and as a melodic instrument, it was gradually substituted by the mandolin, guitar, and other stringed instruments that produced a satisfactory artistic sound, besides the social rank, because they were instruments of the Whites. [Translation mine]

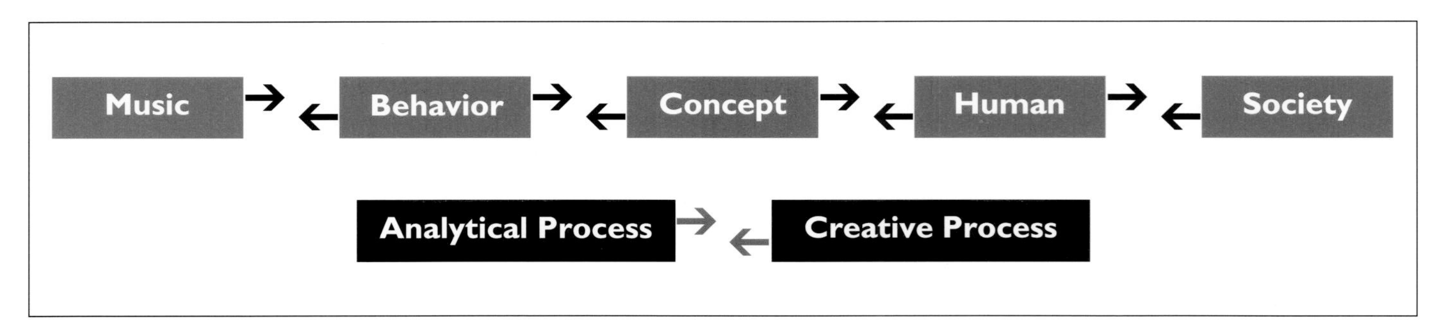

13.3 Linear Analytical Formula.

As slaves, Africans were not brought to the Americas by the Europeans as equals. Therefore, they occupied an inferior position in society, and their cultural practices and beliefs were treated similarly. This is not only true in Latin America but also the deep-seated philosophy of colonialism, in which the continuity of a cultural element/practice in an emerging society resides for the most part on its functionality relative to the needs of the ruling class (see Kazadi wa Mukuna 1994). While Kubik presents a noble argument against ranging cultures into some sort of hierarchy, the application of today's theories to the study of the past often leads to erroneous results.

In light of it's research guideline (quoted above), the "Grupo de Trabajo" compels scholars to recognize and distinguish between the principles of creation and those of innovation:

> The principle of innovation implies that constituent components of a musical expression can be modified or replaced by others independently from each other. . . . Creation, on the other hand, suggests that all of the components which originally composed the total of a musical expression, are replaced by new ones. When these two principles have been distinguished and defined within their conceptual framework, Africanisms in the musics of Latin America and the Caribbean can be evaluated in their proper historical, social, and cultural dimensions. [Kazadi wa Mukuna and Pinto 1990–1991, 48]

Although these principles imply different fields of semantics, the governing principle of organization is common to both of them. This governing principle of organization is the "Africanism," which is not material but conceptual and which underlines the organizational process of musical practices throughout Latin America. It governs the performance of satirical insults through singing found in the Brazilian folk drama *Bumba-meu-Boi*, it constitutes the essence of rhythmic organization in music, and it is an essential element of the norms of aesthetics that govern the styles of vocal production and dance movements of those of African descent throughout Latin America. Writing on this issue, Portia Maultsby concludes with this statement, which also summarizes the present discussion:

> African retentions in African-American music can be defined as a core of conceptual approaches. . . . Black people create, interpret, and experience music out of an African frame of reference—one that shapes musical sound, interpretation, and behavior and makes black music traditions throughout the world a unified whole. [1990, 205]

Conclusion

In this essay I have divided the quest for the "Africanisms" in the music of Latin America into three major categories. These divisions are observed in conjunction with the evolution of "ethnomusicology" as a field of scientific investigation to argue that reports of the presence of African musical materials in Latin America (which dominate the category of "awakening interest") do not constitute studies in ethnomusicology. They are in essence eyewitness accounts by European travelers to Latin America in the eighteenth and nineteenth centuries. In these documents, musical materials and practices are recorded as part of a travelogue without discussion and without interpretation. Nevertheless, they provide valuable information about musical instruments and dances of African origin during an undefined period in Latin American countries, with which to corroborate ethnomusicological scrutiny.

The second category—identification and description—probably the most extended of the three, began during the phase when ethnomusicology was on the defensive to prove the existence of other musical cultures outside of the European tradition and to legitimize its position in the humanities as a field of scientific investigation. Divided into two sometimes overlapping subcategories, the second category focuses on identifying and describing musical material in the Americas and Africa. In the last category—conceptual and contextual analysis—scholars began to approach the study of music holistically, seeking to entertain the question: Why is the music as it is? This quest for the truth led to the adaptation of an interdisciplinary methodology composed of borrowings from sister disciplines in the humanities. The interdisciplinary nature of the new studies has taken into consideration sound, dance, musical instruments, geographic space, and other elements that are integral to the survival, modification, and resilience of African musical material in the "New World." Each of these integral aspects, concrete or conceptual, can be examined separately to cast light on the quest for the meaning of the Africanisms in the "New World." At this scientific stage of intellectual development and activity, it is difficult for a seasoned scholar to comprehend why studies that focus on non-sonic aspects (see Shaw 1999 and Vianna 1999) continue to run the risk of being dismissed as "eth-*no*-musicological" by the "old guard" and the "born-again" ethnomusicologists.

In light of the above discussion, it can be asserted with impunity that ethnomusicology is the humanities par excellence. It summarizes this field and bridges the gap between its disciplines. The objective of its investigation is not the quest for the knowledge about music, for this is only a phase in the process for which the ultimate goal is to contribute to the knowledge about humankind in time and in space, through their musical expression. As such, ethnomusicology needs to be recognized as a valid tool for human understanding and human relations. In Latin America as well as in other parts of the so-called third world, ethnomusicology continues to be insignificant to policymakers who see its need but do not place it high on their list of priorities.

Gerard Behague, recognizing the lack of attention suffered by ethnomusicology in local institutions in Latin America, points out:

> Schools of music, conservatories or music departments in universities recognize the need to provide instruction in local musical traditions, but conceive of the courses as "musical folklore," an exotic subject separate from the main music disciplines traditionally associated with music education. Whenever it is acknowledged as a discipline, ethnomusicology has tended to receive more attention from social scientists than musicians, although this attitude is changing with the younger generation of scholars, trained abroad or in anthropology. [1993, 485]

There are a limited number of ethnomusicological programs that are operational today in Latin America. These programs, meager as they may be, function with the dedication of individual scholars and the support of some local governments, making valuable contributions to fill the gap.

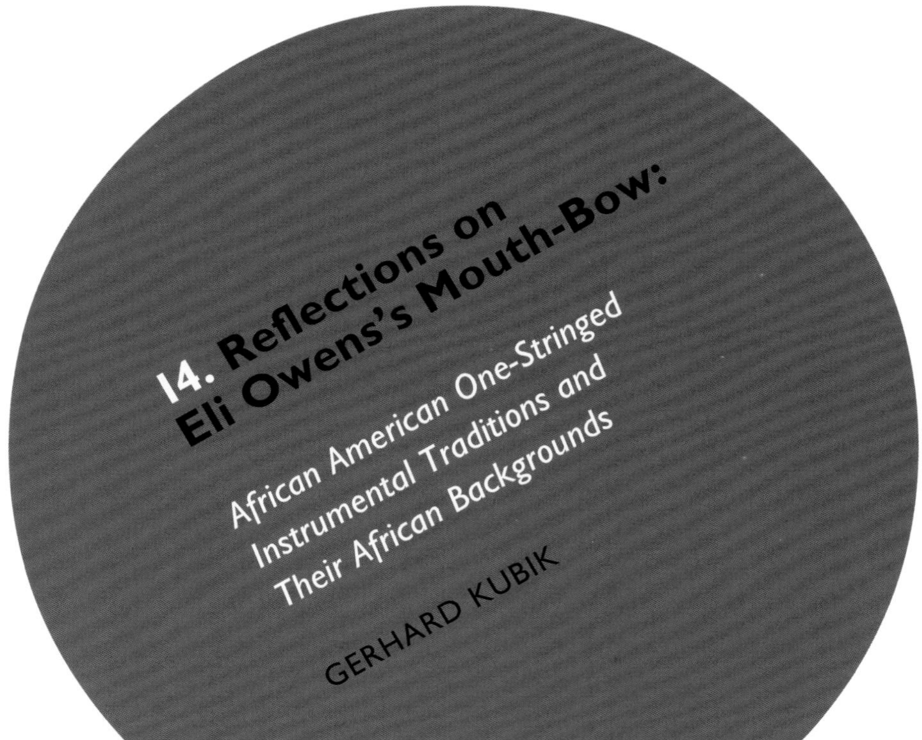

14. Reflections on Eli Owens's Mouth-Bow:

African American One-Stringed Instrumental Traditions and Their African Backgrounds

GERHARD KUBIK

14.1 Napoleon Strickland playing a one-stringed "jitterbug." Constructed on the front of a house, it is made of broom wire and uses snuff bottles for bridges and a slider. Photograph by David Evans, near Senatobia, Mississippi, March 25, 1969.

In the Deep South, the knowledge of musical bows and other one-stringed instruments of African background has survived among African Americans up to the present, particularly among those communities in Mississippi whose progenitors created the blues. David Evans has carried out pathbreaking research on these traditions, and in 1970 he published a stunning account under the title "African-American One-Stringed Instruments." This was followed by the publication of many recordings and by cinematographic documentation.

One type of musical bow, sometimes called a "diddley bow," "bo diddley," "jitterbug," "unitar," etc., is based on the remembrance and development of Central and west central African monochord zithers (fig. 14.1). Like many other African traditions and culture traits, the idea of the monochord zither seems to have smoldered through the nineteenth century in the southern United States. But only since systematic research of southern cultures began in the 1930s has it appeared in the oral tradition of informants. It is first *recalled* from about 1910–1915 (Evans 1970; Evans and Welding 1995, track 2, Big Joe Williams "Talking about Bottleneck").

African monochord zithers, which serve as a children's pastime, are often made of a length of raffia leaf stem, from which a thin strip of the hard epidermis is peeled to form a string. They are played mostly by two (male) youngsters (fig. 14.2), one striking the string with two sticks, the other altering its pitch by stopping the string with a knife, bottle, or other object, often sliding along it (see Djenda 1996, 14, 17; Evans with Graham and Kubik, forthcoming). The use of such zithers in children's games of hide-and-seek has been reported among the Gũ of the Benin coast (Rouget 1982, 310–11).

In the Americas, as a response to different social and historical conditions, African traditions tended to be reconfigured, sometimes trait by trait, generating innovative combinations. Significantly, musical associations of the game of hide-and-seek (as in Gũ-speaking areas of the Republic of Benin) have been reported from the southern United States, though not for a monochord zither or its American derivatives, but for a mouth-resonated musical bow (Evans 1994, 347; see below). And the slider technique reappears in the Deep South in the context of slide guitar playing, as well as one-stringed instruments, such as those played by Napoleon Strickland or Glen Faulkner

14.2 Mono-idiochord zither made from a raffia stalk and performed in a typical arrangement by two Mpyɛmɔ̃ (a Bantu language) speaking boys, Maurice Djenda and Moise Mbongo. One uses two sticks for agitating the string, the other uses a knife as a slider. Photograph by Gerhard Kubik, Bigene village, Nola District, Central African Republic, May 1966.

14.3 Eli Owens playing his unbraced mouth-bow with beer-can attachment. Photograph by Cheryl Thurber, Bogalusa, Louisiana, August 19, 1973.

14.4, 14.5 Eli Owens playing his unbraced mouth-bow. Photograph by Cheryl Thurber, Bogalusa, Louisiana, July 13, 1971.

(Evans and Welding 1995; Evans and Albold 1994, items 4, 12, 16, and 17; Evans 1978, items B2, B3).

In unraveling the remote history of various African American traditions—in South America as well as the Caribbean and the United States—I have adopted the method of "comparison by single traits" between specific American and African traditions (see Kubik 1979; 1999). While it is not possible, for example, to trace the blues as a complex and extremely ramified tradition back to any specific African eighteenth- or nineteenth-century musical genre, the segmentation into single traits of a particular blues style can help to reveal the key areas in Africa that have contributed those traits. Even today, though African antecedents to the blues cannot be reconstructed from any present-day African tradition, almost all the blues characteristics, if split up into single traits can still be traced to specific African areas. This applies also to the one-stringed instrumental traditions in the Deep South, which are related to and often form part of the blues.

In a paper published in 1994, David Evans presented a culture and personality profile of Eli Owens (1909–1980), player of a variety of southern instruments, such as the mouth-bow and quills. Eli Owens of Sandy Hook, Mississippi, was the last representative of a family tradition dating from the nineteenth century. He traced his bow-playing technique to his great grandfather, Andy Owens. Evans has reconstructed Owens's family tree and discussed the various musical influences he probably absorbed as a youngster, including those from his grandfather and his great grandfather, who was probably born between 1827 and 1833. In a lively interview Eli Owens recalled how his great grandfather made and played a mouth-bow, eventually teaching the young Eli, who at that time was not yet fifteen. The great grandfather used to strike the string with a stick, one of the known African techniques.

A look at photographs of Eli Owens (figs. 14.3–14.5), considered against the detailed background information from the interview and Evans's analysis, has stimulated some reflections in me. Obviously, as Evans states, the mouth-bow played by Eli Owens cannot easily be linked to *one* African musical bow tradition; this is a consequence of historical developments, which tended to promote the amalgamation of African musical styles in the United States more than in the Caribbean and in South America. And yet to those of us who have covered large areas of Africa in our fieldwork, Eli Owens's bow contains distinctive traits that we can link with one or the other specific stringed-instrument tradition in Africa.

To put this exercise on a rational basis, it is necessary to analyze such musical tools in terms of single constituent traits as they function together. Thus, Eli Owens's mouth-bow can be characterized as follows:

1. It has a stick (stave) of a rough, somewhat irregular, semicircular shape.
2. The stave is held with the left hand close to the end near the player's mouth.
3. The string of wound nylon fishing line (Evans 1994, 345) is attached to both ends of the stave.
4. The bow is unbraced, i.e., giving just one fundamental.
5. One end of the bow stick is pressed against the right corner of the performer's mouth.
6. The cavity of the mouth is used as a variable resonator. By changing its size, the player can reinforce selected partials.
7. In performance, the bow projects from the player's mouth. In a seated position, the plane formed by the stave and the string is vertical, string up, bow down. The musician's embouchure requires that he incline his head slightly to the left. In a standing position, the plane is closer to horizontal.
8. The musician *plucks* the string with his right index finger.
9. In one performance recorded by David Evans in 1973 (Evans 1994, 347; see also fig. 14.3), Eli Owens capped the far end of the bow with a beer can, firmly attached by expanding the opening of the can, which then covered the ends of both the bow stick and the string. It could be adjusted to give sympathetic vibration.
10. Eli Owens sometimes used *variable string tension*. In one playing position, resting the bow stick on his left knee, he altered the tension of the single string by modifying the pressure against his knee. "Eli stated that his great grandfather would sometimes vary the tension of the string by pressing the far end of the bow against the ground, a wall, or some other object" (Evans 1994, 346)
11. In connection with this pitch variation technique Eli Owens clearly expressed that he had a concept of "talking" ("with the hand and the mouth") and that he associated this practice with children and with two particular verbal phrases: "Catch a goat, nanny goat, and let her go run" or "Catch a goat, nanny goat, yonder let her go." He explained that these phrases were used as directions in the game of hide-and-seek and that children would also talk to one another on their bows, while walking along.

Some of these traits are general, but most are quite specific. In addition, many of them are not necessarily characteristic of African musical bow traditions but can be associated variously with other instrumental practices.

Verbalization of melodic-rhythmic patterns is a universal trait in sub-Saharan musical cultures, especially among the majority of speakers of Niger-Congo (I.A.) languages from Senegal to Mozambique; and not only where such languages are extremely tonal, as for example on the Guinea Coast (the I.A.4, or Kwa family; see Greenberg 1966). In volume 1 of my book *Theory of African Music* (1994a), I have given many examples from eastern Angola showing how syllables or verbal patterns are involuntarily and regularly projected upon "abstract" melodies, particularly in the realm of the children's culture.

As concerns the game of hide-and-seek, however, to date our prominent source reporting a one-stringed instrument used as a talking device to direct a blindfolded child on the path to finding a hidden object is Gilbert Rouget's article of 1982 concerning Gũ children in the Republic of Benin. Most recently, however, I have received information that in 1980 James (Taale) Rosellini made a film of musician Diro Dau from Burkina Faso. Dau uses the musical bow (*kankaramu*) to imitate the rising and falling tones of the Lubi language. He engages children in a hide-and-seek game, directing them with his musical bow. Rosellini is a filmmaker who has made several documentaries on African music and culture. He has spent more than twenty years conducting research in Burkina Faso and has won a number of awards for his films (personal communication from Jacqueline DjeDje, July 6, 1999). There might be more references from other parts of Africa, perhaps also in travelogues, but to recover such information systematically is a task for coordinated teamwork. I myself do not recall having ever come across anything comparable to Gilbert Rouget's find during my own fieldwork. But I did not specifically research hide-and-seek games. My colleague, Moya A. Malamusi, who has systematically covered much of southern Malawi, tells me that hide-and-seek games are common among children in that region. But he could not recall any instance of a musical instrument being used (conversation with Moya A. Malamusi, October 2, 1998).

Tentatively, therefore, we can assume that the trait cluster summarized under item 11 in the above list points to a west central African and/or Guinea Coast heritage in Eli Owens's tradition. At least in part, the same is suggested by trait 10, the principle of *variable string tension*. In May 1966 Maurice Djenda and I recorded the *diyi n'anyɔ*, a children's device, among the Mpyɛmɔ̃, a Bantu-language speaking ethnic group in the upper Sangha River area (southwestern Central African Republic). A steel wire is slung around the pole of one of the village houses equipped with a verandah. The two free ends of the wire are attached to the middle of a wooden bar and held by one of the teenage performers like the handlebars of a bicycle. A resonator is put underneath. By lightly pulling and releasing the stretched double-string, he is able to modify the tension of the wire. The second boy strikes the double-string alternately with two sticks in his hands (Recording B 10866, Djenda/Kubik, Phonogrammarchiv Vienna). A similar instrument was reported from the equatorial zone of the Democratic Republic of the Congo by Laurenty (1960, 10). And from the Côte d'Ivoire, Hugh Zemp (1971, 51–52) reported the Dã mono-idiochord zither in which the glissando effect is not created by using a slider but by varying the tension of the single string through more or less pressing both ends of the string-bearer down.

The other traits I have isolated from Eli Owens's instrument and playing technique, however, point in a totally different direction. Trait 5 (end of the bow stick pressed against the right corner of the performer's mouth) is current particularly in certain areas of southern Africa, especially in women's *umqangala*, a mouth-resonated bow (or rather a stick) from South Africa that spread to Mozambique and Malawi, but only during the second half of the nineteenth century with Angoni migration, when the -Yao and Portuguese slave trade had become more clandestine. It also spread to northern Namibia where it is known as *rugoma* among the -Kwangari in the Okavango River area on the Angolan border (Kubik 1994b, 195).

In one crucial area of Africa, including southern Angola and adjacent lands, something very close to Eli Owens's embouchure is the prominent technique by which the !Kung', often referred to as "bushmen" (see Kubik 1987, 130, 137) and some of their Bantu-language speaking neighbors play a mouth-bow, transforming a hunting bow into a musical instrument. Here, however, the end of the bow stick does not just press at the edge of the mouth (as in Eli Owens's bow and the *umqangala*); rather it is actually inserted in the mouth, pointing against the inside of the player's right cheek (see fig. 14.6). Clearly, all these techniques are to be understood as variants of one and the same basic idea, rather than unrelated developments. Centuries ago, the Ovankhumbi, Ovahanda, and others of Huíla Province in southwestern Angola had adopted this technique from their !Kung' neighbors (see recordings of the *onkhonji* bow of Arturo Branco, thirty, at Munengole/Dinde, July 23, 1965, on Kubik 1973, item 3/side B). Southwestern Angola was a primary slave-recruiting area in the eighteenth century. No speakers of Khoisan languages were taken into slavery, but Ovankhumbi, Ovahanda, Ovacipungu, Ovacilenge, etc., were enslaved in great numbers, as we know from oral tradition (see Kubik 1991, 31–32). Most were taken to Brazil, but some could have reached the United States as well.

In contrast to the southwestern Angolan bow mentioned above, Eli Owens's bow is unbraced (trait 4). Although there are unbraced bows in the area and elsewhere, e.g., the *gubo* of northern Malawi, which is gourd-resonated, or the *mburumbumba* of the -Kwangari in northern Namibia—whose name made it to Cuba (Ortiz 1955, vol. 21)—which is also fitted also with an external resonator (Kubik 1994b, 195), this trait is too widespread to be used as a reliable indicator of historical connections. Most significant, however, is trait 9 (the can attached to the far end of the bow). This very specific and unusual trait is startling because of the can's position (at the end), its function (as resonator *and* as rattler, according to Owens himself), and its association with a *mouth*-resonated bow. I do not remember ever having seen this particular combination of traits anywhere in Africa, but the can at the end of a string-bearer is a significant trait on its own. There is one African area, also in the southwest, where this trait can be found.

14.6 Illustration of one of the mouth-bow embouchures used by musicians in southern Angola, both among Khoisan and Bantu-language speakers. From Kubik 1987, 136.

During fieldwork from 1991 to 1993 in Namibia, Moya A. Malamusi and I documented two instrument types with such a can. One was the *sekampure* (figs. 14. 7, 14.8), a one-stringed friction chordophone known in Namibia and South Africa under various names (see Dontsa 1997; Rycroft 1966; Kubik 1994b, 189), with the top end of the string-bearer always capped by a metal resonator. Even more significantly, we found among the !Ko of the Kalahari a double-braced (though *not* mouth-resonated) bow whose upper end, projecting over the musician's left shoulder, was always capped by a can (Kubik 1994b, 192 and video document no. 4, Kubik/Malamusi in Namibia, archives of the Museum für Völkerkunde, Berlin). The lower end of the bow stick was pressed against a resonator (figs. 14.9, 14.10); in the cases we recorded, the resonator was a plastic pail put upside down on the ground. And associated with this unusual musical bow was another technique mentioned by Eli Owens's great grandfather (trait 10 in our analytical scheme): *variable string tension* "by pressing the far end of the bow against the ground, a wall, or some other object" (Evans 1994, 346). Our performers among the !Ko changed the three pitches produced on their double-braced bows by that method: pressing the bow stick with more or less force against the inverted plastic pail, thereby obtaining two more notes for each string section.

In spite of obvious differences, the !Ko double-braced bow, therefore, displays analogies in two of the most specific traits in Eli Owens's instrument. The question thus raised is: how could such combined knowledge—!Ko double-braced bow characteristics and the !Kung's specific mode of embouchure—have reached the United States? That it could be explained by convergence, independent invention, strains the logic, because these are quite complex traits. The foragers of the Kalahari and southern Angola had, of course, no knowledge of metal prior to the arrival of Bantu-language speakers, and, somewhat later, the Dutch (Boers). The can for capping the upper end of the string-bearer—in contrast to Eli Owens's far end—must therefore be a recent addition to an older tradition. Even gourd resonators were not known among the foragers, because gourds are planted; they used the shell of a bush orange as an external resonator for some of their hunting bows (Kubik 1987, 127). The !Ko could have adopted the idea of capping the end of a string-bearer from the neighboring -Tswana (a Bantu-language speaking people), using their *sekampure* as a model.

Interaction between Bantu-language speaking people and Khoisan speakers in southwestern Africa is well documented.

14.7, 14.8 *Sekampure*, a one-stringed friction chordophone with a characteristic "capped" top end, played by a Tswana musician, Petrus Sechele, sixty-five years old. Photograph by Moya A. Malamusi, Hugus, 12 km south of Aminuis, eastern Namibia, November 8, 1991.

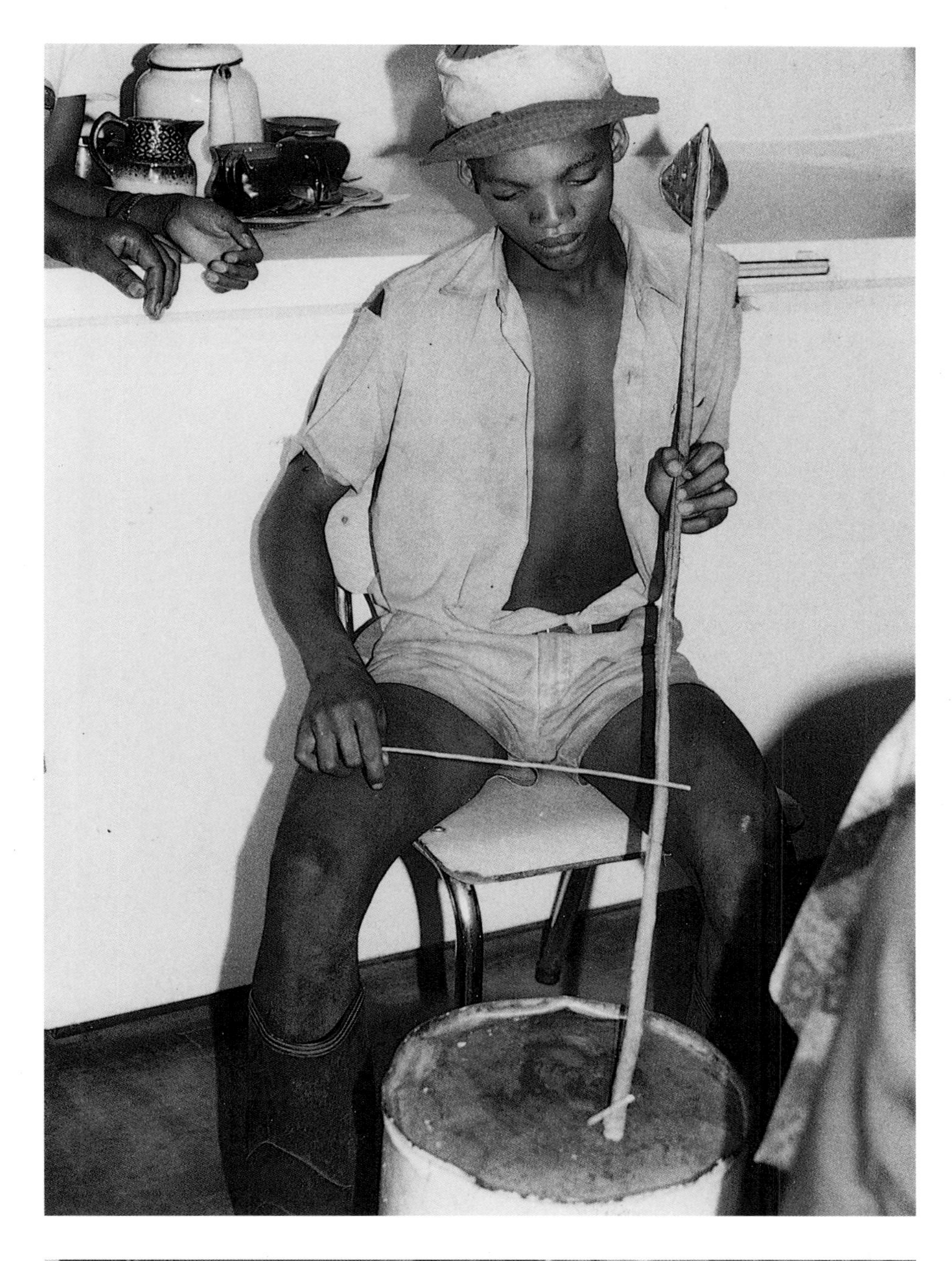

Both parties have exchanged technology and experiences for almost one and a half millennia. For this reason it is not really surprising that musical and technological traits that are associated with the !Kung' of Angola and adjacent areas could have become known in the Americas. The carriers were certainly Bantu-language speakers from those African areas that had absorbed traits from !Kung' music since long before, such as using a hunting bow as a musical bow with one end inserted into the mouth or using reed grass (*Phragmites mauritanus*) for making another type of mouth-resonated instrument, the South African *umqangala* and its derivatives, which also feature the stick end pressed against the corner of the mouth.

Summarizing, we can state that while it is impossible to trace Eli Owens's musical bow and playing style to any specific African bow tradition—in contrast, for example, to the musical bow of Palenque (Colombia) researched by George List (1983)—most of its constituent traits can be traced to somewhere in Africa, either to musical bows or other one-stringed devices. The areas that have crystallized from our investigation include the Republic of Benin, Côte d'Ivoire, the western part of the Central African Republic (Djenda's area of dense tropical forest), and southwestern Angola down to northern and eastern Namibia. Thus, if Eli Owens and his forebears associated their mouth-bow with hunting bows of Amerindians, as we learn from the interview conducted by David Evans (1994, 348), their oral tradition may have pointed in the right direction—though not geographically. Replace the idea "Native American" (hunter-gatherers) with "African hunter-gatherers," and such a historical memory suddenly makes sense psychologically.

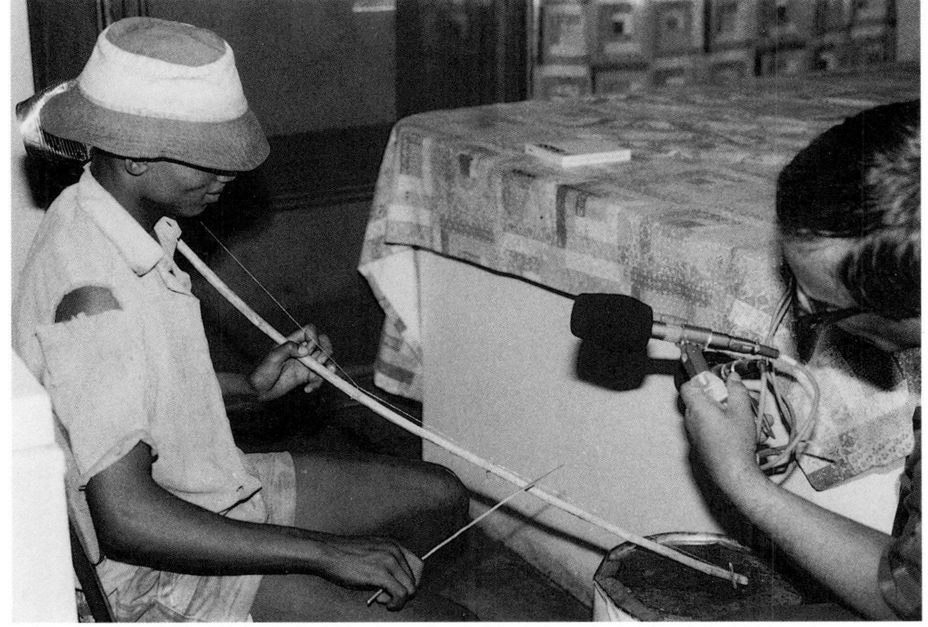

14.9, 14.10 Organology and playing technique of the !Ko (Kalahari foragers) double-braced musical bow with external resonator and buzzing device at the top end. The performer is Thomas Jacob, about twenty years old, a farm worker. Photograph by Moya A. Malamusi, Strydom farm, northeast of Gobabis, east-central Namibia, November 2, 1993.

15. Africa and Jazz:

The Melo-Rhythmic Essence of Warren "Baby" Dodds

EDDIE S. MEADOWS

15.1 Baby Dodds playing a foot solo on "Tea for Two." The photo is a still from a movie that Baby Dodds appeared in, circa 1945. Photograph courtesy of the William Ransom Hogan Jazz Archive, Howard-Tilton Memorial Library, Tulane University.

Of the numerous methodological problems confronting jazz researchers, the search for African origins, precursors, and retentions ranks as one of the most difficult. At the very least, researchers must prove that they are pursuing ideas or concepts that are equivalent and that the phenomena in question survived, albeit in a transformed or reinterpreted state, to the point of comparison. These controls however, will only yield results that can, at best, be labeled "speculative." The search for African antecedents in early jazz is further complicated by the presence of two controversies: the first centers on when or where jazz originated, and the second is related to the fact that most of the evidence, including all of the recordings, dates from the twentieth century. Since the first jazz recording was made in 1917, by which time acculturation had taken place, the task of proving an African connection to early jazz is very difficult. While acknowledging these difficulties, my purpose is to demonstrate an African "family resemblance" in the drumming of Warren "Baby" Dodds (1898–1959) by connecting him with the reinterpreted practices of Congo Square in New Orleans and detailing his use of melo-rhythmic concepts.

Whereas it is not my purpose to draw a direct Africa-to-jazz connection in the case of Dodds's drumming, I believe it is possible to demonstrate what Ernest Brown has labeled "family resemblances" (Brown 1992, 115–35). Since reinterpreted African musical practices were seen as late as the nineteenth century at Congo Square, and since Baby Dodds was connected to these practices via information transmitted by his maternal great grandfather and others, including drummer Walter Brundy, the likelihood of demonstrating such resemblances is plausible. Apropos the subject of family resemblances, Brown, whose research in this area has been seminal, notes that scholars like Hood seem to search for African roots but find African American branches:

> The problem lies in misconceptions of the nature and relationship of African and African American music traditions. First, they are not fixed entities closed to new developments. Second, they are not defined by common properties or characteristics. By that I mean that there is no definitive list of characteristics which all African or African American musics must share or which they only share. These roots and branches are not joined in this way. These music traditions are constantly expanding, developing new songs, styles and instruments, yet they retain their links to each other. New styles are often reinterpretations of old ones. [Brown 1992, 3]

Thus, Brown correctly asserts, and in the process reaffirms J. H. Nketia's belief, that the connection between African and African American musics is deeper than questions of origins, precursors, and survivals (Nketia 1973, 8).

Nketia acknowledges that although problems of unity and diversity are encountered when studying the link between Africa and African American musics, "There is a new trend of thought which is encouraging an integrated approach to the study of African and Afro-American music, a new trend which sees the relationship between African and Afro-American music as dynamic and unbroken at the conceptual level in spite of the differences in materials to which these concepts are applied" (Nketia 1973, 8–9). Nketia asserts that this new paradigm sees African and African American culture as two sides of the same coin, as musical cultures exposed to different formative influence in their respective environments but which share a common conceptual identity in certain vital spheres (Nketia 1973, 9). Within this confluence of indigenous, transformed, or reinterpreted phenomena, Brown believes we can use "the relationship among the diverse traditions of African music as a model for understanding the relationship of African to African-American musics" (Brown 1992, 117), and he quotes Nketia:

> [A] network of distinct yet related traditions which overlap in certain aspects of style, practice, or usage, and share common features of internal pattern, basic procedure, and contextual similarities . . . the most important characteristic of this family of musical traditions is the diversity of expressions it accommodates, a diversity arising from different applications of common procedures and usages. [Nketia 1974, 4]

Relying on common sense and on Wittgenstein's (1984, 31–34) argument that some common properties, like language, "are not defined on the basis of one or more properties that all languages share and that only languages share," Brown espoused a theory of family resemblances to explain the complex relationship that exists between African and African American musics (1992, 120).

Any logical discussion of family resemblances between Africa and jazz should begin by determining whether these phenomena survived up to the time that jazz is believed to have originated. Since my geographical focus is New Orleans, specifically the New Orleans of Warren "Baby" Dodds, I believe that it is necessary to provide an overview of the city and to establish that Africanisms survived up to the time of Dodds's birth.

New Orleans and African Culture: A Case for Family Resemblances

New Orleans has historically cultivated and played a unique role in transmitting African culture. In the past, the sights and sounds of this culture reverberated in what is known today as Louis Armstrong Park. Around 1800 this grass-covered area located behind the Vieux Carré was surrounded by swamp and trees. On Sunday this seemingly unimportant parcel of land was transformed and enlivened with African-derived drumming and dancing. The area was first known as Place Congo; however, as English supplanted French as the dominant language, it became known as Congo Square. By enjoying and participating in these activities on their "free" day, peoples of African origin from throughout the region demonstrated that they had both an African sensibility and cultural memory, albeit transformed and reinterpreted to function as "family resemblances." Historically, New Orleans was unique for a number of reasons, including the relationship between slaves and slave masters. According to Brasseaux, "the lax supervision of slaves on weekends also furnished blacks with the opportunity to gather for social reasons" (1980, 155). The dances at Congo Square continued until the Civil War; they were outlawed during the war and resumed after it until 1885, when local authorities terminated them because they were viewed as disruptive. Evidence of the musical activities at Place Congo and Congo Square permeates the literature.

Henry B. Latrobe and George W. Cable provided eyewitness accounts of the musical activities that were held there. Latrobe, an architect, spent some time in New Orleans between 1818 and 1820. He described the instruments that were used to accompany the dancing as follows:

> The music consisted of two drums and a stringed instrument . . . one of which was a cylindrical drum about a foot in diameter . . . the other drum was an open-staved thing held between the knees . . . they made an incredible noise. The most curious instrument, however, was a stringed instrument which no doubt was imported from Africa. On the top of the finger board was the wide figure of a man in a sitting posture, and two pegs behind him to which the strings were fastened. The body was a calabash. It was played upon by a very little old man,

> apparently eighty or ninety years old. . . . One [instrument] which from the color of the wood seemed new, consisted of a block cut into something of the form of a cricket bat with a long and deep mortise down the center . . . being beaten lustily on the side by a short stick. In the same orchestra was a square drum, looking like a stool . . . also a calabash with a round hole in it, the hole studded with brass nails, which was beaten by a woman with two short sticks. [Latrobe 1971, 21– 23]

Africanisms were also present in the music practiced in Congo Square around 1886, as can be seen from Cable's description:

> One important instrument was a gourd partly filled with pebbles or corn, flourished violently at the end of a stout staff with one hand and beaten upon the palm of the other. Other performers rang triangles, and others twanged from Jew's harps an astonishing amount of sound. Another instrument was the jawbone of some ox, horse, or mule and a key rattled rhythmically along its weather beaten teeth. At times the drums were reinforced by one or more empty barrels or casks beaten on the head with shank bones of cattle. [Cable 1886, 517–32]

Although acculturation had occurred, the evidence strongly suggests that African resemblances had survived in selected New Orleans music and dance practices up to 1886. That Warren "Baby" Dodds, the focus of my research, had contact with and either transformed or reinterpreted African resemblances in his drumming can be demonstrated by means of interviews and an analysis of his drumming techniques.

In an interview Frederic Ramsey Jr. conducted in 1946, Dodds revealed that his maternal great grandfather had played "African Drums" in Place Congo in the mid–nineteenth century (Ramsey 1951, 2). Dodds's statement was later confirmed and expanded on by Rudi Blesh. Blesh quotes Dodds as stating that his maternal great grandfather "talked on them [the drums]" (Blesh 1975, 157). He also revealed that Dodds "proceeded to demonstrate the drum code as it had been traditionally preserved in his family" (Blesh 1975,157). Blesh has summarized the African presence in Dodds's drumming as follows:

> Baby Dodds is still king of the drummers and his percussive instruments are voices in the music, talking as did the drums of his great grandfather in Congo Square, a hundred years ago. His sheer vitality, like the life-force itself, pulses through the polyphony like blood in the veins. His infinite variety, expressed through an incomparable rhythmic sense and an unerring feel for what the music needs at every moment, varies from playful "hokum" to an African and almost demonic dynamism. [Blesh as quoted by Asman 1959, 1]

In my opinion these interviews coupled with the other evidence I have adduced, establish that African drumming techniques survived in New Orleans, that Dodds was familiar with them, and that he transformed and reinterpreted them into his drumming, thereby producing a "family resemblance."

Although we can prove family resemblances survived in New Orleans up to the late nineteenth century, whatever concepts Dodds retained had probably been transformed into new musical expressions due to acculturation. These new musical expressions result from what ethnomusicologists call a "reinterpretation," a process whereby old meanings are ascribed to new musical elements or concepts. The reinterpretation is manifested in the makeup of Dodds's drum set, his accompanying techniques, and his use of what Meki Nzewi has called a "melo-rhythmic essence," a concept he describes as follows:

> I use the term *melo-rhythmic* to refer to a rhythmic organization that is melodically conceived and melodically born. This kind of organisation should be recognized as having a different orientation than the kind in which the rhythm of a music has a more independent derivation and function. In West African folk music, the rhythms of the percussion instruments are firmly rooted in the melo-rhythmic essence, not in the abstract depersonalised percussion function typical of Western percussive style. [Nzewi 1974, 24]

Before I give the specifics of the drum set that enabled Dodds to realize family resemblances, it is important to present a concise description of the drummer's role in early jazz in New Orleans. This role was primarily rhythmic: the drummer provided a metronomelike time line for the melodic instruments. The desire to function as more than a time line probably led drummers to accentuate other ensemble parts, in particular the melody, while continuing a time line. Drum sets began to reflect this changed philosophy, and indoor drum sets began to feature wood blocks, cowbells, toms-toms, and cymbals. Warren "Baby" Dodds was one of the first drummers to utilize this equipment in a melodic context.

It is useful at this point to put Dodds in context in terms of other drummers and of drumming concepts. In an interview conducted in 1961 Alex Bigard revealed that

> the leading drummers in pre-1931 New Orleans were "Red Happy" Bolton, Zutty Singleton, "Bebe Chinee" Foster, James Willigan, Alex Bigard, Baby Dodds, Henry Zeno, Louis Cottrell, Henry Martin, and "Black Benny" Williams. Joe Lindsay was another good drummer. The others such as "Face-o" were of another class of drummers. (Mostly) nonreaders, playing in dance halls and other rougher places. [Allen, Martyn, and Russell 1961, 1]

Bigard also noted that Buddy Petit didn't read music but had a good ear; he could play a lot of Joplin numbers "by head"; and he had a bigger reputation than Louis Armstrong.

Over time the role and function of the drummer changed, as Peter Bocage indicated in an interview of 1962. Concerning the evolution of the drum solo in New Orleans jazz, he stated: " Drum solos were not used in bands in the old days. The practice of featuring certain instruments, such as the drums, began eight or ten years ago, when bands played for entertainment instead of dancing. 'Red Happy' Bolton played drum solos at the Lyric Theater. Another drummer, from Texas, did tricks with his sticks" (Berry 1962, 14). Unfortunately, I cannot verify Bocage's assertion that solos were not included until around "eight or ten years" prior to his 1962 interview. His account of the beginning of the solo phenomenon is contradicted in Natty Dominique's interview with William Russell of 1958:

> WR: I didn't know they ever took drum solos in the old days in New Orleans?
> ND: They did. They did take solos. Give them a Boston, what you call a Boston.
> WR: To the drummer?
> ND: Yes, sir, to the drummer. Had a guitar and bass or either a clarinet playing with them. [Russell 1958b, 18]

According to Dominique, the phrase "Take a Boston" meant "Take a chorus, take a couple of choruses."

> WR: Take a solo?
> ND: Sure, and if you wanted it; get good to ya, raise one finger . . . that mean another one. [Russell 1958b, 5]

In an interview with William Russell, Johnny Wiggs, and Ralph Collins, Albert "Chinee" Foster demonstrated his approach to soloing. Russell noted that

> CF [Chinee Foster] played many solos with bands in the old days; he always hummed the melody to himself as he took his solo. (CF scats the trio of "High Society," accompanying himself by beating two lead pencils on the cover of a tape recorder, to demonstrate (with his foot?) his use of varying number of beats per measure.) (CF continues various demonstrations; he later used drum sticks, adding cymbal effects by hitting a tin box, and tom tom effects by hitting an empty cardboard box.) (CF demonstrates playing on drum sticks only; he shows how he changes the pitch of the stick.) WR mentions Baby Dodds and "nerve beats." [Russell 1961, 3]

The Musical Education of Warren "Baby" Dodds

In terms of early influences, Dodds was inspired by a man named McMurray, Louis Cottrell, Dave Perkins (his teacher), and Walter Brundy, who performed with the Robichaux Band. According to Dodds, Brundy taught him to read music and "he taught me that the right hand was 'mammy,' and the left 'daddy,' and I soon learned how to get my two hands working differently. This was, of course, after I mastered having both hands do the same thing" (Gara 1959, 7–8). In addition to the "mammy" and "daddy" concept, Dodds related that he

> learned that a biff shot was one abrupt fast lick, a flam is a sixteenth note, a flim flam is a thirty-second, and a lick is when you just hit the drum. With a lick you just hit it and with a biff you try to make it sound on something, either the rim or anything else solid. The pickup was the first beat and the rudiments are the things we did with a number to be played. It was just different things we did to make the number go and to make the other fellows play. In other words in a calm, ordinary way you push the number and the other musicians too. [Gara 1959, 9]

Dodds utilized the repertoire of beats fully because he was adept at playing blues and jazz, as well as performing at the halls frequented by Creoles where mazurkas, quadrilles, polkas, and schottisches were preferred. In addition to adapting his drumming to fit specific musical contexts, Dodds could also perform compositions in a distinct New Orleans manner. Ragtime, for example, which was known as "syncopations" in Dodds's time, was performed in a New Orleans style that featured the melody carried by a trumpet, trombone, clarinet, or violin. He was also adept at playing the blues in a "very,very slow" tempo in a Spanish rhythm. Dodds's learning was a hands-on experience, as he related: " I taught myself how tune my drums and how to put the heads on and tuck them in. The skin was wet when I got them and learned how to trim the edges and then tuck the heads on. Today they have regular tuckers but when I started we use to tuck them on with a spoon handle." (Gara 1959, 9). His ability to tune, and put the drumheads on was part of a learning process that dates to the assembling of his first drum set. While working at a bar factory in his youth, he reported that he

> bought the rest of [his] drum set one piece at a time. I bought a bass drum, which was a big high thing with ropes like the drums they used in school bands. I had to pull them to tighten and after they were pulled a while the ropes got slick. Then I would let my fingers slide on the rope. It cost me about ten dollars. It was a big, narrow thing and I had no cymbal, foot pedal or anything else. Finally I got a foot pedal, put the set together, and by gimmy, I come to make a noise. I amused the kids in the neighborhood and was real satisfied with myself. Then I added little traps that I needed like a cymbal, woodblock, and a ratchet and whistles and things of that sort. [Gara 1959, 6]

Dodds hands-on, innovative approach included changing the intonation of the tom-tom and developing both "nerve" and "shimmy" beats. Throughout his career, Dodds developed and experimented with a variety of drumming techniques, including those just noted. He described the origin of the "shimmy beat" as follows:

> It was at Jack Sheen's that I worked out my shimmy beat. It was wartime, around 1918. One night a French soldier came in. When he heard the music he couldn't dance to it, but he just started to shake all over. That's the way it affected me. I saw him do it and I did it too. The people got such a kick out of seeing me shaking like him that they all came around and watched. Then when I saw that it caused such a big sensation and brought credit to myself and my drumming, I continued it. I used to shimmy at the same time I used my press roll and full beat. It was perfect. I slapped my left foot, the right foot was busy, and it worked very nicely. I used it ever since that time and it became a specialty with me. [Gara 1959, 20]

Dodds used the shimmy beat on the Folkways recordings made for Frederic Ramsey Jr. in 1951. He developed and used a concept for which he coined the term "nerve beats" on *Rudiments with Drumstick Nerve-Beats*, recorded in 1946. Dodds played these beats by rattling both drumsticks in the same hand while shaking the arm in a short, agitated manner. Dodds also combined showmanship with drumming concepts (fig. 15.1), he explains one instance of this as follows:

> One time at a jam session at the Congress Casino in Chicago I used a novelty I had worked out using two sticks and my foot to play a solo on my tom-tom. I used to do "Tea for Two" and "Dinah" with that method. I put my foot on the head of the tom-tom and got different tones by moving my foot around in different places. That way I could change the tonation of the tom-tom. I think I worked that out while with Laura Rucker at Tin Pan Alley. While there I used to do different little things for the novelty. [Gara 1959, 86]

Whereas experimentation was a staple of bebop drummers like Denzil Best and Max Roach, Dodds's experiments with change of tonation were both earlier and different. Specifically, bebop drummers used their hands and elbows to evoke pitch differences, and, as previously mentioned, Dodds used his foot, a drumming concept that was used in Congo Square, and an instance of an African family resemblance. The transformation and reinterpretation of the phenomenon in the West Indies has been described by Courlander: "The practice of the player sitting astride the drum and muting the head with a heel is well-known in the West Indies. In Haiti the Juba drum is played in this manner, with a second player beating two sticks against the wood behind the drum. In the Virgin Islands the Bamboula drums are played in this style. All of these characteristics are African" (Courlander, 1954, 2). Since West African drummers are concerned with duration, intensity, and tonal differences in sound production, and since pitch variation can be realized by muting beats—applying pressure on the drumhead with a stick, hand, elbow, or other "trick" beats—it is feasible to assume that Dodds's use of his foot to evoke pitch difference is a reinterpretation of that process, a family resemblance, and akin to the muting concepts described by Jones (1959, 1: 61–67).

Dodds's Drum Language

Ramsey has provided the only recorded interview of Warren "Baby" Dodds (1951, 1–4). Recorded in 1946 and released on Folkways Records in 1951, the interview is significant because it contains both a demonstration of the drumming techniques and drum language used by Dodds (fig. 15.2). Dodds's drum set was put together to achieve certain effects. As an example, he preferred two cymbals, separately mounted on his bass drum, to all mechanical devices, such as the foot-operated cymbal. The following equipment was used on the 1946 recording:

One Bass Drum, originally used by Ben Pollack and presented to "Baby" in 1938 by Ray Bauduc.
One Snare Drum, with "Baby" since 1921, and with Angora Goatskin in the head.
Three Tom-Toms: quarter-tone, half-tone, and whole tone, purchased July, 1945.
Two Cymbals: one large, one small, manufactured by Zildjian, Constantinople, the large one cost $75.00 in 1919.
One Speed Pedal
One Wood Block
One Cowbell Quartet. They've been with Baby since 1916.
One Ratchet
One Tim-Tim
One Pair 4A Drumsticks
One Pair Padded Mauls
All equipment was Ludwig and Ludwig or William F. Ludwig unless otherwise noted. [Ramsey 1951, 2]

15.2 Baby Dodds's drum set. Photographed at 551 East 51st Street, Chicago, Illinois, in 1953 by William Russell. William Russell Collection, photograph courtesy of The William Ransom Hogan Jazz Archive, Howard-Tilton Memorial Library, Tulane University.

Dodds's dictionary of drum terms, as explained during the interview, included the following:

> Biff Shot—one note, say for instance from the right or left hand, hit on the rim and the head. It sounds like a gun. You use biff shots for a pick-up, or in break form, or for an opening or end of a roll. You can introduce or close a drum solo of three or four measures. . . . in other words, how your mind is running.
> Flim-Flam—a flam is a sixteenth, a flim-flam is a thirty-second.
> Lick—any hard blow.
> Mam and Daddy—the left hand is mamma, the hard hand. The right hand is daddy—it's basic.
> Pick-up—anything picked up on the drums after solos. Coming in, if you got a break, you start right in with the bass. Your bass is the pick-up. I used the bass most often.
> Press Roll—it's made up in halves of rolls, two to the measure, and each time over to the next, and so on. You got to make the left hand make 32 counts, and the right hand 32 counts too. They join in, to fill in the measure. It's a double-up of the four beats to a measure, so fast it joins up as a roll, although actually divided.
> Rim Work—sticks beating on the rims.
> Rudiments—comes up from method study of mam and daddy. It's like boot training.
> Shimmy Beat—goes well with the press roll. . . . A contrast of moving your shoulders and stomach while drumming, and not missing a beat. [Ramsey 1951, 2–3]

The Ramsey interview reveals that Dodds's drum set was atypical for its time. Instead of the customary one or two cowbells, Dodds had featured a cowbell quartet since 1916. He also featured three tuned toms-toms (quarter-tone, half-tone, and whole-tone) and the customary wood blocks. Dodds's dictionary of drum terms also provides an interesting insight into his drumming style. For example, he describes a biff shot, (i.e., one rim/head note performed by either the left or right hand) as being different from a lick (any hard blow). Dodds also distinguished between left- and right-hand drumming strokes by using Walter Brundy's "mamma" and "daddy" concept. To Dodds, study and use of mamma and daddy concepts were essential to his drumming.

Dodds's Musical Philosophy

To Dodds, drums were the key to the band. He took great care of his drums, tuned them carefully, and varied his drumming according to the performers and context. Dodds also believed that group improvisation was important because the music was a group project, and musicians should do their best to contribute to the whole. This was part of New Orleans musical dogma, and it underscores the importance that Dodds placed on cooperation and the gestalt concept. When he performed with King Oliver, Dodds had the opportunity to put his cooperative bent into practice because many of Oliver's compositions were group efforts. After the band became famous, however, Oliver focused much of the attention on himself, transforming "the" group into "his" group, a move that led to the eventual breakup of the band.

Dodds also believed that the melody should be heard at all times during a performance and that the drums could carry the melody. Unlike some New Orleans performers, Dodds had no use for the harsh and loud approach used by Buddy Bolden and others, preferring instead, like Jelly Roll Morton, "pretty" or good jazz. Like other New Orleans musicians, however, he believed that a good jazz musician should be able to take any good tune and make it better by putting a little "jump" into it. Also, like his fellow New Orleans musicians, Dodds stressed high musical standards, and to achieve this end he felt that drumming should be clear, not loud. He espoused a clear beat, and with the urging of King Oliver, who brought him a set of wire brushes, a light beat. He later used this light beat on the Jelly Roll Morton Trio recordings, despite the fact that he did not like using wire brushes.

Dodds's ability and willingness to meet the musical demands of both Oliver and Morton are significant; they underscore the importance he placed on adapting to individuals, groups, and differing contexts. He believed that one should be able to play any type of music with any size group—trios, funeral bands, brass bands, or large dance bands. His versatility is demonstrated by the fact that he once accompanied Merce Cunningham, the famed modern dancer; he also once accompanied trombonist Jack Carey at a dance where the other members of the band did not show up. Overall, Dodds believed that a polished drummer should be able to meet any musical demand placed upon him (Gara 1982, 3–4).

Melo-Rhythmic Adaptation

Dodds's ability to adapt his style can be classified according to two broad areas of performance: the first dealing with adjustment to new instrumentation, and the second with adjustment to individuals and groups. When the piano was added to the rhythm section—sometime before 1915—it forced drummers like Dodds to modify their style to compensate for the new sound, a situation that Dodds described as follows:

> Of course in those days the instrumentation was different. When I first started out they had no piano. They most used bass viol, guitar, clarinet, trumpet, trombone, and drums. The guitar carried only rhythms in the bands. Actually you have a much sweeter jazz band when you have a guitar and no piano. In that way the drums couldn't outplay the other guys, because the drummer had to keep in touch with the guitar. The guitar is not a harsh instrument but a very melodious one. When the piano came in it was harsher and louder than the guitar, although in my time we had some guitar players that were awful loud. They were Johnny St. Cyr, Brock Mumford, and Lorenzo Stall. Later they switched to banjo. I think the first to switch was Frankie Duson. They made the change because the banjo was a novelty. And they used two types of banjo, the regulation and the tenor. [Gara 1959, 13]

Dodds as noted above, also adapted his melo-rhythmic concepts to fit the styles of both individuals and groups: "I would have something in mind as a musician went into a solo. And if I found that what I planned didn't seem to work out so well, I'd try something else. I tried my best to work to the advantage of every player. It was hard work because I never knew exactly what the other players would do or what would be best until we actually got into a number" (Gara 1959, 90).

During his impressive career, Dodds adapted his melo-rhythmic expertise to fit the musical styles and philosophies of King Oliver (fig. 15.3), Louis Armstrong, and Jelly Roll Morton. Dodds revealed that although Oliver would sometimes repeat a well-received number as an encore, in most cases he followed a prearranged repertoire of tunes. The length of a composition depended upon its reception or whether Oliver liked or disliked it. The group improvised blues regularly played in very slow tempos. They were speeded up on selected occasions to create musical contrast. Dodds believed that a performer could evince more emotion and meaning from a blues song if it was played slowly. Oliver, however, played blues at a wide

15.3 King Oliver's Creole Jazz Band. Honore Dutrey (trombone), Warren "Baby" Dodds (drums), King Oliver (cornet), Louis Armstrong (kneeling in front with slide trumpet), Lil Hardin Armstrong (piano), Bill Johnson (banjo), and Johnny Dodds (clarinet). Photograph taken by Daguerre, Chicago, Illinois in 1923. Photograph courtesy of the William Ransom Hogan Jazz Archive, Howard-Tilton Memorial Library,Tulane Unversity.

variety of tempos, including waltz (Russell 1958a, 3).

At the Royal Gardens Cafe in the 1920s, the band would set up in a straight line with the bass at one end and the drums at the other. The band also performed in a straight line at the Dreamland and Pekin Theaters in Chicago because Oliver believed it would improve the acoustics and balance of the band. According to Dodds, "the bandstand at the Royal Garden was about four feet high. . . . Oliver believed music is more even when it comes down on people's heads, because it hits the ceiling and comes down on them. He believed the balcony bandstands in some of the New Orleans Halls are good because they were high, and in turn, that the music will sound too far away when the bandstand is too high or too low. And that music from a too-low stand will sound better than from a too-high one. [Therefore] the best place in the room is picked out to set up the band" (Russell 1958a, 3–4). Dodds also recalled that "the Oliver band had all special arrangements, but only after the first recordings were made; before that, every man had contributed his ideas to the music, and that was when it was 'our band'; when the recordings became hits, it became 'King Oliver's band,' and that was the way i.e., the reason it broke up" (Russell 1958s, 6).

Dodds altered his melo-rhythmic concepts for each recording, individual, or group. Dodds and his brother Johnny (a clarinetist) made several recordings with Louis Armstrong's Hot Seven in the spring of 1927. Although the band rehearsed, and Armstrong would tell each person when to solo and when to enter the composition, the group utilized a collective approach with each member contributing ideas for a composition. In fact, Armstrong gave each member maximum freedom to create within an ensemble setting. Dodds described his adaptation to Armstrong's style thus:

> Sometimes when recording with Louis I used the afterbeat cymbal to back him up. I used this on the record we made of "Willie the Weeper." It was my style of playing and I used it often for dancing. Some people think today that my drumming was heavy; it wasn't that at all, but rather it was because my technique was so sharp. Each time I hit the cymbal it was clear and distinct, but it wasn't that I was hitting it hard. I was careful to try to hit the cymbals or rims or even the woodblock, just right, and the way I tried to drum required a good thinking brain and a sharp ear. And it was always necessary to keep a sense of humor, for God's sake, so that if something didn't sound right I could always change it or quickly insert something else in its place. [Gara 1959, 72–73]

Dodds also described Armstrong's rhythmic and instrumentational departure from earlier New Orleans practices:

> With Louis recording outfit we used four beats to the measure. That was different from the older days in New Orleans when we always used two. King Oliver used two also. And Louis used a tuba instead of a string bass. I had started playing with a bass viol and always felt closer to it than to a tuba. It was no harder to drum with a tuba but it always made the group sound brassy to me. It seemed like it was a brass band or street band. Jelly Roll Morton also used a tuba on his records. [Gara 1959, 73]

On June 4, 1927, Dodds and his brother recorded with Jelly Roll Morton's Red Hot Peppers. Unlike Armstrong, Morton did not give individual musicians any leeway. Instead, he outlined in rehearsal the specific roles and functions each musician should follow in recording sessions.

> At rehearsal Jelly Roll Morton used to work on each and every number until it satisfied him. Everybody had to do what Jelly wanted him to do. Doing rehearsal he would say, "Now that's just the way I want it on the recording," and he meant just that. We used his original numbers and he always explained what it was all about and played a synopsis of it on the piano. Sometimes we had music and he would mark with a pencil those places which he wanted to stand out in a number. It was different from recording with Louis. Jelly didn't leave much leeway for the individual musician. You did what Jelly Roll wanted you to do, no more and no less. And his own playing was remarkable and keep us in good spirits. He wasn't fussy, but he was positive. He knew what he wanted and he would get the men he knew could produce it. But Jelly wasn't a man to get angry. I never saw him upset and he didn't raise his voice at any time. He wasn't hard to please and after making a record he would let us know when he was pleased with it. [Gara 1959, 74]

Dodds goes on to describe Morton's attention to detail:

> Although Jelly used to work out all the different parts himself, he often gave us something extra to do, some little novelty or something. When we made "Jungle Blues" he wanted a gong effect and I used a large cymbal and a mallet to produce the effect he wanted. One number that was pretty complicated for me was Jelly's "Billy Goat Stomp." There were places in that where the vocalist made a noise like a billy goat and I had to do something else on the drums at the same time. It was in Spanish Rhythm like so many of the numbers used to be played in New Orleans. I used the cymbal and soft mallet on that number and also on the Chinese tom-tom. Another tricky one was the "Hyena Stomp." It took quite a bit of rehearsing on some of those to get just what Jelly wanted but he told us what he expected and we would do our best to get the right effect. I was very versatile then and picked up the idea when Jelly played it on the piano. [Gara 1959, 74–75]

At the recording, conditions with Morton were conducive to Dodds's musical expression because he was allowed to bring his entire drum set to the session, including a snare drum, suspended cymbal, wood block, Chinese tom-tom, and bass drum. Although he was not the first drummer to take a bass drum to a recording session, it was not a common occurrence in 1927. Four tunes were recorded at the session, three on Victor and one on Bluebird Records, they were "Billy Goat Stomp," "Hyena Stomp," "Jungle Blues," and "Wild Man Blues" (Bluebird). Whereas he displayed excellent drumming skills and a creative approach that complemented both individual musicians and the ensemble on all the recordings, his drumming on "Billy Goat Stomp" is particularly noteworthy. In addition to the use of Spanish rhythm and tom-tom, Dodds took several solo breaks. In the first chorus, he plays an imitative rhythm on Chinese tom-tom, which is answered by the ensemble, thereby producing a call-and-response effect. Although the same rhythmic imitation occurs in the next chorus, Dodds contrasts and varies the rhythm by playing it on the wood block, Chinese tom-tom, and suspended cymbal in combination. Then, he alternates, striking the instruments at random, playing a rhythmic figure first introduced in measure nine of the first chorus

He plays this first on the suspended cymbal, thereafter altering it by playing on the three instruments simultaneously

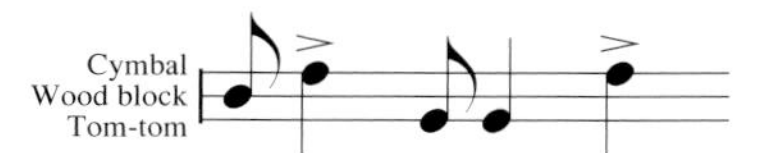

What is interesting is that the varied motif is repeated by all members of the ensemble except Johnny Dodds, who repeats the original rhythm. The same pattern occurs a few measures later where Baby Dodds plays a

rhythm on the previously mentioned instruments; this time, however, Johnny varies the rhythm by adding a note to the motif. It is not clear why Johnny Dodds played the original and the other members played the varied version, nor is it known whether Morton gave them the freedom to choose. By using either or both rhythms within the composition, Dodds provided the generic phenomenon that held the tune together. Later in the composition we hear three solo sections featuring Dodds, the first rather restrained—perhaps because of Morton's influence—on the Chinese tom-tom in a straightforward rhythm

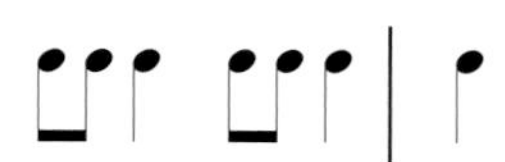

Dodds varies the next two solos. Instead of using the Chinese tom-tom, he plays the next stomp-time solo section on his suspended cymbal using a technique common to most drummers in the 1920s; holding the edge of the cymbal in one hand and striking the stick with the remaining drumstick (Brown, 1976, 233–35). In addition, he varies the cymbal by using both open and closed techniques: releasing the cymbal and allowing it to vibrate and holding the cymbal, when it is struck. His ability to adapt is also evident in the last two choruses where while accompanying the ensemble, he uses a series of eight-note triplets alternating between the Chinese tom-tom, drum rims, and wood block. It is important to acknowledge his ability to adapt to the musical and aesthetic concepts of Morton, as well as to evoke melo-rhythmic concepts by using the Chinese tom-tom, cymbal, drum rims, and wood block at various times.

The Dodds brothers made several trio recordings with Morton four days after the ensemble recordings of June 4. Since the recordings used prerecorded Morton piano solos, Morton added clarinet and drum parts. He wanted these to be felt, not heard. Therefore, at Morton's request, Dodds used wire brushes on "Mr. Jelly Lord." In addition, Johnny Dodds was told to play only in the low register. Yet, on "Wolverine Blues," Dodds used his Chinese tom-toms to create a soundscape that Morton liked and left in the recording. In addition to the aforementioned instructions, Morton was very precise with tempos, an effect that he emphasized by stamping his foot. Once more, Dodds's ability to adapt his drumming to either the musician or ensemble is apparent in his brush techniques, used with a quarter-note backbeat rhythm, accented on two and four. On the same composition, he varied both his rhythm and timbre by using backbeat concepts–Charleston and shuffle rhythms—and the ride-cymbal. Whereas the use of these techniques was not Dodds's alone, his ability to incorporate them into a melo-rhythmic concept appropriate for the individual or group was unique.

Dodds also demonstrated a melo-rhythmic awareness on other recordings (King 1960, 13–14). His earliest recordings were made with King Oliver's Creole Jazz Band in 1923. Here, Dodds was limited to using wood blocks. On "Chimes Blues" he can be heard playing subtle variations on his blocks, syncopating his beat, playing in double time, using shuffle rhythms, and playing rolls. He varied his beat on each theme of "Froggie Moore" by shifting accents and using Spanish rhythms. On

"Canal Street Blues," Dodds featured wood-block interplay with the horns. Behind Johnny Dodds's solo, his wood-block figures first follow the descending runs of the clarinet and then contrast with them during the second half of the chorus. One of the best examples of Dodds's melo-rhythmic awareness can be found on "Mandy Lee Blues," where his accompaniment is constructed from various beats and syncopations that follow the melody. He features double-time figures, always implying contrasting time values above the stated beat. On "Snake Rag," he phrases in unison with the horns; then he can be heard double timing the second theme, changing his beats on the later choruses, and simplifying his patterns for the ride-out. There is a progressive movement from order to excitement and then back to order. Despite the limitations of recording techniques at this early date, Dodds's playing is indicative of a wide vocabulary of beats, a concern for texture, and a sense of swing that implies several contrasting time values simultaneously.

Unfortunately, the whole of Dodds's drumming is not well documented on records. This stems from the fact that only snare-drum rims, bass-drum shells, and wood blocks were used on many of his pre-1930 recordings. In fact, Dodds was not allowed to use either a snare or bass drum on most of the recordings he made while performing with King Oliver and Louis Armstrong. Most of the drumming on pre-1930 New Orleans recordings was overshadowed by either the piano or banjo. Beginning in the early forties, however, Dodds was often recorded using all of the components of his drum set.

After the Oliver recordings, Dodds demonstrated his melo-rhythmic awareness with Louis Armstrong in the 1920s. On the Armstrong Hot Seven recordings, we occasionally hear him playing a wood-block accent or a Charleston beat on the cymbals, but otherwise the drums are inaudible. The same is true of other recordings he made with Armstrong and Johnny Dodds (King 1960, 14); though on a few sides made with his brother, he brings his drumming technique to the washboard. On "Piggly Wiggly," Dodds can be heard using the washboard as an extension of his voice by interweaving figures and accents around the horns, varying his beat with triplets and shuffle rhythms, using off-beats, or playing unaccented straight fours. Further evidence of his melo-rhythmic awareness can be found in selected recordings that he made with Sidney Bechet's Feetwarmers in the early forties. For example, on "Ain't Misbehavin," Dodds used contrasting long and short rolls. He can also be heard to accent the release with his cymbals and to cue in the second chorus with a roll. On the chase choruses he outlined the trumpet part with wood blocks and kept the various breaks melodically different by moving from snare drums to cymbals to wood blocks. Dodds played in unison with the horns on "Blues for You Johnny," mixing nine-stroke rolls with tom-tom accents; behind the vocal he played a basic beat, varying his nine-stroke rolls with twelves and one-beat presses. There are double-time tom-tom punctuations on the release, and on the instrumental choruses, he featured five-stroke rolls played at double time. On "Stompy Jones," Dodds varied his five-stroke rolls with shorter rolls and rim shots. His accents continually shifted the center of the rhythm. He also introduced a type of harmonized riff by performing runs on the drum rims. After the bass solo, Dodds soloed for eight measures in double time. His solo featured accents and a changing tonal pattern. He used two wood blocks and four tuned cowbells.

Another melo-rhythmic concept used by Dodds and other New Orleans drummers is a 2/4 superimposed on a 4/4 melodically conceived, cross-rhythm. Franklin has divided early jazz rhythms into three broad categories (1981, 53–61). None, however, of Franklin's theories have identified the possibility that the 2/4 superimposed on a 4/4 might be either a family resemblance related to an African cross-rhythm or a melo-rhythmic concept. Franklin divided theories of rhythm into the following categories:

a. 4/4 or flat four theory—Leroy Ostransky, Gushee, Eileen Southern Postgate, Michael Budds, Rudi Blesh, John Dankworth, Paul Tanner, and Maurice Gerow.
b. Two beats or emphasis on two and four—Brendt, Newton.
c. A compromise between the 4/4 flat four theory, and the two beat, stress on two and four theory—James Lincoln Collier, Gunther Schuller, and Mark Gridley.

I believe the 2/4 superimposed on a 4/4 rhythm often found in the drumming style of Baby Dodds and others is a family resemblance based on an African cross-rhythm because it can be analyzed as one rhythm that is melodically conceived. Since these interlocking parts (i.e., 2/4 superimposed on 4/4) form one rhythmic pattern, and since the pattern is both conceived and performed as a melo-rhythmic phenomenon, it is a type of cross-rhythm.

Dippermouth Blues

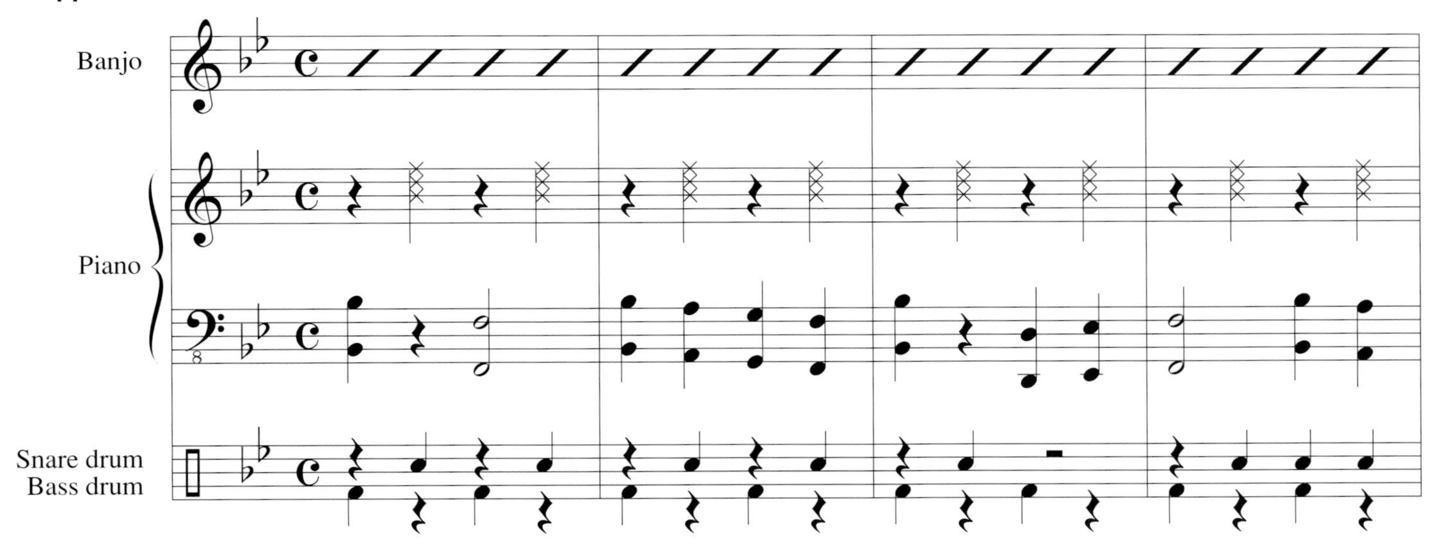

The King Oliver rendition of "Dippermouth Blues" (1923) is a good example of both cross-rhythms and the melo-rhythmic concept that Nzewi described. It is a well-known composition, which was recorded several times by others and again by Oliver under the alternate title "Sugar Foot Stomp," after its first two recordings in 1923. Its primary feature—one that has been widely imitated—is the famous Oliver cornet solo (Dapogny 1978, 407–8).[1] The Oliver recording, on Okeh Records (1923), can be outlined as follows:

a. A four measure, composed introduction, followed by nine choruses with one, two, five, and nine being a statement of the principal melody (ensemble). It ends with a two-measure tag.
b. In choruses one, two, five, and nine the trombonist plays the same line, and the band's dynamics are used aurally to link these ensemble choruses, which surround and provide the principal element for the solo episodes. They function as repetitions.
c.The two clarinet choruses vary somewhat harmonically, e.g., measure two contains a raised supertonic diminished seventh chord. The band accompanies the clarinet choruses with a 4/4 accompaniment.
d. Oliver plays a three-chorus long solo. The band continues to accompany.
e. The song "Oh Play That Thing" occurs at the end of the eighth chorus. A short two-measure tag beyond the normal blues structure ends the recording. The two-measure tag is improvised on tonic harmony.

Beginning in the fifth chorus, one can hear "Baby" Dodds playing on afterbeats. While the principle melody ensemble is being stated, the banjo, piano, and drums are playing the passage shown on the bottom of the previous page (Tirro 1977, 147).[2]

On the surface, the rhythm could be described as follows: the banjo features the rhythmic time line: four equally weighted beats per measure. Lil Hardin's bass line on the piano features a quarter note, quarter rest, and half-note rhythm in the first measure; thereafter, it alternates between quarter-note rhythms, which are only interrupted with a half-note in measure one and four. In addition, Hardin features a two and four rhythm in the right hand; unfortunately, the notes were not discernible. Dodds alternates his rhythm, featuring a one and three on the bass drum and a two and four on the snare drum. Dodds's rhythm features a two feeling, which according to Dodds was Oliver's preference, on two different tonal levels. The combined efforts of Hardin and Dodds form one rhythm that is performed cross-rhythmically and is held together by the time line being performed by Bill Johnson on banjo. As a whole, the rhythms interlock with each other throughout the example.

Both intracross- and intercross-rhythms occur. For example, Dodds features an alternating one and three rhythm on the bass drum and a two and four rhythm on the snare drum, throughout the excerpt. It can be interpreted as an intracross-rhythm that is melodically conceived because there are two tonal levels involved on different beats on two different instruments, the bass and snare drum. Hardin's rhythm, while different when compared to Dodds, can also be described as an intracross-rhythm that is melodically conceived. Hardin's bass line features constant rhythmic movement, with the exception of a half-note in the left hand while the right hand performs on two and four. The result is that a cross-rhythm occurs because different tonal levels are performed on different beats throughout the musical excerpt.

The Dodds and Hardin rhythms combined could also be described as an intermelodically conceived cross-rhythm. For example, both the piano (left hand), and the bass drum began on the first beat, whereas the snare drum and piano (right hand) enter on the second beat, thereby creating both a tonal and rhythmic contrast that is part of the overall rhythm. In turn, these alternating tonal and rhythmic ideas continue in measures two and three between the drum and piano parts. Here the tonal and rhythmic contrasts occur from beat to beat. Beats one and three, with the exception of beat three in measure three, contain equal tonal and rhythmic emphases, whereas beats two and four, with the exception of beat four in measure three, also contain equal tonal and rhythmic emphases. In turn, the alternating tonal and rhythmic contrasts produce a group-against-group feeling. The musical excerpt concludes with a modified retrograde in the piano (left hand), measure four, while the banjo, piano (right hand), and snare drum continue to play the parts that were first introduced in measure one.

Conclusion

While I cannot prove that Dodds purposefully emulated West African rhythmic concepts, it is my belief that the frequency and diversity of his use of melo-rhythmic concepts is a family resemblance based upon drumming. The fact that African musical concepts were employed in Place Congo/Congo Square through the late nineteenth century, ending only two years before Dodds's birth; Dodds's ability to trace his family's musical roots to Congo Square through his maternal great grandfather who taught him African drum language; Dodds's generic use of melo-rhythmic phenomena to fit both individuals and groups; and the make-up of his drum set furnish adequate proof of a family resemblance. Dodds's drumming concepts are, in fact, the strongest indication to date of an African family resemblance in early jazz.

Selected Discography

Recordings with King Oliver (Dodds as Sideman)—1923

Just Gone	Gennett 5133
Canal Street Blues	Gennett 5133
Mandy Lee Blues	Gennett 5134
I'm Going Away to Wear You off My Mind	Gennett 5134
Chimes Blues	Gennett 5135
Weather Bird Blues	Gennett 5132
Dippermouth Blues	Gennett 5132
Froggie Moore	Gennett 5135
Snake Rag	Gennett 5184
Alligator Hop	Gennett 5274
Zulus Ball	Gennett 5275
Working Man Blues	Gennett 5275
Krooked Blues	Gennett 5274
Southern Stomp	Century 3011
Froggie Moore	Riverside SDP11
Snake Rag	OKeh 4933
High Society Rag	OKeh 4933
Sweet Loving Man	OKeh 4933
Sobbin' Blues	Epic NL1012
Jazzin' Babies Blues	OKeh 4975
Room Rent Blues	Epic NL 1012
I Ain't Gonna Tell Nobody'	Epic NL 1012
Working Man Blues	Epic NL 1012

Recordings with Jelly Roll Morton (Dodds as Sideman)—1927

Billy Goat Stomp	Victor 20772
Hyena Stomp	Victor 20772
Jungle Blues	Victor 21345
Wild Man Blues	Bluebird B10256
The Pearls	Victor 20948
Beal Street Blues	Victor 27113
Wolverine Blues	Victor 21064
Mr. Jelly Lord	Victor 21064

Recordings with Louis Armstrong (Dodds as Sideman)—1927

Willie the Weeper	OKeh 8482
Alligator Crawl	OKeh 8482
Wild Man Blues	OKeh 8474
Gully Low Blues	OKeh 8474
Chicago Breakdown	Columbia 36376
Potato Head Blues	Columbia 35660
Melancholy Blues	OKeh 8496
Keyhole Blues	OKeh 8496
Weary Blues	OKeh 8519
That's When I'll Come Back to You	OKeh 8519
Twelfth Street Rag	Columbia 35663
S.O.L. Blues	Columbia 35661

Recordings with the New Orleans Wanderers (Dodds as Sideman)—No date

Perdido St. Blues	Columbia 689-D
Gatemouth	Columbia 689-D

Recordings with Johnny Dodds (Dodds as Sideman)—No Date

Although Baby Dodds performed with his brother, Johnny Dodds, at Kelly's Stable from 1928 to 1930, and then off and on throughout the 1930s in Chicago, I have not been able to ascertain the dates of the following recordings.

Weary Blues	Brunswick 80073
New Orleans Stomp	Brunswick 80073
Wild Man Blues	Brunswick 3567
Melancholy	Brunswick 3567
Come on and Stomp, Stomp, Stomp	Brunswick 3568
After You've Gone	Brunswick 3568
Joe Turner Blues	Brunswick 3997
When Erastus Plays His Old Kazoo	Brunswick 3997
Piggly Wiggly	Brunswick n.n.
Bucktown Stomp	Victor V38004
Weary City	Victor V38004
Blue Washboard Stomp	Victor 21552
Bull Fiddle Blues	Victor 21552
Pencil Papa	Victor V38038
Sweet Lorraine	Victor V38038
Hear Me Talkin' to Ya	Victor V38541
My Little Isabelle	Victor V38541
Goober Dance	Victor 23396
Too Tight	Bluebird B10240

Recordings with Sidney Bechet (Dodds as Sideman)—No Date

Stompy Jones	no label, no date
Ain't Misbehavin	no label, no date
Blues for You Johnny	no label, no date

Recordings with Willie G. "Bunk" Johnson (Dodds as Sideman)—1944

Lowdown Blues	American Music LP 647, American Music 253, Storyville SLP 128, Dan VC-7016
Blue As I Can Be (Vocals by Myrtle Jones)	American Music LP 647, Storyville SLP 205, Dan VC-7018
See See Rider (Vocals by Myrtle Jones)	Storyville SLP 205, Dan VC-7009
Precious Lord (Vocals by Myrtle Jones)	Storyville SLP 205, Dan VC-7009
Life Will Be Sweeter Someday (Vocals by Myrtle Jones)	Storyville SLP 128, Dan VC-7016
St. Louis Blues	American Music 252, Storyville SLP 152, Revival (D) 001, Dan VC-7006
Tiger Rag	American Music Baby Dodds No. 4

Tiger Rag	American Music 251, Storyville SLP 152, Dan VC-7006
New Iberia Blues	American Music Baby Dodds No. 4, Storyville SLP 205, Dan VC-7009
New Iberia Blues	American Music 257, Storyville SLP 152, Dan VC-7006
When the Saints Go Marching In	American Music LP 638, Storyville SLP 203
When the Saints Go Marching In	American Music 252, Storyville SLP 152, Dan VC-7006
Ballin' the Jack	Storyville SLP 205, Dan VC-7009
High Society	American Music Baby Dodds No.4 (last 2:40).
Darktown Strutters Ball	American Music 256 Storyville SLP 152, Dan VC-7006
Lord You're Good to Me	American Music LP 647, Storyville SLP 128, Dan VC-7016
Panama	American Music 256, Storyville SLP 128, Dan VC-7016?
See See Rider	American Music 251, LP 638, Storyville SLP 152, Dan VC-7006
Blues	American Music LP 638, Storyville SLP 205, Dan VC-7009
Weary Blues	American Music unissued
Clarinet Marmalade	Storyville SLP 127, Dan VC-7016
Yes, Yes in Your Eyes	American Music 253, Storyville SLP 206, Dan VC-7009
Streets of the City	American Music 256, Storyville SLP 203, Dan VC-7016
Maryland, My Maryland	American Music Baby Dodds No. 3, Dan VC-7015
Sister Kate	American Music 257, Storyville SLP 128, Dan VC-7016
Weary Blues	American Music 258, Storyville SLP 152, Dan VC-7006
After You've Gone	American Music LP 647
Alabamy Bound	Storyville SLP 205, Dan VC-7009

The following recordings were originally made in 1944 with Bunk Johnson on American Records with no issue numbers: "I Love My Baby," "Honey Gal," "Ballin' the Jack" (an issue was released as LP 643) "Bugle Boy March," "How Long Blues," "Careless Love," and "'Blues." "Muskrat Ramble" was recorded but not issued. In an August 4, 1944, recording session Baby Dodds made several unissued records; they were "Yes, Yes in Your Eyes," "Ole Miss," "You Are My Sunshine," "Tishomingo Blues," "Darktown Strutters Ball," "Ballin' the Jack," "Careless Love," "Panama Blues in C," and "Blues." The following two were released:

Sugar Foot Stomp	American Music LP 643, Storyville SLP 128, Dan VC-7016
When You Wore a Tulip	American Music LP 643, Storyville SLP 152, Dan VC- 006

Recordings with Louis "Kid Shots" Madison (Dodds as Sideman)—1944

High Society	American Music LP 639, Storyville SLP 201, Dan VC-7007
In Gloryland	America Music LP 645, Dan VC-7012
In Gloryland	American Music 530, Storyville SLP 203, Gzl. 1035
Bucket's Got a Hole in It	American Music LP 645, Storyville SLP 127
As Uptown Bump	American Music 529, Gzl. 1034, Dan VC-7012
Dumaine Street Drag	American Music 530 (Cut), America Music LP 645, Gzl. 1035 (Cut), Storyville SLP 127, Dan VC-7012
When You and I were Young Maggie	American Music 529 (Cut), American Music LP 645, Gzl. 1034 (Cut), Storyville SLP 127, Dan VC-7012
Sheik of Araby	American Music LP 646, Storyville SLP 127, Dan VC-7012

Recordings with Willie G. "Bunk" Johnson (Dodds as Sideman)—1945

Tiger Rag	Mnme B. 530, Esq. E. 10-151, EP. 181, Riverside RLP 1047, RLP 12-119, BYG529.-062, Blue Star 222, HOJ 15, Austroton V5164
Weary Blues	Mnme B. 530, Esq. E.10-152, EP. 181, Riverside RLP 1047, RLP 12-119, BYG529-.062, Blue Star 222, HOJ 15, Austroton V5164, Joker SM 3095

Pallet on the Floor	Mnme B. 531, Esq. E. 10-151, EP. 181, Riverside RLP 1047, RLP 12-116, SDP 11, Blue Star 23C, Music JH 1087, Austroton V5167
Careless Love	Mnme B. 531, Esq. E. 10-152, EP. 181, Riverside RLP 1047, RLP 12-116, SDP 11, Blue Star 23C, Music JH 1087, Austroton V5167, Joker SM 3095
Swanee River	American Music 512+, Storyville SLP 202
Swanee River (Drum Solo)	American Music Baby Dodds No. 1, Dan VC-7015
All the Whores Like the Way I Ride	American Music LP 644, Storyville SEP 401
827 Blues	American Music LP 644, Storyville SEP 401
Runnin' Wild	American Music 512, Storyville SLP 202, Dan VC-7011
Margie	American Music 511
You Always Hurt the One You Love	American Music LP 644, Storyville SEP 401
The Sheik of Araby	Storyville SLP 202, Purist PU 7, Dan VC-7011
Listen to Me	American Music 514., American Music Baby Dodds No. 3, Dan VC-7015
Do Right Baby (Ed. Johnson vocals)	American Music 511
Lonesome Road	American Music LP 638, Storyville SLP 201, Dan VC-7016
My Old Kentucky Home	American Music 514, Storyville SLP 202, Dan VC-7011
Golden Leaf Strut	American Music LP 644, Storyville SEP 401
When The Saints Go Marching In	American Music 102, American Music LP 643, Dixie LP 107, Storyville SLP 202, Dan VC-7011
Just a Closer Walk with Thee	American Music LP 638, Storyville SLP 202, Dan VC-7011
Didn't He Ramble	American Music 103, Dixie LP 107, Fkwy FP 57, F. J.2803 Storyville SLP 202, Col. C3L-30, CBS. E. BPG 62234, Dan VC-7011
Just a Little While to Stay Here	American Music 101, American Music LP 643, Dixie LP 107, Storyville SLP 202, 203
Nearer My God to Thee	American Music 102, Baby Dodds No. 1, American Music LP 643, Dixie LP 107, Storyville SLP 202, Dan VC-7011
In Gloryland	American Music 101, Baby Dodds No. 1, Dixie LP 107, Storyville SLP 202, Dan VC-7011
Tell Me Your Dreams	American Music 103, Baby Dodds No. 1, Dixie LP 107, Storyville SLP 202, Dan VC-7011
Maryland, My Maryland	Decca (DE) 25132, Voc. E.V. 1036, Br. E. OE9257, A of H. AH. 140, Br(G) 82568, 12160, 10186, DE (F) MV. 60080, Br/G/F10071 EPB
Alexander's Ragtime Band	DE 25132, Br. E. 04437, OE 9257, A of H. AH 140, DE(F) MV 60080, Br. (G) 82568,12160,10186, Br/G/F 10071 EPB
Tishomingo Blues	DE 25131, DL 8244, Br. E. 04437, OE 9257, Br. E. LAT 8124, A of H. AH 140, DE (F) MV 30535, Br(G) 10186, Br(G/F) 10071EPB, 87003LPBM
You Always Hurt the One You Love	DE 2531, Voc. E. V. 1036, A of H. AH 140, DE (F) MV 30535, Br(G) 10186, Br(G/F)10071 EPB
You Always Hurt the One You Love	DE 25131, Br. E. OE 9257
I Wish I Could Shimmy Like My Sister Kate (Appears Twice)	His Master's Voice (HMV) (Aus) EA 3438, RCA (F) 130.268
" "	Victor (VI). 40-0128, HMV B 9517, B. RCA (F) 75.625, RCA(G) EPA 9696

A Closer Walk with Thee	His Master's Voice 40-127 HMV B 9820 HMV(Aus) EA 3538, RCA (F) 130. 268, RCA LEJ-7
Snag It	His Master's Voice 40-0126 HMV B 9821, HMV (Aus) EA 3400 RCA (F)130.268 (Appears twice on first pressing), RCA (G) EPA 9696
One Sweet Letter From You	His Master's Voice40-0129, HMV (Aus) EA 3438, HMV B 9517
When the Saints Go Marching In	His Master's Voice 40-0126, HMV B 9511, HMV (Aus) EA 3504, RCA (F) 130.268, RCA LEJ-6, 27-0135, EPAT 35, LPT 26, EL. 7MW 107, LPM (S) 2982, HMV 7M141, DLP 1054, RCA (F) 75. 625, RCA RD 7713
High Society	His Master's Voice 40-0127, HMV B. 9820, HMV (Aus) EA 3400, RCA (F) 130. 268, 75.625
Darktown Strutters Ball	His Master's Voice 40-0128, HMV B. 9511, HMV (Aus) EA 3504, RCA (F) 130.268, 75.625, HMV 7M141, RCA EL. 7MW 107, RCA (G) EPA 9696
Franklin Street Blues	His Master's Voice 40-0129, HMV B 9821, HMV (Aus) EA 3538, RCA (F) 130.268, RCA (G) EPA 9696

The following recordings with Bunk Johnson were made on Jubilee Records, but they were never released.

Does Jesus Care	Jubilee 2501, Disc 6038, Mel. E. 1102, Mel. E. 7-52
Does Jesus Care	Asch AA.1, Pioneer AA.1.
The Lord Will Make a Way Somehow	Jubilee 2501, Disc 6039, Mel. E. 1102, Mel. E. 7- 52
Where Could I Go	Jubilee 2502, Disc 6039, MEL. E. 1101, Mel. E. 7-52, Asch AA. 1, Pioneer AA.1.
God's Amazing Grace	Jubilee 2502, Disc 6039, Mel. E. 1101, Mel. E. 7-52

Recordings with Albert Nichols (Dodds as Sideman)—1945

Feelin' at Ease	Blue Note 519, 7021, 6509, 9288
Careless Love	Blue Note 518
High Society (alt.)	Mosaic MR5-114, MD4-114 (CD)
High Society	Blue Note 519
Winin' Boy Blues	Blue Note 518, 7013, 9288
Careless Love (alt.)	Mosaic MR5-114, MD4-114 (CD)
Careless Love (LP)	Blue Note 7021, 65091 9288 JS JSLP50044 Vogue (F) LDE174

Baby Dodds Recordings (Dodds as Leader)—1945

Careless Love	Blue Note 518
Winin' Boy Blues	Blue Note 518
Feelin' at Ease	Blue Note 519
High Society	Blue Note 519
Wolverine Blues	Circle 1001
Buddy Bolden Blues	Circle 1039
Albert's Blues	Circle 1002
Manhattan Stomp	Circle 1002
Drum Improvisation No. 1	GHB 50
Drum Improvisation No. 2	GHB 50

Recordings with Albert Nichols (Dodds as Sideman)—1946

Wolverine Blues	Circle 1001, GHB 50 Riverside RLP12-216, 1039
Buddy Bolden Blues	(EU) J1354, Monkey (F) MY 400230
Albert's Blues	Circle 1002, GHB 50, Riverside RLP 12-216, Concert Hall, (EU) JI354, Monkey (F) MY 400230
Drum Improvisations No. 1	Circle 1001, GHB 50
Drum Improvisations No. 2	Circle 1039

Baby Dodds Recordings (Dodds as Leader)—1946

Title	Label
Rudiments with Drumstick Nerve-Beats	Folkways N: A.

Recordings with George Lewis (Dodds as Sideman)—1946

Title	Label
I Couldn't Hear Nobody Pray (Vocals by Sister Bernice Philips)	Riverside RLP. 12-283
Bill Bailey Won't You Please Come Home (Vocals by Harold Lewis)	Circle J.1068, S. 26, Vg. E. V.2110, Riverside RLP 12-283
The Royal Telephone (Vocals by Lewis and Philips)	Circle R. 3001, S. 26, Riverside RLP. 12-283
Far Away Blues	Circle J. 1068, S. 26, Vg. E. V. 2110, Riverside RLP. 12-283, Revival (D) 001
I Just Can't Keep It to Myself Alone (Vocals by H. Lewis)	Riverside RLP 12-283
God Leads His Dear Children Along (Vocals by Lewis and Philips)	Circle R. 3001, S. 26, Riverside RLP 12-283
Bucket's Got a Hole in It	Circle J. 1012, S. 26, New Orleans Rarities 4
The Girls All Love the Way I Drive	Circle J. 1012, S. 26, New Orleans Rarities 4

Recording with the Original Zenith Brass Band (Dodds plays snare drums)—1946

Title	Label
Fidgety	Circle 1007, S. 25, Esq. E. 10-172, Riverside RLP 12-283
Shake and Break It	Circle 1007, S. 25, Esq. E. 10-172, Riverside RLP 12-283
Bugle Boy March	Circle 1006, S. 25, Esq. E. 10-102, Riverside RLP 12-283, Blue Star 156
Salutation March	Circle 1005, S. 25, Esq. E. 10-101, Riverside RLP 12-12-283
If Ever I Cease to Love	Circle 1005, S. 25, Esq. E. 10-101, Riverside RLP 12-283, Blue Star 156
Taint Nobody's Biz-ness If I Do	Circle 1006, Esq. E. 10-102, Riverside RLP 12-283

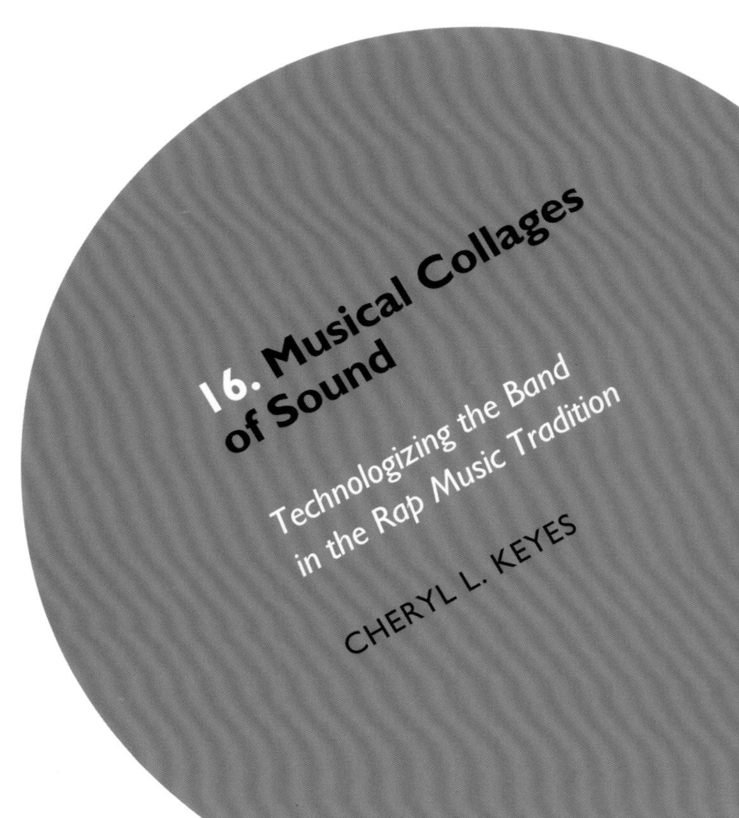

16. Musical Collages of Sound

Technologizing the Band in the Rap Music Tradition

CHERYL L. KEYES

Rap music evolved in the Bronx during the early 1970s as part of a youth arts movement called "hip-hop." Comprised of disc jockeys (DJs), rhymin' emcees or mike controllers (MCs or rappers), break-dancers, and graffiti artists, "hip-hop" also defines an attitude communicated through the use of vernacular speech, stylized dress, and gestures associated with urban street culture. While graffiti and break dancing have not attained the popularity of the other street arts, the rhymin' MCs and the DJs continue to be extremely popular. Their success is predicated on their combined styles of delivery, which have given birth to one of the most vital forms of popular music during the late century, rap. Rap music can be defined as a quasi-song form with street rhymes and rhythmic speech recited over a prerecorded soundtrack. Because of rap's longtime affiliation with the youth arts movement of the Bronx, the terms *hip-hop* and *rap music* are used interchangeably when referring to this nascent popular musical style.

During its early development, rap consisted of a DJ, who mixed prerecorded music alternately on two turntables while simultaneously reciting party phrases to the crowd via a microphone. When mixing records graduated into a competitive art form, however, DJs soon supplemented their verbal performances by hiring MCs. While the art of MCing is based solely on verbal dexterity, DJing demands a comprehensive knowledge of dance music; turntable technique; electronic music-making instruments—digital samplers, drum machines, audio mixers, turntables, and so forth—in order to produce a soundtrack over which the MC raps. Rap music, as one critic asserts, is a complex fusion of orality and postmodern technology (Rose 1994, 85). For this reason, rappers exclaim that rap groups do not need bands, "All we need in order to achieve, is some help from the master; the DJ will give you one-hundred percent " (Whodini 1986). This essay will explore the impact of rap music DJs on musical technology and examine the aesthetic choices they make in producing beats and sounds through electronic means.

Historical Context

Music critics argue that the popularization of disco during the 1970s contributed to transforming the "radio DJ," a persona, into the "club DJ," a performer. Popular music scholar Arnold Shaw states that "disco gave prominence to the record producer and the disc jockey—the former for his skills in manipulating the new sophisticated recording technology, and the latter for his ability to use changes in tempo, volume, and mood to manipulate dancers on the floor" (Shaw 1986, 251). Although record producers and disc jockeys were the movers and shakers of disco, it was the latter who revolutionized the turntable as a musical instrument. This transition was primarily facilitated by Black DJs from the ghetto streets, who were, for the most part, on the periphery of mainstream disco.

The historical precedent for 1970s disco was the work of African American artist Barry White and the musical production of Philadelphia International Records, a Black-owned company started by Kenny Gamble and Leon Huff. Tunes such as White's "Love's Theme" (1973) and "TSOP" (The Sound of Philadelphia; 1973)—the original theme for the television program *Soul Train*—by the group MFSB, are typical of this music. The musical basis of disco was an orchestral arrangement over a rhythm section, soul vocals, and an underlying bass-drum rhythm accenting on all four beats subdivided by the hi-hat cymbals' beats. By the mid-1970s, however, European producers, including Pete Bellotte and Giorgio Moroder, had entered the disco scene and modified it by introducing a pop female soloist, a repetitive bass-line figure outlining the notes of a chord, and a shift in tempo from a moderate to a faster beat. Music critic Nelson George notes that,

> [d]isco movers and shakers were not record executives but club deejays. Most were gay men with a singular attitude toward American culture, black as well as white. They elevated female vocalists like [Donna] Summer, Gloria Gaynor, Diana Ross, Loleatta Holloway, Melba Moore, and Grace Jones to diva status, while black male singers were essentially shunned. Funk, which in the late-70s was enjoying great popularity in the South and Midwest, was rarely on their playlists. It was too raw and unsophisticated, and one thing dear to the hearts of disco fans, gay and straight, was feeling a pseudosophistication. [George 1988, 154]

In the quest for commercial success, creativity had given way to formula, and the very excitement and challenge for which the music makers had long striven were beginning to fade away (Joe 1980, 31). Further removed from its cultural base, 1970s disco became distorted, altered, and less dynamic. It was recognized as "a white, middle-class, youth-to-middle age phenomenon" (Shaw 1986, 250). This radical change was felt among Black youth, particularly those in New York City, as Bill Adler, an independent rap music publicist and critic, has observed:

> In New York City in the mid-70s, the dominant Black popular music was

16.1 This photograph of Grandmaster Flash, Afrika Bambaataa, and Kool "DJ" Herc appeared on the cover of the fiftieth issue of *The Source: The Magazine of Hip-Hop Music, Culture, and Politics* (November 1993). Photograph © Source Magazine.

> disco as it was everyplace else. The difference about New York was that kids were funk fiends who weren't getting their vitamins from disco music. It was "too nervous," in their terminology, which meant, too fast. It was too gay. It was something, but it just didn't move them and so they were thrown back into their own resources and what happened was that they started to . . . play a lot of James Brown. . . . His old records were . . . staples, and Kool and the Gang, and heavy funk like that developed. I mean part of it just had to do with there being a lot of neighborhood parks in New York City . . . and what kind of music played in those parks by the disc jockeys there.[1]

Urban youth's response to disco gave rise to the itinerant disc jockey dubbed the "mobile" or "street DJ," and known today as the "rap music" or "hip-hop DJ."

Hip-hop DJs can trace their roots to the Black radio personality disc jockeys of the 1950s and 1960s. In capturing the persona of these jockeys, early street DJs occasionally chanted partylike phrases to their audiences while simultaneously dovetailing one record after the other. They also included sound techniques popularized by early radio jockeys such as "talking through" and "riding gain" in performances. The former involves lowering the volume of music on an audio board and continuing to talk as the music plays. In "riding gain," the disc jockey boosts or lowers the volume on the audio board in order to accent various parts of a record (Williams 1986, 81). Unlike radio jockeys, street DJs performed primarily in outdoor contexts—school yards, parks, and the streets—thereby creating an outdoor discotheque. As female rap music artist The Real Roxanne has observed: "People used to do jams [parties] outside in the school yard or handball court. Someone used to bring their two turntables out and plug it into the lamppost outside, and that's how they got their power. People would listen and dance to the music out in the streets."[2]

Street DJs were well-known in their own boroughs and were supported by local followers. Popular jockeys included Pete "DJ" Jones of the Bronx and Grandmaster Flowers and Maboya of Brooklyn. They occasionally spoke to their audiences in a legato-mellow style and in street jive reminiscent of early Black radio personality jockeys. According to DJ Hollywood of Harlem, in the early 1970s, street jockeys were evaluated according to the size, quality, and volume of their sound systems, as opposed to being judged solely by their own ability to spin or rap to a crowd:

> Pete "DJ" Jones, Flowers, and Maboya, they weren't microphone DJs. They were DJs that just had big big sound systems and big equipment; and this is what people were into at that particular time. Who had the biggest one, who had the biggest sound. So when I looked back at the concept of what was happening, I said to myself, I wanted to be the best.[3]

Although many street DJs were males, there was one noted female jockey from Brooklyn by the name of Lady J. Music promoter Dennis Shaw recognized Lady J as a pioneer of "lady DJs": "Lady J was definitely a forerunner of lady DJs. She was very adept to picking popular music that people liked. She could mix very well. She was very unique for her time, and she was very capable."[4]

The most innovative of street DJs, and one whose turntable skills were tremendously influential in terms of the future sound direction and production of rap music, was Jamaican-born Clive Campbell, known as Kool "DJ" Herc (figs. 16.1, 16.2). Campbell immigrated to the United States from Kingston, Jamaica, in 1967, at the age of twelve, and lived in the Bronx.

In 1972 Herc began DJing throughout the Bronx; his approach to this form contrasted with that of the United States jockeys. Instead of simply dovetailing one record after another and talking intermittently to the crowd, Herc recited rhymes over the microphone while mixing records from one turntable to the next. Mixing involves the DJ selecting discs and placing each on a turntable; the jockey then attempts to match the speed of each disc with the pitch control device (on the turntable system) until both discs are playing at the same speed. With the use of an audio-mixer, which sits between the turntables, and its cross-fader device, a DJ can smoothly shift from one turntable to the next. In so doing, Herc also added electronic sound effects—"echoing and reverbing back and forth between the vocal and instrument track; [while manipulating] the treble and bass knobs" (Hebdige 1987, 83).

Herc styled his disc jockeying after the dub music jockeys of Jamaica (e.g., Duke Reid and U Roy) by mixing musical fragments, referred to by street jockeys as "breaks" or "break-beats," from various recordings in order to create an entirely new soundtrack. Herc's use of "break-beats" taken from Jamaican dub artists and United States Black artists has been described as follows:

> He took the music of . . . Mandrill, like "Fencewalk," certain disco records that had funky percussion breaks like The Incredible Bongo Band [a Jamaican disco group] when they came out with "Apache" and he just kept that beat going. It might be that certain part of the record that everybody waits for—they just let their inner self go and get wild. The next thing you know the singer comes back in and you'd be mad. [Toop 1991, 60]

That "certain part of the record that everybody waits for " consisted of an African-Latin percussion soundtrack—congas and timbales—called the "break" section. Because of his enormous sound system, Kool Herc could be heard performing at a distance throughout the Bronx. His mixing concept inspired many itinerant jockeys throughout the Bronx area including Afrika Bambaataa, the celebrated godfather of the hip-hop arts movement (see fig. 16.1).[5]

Like Kool "DJ" Herc, Bambaataa incorporated "break-beats"—selective musical passages—in his mixes, eventually perfecting this technique. Some, such as rap music producer Larry Smith, contend that Afrika Bambaataa possessed the most incredible ear for finding beats from all over and making all music work; Smith considers this the reason that Bambaataa earned the title "Master of Records."[6] The "breaks" that contained these beats represented a variety of musical styles, ranging from soul, funk, and disco to commercial jingles and television themes. Most of Bambaataa's favorite break-beat records—including "Funky Drummer" by James Brown, "Take Me to the Mardi Gras" by Bob James, "Think" by Lynn Collins, and "Dance to the Drummer's Beat" by the Herman Kelly Band—have gone on to become the foundation for numerous hip-hop tracks (Fernando 1994, 54). One admirer of Bambaataa notes that

16.2 Several early hip-hop DJs, including (fron left to right) one of the "Nigger Twins," Lovebug Starski, Scorpio, Kool "DJ" Herc, and Melle Mel. Photograph by Ernie Paniccioli.

16.3 Bronx disc jockey Grandmaster Flash. Photograph by Cheryl Keyes, Manhattan, 1993.

> [h]e blended tracks from Germany, Jamaica, the Philippines, Cali[fornia] and the South Bronx into a beautiful collage called hip-hop jams in the park and created a movement that turned into a world-wide musical and cultural revolution, as well as a billion dollar industry. His parties lifted the dancer into a spiritual state of euphoria based on his overstanding of vibrations, rhythms, cadence, tone, melody and mood. [L Ju as quoted by Emery 1998, 26]

Afrika Bambaataa channeled his DJ skills into organizing local "battles," or competitions, throughout the Bronx area.

Another Bronx disc jockey influenced by Kool Herc was Joseph Sadler, better known as Grandmaster Flash (figs. 16.1, 16.3). Flash began his career as a DJ for neighborhood block parties, but he realized his DJ skills were limited because of his audio-mixer board. Flash felt intimidated by Kool Herc's huge sound system and enormous volume, even though he later discerned Herc had less-than-perfect mixing skills.

> With the monstrous power he had he couldn't mix too well. He was playing little breaks but it would sound so sloppy. I noticed that the mixer he was using was a GLI 3800. It was a very popular mixer at that time. It's a scarcity today but it's still one of the best mixers GLI ever made. [Toop 1991, 62]

Flash began going to discotheques to observe other jockeys in performance. At a Manhattan disco club, he met Bronx jockey Pete "DJ" Jones. Although Jones performed for an audience with conservative musical tastes, Flash noticed that Jones was more accurate in mixing records than Kool Herc. Jones was known for his extended-play concept. Commenting on "the way he [Pete] would connect the records," Flash has said that

> some of the DJs I used to watch [back then] used to let the record play all the way to the end then play the next one with the gap in between. I found it quite amazing that Pete kept the record going, going, going, all night long. That's how he acquired the name Pete "with the Funky Beat DJ" Jones.[7]

Jones had a switch on his system that allowed him to hear what was playing on one turntable before playing it aloud. Grandmaster Flash, a student of electronics, later invented a similar apparatus allowing him to cue up a record while another was playing through the speakers. He accomplished this with an external amplifier, headphones (later a one-ear headphone), and a single-pole, double-throw switch, which he glued to his mixer. Through experimenting with this apparatus, Flash pioneered two turntable techniques popularly known as "backspinning," and "phasing."

"Backspinning," which requires having a copy of the same record on two turntables, is accomplished by rotating one record counterclockwise to the desired beat then rotating the second record counterclockwise to the same location, creating a looplike effect. In phasing (also known as "punch-phrasing"), the DJ accents a short phrase of a recording during the playing of a second record by manipulating the turntable's cross-fader. This technique is somewhat similar to the previously discussed "riding gain" technique employed by Black personality radio jockeys of the 1950s, but phasing requires two turntables. While Flash perfected his inventions, other DJs experimented with new mixing concepts.

Grand Wizard Theodore from the Bronx, a protégé of Flash, is credited with inventing another turntable technique called "scratching," moving a record back and forth in a rhythmic manner while the tone

16.4 Afrika Bambaataa (right) with his protégé Afrika Islam. Photograph by Ernie Paniccioli.

16.5 DJ Alladin working a turntable at Stanky Booty. Photograph by Brian Cross, Hollywood, 1992.

arm's needle remains in the groove, thereby producing a scratchlike sound. Although in 1978 Theodore was only thirteen—the youngest of the hip-hop DJs at the time—he was considered one of the few whose skill in mixing records could compare with that of Flash.

New York DJs like Davy DMX and Grandmixer D.ST further perfected Theodore's scratching invention. Grandmixer D.ST is responsible for popularizing scratching as a primary musical feature through the hit single "Rock It" (1983) by Herbie Hancock. Other noted New York street DJs of the time who used various mixing innovations were Junebug, Sweet G., Jazzy Jay, Disco King Mario, DJ Tex, Afrika Islam, Smokey, Kurtis Blow, DJ Hollywood, the Whiz Kid, Charlie Chase, and female jockey RD Smiley.[8]

With the innovations of Herc, Bambaataa, Flash, and Theodore, DJing became an art form. Artists who performed on the turntable began referring to themselves as "turtable technicians" or "turntablists" (White 1996). As the mostly male DJ circuit expanded, some artists underwent apprenticeship with other known DJs. This usually took the form of an exchange wherein the apprentice disassembled the mentor's sound equipment after performances and received all-exclusive professional advice about the art of DJing. Master-student relationships are often indicated by surrogate father-son titles. For instance, DJ Afrika Islam is considered the Son of Bambaataa (fig. 16.4); Joseph "Run" Simmons of Run DMC is considered the Son of Kurtis Blow; and DJ Funkmaster Flex is recognized as the Son of DJ Chuck Chillout.

Most of the early turntablists' recordings are rather difficult to obtain. Some of the most memorable performances can be purchased today only as bootlegged versions or through underground channels. The first commercialized recording by a turntablist was "Grandmaster Flash on the Wheels of Steel" (1981). Recorded by Sugarhill Records, this song contains several break-beats including Blondie's "Rapture," Spoonie Gee's "Monster Jam," Chic's "Good Times," and Queen's "Another One Bites the Dust." Another important turning point in the art of DJing occurred in 1982 with "Planet Rock" by Afrika Bambaataa and his group, Soul Sonic Force, on Tommy Boy Records.

Unlike many DJ mixes, which resorted to essentially manual techniques, "Planet Rock" made extensive use of electronic instruments—synthesizers and drum machines—as its primary soundtrack. Bambaataa was influenced immensely by the computerized sound called "techno-pop," made popular by European and Asian groups. He wanted to experiment with "techno-pop" in rap music because

> basically at the time, a lot of rap records was talking about boasting . . . how many young ladies they could get. . . . I wanted a sound that nobody had before. I looked at all the Black music in the industry, and I said, "there's no electronic or singing group or funk group or whatever style." Techno-pop at the time was only for Europeans from the group Kraftwerk or to the Asian group or Japanese group called Yellow Magic Orchestra. I was influenced a lot from Kraftwerk. . . . The synthesizer, I say, this is the music of the future.[9]

Bambaataa modified the techno-pop sound by fusing it with the funk styles of James Brown and Sly and the Family Stone, thus producing a hybrid that he calls "techno-funk." Additionally, Afrika Bambaataa

ushered in the "battle," a contest in which several of the top DJs in New York City would compete for supremacy. Today this concept has graduated into a national and international venture as best exemplified by the DJ Battles for World Supremacy contests or by the USA DJ Championship and World DJ Championship competitions, sponsored by turntable and electronic music companies Technics and DMC, respectively.

Sound, Aesthetics, and Techniques

Several turntable techniques have already been discussed (figs. 16.5–16.7): mixing, backspinning, phasing or punch-phrasing, and scratching. Other mixing techniques identified by DJs include "cutting" and "blending." The former entails the repetition of a word or musical phrase through selective editing, whereas the latter involves the combination of music or text from two different discs to create a "new" piece of music (White 1996). Ethnomusicologist Miles White (1996) conducted an organological study of the turntable and divided mixing techniques into two categories: single or dual turntable. He found that while backspinning, scratching, and cutting can all be executed on a single turntable, mixing, blending, and punch-phrasing can only occur when using two turntables. With two turntables, DJs can fuse break-beats or collages of sound from prerecorded discs into one cohesive unit.

Developing an acuity for break-beats requires an extensive knowledge of Black dance favorites ranging from percussion-oriented songs such as "Apache" by The Incredible Bongo Band and " It's Just Begun" by Jimmy Castor to heavy funk tunes like "Funky Drummer" by James Brown, "Flashlight" by Parliament-Funkadelic, or the mellow sounds of "Between the Sheets" by the Isley Brothers. The success of a DJ is based on his or her repertory of break-beats and finding them and protecting their identity can be quite tedious. During the 1970s disc jockeys like Afrika Bambaataa and Kool Herc were known to soak record labels off so other jockeys would not recognize their "break-beats." According to Jazzy Jay, a protégé of Afrika Bambaataa, "We'd find these beats, these heavy percussive beats . . . a lot of times it would be a two-second spot, a drum beat, a drum break, and we'd mix that back and forth, extend it, make it 20 minutes long" (Leland and Stein 1988, 26).

In the 1980s, however, shopping for break-beats became less onerous as a result of the recording of compilations. Lenny Roberts, a freelance record collector, compiled over twenty volumes of break-beats called *Ultimate Breaks and Beats* (n.d.). Roberts's series was distributed by the late Stanley Platzer, a well-known hip-hop record dealer, at the famous Music Factory in New York City (Leland and Stein 1988, 26–28). In the 1990s DJs have reversed the trend toward using compilations and instead shifted to finding and using their own beats. Bronx DJ Diamond, for example, who owns thousands of old recordings believes that "there's an art to finding a break that somebody else doesn't know about. . . . It makes people go, 'Oh shit, where'd he get that from.' That's part of the mystique" (Fernando 1994, 54).

Hip-hop DJs are also evaluated on their ability to synchronize various break-beats without interrupting the steady rhythmic flow of the beat. In so doing, rap music DJs broadly conceive of time in an African musical and social sense where a delineation is made between outer and inner time. Outer time is "homogeneous and measurable devices, clocks and metronome" (Stone 1982, 9), and inner time is unmeasurable but consciously experienced. The African notion of outer time and inner time has been applied in the study of African American music forms in the United States. Joyce Jackson, a scholar of the Black sacred music tradition, found there exists an interdependent relationship between outer and inner time. She notes that the reckoning of time "does not totally operate in a Western mode or meter, but rather in an additional internal mode or inner time. Inner timing . . . [is] implied or suggested by outer timing and actions" (Jackson 1987, 171).

For hip-hop music DJs time operates very similarly. It is first realized in an inner sense as "the beat." A rap song must have a certain beat within a tempo if the audience is to dance. Dancing only occurs when the tempo feels right. One audience member indicates that the "right beat" is felt through a certain tempo: "The beat is important. . . . More people like a beat to dance to and rap music has that downbeat to dance to it. It's easier for us to dance to [that beat]; when we go to a garage and hear that fast upbeat music [we] can't dance to that."[10] Here, the "downbeat" refers to a moderately paced tempo which may vary from slow, or 80–88 beats per minutes (bpm), to moderate, or 92–132 bpm. The beat is set by the rap disc jockey who operates as timekeeper. The DJ must have an inner sense that tells just how

16.6 A DJ operating dual turntables at the Attic. Photograph by Brian Cross, South Central Los Angeles, 1992.

fast or slow to set the tempo. As one interviewee remarks, "the DJ is like the drummer. . . . His job is to make sure everything goes steady, and if the beat messes up, everybody is going to know because everybody wasn't on the beat."[11] The disc jockey relies on a pitch control, a built-in mechanism on the turntable, which allows the acceleration or deceleration of the tempo. In this sense, the beat is first internally reckoned through inner timing and later coordinated through outer time by means of the pitch control.

By the mid-1980s, the manual process of mixing music described above had been supplemented by the use of electronic instruments—digital samplers, drum machines, sequencers, and synthesizers. On most samplers there is a built-in sequencer that allows artists to extend the duration of a sound—from long to short fragments—in a looping fashion. "Sampling allows DJs to take bits and pieces of 'breaks' from records, mix and mingle [them] into musical collages of sounds" (Kemp 1989, 68). While some of the most popular samplers like the Akai S900 are hard to find, the sampling drum machines—the Emu SP-1200 and the Roland TR-808—are the most coveted among rap music DJs because of their "raw" sound quality (Fernando 1994, 55) and heavy "kick" or bass-drum sound, respectively.

The aesthetics of sound are not limited to the type of instruments employed but pertain as well to the manner in which timbre and texture are juxtaposed in the musical mix. Rap DJs experiment with and bend the norms of homogeneous timbre and texture in accordance with a non-Western musical aesthetic. Ethnomusicologist Portia K. Maultsby observes that, "the unique sound associated with black music results from the manipulation of timbre, texture and shaping in ways uncommon to Western practice. Musicians bring intensity to their performance by alternating lyrical, percussive, and raspy timbres; juxtaposing vocal and instrumental textures; changing pitch and dynamic levels; alternating straight with vibrato tones; and weaving moans, shouts, grunts, hollers, and screams into the melody" (1990, 191–92). Through digital sampling DJs successfully accomplish the fusing of various timbres and textures—a voluminous bass sound (e.g., bass guitar and drum), strident piercing quality (e.g., high glissandi sounds), static "noise," harmonic dissonance, and a battery of vocal ornamentations from James Brown's yells, grunts, moans, and shouts to speech excerpts. They firmly believe that "you need something [a track] with a heavy beat."[12] According to Cedric Singleton of Black Market Records, Public Enemy (PE) represents the quintessence of the above aesthetic because the group uses "a whole lot of sampling. They get a groove going and build on top of that groove, and build on top of that groove; they just build on top of grooves."[13] PE's music, which is the brainchild of the Bomb Squad (a production team composed of Hank Shocklee, Eric Sadler, et al.), employs dissonant sonorities—booming bass guitar and kick (bass) drum sounds, interlocking speech and music rhythms, and a boisterous-aggressive rap style—as best exemplified in their 1989 song "Fight the Power" (see Keyes 1996, 238).

Qualities of texture and timbre are also unique to geographical regions. For example, in areas like Miami and Los Angeles, where there exists a car culture or low rider culture, the booming bass and closed-kick (short delay in sound) created by the Roland TR-808 tend to dominate in mixes. On the contemporary scene, the proliferation of car culture (e.g., Jeeps and low riders) has impacted rap music to the point where DJs specifically create soundtracks intended not for home stereo systems but rather for automobile stereo systems. It is for this reason that rap musicians have coined the term "jeep beats" when referring to soundtracks with a booming bass quality.[14]

Most hip-hop musicians prefer a certain "noise" level in their finished mix. The preference for certain "noises" or "buzzy-like" musical timbres peculiar to African-derived music represents "an artist's preference . . . for environmental factors as part of the musical event" (Wilson 1974, 70). Environmental sonorities unique to rap mixes are what I refer to as cityscape sounds—sirens, blaring automobile horns, etc. One of the earliest rap songs to incorporate cityscape sounds is "The Message" (1982). In the latter segment of "The Message," Grandmaster Flash incorporates sounds of the urban landscape, ranging from automobile horns to sirens, underscoring a conversation among members of his group, The Furious Five. These sounds, along with the members speaking in street language, intensify the ambience of city life as depicted in the lyrics of this song.

Another factor consistent with the inclusion of environmental sounds and unique to hip-hop music is "popping." When interviewing rap DJs, I discovered, much to my amazement, their knack for replicating "old records for that popping sound" in producing a "dirty" mix.[15] In this tradition, one does not assume that a person who has been professionally trained to mix music on a sound board has the aptitude to mix "dirty" as well. As one rap music producer recalls,

> I had a guy mix it [a rap tune] that does rock. A . . . guy that mixes rock, he's not a rap mixer. I could have mixed the record better than he could 'cause I did the record, and I know what the record's suppose to sound like. They got reverb on stuff that didn't need to have reverb. They got it sounding nice and clean. And every record that I've done since then, I've done on eight tracks. I haven't done it on twenty-four track studio, even though we can afford to do it on twenty-four. We've done it real grimy and dirty, and it works better. The popping on the record . . . [is] the essence of the music. . . . After a while, you listen to some old record, hear that popping; it takes you back. That's really the aesthetic value to it.[16]

Among the many raps that employ the popping sound is "Passin Me By" (1993) by The Pharcyde. In the beginning of this song, auditors hear a sampled excerpt of Quincy Jones's arrangement of Sebastian-Boone-Sebastian's "Summer in the City" (1973), accompanied by a constant popping sound, which is the result of what is seemingly a poorly preserved record. To rappers, however, popping sounds undoubtedly corroborate the essence of "funk"—a return to fundamentals, earthiness as embodied in old scratched-up records.

Despite the fact that dissonant sonorities dominate in a rap music mix, some auditors automatically infer that hip-hop musicians have limited or no knowledge of musical harmony:

> There's no regard for harmonic rules. Like in the case of sampling one harmonic texture and juxtaposing that with another that has the same beat, but is in a totally different key. . . . They're just kind of thrown together. Sometimes when you're ignorant you can do something that no one has done, because you're not aware of what the rules and the habits are. [Norris 1993, 85]

According to Hank Shocklee, lack of knowledge about conventional music harmony has nothing to do with dissonance in rap, rather atonality is a predilection. Shocklee justifies his use of harmonic dissonance in a provocative article by music critic Tom Moon:

> Eric (Chuck D) sings on key, while I'm like, f . . . the key. I'm looking for a mood, a feeling. So some things are purposely out of key. Like Son of Bazerk . . . I work with him by having what's behind him in key, otherwise you lose Bazerk. If I put things in key behind Chuck D, you lose Chuck, because his vocal is smooth. So you have to put it against abrasion. [Moon 1991, 72]

As the above statement implies, ambience ("mood") and the juxtaposition of timbres "(smooth . . . abrasion") interlock to purposely create sound polarities.

By the 1990s, hip-hop DJs began experimenting with soundtracks that narrow the gap between dissonant and harmonic sounds via extended jazz breaks. Mixing jazz with hip-hop music is not a new idea according to Grandmaster Flash, because he used to mix jazz breaks in his music during the early days of rap.[17] In the late 1980s, Flash's concept was advanced by Tribe Called Quest, followed by DJ Premiere of Gangstarr and Digable Planets and US3 in the 1990s.[18]

In the fusing of rap and jazz, DJs maintain a sense of rawness in their mixes by having jazz instrumentalists "play behind the rhymes and over the [jeep] beats" rather than on top of the beats (Norris 1993, 83). Thus, the rap/jazz fusion further demonstrates the juxtaposition of textural polarities from hardcore/rawness (e.g., jeep beats) to smooth/mellowness (e.g., hard and soul jazz) while simultaneously recontextualizing jazz through a hip-hop prism.

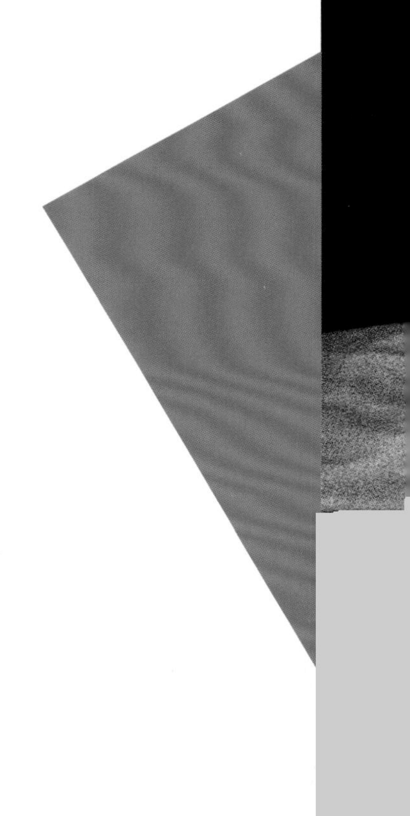

Sampling has undoubtedly revolutionized the art of making music. It is perceived among hip-hop DJs as the most convenient and purest means of recreating past dance favorites. Because of the art of cutting and mixing break-beats, one critic concludes that "[h]ip-hop humanizes technology and makes it tactile" because DJs "make the technology do stuff that it isn't supposed to do, get music out of something that's not supposed to give you music quite that way. [They] squeeze it, rip at it, and do other things with the equipment that mess viciously with [the] warranty" (Allen 1988, 10). When they deem it necessary, DJs rely totally on ingenuity to manipulate, change, or alter state-of-the-art technology by conforming to African-derived cultural practices in search of the perfect beat.

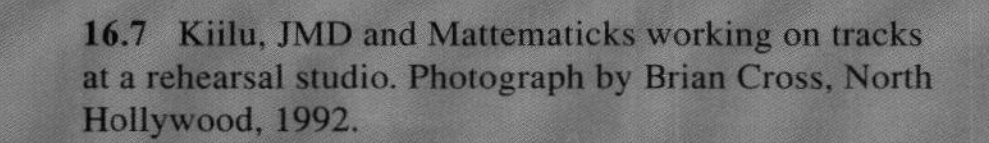

16.7 Kiilu, JMD and Mattematicks working on tracks at a rehearsal studio. Photograph by Brian Cross, North Hollywood, 1992.

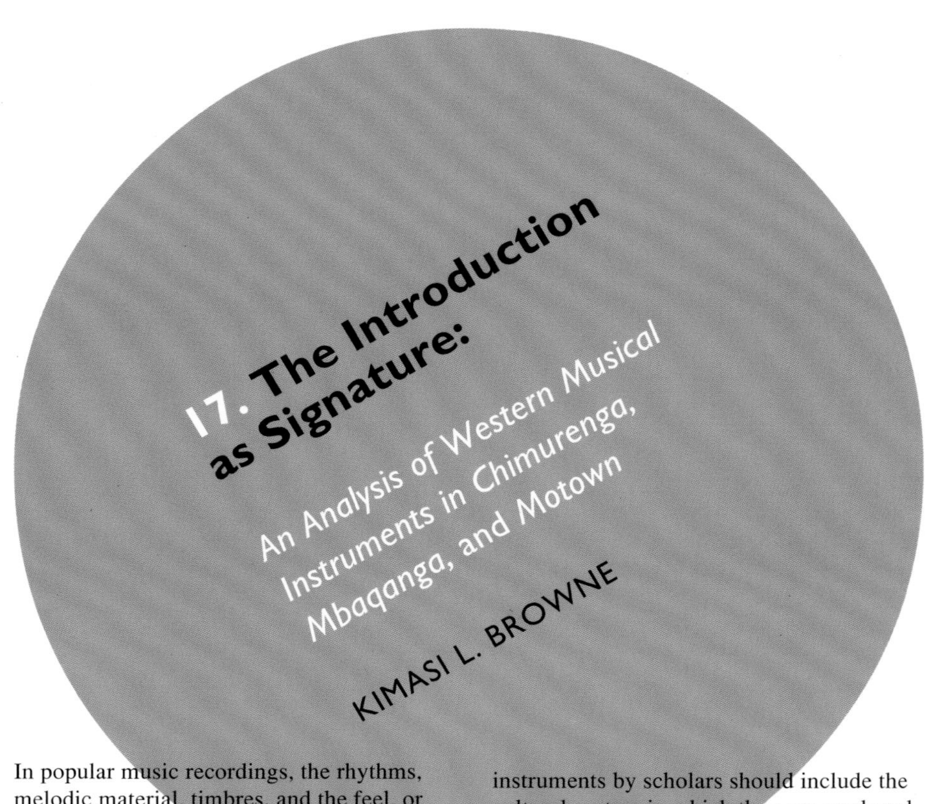

In popular music recordings, the rhythms, melodic material, timbres, and the feel, or "groove," of the first few measures frequently determine whether a radio station will play the record and whether a listener will remain tuned to the station or turn to another. The introduction not only determines whether or not a mass audience will identify with the music; it can also provide the narrative environment in which both tradition and innovation are mediated.

This essay explores the manner in which Western musical instruments are used in the introduction section of commercial recordings in the popular music of Blacks in South Africa, Zimbabwe, and the United States.[1] The nations of South Africa and Zimbabwe have been selected for this study because both have well-developed recording industries and because both have been inspired by African American popular music since the early 1900s. Commercial popular music has been used to protest colonization, apartheid, and racial discrimination. Of the African American genres, particularly rhythm and blues and soul, *motown* was selected for this study because of its similarities to the southern African approach to popular music record production and for the way in which instruments have been utilized.[2]

In this essay similarities between the African American popular music tradition of *motown* and the southern African genres of *mbaqanga* and *chimurenga* will be analyzed and compared.[3] B. A. Aning believes that the study of musical instruments by scholars should include the cultural system in which they are produced (1972, 138). I agree with this notion; therefore, this essay will also examine the function of instruments within their cultural contexts and their commercial applications. There are two important similarities in the popular music of Zimbabwe and South Africa: (1) its development amongst the indigenous people was curtailed because of the racist policies of minority-ruled regimes (Africans regained independence in Zimbawe in 1980 and in South Africa in 1994); and (2) the traditions of popular music in Zimbabwe and South Africa have been heavily influenced by the popular music of African Americans.

A brief discussion of the historical contexts of the *motown* and southern African approaches will illustrate what they have in common when using Western instruments in the introductions of popular music recordings. A detailed comparison of eight musical examples will also be presented; these include four introductions from southern African recordings, two from *chimurenga* (Zimbabwe), two from *mbaqanga* (South Africa), and four from *motown* (United States).

Historical Background and Contexts

> In the late 1400s, the people who spoke Bantu languages were living farther to the north and east of the Cape, and were interacting with the Khoisan peoples. Archeological and linguistic evidence indicates that the Bantu-speaking peoples of southern Africa arrived there from the north within the last thousand years and either overran or pushed aside the indigenous peoples.[4] Many of the Khoikhoi were enslaved by the European settlers, and eventually mixed with Europeans and workers brought from Asia to form what are now called the colored people of South Africa. Though the San were traditionally hunters and gatherers, they are increasingly becoming cattle herders and farmers. [Kaemmer 1998b, 703]

Parallels between South Africa and the United States can be traced back to the earliest presence of European settlers in both lands. In 1607 Captain John Smith landed in Jamestown, Virginia, and established the first permanent English settlement in the "New World," while the first Blacks arrived in Virginia in 1619 (Frederickson 1981, 283–87). The first settlement of Caucasians in South Africa took place at the Cape of Good Hope. When the Dutch East India Company landed in Cape Town in 1652, the Dutch settlers gave names to the diverse people they encountered there (Coplan 1998, 760). They called the pastoral group inhabiting the Cape of Good Hope the Hottentots, while the hunters and gatherers farther north were dubbed the Bushmen. These indigenous peoples referred to themselves as Khoi or Khoikhoi (Hottentots) and San (Bushmen), and as Khoisan when considered together as a group. Their languages include "clicking" sounds, and the peoples differ both linguistically and physically from others in Africa (Kaemmer 1998b, 702–3). "Race relations there, under a system of chattel slavery, set the pattern for the development of South African society" (Coplan 1998, 761). The English settlers arrived in South Africa after armed forces defeated the Dutch, bringing new musical traditions with them (Kaemmer 1998b, 716).

Early on, the colonies in South Africa and the United States categorically banned interracial marriages. As nations, both institutionalized impoverishment for Blacks through legislation. Kimberley, an "instant city" in the area north of the Cape Colony, was a response to the South African diamond rush of the 1870s. Former hunters, both White and Black, migrated to Kimberley to find work in the diamond mines, taking their musical traditions with them. They also created new genres of dance, song, and oral poetry. One genre, the traditional praise poetry of the Xhosa, was used to satirize and flatter the bosses, both

Black and White, who oversaw the mines. The Zulu men's walking-and-courting songs blended the texts of friendship and romantic love, as well as the accompaniment of Western musical instruments, specifically the guitar, concertina, and violin (Kaemmer 1998a, 762).

Today, the San live in Angola, Botswana, and Namibia, and they perform on raft zithers, musical bows, and plucked lamellophones (*likembe* or *mbira*). They sing polyphonic songs and use the hocketing technique;[5] some of their singing involves yodeling. The Khoikhoi, who are mainly found in Namibia, use musical bows as their primary instruments; they too yodel, as do the Shona of Zimbabwe (Kaemmer 1998b, 701). The Nguni people (so named by scholars), the southernmost Bantu-speaking peoples in Africa, include the Xhosa, who come from the Cape of Good Hope region, and the Zulu, from the region near Natal. Together, the Xhosa and the Zula make up the majority of the indigenous people in South Africa. The Xhosa were the first Bantu-speakers to have confrontations with Europeans, which, according to Kaemmer (1998b, 705), weakened them and made them unable to become a strong kingdom like the Zulu and Swazi peoples (Swaziland). Chaka (Shaka) was king of the Zulu from 1816 to 1828; his Zulu kingdom fought against the Boers and the British and was not defeated until 1879, long after his reign had ended. Polyphonic and responsorial choral dance songs are the major form of communal music among the Zulu, and their prominent traditional instrument is the musical bow. While drums are not commonly used in Nguni traditions, a friction drum and a double-headed drum are used in some rituals. Single-tone flutes, found among the Zulu, are used in rituals honoring the harvest of the season's first fruit.

European settlers established a colonial regime in Zimbabwe in 1890 (Southern Rhodesia) that lasted ninety years (Kaemmer 1998a, 744). The music of Zimbabwe is mainly represented by the Shona People. Another large group, the Ndebele, are related to the Zulu people of South Africa (Kauffman 1980, 683). After Europeans arrived in Zimbabwe, Shona music underwent a profound change. People in the central part of the country experienced a stronger European influence than did those in the hotter, less desirable fringe areas. After European music was introduced in Zimbabwe, Shona music was exploited to influence political struggles (Kaemmer 1998a, 745).

Laws were enacted in South Africa, Zimbabwe, and the United States that would systematically oppress and disenfranchise Black Africans on economic, political, and social levels. The 1911 Mine and Works Act of the Union Parliament in South Africa legally separated Blacks from Whites. Whites were either Afrikaners, who spoke the Dutch and German-based Afrikaans language, or English settlers, who spoke the English language. All Blacks, regardless of their traditional heritage, were categorized pejoratively as "Africans." In South Africa this program was called "separate development." Although the formal institution of slavery was abolished in the United States in 1865, the *Plessy vs. Ferguson* Supreme Court decision of 1898 established an equivalent called "separate but equal." Out of these restrictive milieus, musical traditions were transformed and led to the development of the *mbaqanga, chimurenga,* and *motown* genres.

African American Popular Music

Current instrumental traditions in African American popular music grew out of U.S. jazz and blues idioms of the 1920s and 1930s, beginning with "Ethiopian" or Black minstrel troupes and their accompanying bands at the end of the nineteenth century in the southern United States and, in particular, with jazz in New Orleans and bands such as those led by Joe "King" Oliver, Jelly Roll Morton, and Kid Ory, which featured the cornet. Ragtime jazz piano was particularly popular among Europeans and Americans of European descent. Recordings by vaudeville or classic blues singers like Bessie Smith and Ma Rainey featured Black female vocalists accompanied by Western instruments such as the piano, trumpet, guitar, trombone, and drums. The banjo, an African instrument, was also prominent in early jazz and blues music.[6] African American popular music traveled a path of continuous innovation through the swing and big band era, with Black musicians such as Duke Ellington, Louis "Satchmo" Armstrong, and Count Basie, who became pivotal figures in the United States and worldwide. They were especially influential in Europe and Africa. In the 1920s, when popular American music was completely segregated, W. C. Handy and Harry Pace established the first African American-owned recording company, Black Swan Records, whose goal was to record Black artists for Black audiences. Tin Pan Alley was marketed to urban mainstream White audiences, race records to Black audiences, and hillbilly music to rural White audiences.

The contributions of Thomas Dorsey, who began his career as "Georgia Tom" playing blues piano for Ma Rainey, laid the foundation for one of the most prolific traditions in American sacred music. Dorsey, who coined the term *gospel song* and composed some of the earliest standards, was responsible for the budding careers of Mahalia Jackson and the Roberta Martin Singers in the 1930s and 1940s. Meanwhile, rhythm and blues resulted from a combination of the blues and swing-band music. Louis Jordan and His Tympany Five were responsible for establishing one of the first small combo bands in the early 1940s, while Count Basie popularized the Kansas City dance-hall band style and adapted it for radio airplay. Following the end of World War II, rhythm and blues began to receive national airplay, and artists like Fats Domino, Lloyd Price, and Little Richard became exponents of this New Orleans sound. Imitating these sounds in the 1950s, mainstream White recording artists like Pat Boone became popular. The post–World War II generation of youth, unlike their Depression-era parents, had disposable income and became the target audience of the record companies. Rhythm and blues was renamed rock 'n' roll in 1955 by Alan Freed, a White radio disc jockey from Ohio, and it was performed and recorded by White artists and marketed to White urban teenagers. Rock 'n' roll quickly became identifiable with Elvis Presley, after he was packaged as a White singer who could sound Black.[7] Rock 'n' roll waned in the late 1950s when doo-wop and Uptown rhythm and blues, recorded by the Drifters and the Coasters, became popular. Then girl groups took over the pop charts in the early 1960s when Motown Record Corporation entered the marketplace with the Marvelettes, Martha and the Vandellas, and the Supremes. In the mid-1960s the Civil Rights movement became the Black Power movement, which gave rise to soul music performed by James Brown, Ray Charles, Aretha Franklin, and Otis Redding. Motown became an economic icon because of its tremendous financial success in mainstream America and the worldwide recording industries. It also became a cultural institution within the African American community because of its ability to knock down discrimination and racial barriers by marketing its artists and songs as speaking to the hearts of not only African Americans but also audiences across the globe. Motown also became known for its innovative application of instruments during the opening seconds of its hit recordings.

Motown

The Motown Sound,[8] established by Berry Gordy Jr. in 1959, incorporates elements from all of the aforementioned African American styles and genres. Heavily influenced by the regional sound of Detroit, Michigan, the Motown Record Corporation initially marketed its 45 RPM vinyl single records to middle-class African Americans in urban northeastern and midwestern cities.[9] So many of the songs became hits on Black radio stations and record sales charts that they crossed-over, or entered, mainstream charts. White teenagers began purchasing Motown records in large numbers. Eventually, success dictated that this African American-owned company with its unique style of music would permeate the music market worldwide. Motown performers such as Smokey Robinson, the Four Tops, the Temptations, Marvin Gaye, and Michael Jackson have since become international legends. In fact, Motown's sales in the 1960s rivaled those of the Beatles (Fitzgerald 1995).

The *motown* tradition was undergirded by a group of professional jazz musicians who comprised the rhythm section that performed the instrumental backing tracks for nearly all of the hit records released by Motown. Initially these players, who called themselves the Funk Brothers, were led by two musicians: Joe Hunter (piano) first, then Earl van Dyke (piano and organ). The Funk Brothers also included Benny Benjamin (drums), James Jamerson (bass), Robert White (lead guitar), Joe Messina and Eddie Willis (rhythm guitars), Johnny Griffith (keyboards), and Jack Ashford (percussion).

Motown used its commercial leverage to bridge the two USAs (the Union of South Africa and the United States of America). Singer Letta Mbulu and trumpeter Hugh Maskela with his group, the Union of South Africa, recorded for the Chisa label, a company started by Masekela and Stewart Levine; later Chisa became a subsidiary label of the Motown Record Corporation. The B-side song of one of Masekela's Chisa singles was "Shebeen" (Bianco 1988, 169).[10]

The Motown Record Corporation was an active agent in the Civil Rights movement. Although the company's owners and employees were not regarded as marchers and protesters, the company documented some of the major Civil Rights and Black Liberation spokespersons of the era. On its spoken-word label, Black Forum, Motown released compilations of major speeches by Dr. Martin Luther King Jr., Elaine Brown (Black Panther Party), and Stokely Carmichael (SNCC, Student Non-Violent Coordinating Committee). Both Masekela and Carmichael were married to Miriam Mekeba, an important figure in the antiapartheid movement. While living in exile after being banned from her native South Africa, Mekeba recorded songs of protest and performed them all over the world. Her marriages to Masekela and Carmichael identified her with the liberation and freedom movements of Blacks in both South Africa and the United States.

Southern African Popular Music

Popular music in southern Africa developed as a result of cultural turbulence across linguistic and political boundaries, and it encompasses the contributions made by South Africans of European and African origin and by Americans of African descent (Coplan 1998, 759). Beginning in the late 1600s in Cape Town, popular forms of Dutch and British music were introduced to the migrant/ indigenous populations of South Africa. Syncretic genres began to emerge within the colonial context in the late 1800s with the establishment of the diamond mines in Kimberley. All races of the poorer classes and nationalities lived together in shantytowns. There, in canteens, dance halls, honkytonks, and house parties, they blended African, European, and American melodies (Coplan 1998, 762).[11]

Christian missionaries adapted worship songs to indigenous languages and vice versa. These cross-cultural influences led to the development of a South African Christian religious music, which was largely the work of indigenous artists such as Xhosa composers Ntsikana and Bokwe, who blended Xhosa melodies, harmonies, and rhythms with Presbyterian hymnody (Coplan 1998, 763). Bokwe was also active in advancing *makwaya* (choir), a choral style that is popular in southern and eastern Africa.

American blackface minstrelsy was popular with Europeans around the world, especially in South Africa. Negro spirituals, taught in schools and churches set up by Black missionaries sent from the African Methodist Episcopal Church and other Black American denominations, made a big impact on Black South Africans (Coplan 1998, 765). The Virginia Jubilee Singers led by Orpheus "Bill" McAdoo toured South Africa during the 1880s and 1890s. According to Coplan, this religious musical development is highly significant because "until about 1930, Black South African urban popular music had developed only in mission schools, community and voluntary organizations, and neighborhood social events" (1998, 765).

During the 1920s and 1930s, American ragtime and jazz bands influenced the forming of the earliest jazz bands in South Africa. The shebeen—an unlicensed establishment selling beer or liquor—established what would become the most familiar setting for informal music making. African American jazz and blues had a determining effect on South African musicians. The earliest forms of today's popular music in South Africa were intimately tied to that nation's cultural and political events.

> The early introduction of records, mainly American jazz and blues, was another important influence in the development of local music. Johannesburg became the center of modern South African music. Shebeens sprang up to cater to migrant workers, who were usually cut off from their families and communities. Musicians in the shebeens played a mixture of the music they had heard on records with a strong influence of indigenous sounds; choral groups were also popular. The early jazz records by Ellington, Basie and Louis "Satchmo" Armstrong had a huge impact. [Graham 1988, 258]

The indigenous instrument *mbira*, the national instrument of Zimbabwe, is a lamellophone, which is most often associated with the Shona people. All *mbiras* have a soundboard and an assortment of hammered metal lamellae; they also have large half-gourds that serve as resonators with snail shells or metal buzzers attached to them.[12] The *mbira* is played by plucking a metal tongue with the thumb and forefingers. Some believe that the *mbira* began as a portable version of a xylophone (Jones 1971, 34). In Zimbabwe, there are four types of *mbira*. The principal one, the *mbira dza vadzima* (*mbira* of the ancestral spirits), has twenty-two or more wide keys, is associated with the Zezuru people, and is used mainly in spirit possession rituals (Kaemmer 1998b, 746). The *njari*, played singly or in pairs, came from the Zambezi River valley in the 1700s. It has served in rituals involving tutelary (protective or guardian) spirits, but more recently it has been used by elderly men who play it as an accompaniment to nonritual singing. The *mbira* of the Korekore people is referred to as *hera* or *matepe* (Tracey 1970). It has twenty-nine narrow keys; is played with both thumbs and both forefingers; and plays faster music with lower bass notes, more complex rhythms, and a lighter sound than other *mbiras*. The *kalimba*, which is smaller than most *mbiras*, is not used in rituals (Kaemmer 1998b, 746). According to Kauffman, the term *kalimba* designates a group of instruments that were either strongly influenced by or originated from the *kalimba* found in Zambia and Malawi (1980, 684). The *kalimba* is believed to be the oldest form of *mbira* in the region.[13]

There are only a few indigenous instruments in South Africa (Andersson 1981, 15). The most widely known southern African instruments are the musical bows and simple flutes. The people, thus, created surrogates for instruments. According to Mvusi Dlavana, the South African people used their bodies to create new "instruments," transforming their vocal apparatus into imitation instruments.[14] Andersson suggests three major reasons why this occurred: (1) the trees of the Transvaal were not strong enough to make large instruments, (2) instruments were not brought to South Africa during the Bantu migrations, and (3) the men could not bring instruments with them to the mines (1981, 15).

The *Chimurenga* of Zimbabwe

In Zimbabwe in the 1970s American rhythm and blues and soul music were highly popular (Brown 1994).[15] Thomas Mapfumo, the recording artist known as the Lion of Zimbabwe, recorded cover versions of Sam Cooke and Otis Redding. Mapfumo began the *chimurenga* musical style in the 1970s. It originated out of the Shona *mbira* tradition that had been mixed with the guitar styles from the former Zaire region, horns, and rumba-influenced bass.[16] Mapfumo used the Shona language for his lyrics so that everyone in Zimbabwe could understand the music except for the White settlers (Bergman 1985, 119–20). At one point, Mapfumo was arrested for using his recordings to inspire resistance to racial oppression in Zimbabwe (Seligman 1995a). Other important *chimurenga* musicians include Real Sounds, an eleven-piece band; Oliver Mtukudzi, the singer, composer, and leader of the Black Spirits; the Bhundu Boys; and Ephat Mujuru.

According to Coplan, *chimurenga* replicates the structural relationships of *mbira* music by combining two electric guitars and a bass: "*Chimurenga* guitarists prefer a dry, percussive tone which they achieve by using plectra and playing with repeated down strokes, while damping the strings" (1998, 365). Coplan emphasizes how the role of the guitar in African music is highlighted in the literature and on records and compact disks. For example, he points to the guitarists in Mapfumo's band who when performing *chimurenga*, may "play double notes in fourths while deadening the strings at the bridge with the flesh of the palm" (Coplan 1998, 365).

The *Mbaqanga* of South Africa

Mbaqanga, also called township jive, was formed from a combination of jazz, swing and indigenous melodies called *marabi* music.[17] The genre grew out of the South African shebeens established by Black African women as a way to make money after their men were taken away to the mines or cities to work. American ragtime and New Orleans-style jazz were imitated by South African musicians in the 1920s. *Marabi* was popularized during the 1930s in the townships near Johannesburg by Zulu Boy Cele, who became a legend, and groups like the Merry Blackbirds, the Harlem Swingsters, the Jazz Maniacs, and the Rhythm Clouds. Because some *marabi* bands were allowed to perform in Johannesburg concert halls, the music developed a following with the liberal White community (Kivnick 1990, 228). In the 1940s *marabi* gave birth to *kwela* music, characterized by penny whistles accompanied by acoustic guitar and tea-chest bass. These whistles "imitated mission brass bands, European pipe and drum bands, and, brass and reeds" (Kivnick 1990, 229). During the 1950s, the saxophone helped to influence a performance style called saxophone-jive, popularized by Zakes Nkosi. It was Miriam Mekeba, however, who helped to popularize the vocal traditions that arose from the *mbaqanga* show bands.

The combination of American jazz, *marabi*, and *kwela* became the *mbaqanga* tradition made famous by Hugh Masekela (trumpet), Abdullah Ibrahim (known as Dollar Brand, piano), Dudu Pakwana (alto saxophone), Kippie Moeketsi (alto saxophone), and Jonas Gwangw (trombone). The first African musicians to gain international prominence were those associated with the all-Black production of *King Kong* in 1959. The composer, Tod Matshikiza, was Black (Blacking 1980, 197), and Miriam Mekeba was first discovered while performing in the cast. During the show's tour of England in 1960, Mekeba's passport was withdrawn, preventing her return to South Africa. Furthermore, while *King Kong* was a landmark in South African theater history because it was the first South African show to make a large profit, its success resulted in the tightening of apartheid legislation, depriving Blacks of further opportunity to perform before White audiences (Blacking 1980, 198).

Today, the foremost ambassadors of *mbubu* (an a cappella style of *mbaqanga*) is the group Ladysmith Black Mambazo. Led by composer Joseph Shabalala from Ladysmith, Natal, the group is composed of two families, the Shabalalas and the Miziburkos. Their performance technique includes the interpolation of ululations, clicks, and parallel harmonies. Their singing style, *isicathamiya*,[18] represents one of the most complex expressive forms that Zulu-speaking South African migrants have developed since World War I (Erlmann 1989, 35). The style gained international recognition when Ladysmith Black Mambazo performed on Paul Simon's *Graceland* album and world tour.

While *isicathamiya* represents the dominant singing style in South Africa, it is the guitar that has emerged as the dominant instrument. According to Andrew Kaye, the guitar transitioned from a peripheral to a central position in African musical culture somewhere between 1920 and 1965 (1998, 362). Kaye states that "most guitar playing in Africa since the 1960s has been associated with popular urban bands that play contemporary Western or African-American and African-Caribbean popular music. . . . Local rock bands modeled themselves after Western groups. They featured singers, electric guitars, electric bass, and trap drum set, and performed a mix of pop music styles" (1998, 363). Although the *chimurenga* and *mbaqanga* bands were structured in this manner, their music was much more politically charged and the guitar was played in ways that invoked indigenous cultural significance.

The guitar is believed to have come to southern Africa in the nineteenth century when it was introduced by African American minstrel troupes that toured South Africa as early as 1887 (Coplan 1985, 39). South African styles of guitar playing include strumming and plectrum playing (or picking) in a high register.[19] In the 1940s and 1950s acoustic guitars became popular in South Africa, Zambia, Zimbabwe, and Malawi. The guitar-playing styles of these countries became mixed and were heard on Afrikaans recordings, imitating the American "singing cowboy guitarists" (Coplan 1985, 187). "Between about 1956 and 1960, the electric guitar took on an increasingly dominant role in

African music—not entirely displacing the acoustic guitar, but matching it, in its appeal to African youth and the radio-listening and record-buying public" (Kaye 1998, 360). In the 1960s the guitar became the principle instrument in modern African music. In the 1970s and 1980s, in urban areas of Zimbabwe, the solo acoustic guitar mimicked the *mbira*, in both social function and musical relationship (Kaye 1998, 363). The guitar actually became the most popular instrument in South Africa amongst Zulu men who came to town from the country. In *mbaqanga* a preference arose for a clean, "Fender-type" lead guitar sound, with very little distortion effects (Coplan 1998, 364). The guitar has also taken a dominant role in the introductions of African popular recordings. This is especially true in *chimurenga* and *mbaqanga* music.

The Introduction as Signature

The Introduction

The term *introduction* denotes the preparation for presentation of that which is to come. In literature an introduction is the preliminary section of a book. In Western music it is the opening section in the same manner in which a preliminary guide or text introduces information or concepts to the reader. The dictionary definition of the term *prelude* is still more precise: "A thing serving as the introduction to a principal event, action, performance etc., preliminary part; preface; opening" (Webster 1976, 1420). While each of these denotations is applicable, the principal event in each of the introductions seen in this study is when the vocalist(s) enters into the song. The introduction is a preliminary part, or prelude, that prepares us for the vocalist's entrance. An array of extramusical factors, ranging from the record market to the audience to the technology and level of musical expertise in a piece, may help to determine which musical elements are ultimately presented in an introduction. This can be better understood in the approach to organizing introductory materials in *mbaqanga*.

> The principle of parts cutting a cycle at different points is very noticeable in South Africa particularly in *mbaqanga* bands. It is common to have the guitars entering the cycle at one point, the singers starting off at another point, and if there is a frontline brass or sax, their entering at different points too. Each entry demands the next. [Andrew] Tracey feels that this conflict between parts mirrors the relationship between people in a traditional African society. [Andersson 1981, 13]

The *motown* approach to the introduction is similar to the *mbaqanga* principle of cutting a cycle at different points. It is common for a *motown* record to open with a drum fill, followed by hand claps or finger snaps. Within a few seconds of the beginning of a piece, a brass section may enter. A short vocal riff is often used to introduce a part of the instrumental montage being formed. A second drum fill may be used to announce the entrance of the vocal or a lead singer performing text and melody, that is, the principal event. I believe, as Tracey does about South African *mbaqanga*, that the *motown* approach to the introduction section mirrors the relationship between people in the African American community. This overlaying of each item is a form of a call and response, as well as the musical equivalent of the salutory questions asked in African American communal greeting, such as "What's happening, y'all?" or the more contemporary query, "What's up?"

The *motown* approach to organizing the introduction is both similar and different from the African approach mentioned in the quotation above. Unlike the *mbaqanga* version, the *motown* song doesn't follow a continuous groove/ostinato; instead, it reflects an extension of the 32-bar Tin Pan Alley song form: intro—verse—chorus—verse—chorus—verse—chorus. Being both refined and formulaic, the *motown* song does not have the incessant and omnipresent repetition found in most African popular music. The *motown* introductions are similar to *chimurenga* and *mbaqanga*, however, in that the latter are basically short and to the point utilizing the Western drum set, electric bass, and electric guitars in the opening seconds. Another commonality is the way the instruments are grouped to achieve complementary or contrasting timbres. For example, it is common in *motown* introductions to hear hand claps, electric bass, drums, cymbals, tambourine, and the rattling of chains, which provide percussive and contrasting timbres, with an acoustic piano reinforcing harmonic texture. Furthermore, the electric bass often opens the introduction with a solo that is overlaid with plucked electric guitar playing a melody. Finger snaps join in to establish the back beat,[20] thus the ensemble achieves a complementary timbre. The styles of *chimurenga*, *mbaqanga*, and *motown* utilize a variety of these types of organizing schemes to establish a "signature," which is realized within the context of the introductory section.

The Signature

The term *signature* has several denotations, with the most common one being the signing of one's name as a representation of who he or she is. In the earlier part of the twentieth century this term referred to a "musical number or sound effect which opens or closes a radio program" (Webster 1976, 1688). Webster offers several definitions that correspond to the musical function of instruments in this process: as a noun in music, a signature is a sign or signs placed at the beginning of a staff to indicate a piece's key or time. In literature it is a transitive verb indicating to mark or to distinguish; while in printing a signature refers to a large sheet upon which are printed four or a multiple of four pages, and which, when folded and bound, forms a section of a book or pamphlet (Webster 1976, 1688). In the fields of chemistry and physics a signature denotes "a characteristic trace or sign that indicates the presence of a substance or the occurrence of a physical process or event" (Random House 1987, 1770).

It is an ad hoc term such as "signaturing" that perhaps best conveys the idea of a musical event occurring over the duration of the introduction. In so doing, each instrument functions as a signal of the oncoming principal event—the entrance of the vocalist—and, in essence, the true beginning of the musical expression.

The sound sources featured in today's *mbaqanga* recordings include vocals, guitar, bass, drums and percussion, keyboard, accordion, violin, saxophone, whistle, flute, trumpet, and trombone (Kivnick 1990, 230). Similarly, the *motown* records examined here are from the period between 1963 and 1983 and feature vocals that are accompanied by guitar, bass, drums and percussion (especially tambourine), keyboard, full string orchestra, saxophone (especially tenor sax on solos during interludes, and baritone sax used to add raspiness and buzziness in the lower sonic registers), trumpet, trombone, hand claps, and finger snaps. In the introductions both genres use instruments to capture the attention of the listener by organizing sounds so that they are voiced (harmonically or sonorally) in a strident fashion to call attention to themselves.

Analysis

The dominant people in power and the current trends in the commercial music industry frequently determine the type of music that is recorded and which recordings are released into the marketplace. All of the examples examined in this study were released and became commercial hits between 1963 and 1995. As commercially viable products, each was allocated recording, distribution, promotion, and advertising budgets. Motown Record Corporation's Quality Control Department served as a board of judgment for all of its releases. Each recording had to be predetermined as a potential hit song by this evaluation team, and on occasion was required to be a probable "number one" hit before approval was given (Gordy 1994).[21] In South Africa and Zimbabwe the government served as censor, simultaneously controlling the record companies and the radio stations. If the lyrical content of a recording was deemed provocative or in anyway political, it would be officially banned. This is precisely why Mapfumo became so popular (Seligman 1995a). While his intentional use of innuendoes and ambiguous language in his texts was heard and understood by the people, the government missed his meaning. According to Mapfumo, "the message was loud and clear to all Shona speakers, 'We must topple the government.' . . . I kept writing more and more songs about the hardships people were experiencing in the rural areas" (Mapfumo as quoted in Zindi 1985, 34). To an extent, Mapfumo's introductions are declarations or rallying calls to action. The Shona people understood that the principal event—the vocals—would offer them collective hope.

Southern African Popular Music ***chimurenga/mbaqanga***	**African American Popular Music** ***motown***
A1 ***chimurenga*** **"Zvandiviringa (I am in Trouble)"** ***Thomas Mapfumo*** Electric bass guitar Drums Saxophone Guitar	**m1** ***motown*** **"My Girl"** ***The Temptations*** Electric bass guitar Rattle of snare Drum Guitar Finger snaps
A2 ***chimurenga*** **"Zvenyika (Politics)"** ***Thomas Mapfumo*** Drum Guitar Bass Downward melodic movement	**m2** ***motown*** **"Signed, Sealed, Delivered, I'm Yours"** ***Stevie Wonder*** Guitars Drums Tambourines Vocal screams
A3 ***mbaqanga*** **"Shosholoza"** ***Mfiliseni Magubane*** Guitars Drums Synthesizer (mbira sound) Trumpet and trombone Bass	**m3** ***motown*** **"Girl (Why You Wanna Make Me Blue)"** ***The Temptations*** Drum roll Hand claps Trumpet and trombone Bass Piano
A4 ***mbaqanga*** **"No Easy Road"** ***Mzwakhe Mbuli*** Drum solo opening Whistle and flute Guitar melodic ostinato	**m4** ***motown*** **"Nowhere to Run"** ***Martha and the Vandellas*** Drum solo opening Bass ostinato Tambourine Trumpet and trombone

18.1 Comparison of Western instruments in the introduction signatures

Comparison of Examples

The scope of this investigation is limited to those instrumental sound sources that precede the principal event (the entrance of the vocal performance). Although harmonic progressions are discussed in Comparison 1, this project is not an examination of harmonic or melodic elements. The following eight excerpts are short musical examples illustrating how instruments have been used to create signatures in the *chimurenga, mbaqanga,* and *motown* genres (fig. 18.1). The particular introductions in this study were selected because of the similarities in their sound sources and their instrumental groupings, for the specific Western instruments in each ensemble, and because of the comparability of their various timbres and playing techniques. Conversely, they were also selected for their contrasting material, as well as for the recording aesthetics that differed greatly in both their quality and conceptual approaches. In each excerpt it was aurally evident that available technology and regional style were important contributors to the signature sound and character of each introduction. The musical events that are featured within an introduction by and large determine the character and sound that distinguish the identification of a signature.

The musical events featured in introductions often fall into a wide variety of textures ranging from simple to complex. A simple introduction might include hand claps only, whereas a more elaborate one might feature ascending or descending string lines. Introductions can also include linear rhythmical layering. This type of opening might begin with a solo rhythmic line that is progressively added to in layers, ultimately resulting in a complex polyrhythmic texture. After a careful analysis of the excerpts selected for this study, several events or features have emerged. These features occur in at least two of the examples, one from the African American genre and one from one of the two southern African genres. All of the excerpts were then compared for their similarities and differences and then grouped in pairs according to their similarities. Four configurations of features were selected: (1) bass and ostinato (electric bass guitar is the featured instrument and an ostinato is performed by the ensemble; the comparison is between *chimurenga* and *motown*); (2) descending melody (a downward melodic momentum is performed on the guitars; the comparison is between *chimurenga* and *motown*); (3) drum fills and bass riffs (an opening fill on the snare drums is featured, followed by a pronounced melodic prelude performed by a horn section; the comparison is between *mbaqanga* and *motown*); and (4) snare drum tension and ostinato (the drums are used to open the piece and the ensemble immediately establishes a rhythmic ostinato; the comparison is between *mbaqanga* and *motown*). Although there are similarities and differences between them, *chimurenga* and *mbaqanga* excerpts were not analyzed because collectively they enable comparison and contrast between the application of Western instruments in southern Africa and African American popular music styles—the stated goal of this study.

Comparison 1: Bass and Ostinato

The introduction of the first *chimurenga* example, "Zvandiviringa (I am in Trouble)" by Thomas Mapfumo, is thirty seconds long (fig. 18.1—A1). The electric bass enters first, playing a I-IV-V harmonic progression for four seconds. Up front and out in the open, at the first entrance the bass provides a stark melodic motif that is repeated along with the drums that enter with a loud snare snap, announcing the instrumental ensemble's immediate arrival at the fifth second. The ensemble, at the second entrance, begins with the guitar playing an ostinato riff (possibly a transposed *mbira* melody and rhythm), followed four seconds later by the entrance of the alto saxophone that improvises lightly over a groove performed by the entire ensemble for another twenty-one seconds. The point where the entire ensemble is performing can be likened to being "cut" into the cycle referred to by Andersson (1981, 13). Thirty-one seconds into the piece, the vocal enters (fig. 18.2—A1). The use of the term *ensemble* here refers to a grouping of three or more instruments that simultaneously enter into the introduction.

In the *motown* example, "My Girl" by the Temptations, the introduction is only eight seconds long (fig. 18.1—m1). It opens with a deep, resonating bass guitar that plays a V-I-V-I melodic and rhythmic ostinato for four seconds. A sympathetic rattling from the snares beneath a nearby snare drum subtly embellishes the bass line. During the next four seconds a melodic riff is played on the guitar that is juxtaposed over the bass line. The riff is ornamented with percussive finger snaps on the back beat. The use of membranophones and corporophones here to "stack" the backbeat juxtaposes finger snaps and a bright snare-drum strike with the tambourine being played with the palm of the hand and rubbing the skin with the whetted thumb. The vocal enters nine seconds into the introduction (fig.18.2—m1).

Comparison 2: Descending Melody

In the *chimurenga* example "Zvenyika (Politics)," also by Thomas Mapfumo, the introduction is five seconds in length (fig. 18.1—A2). It opens with a drum flam,[22] which announces the ensemble that is then cut into the cycle. The ensemble consists of bass, lead guitar, and rhythm guitar. This combination is a replication of the structural relationship of the *mbira*. The ensemble plays three descending harmonized quarter notes for two seconds. The lead guitar then plays a simple melodic line for three seconds. At the sixth second, the vocal enters (fig. 18.2—A2).

The *motown* hit "Signed, Sealed, Delivered, I'm Yours" by Stevie Wonder has a four-second-long introduction (fig. 18.1—m2). Built with a sequence of entrances, each occurring one second after the other. The piece opens with the lead guitar playing descending quarter notes as the kick drum, tambourine, and rhythm guitar accent the back beat. Only two seconds into the piece Wonder screams "Oh yeah, Baby!" in a gospel style that emphasizes emotional intensity, much like ululation in traditional African music, as an embellishing timbral instrument rather than singing text and melody. This is not the official entrance of the vocal section of the piece; instead, it is an instrumental application of the voice as a signifying instrument, invoking and announcing both the blues and gospel heritage. This results in the musicians and Wonder building the song's opening to a feverish pitch, in the same fashion as an African American folk Baptist preacher might in the height of a Sunday sermon. The brass enters during the third second, followed by a drum fill on second four. Five seconds into the piece the vocal enters (fig. 18.2—m2).

Comparison 3: Drum Fills and Brass Riffs

In the *mbaqanga* example "Shosholoza" by Mfiliseni Magubane, the introduction is a total of sixteen seconds (fig. 18.1—A3). For the first seven seconds one hears a plucked guitar playing a simple, descending melody line accompanied by an ostinato on a synthesizer keyboard (programmed to sound like the *mbira*) and an idiophone. In 6/8 time the drums play an eighth-note fill, ushering in the full ensemble. The rhythm guitar strumming can be heard in the foreground. The larger portion of this

Southern African Popular Music ***Chimurenga/ mbaqanga***	**African American Popular Music** ***motown***
A1 ***chimurenga*** **"Zvandiviringa"** ***Thomas Mapfumo*** Introduction—:30 Total recording—3:48 Durations of events in the introduction :00:04 Electric bass :05:08 Drum snap, guitar :09:30 Saxophone improvisation over ensemble groove :31:00 Vocal enters	**m1** ***motown*** **"My Girl"** ***The Temptations*** Introduction—:08 Total recording—2:56 Durations of events in the introduction :00:04 Electric bass :05:08 Guitar, finger snaps :09:00 Vocal enters
A2 ***chimurenga*** **"Zvenyika"** ***Thomas Mapfumo*** Introduction—:05 Total recording—5:21 Durations of events in the introduction :00:02 Drum flam, bass, lead guitar, rhythm guitar :03:05 Lead guitar :06:00 Vocal enters	**m2** ***motown*** **"Signed, Sealed, Delivered, I'm Yours"** ***Stevie Wonder*** Introduction—:04 Total recording—2:46 Durations of events in the introduction :00:01 Guitars, bass, tambourines :02:00 "Oh yeah, Baby!" vocal :03:00 Brass section :04:00 Drum fill :00:05 Vocal enters
A3 ***mbaqanga*** **"Shosholoza"** ***Mfiliseni Magubane*** Introduction—:16 Total recording—4:08 Durations of events in the introduction :00:07 Guitars, synsethizer, idiophone :08:00 Drum fill :09:16 Trumpets and trombones :17:00 Vocal enters	**m3** ***motown*** **"Girl (Why You Wanna Make Me Blue)"** ***The Temptations*** Introduction—:15 Total recording—2:16 Durations of events in the introduction :00:01 Drum fill :02:07 Trumpets and trombones, hand claps, drums, piano :08:00 Drum fill, trumpets et. al :14:15 Drum fill, trumpets et. al, falsetto vocal "ooo-ooo" :16:00 Vocal enters
A4 ***mbaqanga*** **"No Easy Road"** ***Mzwakhe Mbuli*** Introduction—:54 Total recording—5:28 Durations of events in the introduction :00:05 Drum solo :05:00 Whistle, flute, guitar, trumpet, synthesizer :18:00 Drum fill :19:30 Electric bass added :31:54 Alto saxophone and guitar added :55:00 Vocal enters	**m4** ***motown*** **"Nowhere to Run"** ***Martha and the Vandellas*** Introduction—:06 Total recording—3:00 Durations of events in the introduction :00:02 Drum solo :02:05 Snare drum, kick drum, tambourine, electric bass, rattling chains :06:00 Trombones, piano added :07:00 Vocal enters

18.2 Durations and sequences of events in the introduction signatures

introduction is the brass (trumpets and trombones), which play short melodic riffs from seconds nine through sixteen. The vocals enter seventeen seconds into the piece (fig. 18.2—A3).

The introduction is fifteen seconds long in the third *motown* example, "Girl (Why You Wanna Make Me Blue)" by the Temptations (fig. 18.1—m3). During the opening second there is a snare drum fill of four eighth-note triplets (see fig. 18.3). Two seconds into the piece, technically the second entrance, the rhythm section (piano, bass, and drums), the brass section (trumpets and trombones playing a counter melody), and hand claps begin simultaneously. The drum fill is repeated at the eighth and fourteenth second points. Also at the fourteenth second, while the brass and rhythm sections continue, the voice is used as part of the instrumental build-up. This is where Eddie Kendricks, in a male falsetto voice, interpolates an "ooo-ooo." This is a penultimate announcement that signals the forthcoming principal event. At the sixteenth second the lead vocal enters (fig. 18.2—m3).

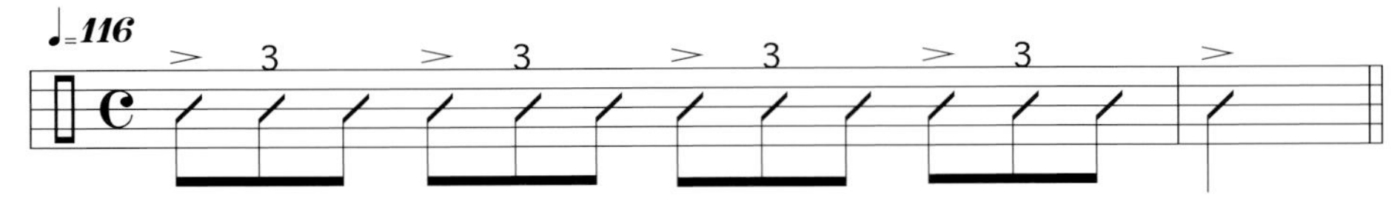

18.3 Drum triplet fill in *motown* example.

Comparison 4: Snare Drum Tension and Ostinato

In the final *mbaqanga* example "No Easy Road" by Mzwakhe Mbuli, the introduction is fifty-four seconds long (fig. 18.1—A4). It opens with a snare-drum solo performing a rhythm for five seconds that is a diminution of the Zulu *indlamu* rhythm, which, according to Ballantine, is a traditional Zulu stomp (1991, 150; see fig. 18.5). At second five the ensemble enters, consisting of the whistle, flute, guitar, trumpet, and keyboard synthesizer. A drum fill ushers in the electric bass adding harmonic and rhythmic support at second eighteen. At second thirty-one the alto saxophone and guitar join the ensemble and play through to second fifty-four. The vocal enters at second fifty-five (fig. 18.2—A4). The *mbaqanga* adaptation of this hiccuplike rhythm dates back to early 1940s when Black South African bands, such as the Harlem Swingsters and the Jazz Maniacs, popularized what has been called an African stomp (fig. 18.4). The coupling of whistles and flutes are remnants of the *kwela* penny whistle tradition.[23] The ostinato performed on the guitar over the *mbaqanga* drum rhythm is a stark attention-grabber, which sets this recording apart from others and thus makes it a probable favorite for radio airplay (fig. 18.4).

In stark contrast to the extensive introduction in the *chimurenga* example "No Easy Road," the fourth and final *motown* example, "Nowhere to Run" by Martha and the Vandellas, has a mere six-second-long introduction (fig. 18.1—m4). It opens with a two-second snare drum solo, a militaristic rhythmic pattern that establishes immediate tension (see fig. 18.6). When this tension is released, there is a heightened expectation of what will come next. From seconds two through five, in 4/4 meter, a steady four beats to the bar ostinato is played. This rhythmic configuration that synchronizes the snare and bass drums is one of the signature characteristics of the Motown sound. The percussive instruments enter first including snare and bass drums, tambourine, electric bass, and an idiophone/rattle that

"No Easy Road"

18.4 *Mbaqanga* drum rhythm.

18.5 Zulu *indlamu* rhythm.

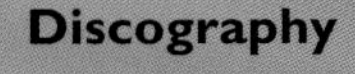

"Girl (Why You Wanna Make Me Blue)"—The Temptations, Gordy 7035, 1964.

Graceland, Paul Simon, Warner Brothers 25447, 1986.

"My Girl"—The Temptations, Gordy 7038, 1964.

"No Easy Road"—Mzwakhe Mbuli, on *South Africa: Only the Poorman Feel It*. EMI-Hemisphere 72438 3286621, 1995, Track 13

"Nowhere to Run"—Martha and the Vandellas, Gordy 7039, 1965.

"Shosholoza"—Mfiliseni Magubane on *South Africa: Only the Poorman Feel It*. EMI-Hemisphere 72438 3286621, 1995, Track 5.

"Signed, Sealed, Delivered, I'm Yours"—Stevie Wonder, Tamla 54196, 1970

"Zvandiviringa (I am in Trouble)"—Thomas Mapfumo, on *The Best of Thomas Mapfumo: Chimurenga Forever*. EMI-Hemisphere 72438 3558232, 1995, Track 5.

"Zvenyika (Politics)"—Thomas Mapfumo, on *The Best of Thomas Mapfumo: Chimurenga Forever*. EMI-Hemisphere 72438 3558232, might be the syncopated rattling of heavy chains. Benny Benjamin of Motown's Funk Brothers rhythm section popularized this style of what studio drummers since the 1960s have referred to as "tight" drumming. The bass, particularly as it is played by James Jamerson, reinforces this four-beat pattern. In 4/4 time in each measure he plays an ostinato pedal on the tonic note on the upbeat of beat two and a quarter note on the downbeat of beat three, an eighth-note on the upbeat of beat four, and a quarter note on beat one of the next measure and repeats the pattern ad infinitum, thus providing the harmonic and rhythmic foundation for the signatory aspects of the introduction. The entrance of the vocal is announced during second six by the addition of the brass (harmonized trombones) and the piano. The vocal enters at second seven (fig. 18.2—m4). There are some aspects present here that are specifically associated with *motown*: (1) the electric bass and the bass drum are synchronized on the downbeats; (2) the tambourine is played with a whetted thumb, rubbed across the perimeter of the skin; (3) a buzzlike texture is produced as the jingles make a continuous sound; and (4) a second tambourine plays on each of the four beats also reinforcing the rhythmic texture. This technique of playing the tambourine is nearly ubiquitous in the Motown sound and is prevalent in contemporary African American gospel choir music (see fig. 18.6).

"Nowhere to Run"

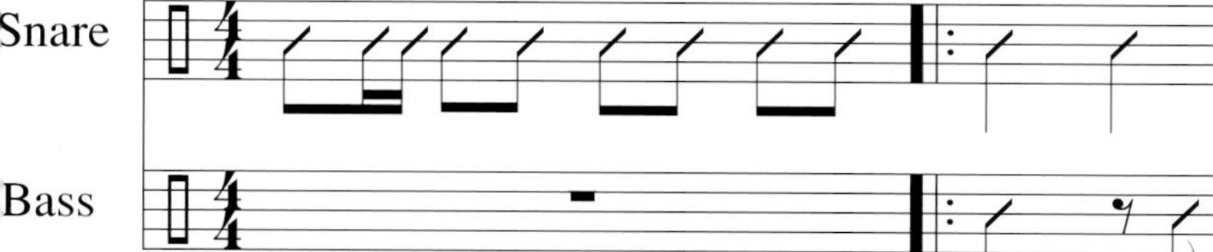

18.6 Snare drum pattern and bass ostinato in *motown*.

Conclusion

Of those elements examined in this study, the African examples exhibited a syncretism of indigenous, European, African, and African American popular music influences. The bass, drums, and guitar are the three instruments that both African genres as well as *motown* used most frequently as solo instruments to begin the opening of the introductions. Recalling Andersson's reference to the *mbaqanga* "principle of parts cutting into a cycle," this principle was observed in both the African and African American genres (1981, 13). The bass, the drum (usually the snare), and the guitar are the instruments most frequently selected to open or begin the "cycle." Instrumental groupings (ensembles) were "cut" into the cycle at the second entrance. Ensemble groupings appear more frequently in African introductions than in *motown* examples most likely, in my opinion, because of the way music functions within traditional African society: the basis of association for music making is communal (Nketia 1974, 21).

All of the African ensembles included guitars. As we have seen, the guitar has a long history of popularity in Africa and has been used regularly as a replacement or substitute for traditional instruments. This is particularly obvious in Zimbabwean *chimurenga*, where two guitars and a bass are grouped to replicate the structural relationship of the *mbira*. The *motown* examples had only one incidence where an ensemble entered the cycle at the second instrumental entrance. This occurred in the introduction to "Girl (Why You Wanna Make Me Blue)" (fig. 18.1—m3), which consisted of acoustic piano, electric bass, and bass drum. The differences in the ways in which membranophones, idiophones, and corporophones are used in the *motown* examples are pronounced.[24] The *chimurenga* and *mbaqanga* examples were void of these idiophones and corporophones, whereas the *motown* examples consistently included them. Some other commonly found characteristics unique to *motown* include finger snaps in "My Girl" (fig. 18.1—m1); the "stacking" of the back beat, which does not occur in the *chimurenga* and *mbaqanga* examples; the technique of playing the tambourine by striking the skin with the palm of the hand and by rubbing the skin with a whetted thumb; and the sound of the bright snare drum.

This essay has explored the manner in which Western musical sound instruments have been used in the introductions of southern African and African American commercial popular music recordings. These instruments have been used to establish signatures by which their respective popular music recordings may be instantly identified. We can conclude that these introductory materials have been organized to make distinctive calls to listeners, dancers, urban and rural peoples, and thus present distinctive signatures. As such, the opening seconds of the recordings serve to mediate expressions of African indigenous musical cultures, *chimurenga* and *mbaqanga*, and expressions of African American musical styles, *motown*, through the use of Western musical sound instruments. The meaning of cultural products to the people they represent, to those who consume them, and to those who claim ownership of them have a significant impact on the structure and development of products. If it is dance music, the first few sounds heard may determine whether people are drawn to dance or leave the event. This prelude segment of the performance can declare what is old or new, or it can refer to that which is yet to come. It functions as an invitation, a salutation, a greeting, or it can "call out" to the hearer and demand a response. Thus, the commercial success of a popular recording is largely dependent on this highly stylized (or simplified) introductory section. By "signing on" at the opening of the recording, the introduction as signature serves as a cultural repository that mediates and preserves tradition and innovation reflecting the historical and immediate reciprocity between these analogous segments of the African Diaspora.

18. The Role of the Gumbe in Popular Music and Dance Styles in Sierra Leone

CHRISTIAN DOWU JAYEOLA HORTON

18.1 The framework of a Jamaican *gumbe* drum. Goatskin is used to cover the drum and an inner square of wood is inserted from below and pushed upward (see fig. 18.2). Drawing from Roberts 1924, 247.

The *Gumbe* and the Feedback Process

The *gumbe* (also spelled *gumbay*, *gombay*, *goombay*, *goombah*, *goombeh*) is a frame drum found in several parts of West Africa and the Caribbean (figs. 18.1, 18.2). In most instances, it consists of a single membrane made of goatskin that is stretched and nailed over a square wooden form, or stool, and raised off the ground on four legs. Cuban scholar Fernando Ortiz (1952) states that the *gumbe* originated in Guinea, but there are no records indicating where in Guinea the instrument might have come into being. If it developed in the region of the Futa Jalon Mountains, then it has a connection to Sierra Leone, as this region belonged to that country until it was ceded to the French by the British government in the late nineteenth century (possibly around 1882). The argument for an origin among the people of Sierra Leone is strengthened by the fact that among the Creole (freed slaves whom the British returned to Africa between the fifteenth and nineteenth centuries),[1] the *gumbe* remains one of the principal instruments used in popular traditional music.

Documentation of the *gumbe* in the Caribbean dates back to the nineteenth century, which suggests that the instrument probably had been used there since the eighteenth century or earlier. Ortiz (1952) states that in Jamaica the drum was known as *gumbe*, in Cuba it was without a name, and the Guinean drum from which the others originated was called *cumbe*. Some linguists (e.g., Hall-Alleyne 1982, 23) believe the term is derived from the Bantu word *ngoma*, a generic term for drum as well as other aspects of music making in Central, East, and southern Africa (DjeDje 1998).

Thus, the name *gumbe* must have been brought from Jamaica to Sierra Leone by various groups who returned to Africa around the late eighteenth and early nineteenth centuries. Some Creoles who arrived in Freetown, Sierra Leone, in the late eighteenth century were freed slaves from Nova Scotia. A number of Maroons from Jamaica arrived in 1800 to form yet another group of Creoles. The last significant additions were peoples from the West Coast of Africa who had been liberated from slave ships destined for the West Indies; they arrived in groups roughly between the years 1800 and 1820. In short, Creoles in Sierra Leone were liberated slaves from differing ethnic backgrounds—chiefly Yorùbá and Igbo. Once arrived in Sierra Leone, these peoples developed a homogenous ethnic entity with their own unique lifestyle and cultural practices. The Creole population became closely knit within Sierra Leone, speaking the same language, Krio, which has since become the country's lingua franca. The Creole people observe rites of passage such as *komojade*—or the introduction of a young child to the world—weddings, and funerals in nearly the same ways. They also employ nearly identical instrumental ensembles for such celebratory occasions.

The arrival of the *gumbe* in Africa around 1800 has far-reaching implications. Significantly, it is the first instance of the reconnection of African expressive culture with its place of birth. The two-hundredth anniversary of this event will be celebrated in the year 2000. John Collins, who has written extensively on the early development of popular music in West Africa, argues that the return of the *gumbe* to Sierra Leone represents the beginning of the feedback process to Africa:

> The earliest "homecoming" is a Jamaican frame-drum dance music known as Goombay (Gumbia) introduced by freed Maroon slaves to Freetown, Sierra Leone, on October 1, 1800, where it is still played and laid the basis of that country's first popular music (c. 1900), known as Asiko (Ashiko).
>
> Goombay and Asiko subsequently spread from Sierra Leone to many West and Central African countries (Mali, Côte d'Ivoire, Ghana, Nigeria, Gabon, Congo, Camerouns, and Fernando Po), creating an important musical building block for various 20th century African popular and neo-traditional music styles: such Maringa, Milo Jazz, Highlife, Juju music, Gube, Gome, Le Goumbe, Simpa, and Gahu. [Personal communication to Jacqueline Cogdell DjeDje, December 28, 1998]

18.2 Jamaican *gumbe* drum. Photograph from Roberts 1924, 248.

The *Gumbe* in Sierra Leone

Sierra Leone is situated in West Africa and bounded by Guinea on the north and east, Liberia on the southeast and south, and the Atlantic on the south and west. Over time, geographical barriers within this tropical rain forest region have precipitated the establishment of small communities (Horton 1979, 1–8). People who originally belonged to the same Western Sudanic linguistic strain developed ideas and vocabulary that contributed to the modifying of their original languages, customs, and traditions. As a result, new languages and subcultures evolved and established their separate identities. Hence today, several ethnic groups and languages exist. Mende, Loko, Vai, Mandingo, Susu, Koranko, and Yalunka have all been classified in the Mande linguistic category, primarily because they share some common words, which, nonetheless, have different meanings (Greenberg 1953). The other ethnic groups and languages include the Temne, Fula, Kissi, Bulom, Krim, Gola, Gallinas, and Sherbro. These groups have been classified in the West Atlantic linguistic group by both Greenberg (1953) and Dalby (1966) for reasons similar to those stated for establishing the Mande linguistic group. Krio, the language of the Creole community is classified as a "pidgin" language by Hall (1976). This is not surprising since, as the brief historical sketch given above has demonstrated, the name "Creole" was given to a group of people made up from a number of ethnic backgrounds.[2]

Gumbe, *maringa*, and *milo* jazz are three important instrumental ensembles associated with the Creole of Sierra Leone. *Maringa* music surpassed *gumbe* in the 1940s, and since the 1970s and 1980s *milo* jazz has become more popular than *maringa*. As a result *maringa* ensembles have altered their instrumentation and playing styles, copying the rather loud musical style of *milo* jazz. Further discussion of each style will help us to understand the distinctions between each.

The *Gumbe* Ensemble

This ensemble took its name from its master drum, the *gumbe,* which was used to perform elaborate improvisations (see figs. 18.1, 18.2). Also included in the ensemble was the bass-box (fig. 18.3). In colonial times this instrument was made from wooden containers used to transport kerosene tins. This container was selected because of the sonority produced by the light wood used to construct it. As containers of this type are no longer used—fuel now being more safely delivered by tanker trucks—a similar lightweight wood would have to be procured to make bass-boxes today if their characteristic sonority were to be preserved. The bass-box was rectangular in shape with square ends, and it was open at the bottom. It was used to keep the time line. The bass-box player would sit astride his instrument and alternate beats between two of its surfaces. Additional beats could be made using the heels of both feet.

The *saw en nef*, or saw, was also a component of the *gumbe* ensemble. Its serrated edges were scraped in rhythm with a knife to create a rasping, rhythmic effect. Over the years, the *gumbe* ensemble typically incorporated a player or two using some form of friction idiophone, for example, rubbing empty milk tins together. This made the tone color of such an ensemble, as one would expect, rather mellow. It was brightened from time to time with the loud improvisatory rhythmic patterns played on the *gumbe* in its role as master drum. The *gumbe* player was also the lead singer of folk tunes, for example, "Lili pepeh lili sal drai bonga go match am" (roughly, "all that it takes to make a quick, cold sauce for eating *fufu* [a staple made from tapioca starch] is to mix pieces of smoked *bonga* fish, hot powdered pepper, salt, and lime"); ballads; and hint songs, for example, "De up na yu garret, lef mi na mi two bai foe" (roughly, "stay up in your storied house, leave me in my small and humble dwelling"). The rest of the ensemble provided appropriate responses to the lead singer. An ensemble of this nature would be best suited to a small outdoor area where all could hear its interacting parts distinctly. If used in a procession, the group would have to be of a moderate size if everyone were to hear and enjoy the interacting roles.

With the advent of the *milo* jazz ensemble—which will be described in greater detail below—in the 1970s, the *gumbe* ensemble was forced to augment its instrumentation to include the *bata* drum (see fig. 18.6) and *koto* (a type of triangle) in order to reach a larger, more youthful dance crowd. In so doing it essentially lost its identity. Hence it has been said that *milo* jazz supplanted the *gumbe* ensemble by virtue of its inclusion of bright sounding instruments, such as the bugle, *koto*, and the two-in-one drum (see fig. 18.6)—instruments capable of appealing to the crowd of dancers it attracted.

The *Maringa* Band of Ebenezer Calender

In the early 1940s Ebenezer Calender—a talented musician who was the son of a Jamaican soldier and a Sierra Leonean mother[3]—played with a *gumbe* ensemble. This suggests that the *gumbe* ensemble was still an integral part of Sierra Leonean culture in the forties and was popular enough to attract a musician of Calender's caliber. However, Calender is best known for originating a style of popular music known as *maringa* in Sierra Leone. *Maringa*, often erroneously equated with the merengue of the Dominican Republic, was actually a lively social dance music in calypso style. As Decca began recording Calender's *maringa* band in 1945, we can also assume that the *maringa* ensemble must have come into existence sometime between 1940 and 1945. This is further supported by the fact that Calender was learning to play the guitar, the lead instrument of the *maringa* band, by 1935. It is not surprising, after all, that the son of a Jamaican father should create music with a Caribbean flavor. With its calypso- and rumba-style music, the *maringa* band is said to have gained popularity over the *gumbe* ensemble in the 1940s (Zensor Musikproduktion 88, 1988).

When *maringa* music came into being in the early 1940s, its instrumentation consisted of the following: acoustic guitar (the guitar player was also the song leader); triangle; *baba*, an octagonal frame drum that is the master drum of the *asiko* ensemble, which accompanies a traditional masquerade known as Alikali;[4] *bombadon*, or bass tuba; and a bass-box like the one used in the *gumbe* ensemble. Calender's music formed part of the "palm-wine" tradition that was introduced to Sierra Leone in the 1920s and was also called ragtime.[5] After making a number of recordings with Decca and His Master's Voice (HMV) in the late 1940s, the ensemble reached its heyday in the 1950s by which time the instrumentation consisted of the *gumbe* drum, which was prominently used during the period; two frame drums, one

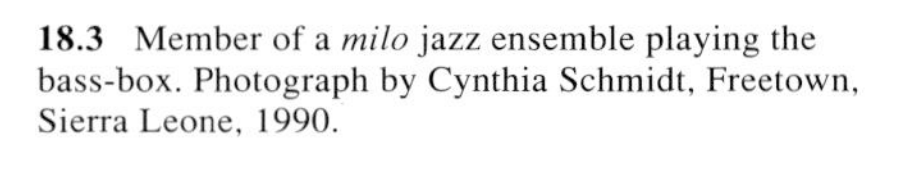

18.3 Member of a *milo* jazz ensemble playing the bass-box. Photograph by Cynthia Schmidt, Freetown, Sierra Leone, 1990.

looking more like a cylindrical tambourine and the other the *baba* mentioned earlier, which has a bar in the frame to serve as a handle for the player who keeps time on the skin with the other hand; and the acoustic guitar—always the principal instrument of the ensemble.

It should be noted that in the 1930s Calender had the opportunity to perform with a renowned flutist of the Sherbro-Mende dialectic-ethnic group. This flutist was so widely known by his nickname "Never Tire" that no one ever bothered to ascertain his real name. He was called "Never Tire" because he could play on his wooden flute for hours without stopping. Because of this association, it is not surprising that Calender also included a transverse flute made from cane wood in his band, which also featured a trumpet, recorder, and the *bombadon* as well. By the 1980s the instrumentation was further transformed to include three drums, or *bata,* as they are called in *milo* jazz, and three percussion instruments including triangles, *agogo* (metal gongs), and milk tins used as a friction idiophone, in addition to the acoustic guitar.[6] The rhythms played by Calender's musicians ultimately became part of the prevailing *milo* jazz style of the 1970s and early 1980s.

The *Milo* Jazz Ensemble

When *milo* jazz came into existence in the late 1970s, the number of skilled *gumbe* players had dwindled, and the traditional instruments of the *gumbe* ensemble were gradually disappearing. At the same time, there was a growing emphasis on the uniqueness of African heritage. This was reflected in the quality and instrumentation of popular bands, which had in the past utilized a number of Western instruments at the expense of their traditional counterparts. The desire among the popular bands of Africa to focus on innovative use of traditional instruments, attire, and languages was clearly growing. This movement witnessed the formation of such bands as Masokoloko, which utilized the slit-log drums (*inkali*) of the Limba ethnic group and the traditional palm-frond attire used by Póró musicians. The group Afro Nationale featured famed vocalist Patricia Koroma, a Mende by ethnicity, who was able to sing a number of popular songs in Mende. The group Sabanoh 75 formed in honor of I. T. A. Wallace-Johnson, a politician, who used the slogan *sabanoh,* meaning "victory," in reference to a high-profile court case in which he had been involved. Dr. Dynamite and his Afro-Rhythms, a band led by Johnson Johnson, was also representative of this time. *Milo* jazz with its bright instrumentational sonority, which sharply contrasted with the mild and rather cool style of the traditional *gumbe* ensemble, completes the list of ensembles that responded directly to the African musical zeitgeist of the late 1970s and early 1980s.

Milo was a nickname for a locally brewed alcoholic drink that was very popular among the working-class people of Sierra Leone. In Nigeria it is known as *ogogoro*, and in Ghana as *apetesi*. Nicknames were necessary as locally brewed spirits were illegal, and anyone caught either distilling or drinking them would be guilty of a crime punishable by fine and or imprisonment. *Milo* jazz (and it should be noted that the term *jazz* is used in the sense of popular music) involves vigorous dancing; with its composition of loud percussion instruments, it is "hot" music that is performed intensely by the instrumentalists. One of the founders of *milo* jazz was Dr. Olo, the nickname for Olorunfeh Johnson (fig. 18.4). The composition of Dr. Olo's ensemble became the standard for other lesser-known *milo* jazz ensembles.

Initially, the ensemble was formed by essentially doubling the number of instruments characterizing the *gumbe* ensemble and adding some more borrowed from other ethnic traditions. Such borrowings included the *kongoma* from the Limba and Loko ethnic groups (fig. 18.5). This is a bass lamellophone composed of a rectangular wooden sound box with a sound hole, over this three pieces of hacksaw are usually fastened. When these metal pieces are plucked with the thumbs and index fingers of both hands, they are amplified in the sound box. The *kongoma* plays the role of string bass sounding a limited number of partials. According to Van Oven (1981), the three-pronged *kongoma* could play basically the tonic chord, restricting the harmonic background role to the sounding of only three pitches of that chord. The *kongoma* falls out of tune every so often resulting in frequent dissonant pitches, including the harsh sounding augmented fourth interval.

A triangle borrowed from the Limba and Loko and known by those groups as the *koto* or *kenten*, respectively, was also used. This instrument is formed of a horseshoe-shaped piece of iron rod used in building construction. It is used to produce the metallic sound effect heard in *milo* jazz. A bass-box, similar to that used in the *gumbe* ensemble, is also featured, as is an answer bass-box. This is essentially a second bass-box, which alternates background rhythms with the first to give the players some respite. The two-in-one drum (fig. 18.6) represents a borrowing from the Fula ethnic group, who call such drums *jimberu*. The two-in-one drum, as its name would imply, is made of a pair of conical conga-type drums. They lack the *jimberu*'s traditional idiophonic attachment of metal strung with wire rings that rattle as the player drums on the skin. The two drums are fastened together to facilitate their playing. The two-in-one drum is the master drum of the *milo* jazz group. Other instruments include various shakers and rattles for producing jingling effects. Originally there was a mouth organ; but this has been superseded by the bugle, which is used to brighten the otherwise dark and shimmering sonority of this predominantly percussion ensemble. The bugle player is usually a novice who can play only two sets of pitches, which are alternated and repeated over and over in a rhythmic sequence, serving to coordinate the players in the absence of a conductor.

18.4 Dr. Olo (Olorunfeh Johnson), a founder of *milo* jazz. Photograph by Cynthia Schmidt, Freetown, Sierra Leone, 1990.

In his essay "Dr. Olo's *Milo* Jazz," Gary Stewart (1987) suggested that Dr. Olo was contemplating adding some additional instruments to his present ensemble. Specifically, he mentioned the electric guitar, as the acoustic guitar was felt to be growing out of style, and the *kondi*, another Limba lamellophone, which plays higher pitches than the *kongoma*, but also experiences the latter's tuning problems. Also mentioned was the *kilii*, or *kalei*, of the Mende ethnic group. This is a log drum with three slits that provide three different tone colors, capable of enhancing the overall sonority of the ensemble. Among the Mende this drum is traditionally used in social dances. Selecting traditional instruments is problematic, however, because it is often difficult to find examples that will stay in tune and thus avoid producing a dissonant sound.

Dance Styles

Gumbe and *maringa*, the oldest of Creole traditional dance styles, are individualized and competitive. The dancer who outlasts the others is hailed as the best and may have currency notes stuck in his or her mouth as an indication of audience approval. The *gumbe* dance style consists of four movements: (1) *olewase* in which the dancer moves rather slowly, swaying the torso to the rhythm, and rests the palms of the hands on the hips; (2) *cut beleh* where the dancer becomes more involved in the dance contracting and expanding the stomach muscles rhythmically and alternating that movement with the first for variety; (3) *shake wase*, the third movement, involves moving the hips and is alternated with the first two movements; and (4) alternation of *cut beleh* and *shake wase* occurs at the climax of the dance when the instrumentalists increase the pace of the music to excite the dancers. At this point the onlookers typically become excited and begin to comment and to applaud those dancers who are displaying their skills to the fullest.

In *maringa* a dancer does not have to go through the four steps of the *gumbe* style. If a dancer joins in the dance when the tempo is already heated, he or she just has to keep the pace and make as much effort as possible to move the hips to the rhythm of the music. In *milo* jazz there is a total disregard of the dance steps described above. The musicians play the music vigorously, and with the bugle controlling the music, it is easy for the dancing to become rowdy with participants bumping into each other. Everyone dances vigorously within minutes of starting. Because the dancing usually lasts much longer than either *gumbe* or *maringa*, most dancers can last for only a single dance. *Milo* jazz has a large following, and many rush to dance as soon as the music starts. Because it ignores the "classic" *gumbe* dance style, however, many of the older generation fear that it is contributing to a loss of tradition.

Historically, *gumbe* and *maringa* were associated with wedding ceremonies among the Creole, but nothing prevented the musicians in those ensembles from making music for an evening's entertainment. *Milo* jazz, however, is primarily performed as recreational music. When social groups, regardless of ethnicity, organize large street dance parades, *milo* jazz with its amplified instrumentation is selected to lead them. In that sense *milo* jazz is serving a wider national function than either the *gumbe* or *maringa*. Nevertheless, each group has its own peculiar music and its supporters. Each attempts to expand and preserve its peculiar identity for posterity as the traditional cultural practices seek ways to adapt to the changing times.

18.5 Members of a *milo* jazz ensemble playing the bell (left) and *kongoma* (center). Photograph by Cynthia Schmidt, Freetown, Sierra Leone, 1990.

18.6 Members of a *milo* jazz ensemble playing the *bata* (left) and the two-in-one drum (right). Photograph by Cynthia Schmidt, Freetown, Sierra Leone, 1990.

Robert Ansah selling cassettes on High Street.
Photograph by Doran H. Ross, Accra, Ghana, 1998.

PART THREE:

Catalog

African musical instruments are aesthetically pleasing, both to the ear and to the eye. Only through an examination of the music, performance contexts, and the instrument itself can we begin to understand what an instrument means to the people who made and played it. The essays in this book are ethnomusicological studies of African music and musical instruments. In this catalog section, we discuss African musical instruments as sculptures from art historical points of view and briefly identify their performance context in the musical life of their respective cultures.

Organizing any group of African artworks in a catalog presents challenges. Rather than a geographical arrangement, we divide African musical instruments into four types: idiophones, or self-sounding instruments; chordaphones, or strings; aerophones, or winds; and membranophones, or drums. Within each type, we recognize subgroups such as whistles and lamellophones.

The works cataloged here are meant to suggest the rich diversity of instrumental types produced by African peoples for their own use. Nevertheless, this presentation should not in any way be viewed as comprehensive and does not include the vast array of Asian and Euro-American instruments that are so vital to many contemporary performance genres.

Unless otherwise noted, all photographs are by Don Cole.

Elisabeth L. Cameron
Doran H. Ross

Idiophones

Catalog Number 1
Lamellophone, or "thumb piano" (*mbira dza vadzimu*)
Shona peoples, Zimbabwe
Wood, metal, shell
H (of *mbira*): 22 cm; Diam (of resonator): 34 cm
FMCH X87.516a,b; Gift of Helen and Dr. Robert Kuhn

The most important of several lamellophones performed by the Shona is the *mbira dza vadzimu*, or "*mbira* of the ancestors." Its most significant performance context is at nightlong rituals called *bira*, which are designed to cure illness or solve other misfortunes brought about by neglected ancestors. The *mbira dza vadzimu* is typically played in ensembles of two or three instruments accompanied by a performer with a pair of gourd rattles (*hosho*) and one or more singers. The music is intended to summon ancestral spirits to possess spirit mediums and the afflicted person, who will not be cured until possessed by the spirit who caused the illness (Berliner 1993, 186–91). The shells on the *mbira* and its resonator produce a buzzing sound that adds complexity to the music (see also Kubik, chapter 1 in this volume).

Catalog Number 2
Lamellophone, or "thumb piano" (*mbira dza vadzimu*)
Shona peoples, Zimbabwe
Wood, metal
H: 23 cm
FMCH X87.521; Gift of Helen and Dr. Robert Kuhn

Instead of shells (see cat. no. 1), this instrument uses bottle caps to produce a buzzing sound. *Mbira*s are not always played with gourd resonators, and given the fragility of the gourds themselves, some musicians have replaced them with fiberglass skeuomorphs of the same color as the gourds (personal communication from William Dewey, 1999). Aside from the *bira* rituals, Shona lamellophones are performed in a variety of popular entertainment contexts, and women performers have now joined what was previously an all-male domain.

Catalog Number 3
Lamellophone, or "thumb piano" (*kasanji*), with resonator (*nkeli*)
Luba peoples, Democratic Republic of the Congo
Wood, gourd, metal, fiber
Diam: 20 cm
FMCH X86.1882; Gift of Helen and Dr. Robert Kuhn

Lamellophones (cat. nos. 3–6) with waisted soundboards and eight keys (cat. nos. 3, 5, and 6 are missing keys) are found among the Luba and the neighboring Tabwa (Laurenty 1995, 53). Luba officials associate the lamellophone, which they refer to as *kasanji*, with a memory device called *lukasa*. A *lukasa* functions to record and transmit the histories that legitimize the current leadership within the kingdom (Reefe 1981, 75–76). Similarly, a lamellophone (*kasanji*) serves "as a memorandum of the past," as one Luba titleholder stated. It is played by court officials called "men of memory" to accompany songs recounting historical events (Roberts and Roberts 1996, 135).

Both types of objects are associated with a tortoise, an animal sacred to the Mbudye association, the institution responsible for the keeping of royal histories. The heads and figures that surmount these instruments evoke the memory of the founding ancestor of the Mbudye association, a woman in the form of a tortoise. When two heads are present, they refer to the twin tutelary spirits of Luba kingship (Roberts and Roberts 1996, 140, 144).

Catalog Number 4
Lamellophone, or "thumb piano" (*kasanji*)
Luba peoples, Democratic Republic of the Congo
Wood, metal
H: 20.4 cm
FMCH X86.1890; Gift of Helen and Dr. Robert Kuhn

Catalog Number 5
Lamellophone, or "thumb piano" (*kasanji*)
Luba peoples, Democratic Republic of the Congo
Wood, metal, bamboo
H: 28 cm
FMCH X86.1933; Gift of Helen and Dr. Robert Kuhn

Catalog Number 6
Lamellophone, or "thumb piano"(*kasanji*)
Luba peoples, Democratic Republic of the Congo
Wood, metal
H: 25.4 cm
The Schorr Family Collection

Catalog Number 7
Lamellophone, or "thumb piano"
Kuba peoples, Democratic Republic of the Congo
Plywood, metal, seedpods
L: 21.8 cm
FMCH X86.1889; Gift of Helen and Dr. Robert Kuhn

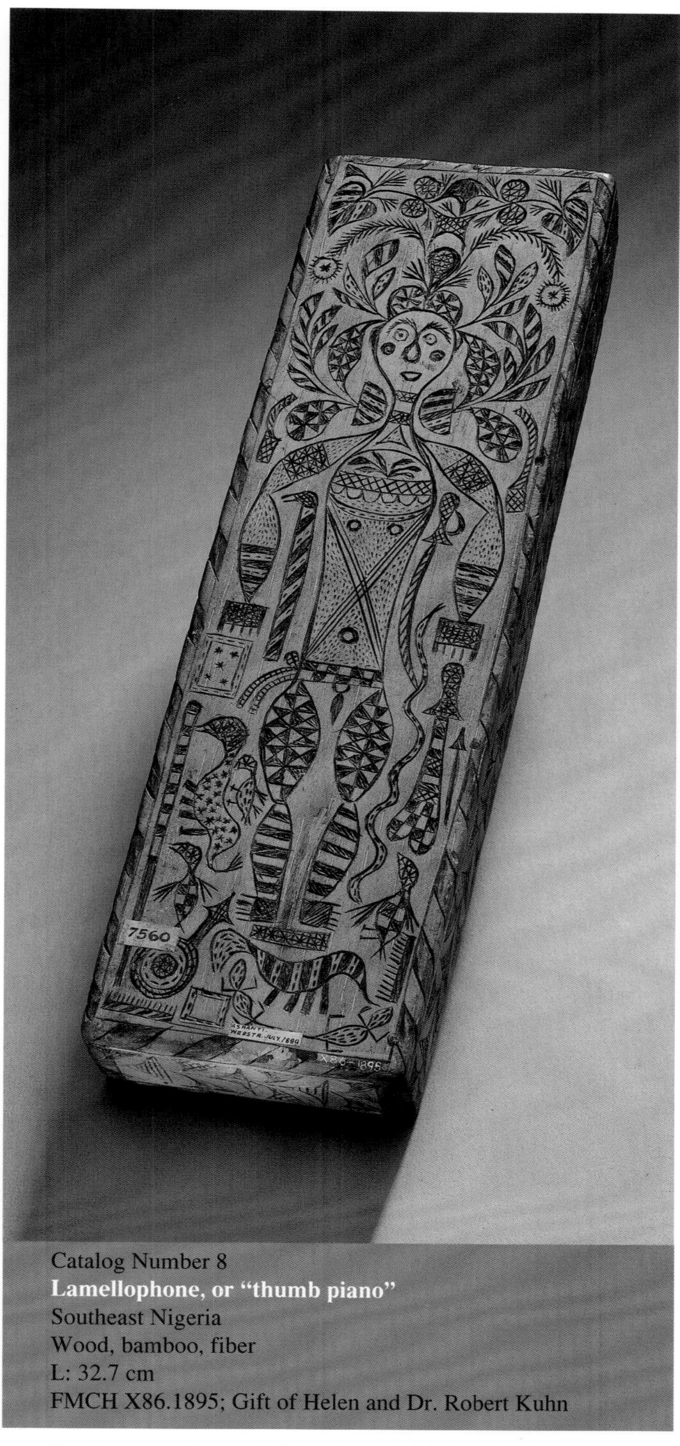

Catalog Number 8
Lamellophone, or "thumb piano"
Southeast Nigeria
Wood, bamboo, fiber
L: 32.7 cm
FMCH X86.1895; Gift of Helen and Dr. Robert Kuhn

This instrument has an old label that reads "Ashanti. Webster. July. 1899." Nevertheless, an Asante attribution must be set aside in favor of a provenance in the Niger Delta and Cross River areas of southeast Nigeria, where a number of similar, pyro-engraved instruments of the same sort have been collected (see Soderberg 1972, 28; Berliner 1993, pl. 3). There is sufficient similarity among this group to suggest a single workshop. None shows any evidence of use, and it is likely that they were made primarily for a European audience.

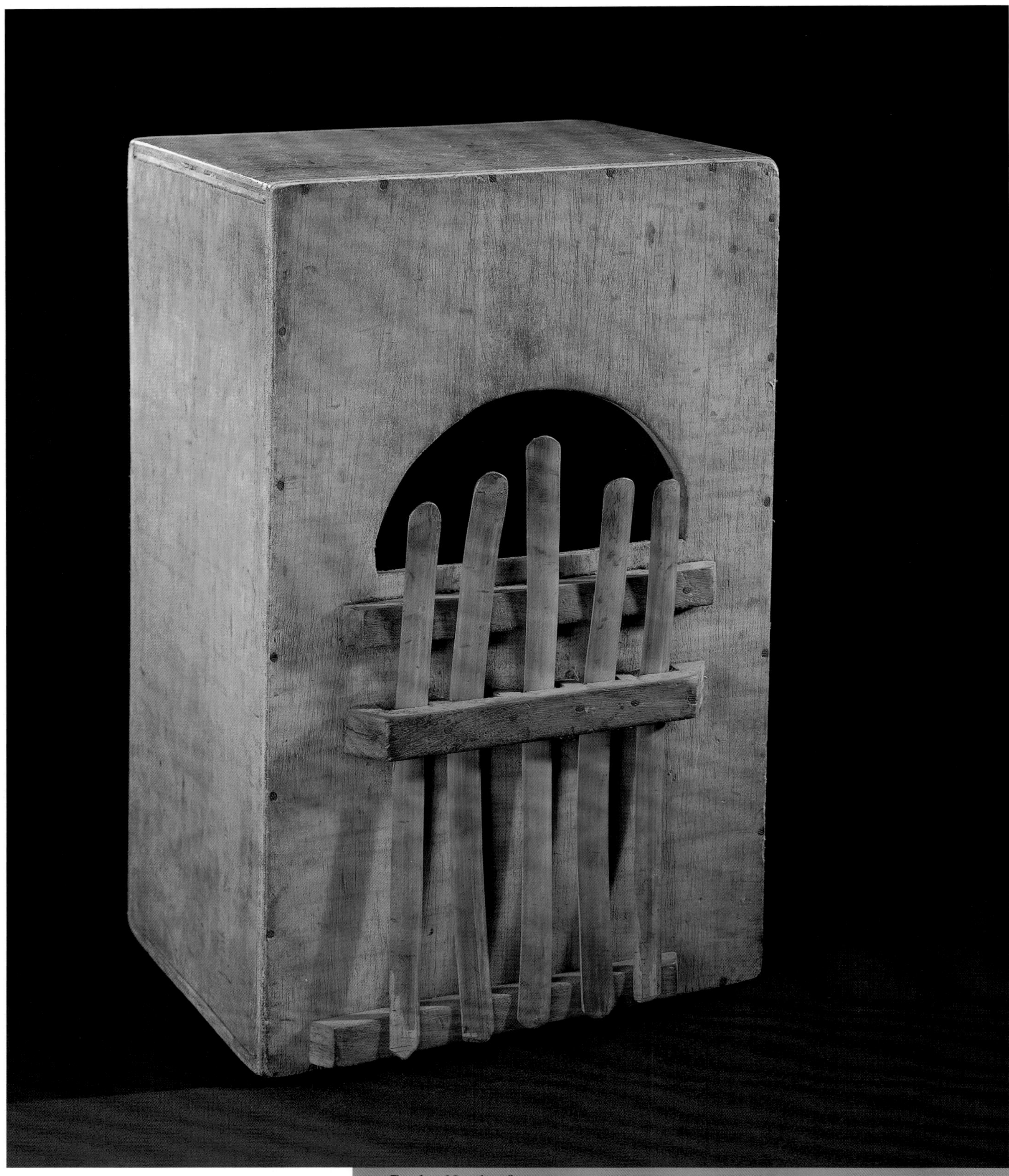

Catalog Number 9
Lamellophone, or "thumb piano"
Mamprussi peoples, Nalerigu, Ghana
Wood, nails, bamboo
H: 57.7 cm
FMCH X98.34.16; Museum purchase

Large box-shaped lamellophones with three to eight keys are found among a number of northern Ghanaian groups, as well as among the Asante peoples of south central Ghana. The musician sits on top of the instrument and plucks the keys, which are between his legs. A three-key example nearly identical to this instrument was played by a Kumase-based Agoro group at the *durbar,* or public festival, held to commemorate the tenth anniversary of Asantehene Opoku Ware II's reign in 1980.

Catalog Number 10
Lamellophone
Unidentified peoples, Africa
Wood, metal
L: 28.5 cm
FMCH X86.1867; Gift of Helen and Dr. Robert Kuhn

Catalog Number 11
Lamellophone, or "thumb piano"
Zande peoples, Democratic Republic of the Congo
Wood, bamboo, fiber
H: 34.9 cm
The Schorr Family Collection

Zande men play lamellophones to the accompaniment of ballads that address common situations, such as the perplexity of love affairs. Lamellophones became popular in the Zande area within the last century, and their artistic form and technical structure have changed through time. One form portrays a person with arms raised, perhaps dancing to the music being played (Schildkrout and Keim 1990, 207–8, 214).

Catalog Number 12
Lamellophone, or "thumb piano"
Boki peoples, Nigeria
Wood, metal, bamboo, fiber
L: 16.5 cm
FMCH X86.1908; Gift of Helen and Dr. Robert Kuhn

Catalog Number 13
One-key xylophone
Luba peoples, Democratic Republic of the Congo
Wood, gourd, resin, hide, fiber
H: 44 cm
FMCH X86.1903; Gift of Helen and Dr. Robert Kuhn

The function of this unusual instrument is not clear. It may serve roles similar to the Luba lamellophone (*kasanji*; see cat. nos. 3–6) as a device for recalling court histories, songs, and praises. The head probably represents a female ancestor as heads do on *kasanji*. Large Luba *balafons* with multiple keys are closely linked to the royal courts, and their tones are thought to summon spirits that safeguard the kingdom.

Catalog Number 14
Xylophone (*bala*)
Made by Yayi Coulibaly in 1947
Soumoukouy, Mali
Wood, gourd, hide, fabric, vegetable fiber, paper
L: 170 cm
FMCH X78.1980a-c; Gift of Dr. and Mrs. Joel Breman.

This twenty-key *bala* was purchased in Ouagadougou, Burkina Faso, and is virtually identical to the instrument played by Wamian Koné in Taale Laafi Rosellini's magisterial film, *Great Great Great Grandparents' Music* (African Family Films, 1997).

Catalog Number 15
Clappers
Asante peoples, Ghana
Wood
L: 34.7 cm
FMCH X76.673a,b; Museum Purchase

Decorated rhythm clappers are rare among the Asante and other Akan peoples, but women play unornamented examples in a variety of popular bands (*agoro*) that perform on special occasions or simply for the entertainment of their members. It is not unusual to see ten or more women playing these instruments in some of the larger groups. The relief carvings on the clappers undoubtedly refer to proverbs. For example, the ladder typically depicts the maxim "The ladder of death is not climbed by one man alone," that is, death is inevitable. Funerals are one of the primary contexts for popular band performances, and thus this imagery reminds members of the ephemeral nature of human life.

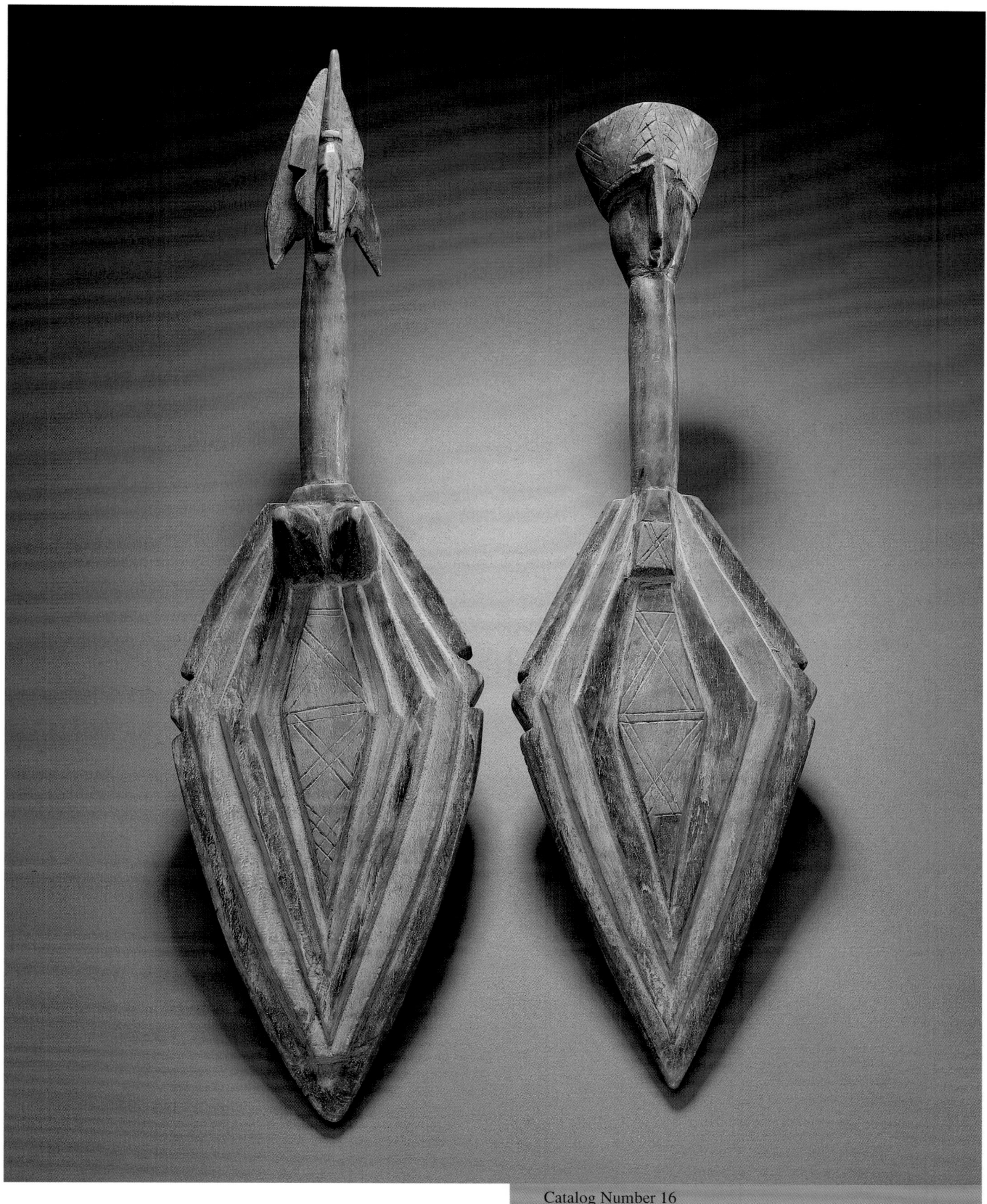

Catalog Number 16
Clappers
Bozo peoples, Mali
Wood, pigment
L: 35.5 cm
FMCH X86.1894a,b; Gift of Helen and Dr. Robert Kuhn

Catalog Number 17
Pair of rattles
Baga peoples (?), Guinea
Gourd, aluminum, metal coins
L (of longest): 56 cm
FMCH X86.2830, X86.2831; Gift of Helen and Dr. Robert Kuhn

Although a Baga attribution has not been firmly established for these rattles, the surface design created by the applied aluminum is consistent with painted designs found on Baga carpentered headdresses (*sibondël*), the development of which was stimulated by Islamic symbolism (see Lamp 1996, 208–13, 229–34). The Muslim star and crescent on each rattle reinforces this association.

Catalog Number 18
Rattle (*kichiboyok*)
Tangala-Waja peoples, Dadiya village, Nigeria
Gourd, metal, pigment, leather, cotton
H: 40 cm
FMCH X83.796; Gift of Barbara Rubin-Hudson

Rattles such as this one are used during the Kal festivals that are held every five years to celebrate the coming of age of young men. According to Berns, "the association of iron regalia with the role of men as protectors and providers has transformed the gourd 'dance rattle' into an emblem of male rather than female status" (Berns and Hudson 1986, 60).

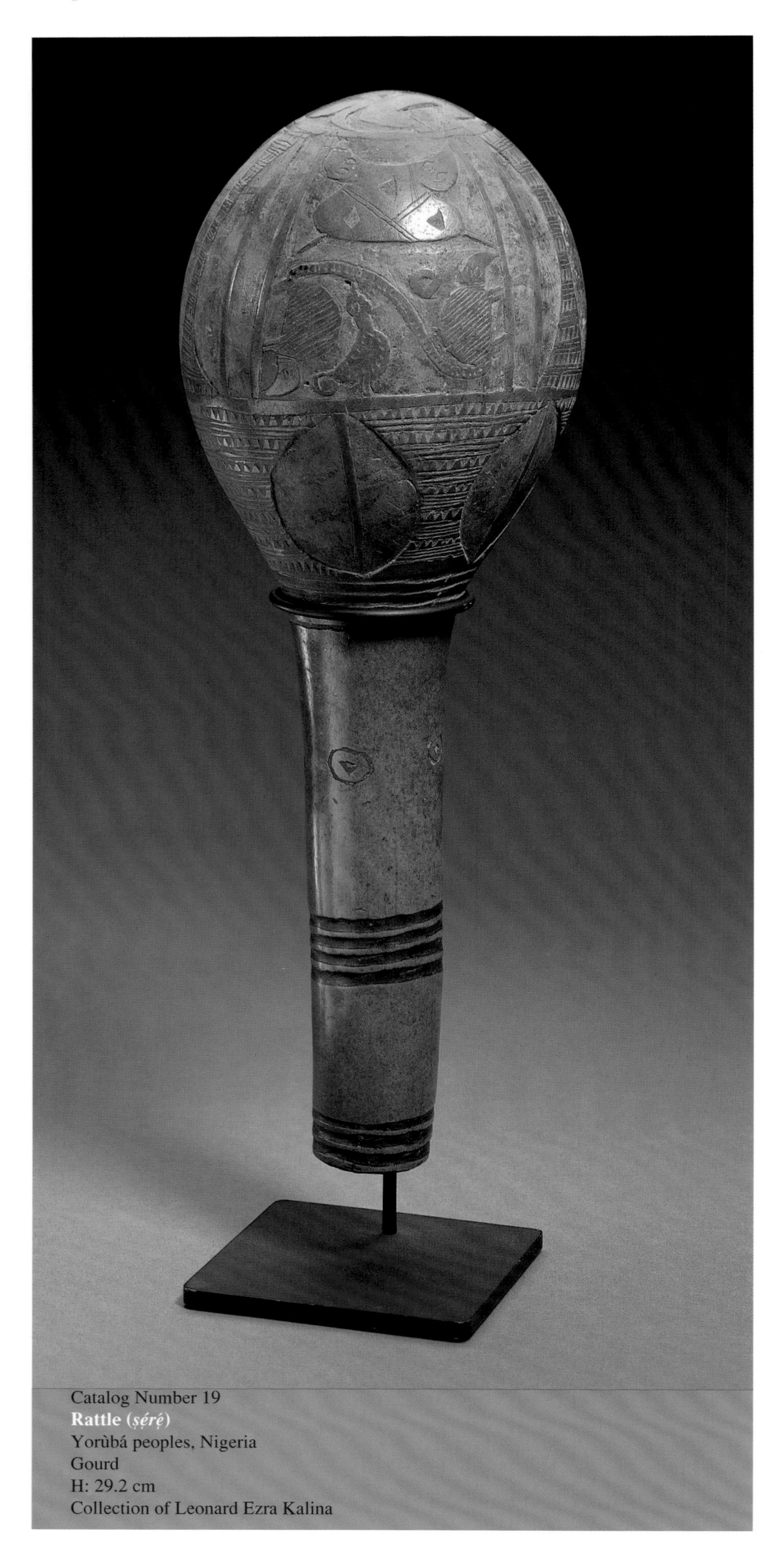

Catalog Number 19
Rattle (ṣẹ́rẹ́)
Yorùbá peoples, Nigeria
Gourd
H: 29.2 cm
Collection of Leonard Ezra Kalina

Catalog Numbers 20–22 (left to right)
Rattles
Unidentified peoples, southern Côte d'Ivoire
Gourd
L (of longest): 26 cm
Two rattles on left: Collection of Diane and Ernie Wolfe III. Rattle on right: FMCH X96.41.41; Anonymous gift

Catalog Number 23
Gourd rattle
Bwa peoples, Burkina Faso
Gourd, fiber, seeds
H: 85 cm
FMCH X86.2502; Gift of Helen and Dr. Robert Kuhn

Catalog number 24
Rattle
Tikar peoples, Cameroon
Bamboo, gourd, seedpods
H: 40 cm
FMCH X86.1887a,b; Gift of Helen and Dr. Robert Kuhn

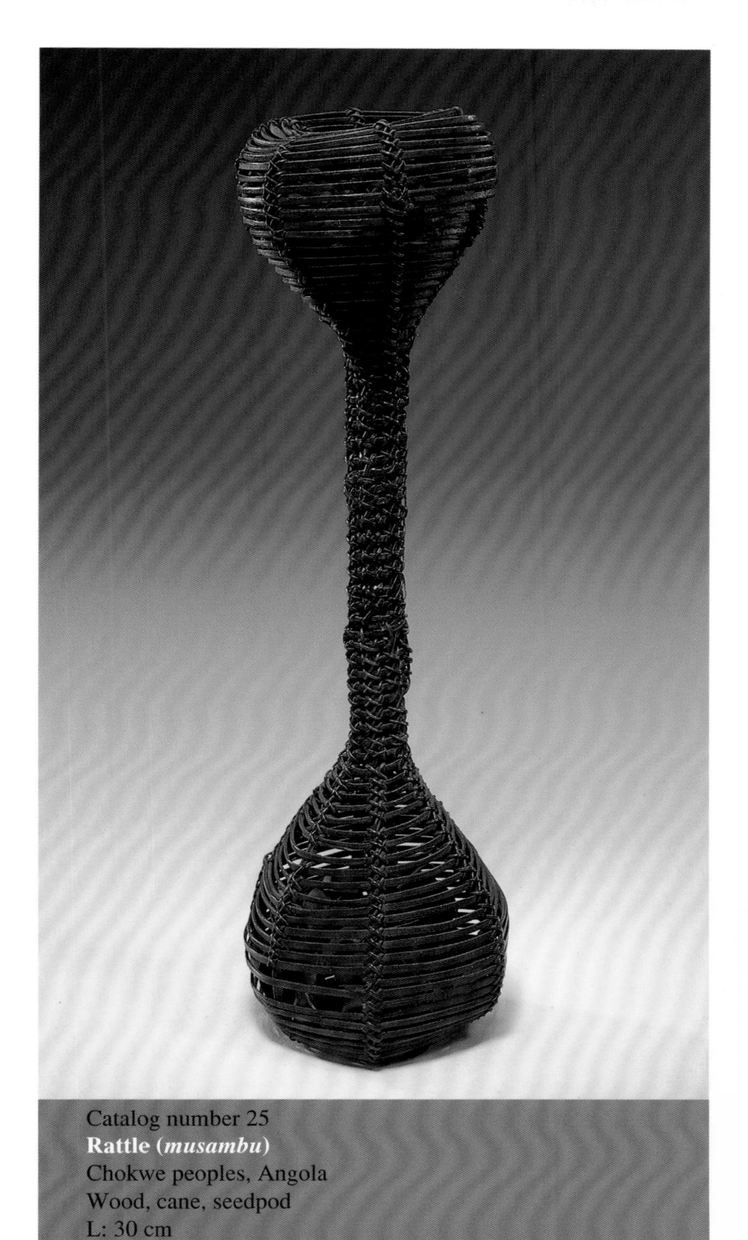

Catalog number 25
Rattle (*musambu*)
Chokwe peoples, Angola
Wood, cane, seedpod
L: 30 cm
FMCH X86.1902; Gift of Helen and Dr. Robert Kuhn

Double-chambered basketry rattles are part of an ensemble used by a Chokwe diviner to diagnose a client's problems. The rattle is used to invoke the diviner's tutelary ancestor (Jordán 1998, figs. 118, 119).

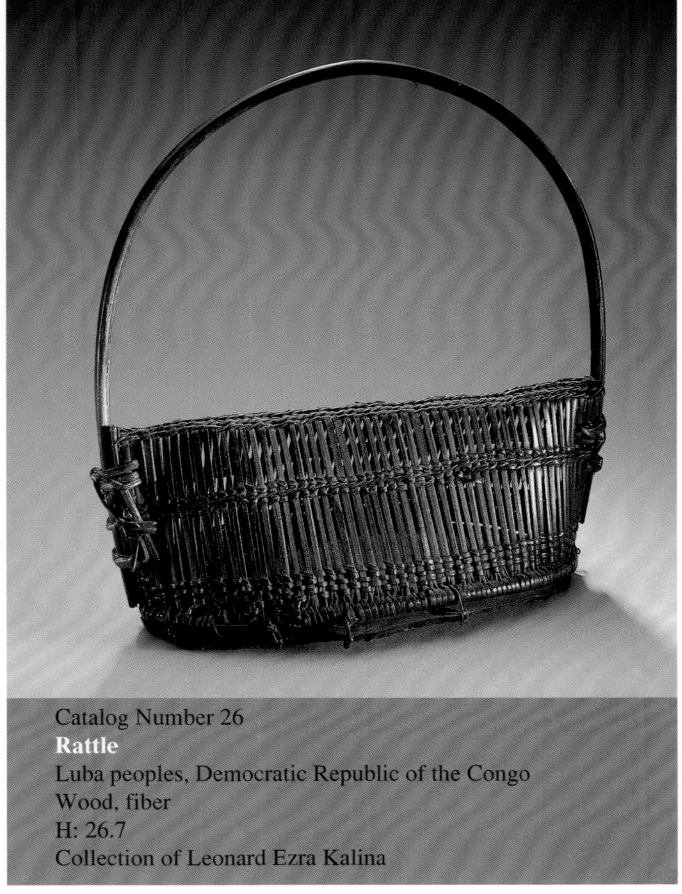

Catalog Number 26
Rattle
Luba peoples, Democratic Republic of the Congo
Wood, fiber
H: 26.7
Collection of Leonard Ezra Kalina

Luba rattles are central to divination practices for healing the sick and reversing misfortune. A Luba diviner enters a state of spirit possession through a combination of percussion and song. Female relatives sing the "Songs for Twins" to invoke the spirits' attention, while shaking rattles and ringing bells. Once the spirit has "mounted" the diviner's head, the women continue to play the instruments in order to maintain the presence of the spirit throughout the duration of the consultation. It is the spirit who guides the diviner to the cure or to the solution for a given problem (Roberts and Roberts 1996, 191).

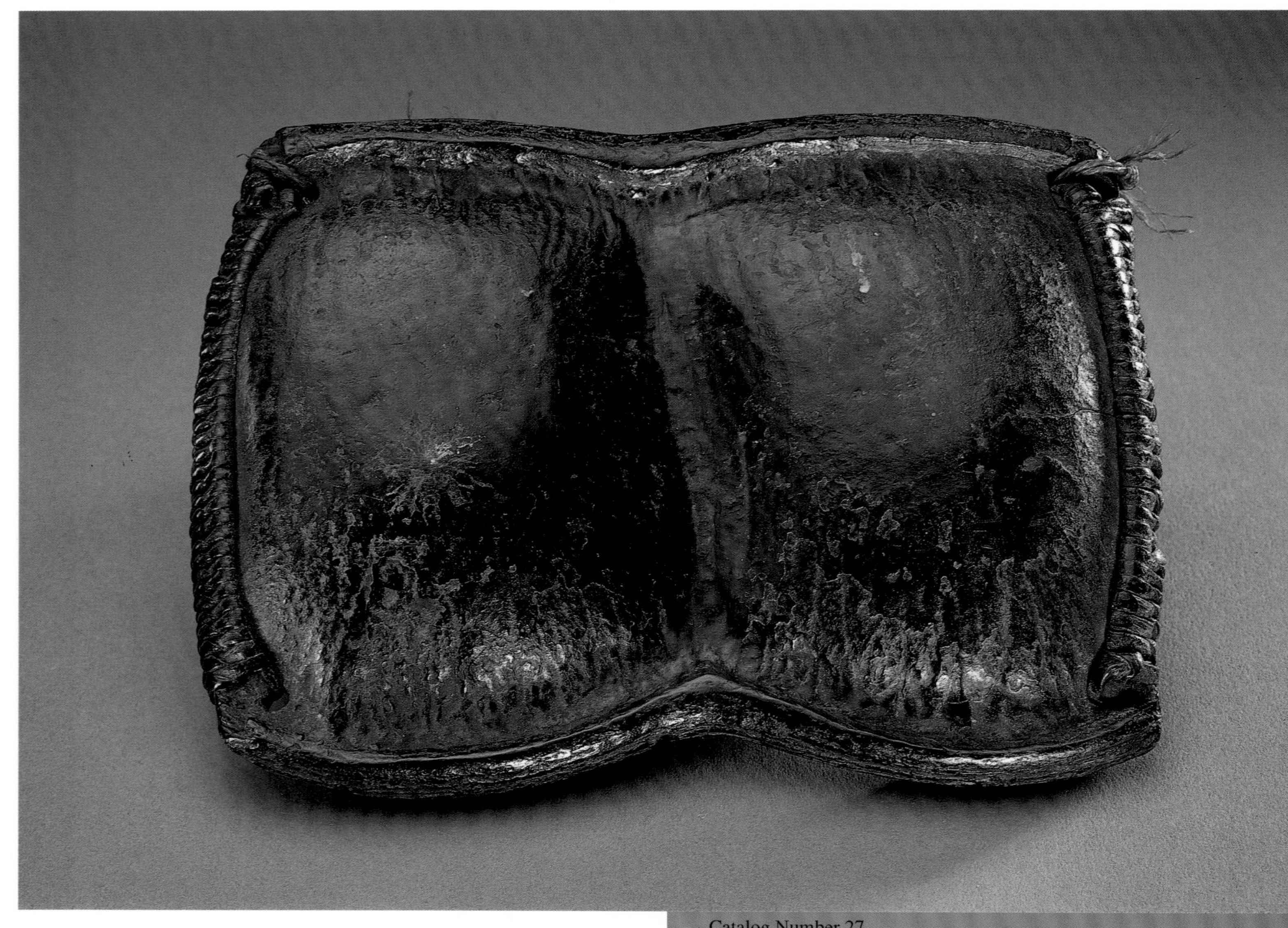

Catalog Number 27
Rattle
Unidentified peoples, Cameroon or Gabon
Seedpod, seeds, fiber
L: 19.5 cm
FMCH X86.1877; Gift of Helen and Dr. Robert Kuhn

Catalog Number 28
Rattle
Acholi peoples, Uganda
Wood, tortoise shell, fiber, metal
L: 30.5 cm
Collection of Leonard Ezra Kalina

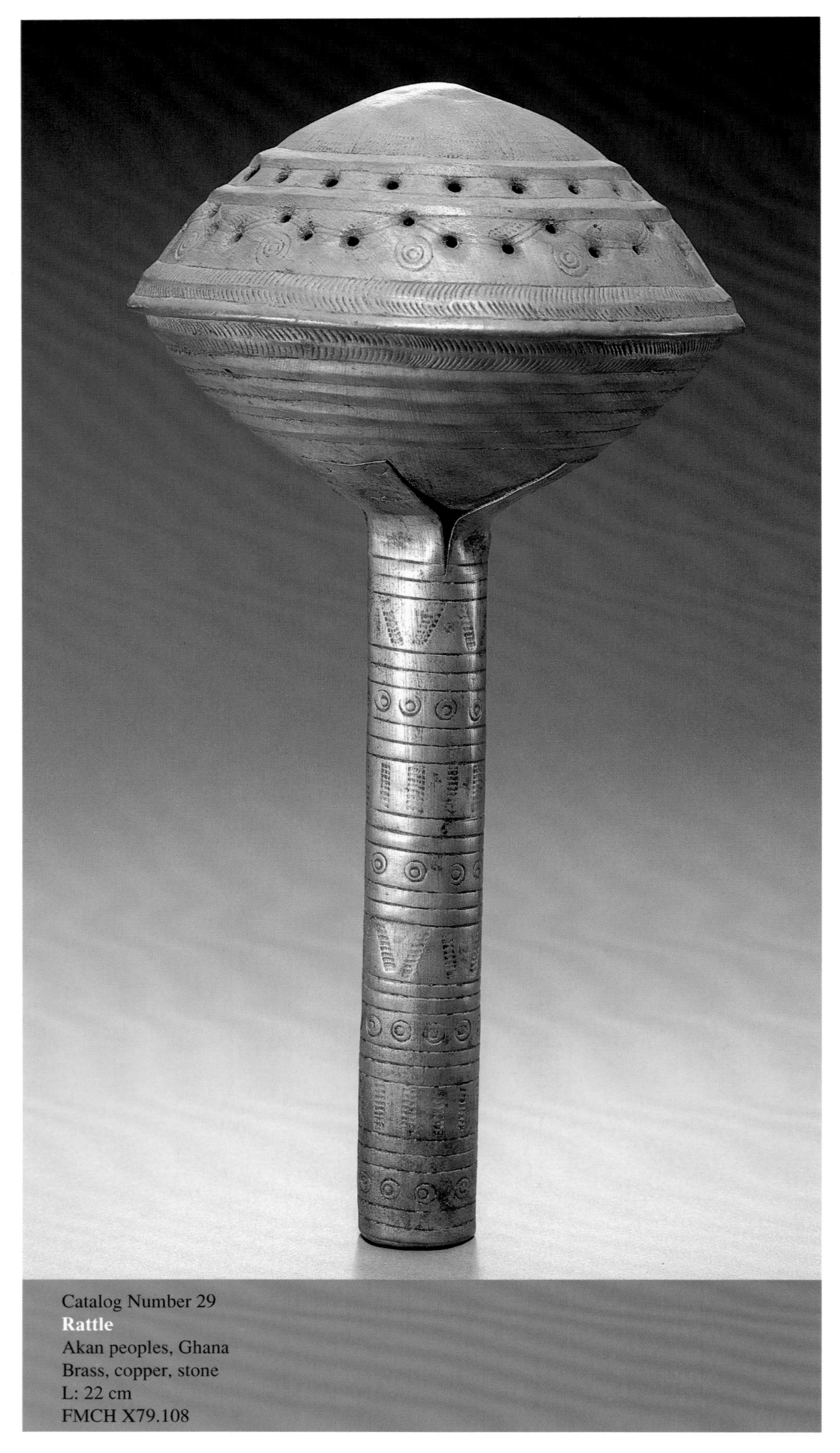

Catalog Number 29
Rattle
Akan peoples, Ghana
Brass, copper, stone
L: 22 cm
FMCH X79.108

Only about a dozen of these rattles have been recorded, and none of them in its indigenous context. The chamber of the rattle is formed from what would otherwise be identified as the lids of repoussé sheet-brass containers (*forowa*) used for shea butter, a vegetable fat that forms a component of medicines and cosmetics (see Ross 1974). The function of these rattles remains unknown.

Catalog Number 30
Rattle
Dengese peoples, Democratic Republic of the Congo
Wood, gourd, seeds, copper
H: 32.4 cm
FMCH X86.1881; Gift of Helen and Dr. Robert Kuhn

The head on this rattle shows the stylistic influence of the Kuba, who are close neighbors to the Dengese. This rattle was probably used by a diviner to call his ancestors.

Catalog Number 31
Bell (*dibu*)
Kongo peoples, Democratic Republic of the Congo
Wood
H: 25.4 cm
Private Collection

These bells (cat. nos. 31–34) were either hung on a hunting dog's collar or used in healing and in rituals to help make hunters successful. The hunter follows the sound of the dog's bell into the forest to catch the animals. Similarly, a Kongo *ng'anga*, or healer, uses a bell when he symbolically enters the spiritual world called "the forest of the ancestors" *(nfinda)* to seek the spirit or ancestor that is causing his client's problems (Thompson 1989, 41).

Catalog Number 32
Bell (*dibu*)
Kongo peoples, Democratic Republic of the Congo
Wood, fiber
H: 14 cm
FMCH X86.1854; Gift of Helen and Dr. Robert Kuhn

Catalog Number 33
Bell (*dibu*)
Kongo peoples, Democratic Republic of the Congo
Wood, fiber
H: 25.4 cm
FMCH X86.1891; Gift of Helen and Dr. Robert Kuhn

Catalog Number 34
Bell (*dibu*)
Kongo peoples, Democratic Republic of the Congo
Wood, leather
H: 16.5 cm
FMCH X78.1813; Gift of Mr. Robert Bronson

Catalog Number 35
Dance rattle
Tikar peoples, Cameroon
Aluminum, cotton
H: 16.5 cm
FMCH X86.1875; Gift of Helen and Dr. Robert Kuhn

Catalog Number 36
Rattle (*thafu ma luangu*)
Kongo peoples, Democratic Republic of the Congo
Wood, fiber, seeds, pigment
H: 41 cm
FMCH X67.870; Gift of the Wellcome Trust

The figures on this rattle represent Maundu and Malanda, the first initiates of the Khimba society, who are responsible for the well-being of the community. They can also represent the double-headed serpent or rainbow god, Mbumba, who protects Khimba initiates. The initiates are hidden from townspeople for several months while they are taught how to live together. The Khimba members hold these rattles in their hands when they dance (Niangi Batulukisi 1995, 53, 65, 106).

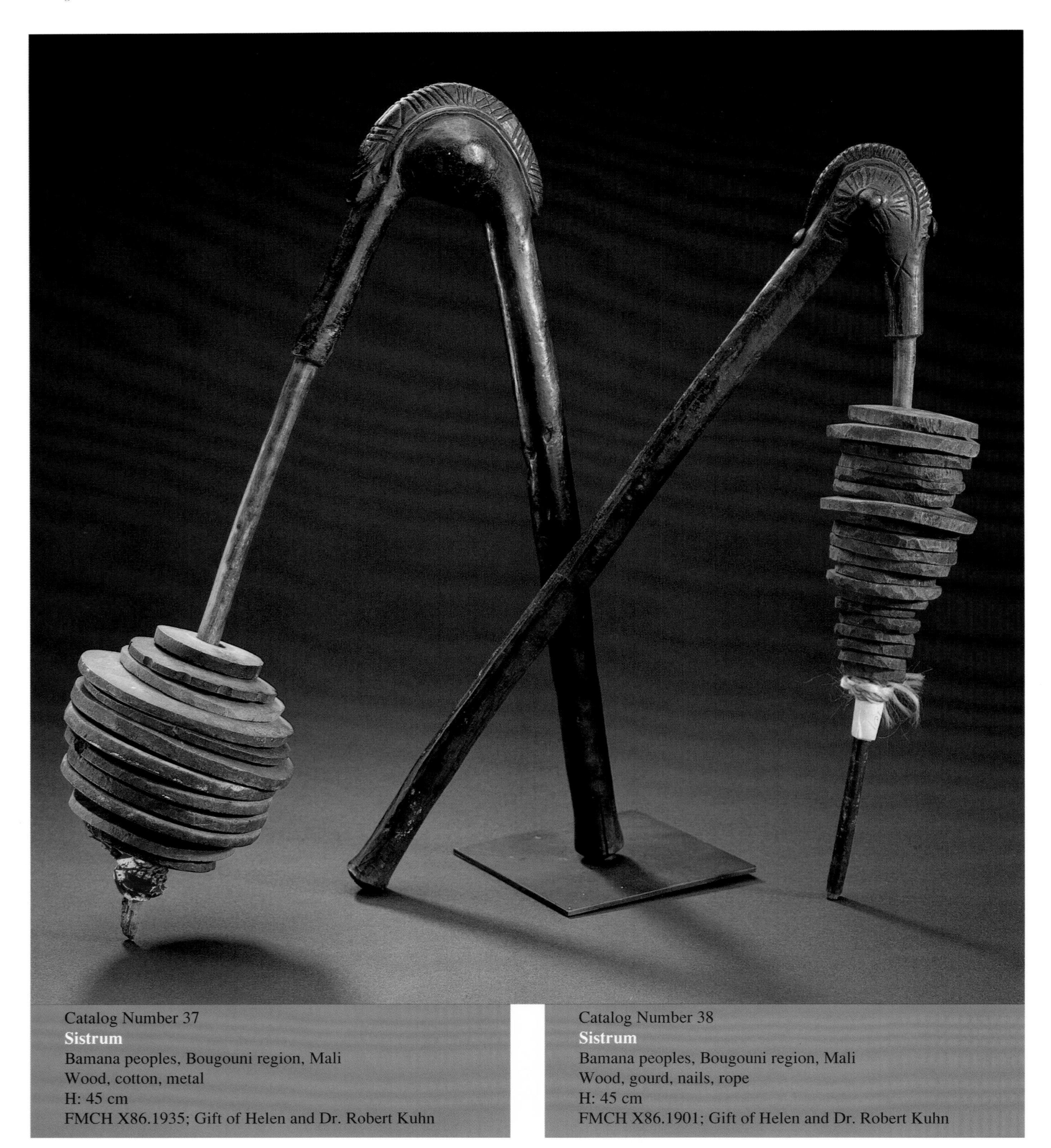

Catalog Number 37
Sistrum
Bamana peoples, Bougouni region, Mali
Wood, cotton, metal
H: 45 cm
FMCH X86.1935; Gift of Helen and Dr. Robert Kuhn

Catalog Number 38
Sistrum
Bamana peoples, Bougouni region, Mali
Wood, gourd, nails, rope
H: 45 cm
FMCH X86.1901; Gift of Helen and Dr. Robert Kuhn

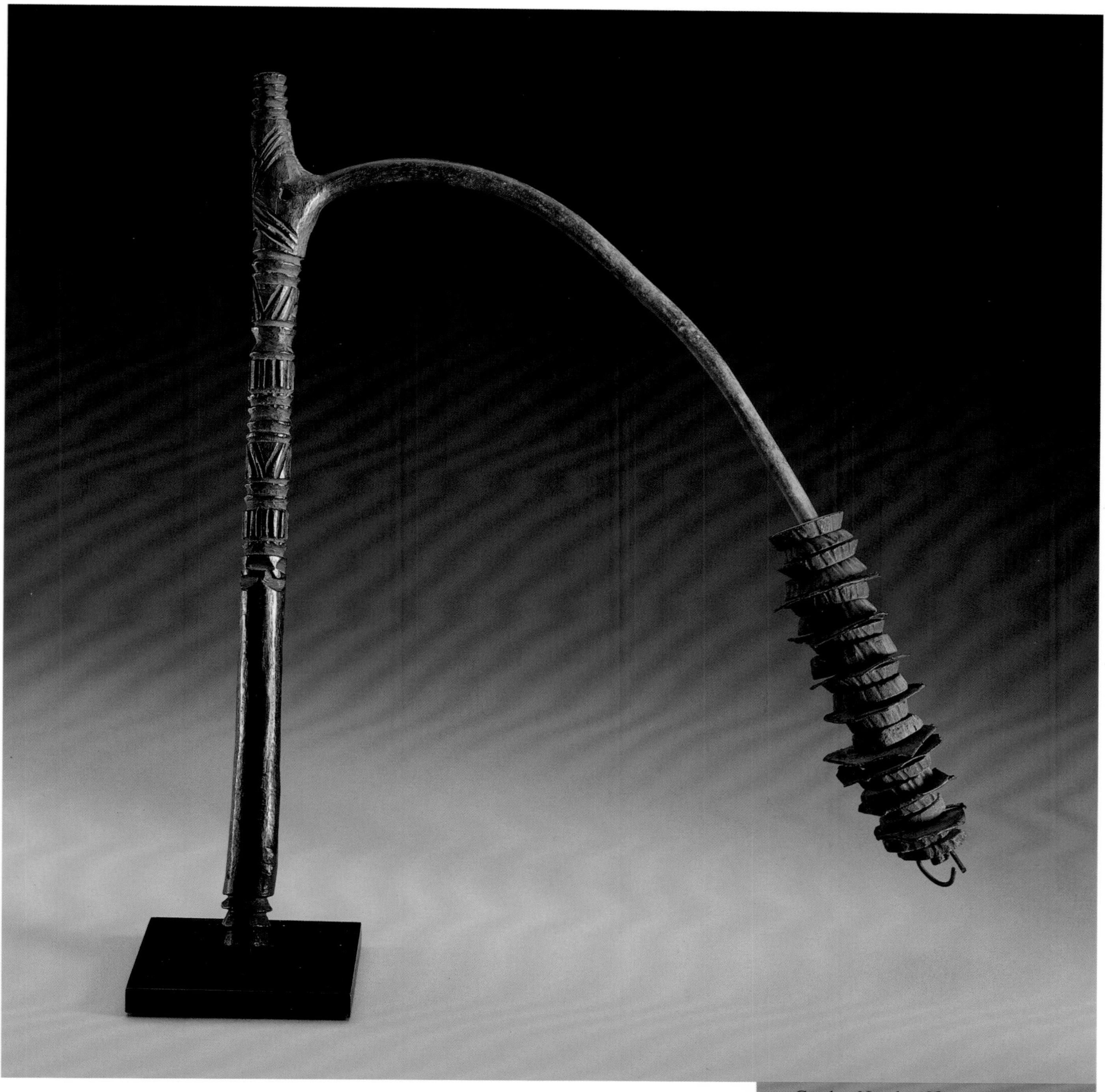

Catalog Number 39
Sistrum
Dogon peoples, Mali
Wood, gourd
H: 33.7 cm
Collection of Leonard Ezra Kalina

Catalog Number 40
Bell
Igbo peoples, Nigeria
Brass
H: 13 cm
FMCH X86.1855; Gift of Helen and Dr. Robert Kuhn

A complex assortment of bronze and brass bells is found in southern Nigeria and serves a variety of functions, from altar and shrine pieces to items of personal adornment and components of masquerade costumes. Bells like the present example are frequently attributed to a famed group of itinerant metalsmiths from Awka who plied their trade throughout Igboland (Cole 1984, 52).

Catalog Number 41
Bells
Dan peoples, Côte d'Ivoire or Liberia
Brass, cloth, coin, plastic
H: 16 cm
FMCH X87.112, X87.113; Gift of Helen and Dr. Robert Kuhn

Catalog Number 43
Bell (*omo*)
Ìjẹ̀bú-Yorùbá peoples, Nigeria
Bronze
H: 85 cm
W. and U. Horstmann Collection; photograph courtesy of Udo Horstmann

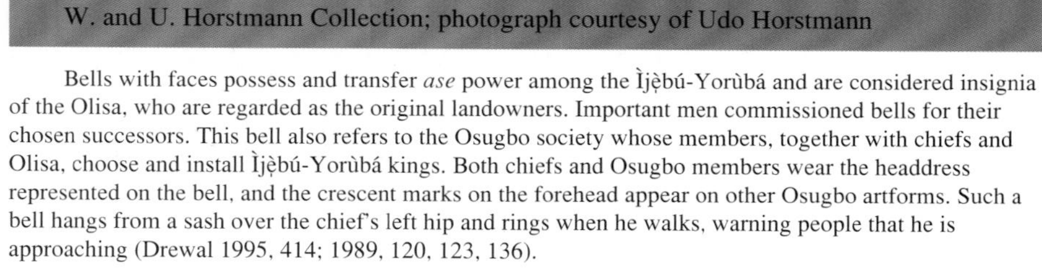

Bells with faces possess and transfer *ase* power among the Ìjẹ̀bú-Yorùbá and are considered insignia of the Olisa, who are regarded as the original landowners. Important men commissioned bells for their chosen successors. This bell also refers to the Osugbo society whose members, together with chiefs and Olisa, choose and install Ìjẹ̀bú-Yorùbá kings. Both chiefs and Osugbo members wear the headdress represented on the bell, and the crescent marks on the forehead appear on other Osugbo artforms. Such a bell hangs from a sash over the chief's left hip and rings when he walks, warning people that he is approaching (Drewal 1995, 414; 1989, 120, 123, 136).

Catalog Number 42
Bell
Kingdom of Benin, Nigeria
Brass
H: 8 cm
FMCH X87.509; Gift of Helen and Dr. Robert Kuhn

Bells in the shape of truncated pyramids are associated with the Benin kingdom of southern Nigeria. Of the 895 Benin brass plaques documented by Philip Dark, 132 have such bells represented on them, usually suspended on the chests of chiefs or retainers (1971, 66, 72–75). The bells are thought to be an indicator of military rank and to protect warriors from danger. They are also placed on ancestral altars (Hess 1983, 103–6).

Catalog Number 44
Gong
Mumuye peoples, Nigeria
Wood, aluminum
H: 82.5 cm
FMCH X86.1125; Gift of Helen and Dr. Robert Kuhn

Catalog Number 45
Bell
Ibibio peoples, Nigeria
Wood
H: 85 cm
FMCH X86.1863; Gift of Helen and Dr. Robert Kuhn

Although the performance context of this instrument is unknown, it represents an example of the tension between aesthetics and musical function: the face carved onto the body of this bell has been damaged by the musician's mallet.

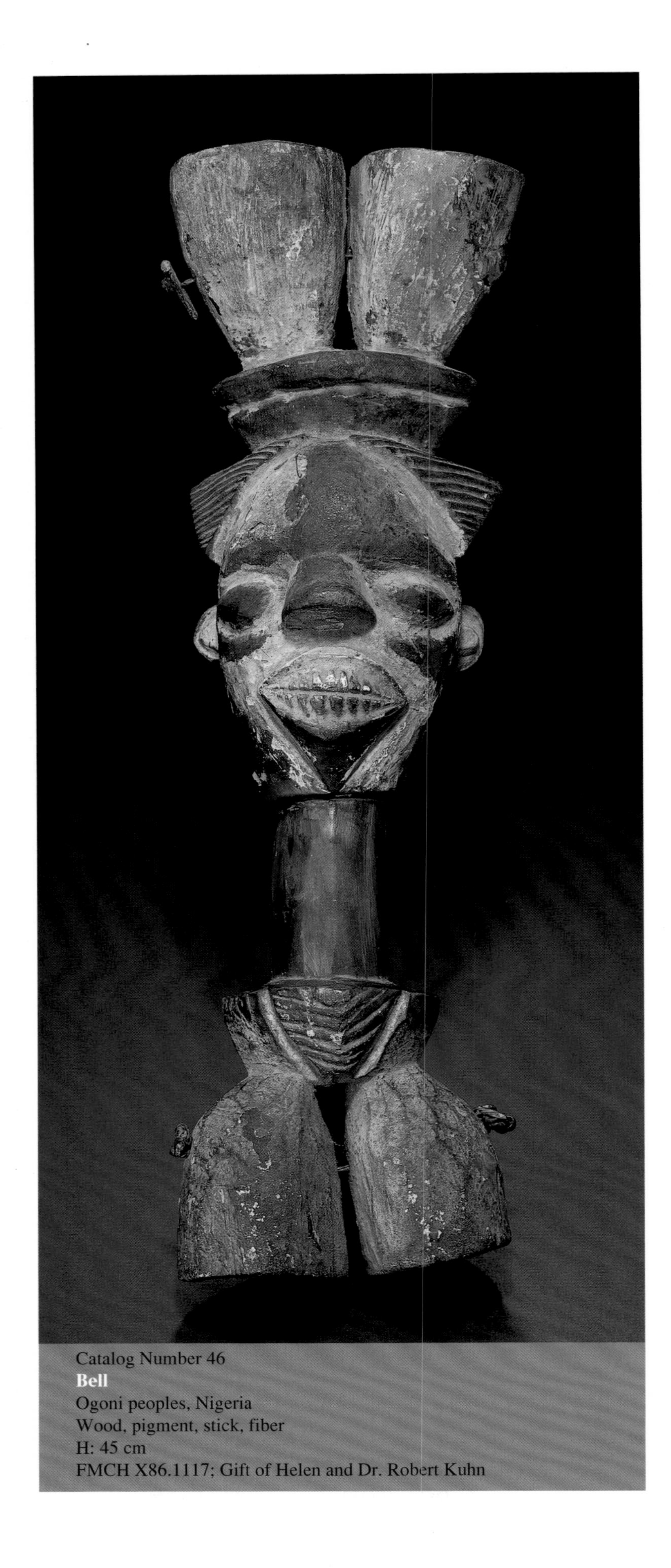

Catalog Number 46
Bell
Ogoni peoples, Nigeria
Wood, pigment, stick, fiber
H: 45 cm
FMCH X86.1117; Gift of Helen and Dr. Robert Kuhn

Catalog Number 47
Gong
Baule peoples, Côte d'Ivoire
Wood, iron
H: 40.7 cm
FMCH X86.1898; Gift of Helen and Dr. Robert Kuhn

Gongs like these have been attributed to but never documented among the Baule peoples. Based on the cheek scarification, it has been suggested that they originate on the northern peripheries of Baule culture areas.

Catalog Number 48
Gong mallet (*lawre waka*) and iron gong (*lawre*)
Baule peoples, Côte d'Ivoire
Wood, fiber, iron
L (of mallet): 27 cm; H (of gong): 19 cm
Mallet: FMCH X64.1450; Museum purchase. Gong: FMCH X75.918b; Gift of Helen and Dr. Robert Kuhn

Bells or gongs such as this one are used by both male and female diviners, who, according to Susan Vogel, "are conditioned to go into a trance state when they hear the steady striking of an iron gong. They enter a trance in private, but they carry the gong and mallet in performance to use if they start to lose the trance during the session, or wish to deepen the trance" (1997, 229). The mallet end is an image of one of the men's sacred helmet masks collectively called *bo nun amuin* (god in the bush); see Vogel 1997, 205–14.

Catalog Number 49
Gong mallet (*lawre waka*) and iron gong (*lawre*)
Baule peoples, Côte d'Ivoire
Wood, iron, cord
H: 22.2
FMCH X86.1883; Gift of Helen and Dr. Robert Kuhn

Baule possession diviners (*komien*) privately enter into a state of trance by rhythmically beating on a hand-held iron gong with an elaborately carved mallet. Waiting clients can hear the beating and anticipate the diviner's arrival. During the session, the diviner holds the gong and mallet in his hand. Susan Vogel points out that only the diviner and his or her heirs see the carvings on the *lawre* (Vogel 1997, 124, 235–37).

Catalog Number 50
Gong
Idoma peoples, Africa
Wood, metal
H: 36.3 cm
FMCH X87.504; Gift of Helen and Dr. Robert Kuhn

Catalog Number 51
Double gong or bell (*dawuro, nnawuta*)
Handle carved by Kwaku Bempah, circa 1925
Asante peoples, Kumase, Ghana
Wood, iron
H: 57.5 cm
FMCH X87.1312; Gift of Elizabeth Lloyd Davis

The Akan twin gong called *nnawuta* is usually performed in connection with drumming associated with warrior groups (*asafo*), but it is also used to send messages (Nketia 1963, 198). It is highly unusual, however, for an *asafo* double gong to have such an elaborately carved handle. It is more likely that this gong was associated with a court or a shrine serving political and religious functions.

Catalog Number 52
Gong or bell (*mokenge*)
Tsogo peoples, Gabon
Wood, iron, pigment
H: 44.5 cm
FMCH X86.1893; Gift of Helen and Dr. Robert Kuhn

This gong type is said to be used in the Tsogo men's initiation association called Evovi, or "judges." The carved head is thought to represent Kombe, the sun and supreme judge. Striking the bell recalls a man's heartbeat (Perrois 1986, 203).

Catalog Number 53
Gong
Bacham peoples, Cameroon
Iron, cloth, bamboo
H: 90.2
FMCH X86.1912; Gift of Helen and Dr. Robert Kuhn

This double gong symbolizes the power of the Kwifoyn society, a regulatory group that is responsible for carrying out the king's decrees, but that also keeps the king's power in check. The gong is sounded when the society is meeting or when they are seeing to the business of the king (Northern 1984, 64).

Catalog Number 54
Slit gong (*nedungu*)
Mangbetu peoples, Democratic Republic of the Congo
Wood, metal
L: 69 cm
W. and U. Horstmann Collection; photograph by A + L Ottiger/Zug, Switzerland

Mangbetu slit gongs are symbols of the king and his power. They are used to communicate between towns, to let people know the king is drinking palm wine, and to announce the visit of important officials. Orchestras also use them for dances. The king would give such slit gongs to his representatives as emblems of their authority (Demolin 1990, 202–3, 210).

Catalog Number 55
Slit gong
Kota peoples, Gabon
Wood, metal
L: 86.4 cm
FMCH X86.1909; Gift of Helen and Dr. Robert Kuhn

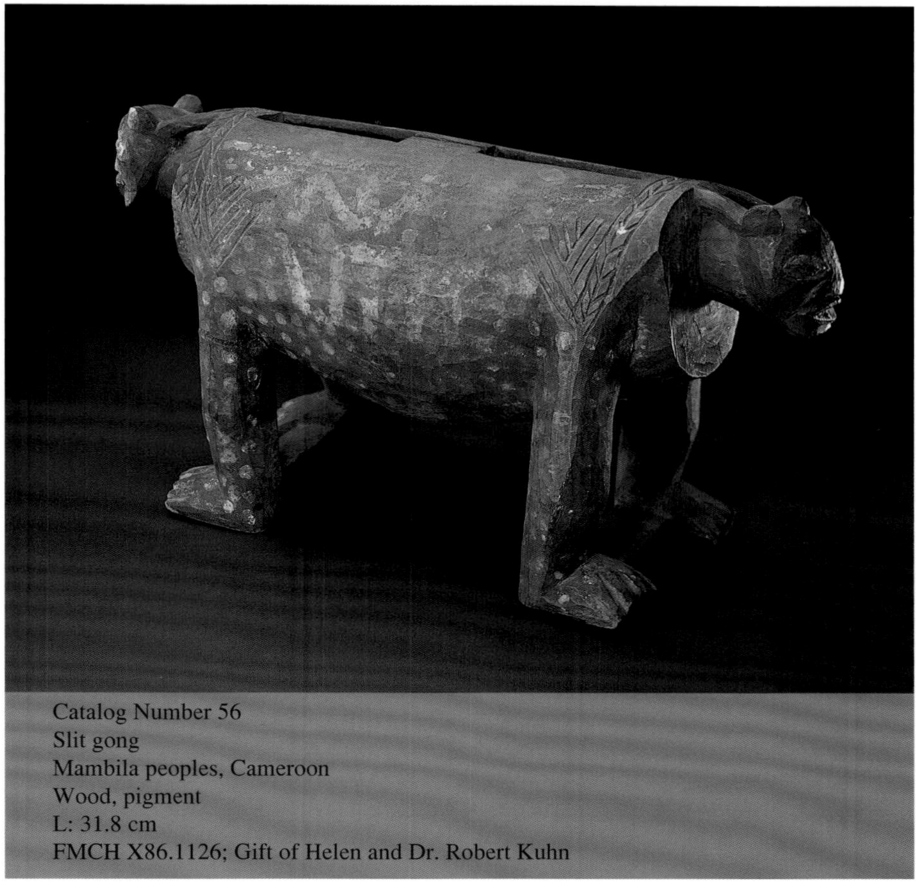

Catalog Number 56
Slit gong
Mambila peoples, Cameroon
Wood, pigment
L: 31.8 cm
FMCH X86.1126; Gift of Helen and Dr. Robert Kuhn

This zoomorphic slit gong may have been used to send signals or gather warriors in time of battle (Geary 1989, 63).

Catalog Number 57
Slit gong
Dan peoples, Côte d'Ivoire
Wood
H: 62.2 cm
FMCH X85.460

The handle of this slit gong is in the shape of a female mask. The instrument is played for ritual masquerade performances as well as for entertainment (Kreamer 1989, 124).

Catalog Number 58
Slit gong
Vili peoples, Democratic Republic of the Congo
Wood
H: 20.3 cm
FMCH X92.47; Gift of Helen and Dr. Robert Kuhn

The Lemba society is a powerful organization that promoted social order, invoked healing processes, and controlled commerce among the Vili peoples. Lemba was (and perhaps is) a cult of affliction, through which people might solve various problems such as child mortality. The teacher played a slit gong like this while training new members. The shape of the gong is that of a crescent moon, a symbol of the world of ancestors. The gong's sound reminds the initiates that they are learning ancestral knowledge (Batulukisi 1995, 53–54, 122; Thompson 1989, 41–43).

Catalog Number 59
Slit gong
Suku peoples, Democratic Republic of the Congo
Wood
H: 42 cm
FMCH X86.1120; Gift of Helen and Dr. Robert Kuhn

Catalog Number 60
Slit gong
Suku peoples, Democratic Republic of the Congo
Wood
H: 47.6 cm
FMCH X86.1876; Gift of Helen and Dr. Robert Kuhn

Among Suku and Yaka peoples, slit gongs (cat. nos. 59, 60) are emblems of healers/ diviners and visual metaphors for the diviners themselves. Combining male and female, the body of the slit gong is phallic in shape while having a womblike interior. Diviners use slit gongs in a variety of ways during a patient's treatment. As they walk to their clients' houses, they play slit gongs so that people know where they are. They continue to play when they arrive. The diviner may sit on the slit gong during sessions with the patient. Small slit gongs can also serve as cups for administering medicine. Finally, when diviners gather for the funeral of a fellow diviner, they play their slit gongs to celebrate the person's life (Bourgeois 1984, 98–101; Devisch 1993, 163).

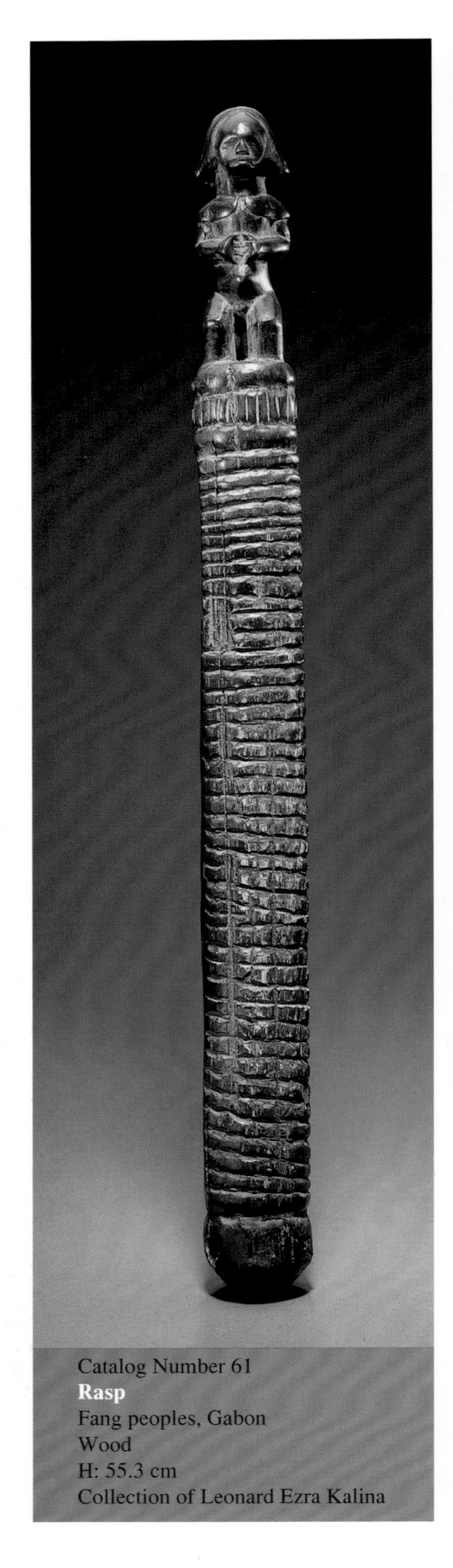

Catalog Number 61
Rasp
Fang peoples, Gabon
Wood
H: 55.3 cm
Collection of Leonard Ezra Kalina

Catalog Number 62
Rasp/gong
Senufo peoples, Mali or Côte d'Ivoire
Iron
H: 55.9 cm
Collection of Leonard Ezra Kalina

Catalog Number 63
Rasp/gong
Senufo peoples, Mali
Iron
H: 28.6 cm
Collection of Leonard Ezra Kalina

Chordophones

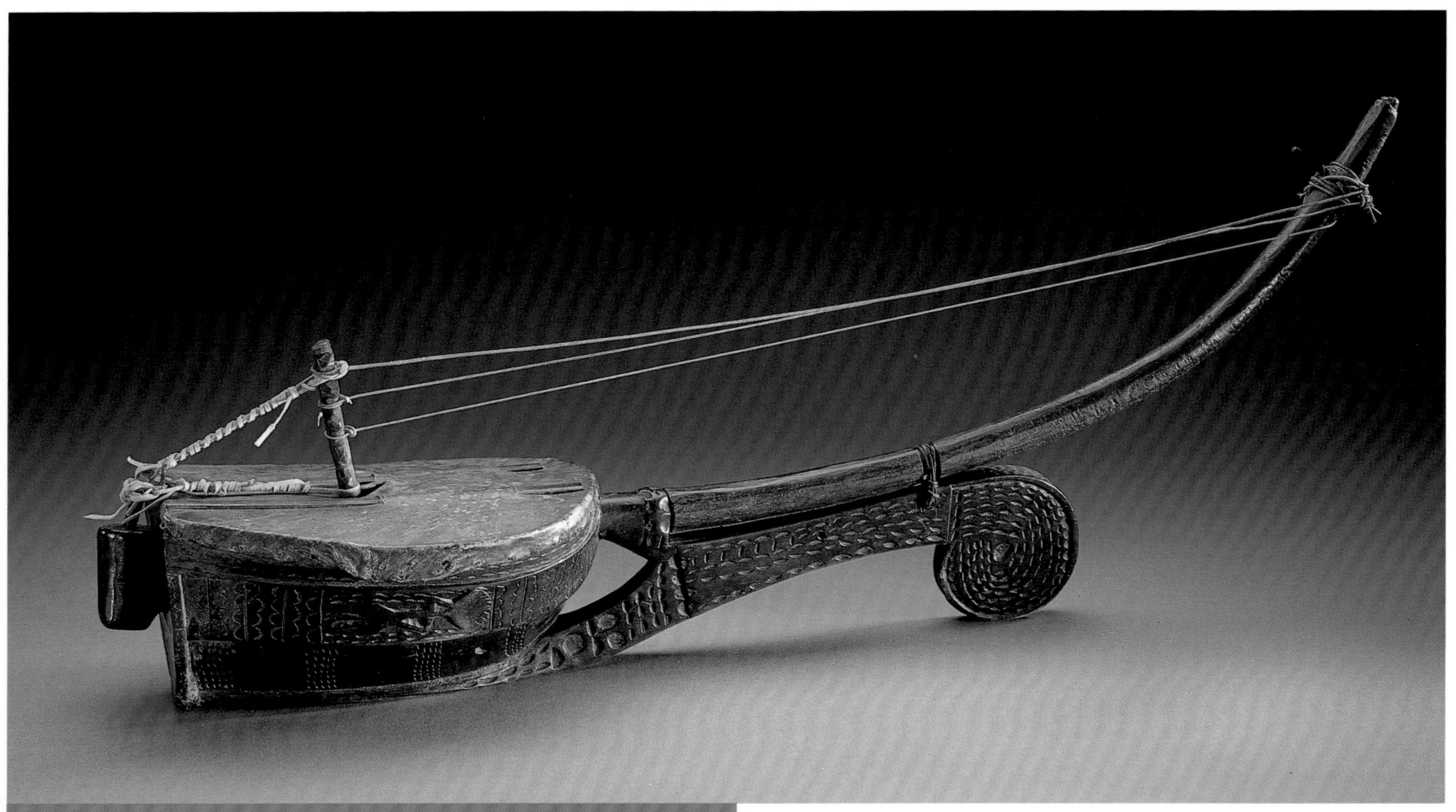

Catalog Number 64
Harp
Kinandas peoples, Zanzibar, Tanzania
Wood, gut, string
L: 78.7 cm
FMCH X86.1852; Gift of Helen and Dr. Robert Kuhn

Catalog Number 65
Harp Lute
Grebo peoples, Liberia
Wood, string, leather
L: 94 cm
FMCH X86.1929; Gift of Helen and Dr. Robert Kuhn

Catalog Number 66
Harp with bridge (*korikaariye*)
Senufo peoples, Mali or Côte d'Ivoire
Wood, gut, string
L: 105.5 cm
FMCH X86.2500; Gift of Helen and Dr. Robert Kuhn

The figure of a woman on this harp reminds men of ideal female beauty, the balance necessary between men and women, the danger of the bush spirits, and the measures required to appease them. Women of the Sandogo divination society possess the power to regulate the conflicting worlds of men and women and of bush and village (Glaze 1981, 176, 179; 1986, 88–89). Instruments such as this one are used by diviners in consultation with the spirit world (Förster 1988, 115, pl. 29).

Catalog Number 67
Harp lute
Tsogo peoples, Gabon
Wood, hide, fiber
L. 48.9 cm
FMCH X67.2162; Gift of the Wellcome Trust

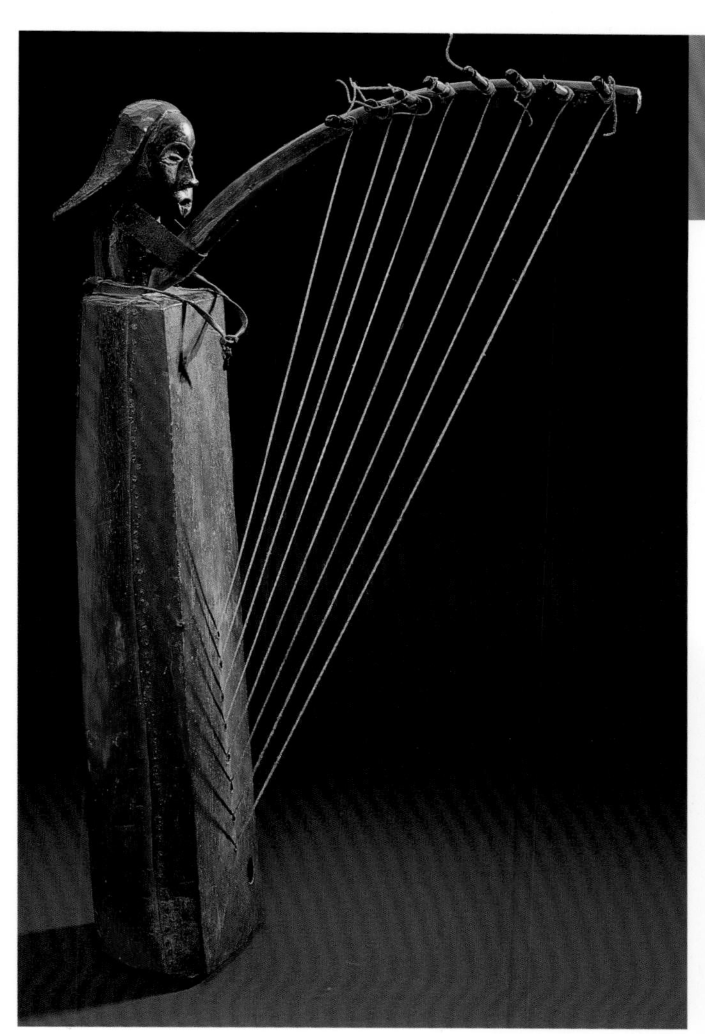

Catalog Number 68
Harp lute (*ngombi*)
Tsogo peoples, Ngounie River region, Gabon
Wood, hide, fiber, metal
H: 78.7 cm
FMCH X85.457; Gift of Helen and Dr. Robert Kuhn

During the early 1900s in response to the rise of Western religions, the *bieri* ancestor cult gave birth to a revivalist religion called Bwiti. Harp lutes came to represent the balance between men and women, and between humankind and the supernatural. The harp itself illustrates the complementarity of male and female: the body is considered female while the neck is male; four strings are male and four are female. Nyingwan Mbege, the Sister of God and a life-giving force, finds form in Bwiti harp lutes: the tuning pegs are her spine and ribs, the strings her tendons and sinews. Harp music is perceived to be the female voice of pity and comfort that keeps foreign evils at bay so that people can communicate with their ancestors (Perrois 1986, 204; Fernandez 1973, 209).

Catalog Number 69
Harp lute
Ndjabi peoples, Gabon
Wood, hide, pigment
L: 58 cm
FMCH X86.1922; Gift of Helen and Dr. Robert Kuhn

Catalog Numbers 70 and 71
Harps *(sati)*
Ngbaka peoples, Democratic Republic of the Congo
Wood, hide, metal, string
H (of tallest): 60 cm
FMCH X85.458a,b; X85.459a b; Gift of Helen and Dr. Robert Kuhn

These harps represent Seto (cat. no. 70) and his sister/ wife, Nabo (cat. no. 71), ancestors of the Ngbaka peoples and messengers to the gods. A seated musician stood such a harp on the ground in front of him and accompanied songs and ballads (Laurenty 1997, 82; Felix 1987, 120).

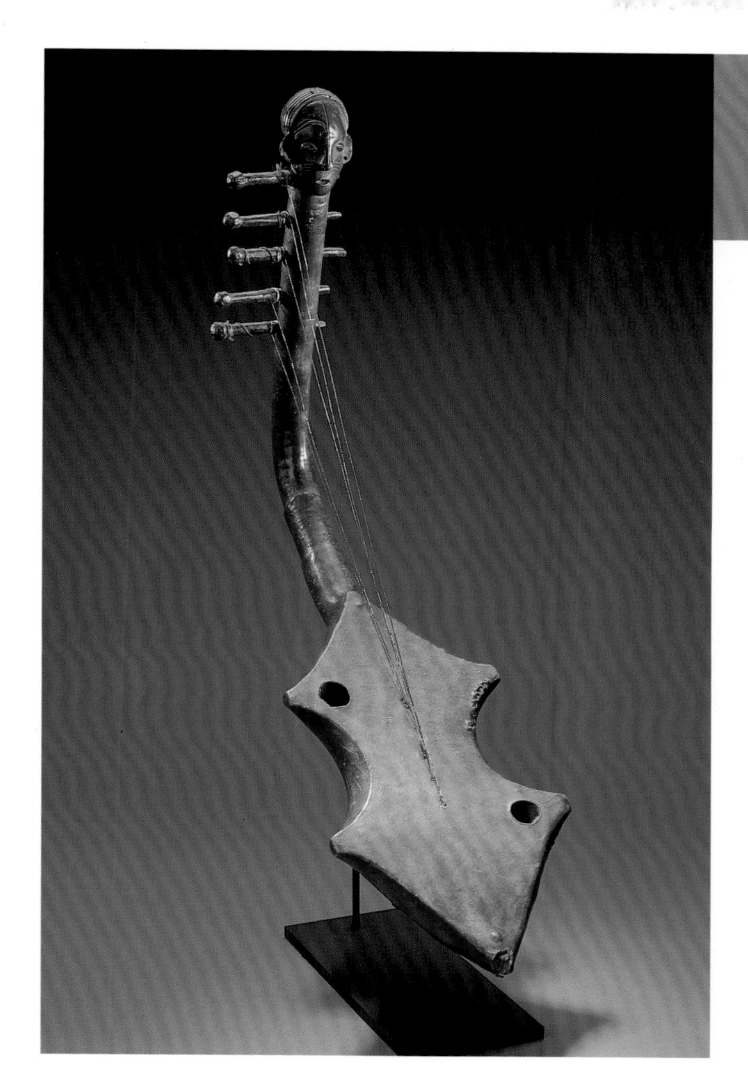

Catalog Number 72
Harp (*kundi*)
Zande peoples, Democratic Republic of the Congo
Wood, gut, leather
L: 66 cm
The Schorr Family Collection

Zande and Mangbetu harps (cat. nos. 72, 73, and 75) can be distinguished by the position of the tuning keys on the neck of the harp: Zande harps have the keys on the left of the neck while Mangbetu ones have the keys on the right. Harps have a longer history among the Zande than their Mangbetu neighbors, who adopted them in the late nineteenth century. While the Zande continue to use harps, they have disappeared from Mangbetu musical ensembles.

Among the Zande, troubadours play harps. An early European account records one harp performer who played for twenty-four hours without stopping except to drink and eat (Schweinfurth 1875, 2: 28). Because Zande musicians depend on their dress and harp to draw an audience, the harps are beautifully decorated.

Harps once owned by Mangbetu court musicians incorporate valuable materials such as ivory or elaborate carvings. On many Mangbetu harps, like catalog number 75, the neck is the full figure of a woman. Scholars suggest that figurative sculpture became pronounced early in the colonial period. Mangbetu elders today claim that figures like this represent Queen Nenzima, who was chief adviser to four kings between 1875 and 1926. (Demolin 1990, 198, 208; Miller 1990, 214; Laurenty 1997, 79-81; Schildkrout and Keim 1990).

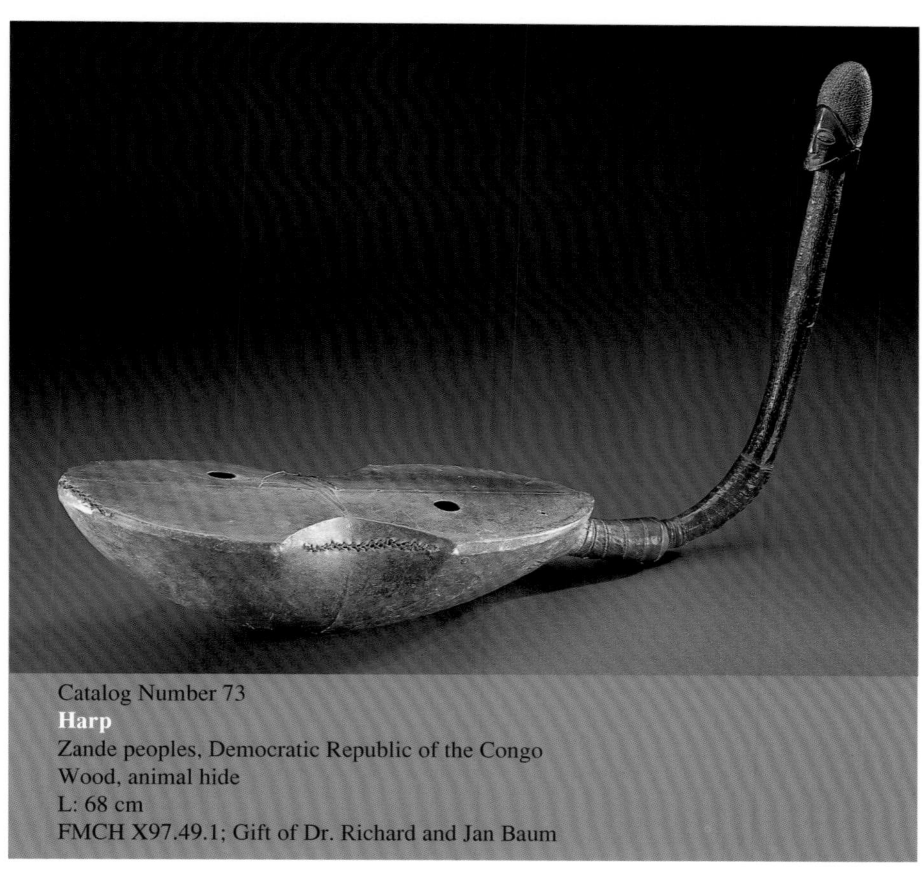

Catalog Number 73
Harp
Zande peoples, Democratic Republic of the Congo
Wood, animal hide
L: 68 cm
FMCH X97.49.1; Gift of Dr. Richard and Jan Baum

Catalog Number 74
Chordaphone (*kalambete* or *kakosh*)
Holo peoples, Democratic Republic of the Congo
Wood, metal, tacks
H: 49.5 cm
FMCH X86.1119; Gift of Helen and Dr. Robert Kuhn

This was originally a two-stringed instrument, with the strings emerging from the mouth and positioned over a soundboard to a bridge, now missing. It could be played at many sorts of events (Laurenty 1997, 92-94).

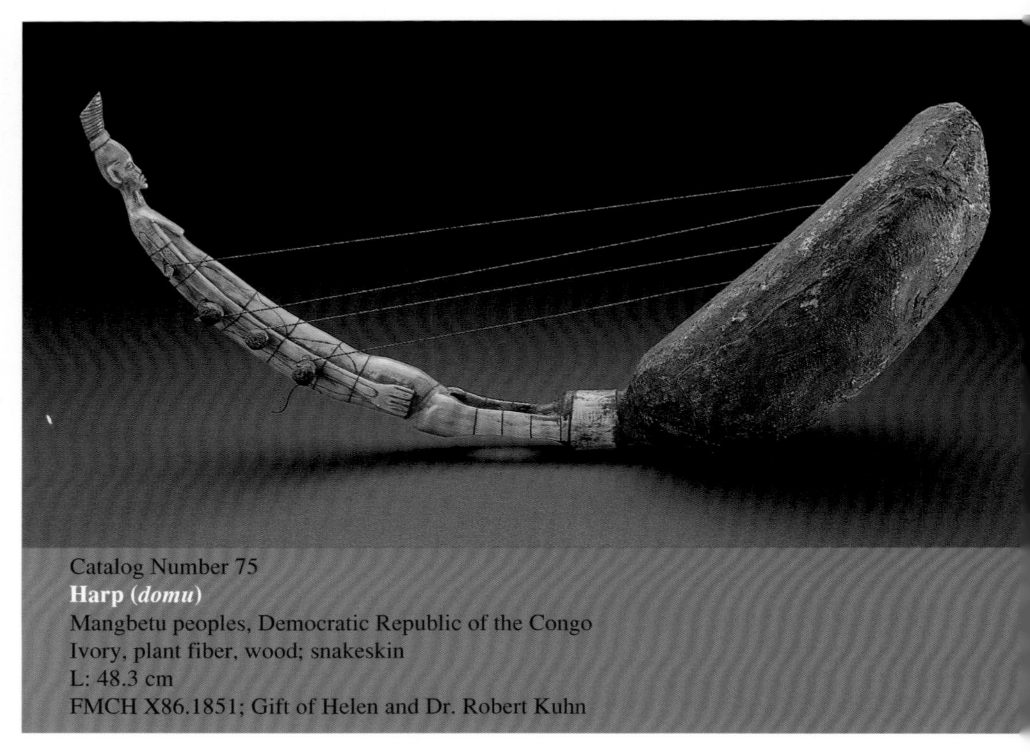

Catalog Number 75
Harp (*domu*)
Mangbetu peoples, Democratic Republic of the Congo
Ivory, plant fiber, wood; snakeskin
L: 48.3 cm
FMCH X86.1851; Gift of Helen and Dr. Robert Kuhn

Catalog Number 76
Lyre (*kissar*)
Tambura peoples, Sudan
Wood, beads, textile, hide, horn
H: 73.7 cm
FMCH X65.5526; Gift of the Wellcome Trust

Tambura musicians often played lyres like this one, accompanied by drums in rituals designed to rid a person of an afflicting spirit (Tobert 1996, 132; see Racy this volume).

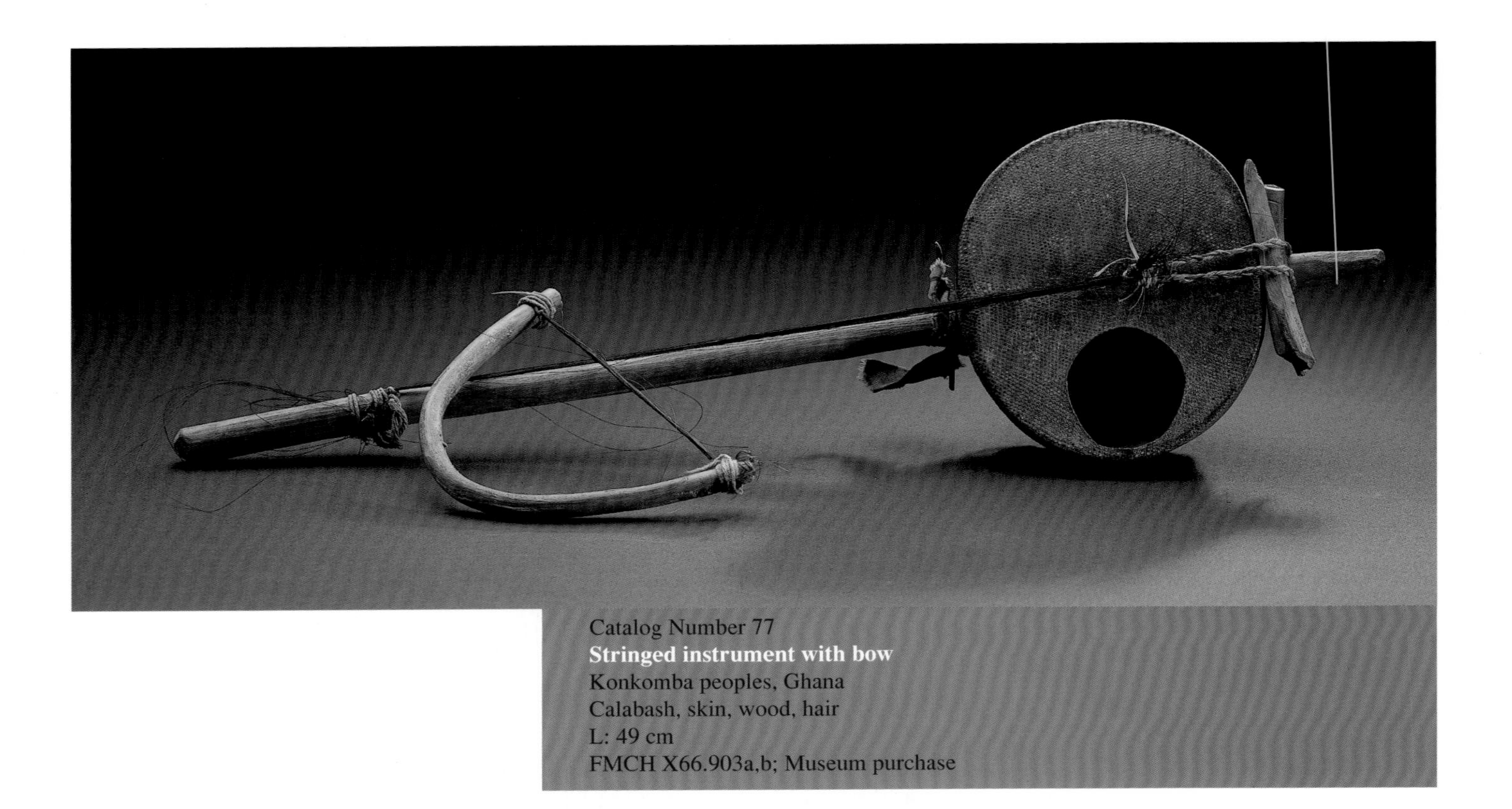

Catalog Number 77
Stringed instrument with bow
Konkomba peoples, Ghana
Calabash, skin, wood, hair
L: 49 cm
FMCH X66.903a,b; Museum purchase

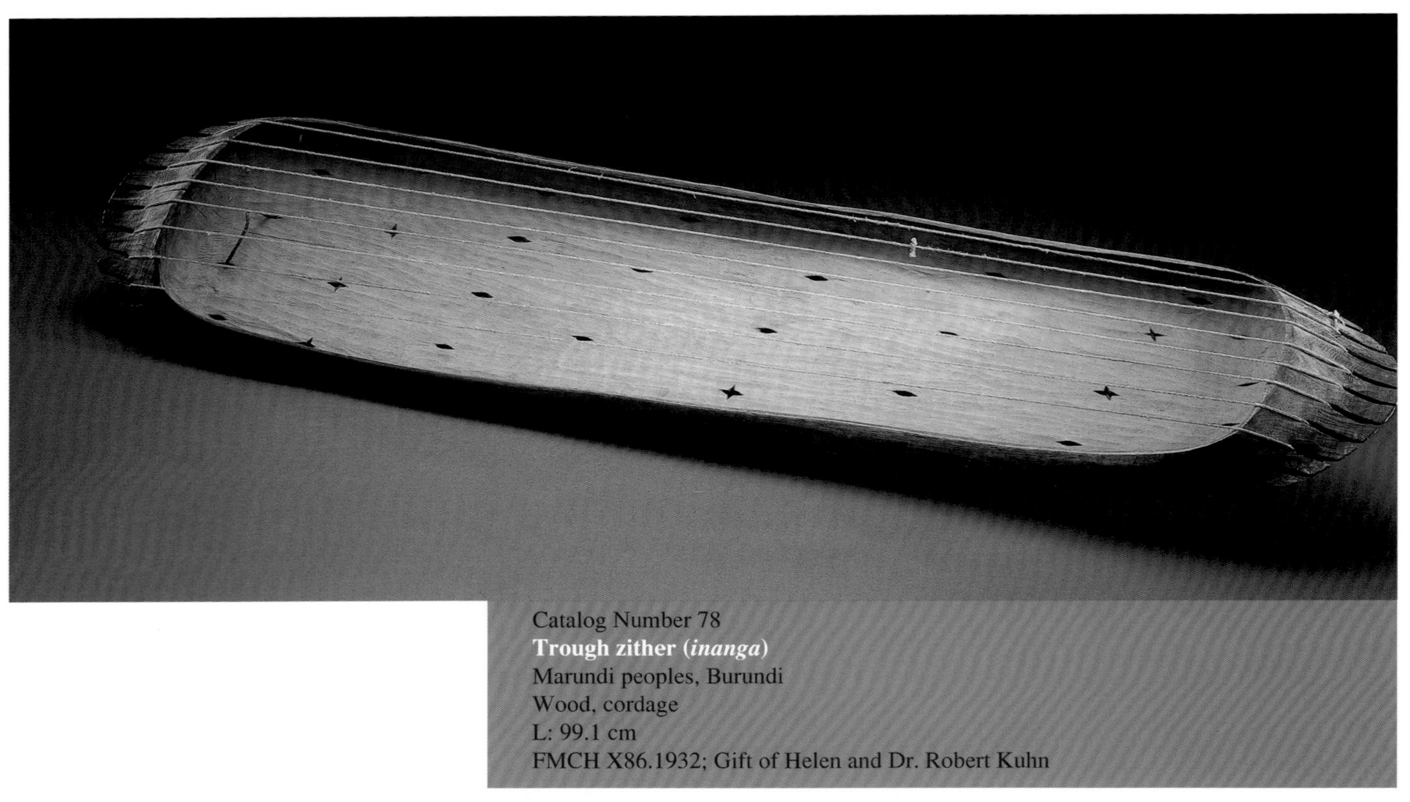

Catalog Number 78
Trough zither (*inanga*)
Marundi peoples, Burundi
Wood, cordage
L: 99.1 cm
FMCH X86.1932; Gift of Helen and Dr. Robert Kuhn

This stringed instrument is played by men to accompany pleasurable vocal performances. Often called "whispered singing," zither music is intimate and is played in the evening for small groups of friends (see Fales 1998).

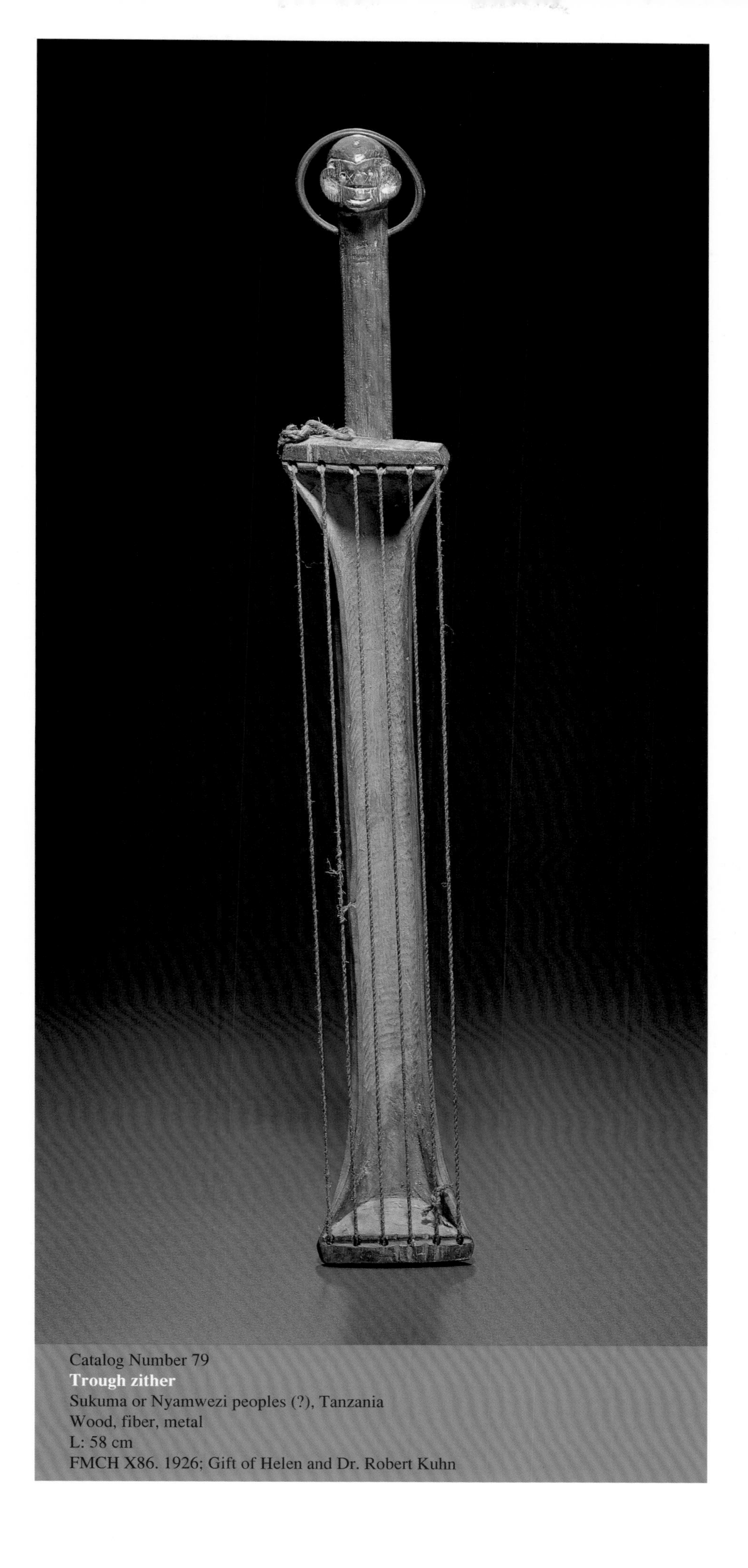

Catalog Number 79
Trough zither
Sukuma or Nyamwezi peoples (?), Tanzania
Wood, fiber, metal
L: 58 cm
FMCH X86. 1926; Gift of Helen and Dr. Robert Kuhn

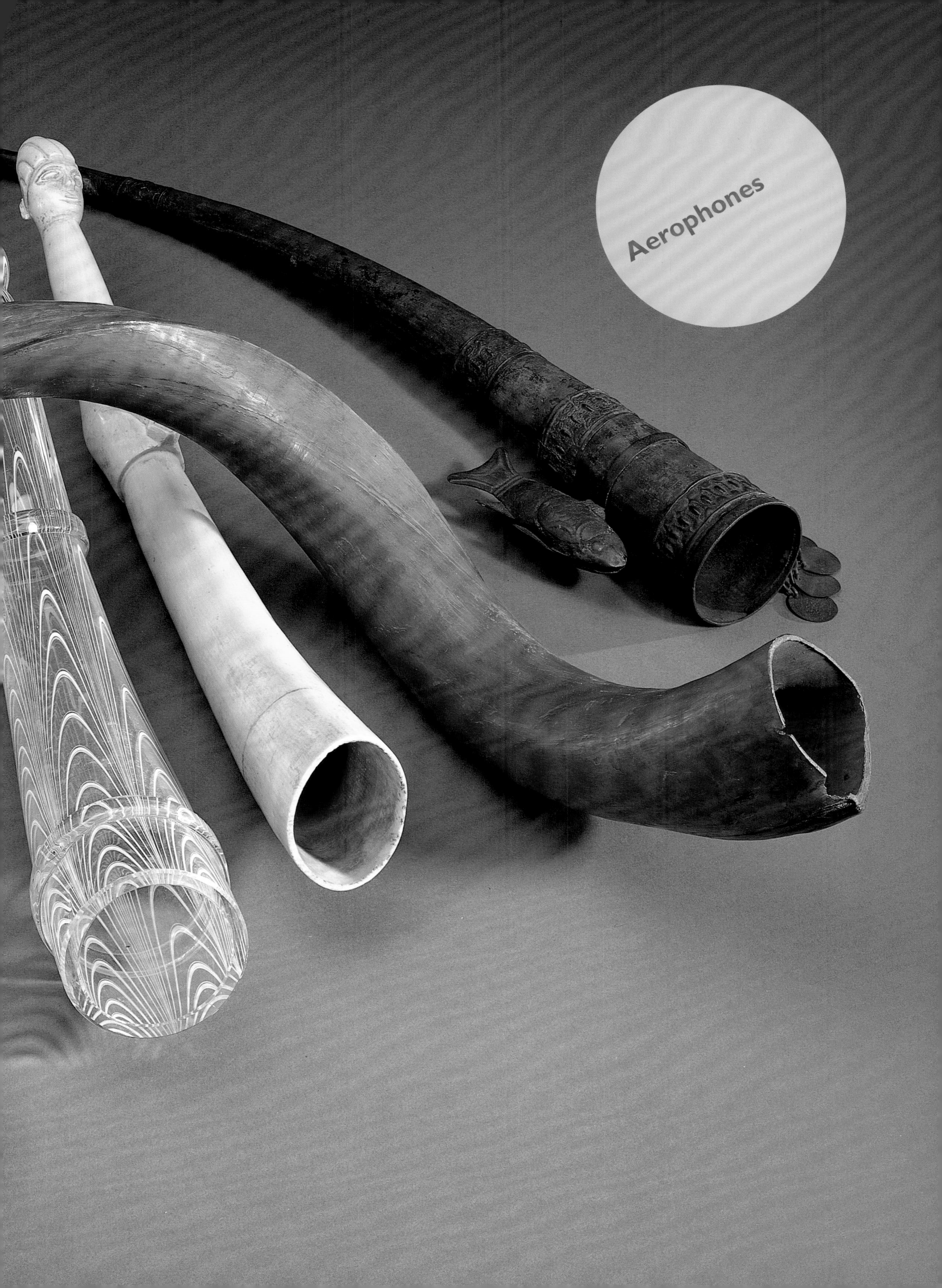
Aerophones

Catalog Number 80
Whistle
Gurunsi peoples
Burkina Faso or Ghana
Wood, string
H: 43.7
FMCH X74.1318; Gift of
Dr. and Mrs. Joel Breman

Catalog Number 81
Whistle
Gurunsi or Frafra peoples,
Burkina Faso or Ghana
Wood
H: 52 cm
FMCH X87.1630; Bequest of
Mary Stansbury Ruiz

Catalog Number 82
Whistle
Bamenda peoples, Cameroon
Wood
H: 22.9 cm
Collection of Leonard Ezra Kalina

Among Bamenda peoples, orchestras of whistles like these play for a special dance called *ndong*. Men and women participate in *ndong* on special occasions, such as a bride's arrival at her new home (Kreamer and Geary, 1989, 170).

Catalog Number 83
Whistle
Nuna peoples, Burkina Faso
Wood
H: 35 cm
The Schorr Family Collection

Whistles or flutes are played in ensembles of instruments during Nuna initiations and funerals, at athletic events, and as signals for hunting and war. While other musical instruments are restricted by ritual roles, any man may play these instruments (Roy 1987, 81–89).

Catalog Number 84
Whistle
Nuna peoples, Burkina Faso
Wood
H: 11.2 cm
Herbert and Lenore Schorr

Men participating in farming contests carry small whistles like this. The first man to finish weeding a given area blows his whistle and wins the contest (Roy 1987, 82).

Catalog Number 85
Whistle
Chokwe peoples,
Democratic Republic of the Congo
Wood
L: 10.5 cm
FMCH X86.1866; Gift of Helen and
Dr. Robert Kuhn

According to Manuel Jordán, the projecting crown on this whistle associates it with royalty. Such whistles are usually carved in male and female pairs with their respective low and high "voices" considered those of the ancestors (1998, fig. 45).

Catalog Number 86
Whistle
Chokwe peoples,
Democratic Republic of the Congo
Wood
H: 12 cm
FMCH X86.1864; Gift of Helen and
Dr. Robert Kuhn

To Chokwe people, the sounds of these whistles are the voices of ancestors, yet whistles may be blown to request that the ancestors help in many different situations: warriors ask for the ancestors' protection while using the whistles to signal to each other during battle; chiefs and other royal dignitaries use whistles to demonstrate that they have the ancestors' support and approval. The ancestors, through these same whistles, call prey so that hunters can catch them.

This whistle portrays a masquerade character named Chikunza, an ancestral spirit responsible for human fertility and success in hunting. The figure's beard, usually found on the masquerade character Chihongo, further associates the whistle with Chihongo's power, wealth, and royalty (Jordán 1998, figs. 131–32).

Catalog Number 87
Whistle
Yaka peoples,
Democratic Republic of the Congo
Wood
H: 13.3 cm
FMCH X86.1865; Gift of Helen and
Dr. Robert Kuhn

Yaka hunters blow whistles or flutes to inform the community of an upcoming hunt. While in the forest, men use whistles to communicate amongst themselves (Bourgeois 1984, 87–90). Whistles are also blown during some rituals, such as when a farmer asks the ancestors to protect his field or a community searches for a thief (Biebuyck 1985, 196). While identified as a Yaka whistle, the style is ambiguous. One head has an upturned nose seen on Yaka *nkhanda* masks; the other head more closely resembles Suku figures and masks.

Catalog Number 88
Sculpture from top of dniker horn whistle
Kongo peoples,
Democratic Republic of the Congo
Wood
H: 12.9 cm
Collection of Saul and Marsha Stanoff

This small sculpture is the top of a dniker horn whistle from the diagnostic equipment of a Kongo *ng'anga* (healer or diviner). After examining a client, the *ng'anga* plays the whistle and contemplates appropriate medicines and treatments. He might compose a verse to strengthen the power of the medicines. An *ng'anga* could possess a set of whistles with different sculptures representing a variety of problems. The problem this sculpture addresses is unclear (Soderberg 1966).

Catalog Number 89
Whistle
Pende peoples,
Democratic Republic of the Congo
Ivory
H: 5.7 cm
FMCH X86.1896; Gift of Helen and Dr. Robert Kuhn

In Central Africa, whistles are versatile instruments. Musicians play whistles during rituals and ceremonies, masquerade performances, and for entertainment. Whistles can be played in orchestras of drums and xylophones. Whistles are often worn on a thong around the neck, resulting in lustrous patinas like that of this ivory example. Pende whistles may have been played in battle or during masquerades (De Sousberghe 1959, 86, 158, 159, and figs. 132–48) or in ensembles of ivory trumpets, iron gongs, and drums that accompanied the building of a chief's ritual house or played on other important occasions (Biebuyck 1985, 246).

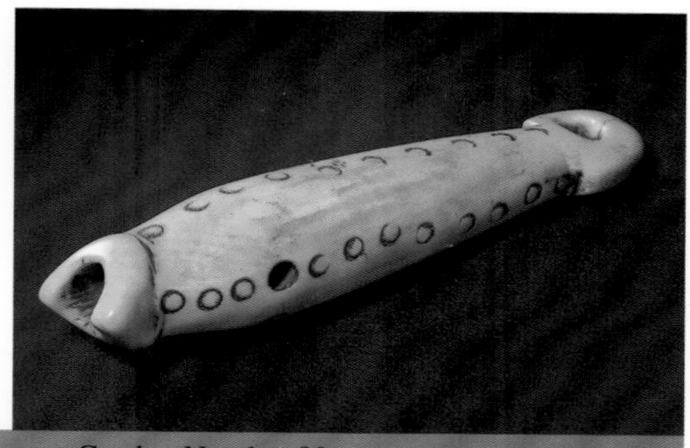

Catalog Number 90
Whistle
Lega peoples,
Democratic Republic of the Congo
Ivory
H: 12 cm
FMCH X86.1892; Gift of Helen and Dr. Robert Kuhn

Lega whistles have multiple uses and meanings depending on the context in which they appear. During Bwami initiations, they may be blown to prevent rainfall. The lead singer during initiations may also use an ivory whistle to give instructions or sing praises. In divination, whistles may refer to malevolent people who use the sound of the whistle to lure their victims away from populated areas. The sound of a whistle can also allow a diviner to identify the guilty (Biebuyck 1986, 201).

Catalog Number 91
Horn
Unidentified peoples, Africa
Brass
L: 30.5 cm
FMCH X86.1916; Gift of Helen and Dr. Robert Kuhn

Catalog Number 92
Trumpet (*mulimu*)
Pere peoples, Democratic Republic of the Congo
Wood, metal
L: 106 cm
FMCH X86.1919; Gift of Helen and Dr. Robert Kuhn

Pere trumpets, generically called *mulimu*, are associated with the *nsindi* initiation, which is related to the Bwami association among Lega. During the initiation, teachers hold the trumpet and explain its anthropomorphic shape and meanings. Because the meanings are restricted to Pere initiated adults, little specific information about the trumpets appears in the literature (Biebuyck 1986, 248–49).

Catalog Number 93
Flute
Malinke peoples, Burkina Faso
Wood
L: 66 cm
FMCH X86.1918; Gift of Helen and Dr. Robert Kuhn

Catalog Number 94
Trumpet
Fon peoples, Republic of Benin
Copper
L: 56 cm
FMCH X87.137; Gift of Helen and Dr. Robert Kuhn

Trumpets such as this were once used in Fon rituals "to promote the reincarnation of royal children" and "during royal funerals and *huetanu* rites" (Blier 1998, 106). Fon arts often include ideographs that can be "read" or that refer to praise names of royal families or particularly storied individuals.

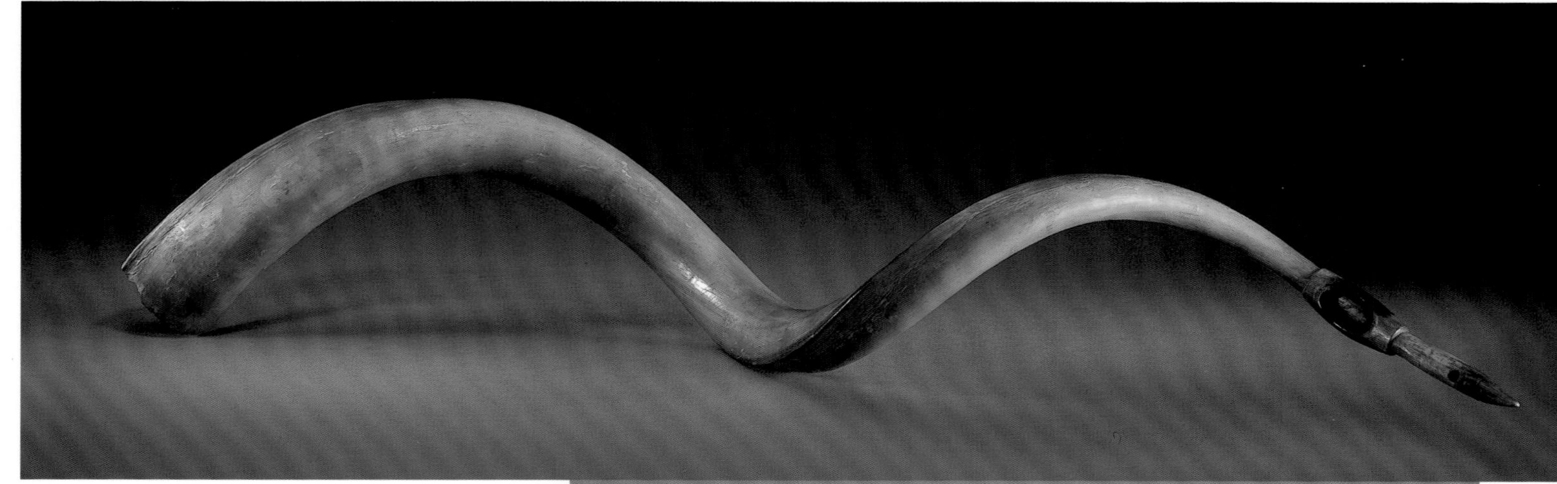

Catalog Number 95
Trumpet
Kilimanjaro region of Tanzania
Kudu horn
L: 89 cm
FMCH X65.2407; Gift of the Wellcome Trust

Side-blown trumpets fashioned from antelope horn are found in many parts of Africa and have been played in a rich variety of political, religious, and social contexts. More common than trumpets carved from elephant ivory, these made from antelope horn are typically not subject to many of the indigenous strictures that reserve ivory for the ruling elite. The loose spiral of this Kudu horn is a particularly dramatic form that may lend symbolic connotations to its music.

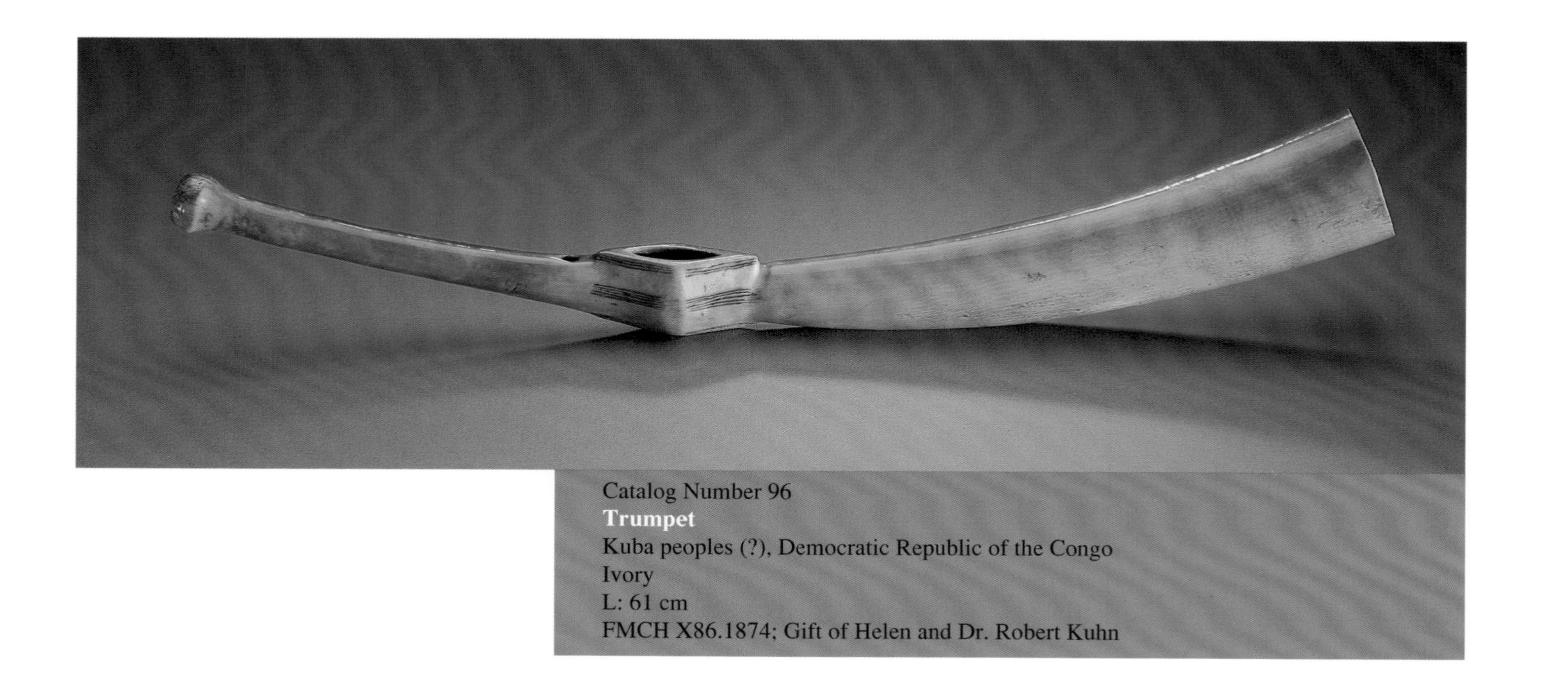

Catalog Number 96
Trumpet
Kuba peoples (?), Democratic Republic of the Congo
Ivory
L: 61 cm
FMCH X86.1874; Gift of Helen and Dr. Robert Kuhn

Catalog Number 97
Trumpet
Zande peoples, Democratic Republic of the Congo
Ivory
L: 12 cm
FMCH X85.455; Gift of Helen and Dr. Robert Kuhn

This ivory trumpet, or oliphant, is an example of a musical instrument commissioned by the Mangbetu royal court from Zande artists. It was played in the court and represents royal power and presence. Often trumpeting accompanied the king and his wife when they performed a dance called *mabolo*. Trumpets also announced the king's movements and his victories. Nowadays, Mangbetu elders claim that the face on many instruments, including ivory trumpets like this one, is a portrait of Queen Nenzima, the advisor to Mangbetu kings between 1875 and 1926 (Schildkrout and Keim 1990, 202–3).

Catalog Number 98
Trumpet
Lega peoples (?), Democratic Republic of the Congo
Ivory
L: 33 cm
FMCH X85.456; Gift of Helen and Dr. Robert Kuhn

Lega associate the elephant with power, leadership, and the Bwami society, whose members are conceptualized as "elephants" (Biebuyck 1976, 343). Members of *kindi*, the highest level of Bwami, are called *nenemulamba*, or "owners of ivory," and they claim ivory for their exclusive use (Biebuyck 1986, 40). In the past, members of Bwami blew ivory trumpets in preparation for battle or an elephant hunt, summoning an elephant's bravery (Biebuyck 1986, 199).

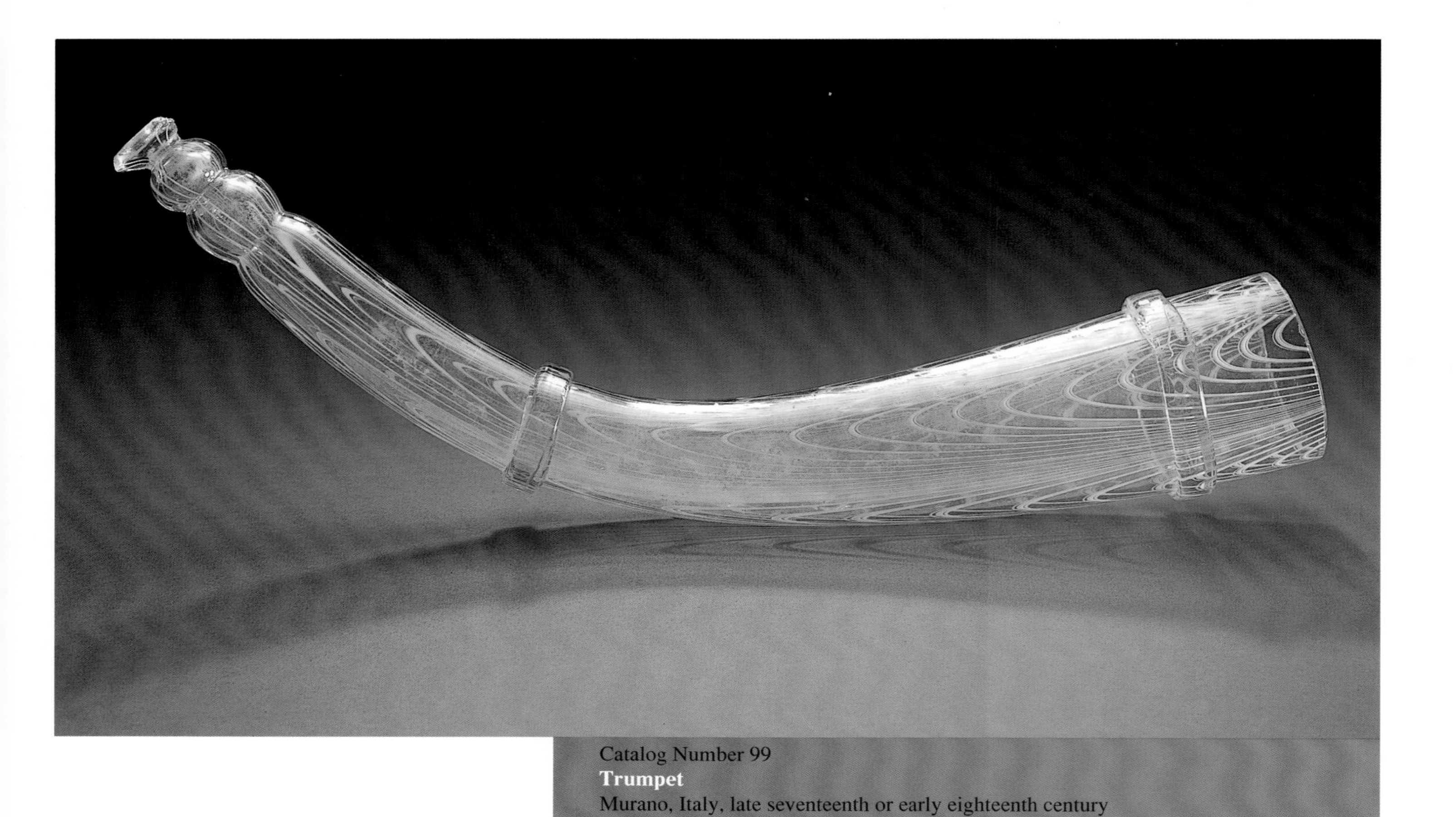

Catalog Number 99
Trumpet
Murano, Italy, late seventeenth or early eighteenth century
Glass
L: 43 cm
FMCH X97.26.1; Anonymous gift

From the seventeenth century to the nineteenth century, Italian blown-glass trumpets were traded into West Africa along with glass canes. Although extant examples are rare, they have been seen on shrines in the regalia of chiefs, and as the property of important merchants. The heirlooms of the nineteenth-century Kalabari leader John Bull, still held by his descendants, include a trumpet somewhat similar to this one but with a more pronounced flare (personal communication from Jo Anne Eicher). Another glass trumpet is in the collection of the J. Paul Getty Museum (Bremer-David 1993, 222).

Catalog Number 100
Hunting horn
Temne/ Bullom peoples, Sierra Leone
Ivory, metal
L: 63.5 cm
Walt Disney-Tishman African Art Collection;
photograph by Jerry L. Thompson

This hunting horn was commissioned from a Bullom or Temne artist by European patrons. It depicts scenes of a European hunt, including men blowing similar horns, men holding dogs, the hunt itself, and successful hunters returning with their kill. Along the bottom of the horn are the royal arms of Portugal and the personal arms of Isabella and Ferdinand V of Spain. Who actually commissioned the horn remains unclear, but William Fagg (1981, 67) suggested that it might have been a present for the wedding of King Manuel I of Portugal to one of the daughters of Ferdinand V of Spain.

Catalog Number 101
Trumpet
Fang peoples (?), Gabon
Wood, hide, fiber
L: 70 cm
FMCH X86.1121; Gift of Helen and Dr. Robert Kuhn

Catalog Number 102
Flute
Malinke peoples, Burkina Faso
Wood, felt, fur, cowrie shell, coins, cord
H: 34.5 cm
FMCH X86.1921; Gift of Helen and Dr. Robert Kuhn

Catalog Number 103
Trumpet
Pende peoples, Democratic Republic of the Congo
Wood, metal, hide
L: 107 cm
FMCH X86.1930; Gift of Helen and Dr. Robert Kuhn

The relief carving on the bell of this trumpet depicts a man wearing a long coat and holding a bow and arrow. A dog faces the man. It is possible this instrument was played in the context of hunting.

Catalog Number 104
Trumpet (*tawong*)
Mambila peoples, Nigeria
Wood, pigment
L: 46.5 cm
FMCH X91.351; Gift of Helen and Dr. Robert Kuhn

Catalog Number 105
Trumpet (*mulimu*)
Pere peoples, Democratic Republic of the Congo
Wood
H: 93 cm
Private Collection, Los Angeles

Tawong trumpets appear in pairs (male and female). They are played at the biannual dances of harvest and planting, periods of diversion when men travel to other villages to participate in sporting events and to renew friendships. According to Gilbert Schneider, "the *tawong* also" begins a period of some license among the Mambila. The young unmarried people are allowed freedom of sexual experimentation, and the time for pairing off is at hand. After the dances there is usually a period during which marriages take place, before all efforts are again devoted to farming (Schneider n.d., 14 15).

Catalog Number 106
Trumpet
Tigong peoples, Cameroon
Wood
H: 49 cm
W. and U. Horstmann Collection;
photograph courtesy of Udo Horstmann

Membranophones

Catalog Number 107
Drum and drumstick
Omdurman, Sudan (?)
Copper, hide
Diam: 38.1 cm
FMCH X65.1708a,b; Gift of the Wellcome Trust

Although its origins are undocumented, this "kettle" drum shares many traits consistent with the metalwork of Omdurman. The Arabic inscription on the drum states that the drum was the "property of Shahin Muhammad 1282 [1865 C.E.]."

Catalog Number 108
Drum (*a-ndëf*)
Baga peoples, Guinea
Wood, hide, pigment
H: 94.6 cm
FMCH X86.1911; Gift of Helen and Dr. Robert Kuhn

Caryatid drums called *a-ndëf* are owned and used by Baga women's important ritual, political, and social societies. Motherhood is a principal criterion for entry. Women play this type of drum at their ceremonies, and its music lets residents of both the supernatural and mundane worlds know about the ceremony. The songs and iconography of individual drums tell of women's power, parenting, and problems in the community.

This sculpture depicts a woman carrying a drum on her head. Women "carry" Baga society. The figure holds a hoe and a cooking spoon in her hands, referring to the constant work that women must do to maintain homes and provide food for their families (Lamp 1996, 122–30).

Catalog Number 109
Drum
Baule peoples, Côte d'Ivoire
Wood, hide, pigment, metal, glass
H: 35.6 cm
FMCH X85.461; Gift of Helen and Dr. Robert Kuhn

Catalog Number 110
Drum
Baule peoples, Côte d'Ivoire
Wood, hide, pigment
H: 62.2 cm
FMCH X85.464; Gift of Helen and Dr. Robert Kuhn

This drum portrays a monkey and may be connected with Mbra, a spirit that is instrumental to one form of trance divination. Mbra provides protection, ensures good health, and helps people to succeed in hunting and farming (Vogel 1997, 224).

Catalog Number 111
***Ntan* drum**
Carved by Osei Bonsu, 1935
Asante peoples, Abofo, Ghana
Wood, pigment
H: 111.7 cm
FMCH X78.136; Gift of Donald Suggs

This instrument was once the principal drum and visual focus of an Asante popular band called *ntan*, one of a number of Akan bands whose music and dance styles have come and gone over the years. The drum is often identified as the "mother" of the group, and the relief carvings represent proverbs about Asante life and culture. These and related bands once provided secular, primarily non-royal, entertainment on a wide variety of occasions including the naming of babies, female puberty celebrations, weddings, the installation of chiefs, and local and national festivals. Funerals were once one of the most important performing contexts, and many musicians and dancers joined these recreational groups to assure a proper send-off at their own funerals (see Ross 1984; 1988).

Catalog Number 112
***Ntan* drum**
Carved by Osei Bonsu, circa 1935
Asante peoples, Ghana
Wood, fiber, pigment
H: 106 cm
Private Collection, Los Angeles

This drum, like catalog number 111, was carved by the famed Asante carver Osei Bonsu and served as the principal drum of a popular band called *ntan*. Both drums have female breasts because such a drum is seen as the "mother of the group"—its focus and gathering point. Like other drums by Bonsu, the relief carvings on the surface represent conventionalized sayings drawn from the enormous corpus of Akan oral literature—proverbs, riddles, boasts, insults, folktales, etc. (see Cole and Ross 1977, 170–76; Ross 1984).

Catalog Number 113
Drum
Carved circa 1920
Fante peoples, Ghana
Wood, hide, pigment
H: 94 cm
FMCH X85.321; Gift of Clayre and Jay Haft

Catalog Number 114
Drum
Fante peoples, Ghana
Wood, resin, wire
H: 62.5 cm
FMCH X89.79; Gift of Helen and Dr. Robert Kuhn

This instrument was once the "master"/"mother" drum of a Fante popular band. Each group was identified with a distinctive style of music and dance, much like popular bands in Euro-American traditions. The large female figure on the front of this drum represents Queen Victoria, whose image continued to play an active role in West African popular culture many years after her death.

Catalog Number 115
Drum
Fante peoples, Ghana
Wood, fiber, skin
H: 71 cm
Private Collection, Los Angeles

Catalog Number 116
Drum
Akan peoples, Ghana
Wood, metal, hide
H: 51 cm
FMCH X83.333; Museum Purchase with Manus Funds

Brass-covered drums are relatively rare in Akan expressive culture. Nketia illustrates a pair of brass-covered *atumpan* drums (1963, pl. 19), which as of 1998 were on display at the Manhyia Palace Museum, Kumase. Herbert M. Cole photographed a drum quite similar to the present example at the Odwira festival in Akuropong in 1972 (see Ross and Garrard 1983, fig. 129). The brass on this instrument was undoubtedly worked by the same artists who produced the Akan sheet-brass containers called *forowa* and the rattle illustrated in catalog number 29. Aside from the Odwira association, it is not clear what other musical contexts utilized these brass-covered instruments.

Catalog Number 117
Tension drum
Dan peoples, Liberia
Wood, hide, cord
L: 49 cm
FMCH X86.1906a,b; Gift of Helen and Dr. Robert Kuhn

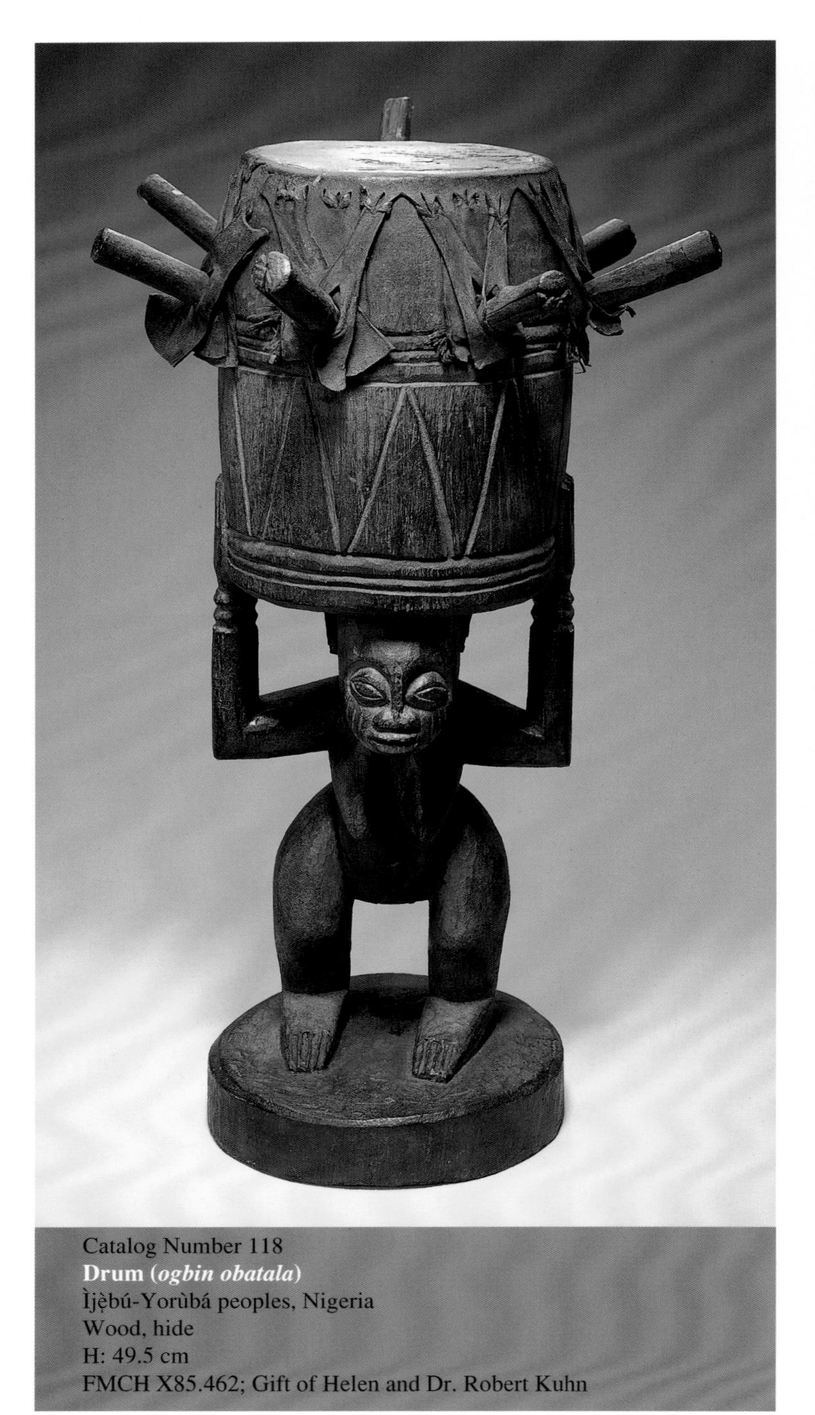

Catalog Number 118
Drum (*ogbin obatala*)
Ìjẹ̀bú-Yorùbá peoples, Nigeria
Wood, hide
H: 49.5 cm
FMCH X85.462; Gift of Helen and Dr. Robert Kuhn

Catalog Number 119
Royal drum (*gbedu*)
Yorùbá peoples, Nigeria
Wood, tin, nails
Dia.: 44.5 cm
FMCH X86.1857a-k; Gift of Helen and Dr. Robert Kuhn

Royal drums called *gbedu* are played during annual rites of rulership. Groups of Yorùbá royal drums are played for the king. Like other lead royal drums (*iya ilu*), this example's motif is a mudfish, symbol of Olukun, the source of wealth and power (personal communication from Henry J. Drewal, 1999; 1989, 132).

Catalog Number 120
Oshugbo society drum (*agba oshugbo*)
Carved by Bandele in 1947
Yorùbá peoples, Ushi-Ekiti area, Nigeria
Wood, hide, pigment
H: 116.5 cm
FMCH X86.2973; Gift of Helen and Dr. Robert Kuhn

This drum, called *agba oshugbo*, was part of a set of drums used by the Oshugbo society to call members to meetings and let the community know of the announcements of upcoming decisions (personal communication from Henry J. Drewal, 1999). The Oshugbo society in Usi-Ekiti commissioned this drum from the artist Bandele for their *iledi*, or meeting place. It was delivered in 1947. The Oshugbo asked for specific motifs to appear on the drum, including a Sango priest holding a rattle and staff. Other motifs show scenes of everyday life including drummers and soldiers (Carroll 1967, fig. 71).

Catalog Number 121
Drum (*ngoma* or *mukupela*)
Chokwe peoples, Democratic Republic of the Congo
Wood, hide, fiber; resin
H: 54 cm
FMCH X85.463a,b; Gift of Helen and Dr. Robert Kuhn

The Chokwe and their neighbors refer to ceremonies in general as "playing the drums." Hourglass-shaped drums like this one were reserved for performances associated with chiefs and, although they could be used at any event, they were identified with Mukanda, the men's initiation society. The face on the side of this drum represents Mwana wa Pwo, a masquerade character representing a young woman who appears in the communities during men's initiations to dance or "play" with the women (Boone 1951, 56; Bastin 1982, 245).

Catalog Number 122
Drum
Luba peoples, Democratic Republic of the Congo
Wood, hide, metal; snakeskin; bamboo
H: 52 cm
FMCH X86.1114; Gift of Helen and Dr. Robert Kuhn

In some Luba areas, there is a close connection between drumming and kingship. The Luba epic tells of a plot by the tyrant king Nkongolo Mwamba to kill his obstreperous nephew Kalala Ilunga. As a trap Nkongolo prepared a large hole filled with upright spears and covered it with a mat. Then he invited Kalala Ilunga to dance before him on the mat. A diviner learned of Nkongolo's duplicitousness and arranged for a drummer to warn Kalala Ilunga with coded rhythms. Kalala eventually defeated Nkongolo and founded the present dynasty. Since his time, royal drums have been played at an enthronement, a king's funeral, or when the Mbudye association sings the kingdom's history. The caryatid female figure represents the king's ancestors and reminds that women are powerful guardians of the knowledge and power of the king (Roberts and Roberts 1996).

Catalog Number 123
Drum
Punu peoples (?), Ngounie River area, Gabon
Wood, hide, pigment
H: 34.2 cm
FMCH X85.465; Gift of Helen and Dr. Robert Kuhn

The three faces on this drum look like *mukudj* masks of the Punu peoples. Alisa LaGamma (1997) convincingly argues that the Punu prominently display this type of mask as "a collective ethnic emblem" in an area of ethnic diversity where being Punu can be politically and economically important. With the *mukudj* masks boldly displayed on the side of this drum, the artist assured that the audience easily identified the musicians as Punu. Leon Siroto (1995, 46) suggests that all drums of this type are by a single unnamed carver and cautions against associating the drum with the performance of the masks depicted on it.

Catalog Number 124
Drum (*ngoma*)
Vili peoples, Democratic Republic of the Congo
Wood, hide, glass, pigment
H: 92.4 cm
FMCH X87.107; Gift of Helen and Dr. Robert Kuhn

Vili associate drums with the presence and voice of ancestors. When an ancestor overcomes a drum, the drum is said to play without human intervention. As a sign of this miraculous occurrence, snakes circle the drum (Fu-Kiau as cited by Thompson 1989, 41). Vili healers and diviners (*ng'anga*) own and use drums in their healing ceremonies, but they can also be played during other important occasions by a drummer with special training about how to respect the ancestral spirit inhabiting the drum (Thompson 1989, 43–44).

Catalog Number 125
Drum
Makonde peoples, Mozambique or Tanzania
Wood, hide, copper, pigment
H: 63 cm
U. and W. Horstmann Collection;
photograph courtesy of Udo Horstmann

Makonde peoples use drums, called *likuti*, to communicate with neighboring towns. One drumbeat might signal a threat such as an attack or a nearby leopard. It has been suggested that since this drum has been anthropomorphized with a female shape, it was used for women's rituals or ceremonies (Kingdon 1996, 174).

Catalog Number 126
Drum (*bulup*)
Kuba peoples, Democratic Republic of the Congo
Wood, metal, leather
H: 79 cm
FMCH X86.1124; Gift of Helen and Dr. Robert Kuhn

Catalog Number 127
Dance drum (*bulup*)
Kuba peoples, Democratic Republic of the Congo
Wood, hide, fiber
H: 111.8 cm
FMCH X86.1913; Gift of Helen and Dr. Robert Kuhn

Each Kuba town has a set of dance drums that are played for entertainment and for ceremonial occasions (cat. nos. 126–129). The decoration on the drums reflects the wealth and prestige of a given community. The handle in the shape of a hand on catalog number 128 is both a visual pun (the drummer's hand and the drum's hand) and a reference to Iyol, the society of soldiers. To join Iyol in the past, a man had to kill an enemy and bring proof to the town council in the form of a severed hand (Boone 1951, 44; Vansina 1978, 377–78).

Catalog Number 128
Drum (*bulup*)
Kuba peoples, Democratic Republic of the Congo
Wood, metal, skin
H: 75 cm
W. and U. Horstmann Collection;
photograph by A + L Ottiger/ Zug, Switzerland

Catalog Number 129
Dance drum (*bulup*)
Kuba peoples, Democratic Republic of the Congo
Wood, leather, metal, raffia
H: 76 cm
Collection of Diane and Ernie Wolfe III

Notes to the Text

Introduction

1. The only people who do not have extensive fieldwork experience on the topics for which they have written essays are the students (Kimasi Browne, Leigh Creighton, and Victoria Simmons) who took my course Seminar in African Music at UCLA in spring 1996, at which time the theme for the course was African musical instruments. Students were invited to submit their essays for inclusion in the volume.

2. Recently, several scholars (historian Edward Alpers and ethnomusicologists Nazir Jairazbhoy and Amy Catlin) at UCLA have been conducting interdisciplinary research on the musical impact of the trans-Indian slave trade on cultures in Asia. On recent field trips to India, Jairazbhoy and Catlin, who are both specialists on Indian music, have discovered musical instruments, events, and terminology that they are able to trace to East Africa. Historian Alpers is using music to explain the presence of African elements in social and political institutions in the Asian world.

3. The research that investigators are pursuing today differs from the work of A. M. Jones (1969; 1971), a prolific scholar who led the debate on the African-Indonesian connection. Whereas Jones emphasized the influence of Southeast Asians on Africa as a result of their migration to the African continent, scholars today are looking at the movements and activities of Africans in Asia and the resultant impact of African culture on the eastern part of the world.

4. See works by Brown, Evans, Holloway, Maultsby, Nketia, and Wilson for some of the scholars who have focused on Africanisms in the Americas.

5. In Los Angeles, Zaire-born Ricardo Lemvo, who grew up listening and performing Kongolese music (which has much Cuban influence) has become very popular among many Latin groups in the Americas. So we have a syncretic Afro-Latin sound (formed on the African continent) now influencing the culture from which this transformed sound was developed. The mother (Africa) reintroduced the language (music) back into the culture of her offspring. They are familiar with some of the language but have lost some. So contact with the mother tongue brings great excitement to the offspring. David Gould (1999), a graduate student in ethnomusicology at UCLA, wrote a paper on Lemvo for a seminar on African music that I gave in spring 1999.

Chapter 1

1. I employ a hyphen for ethnic names in Bantu languages where a plural prefix has been dropped, e.g., -Yao, -Kwangari, etc. The previous tendency was to omit prefixes both singular and plural without any indication that this had been done. This practice was productive of confusion and error, e.g., the Vamakonde people sometimes appeared in literature as Makonde and sometimes as Konde.

Chapter 2

1. In Côte d'Ivoire, the evening news is announced and closed by the sound of xylophones (personal observation, 1990–1991); in Ghana the xylophone opens and closes the news, which is broadcast in the northern languages (personal communication with S. Obeng, 1996); and in Burkina Faso, the national news used the xylophone music of Nani Pale in the same way from the 1960s to the 1980s (Fieloux and Lombard 1993).

2. Since Mali's independence, it is against the law to publish exact figures of ethnic populations within the country. The reason for this is that political leaders believe that the identification of Mali's population by ethnicity encourages ethnic tension and competition as opposed to the desired spirit of national identity.

3. The history of the Lobi people of northern Ghana and southern Burkina Faso presents a fascinating account of this phenomenon. The Lobi people actually include several small ethnic groups, such as the Birifor, Dagara, Lobi, Dian, Gan, Wile, and Pougouli. Ironically, most of the historical information that has been acquired about these people was from European colonial administrators' published works, personal diaries, and photos from the early 1900s. Henri Labouret, the most widely cited of these men, wrote several articles and books about the Lobi from 1916 to 1958, his most famous being *Les tribus du rameau Lobi* (1931). Labouret is reportedly responsible for having finally "pacified" and "conquered" the Lobi after several administrators had failed to do so before him, and it was also Labouret who decided that the term "Lobi" would include all of the above-mentioned ethnic groups in the area.

   According to Jeanne-Marie Kambou-Ferrand (1993), this decision to establish a new ethnic group was based on the fact that the Lobi people (or what is now considered the "pure" Lobi who speak Lobili, Miwaw, or LoWilisi) were the most "savage" and "uncivilized." Since there were too many different ethnic groups and languages in this area for the colonial administrators to keep track of, they needed to create a new basis of categorization and identification. Thus, they divided and identified people according to their esteemed level, or stage of "civilization."

4. The Mande are known in the world music scene for their *griots*—such as Salif Keita and Toumani Diabate—who sing with the xylophone and the *kora* (a harp lute). Although Voltaic xylophone music is rarely found in the world music market, traditional dance and musical theater groups like Farafina, Les Danseurs Logwe, and Kakraba Lobi's Dance Ensemble are popular in Western Europe and Japan.

5. The people who live in the Voltaic region speak a variety of languages, notably Mande and Voltaic-Gur. So two or more language groups exist in this region.

6. This is particularly interesting in terms of ethnicity, because it is an example of how porous ethnicity can be in some areas. The Minyanka in Mali have a different system in which xylophonists learn to play. The Minyanka define themselves as cousins of the Bambara, and they share several religious, social, and agricultural practices with their northern Mande neighbors. They are also eastern neighbors to the Senufo, an important Voltaic group that dwells in northern Côte d'Ivoire, and have assimilated many aspects of Senufo artistic and musical culture. Thus much of their repertoire and performance practice is Bambara (Mande) in nature, while their rules about xylophone players are closer to Senufo (Voltaic) music culture.

7. Beating is an acoustic phenomenon that results when two tones sounding simultaneously produce a third, independent tone. When tones of nearly equal frequency are played together, a canceling out of both waves is created at regular intervals. As a result, one hears beats, that is, loudness fluctuations (Adou 1998, 65).

8. According to this system, the West African xylophones considered in this study can be identified as "1112. .21.12." The first set of numbers (1112.) indicates that the primary resonating material is a struck idiophone (an instrument whose primary resonating body is itself). The next numeric addition (.21) specifies that the idiophone is multitoned and that its sounding body is wood. Thus the combination of these three elements defines the essential features of a xylophone (as opposed to 1112. .22, which is a metallaphone, or sounding body of metal). The final set of numbers (.12) indicates the specific type of foundation, a frame. The classification of Senufo xylophones can be further fine-tuned by a final (1) to indicate "rail xylophones," because the frame hangs from the player's neck on a sling.

Chapter 3

1. Further information on the music of Yorùbá churches will be found in Euba 1992.

2. See, for example, the instrumentation in Aníkúlápó-Kútì 1985.

3. For more information on *jùjú*, see Alájá-Browne 1989 and Waterman 1990.

4. Today there are different types of *highlife* in Nigeria. See, for example Euba 1988, 128–31.

5. Descriptive details of the *duff*, *qānūn*, *'ūd*, and *nay* were obtained from Poche 1984a, 616; 1984b, 169; 1984c, 687; and Hassan and During 1984, 751, respectively.

6. More information on the Yorùbá folk opera will be found in Euba 1989, 31–72.

7. Further details of the rise of neo-African art music will be found in Alájá-Browne 1995, 79–86; Konye 1997; and Ọmọ́jọlà 1995.

8. In traditional culture, there are literally as many different music and dance traditions as there are ethnic groups. In other words, each ethnic group has music and dance traditions peculiar to it, and a knowledgeable person in a given ethnic group does not usually extend his or her expertise beyond the traditions of that group. An Akan person in Ghanaian traditional society, while appreciating the music and dances of other Ghanaian societies as an observer, would be reasonably expected to have performing expertise in Akan traditions only. By contrast, an Akan employed by a national dance ensemble would be expected to develop expertise in Akan as well as non-Akan music and dance traditions.

9. This idea is elaborated in Euba 1990, 89–90.

10. See for example Nketia 1963, 155.

11. See for example Ellingson 1992, 113.

12. This is a rare example of a woman leading an ensemble of this kind. Mrs Nanyonga-Tamusuza is a graduate of the Department of Music, Dance, and Drama, University of Makerere, where she learned to perform various Ugandan musical instruments as a part of the curriculum.

13. The Yorùbá and Hausa of Nigeria also have single-headed varieties called *kóśó* and *kotso* respectively.

14. See for example El-Dabh 1965a.

Chapter 4

1. For an overview of the Póró and Sàndè societies in Liberia, see d'Azevedo (1973, 126–50; 1980, 13–23), Holsoe (1980, 97–109), Johnson (1954, 35–37), and Monts (1984, 321–42).

2. See Holsoe (1966, 1967, 1971, 1977, 1990), d'Azevedo (1962), Johnson (1954, 1961), Jones (1981, 1983), Moore (1955), and Rodney (1970).

3. For brief accounts of the role of music in traditional Vai life, see Ellis (1914, 66–72), Koelle (1854, 144–227), Johnson (1954, 35–37, 47–50), and Ogilby (1670, 379–407).

4. In this part of West Africa, three terms were used to designate men of high political or social importance: king, big man, and chief. According to Jones, the terms should not be confused. "Big man are all those, including chiefs, who hold a strong political and social base, the key factors being 'prestige,' wealth, allies and, above all, a compound made up of relatives and dependents. . . . 'chief' mean[s] the political head of a town or any political unit. . . . King . . . occurs frequently in European documents, although in cases 'overlord' would be more appropriate" (1983, 13). The Vai translate the term *ɓóló mànjà* as "paramount chief" or "country chief," even though, historically, the *ɓóló mànjà* was analogous to Jones's description of "king" or "overlord." These individuals controlled a much larger area than modern Paramount Chiefs, who are elected as heads of petty chiefdoms.

5. In an unpublished paper titled "The First Vai Migration," Holsoe provides a compilation of several traditions pertaining to Vai origins and settlement (1974).

6. For another in-depth discussion of Vai migration and settlement, see Jones (1981, 159–78).

7. See Jones (1981, 159–78) for discussions of the Vai adjustment to a new "cultural focus" in the coastal region.

8. In Liberia, the names Mandingo, Maninka, Manyaka, and Koniaka are often used interchangeably. Liberianist scholars adopted use of the name Manding as a generic term for all these peoples. However, in reference to the Vai, I will use the name Koniaka to designate those Manding people from the Musadu region of modern-day Guinea, who were the main Muslim immigrants into Vai country during this era.

9. Even though the Vai are of Manding origin, ethnohistorians are fairly certain that they arrived on the coast as worshippers of a traditional African religion. See Holsoe (1967, 36–42) and Johnson (1954, 15–17).

10. For example, many Vai chiefs adopted Western names, spoke a European language, and adopted trading practices based on European models (Holsoe 1990, 93–94).

11. The Vai were not fully aware of the specific details of the afterlife. Hence, communion with the ancestors was an important element in the belief system. Rodney Needham's explanation for this phenomenon is indeed applicable: "[O]n the whole there does commonly seem to be a contrast between a relatively patent and apprehensible conception of life and a more obscure and perplexing conception of death. One reason for this readily suggests itself. We have our being in a life we know; we are struck down into a death that we can only surmise" (Needham as cited by Huntington and Metcalf 1979, 58)

12. Boakai Zoludua, interview with the author, June 15, 1989.

13. In societies throughout the world, it is a commonly held conception that birth marks the "beginning" and death the "end." For the Vai, however, death symbolizes both the end *and* the beginning—the end of the physical and the beginning of the metaphysical. A similar theme is echoed by Huntington and Metcalf: "Death is transition. But it is only the last in a long chain of transitions. The moment of death is related not only to the process of afterlife, but also to the process of living, aging, and producing progeny. Death relates to life: to the recent life of the deceased, and to the life he or she has procreated and now leaves behind. There is an eternity of sorts on either side of the line that divides the quick from the dead. Life continues generation after generation, and in many societies it is this continuity that is focused upon and enhanced during the rituals surrounding a death. The continuity of the living is a more palpable reality than the continuity of the dead" (1979, 93).

14. During periods of warfare or intense political strife, the death of warriors and chiefs was commonly kept secret, as this was seen as a period of vulnerability that could result in internal and external turmoil. Warriors were left defenseless without a leader, who often controlled the protective war medicines (*kóndó*), and one's adversaries would seek the opportunity to attack a leaderless opponent. Parsons (1964, 30) adds that "Formerly the interim between the death of a chief and the announcement was used to consolidate and make effective the succeeding authority. The death of a chief was kept secret so that a stable rule might be set up before the shock could disrupt the internal life of the people."

15. These notions derive in part from a belief in malevolent spirits that were capable of harming the living. Huntington and Metcalf (1979, 36) note that "reactions to death express several elements of fear: fear of the afterworld, fear of spirits, fear of not performing the ceremony properly, fear of contagious disease, and fear of witchcraft." Though Islam discourages such beliefs, they remain prominent in the minds of present-day Vai.

16. For a discussion of these protective measures, see Ellis (1914, 85–86) and Koelle (1854, 238–39).

17. Vai oral traditions concerning celebrations of death are fairly accurate in dealing with the recent past. They are understandably deficient, however, in dealing with practices of the distant past.

18. According to Jones (1983, 16), Dapper's account is based on the observations of a Dutch trader who lived in the Cape Mount region around 1640.

19. The procedures described here remain common among neighboring ethnic groups (i.e., the Mende, Gola, Kpelle, and Dei).

20. The burial of important personages was often delayed so that an extended celebration could be held. Temporary graves were often used, with a second and more formal burial rite to take place at a later time.

21. A bit of confusion surrounds the actual number of pre-Islamic funerary celebrations. In former times, the Vai performed a succession of three after-death celebrations: (1) the burial, (2) the wake or "house sitting," and (3) the three- or four-day feast. Written and oral data that are seemingly contradictory intimate that the three- or four-day activities constitute the final formal celebration of death. Yet both pools contain data that indicate that large-scale celebrations occurred two weeks, one to three months, and often a year or two after death. The three- or four-day occasions were in fact the final celebrations, requiring specific ritual procedures, and these rituals—including the burial—were customarily held on those days. However, the deceased person's social and political role in life often required a celebration of increased magnitude. Preparation for such an occasion, however, required weeks and often months. Therefore, though the customary rituals (i.e., burial and sacrifices) were enacted according to the tradition already outlined, the celebratory part of the occasion was often postponed. This explains why different time periods between death and the final celebration appear in the literature. Exceptions even to this were common. In several instances, the body was preserved for up to a year until all the necessary arrangements could be made. At these occasions, a symbolic first burial was followed much later by the more permanent second burial. The social or political status of the deceased required the final burial to occur amid elaborate festivities. Ellis informs us that "in the event that relatives required for the final burial were absent, a temporary grave is made in the house, usually in the kitchen, for two weeks to a year. When all the persons required have arrived, the body of the deceased is buried before the house, generally in the yard. A large feast is spread" (1914, 69). Again, this procedure was most often reserved for kings, warriors, and wealthy persons, who were "buried twice—once in a shallow grave in their 'kitchen' and later in a proper grave" (Jones 1983, 177).

22. These descriptions of past funerary activities are typical of those found in early sources. For the most part, these are accounts of funerals for important men: chiefs, Póró leaders, and the wealthy. Seldom did the early observers write about funerals for common folk. In the literature, ceremonies are depicted as large-scale events. Ceremonies for common people presumably were smaller in scope, yet followed the same basic ritual patterns. Celebrations of death were often combined—that is, a single funerary sequence might be held for people from a family or group of families who had died during a given period of time.

23. Boakai Zoludua, interview with the author, June 20, 1989. Such confessions were not always effective in ridding the person of the troubling ailment. Two days after this confession was made, the man reportedly died.

24. Koelle (1854, 144) called the area a *bámbi*, "a temporary grave in the house or kitchen, where corpses are laid, enveloped all over in many bandages of cloth, from two weeks to one year, before all the relatives can be convened for the final burial, and all be procured that is required for the funeral feast. The *bámbi* is only about two feet deep and two or three wide." By the late nineteenth century, this practice had apparently died out or was reserved only for special persons (Ellis 1914, 69). In some Vai towns the practice of in-town graves is reserved for high-ranking religious and political leaders (see fig. 4.4).

25. Although a *kéngàí* performed duties for a particular locale, it was common for these professional musicians to travel to distant towns to perform at wakes and other social activities.

26. On several occasions, I was forced to cancel the recording of these "old songs," simply because the elderly *kéngàí* could not find women in the town familiar enough with the songs to serve as response singers. Throughout the session, the *kéngàí* admonished the singers for not "holding the song" (responding correctly).

27. I was told that songs were once sung en route to the grave, but that now most of them have been forgotten. Elderly men say that secret society songs (mostly *zìàwá* songs) were performed in this context—Sàndè songs for a woman, and Ɓɛ́lì songs for a man.

28. According to Jones (1983, 177), Dapper (1668, 401–3) mentions the killing of slaves when a chief was buried. Besolow (1891, 129–30) reports that a man's wives volunteered to be buried with the husband, adding that "This is considered to be the highest honor that can be conferred upon a woman." The traditions also speak of a female slave or a Sàndè girl being buried alive as an attendant to a powerful man.

29. The Kono people call this occasion *di boe* (Parsons, 1964, 26), and the Mende call it *kpila-gbualɛi* (Harris and Sawyerr, 1968, 32).

30. Radcliffe-Brown sees such occasions not merely as ritual expressions of sentiments, but as an important element in social integration (Huntington and Metcalf, 1979, 24–25). Participation at these occasions was also built on a form of social reciprocity. It was understood that a person's participation in the funerary activities of another townsperson ensured their participation in his own.

31. Wailing by widows in mourning continued in the "crying house" (*ɗìkɛ́-kèŋ*) where they often remained for thirty days to determine if they were pregnant. Afterwards, those found to be pregnant were cared for by the immediate family; others were given a ritual washing, a dowry was presented to their parents, and they were taken as wives by the deceased's brothers or allowed to remarry outside the family. One of my teachers described such an occasion: "In the early morning, the widows were dressed in white and taken to the creek to be washed. There was a lot of singing and dancing. Everyone rejoiced because they knew the women would be freed from their dead husband. A gun was fired, presumably at the spirit of the deceased. The shooter would say, 'You have no more wives nor children here, nor relatives—do not return here anymore.' One could hear a shrilled voice following the shooting, which was believed to be that of the deceased's spirit being driven away from the widows. The children of the deceased were also washed along with their mothers; even the widow's sisters were washed. No singing went on during the washing, but everyone danced and rejoiced on the way back to town" (Boakai Zoludua, interview with the author, July 20, 1989).

32. Among the ethnic groups in the region, the numbers three and four are associated with women and men respectively. See d'Azevedo (1973, 1980), Johnson (1954, 35), and Moore (1955, 28). According to Sawyerr and Harris (1968, 32), "A woman's spirit is said to reach the river on the third day, and a man's on the fourth."

33. The "singing wife" occupied a privileged position in the polygamous household. She traveled with the king, was at his side at all ceremonial occasions, was exempt from domestic chores, and as a sign of her husband's wealth was given the finest clothes and jewelry.

34. This instrument is named and described as as *támandeŋ* by Koelle (1854, 217), but it is no longer found among the Vai, having declined along with the system of patronage and warfare that sustained its use in the past.

35. Instrumentalists also were brought in from the neighboring Mende and Gola, as were expert dancers and singers. This accounts in part for the high percentage of music materials and of the song repertoire in these languages among the Vai today. Even the speech surrogates used by the Vai on the slit gong (*kèléŋ*)and the conical-shaped drum (*sàŋgbà)* are based on the Mende language (Monts 1982, 106).

36. The *kó kɔ́lɔ́ fɔ́-mɔ̀ɔ̀* at Bulumi (Tombe chiefdom) tells of a small war that started as the result of two brothers fighting over who would rightfully inherit the services of their deceased father's Gola wife, who was a singer.

37. By the mid-nineteenth century, *gbɔ̀njí* groups were sponsored by wealthy patrons. They customarily accompanied their patrons to festive occasions as self-contained entertainment troupes. Masqueraders wearing elaborate costumes were the troupe's main attraction.

38. I observed such a "house visit" in the town of Boloba (Tewɔ chiefdom) in 1977. The proceedings match an elderly informant's descriptions of similar occasions, which were common during the pre-Islamic period.

39. The ability to speak eloquently was—and still is—considered an important attribute in Vai society.

40. For accounts of different funerary activities, see Ellis (1914, 69–70), Parsons (1964, 24–33), Conneau (1976, 328–29), and Johnson (1954, 87–90).

Chapter 6

1. The country is referred to as "The Gambia" to distinguish it from the Gambia River.

2. Concerning the terminology used for the Fulbe, Derrick J. Stenning (1960, 140; 1965, 323) explains: "They are known as Fula [a Mandinka term] in Gambia and Sierra Leone; Fellah by the Arabs of the Western Sudan, Fellaata by the Kanuri and others peoples of the Chad Basin; Peuls [a Wolof term] by the French; and Fulbe in the German literature. Their own term for themselves is Fulbe (sing. Pullo) and their language is Fulfulde. The British in Nigeria use the Hausa term Fulani." In this study, the term Fulbe is used.

3. The Fulbe are among the most widely distributed people on the African continent. Not only are they scattered throughout the savanna belt, they are also among the most populous African peoples, with over fifteen million speaking the Fulbe language (called Fulfulde, Pulaar, Fula, Peul, etc.); see further discussion in Azarya, Eguchi, and VerEecke 1993, 1; and Schultz 1980. In the mid-twentieth century, there were well over six million Fulbe people or speakers of Fulfulde in various African countries, roughly distributed as follows: Nigeria (3,630,000), Mali (850,000), Guinea (720,000), Cameroon (305,000), Niger (269,000), The Gambia (58,700), Benin (54,000), Côte d'Ivoire and Burkina Faso (52,000), Guinea-Bissau (36,000), Senegal and Mauritania (12,000), Ghana (5,000), and Central African Republic (no estimate); see Stenning 1965, 363. Akin Mabogunje (1976, 26) writes that the Fulbe "for the most part are found living as ethnic minorities among such populous groups as the Soninke, Malinke, Bambara, Hausa and Mossi. Others are dispersed among the many smaller tribes of the Voltaic and Plateau Nigerian group. Only in a few discontinuous districts do they constitute the dominant element in the population. These include from west to east, the Senegal valley, Fouta Toro, Fouta Jallon, Kita, Masina, Liptako, Sokoto, Bauchi and Adamawa."

4. Clark (1992, 12) states that Fulfulde was not standardized until a group of UNESCO linguists in 1966 determined a standard orthography, which is now accepted throughout most of francophone West Africa. Because Fulbe live in anglophone, francophone, and lusophone West Africa, not all problems of orthography have been solved completely. The increase of four million speakers of Fulfulde from the 1960s to the 1990s demonstrates that the use of Fulfulde in West Africa continues to grow (Stenning 1965; Clark 1992).

5. Also see Quinn (1967, 40–44; 1972, 20–21). These dialects fall into three general linguistic groupings: (1) Fulbe Firdu, Jombonko, Habobe, Rorobe, Hamanabi (Hammanabi), (2) Torodo, Jawando, Labo, and (3) Fulbe Futa/Fulbe Futo (Quinn 1972, 19).

6. Because the Fulbe constitute one of the largest ethnic groups in Africa and, under Moslem leaders, made themselves political masters over a considerable portion of Sudanic Africa at the time of the arrival of the Europeans, theories of Caucasoid origin were popular during the early part of the twentieth century. The fact that many Fulbe were light-skinned and some were conquerors who owned cattle helped to promote this theory. Some scholars even believed that the Fulbe were a group of Judaeo-Syrians who entered Africa about 200 C.E. and that Fulfulde was Hamitic. Linguistic evidence, however, has demonstrated that the Hamitic theory was based more on racist conjecture than on fact (Greenberg 1970, 24–30).

7. The people of Takrur and their descendants did not use "Tukulor" to refer to themselves; rather, they called themselves "Hal Pulor," speakers of Pulor, that is Fulfulde. The term "Tukulor" is believed to be a corrupted form of "Takruri." Takruri was used by Arab geographers and historians to describe, first, the people of Takrur and later, used loosely and very inaccurately, to describe all Sudanic Muslims (even those who lived as far east as Borno in present-day Nigeria). This "is probably to be accounted for by the fact that West African pilgrims who arrived in Cairo, Mecca and Medina, tended to be referred to by the local peoples as 'Takruri' so the term came to be generally used in this wide sense" (Hiskett 1984, 28).

8. In the literature, several terms are used for the Mande (descendants of the Mali Empire): "Mandinka (Mandingo) of Gambia, the Maninka (Malinké) of Guinea, the Bambara [Bamana] of Mali, and the Dyula of Ivory Coast [Côte d'Ivoire]" (Knight 1983, 37).

9. The Wolof kingdoms included Walo, Cayor, Baol, Sine, and Salum, but they were all dominated by the central kingdom of Jolof.

10. During the nineteenth century, Mandinka landlords were sometimes called "Sonike chiefs." In this case, Soninke did not refer to the people of the ancient Ghana Empire. Rather, "*Sonike* was used as a synonym for the Arabic *kafir* (unbeliever), a term for animists or Muslims who failed to observe Islamic practices. *Marabout*, meaning cleric or teacher, was a term associated with the saint cults of North Africa. In Senegambia it referred to all who accepted a purified form of Islam. The symbol of the differences between the two groups was highly individual and particularized; if a man drank alcoholic beverages he was considered a 'Soninke'; if not, he was a 'Marabout.' Politically, these terms represented a division of the population into two sharply opposed factions which cut across ethnic and traditional political groups. *Soninke* popularly defined the ruling party of aristocratic families and their followers, while *Marabout* referred to all those excluded from land ownership and the highest offices of the state" (Quinn 1972, 53).

11. Quinn (1971, 428) states that Fulbe pastoralists often complained of heavy taxes, extortion, and exploitation. The incident that sparked Alfa Molo's revolt occurred in 1867. According to oral traditions, the "Mandingo king of Jimara one day took a sheep from Molo's herd and refused to return it. Resentment of the Mandingo landlords by this time must have been great, as the dispute, similar to many before it, quickly generalized. As the king of Jimara called on the Mandingo clans throughout the area to help him, the *Fulbe Firdu*, led by Molo, attacked his town and destroyed it. They [Molo and the *Fulbe Firdu*] were joined by groups of 'free' (*Lorobe*) Fulbe and the revolt spread to other districts" (Quinn 1971, 428–29).

    The leaders and location of some of the jihads that took place in the Senegambia area include: Nasir al-Din in Futa Toro (1672–1677), Malik Sy in Bondu or Bundu (1690–1702), Alfa Ba in Futa Jalon (1726–1764), Abd al-Qadir in Futa Toro (1776–1797), Al-hajj Ahmad Umar (1850s–1891), Maba Diakhou in Gambia (1861–1867), Shaykh Amadu Ba in Jolof (1869–1875), and Alfa Molo/Musa Molo in Gambia (1867–1890s).

12. For other works that include discussion of Islamic reform in Senegambia, see Klein (1969, 1972); Curtin (1971); and David Robinson (1973).

13. The Serahuli (also referred to as Sarakole, Sarokolle, Sarakholle, Serahule, and Seraculeh) are related to the Soninke, the rulers of the Ghana Empire.

14. In Senegal, the term *pulaagu* is used, while Fulbe in other areas use the term *pulaaku* (Ogawa 1993, 129).

15. Tamba Kandeh, one of the Fulbe fiddlers who provided me with information about fiddling in The Gambia during my fieldwork in Senegambia in 1990 and 1994, lives in The Gambia. He moved to Lamin (a town approximately ten miles from the capital city, Banjul) from his home of Sarekokeh (a village in the eastern part of The Gambia) during the mid-1970s.

16. Although Ngeya Kandeh is Tamba's cousin, they refer to each other as brothers. Ngeya was born in Suma Kunda Berom (sometimes called Sare Berom), a small town located in the east of The Gambia in the Basse District of the Upper River Division. Originally from the provinces (the eastern region of The Gambia), Ngeya had moved with his family to his present location in the mid-1970s because of his work in the government. After giving up his government job, Ngeya decided to devote his time to farming. Ngeya's compound consisted of two structures: a kitchen area and a residence area with three rooms. Also, there was a courtyard with several large trees that provided shade for people to work and relax.

17. At the wedding was Mamma Kandeh, Ngeya's son, who provided me with background information about his father, the wedding, and the activities that were taking place that day. Mamma also accompanied me to the bride's home.

18. Fulbe men living in this area of The Gambia met each Sunday at Ngeya's compound to discuss business, community affairs, and politics. Like Ngeya and Tamba, they were from the provinces. Because the meetings normally extended from about four o'clock to dusk, everyone knew that the men's discussions would not interfere with the wedding celebrations, which were not expected to begin until later in the evening. Around 5:30 p.m., several men left the meeting and went to get the van that would be used for the wedding. When they arrived at the bride's compound, Ngeya's friends and family members were greeted by the bride's family with drink (water) and talk. When the time for prayers came, all of the men in the compound participated.

    While the men waited in the yard, the bride was making preparations for her departure. When I went inside to see her, she was beautifully dressed in a bright yellow and red *boubou* (African dress). Her bundle of belongings had been carefully packed and placed in a corner of her room. Once she arrived at the groom's house, she would have to stay there for one month before being allowed to return to her parent's home.

19. On the first day, entertainment continued until three o'clock in the morning. On the second day, music making extended until about seven or eight o'clock in the evening.

20. Besides "Supere Demba," "Mamareh ko bengel Kaddy Jakou," and "Jawara," other songs that Tamba performed at the wedding included: "Poromandalli," a criticizing song, composed by Tamba; "Dangingka," a song Tamba adapted from Serahuli lute players; "Burugy warama" (Burugy is killed), a song that documents an incident (the death of a man named Burugy in a market) that took place in the URD during the 1970s; and "Cabral," a praise song composed by Demba Gabbi (a Fulbe fiddler from Guinea Bissau) in honor of Luis de Almeida Cabral (a freedom fighter and former president of Guinea-Bissau).

21. The lack of material on music corresponds with the dearth of ethnographic data concerning the Fulbe in The Gambia. Commenting on this problem, Gamble and Sperling (1979, 157) state, "A vast amount has been written in French about the Fulbe of Senegal, and of Futa Jalon in Guinea, and in Portuguese about the Fulbe of Guinea-Bissau, but little has been written specifically on the Fulbe of The Gambia."

22. For some of the works that include information about music and culture of the Mandinka and Wolof, see Knight, Innes, Darbo, Dalby, King, Coolen, Duran, Gamble, Leymarie-Ortiz, and N'Diaye.

23. Not only have several scholars (P. Eguchi, Erlmann, 'Adama and Erlmann) used the Cameroon Fulani as the primary focus for music studies, a number of researchers (Schaeffner, Belinga, Arnott, Kubik, and M. J. Eguchi) have mentioned Cameroon Fulani in related studies. While a significant amount of information is available on the Fulani in Nigeria (Brackenbury, Reed, Mellor, Anon. 1964, Pfeffer, Abdulkadir, and King), only one or two articles include material about Fulani groups in Niger (Nikiprowetzky 1966) and Burkina Faso (Seydou and Rosellini).

24. Coolen (1994) states, "As for why the Fula aren't discussed so much in Senegambia, I can only guess that it's due in part to the fact that the majority lived much to the east, far from the capitals (and researchers, perhaps), and their presence in the Senegambia is perhaps not as long-standing or pervasive as Cameroon, for example. While in Gambia, I had no sense that the Fulbe were a significant group. Given that Gambia is dominated by the Mandinka and Senegal by the Wolof, maybe that is another reason they've received less attention."

25. Prior to my work on the Dagbamba in Ghana in 1972, little music research had been done on them. But a number of works existed on Ghanaian groups (e.g., Asante, Fanti, Ewe, Ga) that lived in the southern parts of Ghana where Western influence had been extensive. Although the Dagbamba are considered to be one of the most important ethnic groups in northern Ghana, their visibility in southern Ghana is low compared to other groups. I might add, however, that several studies have been published on Dagbamba music since the late 1970s. The lack of visibility, political power, and social influence may also be the reasons little material is available on the Serer and Jola.

26. Much of this may be the result of the emphasis on a nationalist ideology that was prominent among various African countries when they regained their independence during the 1960s and 1970s. Rather than emphasize the differences, nations attempted to unify and build on the similarities that existed among groups in their countries. The use of the term "Gambian" is an indication of this artificial wholeness or oneness. This is also one of the reasons that the power and authority of traditional political leaders were abolished. Leaders of the new political government believed that traditional leaders would defeat the purpose of the federal ideas of the country. Also, the emphasis on the "collective whole" followed the trend of scholarship in earlier years when emphasis was placed on "Culture" with a capital "C." Research today tends to place more emphasis on acknowledging the distinctions that may be apparent, rather than forcing groups and the discussion into a homogenous whole.

27. Henri Gaden's (1931) discussion of Fulbe groups in Futa Toro (Senegal) and Futa Jalon (Guinea) is based on data collected between 1910 and 1912 when he served as governor of the French colonies. Information about Fulbe in Futa Jalon in the Gaden study was collected in 1916 by M. P. Marty. Also see discussion in Arnott 1980, 20, 24.

28. Similar to other world music traditions, the spelling of Fulbe musical terms is not standardized. The spellings used here are taken directly from Gaden (1931). In the literature, other spellings may be used. For example, the term *hoddu* is also spelled *hoDu* (Coolen 1984, 124); the word for the fiddle (listed in Gaden as *nanoru*) also has a number of variants.

29. The information on Gambian Fulbe music was obtained from interviews that I conducted with several Fulbe fiddlers who lived in The Gambia in the early 1990s: Samba Jumba Bah (originally from Guinea), Mamadou Baldeh (a Fulbe Firdu from MacCarthy Island Division in The Gambia), Maulday Baldeh (a Fulbe Firdu from MacCarthy Island Division), Seiniwa Baldeh (originally from Guinea-Bissau), Juldeh Camara (originally from Casamance, Senegal), Ngeya Kandeh (a Rorobe originally from the Upper River Division in The Gambia), and Tamba Kandeh (a Rorobe also from the Upper River Division in The Gambia). Also, I interviewed Ngansumana Jobateh (born in MacCarthy Island Division), a Mandinka *kora* player, as well as several nonmusicians in The Gambia. These individuals ranged in age from thirty to sixty years old. Most were born and raised in the

provinces where they also received their musical training. As performers, they were aware of current musical practices. Their knowledge of the music in the precolonial and colonial periods came from oral tradition that had been passed down by kinsmen. From their statements, it is apparent that changes have occurred in the music culture of the Fulbe since The Gambia regained its independence in the mid-1960s.

30. Tamba Kandeh (1994) stated that while he uses the term *jalijo*, the Fulbe Futa use the term *nyamakala* for a musician. In the liner notes to the recording, *The Griots: Ministers of the Spoken Word*, Samuel Charters (1975, 5) indicates that the word for singer/historian in Fulfulde is "Jelefo." The fact that a variety of terms is used is consistent with cultural practices among Fulbe in The Gambia. Not only are there a variety of Fulbe dialect groups with their own terms and pronunciation, but, like many African languages, the spelling of Fulfulde words is not standardized. In fact, when I ask my interviewees and/or the translators to write terminology, they did it hesitantly because they stated that they do not usually *write* these words; theirs is an oral language.

31. Lynn Jessup's research indicates that the *gawlo* does play a musical instrument. In "Musical Instruments of The Gambia," Jessup (1981, 39) states: "The transverse flute of the Fula *gawulos*—called *serndu*—is longer than the *fuleh*, and it is played in ensembles with other Fula instruments." Unfortunately, the article does not indicate the source of the information.

32. While they are familiar with the terminology used by Fulbe in other parts of Senegambia, the use and meaning of these terms is different. Interestingly, many of their definitions were similar to the meanings found in the literature. All, however, stated that these terms were rarely used by musicians in The Gambia.

33. Although the Fulbe Firdu were politically the most important group in the Gambian region during the nineteenth century, they were looked down upon by "purer" nomadic Fulbe (Quinn 1967, 41–42; 1972, 19).

34. While the Fulbe refer to king as *laamii'do* (pl. *laamii'be*), the Mandinka use the word *mansa*. As noted in the foregoing, Musa Molo was a powerful Fulbe "king" who ruled a large territory in Casamance and the Gambia valley during the late nineteenth century. He lived in Kesserkunda where he was buried in 1931. Scholars (e.g., Innes 1974, 7), as well as the musicians whom I interviewed, state that his court attracted a large number of *griot* families that lived in towns (e.g., Sotuma and Boraba) near Kesserkunda. For a discussion of Mandinka song repertory that relates to the Fulbe, see Knight 1983.

35. When I asked musicians about royal or court traditions, they only related information about musical activity that occurred during the reign of Musa Molo and his descendants. When asked about Fulbe warriors who lived before Musa Molo—e.g., Alfa Molo or Maba Diakhou Ba—all stated that they did not know of any musicians or musical activity associated with these leaders. The Fulbe musicians whom I interviewed were not even familiar with the name Maba Diakhou Ba. The Mandinka *kora* musician thought that Maba Diakhou Ba was a Wolof, probably because Maba's family came from Futa Toro which is now a part of Senegal.

    The responses of the musicians can be interpreted in several ways. First, the role of the Fulbe performer as a court musician only dates back to the nineteenth century when Fulbe warriors rose to power. Second, the reason that oral traditions that associate Gambian musicians with Musa Molo now exist is because Molo is regarded as one of the greatest leaders in Fulbe history. The Fulbe and the Mandinka revere Musa Molo in the same manner that the Mandinka revere Sundiata (the founder of the Mali Empire).

36. In The Gambia, the Mandinka *jalolu* were already established as court musicians because Mandinka landlords politically dominated the Gambian region up until the nineteenth century. In fact, Mandinka *griots* have a long history of serving as court musicians as they trace their origins to the reign of Sundiata who lived during the thirteenth century.

37. The Hornbostel/Sachs figures for such an instrument are 321.311.71 (Hornbostel and Sachs 1961, 23). The placement of the resonating hole is a feature that distinguishes the geographical location of a fiddle. In the Western Sudan, the opening is generally placed in the sound box, whereas the resonating hole in the Central Sudan and Voltaic areas is placed in the skin that covers the body resonator (DjeDje 1998).

38. Wolof "identity" is a topic that has been greatly discussed. Sidibe and Galloway (1975), Gamble (1967), Gamble et al. (1985), and Coolen (1983; 1994) have discussed the significance of language in defining the identity of a Wolof. Coolen (1983, 481) states, "It is common to hear the statement 'there are no people called the Wolof. Wolof is a language. If you speak Wolof, you are Wolof.'" Thus, this association of language with identity makes it difficult to determine if a tradition is actually Wolof or Fulbe. Yet, the issue may be moot. If there are Wolof who play the instrument, they probably have put their identifying mark on it, which now makes it theirs in spite of the fact that it may have been adopted from the Fulbe.

39. Samba Juma Bah settled in The Gambia in the early 1980s; he was thirty-five years old at the time of my interview with him on August 23, 1990. In addition to fiddling, he also was a fire-eater. Bah states that during his travels to other countries in the Western Sudan, Senegal was the only other place, besides Guinea and The Gambia, that he saw the fiddle being played; but he states that the fiddlers in Senegal were Fulbe. In Mali, he saw musicians performing drums and the *balafon* (xylophone).

40. Majaw Bai was born in St. Louis, Senegal. At the time of my interview with him (August 29, 1990), he was living in Charoy Genay Rayi, a suburb of Dakar. While Bai uses the term *nyanyur* for the fiddle, all of the other Senegalese fiddlers whom I interviewed and recorded—Ousainou Chaw and Juldeh Camara—refer to the fiddle as *riti*. Interestingly, Bai stated that he did not know any Wolof fiddlers. Bai's comments are significant for not only is he an urban musician who has spent much time in the Dakar area, he is probably aware of the activities of various groups in the city. For him not to know of Wolof fiddlers implies that the fiddle is not commonly used by Wolof musicians in urban areas such as Dakar and St. Louis. Perhaps Senegalese fiddle musicians may be of Tukulor or Fulbe origin, but speak Wolof.

41. In program notes to performances by Bedouin poets, Dwight F. Reynolds (1993, 4) states that over the centuries, poems and stories of the Bani Hilil Arabs have been woven into "an enormous epic narrative, not by writers, but by poets and storytellers who told and retold the tales. The first scholar to mention the epic poems of the Bani Hilal and to defend them as a rich artistic tradition was none other than the famous 14th century historian Ibn Khaldun." Old and more recent photographs of poets show that all performed the fiddle to accompany their epic poems. However, Reynolds (1993, 6) states, "the tradition of singing the Bani Hilal epic to the accompaniment of the rabab is rapidly disappearing. . . . In the early 1980s, there were fourteen professional epic singers. . . . Now, ten years later, only five singers are left; the older poets have passed away, and several of the younger singers have left the profession to take up more lucrative employment."

42. Visual documentation and brief comments on the use of the fiddle in Mali are found in Felix Dubois's *Timbuctoo: The Mysterious* (1897, 270–74). Dubois does not specify the ethnicity of the fiddle performers. But since the fiddlers are women, we can assume that they are Tuareg. The Tuareg have been more selective in their appropriation of elements from Arab culture. Thus, it is not surprising that women, rather than men, are the primary performers of the fiddle in Tuareg society.

43. Except for statements made by Tamba Kandeh when I interviewed him August 19–25, 1990, there is no other evidence that the Balante and Koniagi play the fiddle. During my visit to Dakar (capital city of Senegal) in

summer 1990, I recorded fiddle music performed by Majaw Bai and Ousainou Chaw (a Serer).

44. Radio news announcements in The Gambia are reported in different languages so that everyone within the country is informed about current events. When announcements are targeted to a specific ethnic group, a short instrumental musical sample associated with that group is performed. For the Fulbe, fiddle music is heard. Even though few people know the history of the fiddle in The Gambia, what they have heard on the media makes them aware of the fact that the fiddle is a symbol of Fulbe identity.

45. Maulday Baldeh, the fiddler who provided the most detailed information about musicians attached to Musa Molo, stated that he acquired his information from his father and grandfathers. At the time of my interview with him December 9, 1994, Maulday was in his mid-thirties. He considered himself to be a professional hereditary fiddler; he received his music training from his father when he was nine years old. Maulday had spent most of his life at his home in the provinces (Fulantang, Macarthy Island Division [MID]), except for short visits to towns in Senegal to perform the fiddle. Maulday moved to the Banjul area in early 1994 to visit his younger brother, Abudullahi Abdoulie Baldeh. Maulday's brother had migrated to Banjul in 1990 to learn to drive and had not returned home. So Maulday traveled to find him.

46. According to Maulday Baldeh, Musa Molo's second name (perhaps he means the middle name) was Balla. So this is the reason the song is called "Balla." "Sorronna" refers to the bow and arrow that Musa used when he went to fight. The literal meaning of "Sodahnam Padeh Jelleh" is "buy high-heeled shoes for me." Composed by Maulday's brother, Abudullahi, "Sodahnam Padeh Jelleh" is in honor of one of Musa Molo's grandchildren because she, at one time, gave Baldeh's brother a bull. At the time the brother decided to praise her for giving him the bull, she was wearing high-heeled shoes. Besides the songs that he recalled, Maulday stated that Fulbe fiddlers in the provinces knew many songs in praise of Musa Molo and still performed them for local chiefs and at rallies for modern political leaders.

47. The information from Maulday Baldeh is confirmed by Ngansumana Jobateh (interview with the author December 10, 1994), a Mandinka *kora* player who was born in 1938 in Boraba in Fuladu, MID). Jobateh stated that he began to take lessons on the *kora* from his father when he was ten years old. He considers himself to be a *jali* (professional musician), and his children actively participate in the profession.

According to Jobateh, Musa Molo was the first and greatest warrior in The Gambia. Molo liked music, and he supported his musicians. Therefore, all types of musicians (praise singers and instrumentalists) played for him. When musicians went to Kesserkunda to entertain Molo, he would always reward them, sometimes with a bull to slaughter. All of the musicians who performed for Musa Molo lived in villages near Kesserkunda, where Musa Molo had appointed different men to serve as district heads or chiefs. While Mandinka musicians lived in Boraba where Dembo Danso was chief, Fulbe musicians lived in Basse where Falai Kora Tamba Sangsang was the political leader. Jobateh indicated that he knew of several Mandinka musicians who played for Musa Molo: Karunkah Jobateh, Jaturr Jobateh, Bamba Suso, Madi Suso. Jobateh also stated that Mandinka musicians had composed many historical songs in honor of Musa Molo, some of which are "Kuruntuh Kelefa," "Golong Jole," "Allah le ya keh," "Jaaka," and "Ntery Jatoe" (see Knight 1983 for discussion of historical songs).

48. In the texts to the songs that they sang, Fulbe fiddlers (e.g, Juldeh Camara and Tamba Kandeh) used the terms *jaleba*, *jalo*, or *jalieya* (spellings provided by Mamma Kandeh).

49. It must be remembered that members of the Rorobe dialect group that Tamba and Ngeya Kandeh belong to were originally cattle herders. As they became more settled, they also began to be involved in farming. More importantly, both Tamba and Ngeya did not become fiddlers until early adulthood (see further discussion below).

50. Tamba Kendeh, interviews with the author, August 19–25, 1990, and December 8–11, 1994. Several of the musicians whom I interviewed explained that they played for politicians. Seiniwa Baldeh, originally from Guinea-Bissau, stated that he first visited The Gambia with a cultural troupe but decided to stay because he found that he could earn more money in The Gambia. Eventually, he became attached to Lamin Tuthi Baldeh, a Fulbe chief in the MacCarthy Island Division, who, according to Seiniwa, selected him to be his *griot*. Whenever the chief traveled, Seiniwa stated that he went with the chief and performed at government programs and other events. Later Seiniwa moved to the Banjul area where he performed at hotels, on ceremonial occasions, and for special programs.

51. Ngeya Kandeh, interview with the author, August 19, 1990. On the first anniversary of The Gambia's independence in February 1966, the country held a national competition to decide on the best cultural troupes to represent the different regions of the country. Four groups from the Basse region competed. Because Ngeya's group won first place, Ngeya eventually became known as the champion fiddler, and his group was often invited to perform on Radio Gambia and at government programs. Ngeya's group was composed of two fiddlers (Ngeya and Tamba) and five women dancers (Metta Baldeh, Kumba Kandeh [Tamba's wife who also won an award in 1966 for the most beautiful Fulbe lady], Subbah Jawo, Daddaa Jawo, and Hawa Barro).

52. Maulday Baldeh stated that around the same time he was taught how to fiddle, he also learned how to play the *tama*. First, a small fiddle was made for him. Then he was taught how to manipulate the fiddle bow. Later he was taught how to coordinate his dance movements; knowing when to step forward and backward in a performance when the women are dancing was important.

Mamadou stated that his teacher, Seidou Windy, was someone who used to visit his home for performances. On one occasion when Windy visited, Mamadou stated that he was interested in learning to fiddle and was allowed to follow the man to his home. Because Windy already had a spare fiddle, Mamadou immediately began his lessons. First, he learned how to bow and then move the fingers. Mamadou stated that when he received his training, no one knew how to fiddle and sing. In fact, his father only performed the fiddle and did not sing. Also, when he learned, he was not taught how to play the *tama*, but *tama* players who accompanied him knew how to sing.

53. Juldeh Camara was twenty-six years old at the time of my interview with him of September 1, 1990. He had four brothers and three sisters. Some of Camara's music appears on a recording (*Ancient Heart: Mandinka and Fulani Music of the Gambia*, 1990) published by Island Records; see discography following the essay for more details.

54. Ngeya Kandeh was able to provide the genealogy for his fiddle training (interview with the author August 19, 1990). Ngeya's teacher was Sambaru Jawo, who lived near a village called Jawo. Sambaru Jawo obtained his fiddle instruction from Jajeh Nyalen, who lived in Sinchu Sambajawo. Jajeh Nyalen learned from Nayang Baldeh, who lived in Sare Timbo. Nayang Baldeh was taught by Samba Janabo, who lived in Sinchu Sara.

55. "Tapa Tura" is a proverbial song. According to Tamba, "In everything, we [the Fulbe] identify first, second, and third class. When you come to bicycles, there are first class, second class, third class. If we're praising somebody by personality, we will praise the person by calling his name and say you will not ride or you will not pedal tapa tura. Tapa tura was third class pedal cycle during those days [in the 1960s]. M. C. Jallowe [one of Tamba's patrons] will not use a tapa tura bicycle because that's a low-class standard. M. C. Jallowe is a person who will use first class in bicycle. Tapa tura is the last standard or class. That's the meaning of the song" (interview with the author August 19–25, 1990).

56. Interview with the author August 19–25, 1990. When I interviewed Tamba, December 8–11, 1994, he stated that his children should make their own decisions about an occupation. He was not going to demand that they enter the fiddle profession.

57. According to Maulday and Mamadou Baldeh (interviews with the author December 9 and 8, 1994, respectively), this is still the most common instrumental organization used in the provinces. On occasion, other instruments may be added. Therefore, it appears that it is only in urban areas that a variety of instruments have been added to fiddle ensembles.

58. The *djembe* is identified with the Mande of Guinea. Because other drums are performed by a variety of ethnic groups in the area, it is not known which, if any, are indigenous to Fulbe culture.

59. The terms *serndu, forrdu, chorumbal* (*tiorumba*) and *tambing* are used interchangeably by the Fulbe in The Gambia. The large number of Fulbe dialect groups that reside in The Gambia is probably the reason that a variety of terms is used.

60. Written documentation on the lute in West Africa dates back to the fourteenth century when Ibn Battuta mentions its use in the Mali Empire. Farmer (1928, 27) believes that a folk version of the lute was already in existence when the Arabs arrived. Information about the use of the lute among the Fulbe, however, is more scarce. For a general discussion on the development of lutes in West Africa, see Coolen 1991, 10–11.

61. The Fulbe plucked lute (*hoddu*) is found in the following countries: The Gambia, Guinea, Senegal, Sierra Leone, Mali, Niger, and Burkina Faso. Although he does not specify a term, King (1980, 241) indicates that Fulani who reside in the middle belt of Nigeria perform a plucked lute.

62. The *molo* is found among Fulbe in The Gambia, Guinea, Senegal, Mauritania, Mali, and Burkina Faso. Not only did I personally see a Tukulor performer in Senegal (Majaw Bai) who used the *molo*, I recorded a Fulbe performing the *molo*.

63. The *buusawru* (a horn), along with several other instruments, was adopted by the Fulani during the founding of the state in Diamaré. The *buusawru*, only found in three specimens at the court of the *laamii'do* of Maroua and considered to be the paramount instrument associated with kingship, is played by the chief of all court musicians. Originally, the *buusawru* was widespread among non-Muslims of the Chad area (Erlmann 1983a, 23).

64. According to Arnott (1980, 25), in addition to other instruments, cattle Fulani play a type of Jew's harp: "A jew's harp played in interludes between songs by a youth from Maroua (north-west Cameroon) was fashioned from pieces of wood, palm frond, guinea-corn stalk and tough grass."

65. Interview with the author December 8, 1994. This performance organization is similar to the Hausa. The Hausa fiddler *rarely* sings; in performance he is only responsible for performing the fiddle.

66. Although some of the songs that Tamba Kandeh played at his brother's wedding were the same as the ones that he played for me in his courtyard, I observed that his behavior was different in each context. He did not dance in either situation, but at the wedding he stood and was more physically involved in the performance.

67. When Juldeh Camara performed for me in Tamba Kandeh's courtyard, he was the only fiddler, but he brought along a *tama* player to provide rhythmic accompaniment. Before his performance, Camara changed from his street clothing (Western-style pants and shirt) and put on a special costume. For the performance, he wore a bright red, blue, and white vest over a white T-shirt. He also wore wide-legged trousers that were long and full in the middle, characteristic of clothing worn by people in Sudanic Africa. He tied a wide leather band around his head and forehead. The headdress was intricately designed with several cowry shells. A horsetail was attached to the headdress so that it was in the middle of the forehead (see Camara in fig. 6.7). When I observed other fiddlers in performance, their clothing—a T-shirt with Sudanic-style trousers—was not different from the clothing worn by members of their audience.

68. This is the typical instrumentation of ensembles that perform at luxury hotels.

69. Interview with the author December 8, 1994. From these comments, it is apparent that Fulbe fiddlers associate fire-eating and acrobatics with traditional religious practices, which obviously preceded the use of the fiddle in Fulbe society.

70. See *The Griots: Ministers of the Spoken Word* (1975) for two historical songs—"Alifa Ya Ya" and "Moro"—played on the fiddle.

Chapter 7

1. *Lunsi* can mean either many *luŋa* players or many *luŋa* drums.

2. I heard a similar version of this story from Abubakari Lunna on September 27, 1993.

3. Abubakari Lunna, interview with the author, September 27, 1993.

Chapter 8

This article is a revised version of an oral presentation given at the 32nd International Council of Traditional Music World Conference held in Berlin, June 16–22, 1993. Amharic words are italicized and are given in English transliteration for the most part according to the technique outlined by Wolf Leslau in his *Amharic Textbook* (1968). Variations in spelling occur because written Amharic is syllabic and does not use the Latin alphabet. In view of this, I have chosen to employ commonly used spellings of some Amharic words and geographical locations based on five other sources: T. P. Ofcansky and L. Berry, *Ethiopia: A Country Study* (1980 and 1993 editions); the National Democratic Institute for International Affairs, *An Evaluation of the June 21, 1992, Elections in Ethiopia* (1992); Chris Prouty and Eugene Rosenfeld, *Historical Dictionary of Ethiopia and Eritrea* (1994); and Tom Killon, *Historical Dictionary of Eritrea* (1998).

1. These regions were formerly known as Tigre, Begemder, and Wallo Provinces, and the city of Addis Ababa, respectively.

2. Both of these actors were born in the United States although it is often assumed that Lee was born in Hong Kong because he lived there for a time. They gained their reputations first as martial arts experts and later as actors in action films. Although media censorship during the Mengistu regime was extensive, action films like those made by Lee and Norris were acceptable because the dialogue was secondary to action, and translation into the various Ethiopian languages was therefore not essential to a basic understanding of the plot.

3. Additional examples of group singing using the "call-and-response" format were recorded on twenty-three tape cassettes made in the early 1980s containing songs of the Eritrean freedom fighters. The tapes are currently are housed at the Africana Library, Stanford University, California.

4. The Tigrayan People's Liberation Front (TPLF) was the principal political party to help the Eritrean People's Liberation Front (EPLF) to overthrow Mengistu Haile Mariam and gain control of Ethiopia in May 1991. The current president of Ethiopia, Meles Zenawi, is an EPLF member. Another important result of the EPLF victory is that on May 24, 1993, the former Ethiopian province of Eritrea officially became an independent country.

5. Like men, women soldiers, or freedom fighters as they were often called, wore rock and heavy metal music T-shirts along with slacks or jeans and sandals or tennis shoes rather than the traditional Tigre dress. In addition, they wore their hair in an Afro as opposed to the traditional cornrows characteristic of Tigre and Eritrean women.

6. If a noted performer legally produced a number of cassette tapes for sale on the open market, virtually the only way the customer could identify the "latest" release was by the cover photograph of the artist. Each succeeding tape could have a different cover photograph. Use of different photographs is an effective method of identifying artists as well as a way the customer can place each recording in sequence if the date is not noted.

7. The tank parts are technically "bells," and the rock gong sets are technically "gongs" as determined by where and how the object is struck. A gong is struck at its center, and the vibration is strongest at the vertex. A bell is struck at its edge and the vibration is weakest at the vertex (Hornbostel and Sachs 1914, 15). When each tank component was struck, the intervals sounded approximated a fundamental and a perfect fifth and an octave above the fundamental.

8. Symbols were provided by the Polling Station Electoral or district committee and registered in the candidate's names (The Election Commission of the Transitional Government of Ethiopia 1992a, 4–5).

Chapter 9

This essay originally appeared in *Al-Ma'thurat Al-Sha'biyyah* 27 (July 1992): 7–17.

1. The information upon which this essay is based was gathered in 1988 during a six-month period of fieldwork in Qatar and the United Arab Emirates. This research was sponsored by the Arab Gulf States Folklore Center in Doha, Qatar.

2. For further information about the tunings and repertoire of the Gulf *tanbūrah*, see the author's text in a booklet accompanying a field recording of *tanbūrah* music released throught the Arab Gulf States Folklore Center (Racy 1988).

3. The close resemblance between the Gulf *tanbūrah* and its Egyptian counterpart is confirmed by Barbara Racy's field research on *tanbūrah* practice in Cairo conducted during the summer of 1989. See the included photograph from Egypt (fig. 9.6).

Chapter 10

1. In this document, I refer to the official and unofficial celebrations in Port of Spain, Trinidad's capital as Carnival '96; but that is not its official name. Carnival, per se, has no official name. There are official celebrations in Port of Spain, and in other cities, which have official parade routes and judging stands; but not everyone sticks to these routes, and these official celebrations are merely one layer in a multilayered people's celebration. In that sense, Carnival is like New Year's Eve. There are celebrations in many cities and towns. Some are public while others are private. Furthermore, official celebrations are "Johnny-come-lately" additions to something that existed long before. The ownership of Carnival is firmly in the public domain. Thus, Trinidadians commonly ask, "How was your Carnival?" meaning "How was your personal experience of Carnival?" or "What did you do for Carnival?"

2. Casual conversation with members of the Callaloo Company, Peter Minshall's *mas* band, at their *mas* camp in Chaguaramas, December 1996.

3. Private conversation with Philip Kasinitz of the City University of New York, circa 1991. Kasinitz (1992) has written a study of Trinidadian immigrants in New York City.

4. A pan is made by tuning the end of a fifty-five-gallon oil drum. Pan design is not standardized, but a typical steelband contains about eight different types of pan, each having differences of range, tone quality, volume, and musical function. The highest pitched pan, the tenor, is really in the soprano range and contains about thirty notes on one steeldrum. The lowest pan, the bass, has only three or four notes per pan but may include six, eight or nine steeldrums arranged in a circle to give one player access to the notes he needs.

5. In most countries, a brass band is a musical ensemble composed primarily of brass instruments, but not in Trinidad where the term is used for any ensemble that has a horn section.

6. *Soca* is the contemporary, electronic form of calypso. Derived from the phrase, "soul of calypso," it has been influenced by various musics including calypso, soul music, funk, disco, and Trinidad's East Indian music traditions.

7. The word *Jouvay* comes from the French *jour ouvert*, opening day.

8. Social commentary and criticism is not exclusively an African tradition, being found in many Carnivals in Europe. However, Africans did bring to Carnival their own traditions of social criticism, which were often turned against their former European masters.

9. Interview with John Cupid of the National Carnival Commission, Port of Spain, December 1996.

10. A *cuatro* is a small four-stringed, guitarlike instrument that originated in Venezuela.

11. I am grateful to Carol Marks of New York University, one of the visiting scholars at Carnival '96, for the juggernaut metaphor.

12. Interview with Earl Crosby, Port-of-Spain, December 1996.

13. Casual conversation with Roy "Diablo" Jobity, member of San Jose Serenaders, a top *parang* band, and former member of Sound Revolution, one of Trinidad's top brass bands, Port of Spain, December 1996.

14. In Trinidad, a band singer is someone who performs regularly with the same band in concerts, clubs, or parties. They are distinct from calypsonians in that they perform other people's songs. True calypsonians compose and perform only their own songs. Now, however, many band singers write their own material and have blurred the line between themselves and calypsonians. Band singers are also distinct from calypsonians in that they perform with the same band. Most calypsonians do not have their own bands. They use pickup bands for performances and studio musicians for recordings. In addition, most calypsonians do not work as often as band singers do, since band singers perform a wider variety of material and interest in calypso is largely confined to the Carnival season in Trinidad.

15. Separate conversations with the calypsonian, Rootsman, and the *mas* band leader, Peter Minshall, Port of Spain and Chagauramas, respectively, December 1996.

16. Interview with the calypsonian, Rootsman, Port of Spain, December 1996.

17. "To wine" is a Trinidadian expression meaning to dance with very fluid pelvic rotations, a typical African movement style. "Wine" is a contraction of "wind."

18. The Midnight Robber is a traditional character who roamed the streets at Carnival. He often wore a large black *sombrero* and an ornate cape. He would blow his whistle loudly to make passers-by stop. Then he would impress them with his boastful rap talking about his lineage, his victims, and his power before asking for them for small sums of money. You could not refuse a Midnight Robber on the streets.

Chapter 12

1. Geertz states that religion is a system of symbols that produces powerful, long-lasting, pervasive moods and motivations in the members of a given culture. Thus, music is also part of this system of symbols.

2. Mulattoes are persons of European and African descent.

3. The Pelourinho, the oldest area in Salvador, is the place where slaves were tortured and sold (the term translates as "whipping post"). The old slave-auction site on Largo do Pelourinho has now been converted into the Fundacão Casa do Jorge Amado (Jorge Amado Museum).

4. Gilberto Freyre, one of Brazil's most prominent scholars, emphasized that the

impact of African culture on Brazil was so great that every Brazilian, even the fairest blonde, bears in his/her soul a lasting imprint of the African. See Freyre 1936, 33.

5. Curtin presents a table of the Brazilian slave trade from the British Foreign Office from 1871. The imports into Brazil by African origin include: Bight of Biafra, 12,600; Bight of Benin, 1,200; Congo North, 26,000; Angola, 4,100; Mozambique and Madagascar, 2,300; São Tomé and Principe, 600; unknown origins, 8,000.

6. The designations of "Sudanese" and "Islamized" to identify ethnic groups in parts of Africa are concepts that were used by Arthur Ramos (1934). Currently, scholars are using other concepts to describe the various ethnic groups in these areas.

7. The Christian elements of Candomblé also include the use of the Bible, Catholic prayers and invocations, crosses and crucifixes, candles, pictures of saints, and the use of altars. See Béhague 1977.

8. *Feijoada* is a Brazilian dish consisting of various types of meats, rice, and black beans.

9. The *orixá* Omolú is also known by the names Obaluaiye, Xapanã, and Soppona. See Omari 1984.

10. The *orixá* Nanan is also known by the names Nana and Buruku.

11. The *orixá* Yansan is also known by the name Oya.

12. The *orixá* Oxum is also known by the name Oxun.

13. Oxalá is also known by the names Oxaguian (syncretized with the adolescent Jesus Christ) and Oxalufon (syncretized with the mature Jesus Christ). Oxalá is also the father of all *orixás*.

14. Exú is one of the most important *orixás* and serves as an intermediary between the gods, ancestors, and humans. Exú, also called Elegbara or Legba by the Fon, is considered the messenger of the *orixás* and guardian of the temples, houses, roads, and crossroads. Also, Exú is always the first deity to be celebrated in any *candomblé* ritual. See Béhague 1977.

15. Mikelle Smith Omari obtains this information from Castro 1976, which is basically a dictionary that traces the etymology of words used in Afro-Brazilian religions.

16. The term *orìsà* refers to Yorùbá deities; *orixá* refers to the deities of Afro-Brazilian *candomblé*.

17. Béhague states that although the cult leader appears to be the supreme authority on musical matters, he/she may not be a performer.

18. In *candomblé* an initiate is called *abian* during the initiation, *iaô* up to the seventh year after initiation, and *ebomin* thereafter. See Béhague 1977.

19. Initiation involves the preparation of sacred liquids (*abô*), special cloths (*kelê*), and braided threads made of straw and cowry shells (*contregun*) worn around the arms as protection from spirits of the dead. The initiation also includes a *bori*, an offering given to reinforce spiritual strength.

20. The same power that is believed to be in the drums is said to exist in the sticks.

21. Among the Yorùbá, sacrifice is referred to as *ebô* and is used in a religious context. Sacrifice has both a positive (atonement) and negative side (witchcraft, sorcery, etc.). On the positive side, it is believed that life should be preserved and that its preservation and continuation are dependent on the favor of certain beings who have the power to sustain or destroy it. Like many other nations, the Yorùbá attribute human qualities to the divinities and spirits to whom offerings are made. Sacrifice also springs from a longing on the part of a person to establish, renew, and maintain communication with supernatural beings and to share and enjoy communicating with them. In the Candomblé of Bahia, animal and food sacrifice are used and conceived as a positive way of communicating with the *orixás*. See Shapiro 1995 and Wafer 1991.

22. Covering the drum bodies with the feathers of the sacrificial animal is also an important part of the ritual. See Béhague 1977.

23. The musicians of Candomblé also undergo an initiation process. This involves ritual bathing, seclusion in the *candomblé* house for a period of time, etc.

24. *Forró* is a rural type of music that is predominant in the northeastern part of Brazil. *Axé* music is one of the most popular styles in Brazil today.

25. The *berimbau* is a musical instrument that originated in the Congo. Ethnomusicologists refer to it as a musical bow for it is constructed with a long metal string attached to a wooden pole. The sound of the instrument is resonated through a gourd that is attached to the pole. This instrument is associated with the Brazilian martial art that is called *capoeira*.

26. *Favelas* are slum areas, especially in Salvador and Rio de Janeiro.

27. In Candomblé each person is said to have an *orixá* that provides protection throughout life. The *orixá* for each person is identified after a *pãi de santo* or *mãe de santa* makes successive throws with a handful of *búzios* (shells). The position of the shells is used to interpret one's luck, future, and past relation with the *orixás*.

28. The entire system of Candomblé resulted from the oppressive social and cultural context of slavery. The *orixás* served as entities that were responsible for the elements and dynamics of natural and human reality on soil distant from the African homeland. Moreover, Candomblé as a religious system took precedence over other African religious influences in Brazil, partly due to the late arrival of large numbers of Yorùbá slaves in northeastern Brazil. Among these were priests, priestesses, and initiates of the cults of the various *orixás*, who desired to maintain the cultural and spiritual foundations of their African heritage.

29. In Candomblé it is believed that Exú does not enter the Candomblé house but remains outside. The ceremony, however, always begins with songs to Exu.

30. At the Ilê Axé Opô Afonjá many of the initiates live on the Candomblé premises during annual rituals and initation cycles. They commonly refer to this residence as the *roça* (a Portuguese term meaning country, region, or backwood plantation). See Omari 1984, 16–18.

31. Unfortunately there is no illustration of this instrument, which is used only in the ceremonies at Ilê Axé Opô Afonjá.

32. The Bonfim church is considered to be the church of the *orixá* Oxalá, who is syncretized with Jesus Christ.

Chapter 13

1. See the sketches by the French artist Jean-Baptiste Debret (1949), who visited Brazil from 1816 to 1831; see also various illustrations of street scenes by Johann Moritz Rugendas (1835) and Lieutenant Chamberlain (1822).

2. *Webster's Third New International Dictionary* defines *ethnology* as a science that deals with the division of mankind into races, with their origin, distribution, and relations, and with the peculiarities that characterize them.

3. The "Grupo de Trabajo" is a research task force created by the Concejo Interamericano de Musica (CIDEM), music division of the Organization of American States (OAS), in collaboration with the International Music Council (IMC) of the United Nations Educational, Scientific, and Cultural Organization (UNESCO) to oversee and coordinate research on the impact of African music on the music of Latin America and the Caribbean.

Chapter 15

This paper has been revised and expanded from an original version that was presented at the Society for Ethnomusicology meeting held at the Eastman School of Music on October 17, 1986.

1. My analysis coincides with Dapogny (1978).

2. This transcription differs from Tirro's (1977, 147) because I could not clearly hear notes played by the piano (right hand).

Chapter 16

1. Bill Adler, interview with the author, Manhattan, May 23, 1986.

2. The Real Roxanne, interview with the author, Brooklyn, July 30, 1986.

3. DJ Hollywood, interview with the author, Manhattan, August 18, 1986.

4. Dennis Shaw and Lumumba Carson, telephone interview with the author, Brooklyn, July 12, 1986.

5. Between the late 1950s and the early 1970s, New York City had a massive and violent youth gang problem. By the 1960s Bambaataa had become a member of the notorious Black Spades, but by the 1970s, he had conceived of a way to deter youth from competing violently, instead directing them toward expressing themselves in an artistic way through various street arts: graffiti, break dancing, DJing, and MCing. Bambaataa started a youth organization called Zulu Nation, whose membership consisted of various street artists. He refers to the galvanization of the various arts as "hip-hop," a catchall phrase once used by veteran Bronx DJ Lovebug Starski.

6. Larry Smith, telephone interview with the author, Brooklyn, July 12, 1986.

7. Grandmaster Flash, interview with the author, Manhattan, March 4, 1993.

8. By the 1980s hip-hop DJing—considered up to that point as a primarily male-dominated craft—had expanded to include female artists such as Jazzy Joyce (who studied with Whiz Kid), DJ La Spank, Cocoa Chanel, and Latoya "Spinderella" Hanson (the original DJ for Salt-N-Pepa).

9. Afrika Bambaataa, interview with the author, Manhattan, July 10, 1986.

10. Vicki and Valerie, interview with the author, Manhattan, July 15, 1986.

11. Dynasty, interview with the author, Manhattan, May 23, 1986.

12. Cut Master DC et al., interview with the author, Brooklyn, July 21, 1986.

13. Cedric Singleton, interview with the author, Manhattan, October 12, 1992.

14. Rap producer Marley Marl contends that rap is music made for steering (cruising) as captured in volumes 1 and 2 of his album *Steering Pleasure*. Marl states that he made this album "for people who wanna have som'n cool playin' in their rides. [Moreover] You won't get the same effect if you play the tracks through a regular system; you need a hype car system. The beats are programmed to make the speakers howl, you know what I'm sayin'" (Nelson 1991, 39).

15. Cedric Singleton, interview with the author, Manhattan, October 12, 1992.

16. Cedric Singleton, interview with the author, Manhattan, October 12, 1992.

17. Grandmaster Flash, interview with the author, Manhattan, March 4, 1993.

18. Although the jazz-rap fusion was first labeled among English DJs as "acid jazz" in the 1980s, US-based artists do not use this term. However, the hybrid "trip-hop," an instrumental form of rap music, incorporates elements of hard and soul jazz, funk styles, and techno-pop over a simulated drum beat or hip-hop beat.

Chapter 17

1. This essay could not have been completed without the guidance of my mentor, Dr. Jacqueline Cogdell DjeDje. It began as a research project when I was a doctoral student in her seminar on African musical instruments held in the Department of Ethnomusicology at the University of California, Los Angeles, during spring of 1996.

2. The term *motown* has two referents. The first is the Motown Record Corporation founded in 1959 in Detroit, Michigan; the second is the stylistic tradition of African American popular music that was first popularized in the United States and then in Europe in the 1960s. In this essay references to the musical tradition will be indicated by use of italics and a lowercase *m (motown)*. References to the corporate entity will appear in roman type with a capital *M* (Motown).

3. For a detailed discussion of the *chimurenga* and *mbaqanga* traditions, see Eyre (1988). The term *mbaqanga* means "steamed mealy bread or mealy porridge," a quick-to-prepare staple in the South African diet. As a musical term it was coined by Mike Xaba who used it to mean "quick money" (Andersson 1981, 13). The term *chimurenga*, which means "music of struggle," was coined by Thomas Mapfumo. With his guitarist, Jonah Sithole, Mapfumo "took *mbira* rhythms and transposed them onto guitar, working its two most prominent figures—the repetitive, rhythmic pattern of *kutshinhira* and the more melodic *kushaura*—into a new, electric mix. Meanwhile, the high-hat and bass drum reproduced the traditional *honsho* (gourd rattle) rhythms. Mapfumo took what was best from the West and used it to interpret his own traditions" (Seligman 1995a). See also Bergman (1985, 119–20).

4. Phillipson 1985, 208 (as quoted in Kaemmer 1998b, 703).

5. Hocketing is performed using separate rhythmic and/or melodic interlocking parts at specified times. By interlocking the individual parts of the melody, it is possible to hear the melody and any harmony that occurs as a result. For further disussion of the hocketing technique, see Nketia (1974, 167) and Titon (1992, 73, 96, 386, 387).

6. For a detailed account of the African roots of the banjo, see Conway (1995). See Brown (1994) for a discussion on the guitar in contemporary Zimbabwe.

7. For more on Elvis Presley, see Guralnick (1971 and 1976); and Garofalo (1997, 131–41).

8. The musical basis of the sound that emanated from the Motown Record Corporation was established by the company's founder, Berry Gordy Jr., in the late 1950s. It included elements first popularized in the 1940s by Louis Jordan and His Tympany Five, such as four beats to the bar, up-tempo, horn riffs, walking bass line, honking saxophone solos, gospel vocal leads singing in their upper registers, and soprano backing vocals. These elements can be heard in Gordy's pre-Motown compositions and productions performed by Jackie Wilson ("Reet Petite," "To Be Loved," and "Lonely Teardrops"). But it was the songwriting and producing team of Edward Holland, Lamont Dozier, and Brian Holland, along with singer, songwriter and producer William "Smokey" Robinson, who were primarily responsible for shaping the Motown sound. Trademarked as the "Sound of Young America," the music spoke for lower- and middle-class African American teenagers (like many of Motown's recording artists) and spoke to middle-class White American adults and teenagers (who became the primary consumers of this music). For further reading see George (1985); Gordy (1994); and Fitzgerald (1995). These sources refer to Gordy's pre-Motown period, but also include discussions on Motown in general. For more on Motown, see Benjamin (1979); Bianco (1988); Browne (1995; 1998); Early (1995); Fitzgerald (1995); Garofalo (1997); Dr. Licks (1989); Stephens (1984); Wimer and Marks (1986); and Waller (1985).

9. African American popular music associated with other regions—Memphis (Aretha Franklin, Sam and Dave, Booker T. and the M.G.s), Philadelphia (the Ojays, Teddy Pendergrass, Lou Rawls), and Chicago (the Dells, the Chi-Lites, B.B. King)—are not included in this study because they were not stylistically homogeneous and, as in the case of Philadelphia International Records, were heavily influenced by *motown*.

10. A shebeen was "an unlicensed business (usally a private residence), whose owners illegally brewed and sold beer and liquor. The origins of this institution apparently go back to seventeenth-century Cape Town, where Dutch colonists sold liquor to Black servants and slaves, and sometimes provided rooms to drink it in. The term *shebeen* apparently came from the speech of immigrant Irish vice police in early twentieth-century Cape Town" (Coplan 1998, 766). For more on the social, cultural, and political roles of music in South Africa, see Byerly (1998); Coplan (1985); Hamm (1988); Kinloch (1972); Kivnick (1990); Erhlmann (1996); Seligman (1995b); Wachsmann (1977); and Zindi (1985).

11. On the violin and guitar, blends were created in Khoi, Cape-Malay-Afrikaans, British, and American popular melodies (Coplan 1998, 762). For studies on the role that musical instruments have played in South African society, see Kirby (1934) and Wachsmann (1952). For more on the fusion of African and African American styles, see Hamm (1988) and Waterman (1952).

12. According to Kaemmer, "in pre-European times, blacksmiths made lamellae from smelted iron, in the late twentieth century, people pounded them from nails, or from wire" (1998a, 245).

13. The *kalimba* was introduced into the African American funk genre in the mid-1970s by Maurice White while he was the leader of the group Earth, Wind and Fire.

14. Mvusi Dlavana, telephone interview, June 4, 1996.

15. According to Zindi (1985, 17): "Soul music seemed to have a cross-section of listeners of all ages and all races. Many bands and individual musicians began to sound like Otis Redding, Arthur Conley, Wilson Pickett or Sam and Dave to the extent that musicians added soul labels to their names. For example, the lead singers of some of the most popular groups were: Soul Evans, Soul Sam, Soul Amos and Hylton Mambo—'the Soulman' . . . A new breed of soul musicians [circa 1985] play funk and disco music emulated from musicians such as the Gap Band, Kool and the Gang, Shalamar, Stevie Wonder, Melba Moore, Sharon Reid, Grandmaster Flash, Melle Mel, Michael Jackson, Commodores and Lionel Ritchie. Funk groups in Zimbabwe include Movement, Rusikes, Grabb, Celebration and Wells Fargo."

    For more on soul music, see Bowman (1993 and 1997); Browne (1995); George (1988); Garofalo (1997); Guralnick (1986); Haralambos (1985); Hirshy (1984); Maultsby (1983); and Stephens (1984). For a detailed discussion of the history of hip-hop/rap cultures, see Keyes (1996) and Toop (1991).

16. Congolese is a popular music in Central Africa. It grew out of a blend of styles made famous by the group African Jazz in the 1950s. By blending Latin rhythms such as the Cuban cha-cha-cha, mambo, and rumba; the Brazilian samba; and the Colombian merengue, with indigenous forms of tom-toms, drums, and cowbells. Particularly during the 1960s, an enormous amount of Congolese music was produced in Zaire (Democratic Republic of the Congo). For further reading see Graham 1992, 107–33. According to Zindi (1985, 12), the rumba was brought to Zimbabwe by Zaireans between 1954 and 1984 (1985, 12). He states that "this is the same music which was taken by the French to Europe, and the slaves to latin America and Cuba in the 17th and 18th centuries when slavery was at its peak." For further reading on the development of traditional and popular music in Zimbabwe, see Berliner (1981); Brown (1994); Kubik (1988); Seligman (1995a); Tracey (1970); and Zindi (1985).

17. For further details on the shebeens and *marabi* music, see Andersson (1971, 23–35); Coplan (1985); Graham (1988, 258); Kivnick (1990, 226–29); and Rörich (1989, 78–101). For further discussion of popular music in South Africa, see Ballantine (1991); Benson (1996); Blacking (1980); Byerly (1998); Collins (1985); Coplan (1985); Erlmann (1989, 1991, 1996); Eyre (1988); Graham (1988, 1992); Hamm (1988); Kivnick (1990); Magubane (1990); Manuel (1988); Mekeba (1988); Rycroft (1977); Seligmann (1995b); and Zindi (1985).

18. *Isicathamiya* means "a stalking approach" or "a surprise attack" (Coplan 1985, 188). For a detailed study of the history and criticism of *isicathamiya*, see Erlmann (1996).

19. This is to enable "high-on-the-fretboard guitar work" (Eyre 1988, 85, as quoted in Coplan 1998, 351).

20. The back beat is the second and fourth beats in duple meter (beats counted in groups of two; i.e., 1–2, 3–4, 5–6, 7–8) in 4/4 time. It is usually referred to when beats two and four are accented; in *motown*, they are heavily accented. A typical *motown* approach is to accent beats two and four using hand claps, foot stamps, the snare drum, and several other instruments, such as two guitars, each simultaneously plucking different chord tones or the same notes at an octave's distance. This procedure is referred to as "stacking" the back beat.

21. For further discussion on Motown's Quality Control Department, see Benjamin (1979); George (1985); Waller (1985); Gordy (1994); and Browne (1995 and 1998).

22. A flam is a common stroke on the snare drum played with the two hands in quick succession (Randel 1983, 310).

23. According to Nettl, simultaneous contrast can also be shown in the prominence of heterogeneous instrumental ensembles; for example, in Zimbabwean traditional music the *mbira*, drums, horns, and flutes may play together (1986, 19).

24. Corporophones produce sound by striking human body parts against other human body parts, such as hand claps and thigh slaps.

Chapter 18

1. The name "Creole" was probably derived from the French *creole* or the Spanish *criollo* —terms used in the West Indies and in Spanish America to indicate a native of those regions not of indigenous blood.

2. When the Jamaican Maroons (Africans in the Americas who ran away from European slaveholders and established their own communities) signed treaties with the British in 1738, they found themselves under British control. Later in the eighteenth century some Maroons revolted against the British, which led to their forced deportation to Nova Scotia and eventually to Sierra Leone (DjeDje 1998; Furness 1965).

3. When soldiers from the West Indian Regiment were stationed in Freetown during World War I, the intermarriage and/ or mixing of the two groups increased the Creole population. Ebenezer Calender was the son of one of these soldiers and a Sierra Leonean woman.

4. *Alikali* is a word of Islamic origin meaning a "town elder" but also suggesting a "native speaker" or "interpreter." The masquerade involves masked devils of different sizes. Some of these wear headpieces and masks symbolizing leadership. The instrumental ensemble that provides appropriate accompaniment for the masquerade is composed of four drums: *bel* and *marine*, which alternate beats to provide the time line; *rolin*, which embellishes the time line; and *baba*, which functions as the master drum. All are octagonal frame drums. *Bel* and *marine* are the largest; *baba* is roughly two-thirds of the size of *bel* or *marine*; *rolin* is the smallest.

5. The "palm-wine" tradition in Sierra Leone and other West African countries is long standing. Typically in rural areas, men would gather in the evenings to relax while drinking wine made from the sap of a tropical palm. This activity was accompanied by music featuring guitar or traditional instruments.

6. *Bata* and *agogo* are Yorùbá names. Given that many Creole people are of Yorùbá or Igbo descent, it is not surprising that many terms of Yorùbá and Igbo origin appear in the Krio language.

References Cited

Abdulkadir, Dandatti
1975 "The Role of the Oral Singer in Housa/Fula Society: A Case Study of Mamman Shata." Ph.D. Diss., Indiana University.
Adama, Souleymane, and Veit Erlmann
1986 "Konu Raabe: A Fulbe Booku Song on Rabih b. Fadlallah." *Africana Marburgensia* 19 (2): 79–94.
Adamu, Mahdi
1986 "The Role of the Fulani and Twareg Pastoralists in the Central Sudan, 1405–1903." In *Pastoralists of the West African Savanna: Selected Studies Presented and Discussed at the Fifteenth International African Seminar held at Ahmadu Bello University, Nigeria, July 1979*, edited by Mahdi Adamu and A. H. M. Kirk-Greene, 55–61. Manchester: Manchester University Press with the International African Institute.
Ade, King Sunny
1986 *Sweet Banana*. One 33 1/3 LP. Atom-Park APLPS 1.
Adegbite, Ademola
1988 "The Drum and Its Role in Yoruba Religion." *Journal of Religion in Africa* 8 (1): 15–26.
Adou, Heather A.
1996 "The Politics of Music and Identity: A Study of the 'Lobi' Xylophone as Symbol of Ethnic and National Identity in Ghana and Burkina Faso." Unpublished paper, Indiana University.
1998 "The Xylophone as an Intensifier of Musical Interaction: The Bala in Minynakala, Mali." Master's Thesis, Indiana University.
Alájá-Browne, Afọlábí
1989 "A Diachronic Study of Change in Juju." *Popular Music* 8 (3): 231–42.
1995 "A History of Intercultural Art Music in Nigeria." In *Intercultural Music*, vol. 1, edited by Cynthia Tse Kimberlin and Akin Euba, 79–86. Bayreuth: Bayreuth African Studies Series.
Alexander, Herbert B.
1922 "Brazilians and United States Slavery Compared." *Journal of Negro History* 7 (4): 349–64.
Alldridge, Thomas J.
1901 *The Sherbro and Its Hinterland*. London: Macmillan.
1910 *A Transformed Colony, Sierra Leone, As It Was, and As It Is: Its Progress, Peoples, Native Customs, and Undeveloped Wealth*. London: Seeley.
Allen, Harry
1988 "Invisible Band." *The Village Voice* (Consumer Electronics Special) 1 (1): 10–11.
Allen Richard, Barry Martyn, and Graham Russell
1961 Interview with Alex Bigard. Hogan Jazz Archive, Tulane University, February 7.
Al-Naqar,'Umar
1969 "Takrur: The History of a Name." *Journal of African History* 10 (3): 365–74.
Andersson, Muff
1981 *Music in the Mix: The Story of South African Popular Music*. Johannesburg: Raven Press.
Andrade, Mario de
1959 *Dancas dramaticas do Brasil*. Sao Paulo: Livraria Martins Editora.
Aníkúlápó-Kútì, Fẹlá
1985 *Shuffering and Shmiling*. One 33 1/3 LP. Celluloid Records CELL 6117.
Aning, B. A.
1972 "Sociocultural Systems and Their Relationships with Musical Instruments in Africa." In *Report of the Eleventh Congress of the International Musicological Society*, vol. 1, edited by Henrik Glahn, Soren Sorensen, and Peter Ryom, 137–83. London, J. & W. Chester.
Ankermann, Bernhard
1901 "Die afrikanischen Musikinstrumente." *Ethnologisches Notizblatt* 3 (1): I–X, 1–132, pls. I–III. Reprint, Leipzig: Zentralantiquariat, 1976.
Anonymous
1964 "Sharo—a Fulani Test of Endurance." *Nigeria Magazine* 82 (September): 200–209.
Anonymous
1966 *Amariñña Qene* (1958 E.C.)[compilation of sayings and proverbs in Amharic]. Addis Ababa: n.p.
Apter, Andrew
1992 *Black Critics and Kings: The Hermeneutics of Power in Yoruba Society*. Chicago: University of Chicago Press.
Arnott, D. W.
1980 "Fulani Music." In *The New Grove Dictionary of Music and Musicians, Volume 7*, edited by Stanley Sadie, 23–25. London: Macmillian Publishers Limited.
Asman, James
1959 "Baby Dodds." *Jazz News* (April 24): 1.
Azarya, Victor, Paul Kazuhisa Eguchi, and Catherine VerEecke
1993 "Introduction." In *Unity and Diversity of a People: The Search for Fulbe Identity*, edited by Paul Kazuhisa Eguchi and Victor Azarya, 1–9. Osaka, Japan: National Museum of Ethnology.
Bâ, Amadou Hampate
1966 "The Fulbe or Fulani of Mali and Their Culture." *Abbia: Cameroon Cultural Review* 14–15 (July–December): 55–87.
Babalola, Adeboye
1989 "A Portrait of Ògún As Reflected in Ìjálá Chants." In *Africa's Ogun: Old World and New*, edited by Sandra T. Barnes, 147–72. Bloomington: Indiana University Press.
Baines, Anthony, and Klaus P. Wachsmann, trans.
1961 "Erich M. von Hornbostel and Curt Sachs Classification of Musical Instruments. Translated from the Original German." *The Galpin Society Journal* 14: 3–29.
Ballantine, Christopher
1991 "Music and Emancipation: The Social Role of Black Jazz and Vaudeville in South Africa between the 1920s and the Early 1940s." *Journal of Southern African Studies* 17: 129–52.
Barbosa, Adriano
1989 *Dictionário Cokwe-Português*. Coimbra: Publicações do Centro de Estudos Africanos, Instituto de Antropologia, Universidade de Coimbra.
Barnes, Sandra T., ed.
1989 *Africa's Ogun: Old World and New*. Bloomington: Indiana University Press.
Barrett, Leonard
1977 "African Religion in the Americas: The Islands in Between." In *African Religion: A Symposium*, edited by Newell S. Booth, Jr. New York: NOK Publishers, Limited.
Bastide, Roger
1978 *The African Religions of Brazil: Toward a Sociology of the Interpenetration of Civilizations*, translated by Helen Sebba. Baltimore: Johns Hopkins University Press.
Bastin, Marie-Louise
1961 *Art décoratif Tshokwe*. Lisbon: Diamang.
1982 *La sculpture Tshokwe*, translated by J. B. Donne. Meudon, France: Alain et Francoise Chaffin.
1983 "Instruments de musique, chants et danses des Tshokwe (région de Dundo, district de la Lunda, Angola)." *African Musicology* 1 (1): 45–66.
1992 "Musical Instruments, Songs and Dances of the Chokwe (Dundo Region, Lunda District, Angola)." *African Music* 7 (2): 23–44.
Batulukisi, Niangi
1995 "Societe initiatiques" and "Yombe." In *Art and Kongos: Les peuples Kongophones et leur sculpture Biteki bia Bakongo*, edited by Marc Leo Felix, 51–62 and 99–108. Brussels: Zaire Basin Art History Research Center.
Beauvoir-Dominique, Rachel
1995 "Underground Realms of Being: Vodoun Magic." In *The Sacred Arts of Haitian Vodou*, edited by Donald J. Cosentino, 153–77. Los Angeles: UCLA Fowler Museum of Cultural History.
Behague, Gerard
1975 "Notes on Regional and National Trends in Afro-Brazilian Cult Music." In *Traditions and Renewal: Essays on Twentieth-Century Latin American Literature and Culture*, edited by Merlin H. Forster, 68–80. Chicago: University of Chicago Press.
1984 "Patterns of *Candomblé* Music Performance: An Afro-Brazilian Religious Setting." *In Performance Practice: Ethnomusicological Perspectives*, 222–54. Westport, Conn: Greenwood Press.
1993 "Latin America." In *Ethnomusicology: Historical and Regional Studies*, edited by Helen Myers, 472–94. New York: W. W. Norton and Company.
Belinga, M. Samuel Eno
1972 "The Traditional Music of West Africa: Types, Style, and Influences." In *African Music: Meeting in Yaoundé (Cameroon), 23–27 February 1970*, 71–75. Paris: La Revue Musicale.
Ben-Amos, Dan
1975 *Sweet Words: Storytelling Events in Benin*. Philadelphia: Institute for the Study of Human Issues, Inc.

Ben-Amos, Paula, and Arnold Rubin, eds.
1983 *The Art of Power, The Power of Art: Studies in Benin Iconography*. Museum of Cultural History, UCLA, Monograph Series, no. 19. Los Angeles: Regents of the University of California.
Bender, Wolfgang
1991 *Sweet Mother: Modern African Music*. Chicago: University of Chicago Press.
Benjamin, Peter
1979 *The Story of Motown*. New York: Grove Press.
Benson, Herman
1996 "Hugh Masekela: His Assimilation of Traditional African Music with Modern Jazz Music." Unpublished Paper, UCLA.
Bergman, B.
1985 *Goodtime King's Emerging African Pop*. New York: Quill.
Bergman, B. et al.
n.d. *Hot Sauces: Latin and Caribbean Pop*. New York: Quill.
Berliner, Paul
1975 "The Vocal Styles Accompanying the Mbira dza Vadzimu." *Zambezia* 9: 103–4.
1976 "The Poetic Song Texts Accompanying the Mbira dza Vadzimu." *Ethnomusicology* 20 (3): 451–81.
1978 *The Soul of Mbira: Music and Traditions of the Shona People of Zimbabwe*. Berkeley: University of California Press.
1980 "John Kunaka, Mbira Maker." *African Arts* 14 (1): 61–64.
1981 *The Soul of Mbira: Music and Traditions of the Shona People of Zimbabwe*. Berkeley: University of California Press.
Berliner, Paul
1993 *The Soul of Mbira*. Chicago: University of Chicago Press.
Berns, Marla C., and Barbara Rubin Hudson
1986 *The Essential Gourd: Art and History in Northeastern Nigeria*. Los Angeles: Museum of Cultural History.
Berry, Jason
1962 Interview with Peter Bocage. *Hogan Jazz Archive*, Tulane University, February 6.
1988 "African Cultural Memory in New Orleans." *Black Music Research Journal* 8 (1): 3–15.
Besolow, Thomas
1891 *From the Darkness of Africa to the Light of America: The Story of an African Prince in Exile*. Boston: F. Wood.
Bianco, David
1988 *Heat Wave, The Motown Fact Book*. Ann Arbor: Popular Culture.
Biebuyck, Daniel
1976 " The Decline of Lega Sculptural Art." In *Ethnic and Tourist Arts: Cultural Expressions from the Fourth World*, edited by Nelson H. Graburn, 334–39. Berkeley: University of California Press.
1985 *The Arts of Zaire. Volume I: Southwestern Zaire*. Berkeley: University of California Press.
1986 *The Arts of Zaire. Volume II: Eastern Zaire*. Berkeley: University of California Press.
Blacking, John
1961 "Patterns of Nsenga *Kalimba* Music." *African Music* 2 (4): 26–43.
1977 "Some Problems of Theory and Method in the Study of Musical Change," *Yearbook of International Folk Music Council* 9: 1–26.
1980 "Trends in Black Music of South Africa, 1959–1969." In *Musics of Many Cultures: An Introduction*, edited by Elizabeth May, 195–215. Berkeley: University of California Press.
Blench, Roger
1987 "Idoma Musical Instruments." *African Music* 6 (4): 42–52.
Blesh, Rudi
1975 *Shining Trumpets*. New York: DaCapo Press.
Blier, Suzanne Preston
1998 *Royal Arts of Africa: The Majesty of Form*. London: Calmann and King Ltd.
Blyden, Wilmot E.
1974 " Remarkable Condition of the African Field." In *The People of Africa: A Series of Papers on Their Character, Condition, and Future Prospects*, edited by Henry M. Schieffelin, 2d ed, 99–129. Ibadan: Ibadan Univerisity Press.
Bonanni, Filippo
1723 *Gabinetto armónico*. Rome: Giorgio Placho. Rev. ed., with introduction and captions by Frank W. Harrison and Joan Rimmer, *Antique Musical Instruments and Their Players*. New York: Dover Publications, 1964.
Boone, Olga
1951 *Les tambours du Congo belge et du Ruanda-Urundi*. Annales du Musée du Congo belge, n.s. 4. Tervuren.
Borel, François
1986 *Collections d'instruments de musique: Les sanza*. Neuchâtel: Musée d'Ethnographie.
Bourgeois, Arthur P.
1984 *Art of the Yaka and Suku*. Meudon, France: Alain and Francoise Chaffin.
Bowman, Robert
1993 "Stax Records: A Historical and Musicological Study." Ph.D. diss., Memphis State University.
1997 *Soulsville U.S.A.: The Story of Stax Records*. London: Macmillan.
Brackenbury, E. A.
1924 "Notes on the 'Bororo Fulbe' or 'Cattle Fulani.'" *Journal of the African Society* 23, 91 (April): 208–17; 23, 92 (July), 271–77.
Brasseaux, Carl
1980 "The Administration of Slave Regulations in French Louisiana, 1724–1766." In *Louisiana History* 20: 139–58.
Bremer-David, Charissa
1993 *Decorative Arts: An Illustrated Summary Catalogue of the Collections of the J. Paul Getty Museum*. Malibu: J. Paul Getty Museum.
Brincard, Marie-Thérèse, ed.
1989 *Sounding Forms: African Musical Instruments*. New York: The American Federation of Arts.
Brown, Diana de G., and Mario Bick
1987 "Religions, Class, and Context: Continuities and Discontinuities in Brazilian *Umbanda*." *American Ethnologist* 35: 74–93.
Brown, Ernest D.
1987 "Musical Nation." In *Trinidad and Tobago*, edited by Elizabeth Saft, 229–49. Insight Guides Series. Singapore: APA Productions.
1992 "The African/African American Idiom in Music: Family Resemblances in Black Music." In *African Musicology: Current Trends*, vol. 2, edited by Jacqueline Cogdell DjeDje, 115–35. Los Angeles: UCLA International Studies and Overseas Program, The James S. Coleman African Studies Center, and Crossroads Press: African Studies Association.
1994 "The Guitar and the Mbira: Resilience, Assimilation, and Pan-Africanism in Zimbabwean Music." *World of Music* 36: 73–117.
Brown, Karen McCarthy
1989 "Systematic Remembering, Systematic Forgetting." In *Africa's Ogun: Old World and New*, edited by Sandra T. Barnes, 65–89. Bloomington: Indiana University Press.
1991 *Mama Lola: A Vodou Priestess in Brooklyn*. Berkeley: University of California Press.
Brown, Theodore D.
1976 "A History and Analysis of Jazz Drumming to 1942." 2 vols. Ph.D. diss., University of Michigan.
Browne, Kimasi L.
1995 "Variation in the Vocal Style of Brenda Holloway: Soul Singer and 1960s Motown Recording Artist." M.A. thesis, University of California, Los Angeles.
1998 "Brenda Holloway: Los Angeles' Contribution to Motown." In *California Soul: Music of African-Americans in the West*, edited by Jacqueline Cogdell DjeDje and Eddie S. Meadows, 321–51. Berkeley: University of California Press.
Browning, Barbara
1995 "Daughters of Gandhi: Africanness, Indianness, and Brazilianness in the Bahian Carnival." *Women and Performance: A Journal of Feminist Theory* 7 (2): 151–69.
Burns, E. Bradford
1993 *A History of Brazil*, 3d ed. NewYork: Columbia University Press.
1994 "Brazil." In *The New Encyclopedia Britannica*, 15th ed., edited by Peter B. Norton, 3: 185–209. Chicago: Encyclopedia Britannica, Inc.
Büttikofer, Johann
1890 *Reisebilder aus Liberia*. 2 vols. Leiden: Brill.
Byerly, Ingrid Bianca
1998 "Mirror, Mediator, and Prophet: The Music *Indaba* of Late-Apartheid South Africa." *Ethnomusicology* 42 (1): 1–44.
Cable, George Washington
1886 The Dance in Place Congo." *Century Magazine* 31 (February): 517–32.
Calixte, Colonel D. P.
1939 *Haiti: The Calvary of a Soldier*. New York: Negro Universities Press.
Candler, John
1842 *Brief Notices of Hayti*. London: Thomas Ward & Co.

Capello, H., and R. Ivens
1881 *De Benguella ás terras* de Iácca. *Descripção de uma viagem na Africa Central e Occidental. Expedição organisada nos anos de 1877–1880*. 2 vols. Lisbon: Imprensa Nacional.
Carneiro, Edison
1940 "The Structure of African Cults in Bahia." *Journal of American Folklore* 53: 271–78.
1961 *Samba de Umbigada*. Rio de Janeiro: Cia. de Defesa do Folclore Brasileiro.
Carroll, K. C.
1966 *Yoruba Religious Carving*. London: Geoffrey Chapman.
Carvalho, Gerardo A.
1948 "Os instrumentos musicais primitivos Afro-Brasileiros no Museu Histórico Nacional." *Anais do Museu Histórico Nacional* 9: 139–57.
Castro, Ieda P.
1976 "De l'integrations des apports africaines dans les parlers de Bahia au Brésil." Ph.D. diss., Université Nacional du Zaïre.
Cates, J. B.
1819 " Journal of a Journey by J. B. Cates and Others in February, March–April, 1819." Manuscript CA/E7A9,99–129. Church Missionary Society, London.
Chaillu, Paul B. du
1861 *Equatorial Africa*. London: John Murray.
Chamberlain, Lieutenant
1822 *Views and Costumes of the City and Neighbourhood of Rio de Janeiro, Brazil*. London: Columbian Press,.
Charters, Samuel
1975 Liner notes. *The Griots: Ministers of the Spoken Word*. Folkways Records FE 4178.
Chauvet, Stephen
1929 *Musique Nègre*. Paris: Société d'éditions géographiques, maritimes et coloniales.
Church, R. J. Harrison
1994 "The Gambia: Physical and Social Geography." In *Africa South of the Sahara, 1994*, 23rd ed., 392. London: Europa Publications Limited.
Clark, Andrew F.
1992 "The Challenges of Cross-Cultural Oral History: Collecting and Presenting Pulaar Traditions on Slavery from Bundu, Senegambia (West Africa)." *The Oral History Review* 20 (spring–fall, nos. 1–2):
Cole, Herbert M.
1984 *Igbo Arts Community and Cosmos*. Los Angeles: Museum of Cultural History.
Cole, Herbert M., and Doran H. Ross
1977 *Arts of Ghana*. Los Angeles: UCLA Museum of Cultural History.
Collaer, Paul
1968 *Enquête sur la vie musicale au Congo Belge, 1934–1935* (Questionnaire Knosp). Tervuren: Musée Royal de l'Afrique centrale.
Collins, John
1985 *African Pop Roots: The Inside Rhythms of Africa*. London: W. Foulsham & Co.
1987 "Jazz Feedback to Africa." *American Music* 5, 2 (summer):176–94.
Conneau, Theophile
1976 *A Slaver Log Book; or, Twenty Year's Residence in Africa*. Englewood Cliffs: Prentice Hall.
Conniff, Michael L., and Thomas J. Davis
1994 *Africans in the Americas: A History of the Black Diaspora*. New York: St. Martin's Press.
Conway, Cecilia
1995 *African Banjo Echoes in Appalachia: A Study of Folk Tradition*. Knoxville: University of Tennessee Press.
Coolen, Michael T.
1982 "The Fodet: A Senegambia Origin for the Blues." *The Black Perspective in Music* 10 (spring, no. 1): 69–84.
1983 "The Wolof Xalam Tradition of the Senegambia." *Ethnomusicology* 27 (September, no. 3): 477–98.
1984 "Senegambia Archetypes for the American Folk Banjo." *Western Folklore* 43 (April, no. 2): 177–32.
1991 "Senegambia Influences on Afro-American Musical Culture." *Black Music Research Journal* 11(spring, no. 1): 1–18.
Coplan, David B.
1985 *In Township Tonight!: South Africa's Black City Music and Theatre*. London: Longman.
1998 "Popular Music in South Africa." In *The Garland Encyclopedia of World Music: Africa*, vol. 1, edited by Ruth Stone, 719–80. New York: Garland Publishing.
Coquilhat, Camille
1888 *Sur le Haut-Congo*. Paris: Lebègue.
Costa, Peter da
1990 "The Gambia: Carnival in Banjul. Independence Silver Jubilee Fiesta." *West Africa* 3784 (March 5–11): 361.
Courlander, Harold
1954 Liner notes. *African and Afro-American Drums*. Folkways FE 4502, 1–4.
Curtin, Philip D.
1969 *The African Slave Trade: A Census*. Madison: University of Wisconsin Press.
1971 "Jihad in West Africa: Early Phases and Inter-Relations in Mauritania and Senegal." *Journal of African History* 12 (1): 11–24.
1976 "Discussion: Measuring the Atlantic Slave Trade." *Journal of African History* 17(2): 595–627.
Dagan, Esther A.
1993 *Drums the Heartbeat of Africa*. Montréal: Galerie Amrad African Art Publications.
Dalby, T. B.
1966 "Languages." In *Sierra Leone in Maps*, edited by John I. Clarke, 38–39. London: University of London Press.
Dalby, Winifred
1980 "Mali: Music and Society/Manding Music." In *The New Grove Dictionary of Music and Musicians*, vol. 11, edited by Stanley Sadie, 573–75. London: Macmillian Publishers Limited.
Daniel, Oliver
1980 "El-Dabh, Halim." In *The New Grove Dictionary of Music and Musicians*, vol.6, edited by Stanley Sadie. London: Macmillan.
Dapogny, James
1978 Book review of *Jazz: A History* by Frank Tirro. *The Musical Quarterly* 64, 6 (July): 407–408.
Dapper, O.
1668 *Naukeurige beschrijvinge der afrikaensche gewesten. Van Egyptien, Barbaryen, Libyen, Biledulgerid, Negroslavit, Guinea, Ethiopiën, Abyssine* [. . . .]. Amsterdam: J. Van Meurs.
Darbo, Seni
1976 *A Griot's Self-Portrait: Origins and Role of the Griot in Mandinka Society as Seen from Stories Told by Gambian Griots*. Banjul: Gambia Cultural Archives.
Dark, Philip John Crosskey
1971 "Musical Instruments on Benin Plaques." *In Essays on Music and History in Africa*, edited by Klaus Wachsman. Evanston.
Dark, Philip, and Matthew Hill
1971 "Musical Instruments on Benin Plaques." In *Essays on Music and History in Africa*, edited by Klaus Wachsmann, 67–78. Evanston: Northwestern University Press.
Davidson, Basil
1984 *The Story of Africa*. London: Mitchell Beazley Publishers and Television.
Davidson, Marjory
1970 "Some Music for the Lala *Kankobele*." *African Music* 4 (4): 103–13.
Davis, Ruth
1990 Review of *Taarab, the Music of Zanzibar*. (Produced by Ben Mandelson, 1988. Two 33 1/3 LPs. Globe Style Records ORBD 032 and 033.) *Ethnomusicology* 34 (1).
D'Azevedo, Warren L.
1962 "Some Historical Problems in the Delineation of a Central West Atlantic Region." *Annals of the New York Academy of Sciences* 96 (2): 512–38.
1970/71 "A Tribal Reaction to Nationalism." *Liberian Studies Journal* 1 (2): 1–22; 2 (1): 43–63; 2 (2): 99–115; 3 (1): 1–19.
1973 "Mask Makers and Myth in Western Liberia." In *Primitive Art and Society*, edited by Anthony Forge, 126–50. London: Oxford University Press.
1980 "Gola Poro and Sande: Primal Tasks in Social Custodianship." *Ethnologische Zeitschrift Zurich* 1: 13–23.
Debret, Jean-Baptiste
1834 *Voyage pittoresque et historique au Brésil; ou, Séjour d'un artiste français au Brésil depuis 1816 jusqu'en 1831 inclusivement*. Paris: Firmin Didot Frères.
1949 *Viagem pitoresca e historica ao Brasil: 1816–1831*. São Paulo: Edições Melhoramentos.
Demolin, Didier
1990 " Music and Dance in Northeastern Zaire. Part I: The Social Organization of Mangbetu Music." In *African Reflections: Art from Northeastern Zaire*, edited by Enid Schildkrout and Curtis A. Keim, 198–208. Seattle: University of Washington Press.
Deren, Maya
1953 *Divine Horsemen: The Living Gods of Haiti*. Kingston, New York: DocumenText (McPherson and Company).
de Sousberghe, Leon.
1959 *L'art Pende*. Belgium: Editions J. Duculot and S. A. Gembloux.

Devisch, Rene
1993 *Weaving the Threads of Life: The Khita Gyn-Eco-Logical Healing Cult Among the Yaka*. Chicago: The University of Chicago Press.
Diallo, Yaya
1989 *The Healing Drum: African Wisdom Teachings*. Rochester: Destiny Books.
Dias, Margot
1970 "Gruppenbildende und individuelle Musikinstrumente in Moçambique." In *VIIme Congrès International de Sciences Antropologiques et Ethnologiques, Moscovo, 1964*, vol. 3, 293–308. Moscow.
1986 *Os instrumentos musicais de Moçambique*. Lisbon: Instituto de Investigação Cientifica Tropical, Centro de Antropologia Cultural.
1988 "Chitatya e ulimba: Algumas notas sobre lamelofones ao Sul do Rovuma (Moçambique) e ao Norte do Rovuma (Tanzânia)." In *Livro de homenagem a Orlando Ribeiro*, 583–94. Lisbon: Centro de Estudos Geográficos.
DjeDje, Jacqueline Cogdell
1978 'The One String Fiddle in West Africa: A Comparison of Hausa and Dagomba Traditions." Ph.D. diss., University of California, Los Angeles.
1982 "The Concept of Patrongage: An Examination of Hausa and Dagomba One-String Fiddle Traditions." *Journal of African Studies* 9(3):116–27.
1992 "Music and History: An Analysis of Hausa and Dagbamba Fiddle Traditions." In *African Musicology: Current Trends*, vol. 2, edited by Jacqueline Cogdell DjeDje, 151–79. Los Angeles and Atlanta: UCLA International Studies and Overseas Program (ISOP)/The James S. Coleman Center African Studies Center and African Studies Association.
1998 "Remembering Kojo: History, Music, and Gender in the January Sixth Celebration of the Jamaican Accompong Maroons," *Black Music Research Journal* 18, nos. 1/2 (spring/fall): 67–120.
1998 "West Africa: An Introduction." In *The Garland Encyclopedia of World Music*, vol. 1, edited by Ruth M. Stone, 442–70. New York and London: Garland Publishing, Inc.
Djenda, Maurice
1996 "L'importance de la fonction musicale pour la classification des instruments de musique en langue Mpyɛmɔ̃," *African Music* 7 (3): 11–20 (with English summary).
Djenda, Maurice, and Gerhard Kubik
1966 Recording B 10866. Phonogrammarchiv Vienna.
Dontsa, Luvuyo
1997 "The Incredible Voices of Igongqo." In *Symposium on Ethnomusicology Number 14, Rhodes University 1996*. Grahamstown: International Library of African Music, 70–80.
dos Santos, Deoscóredes Maximiliano
1994 *História de um Terreiro Nagô*. São Paulo: Címara Brasileira do Livro.
Drewal, Henry John
1989 "Art and Ethos of the Ijebu." In *Yoruba: Nine Centuries of African Art and Thought*, edited by Henry John Drewal and John Pemberton III, 117–45. New York: The Center for African Art in association with Harry H. Abrams Inc., Publishers.
1995 "Face Bell." In *Africa: Art of the Continent*, edited by Tom Phillips, 414. Munich: Prestel.
Dubois, Felix
1897 *Timbuctoo: The Mysterious*, translated from the French by Diana White. London: William Heinemann.
Dūkhī, Yūsuf Farhān
1984 *Al-Aghānī al-Kuwaytiyyah*. Doha, Qatar: Markaz al-turāth al-sha'bī li-duwal al-Khalīj al-'Arabiyyah.
Dunham, Katherine
1983 *Dances of Haiti*. Los Angeles: Center for Afro-American Studies, University of California, Los Angeles.
Duran, Lucy
1978 "Introduction: The Music." In *Kelefa Saane: His Career Recounted by Two Mandinka Bards*, edited and translated by Gordon Innes, 16–26. London: School of Oriental and African Studies University of London.
1981 "A Preliminary Study of the Wolof Xalam (with a list of recordings at the BIRS)." *Recorded Sound: The Journal of the British Institute of Recorded Sound* 79 (January): 29–50.
1987 "On Music in Contemporary West Africa: Jaliya and the Role of the Jali in Present Day Manding Society." *African Affairs: Journal of the Royal African Society* 86 (April, no. 343): 233–36.
Early, Gerald
1995 *One Nation under a Groove: Motown and American Culture*. Hopewell, New Jersey: Ecco Press.
Eguchi, Miriam Joy
1973 "Aspects of the Life Style and Culture of Women in the Fulbe Districts of Maroua." *Kyoto University African Studies* 8: 17–92.
Eguchi, Paul Kazuhisa
1973 "The Chants of the Fulbe Rites of Circumcision." *Kyoto University African Studies* 8: 205–31.
1984 "'Let Us Insult Pella': Fulbe Mbooku Poem." *Senri Ethnological Studies* (Osaka) 15 (August): 197–246.
El-Dabh, Halim
1965a *Hindi-Yaat* no. 1. New York: C. F. Peters.
1965b *The Derabuccca: Hand Techniques in the Art of Drumming*. New York: C. F. Peters.
Elder, J. D.
1969 *From Congo Drum to Steelband: A Socio-Historical Account of the Emergence and Evolution of the Trinidad Steel Orchestra*. St. Augustine, Trinidad: The University of the West Indies.
The Election Commission of the Transitional Government of Ethiopia.
1992a *International Observers Handbook on the Electoral Rules of Implementation of the Transitional Government of Ethiopia*. Addis Ababa.
1992b Samples and copies of election materials. Addis Ababa.
Ellingson, Ter
1992 "Transcription." In *Ethnomusicology: An Introduction*, edited by Helen Myers, 110–52. New York and London: W. W. Norton.
Ellis, Alexandre John
1885 "On the Musical Scales of Various Nations," *Journal of the Society of Arts* 33 (March 27): 485–527; (October 30): 1102–11.
Ellis, George W.
1914 *Negro Culture in West Africa*. New York: Neale. (Reprint, New York: Johnson Reprint Corporation, 1970).
Elmer, Laurel
1983 *The Gambia: A Cultural Profile*. Banjul, The Gambia: The American Embassy.
Emery, Andrew
1998 "The Best DeeJay in the World." *Hip-Hop Connection* (May): 26–28.
Erlmann, Veit
1983a "Notes on Musical Instruments Among the Fulani of Diamare (North Cameroon)." *African Music* 6 (3): 16–41.
1983b "Marginal Men, Strangers, and Wayfarers: Professional Musicians and Change Among the Fulani of Diamare (North Cameroon)." *Ethnomusicology* 27 (May, no. 2): 187–225.
1985 "Model, Variation, and Performance: Ful'be Praise-Song in Northern Cameroon." *Yearbook for Traditional Music* 17: 88–112.
1988 *Essays on Music in Africa 1*. Bayreuth: Iwalewa-Haus.
1989 *Essays on Music in Africa 2: Intercultural Perspectives*. Lagos and Bayreuth: Elékóto Music Centre and Bayreuth African Studies Series.
1989 "A Conversation with Joseph Shabalala of Ladysmith Black Mambazo: Aspects of an African Performer's Life Stories." *World of Music* 31 (1989): 31–57.
1990 *Yorùbá Drumming: The Dùndún Tradition*. Bayreuth and Lagos: Bayreuth African Studies Series and Elékóto Music Centre.
1991 *African Stars: Studies in Black South African Performance*. Chicago: University of Chicago Press.
1992 "Yoruba Music in the Church: The Development of a Neo-African Art among the Yoruba of Nigeria." *In African Musicology: Current Trends: A Festschrift Presented to J. H. Kwabena Nketia*, vol. 2, edited by Jacqueline Cogdell DjeDje, 45–63. Atlanta, Georgia: Crossroads Press.
1996 *Nightsong: Performance, Power, and Practice in South Africa*. Chicago: Univeristy of Chicago Press.
Evans, David
1970 "Afro-American One-Stringed Instruments." *Western Folklore* 29: 229–45.
1978 "African Elements in Twentieth-Century United States Folk Music," *Jazzforschung* (10): 86–88.
1978 *Afro-American Folk Music from Tate and Panola Counties, Mississippi*. LP with notes. AFS L67. Library of Congress.

1994 "The Music of Eli Owens: African Music in Transition in Southern Mississippi." In *For Gerhard Kubik: Festschrift on the Occasion of His Sixtieth Birthday*, edited by August Schmidhofer and Dietrich Schüller, 329–59. Frankfurt: Peter Lang.

Evans, David, and Volker Albold

1994 *The Spirit Lives On: Deep South Country Blues and Spirituals*. CD with notes. Hot Fox Records, HF-CD-005. Kahla and Pfullendorf: Concert Direction Volker Abold and Uwe Gleich.

Evans, David, with Richard Graham and Gerhard Kubik

Forthcoming *Evolution and Invention: African and African-American One-Stringed Zithers and Their Derivatives*. Manuscript with David Evans, University of Memphis, Department of Music.

Evans, David, and Pete Welding

1995 *Bottleneck Blues*. CD with notes. Testament Records, TCD 5021. Oakland, CA: Hightone Records.

Ewbank, Thomas

1856 *Life in Brazil; or, A Journey to the Land of the Cocoa and the Palm*. New York: Harper and Brothers.

Ewens, Graeme, ed.

1991 *Africa O-Ye! A Celebration of African Music*. Enfield, Middlesex: Guinness Publishing Limited.

Eyre, Banning

1988 "Soukous, Chimurenga, Mbaqanga, and More: New Sounds from Africa." *Guitar Player* 22 (10): 80–88.

Fagan, Brian

1965 *Southern Africa during the Iron Age*. London: Thames and Hudson.

Fagg, William

1981 "Hunting Horn, Sierra Leone." In *For Spirits and Kings: African Art from the Tishman Collection*, edited by Susan Vogel, 64–68. New York: Metropolitan Museum of Art.

Fales, Inanga Chuchotée Cornelia

1998 "Issues of Timbre." In *The Garland Encyclopedia of World Music: Africa*, edited by Ruth M. Stone. New York: Garland Publishing.

Farmer, Henry George

1928 "A North African Folk Instrument." *The Journal of the Royal Asiatic Society of Great Britain and Ireland*, 25–34.

Felix, Marc

1987 *100 Peoples of Zaire and their Sculpture*. Brussels: Tribal Arts Press.

Fernandez, James

1973 "The Exposition and Imposition of Order: Artistic Expression in Fang Culture." In *The Traditional Artist in African Society*, edited by Warren L. d' Azevedo, 194–220. Bloomington: Indiana University Press.

Fernando, S. H.

1994 "Spinning Isn't Everything." *The Source: The Magazine of Hip-Hop Music, Culture, and Politics* (September): 54–56.

Ferreira, Alexandre Rodrigues

1971–74 *Viagem filosófica pelas Capitanias do Grão Pará, Rio Negro, Mato Grosso e Cuiabá, 1783–1792*. Rio de Janeiro: Conselho Federal de Cultura.

Fitzgerald, Jon

1995 "Motown Crossover Hits 1963–1966 and the Creative Process." *Popular Music* 14: 1–11.

Flores, Juan

1993 "Puerto Rican and Proud, Boyee!" *Centro de Estudios Puertorriqueños* 5 (1): 22–32.

Förster, Till

1988 *Die Kunst der Senufo*. Zurich: Museum Rietberg Zürich.

Franklin, A. David

1981 "Meter in Early Jazz." In *Jazz Research Papers*, edited by Charles T. Brown, 53–61. Manhattan, Kansas: National Association of Jazz Educators Publications.

Franklin, James

1828 *The Present State of Hayti*. London: John Murray.

Fredrickson, George M.

1981 *White Supremacy: A Comparative Study in American and South African History*. New York: Oxford University Press.

Freyre, Gilberto

1936 *Casa Grande Senzala*. Rio de Janeiro: Schmidt.

Furness, A. E.

1965 "The Maroon War of 1795." *Jamaican Historical Review* 5 (2): 30–49.

Gaden, Henri

1931 *Proverbes et maximes Peuls et Toucouleurs: Traduits, expliqués et annotés*. Paris: Institute d'Ethnologie.

Galembo, Phyllis

1993 *Divine Inspiration from Benin to Bahia*. Albuquerque: University of New Mexico.

Gamble, David P.

1949 *Contributions to a Socio-Economic Survey of the Gambia*. London: Research Department, Colonial Office.

1967 *The Wolof of Senegambia, Together with Notes on the Lebu and the Serer*. 2d ed. London: International African Institute.

Gamble, David P., and Meri Ouma Baldeh

1981 *Gambia Fula-English Dictionary (Firdu Dialect)*. Gambian Studies, no. 12. San Francisco: D. P. Gamble.

Gamble, David P., Linda K. Salmon, with Alhaji Hassan Njie

1985 *Peoples of the Gambia. I. The Wolof*. San Francisco: San Francisco State University, Anthropology Department.

Gamble, David P., and Louise Sperling

1979 *A General Bibliography of The Gambia (Up to 31 December 1977)*. Boston: G. K. Hall and Co.

Gansemans, Jos

1980 *Les instruments de musique Luba (Shaba, Zaïre)*. Annalen in-8, no. 103. Tervuren: Musée Royal de l'Afrique Centrale.

1989 "Le marimbula, un lamellophone africain aux Antillees Néerlandaises." *Cahiers de Musiques Traditionnelles* 2: 125–32.

Ganseman, Jos, and Barbara Schmidt-Wrenger

1986 *Zentralafrika*. Vol. 1, book 12 of *Musikgeschichte in Bildern*. Leipzig: Deutscher Verlag für Musik.

Gara, Larry

1959 *The Baby Dodds Story*. Los Angeles: Contemporary Press. Reprint, Baton Rouge and London: Louisiana State University Press, 1992.

1982 "Baby Dodds Remembered." *Mississippi Rag* 10 (2): 1–4.

Garcia, Rodolfo

1935 "Vocabulario Nagi." In *Estudos Afro-Brasileiros*, edited by E. Roquette-Pinto, 1: 21–27. Rio de Janeiro: Ariel Editôria Ltda.

Garlake, Peter S.

1973 *Great Zimbabwe*. London: Thames and Hudson.

Garofalo, Reebee

1997 *Rockin' Out: Popular Music in the USA*. Boston: Allyn and Bacon.

Geary, Christraud M.

1989 "Slit Gongs in the Cameroon Grassfields: Sights and Sounds of Beauty and Power." In *Sounding Forms: African Musical Instruments*, edited by Marie-Terese Brincard, 63–72. New York: The American Federation of Arts.

Geertz, Clifford

1966 "Religion as a Cultural System." In *Anthropological Approaches to the Study of Religion*, edited by M. Banton, 204–15. London: Tavistock Publications.

George, Nelson

1985 *Where Did Our Love Go: The Rise and Fall of the Motown Sound*. New York, St. Martin's Press.

1988 *The Death of Rhythm and Blues*. New York: Pantheon Press.

1998 *The Death of Rhythm and Blues*. New York: Plume.

Glaze, Anita J.

1981 *Art and Death in a Senufo Village*. Bloomington: Indiana University Press.

1986 "Dialects of Gender in Senufo Masquerades." *African Arts* 19 (3): 30–39.

Gnielinski, Anneliese von

1986 *Traditional Musical Instruments of Tanzania in the National Museum*. Occasional Paper, no. 6, National Museum of Tanzania. Dar es Salaam: Kiuta-NPC.

Goddard, Keith

1996 "The *Soul of Mbira* Twenty Years On: A Retrospect." *African Music* 7 (3): 76–90.

Goffman, Ervin

1967 *Interaction Ritual*. New York: Pantheon.

Gonzalez, Sylvia

1978 *Steelband Saga: A Story of the Steelband—the First Twenty-Five Years*. Port of Spain, Trinidad: Ministry of Education and Culture.

Goodman, Walter

1873 *The Pearl of the Antilles; or, An Artist in Cuba*. London: Henry S. King.

Gordy, Berry Jr.

1994 *To Be Loved the Music, the Magic, the Memories of Motown, An Autobiography*. New York: Warner Books.

Gould, David A.

1999 "Another Round on the Feedback Loop: Ricardo Lemvo and the Ongoing Relationship between African and Latin Musics." Unpublished paper.

Graham, Ronnie

1988 *The Da Capo Guide to Contemporary African Music*. New York: Da Capo Press.

1992 *The World of African Music: Stern's Guide to Contemporary African Music*, vol. 2. London: Pluto Press.

Gray, J. M.
1940 *A History of the Gambia*. London: Cambridge University Press.
Greenberg, Joseph H.
1953 "The Languages of Africa," *International Journal of American Linguistics* 29 (1): part 2.
1960 [1941] "Some Aspects of Negro-Mohammedan Culture-Contact Among the Hausa." In *Cultures and Societies of Africa*, edited by Simon and Phoebe Ottenberg, 477–88. New York: Random House.
1966 *The Languages of Africa*. Bloomington: Indiana University.
1970 *The Languages of Africa*. Bloomington: Research Center for the Language Sciences.
Guralnick, Peter
1971 *Feel Like Going Home: Portaits in Blues and Rock 'n' Roll*, 140. New York: E. P. Dutton.
1976 "Elvis Presley." In *The Rolling Stone Illustrated History Rock 'n' Roll*, edited by H. Miller, 35. New York: Rolling Stone Press.
1986 *Sweet Soul Music*. New York: Harper & Row.
Guthrie, Malcolm
1948 *The Classification of Bantu Languages*. London: Oxford University Press for the International African Institute.
Haiti Government Tourist Bureau
1954 *A Guide to Haiti: The Star of the Caribbean*. New York: Haiti Government Tourist Bureau.
Hall, Robert A.
1976 "Pidgin Languages." In *Collier's Encyclopedia*, vol. 19, 37. New York: Macmillian.
Hamm, Charles
1995 *Afro-American Music, South African, and Apartheid*. New York: Institute for Studies in American Music, CUNY.
Haralambos, Michael
1985 *Soul Music: The Birth of a Sound in Black America*. New York: Da Capo Press; reprint of 1979 edition.
Harris, Laura A.
1992 "The Play of Ambiguity in Praise-Song Performance: A Definition of the Genre Through an Examination of Its Practice in Northern Sierra Leone." Ph.D. diss., Indiana University.
Harris, W. T., and Harry Sawyerr
1968 *The Springs of Mende Belief and Conduct*. Freetown: Sierra Leone University Press.
Harro-Harring, Paul
1965 *Tropical Sketches from Brazil, 1840*. Rio de Janeiro: Instituto Histórico e Geográfico Brasileiro.
Hassan, Schéhérazade Qassim
1980 *Les instruments de musique en Irak*. Paris: Mouton Editeur.
Hassan, Schéhérazade Qassim, and Jean During
1984 "Nay." In *The New Grove Dictionary of Musical Instruments*, vol.2, edited by Stanley Sadie, 751–72. London: Macmillan.
Haydon, Geoffrey, and Dennis Marks, eds.
1985 *Repercussions: A Celebration of African-American Music*. London: Century Publishing.
Hebdige, Dick
1987 *Cut n Mix: Culture, Identity, and Caribbean Music*. London: Methuen.
Herskovits, Melville J.
1938 *Dahomey: An Ancient West African Kingdom*, vols. 1 and 2. New York: J. J. Augustin.
1944 "Drum and Drummers in Afro-Brazilian Cult Life." *Musical Quarterly* 30 (4): 477–92.
Hess, Catherine
1983 "Quadrangular Bells." In *The Art of Power, The Power of Art : Studies in Benin Iconography*, edited by Paula Ben-Amos and Arnold Rubin. Los Angeles: Regents of the University of California.
Hill, Errol
1972 *The Trinidad Carnival*. Austin: University of Texas Press.
Hirshey, Gerri
1984 *Nowhere to Run*. New York: Times Books.
Hiskett, Mervyn
1984 *The Development of Islam in West Africa*. London and New York: Longman Group Limited.
Hollis, A. C.
1909 *The Nandi: Their Language and Folklore*. London: Oxford University Press.
Holloway, Joseph E., ed.
1990 *Africanisms in American Culture*. Bloomington: Indiana University Press.
Holsoe, Svend E.
1966 "The Condo Confederation in Western Liberia." *Liberian Historical Review* 3: 1–28.
1967 "The Cassava-Leaf People: An Ethnohistorical Study of the Vai People, with Particular Emphasis on the Tewõ Chiefdom." Ph.D. diss., Boston University.
1971 "The Manipulation of Traditional Political Structures in Western Liberia During the Nineteenth Century." *Ethnohistory* 21: 158–67.
1974 "The First Vai Migration." Unpublished paper presented at the annual conference of the Liberian Studies Association, Madison, University of Wisconsin.
1977 "Slavery and Economic Response among the Vai (Liberia and Sierra Leone)." In *Slavery in Africa: Historical and Anthropological Perspectives*, edited by S: Miers and I. Kopytoff, 287–303. Madison: University of Wisconsin Press.
1989 "Notes on the Vai Sande Society in Liberia." *Ethnologische Zeitschrift Zurich* 1: 97–109.
1990 "Zolu Duma, Ruler of the Southern Vai, 17??–1828: A Problem in Historical Interpretation." *Liberian Studies Journal* 15: 91–107.
Hood, Mantle
1957 "Training and Research Methods in Ethnomusicology," *Ethnomusicology Newsletter* (11): 2–8.
Hornbostel, Erich Moritz von, and Curt Sachs
1914 "Systematik der Musikinstrumente: Ein Versuch." *Zeitschrift für Ethnologie* 4–5. [English translation by A. Baines and K. P. Wachsmann in *Journal of the Galpin Society*, vol. 14, 1961: 14–29.]
1961 "Classification of Musical Instruments, Translated from the Original German by Anthony Baines and Klaus P. Wachsmann." *Galpin Society Journal* 14: 3–29.
Horton, Christian Dowu
1979 "Indigenous Music of Sierra Leone: An Analysis of Resources and Educational Implications." Ph.D. diss., University of California, Los Angeles.
Horton, James Africanus
1969 *West African Countries and Peoples*. Edinburgh: University Press.
Hughes, Arnold
1994 "The Gambia: Recent History." In *Africa South of the Sahara, 1994*. 23d ed., 392–94. London: Europa Publications Limited.
Huntington, Richard, and Peter Metcalf
1979 *Celebrations of Death: The Anthropology of Mortuary Ritual*. Cambridge: Cambridge University Press.
Husmann, Heinrich
1936 "Marimba und Sansa der Sambesikultur." *Zeitschrift für Ethnologie* 68 (1–3): 197–210.
Hyslop, Graham
1974 "The Kizarano Marimba." *Tanzania Notes and Records* (Dar es Salaam) 74: 19–30.
Innes, Gordon
1974 *Sunjata: Three Mandinka Versions*. London: School of Oriental and African Studies University of London.
1976 *Kaabu and Fuladu: Historial Narratives of the Gambian Mandinka*. London: School of Oriental and African Studies University of London.
1978 *Kelefa Saane: His Career Recounted by Two Mandinka Bards*. London: School of Oriental and African Studies University of London.
Institute of Ethiopian Studies
1988 *Vistor's Manual*. Addis Ababa: Addis Ababa University.
Ismail, Mahi
1980 "Sudan." In *The New Grove Dictionary of Music and Musicians*, vol. 18, edited by Stanley Sadie, 327–31. London and New York: Macmillan and Company.
Jabir, Jum'ah
n.d. *Al-Mūsīq'a al-Sudaniyyah*. Khartoum, Sudan: Sharikāt al-Farabi.
Jackson, Joyce
1987 "The Performing Black Quartet: An Expression of Cultural Values and Aesthetics." Ph.D. Diss., Indiana University.
Jessup, Lynne
1981 "Musical Instruments of The Gambia." *Gambia Museum Bulletin* (February): 39–42.
Joe, Radcliffe A.
1954 *Traditional History, Customary Laws, Mores, Folkways, and Legends of the Vai Tribe*. Monrovia: Department of the Interior.
1961 *The History and Folklore of the Gola Tribe in Liberia*. 2 vols. Monrovia: Department of the Interior.
1980 *The Business of Disco*. New York: Billboard Books/Watson-Guptill.

Johnson, William J.
1992 *The Epic of Son-Jara: A West African Oral Tradition.* Bloomington: Indiana University Press.
Jones, Adam
1981 "Who Were the Vai?" *Journal of African History* 22: 159–78.
1983 *From Slaves to Palm Kernals: A History of the Galinhas Country (West Africa).* Wiesbaden: F. Steiner.
Jones, Arthur M.
1949 *African Music in Northern Rhodesia and Some Other Places.* The Occasional Papers of the Rhodes-Livingstone Museum, 4. Manchester: Manchester University Press.
1950 "The Kalimba of the Lala Tribe of Northern Rhodesia." *Africa* 20: 324–34.
1959 *Studies in African Music*, 2 vols. New York: Oxford University Press.
1963 "Experiments with a Xylophone Key." *African Music* 3 (2): 6–10.
1964 *Africa and Indonesia: The Evidence of the Xylophone and Other Musical and Cultural Factors.* Leiden: E. J. Brill. 2d ed., 1971.
1969 "The Influence of Indonesia: The Musicological Evidence Reconsidered." *Azania* (4): 131–45.
1970 "On Using the Stroboconn." *African Music* 4 (4): 122–24.
1973/74 "Letters to the Editor." *African Music* 5 (3): 96–97.
Jordán, Manuel
1998 *Chokwe! Art and Initiation among Chokwe and Related Peoples.* New York: Prestel.
Kaemmer, John E.
1998a "Music of the Shona of Zimbabwe." In *The Garland Encyclopedia of World Music: Africa*, vol. 1, edited by Ruth Stone, 744–57. New York: Garland Publishing.
1998b "Southern Africa: An Introduction." In *The Garland Encyclopedia of World Music: Africa*, vol. 1, edited by Ruth Stone, 700–721. New York: Garland Publishing.
Kambou-Ferrand, Jeanne-Marie
1993 *Peuple Voltaiques et Conquete Coloniale, 1885–1914.* Paris: L'Harmattan.
Kanyoro, Rachel A.
1983 *Unity in Diversity: A Linguistic Survey of the Abaluyia of Western Kenya.* Vienna: Afro-pub.
Kasinitz, Philip
1992 *Caribbean New York: Black Immigrants and the Politics of Race.* Ithaca, New York: Cornell University Press.
Katz, Bernard, ed.
1969 *The Social Implications of Early Negro Music in the United States.* New York: Arno Press and The New York Times
Kauffman, Robert A.
1969 "Some Aspects of Aesthetics in the Shona Music of Rhodesia." *Ethnomusicology* 13: 507–11.
1980 "Zimbabwe." In *The New Grove Dictionary of Music and Musicians*, edited by Stanley Sadie, 683–85. London: Macmillan.
Kaye, Andrew L.
1998 "The Guitar in Africa." *In The Garland Encyclopedia of World Music*, vol. 1, edited by Ruth Stone, 350–69. New York: Garland Publishing.
Kebede, Ashenafi
1977 "The Bowl-Lyre of Northeast Africa. Krar: The Devil's Instrument." *Ethnomusicology* 21 (3): 379–95.
1995 *Roots of Black Music.* Trenton, New Jersey: African World Press, Inc.
Kemp, Mar
1989 "Name That Tune: Sampling—Whose Music Is It Anyway?" *Option* (May–June): 66–69, 129.
Keyes, Cheryl L.
1996 "At the Crossroads: Rap Music and Its African Nexus." *Ethnomusicology* 40 (1): 223–48.
Killion, Tom
1998 *Historical Dictionary of Eritrea.* African Historical Dictionaries, no. 75. Lanham, Maryland, and London: The Scarecrow Press.
Kimberlin, Cynthia Mei-Ling
1976 "Masinqo and the Nature of Qañat." Ph.D. diss., University of California at Los Angeles, Department of Music.
Kimberlin, Cynthia Tse
1978 "The Baganna of Ethiopia." *Ethiopianist Notes* (2) 2: 15–32.
1983 "The Music of Ethiopia." In *The Musics of Many Cultures*, edited by Elizabeth May, 232–52. Berkeley, Los Angeles: University of California Press.
Kimberlin, Cynthia Tse, and Jerome Kimberlin
1984 "The Morphology of Ethiopia's Bowed Spiked Fiddle." *Selected Reports in Ethnomusicology* 5, 249–62. Los Angeles: University of California.
1995 "Ethiopian Music Traditions and Transitions: Event as Catalyst for Change." *Intercultural Music*, edited by C. T. Kimberlin and A. Euba, 1: 131–42. Bayreuth: E. Breitinger and Bayreuth University.
King, Anthony
1974 "Music: the Performance Modes" and "Music: the Instrumental Accompaniments." In *Sunjata: Three Mandinka Versions*, edited and translated by Gordon Innes, 17–27. London: School of Oriental and African Studies, University of London.
1980 "Nigeria." In *The New Grove Dictionary of Music and Musicians, Volume 13*, edited by Stanley Sadie, 235–43. London: Macmillian Publishers Limited.
King, Bruce
1960 "The Gigantic Baby Dodds." *Jazz Review* 3, 7 (August): 13–14.
Kingdon, Zachary
1995 "Drum (*likuti*)." In *Africa: Art of the Continent*, edited by Tom Phillips, 174. Munich: Prestel.
Kinloch, G. C.
1972 *The Sociological Study of South Africa: An Introduction.* London: Macmillan.
Kirby, Percival R.
1934 *The Musical Instruments of the Native Races of South Africa.* Johannesburg: Witwatersrand University Press.
Kivnick, Helen Q.
1990 *Where Is The Way: Song and Struggle in South Africa.* New York: Penguin Books.
Klein, Martin A.
1969 "The Moslem Revolution in Nineteenth Century Senegambia." In *Western African History*, edited by Daniel F. McCall, Norman R. Bennett, and Jeffrey Butler, Boston University Papers on Africa, vol. 4, 69–101. New York: Frederick A. Praeger, Publishers.
1972 "Social and Economic Factors in the Muslim Revolution in Senegambia." *Journal of African History* 13 (3): 419–41.
Knight, Roderic C.
1975 "The Jali, Professional Musician of West Africa." *The World of Music* 17 (2): 8–13.
1976 "Record Review. The Griots: Ministers of the Spoken Word. Recordings and Notes by Samuel Charters." *African Arts* 10 (October, no. 1): 92–93, 100.
1980 "Gambia." In *The New Grove Dictionary of Music and Musicians, Volume 7*, edited by Stanley Sadie, 139–42. London: Macmillian Publishers Limited.
1983 "Manding/Fula Relations as Reflected in the Manding Song Repertoire." *African Music* 6 (2): 37–47.
1984a "Music in Africa: The Manding Contexts." In *Performance Practice: Ethnomusicological Perspectives*, edited by Gerard Béhague, 53–90. Westport, Connecticut: Greenwood Press.
1984b Mandinka Drumming. *African Arts* 7 (4): 24–35.
1991 "Music Out of Africa: Mande Jaliya in Paris." *The World of Music* 33 (1): 52–69.
Koelle, S. W.
1854 *Outlines of a Grammar of the Vei Language.* London: Church Missionary House.
Konye, Paul
1997 "Twentieth Century Nigerian Art Music: Social, Political, and Cultural Factors Involved in Its Evolution and Practice." Ph.D. diss., University of Kentucky.
Koster, Henry
1817 *Travels in Brazil.* Philadelphia: M. Carey & Son; reprint, Carbondale: Southern Illinois University Press, 1966.
Kramer, Karen
1986 *Legacy of the Spirits.* Film. New York: Erzulie Films.
Kreamer, Christine M.
1989 "Slit Gong. Cote d'Ivoire, Dan." In *Sounding Forms: African Musical Instruments*, edited by Marie-Terese Brincard, 124. New York: The American Federation of Arts.
Kreamer, Christine M., and Christraud Geary
1989 "Whistle. Cameroon, Bamenda." In *Sounding Forms: African Musical Instruments*, edited by Marie-Terese Brincard, 170. New York: The American Federation of Arts.
Kubik, Gerhard
1964a "Recording and Studying Music in Northern Mozambique." *African Music* 3 (3): 77–100. Corrigenda in *African Music* 4 (4): 136–37 (1970).
1964b "Generic Names for the Mbira." *African Music* 3 (3): 25–36 (part 1). Corrigenda in *African Music* 4 (4) 137 (1970).
1965 "Generic Names for the Mbira." *African Music* 3 (4): 72–73 (part 2).

1966a "Probleme der Tonaufnahme afrikanischer Musiker." *Afrika heute* 15/16 (August 1): 227–33.
1966b "Music in Uganda: A Synopsis—La musique en Ouganda: Un aperçu général." *Afrika* (Bonn) 7 (6): 42–45.
1966c "Musique camerounaise: Les timbili des Vute." *Abbia* (Yaoundé) 14–15 (July-December): 153–63.
1968 "Ethnomusicological Research in Southern Parts of Malawi." *The Society of Malawi Journal* 21 (1): 20–32.
1971 "Carl Mauch's Mbira Musical Transcriptions of 1872." *Review of Ethnology* 3 (10): 73–80. Reprinted in *Ethnohistory in Vienna*, edited by Karl Wernhard, 165–72. Edition Herodot, Forum 9. Aachen: Rader, 1987.
1973 *Humbi en Handa—Angola*. LP with notes, no. 9 of the series. Tervuren: Musée Royal de l'Afrique Centrale.
1978a "Recording Utamaduni in Tanzania—A Field Report from Iringa and Mbeya Regions, Oct. 19–Dec. 14, 1976." *Review of Ethnology* 5 (11–14): 81–107.
1978b "Uganda Music of the Past: An Interview with Ephraim Bisase." *African Musicology* (Nairobi)1 (1): 22–30.
1979 *Angolan Traits in Black Music, Games, and Dances of Brazil: A Study of African Cultural Extensions Overseas*. Estudos de Antropologia Cultural 10. Lisbon: Junta de Investigações Cientificas do Ultramar
1980 "Cameroon." In *The New Grove Dictionary of Music and Musicians*, vol. 3, edited by Stanley Sadie, 647–49. London: Macmillian Publishers Limited.
1986 "African Graphic Systems: With Particular Reference to the Benue-Congo or 'Bantu' Languages Zone." *Muntu—Revue Scientifique et Culturelle du CICIBA, Libreville* (Gabon) 4–5: 71–135.
1987 "Das Khoisan-Erbe im Süden von Angola: Bewegungsformen, Bogenharmonik und tonale Ordnung in der Musik der !Kung' und benachbarter Bantu-Populationen." In *Musikkulturen in Afrika*, edited by Erich Stockmann. Berlin: Verlag Neue Musik, 82–196.
1988 "Nsenga/Shona Harmonic Patterns and the San Heritage in Southern Africa." *Ethnomusicology* 32 (2): 39–76.
1989 "Subjective Patterns in African Music." In *Cross Rhythms: Papers in African Folklore*, edited by Susan Domowitz, Maureen Eke, and Enoch Mvula, vol. 3, 129–54. Bloomington: African Studies Program, Trickster Press.
1991 *Extensionen Afrikanischer Kulturen in Brasilien*. Gottingen: Alano Verlag.
1994a *Theory of African Music*. Vol 1. International Institute for Traditional Music Berlin. Wilhelmshaven: Florian Noetzel.
1994b "Namibia-Survey, 1991–1993, Gerhard Kubik/Moya A. Malamusi: Landesweite Bestandsaufnahme von Musiktraditionen und Oralliteratur." *EM—Annuario degli Archivi di Etnomusicologia dell'Academia Nazionale di Santa Cecilia* 2: 151–209.
1997 "Cultural Interchange between Angola and Portugal in the Domain of Music since the Sixteenth Century." In *Portugal and the World: The Encounter of Cultures in Music*, edited by Salwa El-Shawan Castelo-Branco, 407–30. Lisbon: Publicações Dom Quixote.
1998 "Intra-African Streams of Influence." In *Africa*, edited by Ruth M. Stone, vol. 1 of *The Garland Encyclopedia of World Music*, 370–82. New York: Garland, Inc.
1999 *Kalimba, Nsansi, Mbira—Lamellophone in Afrika*. Berlin: Museum für Völkerkunde.
1999 *Africa and the Blues: Connections and Reconnections*. Jackson: University Press of Mississippi.

Kubik, Gerhard et al.
1982 *Ostafrika*. Musikgeschichte in Bildern, vol. 1, book 10. Leipzig: VEB Deutscher Verlag für Musik.
1989 *Westafrika*. Musikgeschichte in Bildern, vol. 1, book 11. Leipzig: VEB Deutscher Verlag für Musik.

Kubik, Gerhard, and Moya A. Malamusi
1989 *Opeka Nyimbo: Musiker-Komponisten aus dem südlichen Malawi*. Double-Album, MC 15, Museum Collection. Berlin: Museum für Völkerkunde, Abteilung Musikethnologie.

Kubik, Gerhard, Moya A. Malamusi, and Lidiya Malamusi
1985–87 *Nachdokumentation und Katalogisierung der Sammlung afrikanischer Musikinstrumente im Musikinstrumentenmuseum/ Münchener Statdtmuseum*. Manuscript (673 pages) deposited in the Münchner Stadtmuseum.

Lagamma, Alisa
1997 "The Art of the Punu *Mukudj* Masquerade: Portrait of an Equatorial Society." Ph.D. diss., Columbia University, New York.

Lamb, David
1984 *The Africans*. New York: Vintage Books.

Lamp, Fredrick
1996 *Art of the Baga: A Drama of Cultural Reinvention*. New York and Munich: Museum for African Art and Prestel.

Landes, Ruth
1940 "Fetish Worship in Brazil." *Journal of American Folklore* 53: 261–70.
1947 *The City of Women*. New York: Macmillan Press.

Latrobe, Benjamin
1971 *The Journal Latrobe: Being the Notes and Sketches of an Architect, Naturalist, and Traveler in the United States from 1796 to 1800*. New York: Burt Franklin.

Laurenty, Jean-Sebastien
1960 *Les chordophones du Congo Belge et du Ruanda-Urundi*. In *Annales du Musée Royal du Congo Belge, Tervuren*, n.s. in-4. Sciences de l'Homme, vol. 2. Tervuren: Musée Royal de l'Afrique Centrale.
1962 *Les sanza du Congo*. 2 vols. Annales du Musée Royal de l'Afrique Centrale Tervuren, n.s. in-4. Sciences Humaines 3. Tervuren: Musée Royal de l'Afrique Centrale.
1995 *L'organologie du Zaire. Tome II: Les sanza-Les xylophones-Les tambours a fente*. Musee Royal de l'Afrique Centrale, Annales Sciences Humaines, no. 147.
1997 *L'Organologie du Zaire. Tome IV: Les Cordophones*. Musee Royal de l'Afrique Centrale, Annales Sciences Humaines, no. 158.

Lavergne, Barbara, and José Flavio Pessoa de Barros
1986 "Chants sacrés et plantes liturgiques dans le *Candomblé* brésilien." *Cahiers du Monde Hispanique et Luso-Brasilien* 47: 25–39.

Lee, Linda
1991 *The Bruce Lee Story*. Santa Clarita, California: Ohara Publications, Inc.

Leland, John, and Steve Stein
1988 "What Is It?" *The Village Voice* (special section on "Hip Hop Nation") (January 19): 26–30.

Leslau, Wolf
1968 *Amharic Textbook*, 1–7. Berkeley: University of California Press.

Leyburn, James G.
1941 *The Haitian People*. Westport, Connecticut: Greenwood Press.

Leymarie-Ortiz, Isabelle
1979 "The Griots of Senegal and Change." *Africa (Rome)* 34 (September): 183–97.

Licks, Dr.
1989 *Standing in the Shadows of Motown: The Life and Music of Legendary Bassist James Jamerson*. Wynnewood, Pennsylvania: Dr. Licks Publications.

Lindon, Thomas
1990 "Oríkì Orìsà: The Yoruba Prayer of Praise." *Journal of African History* 2: 205–24.

List, George
1968 "The Mbira in Cartagena." *Journal of the International Folk Music Council* 20: 54–59.
1983 *Music and Poetry in a Colombian Village: A Tri-Cultural Heritage*. Bloomington: Indiana University Press.

Little, Kenneth L.
1951 *The Mende of Sierra Leone: A West African People in Transition*. London: Kegan Paul, Trench, Trubner.

Livingstone, David, and Charles Livingstone
1865 *Narrative of an Expedition to the Zambesi and Its Tributaries; and of the Discovery of the Lakes Shirwa and Nyassa, 1858–1864*. London: John Murray.
1875 *A Popular Account of Dr. Livingstone's Expedition to the Zambesi and Its Tributaries; and of the Discovery of Lakes Shirwa and Nyassa, 1858-1864*. London: John Murray.

Liyounet, Demis
1996 "Shibsheba Choir and the Origin, Quality, and the Nature of Their Songs." Unpublished paper, Addis Ababa University, Theater Arts Department.

Locke, David, featuring Abubakari Lunna.
1990 *Drum Damba: Talking Drum Lessons*. Crown Point, Indiana: White Cliffs Media Company.

Mabogunje, Akin
1976 [1971] "The Land and Peoples of West Africa." In *History of West Africa, Volume 1* (2nd ed.), edited by J. F. A. Ajayi and Michael Crowder, 1–32. London: Longman Group Limited.

MacKenzie, Charles
1830 *Notes on Haiti*, vol. 2. London: Henry Colburn & Richard Bentley.
Maes, J.
1921 "Le sanza du Congo Belge." *Congo* 1 (4): 542–72.
Magubane, Bernard Makhosezwe
1990 *The Political Economy of Race and Class in South Africa*. New York: Monthly Review Press.
Mahy, Judith.
1974 "Mali, Kolokani, Bamana, 1974–76." Ph.D. diss. Bloomington: Archives of Traditional Music.
Malamusi, Moya Aliya
1993 "Kambazithe Makolekole Valimba Band." *Perkussionale '93*. Program brochure. Berlin: Haus der Kulturen der Welt
Manuel, Peter
1988 *Popular Musics of the Non-Western World: An Introdutory Survey*. New York: Oxford University Press.
Marcuse, Sibyl
1975 *A Survey of Musical Instruments*. New York: Harper and Row Publishers.
Maret, Pierre de
1978 "Chronologie de l'Age du Fer dans la dépression de l'Upemba en République du Zaire." Ph.D. Diss., Université Libre de Bruxelles.
Martins, Bayo
1983 *The Message of African Drumming*. Heidelberg: P. Kivouvou Verlag-Editions Bantoues.
Martius, Carl Friedrich Phillip von, and Johann Baptist von Spix
1966–1967 *Atlas zur Reise in Brasilien (1817-1820)*. 4 vols. Stuttgart: Antiquarium.
Mason, John
1992 *Orin Orisa: Songs for Selected Heads*. New York: Yoruba Theological Archministry.
Massa, Gabriel, and Y. Georges Madiega, eds.
1995 *La Haute-Volta coloniale: Temoignages, recherches, regards*. Paris: Editions Karthala.
Mattoso, Katia M. de Queiros
1988 "Slave, Free, and Freed Family Structures in Nineteenth-Century Salvador, Bahia." *Luso-Brazilian Review* 25 (1): 69–88.
Mauch, Carl
1869–72 *Afrikanisches Tagebuch, 1869–1872*. Manuscript deposited in Linden-Museum, Stuttgart.
1969 *The Journals of Carl Mauch: His travels in the Transvaal and Rhodesia, 1869–1872*. Transcribed from the original by Mrs. E. Bernhard, translated by F. O. Bernhard. Salisbury: National Archives of Rhodesia.
Maultsby, Portia K.
1990 "Africanisms in African-American Music." In *Africanisms in American Culture*, edited by Joseph E. Holloway, 185–210. Bloomington: University of Indiana Press.
1983 "Soul Music: Its Sociological and Political Significance in American Popular Culture." *Journal of Popular Culture* 17 (2): 51–60.
Medeiros, José
1957 *Candomblé*. Rio de Janeiro: Edições o Cruzeiro.
Mekeba, Miriam
1988 *My Story*. Johannesburg: Skotaville Press.
Mellor, Captain
1936 "Strange People and Customs of Northern Nigeria. The Fulani Dance." *The Saturday Review of Politics, Literature, Science and Art* (October 31): 571.
Merriam, Alan P.
1964 *The Anthropology of Music*. Evanston, Illinois: Northwestern University Press.
Métraux, Alfre
1972 *Voodoo in Haiti*. 1st English ed. New York: Schocken Books.
Miller, John Ross
1990 "Music and Dance in Northeastern Zaire. Part II: Collecting Culture: Musical Instruments and Musical Change." In *African Reflections: Art from Northeastern Zaire*, edited by Enid Schildkrout and Curtis A. Keim, 209–16. Seattle: University of Washington Press.
Miller, Joseph C.
1992 "The Numbers, Origins, and Destinations of Slaves in the Eighteenth-Century Angolan Slave Trade." In *The Atlantic Slave Trade Effects on Economics, Societies, and Peoples in Africa, the Americas, and Europe*, edited by Joseph E. Inikori and Stanley L. Engerman, 77–115. Durham: Duke University Press.
Moon, Tom
1991 "Public Enemy's Bomb Squad." *Musician* (October): 69–72, 76.
Moore, Bai T.
1955 *The Tribes of the Western Province and the Dewoin People*. Monrovia: Department of the Interior, Republic of Liberia.
Monts, Lester P.
1982 "Music Clusteral Relationships in a Liberian Sierra Leonean Region: A Preliminary Analysis." *Journal of African Studies* 9: 101–15.
1984 "Conflict, Accommodation, and Transformation: The Effect of Islam on Music of the Vai Secret Societies." *Cahiers d'Etudes Africaines* 95: 321–42.
Morais, João M. F.
1986 "An Annotated Bibliography of Mozambican Archaeology." *Working Papers in African Studies*, 30. Uppsala: African Studies Programme.
1988 *The Early Farming Communities of Southern Mozambique*. Studies in African Archaeology, 3. Maputo: Eduardo Mondlane University.
Mukuna, Kazadi wa
1979 *Contribuicao Bantu na Musica Popular Brasileira*. Sao Paulo: Global Editora.
1994 "Resilience and Transformation in Varieties of African Musical Elements in Latin America." In *For Gerhard Kubik: Festschrift on the Occasion of His 60th Birthday*, edited by August Schmidhofer and Dietrich Schuller, 405–12. Vienna: Peter Lang.
1994 "Sotaques: Style and Ethnicity in a Brazilian Folk Drama." In *Music and Black Ethnicity in the Caribbean and South America*, edited by Gerard Behague, 207–24. London: Transaction Publisher.
(Forthcoming) "The Rise of Bumba-meu-Boi in Maranhao: Resilience of African-Brazilian Cultural Identity." In *Black Brazil: Culture, Identity, and Social Mobilization*, edited by Larry Crook and Randal Johnson.
Mukuna,Kazadi wa, and Tiago de Oliveira Pinto, eds.
1990–91 "The Study of African Musical Contribution to Latin America and the Caribbean: A Methodological Guideline," *Bulletin of the International Committee on Urgent Anthropological and Ethnological Research* (32–33): 47–48.
Murdock, George P.
1959 *Africa: Its People and Their Culture History*. New York: McGraw Hill Book Co.
Musambi, J. K. L. Khadambi
1994 "*Vukhulu* Circumcision Song and Dance of the Abatirichi People." Unpublished paper.
Myers, Helen
1992 *Ethnomusicology*. New York: W.W. Norton.
National Democratic Institute for International Affairs (in conjunction with the African American Institute)
1992 *An Evaluation of the June 21, 1992, Elections in Ethiopia*. National Democratic Institute: Washington, D.C.
N'Diaye, Diana Baird
1990 "Tradition and Cultural Identity in Senegal." In *Festival of American Folklife (1990), June 27–July 1/July 4–8*, edited by Peter Seitel, 38–47. Washington, D.C.: Smithsonian Institution.
Nelson, Harold D., and Irving Kaplan, eds
1981 *Ethiopia: A Country Study*. Foreign Area Studies. The American University, Washington, D.C.
Nelson, Havelock
1991 "Marley Marl: Soul Controller, Sole Survivor," *The Source: The Magazine of Hip-Hop Music, Culture, and Politics* (October): 36–39.
Nettl, Bruno
1986 "Africa." In *The New Harvard Dictionary of Music*, ed. Don Randel, 16–24. Cambridge: Belknap Press of the Harvard University Press.
Nicholls, David
1979 *From Dessalines to Duvalier: Race, Colour, and National Independence in Haiti*. Cambridge: Cambridge University Press.
Nikiprowetzky, Tolia
1963 "The Griots of Senegal and Their Instruments." *Journal of the International Folk Music Council* 15: 79–82.
1966 *Trois aspects de la musique Africaine: Mauritanie, Sénégal, Niger*. Paris: Offica de Coopération Radiophonique, OCORA.
1980 "Senegal." In *The New Grove Dictionary of Music and Musicians*, vol. 17, edited by Stanley Sadie, 127–29. London: Macmillian Publishers Limited.
Njie, Saihou
1970a "A Look at Gambian Praise Songs and Singers, Part One." *The Gambia News Bulletin* 8 (August 6): 73.
1970b "Praise Song for the Great Man of the Village, Part Two." *The Gambia News Bulletin* 8 (August 8): 32.

1970c "Wedding Praise Song, Part Three." *The Gambia News Bulletin* 8 (August 11): 93.
Nketia, J. H. Kwabena
1963 *Drumming in Akan Communities of Ghana.* Edinburgh: Thomas Nelson.
1973 "The Study of African and Afro-American Music," *The Black Perspective in Music* 1 (1): 7–23.
1974 *The Music of Africa.* New York: W.W. Norton and Co., Inc.
1979 "African Roots of Music in the Americas: An African View." *Jamaica Journal* 43 (March): 12–17.
1982 "On the Historicity of African Music in African Cultures." *Journal of African Studies* 9: 90–100.
1988 "The Intensity Factor in African Music." *Performance in Contemporary African Arts.* Bloomington: Indiana University Press.
Nodal, Roberto
1983 "The Social Evolution of the Afro-Cuban Drum." *The Black Perspective in Music* 11 (2): 157–77.
Norris, Chris
1993 "Old School, New School, Cool School." *Option* (September/October): 82–87.
Norris, Chuck, with Joe Hyams
1988 *The Secret of Inner Strength: My Story.* Boston: Little Brown and Company.
Northern, Tamara
1984 *The Art of Cameroon.* Washington, D.C.: National Museum of Natural History.
Nurse, George T.
1970 "Cewa Concepts of Musical Instruments." *African Music* 4 (4): 32–36.
Nzewi, Meki
1974 "Melo-Rhythmic Essence and Hot Rhythm in Nigerian Folk Music," *The Black Perspective in Music* 2 (1): 23–28.
Ofcansky, T. P., and L. Berry
1993 *Ethiopia: A Country Study.* 4th ed. Country Studies/Area Handbook Program. Washington D.C.: Library of Congress, Federal Research Division.
Ogawa, Ryo
1993 "Ethnic Identity and Social Interaction: A Reflection of Fulbe Identity." In *Unity and Diversity of a People: The Search for Fulbe Identity*, edited by Paul Kazuhisa Eguchi and Victor Azarya, 119–37. Osaka: National Museum of Ethnology.
Ogilby, Johann
1670 *Africa, Being an Accurate Description of the Regions. . . .* London: T. Johnson.
Okelo, Anthony
1976 *"Kyrie from Missa Maleng" for Choir and African Instruments.* Ile-Ife: University of Ife Press.
Olsen, Poul Roving
1967 "La musique Africaine dans le Golfe Persique." *Journal of the International Folk Music Council* (19): 28–38.
1980 "Arabian Gulf." In *The New Grove Dictionary of Music and Musicians*, edited by Stanley Sadie, vol. 1, 513–14. London: Macmillan and Company.
Omari, Mikelle Smith
1984 *From the Inside to the Outside: The Art of Bahian Candomblé.* Museum of Cultural History, Monograph Series No. 24. Los Angeles: University of California Press.
Ọmọ́jọlà, Bọ̀dé
1995 *Nigerian Art Music.* Ibadan: Institut Français de Recherche en Afrique.
Opefeyitimi, Ayo
1975 "Owuré: Medium of Communicating the Desires of Men to the Gods of Yorubaland." *Journal of Religion in Africa* 4: 15–30.
Oppong, Christine
1973 *Growing Up in Dagbon.* Tema, Ghana: Ghana Publishing Corporation.
Ortiz, Fernando
1950 *La Africania de la musica folklorica de Cuba.* Havana: Ed. Cardenas y Cia.
1952 *Los Instrumentos de la Musica Afrocubana.* 5 vols. Havana: Direccion de Cultura del Ministerio de Educacion.
1955 *Los instrumentos de la música afro-cubana*, vols. 1–4. Habana: Cárdenas.
Oven, Cootje van
1973/74 "The Kondi of Sierra Leone." *African Music* 5 (3): 77–85.
1980 "Sierra Leone." In *The New Grove Dictionary of Music and Musicians*, vol. 17, edited by Stanley Sadie, 302–4. London: Macmillian Publishers Limited.
1981 *An Introduction to the Music of Sierra Leone.* Wassenaar, Netherlands: Cootje van Oven.
Pan-American Union
1947 *Haiti.* Washington, D.C.: Pan-American Union.
Parrinder, G.
1947 "Yoruba-Speaking Peoples in Dahomey." *Africa* 17 (2): 122–29.
Parsons, Robert T.
1964 *Religion in an African Society.* Leiden: E. J. Brill.
Pemberton, John, III
1989 "The Dreadful God and the Divine King." In *Africa's Ogun: Old World and New*, edited by Sandra T. Barnes, 65–89. Bloomington: Indiana University Press.
Perrois, Louis
1985 *Ancestral Art of Gabon from the Collections of the Barbier-Mueller Museum.* Geneva: Barbier Mueller Museum.
Pfeffer, G.
1939 "Prose and Poetry of the Ful'be." *Africa: Journal of the International African Institute of Languages and Cultures* 12 (July, no. 3): 285–30.
Phillips, Tom, ed.
1995 *Africa: The Art of a Continent.* London Royal Academy of Arts.
Phillipson, David W.
1977 *The Later Preshistory of Eastern and Southern Africa.* London: Heinemann.
1985 *African Archaeology.* Cambridge: Cambridge University Press.
Pierson, Donald
1942 *Negro in Brazil: A Study of Race Contact at Bahia.* Chicago: University of Chicago Press.
Pinto, Tiago de Oliveira, ed.
1986 *Brasilien: Einführung in Musiktraditionen Brasiliens.* Mainz: Schott.
Pinto, Tiago de Oliveira
1991 *Capoeira, Samba, Candomble: Afro-brasilianische Musik im Reconcavo, Bahia.* Berlin: Museums fur Volkerkunde.
1991 "Making Ritual Drama: Dance, Music, and Representation in Brazilian *Candomblé* and *Umbanda.*" *World of Music* 33 (1): 70–87.
Pitman, Andrew
1972 "Kings Abroad: Maybe—But We're Beggars at Home." *The Daily Express* 1, 16: 16–17.
Poche, Christian
1984a "Duff." In *The New Grove Dictionary of Musical Instruments*, vol. 1, edited by Stanley Sadie, 616–17. London: Macmillan.
1984b "Qānūn." In *The New Grove Dictionary of Musical Instruments*, vol. 3, edited by Stanley Sadie, 169–71. London: Macmillan.
1984c "'Ūd." In *The New Grove Dictionary of Musical Instruments*, vol. 3, edited by Stanley Sadie, 687–93. London: Macmillan.
Pollak-Eltz, Angelina
1978 "The Marimbula: An Afro-American Instrument." *Review of Ethnology* 5 (4): 28–30.
Póvoas, Ruy do Carmo
1989 *A linguagem do Candomblé níveis sociolingüísticos de integração Afro-Portuguesa.* Rio de Janeiro: Livraria José Olympio Editôra S. A.
Powne, Michael
1968 *Ethiopian Music.* London: Oxford University Press.
Prichard, Hesketh
1971 *Where Black Rules White: A Journey Across and About Hayti.* Freeport, New York: Books for Libraries Press. (Reprint of 1900 ed.)
Prouty, Chris, and Eugene Rosenfeld
1994 *Historical Dictionary of Ethiopia and Eritrea.* 2d ed. African Historical Dictionaries no. 56. Lanham, Maryland, and London: The Scarecrow Press.
Querino, Manoel Raymundo
1938 *Costumes Africanos no Brasil.* Rio de Janeiro: Civilização Brasileira, S. A.
Racy, Ali Jihad
1986a "Folk Instruments of the Arab Near East: Toward the Study of Cross-Mediterranean Links," *Viltis Magazine* 45 (1): 4–6.
1986b "The Interconnection of Elements in Gulf Folk Arts: Implications for Folk Research," *Al-Ma'thūrāt al-Sha'biyyah*, 1 (2): 27–29.
1988 *Tanburah Music of the Gulf* (Gulf Music Cassette, vol. 2). Doha, Qatar: Arab Gulf States Folklore Centre.
Ramos, Arthur
1937 *As culturas Negras no Novo Mundo.* Rio de Janeiro: Civilizacao Brasileira.
1939 *The Negro in Brazil*, translated by Richard Pattee. Washington, D. C.: Associated Publishers, Inc.
1954 *O folclore Negro do Brasil*, 2d ed. Rio de Janeiro: Livaria Editôria Casa do Estudante do Brasil.
1988 *O Negro Brasileiro: Etnografia Religiosa e Psicanālise*, 2d ed. Recife: Fundação Joaquim Nabuco, Editora Massangana.
Ramsey, Frederic, Jr.
1951 "Baby Dodds: Talking and Drum Solos in Footnotes." In *Jazz, Vol. 1.* Folkways Records FJ 2290: 1–4.

Randel, Don
1986 *The New Harvard Dictionary of Music*, edited by Don Randel. Cambridge: Belknap Press of Harvard University Press. Random House
1987 *Random House Dictionary of the English Language*. New York: Random House.
Rashīd, Subhī Anwar
1975 *Al-Alāt Al-Mūsīqiyyah fī al-'Usūr al-Islāmiyyah*. Baghdad: Dār al-Hurriyyah.
1989 "Al-Tanbūrah fī al-Basran, Alah Turāthiyyah," *Al-Turāth al-Sha'bī* 3: 56–66.
Reed, L. N.
1932 "Notes on Some Fulani Tribes and Customs." *Africa: Journal of the International Institute of African Languages and Cultures* 5 (October, no. 4): 422–54.
Reefe, Thomas Q.
1981 *The Rainbow and the Kings: A History of the Luba Empire to 1891*. Berkeley: University of California Press.
Reynolds, Dwight F.
1993 *Sirat Bani Hilal: A Guide to the Epic and Its Performance*. Detroit: ACCESS Cultural Arts Program.
Riesman, Paul
1977 [1974] *Freedom in Fulani Social Life: An Introspective Ethnography*, translated by Martha Fuller. Chicago: The University of Chicago Press. Originally published as *Société et liberté chez les Peul Djelgôbé de Haute-Volta*.
Rigaud, Milo
1969 *Secrets of Voodoo*. San Francisco: City Lights Books.
Rimmer, Joan
1969 *Ancient Musical Instruments of Western Asia*. London: The Trustees of the British Museum.
Roberts, Helen H.
1924 "Some Drums and Drum Rhythms of Jamaica." *Natural History* 24 (2): 241–51.
Roberts, John Storm
1998 *Black Music of Two Worlds*. 2nd ed. New York: Praeger Publishers.
Roberts, Mary Nooter, and Allen F. Roberts
1996 *Memory: Luba Art and the Making of History*, edited by Mary Nooter Roberts and Allen F. Roberts. New York: The Museum for African Art.
Robinson, David
1973 "Abdul Qadir and Shaykh Umar: A Continuing Tradition of Islamic Leadership in Futa Toro." *The International Journal of African Historical Studies* 6 (2): 286–303.
Robinson, Eugene
1997 "Pulsations." *Washington Post Magazine* (September 28): 11–14.
Rodney, Walter
1970 *A History of the Upper Guinea Coast, 1545–1800*. Oxford: Oxford University Press.
Rodrigues, Nina
1988 *Os Africanos no Brasil*, 7th ed. São Paulo: Cia Editôria Nacional.
Rörich, Mary
1989 "Shebeens, Slumyards, and Sophiatown: Black Women, Music, and Cultural Change in Urban South Africa c. 1920–1960." *World of Music* 31: 78–101.
Rose, Tricia
1994 *Black Noise: Rap Music, and Black Culture in Contemporary America*. Hanover: Wesleyan University Press.
Rosellini, James
1980 *Dira and His Talking Musical Bow*. African Family Films.
1980 "Upper Volta." In *The New Grove Dictionary of Music and Musicians*, vol. 19, edited by Stanley Sadie, 456–60. London: Macmillian Publishers Limited.
Ross, Doran H.
1974 "Ghanaian Forowa." *African Arts* 8 (1): 40–49.
1984 "The Art of Osei Bonsu." *African Arts* 17 (2) 28–40, 90.
1988 "Queen Victoria for £25 : The Iconography of a Breasted Drum from Southern Ghana." *College Art Journal* 47 (2): 114–20.
1992 *Elephant: The Aminal and Its Ivory in African Culture*. Los Angeles: University of California, Los Angeles, Fowler Museum of Cultural History.
Ross, Doran H., and Timothy F. Garrard, eds.
1983 *Akan Transformations: Problems in Ghanaian Art History*. Los Angeles: UCLA Museum of Cultural History.
Rouget, Gilbert
1980 "Guinea." In *The New Grove Dictionary of Music and Musicians*, vol. 7, edited by Stanley Sadie, 819–22. London: Macmillian Publishers Limited.
1982 "Cithare et glissando: Nouvelles données sur le chromatism au Bénin," *Revue de Musicologie* 68 (1–2): 310–24.
1985 *Music and Trance*. Chicago: The University of Chicago Press.
Rower, William, and Vivian Schelling
1991 "From Slavery to Samba." In *Memory and Modernity: Popular Culture in Latin America*, edited by William Rower and Vivian Schelling, 122–27. London and New York: Verso.
Roy, Christopher D.
1987 *Art of the Upper Volta Rivers*. Meudon: Chaffin.
Rugendas, Johann Moritz
1835 *Malerische Reise in Brasilien*. Paris: Engelmann & Cie.
Russell, William
1958a Interview with Warren "Baby" Dodds. Hogan Jazz Archive, Tulane University, May 31.
1958b Interview with Natty Dominique. Hogan Jazz Archive, Tulane University, May 31.
1959 Interview with Nappy Lamare and Ray Bauduc. Hogan Jazz Archive, Tulane University, September 9.
Russell, William, Johnny Wiggs, and Ralph Collins
1961 Interview with Albert "Chinee" Foster. Hogan Jazz Archive, Tulane University, March 9.
Rycroft, David
1966 "Friction Chordophones in South-Eastern Africa," *Galpin Society Journal* 19: 84–100.
1977 "Evidence of Stylistic Continuity in Zulu 'Town' Music." In *Essays for a Humanist: An Offering to Klaus Wachsmann*, 216–60. New York: Town House Press.
Sachs, Curt
1940 *The History of Musical Instruments*. New York: W. W. Norton and Co.
Sadie, Stanley, ed.
1980 The New Grove Dictionary of Music and Musicians, vol. 19. London: Macmillan.
St. John, Sir Spenser
1889 *Hayti, or The Black Republic*. London: Smith, Elder & Co.
Samnadda, Elizabeth
1970 "At One Time Carnival Was an Orgy Indulged in by the Lower Classes." *The Daily Express* 2, 8: 11.
Sandy, Jude
1997 "3 Canal Turns 'Blue': Obscure Performing Arts Entity, Made Up of a Few Familiar Faces, Surprises All with a Catchy Carnival Debut." *Trinidad Guardian* 1, 18: 16.
Sangree, Walter H.
1966 *Age, Prayer and Politics in Tiriki, Kenya*. London: Oxford University Press.
Santos, Frei João dos
1609 *Ethiopia Oriental*. Evora. 2d ed., Biblioteca de Clássicos Portugueses. 2 vols. Lisbon: Mello de Azevedo, 1891.
Santos, Orlando
1993 *O Ebó no Culto aos Orixás*. Rio de Janeiro: Pallas.
Santos Jr., Norberto
1958 "Contribuição para o estudo dos instrumentos musicais dos indígenas de Moçambique—A chitata." *Garcia de Orta—Revista da Junta das Missões Geográficas e de Investigações do Ultramar* 6 (2): 347–64.
Sawyerr, Harry, and W. T. Harris
1968 "The Significance of the Numbers Three and Four among the Mende of Sierra Leone." *Sierra Leone Studies* 26: 31–36.
Schaeffner, Andre
1960 "Situation des musiciens dans trois sociétés Africaines." *Les Colloques de Wégimont III (1956). Ethnomusicologie* 2: 33–50.
Schildkrout, Enid, and Curtis A. Keim
1990 *African Reflections: Art from Northeastern Zaire*. Seattle: University of Washington Press.
Schmidt, Cynthia
1998 "Kru Mariners and Migrants of the West African Coast." In *Africa*, vol. 1 of *The Garland Encyclopedia of World Music*, edited by Ruth M. Stone, 370–82. New York: Garland Inc.
School of Oriental and African Studies
1972 *Conference of Manding Studies*. London: University of London.
Schultz, Emily A.
1980 "Introduction." In *Image and Reality in African Interethnic Relations: The Fulbe and Their Neighbors*, edited by Emily A. Schultz, v–xiv. Williamsburg, Virginia: Department of Anthropology, College of William and Mary.
Schwartz, Nancy Beth A.
n.d. *Mambilla—Art and Material Culture*. Publications in Primitive Art 4. Milwaukee: Milwaukee Public Museum.
Schweinfurthe, Georg
1875 *The Heart of Africa: Three Year's Travels and Adventures in the Unexplored Regions of Central Africa, from 1868 to 1871*. 2 vols. London: n.p.

Seabrook, W. B.
1929 *The Magic Island*. New York: Harcourt, Brace & Co.
Seligman, Gerald
1995a *Chimurenga Forever: The Best of Thomas Mapfumo*. CD Liner Notes. EMI Hemisphere 72438 3558223.
1995b *South Africa: Only the Poorman Feel It*. CD Liner Notes. EMI Hemisphere 72438 3286621.
Seydou, Christiane
1972 *Silamaka and Poullori: Récit epique peul raconté par Boubacar Tinguidji*. Paris: Armand Colin.
Shapiro, Dolores J.
1995 "Blood, Oil, Honey, and Water: Symbolism in Spirit Possession Sects in Northeastern Brazil." *American Ethnologist* 22 (4): 828–47.
Shaw, Arnold
1986 *Black Popular Music in American: From the Spirituals, Minstrels, and Ragtime to Soul, Disco, and Hip-Hop*. New York: Schirmer Books.
Shaw, Lisa
1999 *The Social History of the Brazilian Samba*. Brookfield, Vermont: Ashgate Publishing Company.
Sidibe, B.K., and Winifred F. Galloway
1975 *Senegambian Traditional Families: An Occasional Paper*. Banjul: Gambia Cultural Archives.
Simon, Artur, ed.
1983 *Musik in Afrika: 20 Beiträge zur Kenntnis traditioneller afrikanischer Musikkulturen*. Veröffentlichungen des Museums für Volkerkunde Berlin, n.s. 40, Abteilung Musikethnologie IV. Berlin: Staatliche Museen, Preussischer Kulturbesitz.
Siroto, Leon
1995 *East of the Atlantic West of the Congo: Art from Equatorial Africa*. Seattle: The University of Washington Press.
Small, Christopher
1987 *Music of the Common Tongue: Survival and Celebration in Afro-American Music*. London: John Calder; New York: Riverrun Press.
Söderberg, Bertil
1956 *Les instruments de musique au Bas-Congo et dans les régions avoisantes*. Monograph Series, no. 3. Stockholm: Ethnographical Museum of Sweden.
1966 "Antelope Horn Whistles with Sculptures from the Lower Congo." *Ethnos* (3): 5–33.
1972 "The Ornamentation of the Sanza." *African Arts* 5 (4) 28–32.
Sow, Abdoul Aziz
1993 "Fulani Poetic Genres." *Research in African Literatures* 24 (summer, no. 2): 61–77.
Stenning, Derrick J.
1960 "Transhumance, Migratory Drift, Migration: Patterns of Pastoral Fulani Nomadism." In *Cultures and Societies of Africa*, edited by Simon and Phoebe Ottenberg, 139–59. New York: Random House.
1965 "The Pastoral Fulani of Northern Nigeria." In *Peoples of Africa*, edited by James L. Gibbs Jr., 363–401. New York: Holt, Rinehart and Winston, Inc..
Stephens, Robert W.
1984 "Soul: A Historical Reconstruction of Continuity and Change in Black Popular Music." *Black Perspective in Music* 12 (10): 21–48.
Stevenson, Robert
1968 "Some Portuguese Sources for Early Brazilian Music History." *Inter-American Institute for Musical Research Yearbook* 4: 21–68.
Stewart, Gary
1987 "Dr Olo's *Milo* Jazz," *West Africa* 22 (June): 1202–3.
Stone, Ruth M., ed.
1998 *Africa: The Garland Encyclopedia of World Music*, vol. 1. New York: Garland Publishing.
Stone, Ruth M.
1982 *Let the Inside Be Sweet: The Interpretation of Music Event Among the Kpelle of Liberia*. Bloomington: Indiana University Press.
Stuempfle, Stephen
1995 *The Steelband Movement: The Forging of a National Art in Trinidad and Tobago*. Philadelphia: The University of Pennsylvania Press.
Sunday Express
1972 "Sunday Opinion: We Must Do Something for Calypso." 1, 23: 4.
Suret-Canale, J., and Boubacar Barry
1976 [1971] "The Western Atlantic Coast to 1800." In *History of West Africa, Volume 1* (2nd ed.), edited by J. F. A. Ajayi and Michael Crowder, 456–511. London: Longman Group Limited.
Swift, Lloyd B., Kalifu Tambadu, and Paul G. Imhoff
1965 Fulai Basic Course. Washington, DC: Foreign Service Institute.
Tesfaye Lemma
1975 *Ethiopian Music Instruments*. 1st ed. Addis Ababa, Ethiopia: n.p.
Thieme, Darius L.
1967 "Three Yoruba Members of the Mbira-Sanza Family." *Journal of the International Folk Music Council* 19: 42–48.
1970 "A Summary Report on the Oral Traditions of Yoruba Musicians." *Africa* 40 (4): 359–62.
Thiermann, David
1971 "The Mbira in Brazil." *African Music* 5 (1): 90–94.
Thompson, Donald
1971 "The Marimbula: An Afro-Caribbean Sanza." *Yearbook for Inter-American Musical Research* 7: 103–16.
1975/76 "A New World Mbira: The Carribean Marimbula." *African Music* 5 (4): 104–8.
Thompson, Robert Ferris
1989 "Kongo Civilization and Kongo Art." In *The Four Moments of the Sun: Kongo Art in Two Worlds*. edited by Robert Farris Thompson and Joseph Cornet, 34–140. Washington, DC: National Gallery of Art.
1995 "From the Isle Beneath the Sea: Haiti's Africanizing Vodou Art." In *The Sacred Arts of Haitian Vodou*, edited by Donald J. Cosentino, 91–119. Los Angeles: UCLA Fowler Museum of Cultural History.
Tirro, Frank
1977 *Jazz: A History*. New York: W. W. Norton and Company (reprint, 1993).
Titon, Jeff Todd
1992 *Worlds of Music: An Introduction to the Music of the World's Peoples*, edited by Jeff Todd Titon. New York: Schirmer Books.
Tobert, Natalie
1995 "Lyre (kissar)." In *Africa: Art of the Continent*, edited by Tom Phillips, 132. Munich: Prestel.
Toop, David
1991 *Rap Attack 2: African Rap to Global Hip Hop*. Revised and expanded edition. New York: Serpent's Tail.
Tracey, Andrew
1961 "Mbira Music of Jege A Tapera." *African Music* 2 (4): 44–63.
1963 "Three Tunes on the Mbira dza Vadzimu." *African Music* 3 (2): 23–26.
1970 "The Matepe Mbira Music of Rhodesia." *African Music* 4 (4): 37.
1969 "The Tuning of Mbira Reeds: A Contribution to the Craft of Mbira Making." *African Music* 4 (3): 96–100.
1970a *How to Play the Mbira dza Vadzimu*. Roodeport: International Library of African Music.
1970b "The Matepe Mbira Music of Rhodesia." *African Music* 4 (4): 37–61.
1972 "The Original African Mbira?" *African Music* 5 (2): 85–104.
1989a "The System of the Mbira." In *Papers Presented at the Seventh Symposium on Ethnomusicology*, 43–55. Department of Anthropology and Ethnomusicology, University of Venda, September 3–5, 1988. Grahamstown: International Library of African Music.
1989b "Music in Moçambique: Structure and Function." In *Novas Perspectivas em Etnomusicologia*. Instituto de Investigação Cientifica Tropical, Lisbon, seminar 16– 20 May 1983. Lisbon: Museu de Etnologia, 69–82.
1991 "Kambazithe Makolekole and His *Valimba* Group: A Glimpse of the Technique of the Sena Xylophone." *African Music* 7 (1): 82–104.
Tracey, Hugh T.
1948 *Ngoma*. London: Longmans, Green & Co.
1948a *Handbook for Librarians*. Roodeport: African Music Society.
1948b *Chopi Musicians: Their Music, Poetry and Instruments*. London: Oxford University Press. Rev. ed., 1970.
1953 "Review of 'Tribal Crafts of Uganda' (Trowell and Wachsmann, 1953)." *African Music Society Newsletter* 1 (6): 78–79.
1961 "A Case for the Name Mbira." *African Music* 2 (4): 17–25.
1969 "The Mbira Class of Instruments in Rhodesia, 1932." *African Music* 4 (3): 78–95.
1973 *Catalogue of the Sound of Africa Recordings. 210 Long Playing Records on Music and Songs from Central, Eastern and Southern Africa by Hugh Tracey, Vol. I and II*. Roodepoort: The International Library of African Music.

Tremmel, Erich
1986 "Die Sammlung afrikanischer Musikinstrumente im Missionsmuseum Sankt Ottilien." *Augsburger Jahrbuch für Musikwissenschaft* 3: 7–50.
Turner, Lorenzo D.
1942 "Some Contacts of Brazilian Ex-Slaves with Nigeria, West Africa." *Journal of Negro History* 27: 55–67.
Valdman, Albert
1981 *Haitian Creole-English-French Dictionary*. Bloomington: Indiana University, Creole Institute.
Vansina, Jan
1978 *The Children of Woot: A History of the Kuba Peoples*. Madison: University of Wisconsin Press.
Vassberg, David E.
1976 "African Influences on the Music of Brazil." *Luso-Brazilian Review* 13 (1): 35–54.
VerEecke, Catherine
1993 "Sub-National Fulbe Identity in Nigeria? Responses to Political Change in Post-Independence Times." In *Unity and Diversity of a People: The Search for Fulbe Identity*, edited by Paul Kazuhisa Eguchi and Victor Azarya, 163–79. Osaka: National Museum of Ethnology.
Verger, Pierre
1957 *Notes sur le Culte des Orisa et Vodun à Bahia, la Baie de tous les Saints, au Brésil et à l'ancienne Côte des Esclaves en Afrique*. Dakar: L'Institut Français D'Afrique Noire.
Vianna, Hermano
1999 *The Mystery of Samba: Popular Music and National Identity in Brazil*. Edited and translated by John Charles Chasteen. Charlotte: The University of North Carolina Press.
Villoteau, M.
1923 "Description historique, technique et littéraire, des instruments de musique des orientaux." In *Description de L'Egypt*, vol. 13, 2nd ed., 221–568. Paris: Imprimerie de C. L. F. Panckoucke.
Vogel, Joseph O.
1971 *Kumadzulo: An Early Iron Age Village Site in Southern Zambia*. Museum Papers 3. Livingstone: Livingstone Museum.
Vogel, Susan
1997 *Baule: African Art/Western Eyes*. New Haven: Yale University Press.
Wachsmann, Klaus P.
1971 "Musical Instruments in the Kiganda Tradition and Their Place in the East African Scene." In *Essays on Music and History in Africa*, edited by Klaus P. Wachsmann, 93–134. Evanston: Northwestern University Press.
1972 "Social Roles for Musical Instruments and Their Interaction with Musical Form in Africa." In *Report of the Eleventh Congress of the International Musicological Society*, vol. 1, edited by Henrik Glahn, Soren Sorensen, and Peter Ryom, 135. London, J. & W. Chester.
Wachsman, Klaus et al.
1980 "Lyre." In *The New Grove Dictionary of Music and Musicians*, edited by Stanley Sadie, vol. 11, 397–401. London: Macmillan and Company.
Wafer, Jim
1991 *The Taste of Blood Spirit Possession in Brazilian Candomblé*. Philadelphia: University of Pennsylvania Press.
Walker, Shelia S.
1990 "Everyday and Esoteric Reality in Afro-Brazilian *Candomblé*." *History of Religion* 30 (2): 108–11.
Waller, Don
1985 *The Motown Story*. New York: C. Scribner.
Waterman, Christopher Alan
1990 *Jùjú: A Social History and Ethnography of an African Popular Music*. Chicago and London: The University of Chicago Press.
Waterman, Richard
1952 "African Influences on the Music of the Americas." In *Accultration in the Americas*, edited by Sol Tax, 207–18. Chicago: University of Chicago Press.
Webster, Noah
1976 *Webster's New Twentieth Century Dictionary of the English Language*, 2nd edition. N.p.: William Collins and World Publishing Co.
Weil, Thomas E.
1973 *Area Handbook for Haiti*. Washington, D.C.: U.S. Government Printing Office.
Welmers, William E.
1960 *The Mande Languages*. Georgetown University Monograph Series in Languages and Linguistics 11: 9–24. Washington: Georgetown University Press.
1971 "Niger-Congo Mande." *Current Trends in Linguistics* 7: 113–40.
Welmers, William E., and Christopher Kandakai
1970 *A Vai-English Dictionary*. Manuscript
1974 *A Dictionary of Vai*. Unpublished manuscript.
Were, Gideon
1967 *A History of the Abaluyia of Western Kenya*. Nairobi: East African Publishing House.
Wetherell, James
1860 *Stray Notes from Bahia*. Liverpool: Birkenhead Advertiser.
Weule, Karl
1908 *Wissenschaftliche Ergebnisse meiner ethnographischen Forschungsreise in den Südosten Deutsch-Ostafrikas*. Berlin: Ernst Siegfried Mittler and Sohn.
White, Miles
1996 "The Phonograph Turntable and Performance Practice in Hip Hop Music: Classifactory, Analytic, and Applied Aspects of Organological Inquiry." Paper presented at the 41st Annual Meeting of the Society for Ethnomusicology, Toronto, Canada, October 31–November 3.
Whodini
1986 "Funky Beat." *Back in Black*. Jive/Arista JCB-8407.
Willet, Frank
1977 "A Contribution to the History of Musical Instruments among the Yoruba." In *Essays for a Humanist: An Offering to Klaus Wachsmann*, 350–89. New York: The Town House Press.
Williams, Gilbert
1986 "The Black Disc Jockey as a Cultural Hero." *Popular Music and Society* 10 (3): 79–90.
Wilson, Olly
1974 "The Significance of the Relationship between Afro-American Music and West African Music." *Black Perspective in Music* 2 (spring): 3–22.
Wilson, Ruth Danenhower
1957 *Here Is Haiti*. New York: Philosophical Library.
Witmer, Robert E.
1986 "Afro-American Music." In *The New Harvard Dictionary of Music*, edited by Don Randel. Cambridge: Belknap Press of the Harvard University Press, 24–25.
Wittgenstein, Ludwig
1984 *Philosophical Investigations*. Oxford: Basil Blackwell.
Yankah, Kwesi
1989 *The Proverb in the Context of Akan Rhetoric*. New York: Peter Lang.
1995 *Speaking for the Chief: Ɔkyeame and the Politics of Akan Royal Oratory*. Bloomington : Indiana University Press.
Zemp, Hugo
1971 *Musique Dan: La musique dans la pensée et la vie sociale d'une société africaine*. Cahiers de l'homme, n.s. 11. The Hague: Mouton.
Zenkovsky, S.
1950 "Zar and Tanbura as Practiced by the Women of Omdurman," *Sudan Notes and Records* 31 (1): 65–81.
Zensor Musikproduction 88
1988 "Sierra Leone Music: West African Gramophone Records Recorded in Freetown in the 1950s and early 1960s." Pamphlet accompanying recording by Zensor Musikproduktion 88.
Zindi, Fred
1985 *Roots Rocking in Zimbabwe*. Gweru, Zimbabwe: MamboPress.
Zubko, Galina V.
1993 "Ethnic and Cultural Characteristics of the Fulbe." In *Unity and Diversity of a People: The Search for Fulbe Identity*, edited by Paul Kazuhisa Eguchi and Victor Azarya, 201–14. Osaka: National Museum of Ethnology.

Contributors

Ernest D. Brown Jr. is an associate professor in the Department of Music at Williams College, Williamstown, Massachusetts

Kimasi L. Browne ia a doctoral candidate in the Department of Ethnomusicology at UCLA and a lecturer in the Department of Black Studies at California State University, Long Beach.

Leigh Creighton is a graduate student in the Department of Ethnomusicology at UCLA.

Jacqueline Cogdell DjeDje is a professor in the Department of Ethnomusicology at UCLA.

Akin Euba is Andrew W. Mellon Professor of Music in the Department of Music at the University of Pittsburgh.

Clarence Bernard Henry is an assistant professor in the Department of African and African American Studies at Indiana State University, Terre Haute.

Christian Dowu Jayeola Horton is an adjunct professor in the Music Department at Macon State College, Georgia.

Cheryl L. Keyes is an assistant professor in the Department of Ethnomusicology at UCLA.

Jean Ngoya Kidula is an assistant professor in the School of Music at the University of Georgia, Athens.

Cynthia Tse Kimberlin holds a doctorate in ethnomusicology from UCLA and is executive director of the Music Research Institute and publisher of MRI Press, Richmond California.

Gerhard Kubik is a professor of cultural anthropology at the University of Mainz and professor of ethnomusicology and cultural anthropology at the University of Vienna.

Heather A. Maxwell is a graduate student in ethnomusicology in the Folklore Institute at Indiana University, Bloomington.

Eddie S. Meadows is a professor in the School of Music and Dance at San Diego State University.

Lester P. Monts is a professor in the School of Music and Associate Provost for Academic Affairs at the University of Michigan, Ann Arbor.

Kazadi wa Mukuna is an associate professor of ethnomusicology in the School of Music at Kent State University.

Ali Jihad Racy is a professor in the Department of Ethnomusicology at UCLA.

Victoria Simmons is a doctoral candidate in the Folklore and Mythology Program at UCLA.